Slovenly Peter, or Pleasant Stories and Funny Pictures, Hoffman-Donner, Heinrich, New York (entry no. 1133).

Pictured from left: *A Collection of the Most Approved Entertaining Stories*, Solomon Winlove, Esq. London: 1770 (entry no. 636); *A Museum for Young Gentlemen and Ladies*, Anonymous, Salisbury; (1750 or earlier) (entry no. 1620) and *The New Robinson Crusoe, Designed for the Amusement and Instruction of the Youth of Both Sexes*, Joachim Heinrich Campe, London: 1790 (entry no. 485).

The

David McCandless McKell

Collection:

A Descriptive Catalog of

Manuscripts, Early Printed Books, and Children's Books

by

Frank B. Fieler

assisted by

John A. Zamonski and Kenneth W. Haas, Jr.

G. K. HALL & CO., 70 LINCOLN STREET, BOSTON, MASS.

1973

Library of Congress Cataloging in Publication Data

Fieler, Frank B
    The David McCandless McKell collection.

    1. Children's literature--Bibliography--Catalogs.
2. McKell, David McCandless, 1881-   --Library.
I. Title.
Z1037.F49   028.52   72-11797
ISBN 0-8161-0993-1

This publication is printed on permanent/durable acid-free paper.

ISBN 0-8161-0993-1

TABLE *of* CONTENTS

INTRODUCTION

In the spring of 1967 I made an appointment with Mr. Eugene D. Rigney, Director of the Ross County, Ohio, Historical Society to view a collection of rare books brought together by Col. David McKell of Chillicothe, Ohio, which had come to the Historical Society. I was, at the time, engaged in a study of sixteenth-century emblem books, and was hopeful that the collection included some examples I hadn't seen. Three hours on a Saturday morning with the books indicated that although no emblem books were present there were indeed a great number of rare items in the collection, including some unique copies of printed books and a small group of fine illuminated manuscripts. Upon learning that the Ross County Historical Society had neither resources nor plans for cataloging the books, I suggested to Mr. Rigney that perhaps Ohio University could be persuaded to undertake the cataloging of the collection. Ohio University could and was persuaded. So, in the summer of 1967, with two graduate assistants and a certain sense of trepidation, I began cataloging the McKell Collection.

Books were transported to Ohio University in Athens, Ohio, where a gallery in the Library was reserved for our use and where we could use the bibliographical resources of the University Library while cataloging. The manuscripts and the most valuable printed books remained in Chillicothe. Our procedure was as follows. Every Tuesday we would drive the fifty-five miles from Athens to Chillicothe to return the books cataloged during the previous week and to pack up the books to be cataloged the following week. While my assistants were checking in the books returned, listing and packing up the books to go to Athens, I would work on the manuscripts and incunables which could not be removed from Chillicothe.

By the end of that first summer we had completed bibliographical descriptions of most of the books but were a long way from finishing the project. The press of teaching responsibilities effectively stopped any work on the collection from September to June. A Baker Award enabled me to devote full time to the collection during the summer of

1968 and Ohio University again supplied graduate assistants and space in the library. As a result, we were able to complete the bibliographical descriptions and start putting our cards in a final order by the time the fall term began. All that remained was retyping of certain cards for formal consistency, completing biographical information on some of the authors or illustrators, and devising some indices which would enhance the value of the catalog for users. These tasks were completed early in the summer of 1969 and by August 1 of that year duplicate sets of cards were placed with the McKell Collection, in Chillicothe, and in Alden Library, at Ohio University, in Athens.

In the spring of 1971, G. K. Hall & Company expressed interest in publishing the catalog. My current administrative and teaching responsibilities as chairman of the English department at Ohio University made impossible my devoting anything more than minimal time to preparing the card catalog for publication in book form. My former graduate assistants, Mr. Haas and Mr. Zamonski, who by now had taken their Ph. D. 's in English at Ohio University and were assistant professors of English at Ohio University at Lancaster and Wright State University respectively, volunteered to prepare the catalog for publication. This they have done and in the process have corrected a number of errors of omission, oversight, typing and fact. They also completely revised the indices. The degree of accuracy contained in the descriptions is largely the result of their labors during the past year.

The motive for preparing a catalog of the McKell Collection was, and remains, threefold: (1) to record the contents of a valuable collection, particularly of children's books, which, except locally, might otherwise disappear from sight; (2) to bring together on cards bibliographical information sufficiently complete to enable the Ross County Historical Society to answer queries from scholars and collectors concerning items in the collection; and (3) to aid students who have occassion to study the contents of the collection.

Organization of the Catalog

The contents of the Collection dictated the plan of organization. The great majority of the items, mainly children's books, came from the eighteenth and nineteenth centuries. There were approximately fifty earlier books which were about evenly divided between examples of book illustration and books written either for children or concerned with the education of children. And there was a smaller group of twenty-three medieval and illuminated manuscripts.

The catalog was divided into three parts. First the manuscripts were brought together and placed in chronological order. The second part of the catalog contains in chronological order the fifty-four books in the Collection printed before 1700. Our belief was that the relatively small number of items in this part did not necessitate an alphabetical order and a chronological order offered the advantage of suggesting the early historical development of both book illustration and books for and about children. The third part of the catalog contains over 2200 items published from 1700 to the present in alphabetical order. Anonymous works in this section are listed alphabetically by title. Cross-reference cards were made for pseudonyms and identifiable authors of anonymous works. All items in the catalog are numbered serially in the upper right-hand corner of the initial card. For purposes of publication we did not include approximately six hundred catalog cards for McKell books which are neither children's books nor examples of book illustration. In every case the books not included are either ordinary general literature or standard studies concerned with Col. McKell's collecting interests. To increase the usefulness of the catalog three indices, keyed to the numbered items, were made: a subject index, an index of illustrators and engravers, and an index of publishers, printers, and booksellers.

Catalog Entries -- Manuscripts

Descriptions of medieval and illuminated manuscripts are as complete as we could make them within the physical limitations of a card catalog. Each entry is divided into four or more sections. In the first is contained identifying information: author, title, language, place, and date. The second section contains a description of physical characteristics: number of leaves and size, foliation, material, scribal hand, ink, number of columns and lines to page. The third section on the card describes the illustrations found in the manuscript. A simple description of the binding is given in the fourth section. Following these sections is a statement of former owners (if known), and when applicable additional notes, for example, contents of a colophon, existence of early marginalia, etc. In a few instances where the title alone seemed insufficient a description of the textual contents is given following the description of the physical characteristics.

Catalog Entries -- Books

Descriptions of books published before 1861 are fairly full. Entries for these books are divided into four sections. The first contains title page information: author, title, place, publisher, and date. Books printed in a type face other than Roman are so indicated (BL = Black Letter). The second section contains format and collational formula following the practice advocated by Fredson Bowers in his Principles of Bibliographical Description (Princeton, 1949). The third section deals with illustrations and plates. Notes are contained in a fourth section. On many cards a short description of the binding precedes the notes.

Format and collational formulae are not given for books published after 1860. Instead, a statement of pagination follows the title page information.

Catalog Entries -- General

Abbreviations used on all cards are common enough not to be misinterpreted by the reader. Bibliographies and source material used in preparing the Catalog and referred to in the entries will be found in "A Source Bibliography" printed at the back. Col. McKell's correspondence concerning his books is kept with the Collection and is keyed to the Catalog at the end of relevant entries, e.g., "S 4-25-49."

Acknowledgments

It is a distinct pleasure to acknowledge publically the help received during the cataloging of the McKell Collection. First, I must register my great sense of gratitude to Ohio University for making possible the project in the first place and its continuing material support. Particularly I am grateful to Mr. Walter Wright, the former Director of Libraries and Mr. Thompson Little, the present Director, for their enthusiastic and wholehearted support, aid, and advice throughout the life of the project. Without the complete and sympathe-

Introduction

tic cooperation of Mr. Eugene Rigney, Director of the Ross County Historical Society, the job of cataloging would never have been completed.

My colleagues, Professor B.A. Park, R. Vance Ramsey, and Barry Thomas, were helpful in deciphering some particularly difficult late medieval hands. My students Claude Brew, Dorothea Kehler, Robert Lysiak, and William Wallace also helped.

Much of the faculty research at Ohio University is supported by the John C. Baker Fund, through the enlightened generosity of Edwin and Ruth Kennedy. I owe a great debt to Mr. and Mrs. Kennedy, for it was a Baker Award which enabled me to spend the summer of 1968 completing the bibliographical descriptions of the Collection.

Preparations for publication were greatly aided by a summer grant to Mr. Haas from the Regional Higher Education Grants Committee, and a travel grant to Mr. Zamonski from the College of Liberal Arts, Wright State University.

Mr. Charles F. Tomastik took the photographs for the plates in this volume.

FRANK B. FIELER
Athens, Ohio

August 15, 1972

Manuscripts

1

GREGORY OF NAZIANZUS (329-389)
MS Apologeticum, prologue and eight books, Latin
trans., Abbey of Cadouin (Dordogne, So. France),
ca. 1130-1140.

81 leaves (23 X 13 cm.), unnumbered, vellum, Gothic
miniscule by several hands, bistre ink, chapter
headings and paragraph marks in red, single columns.
There are 35 lines to a page.
Large initial "P" formed of two beasts, 8
calligraphic initials in colors.

Contemporary parchment covering thick oak boards,

MS Apologeticum,   2.

missing single clasps.

Text is complete and varies considerably from
that in Migne PG.

2

BIBLE
MS Old and New Testament, Latin (Parma?), ca. 1180-
1200.

440 leaves (21 X 13 cm.), unnumbered, vellum, small
Gothic miniscule by several hands, brown and black
inks, with initials, page headings, and chapter
numbers in alternate red and blue, double columns,
36-63 lines in column.

Full page Romanesque miniature in colors (fol. 354^V)
of Crucifixion, with Mary and John under the cross,
and compassionate faces of sun and moon in upper
spaces.

BIBLE 440 LL.   2

4 historiated initials: God the Father creating
the world (fol. 1); Isiah (fol. 181); angel of
St. Matthew (fol. 288); St. Matthew writing
Gospel (fol. 288^V).

8 ornamental illuminated initials: fols. 26, 47,
62^V, 84, 99, 110, 114^V, 121.

Marginal extensions and penwork ornaments in left
and center margins usually on every page.

BIBLE 440 LL.   3

Old calf back (spine?) over old wooden boards,
metal clasps; title BIBLIA SACRA gilt stamped
on back (spine) within a gilt border.

Bookplate of A. Hachette. The ms is North
Italian, probably from Parma.

3

PSALTER, WITH CALENDAR (Benedictine)
MS Latin, Bavaria, ca. 1225-1250.

64 leaves only (18.4 X 15 cm.), unnumbered, vellum,
Romanesque hand, black ink with rubrication, single
column, 22 lines to page.

Full page miniature of Resurrection in gold and colors
(fol. 33^V). 2 historiated initials in gold and colors:
St. Michael killing the dragon (fol. 34); a sainted
bishop (fol. 62). 12 signs of the Zodiac in colors
within gold roundel (fols. 1-6). Each page of
calendar written within arched borders. 5 illuminated
initials in gold and colors: fols. 7, 34^V, 38

PSALTER, 64 LL.   2.

(in likeness of dragon), 49^V, 61.

Sixteenth century calf, roll-tooled in blind, with
two clasps.

Manuscript is incomplete. Once owned by Barnet
J. Beyer, Inc.

4

PSALTER, WITH CANTICLES
MS Latin, Netherlandish, c. 1280-85.

221 leaves only (10.6 X 7.8 cm.), unnumbered, vellum
small Gothic hand, black ink, single column, 14 lines
to page.

Large miniature in gold and colors representing the
Anointing of David (fol. 48^V). 95 illuminated pages,
in gold and colors. 65 illuminated initials. 35
contain heads of men and women, typical Netherlandish
faces, young and old, handsome and ugly, laymen,
monks, and nuns. 30 initials contain human heads

MS PSALTER, 221 LL.   2.

with animal bodies, and parrots, dogs and monkeys.
Initial cut out on fol. 90. Margins contain men and
animals playing contemporary musical instruments,
couples kissing, armored knights fighting, women, boys,
animals, all wittily and realistically observed, but
also betraying an exuberant fantasy. Small gold
initials with blue pen ornaments alternating with
blue capitals against red penwork, at beginning of
each verse.

Seventeenth century red velvet over boards, gilt
edged, gauffered.

MS PSALTER, 221 LL.   3.

Bookplate of Wilfred Merton (Merton MS. 6).

For related manuscripts, cf. BM Stowe MS. 17, the
Psalter of Guy de Dampierre in Royal Library at
Brussels, and Psalter of Margaret of Flanders
(H.P. Kraus, Cat. 75, No. 88).

#5

KORAN. MS. Arabian, 1327.

5 loose leaves (45 X 32.7 cm.) only, polished paper,
Thuluth script, black ink, single column.

5 illuminated headings, in gold and colors, Kufic
lettering with intricate scroll and vine work
20 medaillons in gold and colors.

Colophon leaf retained by Philip Duchnes the
bookseller

(

#7

BIBLE
MS Old and New Testaments, Latin, Italy, ca. 1350-1380.

476 leaves (24.5 X 18.5 cm.), unnumbered, vellum,
Gothic miniscule, black ink, with initials in red
or black, double columns, 45 lines in column.

18 large illuminated initials in colors with
marginal extentions.

123 large initials (2" or 1" square) in gold and colors

17th century brown calf, elaborately blind tooled
and ruled, 4 clasps missing.

(

#6

MISSAL (with Franciscan calendar, for Paris use by
a bishop)
MS Latin, Paris, ca. 1350-1360.

228 leaves (20.3 X 14 cm.), fols. 8-217 numbered
I-CCX, fols. 220-221 numbered CCXI-CCXII, vellum,
Gothic hand (2 sizes), brown and brown-black inks
with rubrication, 2 columns, 37 lines to column.

Full page miniature in gold and colors of
Crucifixion (fol. 81^v): Mary and John on either
side of cross, with sun and moon appearing over arms
of the cross. The four corners of the frame terminate

(

#8

INNOCENT VI Étienne Aubert (d. 1362)
MS Papal Supplication, Latin, Avignon, 1357

1 leaf, vellum, late Gothic script, black ink.

1 large historiated initial in gold and colors,
depicting St. Clare and Christ, with leaf-work
extending along inner and upper margins. Four of
originally twelve episcopal seals.

Contents:　A supplication directed to twelve
　　　　　　bishops for　donations of gold,
　　　　　　　　　　　　　　(cont'd)

MS MISSAL, 228 LL. 2.

in gold bosses from which sprout ivy sprays. 5
historiated initials with ivy ornament: priest
lifting up a small child (fol. 8); Nativity
(fol. 16^v); Resurrection (fol. 86); Pentecost
(fol. 103^v); Ascension of Christ (fol. 173^v).
3 large illuminated initials in burnished gold and
colors on fols. 19, 82, 192^v. Fine ornamental
penwork throughout.

Fifteenth century brown calf, blind stamped, over
bevelled oak boards. Sides are divided into three
panels by triple vertical and horizontal fillets.

(

INNOCENT VI
MS Papal Supplication

　　　　　silver, vestments, books, chalices for
　　　　　the Order of St. Clare, at Trier, Arch-
　　　　　diocese of Luxemburg.

(

MS MISSAL, 228 LL. 3.

Four rectangular stamps are used: a stag courant
faced by two demi fleur de lis, a lion passant, a
flower reversed, and a trefoil.

Armorial bookplate of Alfred Thomas Townshend, 5th
Baron de Braye (1849-1928).

Manuscript and fly leaves contain prayers in Latin,
and Latin and French inscriptions by previous
owners dating from 15th through 19th centuries.

Miniature on fol. 78^v is closely related to miniature
(

#9

ROTVLVS DOMORVM AC TERENOR D NICOLAI AC D
FRANCISCI DE CANDIDIS AB
ANN. CHR. MCCCLXXXXIIII
MS Property book in Italian, Italy, 1393-1403, 1544-
1552, 1557.

115 leaves (30 X 22.4 cm.) unnumbered, paper, brown
and black inks. Entrees dated 1393-1403.

Sheepskin, with leather hinges and belt.

Fols. 38, 72-73 blank.

6 leaves at end bound in upside down. 7 leaves of

MS MISSAL, 228 LL. 4.

of the Crucifixion in an earlier missal executed
for the Paris church of St. Geneviève (Ms. 1259),
reproduced in Bulletin de la Société de Reproduction
de Manuscrits (Paris, 1921), p. 75, pl. xxi.

(

MS ROTVLVS 2.

various sizes loosely inserted throughout. 5
loose leaves (watermark differs from that on bound
leaves) at end, containing entrees dated 1544-1552.
A marginal addition dated 1557.

5-11-15-50B

( )

VEGIO, MAFFEO (1407-1458) # *10*

MS Fragment. De Educatione Liberorum et eorum Claris
Moribus. Consists of Book IV, Chap.13 (from "Non est
obscurum filiam & neptes Augusti ua ab eo institutas
. . .."), Book V (lacks beginning to "data ab omnibus
pudicicia ut luman. . . ."; and 2 leaves between
". . . deus laudaturus atque exoraturus accedit.
Verum" and "Qui moderatur enim sermones suos ut
sacer auctor inquit doctus . . . ."), and Book VI,
Chap. 1 (ending "Labitae uero quos cum Perithoo
& Theseo pugnantes describit Naso: ubi sipo").
Latin, Italy, ca. 1450.

)

MS VEGIO   2.

23 leaves (28.4 X 21.6 cm), vellum rounded Roman
script, black ink, chapter headings in red, 35
lines to page.

4 illuminated initials, gold on white-vine gounds.

Archaic foliation: 84-86, 89-108

Complete text with analysis, found in <u>Studies in
Medieval and Renaissance Latin</u>, Catholic Univ. of
America, Vol I, fasc. I-II (Washington, D. C. , 1933-
1936).

)

TERENTIUS AFER, PUBLIUS (185-159 B.X.C.) # *11*
MS Comoediat, Latin, Central Italy, ca. 1440-1450.

162 leaves (18 X 11.8 cm.), vellum, Humanistic
miniscule, black and red inks, 24 lines to page.

2 large burnished gold initials and an unfilled
armorial wreath within an elaborate white vine
scrollwork border in gold and colors (Fol. 1).
17 initials of similar design in text. Smaller
initials in blue and red.

Fols. 1-162: Andria, Eunucus, Heatuntumer, Adelphos,
Hechira, Phormio.

)

MS TERENTIUS   2.

Binding by C. Lewis: mid 19th century purple morocco,
gilt fillets with corner gilt roses, richly gilt spine
with floral ornaments and title (M.S. Super Membranis)
in compartments.
Previous owners: Dr. E. C. Hawtrey, Tite, Sir Eric
Millar, Samuel Allen.

)

SENECA, LUCIUS ANNAEUS (4 B.C.?-65 A.D.) # *12*
MS De Beneficiis. Italian, Florence, ca. 1460-65.

102 leaves (21.8 X 15.3 cm.), unnumbered, vellum,
Humanistic miniscule, light brown ink, chapter headings
in red, 26 lines to page.

Large illuminated initial within elaborate scrollwork
border in gold and colors (Fol. 1). Coat of arms in
silver with three fleur-de-lys within scrollwork
border in gold and colors (Fol. 1). 7 large initials
in gold and colors in text.

Fol. 101 contains a conclusion by an unnamed editor.

)

MS SENECA   2.

Contemporary brown calf, elaborately blind tooled,
gilt edged.

MS contains two names: Jacopo Terzell (Fol. 1)
and Joho usato (Fol. 102^V).

)

ASTROLOGICAL MANUSCRIPT # *13*
MS Latin, Germany, 1463

10 leaves (17 X 12.4 cm.), vellum, late Gothic script,
black and red inks, some initials in gold.

<u>Contents</u>: Tabula paschalis for various years between
1437 and 2081. Calendar of months for the years
1463, 1482, and 1501. Oppositions for years 1463-1519.
Tables indicating planetary influences.

18th century half-calf over marbled boards. 4 blank
leaves and 34 paper leaves bound in.

)

PETRARCA, FRANCESCO (1304-1374) # *14*
MS I Trionfi Italian, ca. 1470

47 leaves (20.9 X 13.5 cm.), vellum, Humanistic
miniscule, black ink, 24 lines to the page.

Title page: Title in burnished gold, within an elaborate
three-sided border of white vine scrollwork, with
nine putti in various allegorical attitudes, one
mounting a fawn, four forming a wreath designed to
hold arms (now blank), the whole forming a Tree of
Life pattern. Above title is a miniature (7.1 X 7.8 cm)
depicting the poet in red robe and hat and blue
doublet at a writing stand before a symbolic landscape.

)

I Trionfi MS   2

Large gold initial ornamented in white vine manner
with green, red, and blue background at beginning of
each triumph. 8 smaller ornamented initials.

17th century brown calf. elaborately tooled in gold
and silver, recased in 19th century calf.

Formerly owned by Federico Patella, who acquired it
from Hoepli in Milan in 1936. Bookplates of the
Sanvitale Collection and an old princely collection
(initials L.S. under a crown[black and green]).

)

HORAE BEATAE VIRGINIS MARIAE. CUM CALENDRIO # *15*
MS Dutch, Netherlands, ca. 1480

168 leaves (18.2 X 12.7 cm.) vellum, Gothic script,
black and red inks, 22 lines to the page.

19 miniatures in gold and colors: Annunciation (Fol.
8^V), Virgin and Child (9), Mary and Elizabeth (16),
Nativity (22^V), Angel appearing to shepherds (25^V),
Circumcision (28), three Kings at Manger (30^V),
Presentation in Temple (33), Flight into Egypt (37^V),
Betrayal (41^V), Christ before Herod (42), Crowning
of the Virgin (64^V), Elevation by Pope at Mass (85^V),

)

HORAE 168 LL. 2.

Assumption of Virgin (91^v), Virgin, Child, and St. Anne (93), Pentecost (100^v), Last Judgment (121^v), Harrowing of Hell (139^v), Flowers, bird, grotesque, and butterfly (140). All with highly imaginative borders containing a rich profusion of flowers, birds, animals, insects and grotesques. 23 historiated initials in gold and colors. Small initials in burnished gold and colors, red and blue throughout.

Full brown levant, elaborately blind-tooled in geometric pattern, gilt edged, by Wallis. Full levant solander case by Riviere.

BREVIARY, WITH CALENDAR   # 16
MS Dutch, Utrecht?, 1482

322 leaves (17.1 X 12 cm), vellum, Qothic script, red and black inks, double-columns, 29 lines to the column.

5 illuminated pages with borders of calligraphic decoration, comprising feathery stems, leaf forms, and formal flowers with gold studs; also half-figures of man and angel, peacock, birds, and chalice. Large initials in red and blue, with pen-drawn fillings. Easter initial is historiated, Christ rising.

17th century red morocco, gilt borders and center tooling in form of a cross

---

BREVIARY 322 LL. 2.

Bookplate of Ambrose Lisle Phillipps.

BIBLE, New Testament   # 17
MS Tetraevangelium, Armenian, 1495

302 leaves (27 X 18.2 cm.), glazed paper, Armenian round hand, black, chapter heads and initials in red, double column. 21 lines to a column.

Fol. 1^{r}2: Letter of Eusebius to Karpianus; 2^v-6: Ten canons of Eusebius; 6^v-7: blank; 7^v: Preface to Matthew; 8-9^v: Table comparing chapters in Matthew with other gospels; 9^v-10: Concordances; 10^v: blank; 11-93: Matthew; 93^v-94: Preface to Mark; 94^v- 95^v:

Table relating chapters in Mark with contents of other Gospels; 96-148: Mark; 148^v: the false end of Mark

---

MS Tetraevangelium 2.

(one column only); 149: Preface to Luke; 149^v-150^v: Table relating chapters in Luke with contents of other gospels; 151-235: Luke; 235^v: Preface to John; 236-236^v: Table relating chapters in John with contents of other gospels; 237-300: John; 300-300^v: Supplement to the apocryphal "Adultera"; 301-302: scribal inscription; 302^v: blank.

3 full-page miniatures in red, blue, green, violet and gold: Christ appearing to eleven apostles in Galilee after Resurrection (Fol. 92), Christ's entry into Jerusalem (129^v), and the Nativity (157^v). 2 full-

---

MS Tetraevangelium 3.

page pen drawings: Last Judgment and Hell (79) and Pentecost (92^v). 2 smaller miniatures: Repentance of St. Peter (86^v) and Mary and Elizabeth (154). Elaborate ornaments at beginning of each gospel. Many ornamented figures in red and blue in margins.

Inscription: "In the year of our nation 944 [i.e., A.D. 1495] this holy Gospel was completed . . . for the pious Christian, the pilgrim Khodja Hovannes who received it with great love as a memorial for his soul and that of his parents, his father Arev, his mother Markarid, his brothers Karim, Azdan Baghshi and his

---

MS Tetraevangelium 4.

sons, the pilgrim Amir and Mkhitar and Sinan and his wife Shah Pasha and all his other relatives. He preferred this to all other worldly benefits . . . and he had it written with great love and faith by the hand of the sinful priest Abraham. . . . This Gospel was completed in the metropolis called Constantinople, at the church of the Holy Virgin now called Sulu Manastir, during the primacy of Der Sarkis and when Der Garabed of Caffa was the archbishop . . ."

Contemporary blind-tooled, brown leather, showing an elaborately punched cross within a border on front, blind-tooled leather flap over foreedge. Five (4small)

MS Tetraevangelium 5.

crosses (brass?) missing from front and one from back.

Front and back endpapers are two leaves of 10-11th century MS, written in an Armenian middle-uncial script, containing a homily on baptism.

ANON.   # 18
MS. Teth Kera. Persian, 16th century.

146 leaves (20.3 X 13.3 cm.), unnumbered, paper, Nastaliq hand, black ink with red for quotations from the Koran, 16 lines to the page.

No illustration.

Sixteenth century brown morocco, blind tooled and stamped, rebacked in brown calf.

Colophon reads in part "finished with the help of Almalek Almenan."

NIZAMI (1141-1202)   # 19
MS. Poems, Persian, Isfahan, 1571.

224 leaves (26.7 X 17.4 cm.), unnumbered, pink-tinted polished paper, Nastaliq hand, black ink. 12 lines to a page within gold, red, and green borders. 4 miniatures in gold and colors, in a frame of gold and colors, within large margins elaborately flowered in gold, and including exotic birds, dragon, lion, leopard, deer, and rabbit: Fols. 49, 82, 223^v, 224, 16 medaillons in gold and blue: fols. 1, 13, 20, 29, 35, 44, 55, 66, 79, 87, 93, 103, 181, 189, 196, 208. Text on each page within a border of gold and colors. Vine and leaf decoration in gold and colors on every leaf.

MS NIZAMI 2.

Near contemporary polished calf, dark brown on outer sides, dark red on inner sides, dark green edges and back, gilt tooled and stamped, gold and blue doublures on inside.

Colophon, in part, states that the manuscript was completed through the efforts of Faghir Baba Shah Esfahani Ghafrolah Zanobi and Setapr Ayube.

Once owned by William Cleary. In the top margin at the head of the text is written in Persian "From the books of Mohamad Katebsepah."

20

MEGILLAH
MS Scroll Book of Esther, Hebrew, Italy, ca. 1600

19 panels on five rectangular sheets of thick vellum of unequal lengths sewn together, 16th century Hebrew calligraphy, black ink. 21 lines to a panel.

On original turned fruitwood roller.

[D-11-1-55B]

21

Paper Manuscript
MS Latin, Italy, 16th century

4 leaves (45.5 x 29.8cm), paper, sewn end to end, secretary script, brown and black inks.

Written by at least three different hands, on both sides of leaves.

22

OMAR KHAYYAM (d. ca. 1123)
MS. Rubaiyat. Persian, Isfahan, 1613.

28 leaves (15.3 X 9.2 cm.), unnumbered, polished paper, Nastaliq hand, black ink. 10 lines to a page.

5 miniatures by Reza Abasi in gold and colors on fols. 3^V, 8, 13^V, 19, 23^V (each containing 5 or 6 human figures). 4 medaillons in gold and blue or gold and red on fols. 3^V, 8, 13^V, 19. Text on each page written within an elaborately floral margin in gold or gold and colors.

MS Rubaiyat 2.

Contemporary dark brown morocco, edges red morocco, gilt tooled and stamped, rebacked with red morocco.

Colophon states that the manuscript was completed by Mohamad Reza Alabasi for Homayoun Zolalahi Arvah Alalamin.

Formerly owned by Kermit Roosevelt, who brought it out of Persia in 1922.

MS N.T. Armenian 2.

New Testament figures and scenes.

Scribal Inscription: "This holy Gospel was written by the hand of the scribe Hovannes, in the year of the Armenians 1095 [i.e., A.D. 1646] at the request of the pious Khatcho who places it, as a memorial, in the church of the Holy Virgin. I beseech you all, who read, copy or casually look at this book, to remember in your pure prayers Khatcho and his wife Sara Khatun, and his father Khodja Krikor, and his mother Gülzade, and his son Hohannes, and his deceased sons Krikor, Asdvadzadur and David.

23

BIBLE, New Testament
MS Armenian, 1646

286 leaves (20.3 X 15.2 cm.), parchment, Armenian round hand, black ink, chapter heads and initials in red, double-columns, 22 lines to column.

Total of 47 illuminated pages. 18 full-page illuminations, including one of each Evangelist in gold and colors (Fols. 13^V, 92^V, 142^V, and 222^V). Fols. 1-10 contain elaborately decorative scrollwork; 1^V-2 with half-figures of Evangelists; 3^V-6 with exotic birds and trees; 7-10 with exotic lions, birds, and trees. Many marginal miniatures in gold and colors depicting

Early Printed Books Before 1700

MS. N.T. Armenian · 3.

17th century calf, gilt tooled, gilt edged; red leather on spine NOVUM TESTAMENTUM | MSS. | SYRO-PHOENICIUM

Fasciculus Temporum

Notes: a2–a8 are badly clipped and worn, pasted to new stubs by binder; K7–U7 are pasted to new stubs by binder; U8 is pasted to new leaf supplied by binder. Fols. CCCix–CCCxx bound out of order, following Fol. xvi.

#24

CAESAR, CAIUS JULIUS (100–44 B.C.). Commentarios Belli Gallici. Venice: Nicholas Jenson, 1471. (Roman)

Coll.: 2^0: a–b^{10}c–e^{8}f–i^{10}k–m^{8}n^{10}o^{8}p^{10}q^{12}. 148 Leaves, unnumbered.

Contents: See Gesamtkatalog der Wiegendrucke 5864. This copy lacks ornamental initials.

Binding: 19th c. calf with colored leather inlays, gilt edged.

S 1–28–53, 2–7–53 B, 2–10–53.

#27

BIBLIA GERMANICA, 2 vols. Nuremberg: Anton Koberger, Montag nach Invocavit 17 February 1483. (in German, BL)

Coll.: 2^0: Vol. I: [a^{12}b–c^{8}d^{6}e–z^{8}A–N^{8}O^6]. 296 Leaves, numbered I–CCXCV, last leaf blank (CXXVIII misnumbered CXXIX, CXLII misnumbered CXLIIII). Vol. II: [2a–2z, 2A–2L^{8}2M–2O^6]. 290 Leaves, numbered CCXCVI–CCCCLXXXIII, first and last leaves blank (CCCLXXV misnumbered CCCLXXVI, CCCCLXVII misnumbered CCCCLXVIII, CCCCLXXXIII misnumbered CCCCLXXVIII).

102 hand-colored woodcuts; 3 large illuminated initials in gold and colors, with floriation extending down margins; numerous large initials handpainted in blue and/or red; all other initials rubricated. Chapter

---

#25

ZAMORENSIS, RODERICUS VON [SÁNCHEZ DE ARÉVALO, RODRIGO] (1404–1470). Der Spiegel des Menschlichen lebens (German translation by Heinrich Steinhowel of Zamoren-sis' Speculum humanae vitae) Augsburg: Gunther Zainer, ca. 1475–76]. (BL)

Coll.: 2^0: [a–k^{10}l^{8}m–q^{10}r–s^8]. 174 Leaves, numbered [1–10] i–clxiiij (cxxi misnumbered cxxiii, cxxvi misnumbered cxxiv).

54 hand-colored woodcuts, 76 hand-colored initials, chapter heading on Fol. 109 printed with red ink.

Biblia German. 1483

headings and headlines rubricated on fols. CXXIV^v and CXXX only.

Binding: blind-tooled contemporary brown calf.

Notes: McKell copy lacks fols. V–XII (8 leaves). Bookplate of James Mason Hoppin on front paste-down endpaper in each volume.

Der Spiegel

Binding: Contemporary pink embossed pigskin over wooden boards, metal clasp, brass knobs on both covers.

S 12–10–51 L, 12–26–51 B.

#28

Anon. REGIME SCHOLARIŪ [?Leipzig: Martin Lansberg, 1488].

Coll.: 4^0: [A^8].

Bound in modern boards.

Lacks A7. Possibly the only copy extant. Hain 13764, now in the Bavarian State Library in Munick (Bayer. Staatsbibliothek Munchen: Inc. s.a. 1550), is a later type setting based upon this edition. A photostat copy of Hain 13764 accompanies McKell copy.

S 8–23–44L, 9–1–44–L, 12–15–50–L, 2–23–51–L, 3–0–51–L, 6–16–51–L, 12–10–51–L (p.2).

#26

ROLEWINCK, WERNER (1426–1502). Dat boek dat men hiet Fasciculus Temporum. Utrecht: Jan Veldener, 14 February 1480. (in Dutch, BL)

Coll.: 2^0: [a^8(–a1)b–z^{8}A–F^{8}G^{6}H^{8}I^{4}K–U^8]. 337 Leaves, Fols. [2–8,] ii–Clxxxiiii, Clxxxvi–CClviii, CClviii–CCCxx.

Contents: See BM Cat. of 15th C. books.

31 woodcuts (3 in color); 249 decorative, small coats of arms; large decorative woodcut initial G, with decorative border (a2); printer's device (U8).

Binding: early 19th c. marbled calf, gold tooling.

#29

Anon. CHRONIQUES ABRÉGÉES DES ROIS DE FRANCE [Chronicle of Saint Denis]. Paris: Jean Treperel, 4 February 1492. (BL)

Coll.: 4^0: a^{6}A^{8}b–c^{8}d e–f^{8}g–k^{8}l^{6}m^8. 92 Leaves (missignings: A2 for a2, i4 for i3, i3 for i4).

Contents: See Gesamtkatalog der Wiegendrucke 6683.

53 woodcuts, printed from five blocks.

Bound in contemporary vellum.

Chroniques Abrégées

Notes: McKell copy lacks A1 and M8 (M8 is blank, M8 contains printer's device only). a1 (TP) signed "SECOUSSE" (Denis François Secousse, friar, who fl. 1495, author of the Ordonnances of the Kings of France). Only other recorded copy of this book is in Moulins at the Bibliotheque et Archives Municipales, which lacks all of Quire a.

S 2-19-48 L, 3-13-48 B.

 # 30

Anon.
REGULE CONGRUITATUM MEDIOCRES. Reuttlingen: Michaelem Greyffen, n.d. [ca. 1493].

Coll.: 4^0: $A^8 B^6$. 14 leaves.

Hand-tinted woodcuts on A1 (TP) and B6^V. Decorative printed initials.

Bound in contemporary vellum.

SCHEDEL, HARTMAN (1440-1514). **#31**
Liber chronicarum. Nuremberg: Anton Koberger, 12 July 1493. (BL)

Coll.: $[2^0: 2_6^6 2_6^6 3 8_A^6 B-D^4 E_7 H^6 I^2 K^4 L-N^6 O_4^2 P-Q^6 R-Y^4 Z-2C^6 2D^2 2E^4 2F^4 2G-2I^6 2K^4 2L^6 2M-3K^6 3L^4]$.

320 Leaves. Fols. 21-319 numbered I-CCXCIX.

1809 Woodcuts, printed from 645 blocks by Wolgemut and Pleydenwurff, entirely untouched with color. No color supplied to the initials. No rubrication except for paragraph mark and underline on Fol. 2, line 1.

Nuremberg Chronicle

Binding: 19th c. blind-stamped pigskin, gilt edged and tooled.

Notes: Blank spaces, as usual, for initials on Fols. 2-21, 28s, 321, printed initials elsewhere. Fols. 279-281, except for headlines, are blank, as usual. Misprints on Fols. 7 and 182 are not corrected. McKell copy apparently represents an earlier state than that commonly found. See BM Cat. of 15th c. books, II, 437.

Bookplate of Joseph Neeld.

SAVONAROLA, HIERONYMUS (1452-1498). **# 32**
Expositione del pater noster . . . traducta . . . da uno suo amico in vulgare. Epistola della comunione. Florence: Antonio Mischomini, 1494. (Roman)

Coll.: 4^0: $a-c^8 d^2$. 26 Leaves

Contents: See BM Cat. of 15th c. books.

SAVONAROLA, HIERONYMUS (1452-1498). **# 33**
Tractato del sacramento & de mysterii della messa & Regola utile composta da frate Hieronymo da ferrara. [Florence: Bartolommeo di Libri, ?1495]. (Roman)

Coll.: 4^0: $[a^4]$. 4 Leaves ([a3] contains 34 lines of type).

Woodcut (12.3X11.2 cm.) within a strapwork border, depicting crucified Christ, Mary and John, on TP.

BRANT, SEBASTIAN (1458-1520). **# 34**
Stultifera Nauis . . . [Das Narrenschiff. Translated into Latin by Jacob Locher, with additions by Thomas Beccadelli]. Basel: Johann Bergmann de Olpe, August 1497. (Rom. and BL)

Coll.: 4^0: $a-e^{8/4} t-y^4$, 164 Leaves. Fols. I-CXLIII [A] CXLV-CLIX [CLX].

Contents: See *Gesamtkatalog der Wiegendrucke* 5061. Quire f represents a variant state.

119 woodcuts, some possibly by Dürer.

Brant, Stultifera Nauis

Binding: Tan pigskin over oak boards, blind-stamped panels in four concentric rectangles on front and back. On front are stamped the initials C H and the date 1540.

Notes: Contains much underlining and Latin annotation of the text in brown ink, predating the binding. Sig. y3^V contains seven lines of Latin moral verses in dactylic hexameter, in a contemporary hand. Sig. y4 contains in a contemporary hand what seems to be the curriculum for the M.A. at the University of Leipzig (in Latin). Sig. y4^V contains an unidentified 34-line poem in German, predating the binding, entitled "Eyn oberschrifft ober eines turgkischen kaysers grabe."

DÜRER, ALBRECHT (1471-1528) **#35**
Title: EPITOME IN DIVAE PARTHENICES MARI|AE HISTORIAM AB ALBERTO DVRERO | NORICO PER FIGVRAS DIGES | TAM CVM VERSIBVS ANNE | XIS CHELIDONII [woodcut (20.3 X 19.3cm) of Mater Coelis] | Quisquis fortunae... [10 lines, ending]...O homo supplicijs|

Coll.: 2^0: $A^8 B^6 C^6$ 20 leaves (44.1 X 31cm)

Contents: A1: Title, as above. A1^V-C6: Text on verso, woodcuts on recto. C6: Colophon, as below (verso blank)

Colophon: Impressum Nürnberge per Albertum Dürer Pic-

DÜRER   **2**

EPITOME IN DIVAE PARTHENICES MARI

torem. Anno Christiano Millesi| mo quingentisimo vndecimo. | Heus tu insidiator:ae alieni laboris:& ingeni j:surreptor:ne manus temerarias |his nostris operibus inicias.caue:Scias enim a gloriosissimo Romano | rum imperatore.Maximiliano nobis concessum esse:ne quis| suppositicijs formis:has imagines imprimere:seu | impressas per imperij limites vendere aude:at:q si per cotemptum;seu auaricie cri | men:sec feceris:post bonorū co |fiscatioem:tibi maximum pe | riculu subeundum |esse certissime |scias.

Woodcuts: 20 by Dürer

DÜRER **8**

EPITOME IN DIVAE PARTHENICES MARI

Binding: Bound in vellum

Notes: Leather bookplate of Carl J. Ulmann. McKell #
S 4-1-52L, S 4-16-52B

OVIDIUS **3**

Metamorphosis Libri Moralizati. 1524.   (Cont'd)

operibus luculenter collecta: in lucem exiliunt.|
1524 [date in red]||woodcut, 8.2 X 6.6cm., of Guilla-
ume Boulle's publisher's device||Laus tibi christe|
Et uirgini matri. [last two lines in red]

Coll: 4°: a⁶b⁻(2)C⁸D⁶C⁶. 218 leaves. $1,2,3,4, except on t1.

Foliation: b1-D6 numbered Fo. I-CCVI.

Contents: a1:title, as above. a1ᵛ: Vita et opera. a4ᵛ:
epistle to Franciscus Gonzaga. a6: epigram to
(cont'd)

BRASSICANI, IOANNIS (1500-1539). # 36
Institutiones grammaticae elimatissimae. Hagenau:
Thomas Anshelmi Badensis, 1519. (Roman)
Coll.: 4°: a⁴a-d⁴e⁸f-g⁴h⁸i-k⁴l⁸m-n⁴o⁸p-q⁴r⁸s-t⁴v⁸x⁸.
116 Leaves (20.7X15 cm.), unnumbered.

Binding: Contemporary blind-tooled quarter-calf over
wooden boards. Original flyleaves bound in after the
first and before the final gatherings.

Notes: x8: "Impressum Hagnoae in aedibus Thome Anshelmi
Badensis. Mense Iunio. Anno. M.D.X.VIII." 1a1 (TP):
in brown ink, "Est Joannis Wolfi a Glauburg" and "Jacobi
Margourdt a Glauburg." x8ᵛ: in black ink, "hans Brumia."

OVIDIUS **4**

Metamorphosis Libri Moralizati. 1524.   (Cont'd)

Petrus Lavinius. b1-D6ᵛ: text. E1: Index.
E6: blank. E6ᵛ: printer's device of
Jaques Mareschal (5.8 x 4.7cm).

Illus: Cosmological diagram (a6ᵛ) plus 15 woodcuts in
text; large initials.

Binding: Red levant with Maxwell device blind stamped
on front and back. In gilt on spine (BL):
(cont'd)

PFINTZING, MELCHIOR (1481-1535). # 37
Die geuerlichkeiten und einsteils der geschichten des
loeblichen streitbaren und hochberuembten helds und
Ritters Tewrdannskhs. Augsburg: Hans Schoensperger,
1519 (BL)
Coll.: 2°: a-c⁸d⁶e-h⁸i⁶k-n⁸o⁶p-s⁸r⁶s-t⁸u⁶x-y⁸z⁶
A-B⁸C⁶D-E⁸FG-H³I⁶K-L⁸M⁶N⁸O⁶P⁸2A⁸. 290 Leaves,
unnumbered.

118 woodcuts by Leonhard Beck, Hans Burgemair, Hans
Schaeuffelein, Wolf Traut, and others.

Binding: 17th c. half calf, gilt back with labels and
floral ornaments in compartments, red edges.

OVIDIUS **5**

Metamorphosis Libri Moralizati. 1524   (Cont'd)

P. | Ovidii | Nasonis | Meta-| morphosis |
Libri | LVGDVNI | M.D.XXIV |

Notes: Bookplate of William Stirling Maxwell

OVID. (PUBLIUS OVIDIUS NASO)   43 B.C.-17 A.D. # 38
Metamorphosis Libri Moralizati cum pulcherrimis fabularum
principalium figuris. Lyons: Printed by Jacques Mareschal
for Guillaume Boullé, 1524.

Title: [within a woodcut border]: P. Ouidij Nasonis Meta-
morpho⁴ [in red]||sis Libri moralizati cum pulcherri-
mis fabularum principalium figuris.| O [woodcut
initial] Vidij Nasonis Metamorpho [in red except for
initial]|seos quindecim librorum preclarum opus:
docte ac diligenter | familiaribus commentarijs:
caracteribus grecis modo excussis | expositum: [last
five words plus colon in red] et ab omni erroru
cumulo elimatum: una etiam cum | preclarissimis
(cont'd)

GUNTHERUS, RUFFUS # 39
Compendaria scribendarum epistolarum ratio. Nuremberg:
Fridericus Peypus, 1528. (Italic)

Coll.: 8°: A-C⁸. 24 Leaves (14.4X9.6 cm.).

Binding: Modern boards reproducing early printed page.

S 6-6-47 L&B

OVIDIUS **2**

Metamorphosis Libri Moralizati. 1524.   (Cont'd)

doctissimi uiri Lactantij firmiani. [last two words
plus period in red] Cocli in singulas | fabulas
argumentis (ut uno intuitu insigniter poete sententia
pateat) suis locis | collocatis. Necnon et tropologica
nonullarum fabularum enarratione per reue | rendum
patrem magistrum Petrum Lauinium [name and paren-
thesis mark in red]ordinis predicatorum in philo⁴
sophia ac poesi non mediocriter eruditum adiccia.|
¶ [in red] Denuo Raphaelis Regij | [name and vertical
mark in red] secunde enarrationes: cum alijs pluribus
adnotatio | nibus: ad limam ex omni parte ab erroribus
castigate: una cum ipsius poete uita | ex eius
(cont'd)

PALATINO, GIOVANBATTISTA (fl. 1540) # 40
Libro di M. Giovanbattista Palatino. Rome: Antonio
Blado Asolano, 1548.
Coll.: 4°: A-H⁸. 64 Leaves.

Bound in 19th c. green morocco.

Notes: Blocks on B8 and D1 dated 1540, on C1ᵛ, C2,
D2, D3, D3ᵛ, D6, D6ᵛ, D7ᵛ, E3 dated 1545. Rebus in
Italian supposedly the work of Leonardo da Vinci.
Bookplate of Bernard Sancholle-Henraux.

S 4-28-45 L.

DIETRICH, VITUS (1506-1549).   # 41
Summaria christlicher lehr für das junge volck. Nuremberg: Johann vom Berg und Ulrich Newber, 1550.   (BL)

Coll.: 8⁰: A⁸-T⁸. 152 Leaves (15X9.7 cm.)

79 woodcuts.

Binding: Blind-stamped, light-brown calf over wood
boards, elaborately decorated in three concentric
rectangles within three rules. Outer rectangle contains
eight cameos of four humanists (Erasmus, Luther,
Melancthon, and Reuchlin). Middle rectangle has panels
top and bottom: top panel stamped with title,

            Dietrich, Summaria

"Sumaria" (BL), bottom panel is blank, inside are six
flower faces. Inside rectangle contains three acorns.

Note: Dedication (A5ᵛ) to Johann Newdörffer is dated
1548.

S 3-3-47.

CHAUCER, GEOFFREY   c.1340-1400   # 42

The Woorkes of Geffrey Chaucer, newly printed,
with diuers addicions, whiche were neuer in printe
before: with the siege and destruccion of the
worthy citee of Thebes, compiled by Jhon Lidgate,
monke of Berie. Imprinted at London, by Jhon
Kyngston, for Jhon Wight . . . Anno. 1561.

Coll: 2⁰ ¶⁴A-Vᵛ⁶ 2A-2Tᵛ⁶ 2V-2Xᵛ⁸ 2Y-3Tᵛ⁶ 3vᵛ⁸
388 leaves $1,2,3,4 (-¶1, ¶4, A1, 2A1;
+ 2V5, 2X5, 3V5) ff. B1-3V5 numbered
                         (cont'd)

Chaucer. Woorkes. . . . . 1561.   (Cont'd)

i-ccclxxviij, (Ciii for Ciiii, Cxli for Cli,
CCxxv for CCxxiiii, ccxxxij-ccclxxxix for
ccxxxiiii-ccclxvi, ccclxiij for ccclxii)
Woodcuts: Title, ¶T (2),+1. Woodcut initials
      throughout.
Binding: ¶ 1-5 pasted to stubs supplied by
      binder.
Notes: Bookplate of Henry James Blakeley. TP con-
      tains signatures of Jimmy Cunningham, Har-
      riot Neale, and Samuel Bond.

ASCHAM, ROGER   1515-1568   # 43

The Scholemaster. Or, plaine and perfite way of
teachyng children, to understand, write, and
speake, the Latin tong, etc. London: Printed by
John Day, 1570.

Coll.: 4⁰ A² B-T⁴ 74 leaves
     ff. [1-6] 1-67 [68]
Contents: A: title; A1ᵛ: blank; A2-A2ᵛ: dedication
      to"Sir William Cecil, principall Secre-
      tarie to the Queens most excellent ma-
                    (cont'd)

Ascham.   (Cont'd)

      iestie" by Margaret Ascham; B-B4ᵛ: Preface;
      C-T3ᵛ: text; T4: woodcut colophon; T4ᵛ:
      blank.

[GUNTHERUS, RUFFUS]   # 44
Onomasticon puerile Argentinense. II. Argentorati
[Strassburg]: Iosias Rihelius, 1571.   (BL)

Coll.: 8⁰: A⁸-C⁸ [D⁹(D⁸+1)]. 33 Leaves (15.5X9.8 cm.)

Binding: Modern boards reproducing early printed page.

Notes: Quire D may or may not have been added in binding.
All the leaves were originally blank and in this copy
are now covered with Latin paradigms and notes on Latin
grammar in various hands. D9 has been laid in and
pasted to loose flyleaf by latest binder; verso contains

           Gunther, Onomasticon

two names: "Pertinax _____ " and "Sigismundus
Stein(r?)peis, Anno I.VI.XIII." D9 may originally
have been a flyleaf which in a later binding was given
its present place.

S 6-6-47 L&B

TABULAE ABCDARIAE PUERILES   # 45

Printed on a half-sheet (33.2 x 21.3cm) within a
decorative border: 3 alphabets (upper case Roman,
lower case Roman, lower case Black Letter); vowels,
dipthongs, consonants (in Roman); syllabulary (in
Black Letter); Pater Noster (in black Letter).
[1544].

Notes: McKell #S-3-16-55.

Anon.   # 46
REYNEKE VOSS de olde nye gedrucket/mit sidlykein vor-
stande unde schonen Figuren/erlüchtet unde vorbetext.
Rostock: Stephan Molleman. In Vorlegginge Laurentz
Albrechts/Bockhandler in Lübeck. 1592.

Coll: 4⁰: (in 8's) A-2L⁸ 272 leaves. Fols. 3-272 num-
     bered III-CCLXXI, CCLXXIII. (19 x 14.7cm)

Illus: Woodcut title page, 44 woodcuts (many repeats),
     and 54 woodcut figures (mainly repeats).

Notes: Bookplate of Heinrich Grote, Reichs-Fryherr zu
     Schauen.

Aesop.   619-564 BC   # 47

Les Fables et sa vie d'Esope, en François & Allemand.
[Lyons:] Jean de Tournes, 1606.

Title: LES FABLES | et sa vie d'Esope, | [printer's dec-
oration] | En François & Allemand, pour l'uti-|
lite & recreation de ceux qui se plai-|sent esdites
deux langues, ou qui les | veulent apprendre,
[preceding four lines in italic] | Avec trois amples
indices | [printer's device] | PAR IEAN DE TOVRNES
[a short rule] | M. DC. VI.

Coll: 16°: ¶8 2¶4 A-Z8 a4 200 leaves (11.9 X 7.5cm)
Pp. i-xxiv 1-376

(cont'd)

Aesop.   (Cont'd)

Les Fables et sa vie d'Esope. 1606.

Contents: ¶1: Title, as above. ¶1v: Jean de tournes au
Lecteur. ¶2v: Tables du Fables. ¶6: Register du
Fabeln Esopi. ¶8v: Table des bonnes instruc-
tions...." A1: La Vie D'Esope, composee en
Grec par Maxime Planndes...& depuis translatee
en Francois....Das Leben Esopi...vud auss dem
Franzosischen in Deutsche sprach gestelt,
[French and German in parallel columns]. K6:
Les Fables....Die Fabeln....[French and German
in parallel columns].

(cont'd)

Aesop.   (Cont'd)

Les Fables et sa vie d'Esope. 1606.

Illus: 97 woodcuts in text of the fables.

48

Topsell, Edward   (d. 1638?)

The Historie of Foure-footed Beastes. London:
Printed by William Jaggard, 1607.

Coll: 2° A6 ¶6 2¶10 B-V6 3A-3X6 3Y8 $1,2,3
(2V2 for 2V2, 2X3 for X3, 2Y2 for 2Y; -A1, A2,
L2, ¶1, 3P2;±2 ¶4, 3Y4) 408 leaves . Pp.[i-
xliv] 1-228 [229] 230-445[446] 447-720 [721]
722-757 [758-772] (59 for 56, 101 for 100, 435
for 437, 436 for 438, 551-553 for 521-523, 550-
551 for 549-550, 580 for 586, 193 for 593, 732 for
632, 643 for 644 , 741 for 704, 722 for 723).

(cont'd)

Topsell. Historie of Foure-footed Beastes. 1607
(Cont'd)

Illus: Numerous woodcuts in text.

Binding: Bound together with Topsell's Historie
of Serpents, 1608. q.v.

Notes: McKell copy lacks A1, 3Y8. STC 24123.

Topsell, Edward   (d. 1638?)   # 49

The Historie of Serpents. Or, The second Booke of
living Creatures. London: Printed by William
Jaggard, 1608.

Coll: 2° A-V6 2A-2H6 168 leaves $1,2,3,4(L3 for
L2, A4 for 2A4, B4 for 2B4, F3 for 2F3; -A1,
A2, B2, B4, C4, M4, E4, F4, 2H4). Pp. [i-xii]
1-2 [3] 4-233 [234] 235-315 [316-324] (59 for
89, 73 for 93, 141 for 149, 193 for 195, 282
for 283).

Illus: Numerous wood   cuts in text.

(cont'd)

Topsell. Historie of Serpents. 1608 (Cont'd)

Binding: Bound with Topsell's Historie of Foure-
footed beastes. 1607. q.v.

Notes: STC 24124

50

Withals, John   fl. 1553-

A Dictionarie in English and Latin for Children, and
young beginners: compiled at the first by John
Withals, (with the phrases, and rythmicall, and pro-
verbiall verses & c, which have bin added to the
same, by Levvis Evans, and Abr. Fleming, successively.)
And (newlie) now augmented . . . By William Clerk.
London: Printed by Thomas Purfoot, 1608.

Coll: sm 8° A4 B-Gg8 Hh3 239 leaves (15 x 8.9cm)
Pp. [i-viii, 1] 2-146 ("147" mispaginated 174)

(cont'd)

Withals, John   A Dictionarie . . . . (Cont'd)

148-277("278" mispaginated 678) 279-356 ("357"
mispaginated 337) 358-414 ("415" mispaginated
405) 416-458 ("459" mispaginated 457) 460-461
("462" mispaginated 464) 463-464 [465-466, 467-
470: the table].

Binding: Rebound in full speckled calf, gilt borders.
Notes: STC # 25885. Bookplate of "Evln P H Shirley
De Eatington."

Johnson, Richard   1573-1659   # 51

The Famous Historie of the Seaven Champions of
Christendome, 2 parts.

Part I:
THE FAMVS HISTORIE OF the Seauen Champions of
Christendome. Saint GEORGE of England . . . (4 lines)
Shewing their Honourable Battels . . . (7 lines)
whereunto is added by the first Author, the true manner
of their deaths . . . (3 lines). a rule   The
first Part. a rule LONDON, Printed by William
Stansby.

(cont'd)

The Famous Historie of the Seuen Champions of
Christendome. Part I.   (Cont'd)

Coll: 4°   A-2E⁴   112 leaves.

Contents: A1: Title (verso blank); A2: author's
epistle "To all courteous readers,"; A2ᵛ:
"The Authors Muse Vpon the History,"; A3:
Text; 2E3ᵛ: "Thus gentle Reader, hast thou
heard the first part . . . which if . . .
thou accept of, my weary Muse shall take in
hand the second part. . . . From my house at
London, the two and twenty day of May 1616."

(
                        (cont'd)

The Famous History . . . . Part I.   (Cont'd)

Notes: U2 and U3 are reversed in order. McKell copy
lacks 2E4. STC (14682) lists an edition of both
parts by Stansby in 1626.

Part II:
THE FAMOVS HISTORY OF the Seven Champions of
Christendome. a rule The Second Part. a rule
LIKEWISE Shewing the Princely Prowesse of Saint
GEORGES three Sonnes, the lively   Sparks of Nobility.
a rule Whereunto is added by the first Author, the
true   manner of their deaths, being seven famous

(
                        (cont'd)

The Famous History . . . . Part II.   (Cont'd)

tragedies: and how they came to be called the seven
Saints of Christendome. ornament LONDON, Printed
by Richard Bishop.

Coll: 4°   A-2C⁴   104 leaves

Contents: A2: Title (verso blank); A3: Dedication to
Lord William Howard; A4: Epistle to the
gentle reader; B1: text

Notes: McKell copy lacks A1 and 2C4. STC (14683) lists
a 1639 edition of both parts by Bishop.

(
                        (cont'd)

The Famous History . . . . Parts I & II (Cont'd)

Binding: Bound together in 18th century Russian. BMC
(v. 117, col. 837) lists a copy of these two
in one binding, and gives a probable date of
1620.

(

#52

Stevens, Charles and John Liebault

Maison Rustique, or, The Country Farme. Translated
into English by Richard Surflet. Now newly re-
viewed, corrected, and augmented with divers large
additions . . . . And The Husbandrie of France,
Italie, and Spaine, reconciled and made to agree
with ours here in England. By Gervase Markham.
London: Printed by Adam Islip for John Bill, 1616.

Coll: 2° ¶³ A-3R⁶ 3S⁵ $1,2,3 386 leaves (28.5 x
18.6cm) Pp. [1-xviii] 1-732 [733-754]

(
                       (cont'd)

Stevens and Liebault. Maison Rustique. 1616.
(Cont'd)

Binding: By Rivierre & Son, designed by Mary Houston.
Green morocco, gilt tooled leaves and
flowers within gilt lines forming decorative geometric forms. Seven blind stamped
cameos depicting young man engaged in
various seasonal activities in brown morocco inlays. Title, date, and authors'
names gilt stamped on red morocco inlays.
Gilt edged.
Notes: Bookplate of   Clarence E. Bemens

(

#53

Heywood, Thomas   1574?-1641

Tunaikeion: or, Nine Bookes of Various History
Concerninge Women . . . . London: Printed by Adam
Islip, 1624.

Coll: 2°   A-2Q⁶ 2R⁵ 239 leaves (28.5 x 18.1cm)
Pp. [1-xii] 1-466.
Illus: Engraved title page.
Notes: McKell copy lacks A1; A2-E4 repaired at
outer edges. #8-2-27-46.

(

#54

Denison, Stephen.

The White Wolfe or, A Sermon Preached at Paul's Cross,
Feb. 11 . . . 1627 . . . . London, Printed by George
Miller, for Robert Milbourne, 1627.

THE | WHITE WOLFE | OR, | A Sermon Preached at Pavls |
Croffe, Feb. 11. being the laft Sunday in Hillarie |
Tearme, Anno 1627. and printed fomewhat more largely |
then the time would permit | at that prefent to deliuer. |
Wherein Faction is vnmasked, and iustly taxed |
without malice, for the fafetie of weake | Christians. |
Efpecially, the Hetheringtonian faction growne | very

O
                       (cont'd)

The White Wolfe . . . .   (Cont'd)

impudent in this Citie of late | yeeres, is here
confuted. | [a rule] | By Stephen Denison, Minifter of
Katherine | Cree-Church, London. | [a rule] | I. Tim. I.
3. | As I befought thee to abide ftill at Ephefus, when
I went into Macedonia, that | thou mighteft charge fome,
that they teach no other Doctrine. | Hier. aduerf.
LVCIFERIAN. | Quomodo deftructae | funt Diaboli Ciuitates,
& infina, hoc eft in feculorum | confummatione, idola
corruerunt | [a rule] | [device] | London, | Printed by
George Miller, for Robert | Milbovrne, 1627.

(

The White Wolfe . . . .   (Cont'd)

Coll: 4° (8's ?) [1] A⁶ B-K⁴ L²   44 leaves
Pp. [xii] 1-76.

Illus: Woodcuts: A6ᵛ, "The Wolfe in a | fheepes skinne."
and F2ᵛ, "The Wolfe in his | owne skinne."

Binding: Tan calf.

Contents: A1: Title page, within a decorative border;
A2: "TO THE HIGH And Mighty Prince CHARLES
. . . ."; A5: "To the Chriftian Reader.";
B1: Text; 12ᵛ: ". . . The Fecond Im-
O
                       (cont'd)

The White Wolfe . . . . (Cont'd)

     pression. FINIS."

Notes: Nameplate of G. Harold Culshaw, Coll. Exon.
Oxon. in inside front cover. After L2 is inserted a stub of a leaf to which is pasted a
fragment of a sheet containing Ms note concerning the contents of at least 2 books.

Johnson, Richard   1573-1659   **# 55**

JOHNSON, RICHARD. The Famous Historie of the Seaven
Champions of Christendome. . . . The first Part.
London: Printed by William Stansby, n.d.[1626?].

Coll: 4°: A-2E⁴. 112 leaves.

McKell copy lacks 2E4.

Johnson, Richard   1573-1659

JOHNSON, RICHARD. The Famous Historie of the Seaven
Champions of Christendome. . . . The first Part.
London: Printed by William Stansby, n.d.[1626?].

Coll: 4°: A-2E⁴. 112 leaves.

McKell copy lacks 2E4.

55

Johnson, Richard   1573-1659   **# 56**

JOHNSON, RICHARD. The Famous History of the Seven
Champions of Christendome. The Second Part.
. . . London: Printed by Richard Bishop, n.d.
[1639?].

Coll.: 4°: A-2C⁴. 104 leaves.

McKell copy lacks A1 and 2C4. Bound together in 18th
c. russian. BM Cat., v. 117, col. 837, lists a copy
of these two in one binding, and gives a probable
date of 1620. McKell # R-2-21-44-B

 # 56.1

Da Vinci, Leonardo 1452-1519

TRATTATO | DELLA PITTVRA | DI LIONARDO | DA VINCI, |
Nouamente dato in luce, con la vita dell'istresso
autore, scritta | DA RAFAELLE DV FRESNE. | Si sono
giunti i tri libri pittura, & il trattato della
statua | di Leon Battista Alberti, con la vita
medesimo [rectangular engraving, 17.2 x 14.2cm]
IN PARIGI, | Giacomo Langlois, stampatore ordinario
del rè Christianissimo, al | monte S. Genovesa, dirim-
petto alla fontana, all' insegna della Regina di
pace. | [a rule | M.DC.LI. | CON PRIVILEGIO DEL RE.
             (cont'd)

DaVinci, Leonardo. TRATTATO. (Cont'd)

Coll: 2° a̅4 a̅² ¹4 A-o⁴ [F]² q² R⁴ x² 2e̅² 2I²,
a-h⁴ 112 leaves. $1,2,3 (-C3, K3, Q2, 2e,
2I2. Pp. [i, ii, iii, iv, v-vi, vii-viii, ix-
xvii, xviii-xx]:(a list of art books printed in
Europe from 1549-1649) 1-58 (59-62 mispaginated 61-64) 63-104 (105-106 mispaginated 103-
104) 107-112 [113-126] [i, ii, iii-xii]:
(Life of Alberti by DuFresne including a list
of Alberti's printed works)[1] 2-18 (61 for
19) 20-47 [48] 49- 62 [63-64]
             (cont'd)

DaVinci, Leonardo TRATTATO (Cont'd)

Plates: Engraved portrait of Alberti (following
     1). 97 in the text, including diagrams,
     headpieces and tailpieces. All by R.
     Lochon. Copper and wood.
Binding: Contemporary vellum over boards, gilt
     stamped, title and flowers on spine.
Notes: R3ᵛ-R4ᵛ and h4-h4ᵛ are blank; H1 was
     machined after engraving; R4ᵛ picked up
     surplus ink from forme for R1ᵛ. Heraldic
     bookplate of Rolle : "Nec Rege, Nec Populo
     Sed Utroque."

 # 57

Codrington, Robert, M.A.

Aesop's Fables with his Life: in English, French,
and Latin by Rob. Codrington M. A. Illustrated with
One Hundred and Twelve Sculptures by Francis Barlow.
London: Printed by William Godbid for Francis
Barlow, and are to be sold by Ann Seile . . . and
Edward Powell . . . . MDCLXVI.

Coll: 2° [a]², b², B-L², B-I², B-R², [2] R²,
S-T² Pp. [i-viii,] 1-40, 1-31 [32], 1-17,
2-221 [222-223, 224]. (35.1 x 23cm)
             (cont'd)

Codrington. Aesop's Fables. 1666. (Cont'd)

Illus: Engraved frontispiece, title page, + 110 in
     text by Francis Barlow.
Notes: The engraved title page gives 1665 as date
     and refers to 110 sculptures by Barlow.
     McKell #S-1-30-51-B Pp. [222-223]: table of
     contents; p. [224]: blank.

Comenius, Joh[annes] Amos. 1592-1670   **# 58**

Orbis Sensualium Pictus Quadrilinguis, Hoc est, Omnium
fundamentalium in mundo rerum, & in vita actionum, Pic-
tura & Nomenclatura, Germanica, Latina, Italica, et
Gallica. Cum titulorum juxta, atq[ue] Vocabulorum Indice.
Noribergae [Nüremberg]: Sumptibus Michaelis & Johan.
Friderici Endterorum, 1666.

Coll: 8°:)(⁸ 2)(⁸ A-3M⁸ 3N⁴ 484 leaves (16.5 X 11cm)
     Leaves A1-2P6 are paginated [1] 2-601

Illus: 152 woodcuts

Notes: Bookplated Emericus Fredericus, Baron de Walderdorf
     [S-12-14-1950-B
     12-15-1950C]

Anon.   #59

The Memories of Monsieur du Vall: Containing the History
of his life and death. Whereunto are annexed his last
speech and epitaph. London: Printed for Henry Brome, at
the Gun near the West-end of St. Paul's, 1670.

Coll: 4°: A-C⁴ 12 leaves Pp. [i-ii] 1-21 [22]

Binding: Rebound

Notes: Bookplate of Howard Pyle

Commenius -2-

Plates: Frontispiece + 155 cuts in text.

Wing C5524. Bookplate of Robert Spearman of
Oldacres, Durham.

Charles Hoole, M.A. 1610-1667

Commenius, Johannes Amos   1592-1670   #60

COMMENIUS, JOHANNIS AMOS. Orbis Sensualium Pictus
. . . The Visible World: or, A Picture and
Nomenclature of all the chief Things that are in
the World; and of Mens Employments therein.
. . . translated into English, By Charles Hoole, M.A.
For the Use of Young Latine-Scholars. London:
Printed by T.R. for S. Mearne, 1672.

Coll.: 8°: A-X⁸. 168 leaves. [xvi], 309 + [11]pp.

                                                        #61

Janeway, James (Jacob Janneway, pseud. 1636?-1674)

A Token For Children. 2 Parts. London: Printed
for Dorman Newman, 1672.

Part I: A Token For Children; Being An Exact
  Account of the Conversion, Holy and Exemplary
  Lives and Joyful Deaths of several young Children.
  . . . London: Printed for Dorman Newman, 1672.

Coll: 12° A⁸ χ² (-χ2) B-D¹² 45 leaves (12 x
6.6cm)
                                         (cont'd)

Janeway. Token for children. 1672.   (Cont'd)

Part II: A Token For Children: The Second Part.
  Being a further Account . . . not published in the
  First Part. . . . London: Printed for D. Newman,
  1672.
  Coll: 12° A⁶ B-F¹² 66 leaves (11.9 x 6.6cm)

Binding: Bound together in 19th century cloth.
         Binder of McKell copy mistakenly exchanged
         quires G-F, Part II, for C-D of Part I.

Notes: No STC #.

Nostradamus, Michael (Michel de Nostredonne,
1503-1566)   #62

The True Prophecies or Prognostications of
Michael Nostradamus, Physician to Henry II.
Francis II. and Charles IX. Kings of France,
And one of the best Astronomers that ever were.
A Work full of Curiosity and Learning. Trans-
lated and Commented by Theophilus de Garencieres,
Doctor in Physick Colleg. London. London,
Printed by Thomas Ratcliffe, and Nathaniel Thomp-
son and are to be sold by John Martin, at the
                                         (cont'd)

Nostradamus   (Cont'd)   2

Bell in St. Pauls Church-yard, Henry Mortlack at
the White Hart in Westminster-Hall, Thomas
Collins, at the Middle-Temple Gate, Edward Thomas,
at the Adam and Eve in Little Britain, Samuel
Lowndes over against Exeter-house in the Strand,
Rob. Bolter, against the south door of the Ex-
change, Jon. Edwin, at the Three Roses in Ludgate
Street, Moses Pits at the White Hart in Little
Britain, 1672.

Coll: 2° (4's) π²a-b² c-e⁴ B-Uuu⁴ 279 leaves
                                         (cont'd)

Nostradamus   (Cont'd)   3

$1,2 (Uuu2 missigned Vvv2; - a1, 2; -b2)
(29.5 x 18.8cm) Pp. [i-ii, iii-iv, v-vi, vii-
viii, ix-xii, xiii-xvi, xvii-xxix, xxx-xxxvi]
1-173 ("174" mispaginated 147) 175-256 ("257"
mispaginated 256) 258-378 (379-380, 381-382
on transposed leaves) 383-488 ("489" mispaginated
881) 490-494 ("495" mispaginated 465; "496"
mispaginated 456) 497-522.

Notes: Ccc2-Ccc3 folded around instead of inside
Ccc1-Ccc4.

Kircher, Athanasius   #63

Arca Noë, in tres libros digesta . . . . Amsterdam:
John Jansson à Waesberge, 1675.

Coll: 2° π-**4 A-2I⁴ 136 leaves $1,2,3 (-*1)
      Pp. [i-xvi] 1-240 [241-256]
Plates: HT, one rold-out, eleven double-leaf, three
  leaf, 2 half-leaf, plus innumerable other
  woodcuts in text. Possibly by G. Decker.
Notes: Half-title pasted on leaf supplied by binder.
  Unless HT was *1, McKell copy lacks *2.

Basile, Giovan[i] Battista   1575 ? - 1632   #64

Il Pentamerone Del Cavalier Giovan Batt Ist a Basile,
Quero Lo Cunto De Li Cunte Trattenemiento de li Pecceril-
li Digian Alesio Abbattritis. Nuamente restampato, e co
tulte le zevemonie corrietto. Al Illustrissimo Sig. e
Padron. Coll. Il Signor Guiseppe Spada. In Roma, M.
D.C. LXX IX, Nella Stamperia de Bartolomeo Lupardi
Stampator Camerale. Con Licenzd de' Superiori.

Coll: 12° a3⁶, A-Cc¹², Dd⁶ 324 leaves (13.3 x 7.2cm)
  Pp. [i-xii] 1-370 ("371" mispaginated 351) 372-
  465 ("466" mispaginated 465) 467-633 [634-636].

Illus: 6 woodcuts + numerous decorations.
                                         (cont'd)

Il Pentamerone Del Cavalier . . . . (Cont'd)

<u>Binding</u>: Vellum covers. Free endpapers front and back.

<u>Notes</u>: McKell # S-6-19-44. "a⁴" missigned a³. Σ 6-7 not
        sewn but inserted. Σb signed.

#65

Godwyn, Tho[mas]   1587-1643

Romanae Historiae Anthologia Recognita et Aucta
An English Exposition of the Roman Antiquities . . .
London: Margaret White for R. Chiswel, 1680.

<u>Coll</u>: 4° A-Oo⁴   148 leaves   (19.1 x 14.2cm)
        Pp. [1-11], iii-iv, v, vi] 1-270, [1-20]
<u>Contents</u>: A: title; A1ᵛ: blank; A2-A2ᵛ: Viro Colen-
        dissimo P. Zohanni Young . . . Decano
        Ornatissimo; A3: Benevololectori; A3ᵛ: a
        short table shewing the argument of every
                                        (cont'd)

Godwyn. Romanae . . . . 1680.   (Cont'd)

        book and section; A4-Mm2ᵛ: text; Mm3-Oo4ᵛ:
        Index rerum et verborum.

<u>Binding</u>: Rebound in red, ½ calf. Marbled endpapers;
        free and paste-down front and rear; 2
        other free endpapers front and rear.

<u>Notes</u>: $1,2 (A1), horizontal chains. Thirteenth
        edition? see STC G. 995. BMC #7702 b2b.
        On [A1] appears "Jno Anby" handwritten in
        ink, and also the inscription "Mrs. Angier,
        1753."

#66

[Shirley, John]

The Most Delectable History of Reynard the Fox.

(1) The Most Delectable | HISTORY | OF | Reynard the Fox. |
        Newly Corrected and Purged, from all grossness | in
        Phrase and Matter. | Augmented and Enlarged with
        sundry Excellent | Morals and expositions upon every
        several Chapter. | To which may now be added a
        Second Part of the said History: | As also the
        Shifts of Reynardine the Son of Reynard the FOX, |
        Together with his Life and Death, &c. | [woodcut
        (7.5 x 10.4cm), signed "EB"] | LONDON, Printed by
                                        (cont'd)

The Most Delectable History of Reynard the Fox. (Cont'd)

T. Ilive, for Edward Brewster, at the | Sign of the
Crane in St. Pauls Church-Yard. 1681.

<u>Coll</u>: 4° A-U⁴   80 leaves $2 (except A1).

<u>Illus</u>: 56 woodcuts signed "EB"; cut on title page
        repeated on A3ᵛ. On C1 woodcut is turned.

<u>Contents</u>: A1: Title (verso blank); A2: Epistle to the
        Reader. A3: Text; U3: Table of Contents;
        U4: "Books printed for, and sold by Edward
                                        (cont'd)

The Most Delectable History of Reynard the Fox. (Cont'd)

        Brewster at the Crane in St. Pauls Church-
        yard, 1701"

<u>Notes</u>: STC (S3509A) lists only a 1667 edition by T.
        Ilive for Edward Brewster.

(2) THE | Most Pleasant and Delightful | HISTORY | OF |
        REYNARD the FOX. | THE SECOND PART. | Containing Much
        Matter of Pleasure and Content. | WRITTEN For the
        Delight of young Men, Pleasure of the | Aged, and
        Profit of all. | To which is added many Excellent
                                        (cont'd)

The Most Delectable History of Reynard the Fox (2)
        (Cont'd)

Morals. | [a rule] | Here read the FOX . . . (3 couplets,
6 lines, in italic). . . and did for his Treason die. |
[a rule] | LONDON, Printed by A.M. and R.R. for Ed-|
ward Brewster, at the Sign of the Crane in St. | Pauls
Church-yard, 1681

<u>Coll</u>: 4° A-O⁴   56 leaves $2 (except A1)

<u>Illus</u>: 15 woodcuts, all from the first part.

<u>Contents</u>: A1: Title (verso blank); A2: To the reader;
                                        (cont'd)

The Most Delectable History of Reynard the Fox (2)
        (Cont'd)

        A3: Contents; B1: Text; O4: Postscript;
        O4ᵛ: "Books printed for, and sold by Edward
        Brewster . . . 1681."

<u>Notes</u>: STC # (?): S3512

(3) THE SHIFTS of | REYNARDINE | The SON of | Reynard the
        Fox, | Or a Pleasant | HISTORY | OF HIS | LIFE and DEATH
        . | Full of Variety, &c. And may fitly be applied | to
        the Late Times. | Now Published for the Reformation
                                        (cont'd)

The Most Delectable History of Reynard the Fox (3)
        (Cont'd)

of Mens | Manners. | [a rule] | Rare antecedentem . . .
(2 lines) | [a rule] | LONDON, | Printed by T. F. for
Edward Brewster at the | Crane in | St. Pauls-Church-Yard,
and Thomas Passenger at the | Three Bibles on London-
Bridge. 1684.

<u>Coll</u>: 4° A-X⁴   84 leaves Pp. viii [1] 2-160.

<u>Contents</u>: A1: Title; A2: To the reader; A3: Contents;
        B1: Text.

                                        (cont'd)

The Most Delectable History of Reynard the Fox (3)
        (Cont'd)

<u>Binding</u>: The three preceding titles are bound together.

Anon   #67

The Life and Death of Mother Shipton . . . Licens'd and Entred according to Order. London: Printed for W. Harris, and are to be sold by him in Dunnings-Alley, without Bishops-Gate, 1687.

Coll: 4°   A⁴-B³ C⁴ D³ E¹ D³ 18 leaves (21 x 16.7cm) Pp. [i-vi] 1-30

Illus: Woodcut frontispiece (with horizontal chain lines).

Binding: Rebound

(cont'd)

Life and Death of Mother Shipton. 1687 (Cont'd)

Notes: Except for the frontispiece, the book has vertical chain lines. The rebinding has prohibited a truer collation. Bookplates of Howard Pyle.

Behn, Mrs. A [phra].   1640-1689   #68

The Widdow Ranter, or, The History of Bacon in Virginia A Tragi-Comedy, Acted by their Majesties Servants. London: James Knapton, 1690.

Coll: 4°   A-H⁴ $1,2 (-A1) 32 leaves. (19.9 x 15cm) Pp. [i, ii, iii-iv v-vi, vii, viii] 1-56.

Contents: A: title; A^v: blank; A2-A2^v: to the much honoured Madam Welldon, signed G[eorge] J [enkins?] ; A3-A3^v: Prologue and epilogue

(cont'd)

Behn. Widdow Ranter . . . . 1690.   (Cont'd)

by John Dryden; A4: dramatis personae; A4^v: books newly printed for James Knapton; B2-H4^v: text.

Binding: Rebound in full calf. Marbled free and paste-down endpapers.

Notes: STC 1774.

Le Clerc, Seb [astian]   1637-1714   #69

Figures De La Passion D. N. S. Iesus Christ. Presentees a Madame Madame De Maintenon, Par son tres humble et tres obeiss? Serviteur Seb. le Clerc. Paris: Chez Audran Graveur Ordinaire du Roy rue S¹ Jacques aus deux Piliers d'or Avec Privilege. [ca 1692].

Coll: 8° π², 2π,1⁶, 2A, 3-5⁶, 6A, 7³ (7.1,+7.2-7.3) 38 leaves (14.6 x 23.6cm) Ff. 38. Unpaginated.

Plates: A book of pasted down plates: each is approx. 5.5-6.0 x 9cm. Title page is a woodcut, unnumbered but conside red #1; the others are

(cont'd)

Figures De La Passion D. N. S. Iesus Christ.   (Cont'd)

numbered consecutively from 2-36. Collation refers to leaves not plates.

Notes: Bookplate of Arthur Perigal.

[Perrault-D'armancour, Pierre]   (1678-1700)   #70

Recueil de Pieces Curieuses et Nouvelles, Tant en Prose qu'en Vers. Thirty parts in Five volumes. La Haye: Adrian Moetjens, 1694-1701.

I...1694. Coll: 12°: *⁴ A-D¹² E⁸ | F-K¹² | L-P¹² | Q-V¹² X-2B¹² 2C-2G¹² 360 leaves (14.8 X 8.0cm) Pp. [i-viii] 1-111 [112] [113-114] 115-230 [231-232] [233-234] 235-351 [352] [353-354] 355-470 [471-472] [473-474] 475-496, 493-586 [587-588] [589-590] 591-698 [699-708]

II...1694. Coll: 12°: A-D¹² E¹⁰ | F-K¹² | L-P¹² | Q-V¹² | X-2B¹² | 2C-2G¹² 358 leaves (14.8 X 8.0cm) Pp. [1-4]

[Perrault-D'armancour]

Recueil de Pieces Curieuses, five vol., 1694-1701.

5-114 [115-116] [117-118] 119-234 [235-236] [237-238] 239-354 [355-356] [357-358] 359-474 [475-476] [477-478] 479-594 [595-596] [597-598] 599-706 [707-716]

III...1695. Coll: 12°: A-D¹² E²P-I¹²K⁸ | F-I¹²K⁸ | L-O¹²P⁸ | Q-T12V⁸ | X-2A¹²2B⁸ | 2C-2F¹²2G⁸ 336 leaves (14.8 X 8.0cm) Pp. [1-4] 5-110 [111-112] [113-114] 115-222 [223-224] [225-226] 227-334 [335-336] [337-338] 339-446 [447-448] [449-450] 451-558 [559-560] [561-562] 563-662 [663-672]

[Perrault-D'armancour]

Recueil de Pieces Curieuses, five vol., 1694-1701.

IV...1695. Coll: 12°: A-E¹² | F-K¹² | L-P¹² | Q-V¹² X-2A¹² 2B⁸ | 2C-2G¹² 356 leaves (14.8 X 8.0cm) [1-2] 3-117 [118-120] [121-122] 123-238 [239-240] [241-242] 243-358 [359-360] [361-362] 363-477 [478-480] [481-482] 483-591 [592] [593-594] 595-705 [706-712]

V...1696-1701. Coll: 12°: A-E¹² | F-K¹² | L-P¹² | Q-V¹² | X-2B¹² | 2C-2G¹² 360 leaves (14.8 X 8.0cm) Pp. [1-2] 3-118 [119-120] [121-122] 123-238 [239-240] [241-242] 243-357 [358-360] [361-362] 363-432,431-476 [477-478] [479-480] 481-597 [598] [599-600] 599-708

[Perrault-D'armancour]

Recueil de Pieces Curieuses, five vol., 1694-1701.

Binding: Bound by Trautz-Bauzounet in full green crushed levant morocco, with gilt monogram of Comte de Lurde in the corners and repeated four times on spine.

Notes: Six parts in each volume, each part with a separate title page. Table des pieces at the end of each volume. Bookplate of Baron de Lurde.

DENNE, [HENRY] (b. 1671). # 71

Poem on the taking of Namur by his majesty. London:
R. Cumberland, 1695.

Title Page: [A1] : Within double rules: A | POEM | ON THE |
TAKING | OF | NAMUR, | By His MAJESTY. | [a rule] | - - - - Tu
maximus Ille es, | Vnus qui nobis cunctando restituis
Rem. | Virgil | [a rule] | By Mr. DENNE | [a rule] | LONDON, |
Printed for R. Cumberland, at the Angel in | St. Paul's
Church-yard, 1695.

Coll.: 2⁰: [A²] B-C². 6 Leaves (30.1X18.3 cm.).
Pp. [i-iv] 1-8 (pp. in parens centered in hdl.)

Denne, Poem 2

Contents: [A1] : TP (verso blank). [A2] : Dedication to
Lord Cutts (and on verso). B1: [a double rule] | ON THE |
SIEGE | OF | NAMUR. | [2] 1i: "Once more, my Muse, thy
William is thy Theme,". C2ᵛ: . . . [a rule] | FINIS. |
[a rule]

Unbound.

Notes: Not listed by Wing. Dedication signed Henry
Denne, Trinity College, Cambridge. Probably the
Henry Denne who, according to Venn, was born 1671,

Denne, Poem 3

son of Thomas B. Denne, educated at St. Paul's,
matriculated Trinity, April 5, 1689; Scholar, 1693;
B.A. 1693-4.

Jole, W. # 72

The Father's Blessing Penned for the Instruction
of His Children. London: Printed for Hugh
Newman, 1696.

Coll: 12⁰ A-D¹² 48 leaves (5.5 x 10.7cm). 96pp.
Illus: small woodcuts in text
Contents: D4: "Youth's Recreation" (a dialogue of
         questions and answers in verse form)
Notes: McKell copy lacks D12, which has been re-
       placed by photostats of D12 from later
       edition. Not in Wing. #S-5-12-51-B

[Perrault, D'armancour, Pierre] 1678-1700 # 73

Histoires ou Contes du tems passe. Avec des
Moralitez. A Trevoux: de l'Imprimerie de S.A.
Seren. Mons. Prince Souverain de Dombre. 1697.

Coll: 12⁰ a⁴ A-G¹² H⁸ 96 leaves (14.05 x 7.7cm)

Illus: Woodcuts used as headpieces to each of the
       tales depict seasonal occupations and have
       no connection with the tales.
Notes: This is a poor, unauthorized edition of that
       of Paris of the same year.

H [arris] B [enjamin, Sr.] (fl 1673-1716) # 74

The Holy Bible; Containing, The Old and New
Testaments, with the Apocrypha. Done into Verse
by B.H. for the Benefit of weak Memories. London:
Printed for Benj. Harris, Senior, 1698.

Coll: 32⁰ A-D⁸ (-D7, D8) 30 leaves (7.3 x 5.4cm)

Plates: 3 woodcuts.

Notes: No STC #.

THE HOLY BIBLE. Containing the Old and New Testament. # 75
London: Printed by Charles Bell and the Executrix of
Thomas Newcomb, 1698.

Coll: A-2E¹⁸ 504 leaves (12.5 X 6.6cm). $10: A-DFLOPY
(Y6 unsigned); $11: EG-KMNQ-XZ-2E.

Notes: Wing B2373, but not on Y6 title page for New Testa-
       ment is dated 1699. McKell copy lacks G4, 2E17,
       2E18.

HORNBOOK (IVORY) # 76

Paddle-shaped ivory. 17th century English. (9 x 4.4cm)
With handle (2.3cm in length). Lower case letters plus
ampersand cut in one side, upper case on the other.
Both sides of handle decorated with flower.

Notes: Lower edge, and part of handle broken.
       Belonged to the Larwell family, who emigrated
       Deptford, Kent, and settled in Wooster, Ohio.
       #M-10-1-47-B

HORNBOOK (SILVER) # 77

Printed in Roman on paper with filigree silver frame.
17th century English. (8.8 x 6cm) With handle (3.2cm
in length). Contains lower case alphabet, vowels,
upper case alphabet, combinations of vowels with b, c,
and d, in anterior and post position, sign of the Cross,
and Pater Noster.

Children's Books Dating From 1700

78

[Abbott, Jacob]   1803-1879

Bruno; or, lessons of fidelity, patience, and self-
denial taught by a dog. New York: Harper and
Brothers, [entered 1854].

Coll: 8° A-K⁸   80 leaves (16.8 x 13.2cm) Pp.[1-
vii] viii [ix-xii, 13] 14-160.

Plates: Frontispiece by J. W. Orr, Sc., N.Y.; and
numerous wood engravings.

Notes: Harper's Story Books series. Bookplate of
Henry Matier   )& Co., Belfast.

79

[Abbott, Jacob]   1803-1879

The Harper Establishment; or, how the story books
are made. ["Harper's Story Books Series."] New York:
Harper & Brothers, Publishers, n.d. [1855?].

Coll: 8° A-K⁸   80 leaves (16.7 x 13.3cm) Pp.
[1-vii] viii [ix-xii, 13] 14-160.

Plates: Frontispiece +woodcuts.

Binding: Yellow free and paste-down endpapers.

80

Abbott, Jacob   1803-1879

Learning to Talk; or, entertaining and instructive
lessons in the use of language. Illustrated with
one hundred and seventy engravings. "Harper's
Picture Books for the Nursery, The Little Learner."
New York: Harper & Brothers, 1874. Pp.[1-vii] viii
[ix] x [11] 12-192.

Illus: Frontispiece + numerous black and
white illus. throughout

81

Abbot, Jacob. 1803-1879

The Little Philosopher, For Schools and Families; designed to teach children to think and to reason about
common things; and to illustrate for parents and
teachers methods of instructing and interesting children. With a copious introduction, explaining fully the
method of using the book. By Jacog Abbot, principal
of Mount Vernon School. London: L. B. Seely, 1833.
                    6
Coll: 12° A-L [M]M2- P⁶ 90 leaves (14x8.9cm) Pp. []-2,
3] 4-6 [7] 3-16 []7] 18-43 [44] 45-70 [7]] 72-97

(cont'd)

Abbot, The Little Philosopher... (Cont'd)

Coll:(Cont'd) [98] 99-120 [121] 122-146 [147]
148-177 [178-171; blank]

Illus: Engraved frontispiece

Notes: M₁ unsigned.

82

[Abbott, Jacob]   1803-1879

Mary Bell; a Franconia story, by the author of the
Rollo Books. New York: Harper & Brothers, [1850].

Coll: 8° [A]⁸ B-C⁸ [D]⁸ E-N⁸ 104 leaves (16.3 x
10.8cm) Pp. [1-x] 11-204,[1] 2-4: adverts.

Illus: Frontispiece +numerous engravings in text
by W. Roberts.

83

[Abbott, Jacob]   1803-1879

Orkney The Peacemaker; or, the various ways of
settling disputes. ["Harper's Story Books."] New
York: Harper & Brothers, Publishers, n.d. [1857?]

Coll: 8° A-K⁸   80 leaves (16.8 x 13.5cm)
Pp.[1]-xiii, 14-160.

Plates: Frontispiece,+woodcut vignette title page;
several full-page illus. included in pp.

84

[Abbott, Jacob]   1803-1879

Rollo at School. Boston: Weeks, Jordan, and
Company, 1839.

Coll: 12° (6s) [1⁶ 2-16 6 17³ 99 leaves (16.5 x
10.3cm) Pp. [1-7] 8-10 [11-12] 13-44 [45-46]
47-134 [135-136] 137-166 [167-168] 169-197
[198].

Illus: Engraved frontispiece + 3 full page engravings.

Notes: First ed.

85

[Abbott, Jacob]   1803-1879

Rollo in Switzerland. "Rollo's Tour in Europe."
Boston: W. J. Reynolds and Company, 1854.

Coll: 8° [1]⁸ 2-5⁸ [6-7]⁸ 8-13⁸ 104 leaves
(16.3 x 11.1cm) Pp. [1-6] 7-8 [9-10] 11-197
[198]+7: adverts + 3: blank.

Plates: Frontispiece + engraved series title page+3;
numerous engravings throughout text by
Baker-Andrew.

86

Abbott, Jacob.   1803-1879

Rollo in Switzerland. Frontispiece by John More.
["Rollo's Tour in Europe Series."] New York:
Sheldon and Company, 1864. Pp.[1-6] 7-221 [222].

Plates: Frontispiece,+series title +1: engraved by
Baker-Smith-Andrew. 11 other engravings in
text. Series title and title page are
cancels.

Notes: Not a first ed.

[Abbott, Jacob]   1803-1879   #87

Rollo on the Atlantic. ["Rollo's Tour in Europe."]
Boston: W. J. Reynolds and Co., 1853.

Coll: 8° [A]⁸ B-I⁸ J-N⁸ 112 leaves (16.6 x 11cm)
Pp. [1-4] 5-220 + 4: adverts.

Illus: Frontispiece, title page and numerous other
engravings throughout text by Baker-Smith-
Andrew.

Notes: Not a first ed.

[Abbott, Jacob]   1803-1879   #88

Rollo's Experiments. Boston: Weeks, Jordan, and
Company, 1839.

Coll: 12° (6s) 1⁴ 2-15⁶ 88 leaves (16.5 x 10.5cm)
Pp. [i-vi, 11] 12-180.

Illus: "Frontispiece" woodcut +4 others.
Binding: Stabbed.
Notes: First ed.   1964.70

[Abbott, Jacob]   1803-1879   #89

Rollo's Philosophy. (Fire). New York: Sheldon
and Company, [1868]. Pp. [1-5] 6 [7] 8 [9] 10-92

Plates: 3 by Baker-Andrew

Binding: Fly leaves and free and paste-down endpapers
front and back.
Notes: Not a first ed.

[Abbott, Jacob]   1803-1879   #90

Rollo's Travels. Boston: William Crosby and
Company, 1840.

Coll: 12" (6s) 1-15⁶ 16⁵ (16·1+4) 95 leaves
(15.8 x 10.5cm) Pp. [i-vi, 7] 8-189 [190].

Illus: Frontispiece woodcut +3.
Binding: Stabbed
Notes: First ed.

ABC-Books

    see also

        Henkel, Ambrosius. *Das Kleine ABC-Buch.*
           Newmarket, Va., 1819.

        Neues Unterhaltendes ABC Sillabir-und Lese-
           buch von I.X.N. Nurnberg, 1820.

        The New Royal ABC Book . . . . J.L. Marks.

        Rebus ABC. McLoughlin Bros.

                        (cont'd)

ABC-Books (Cont'd)

    see

        The Young Child's ABC; or, First Book.
          New York & Baltimore, 1820.

    and see under

        Alphabet.

                             #91

The ABC Both in Latyn & Englyshe: being a
Facsimile reprint of the earliest extant English
Reading Book. With an introduction by E.S.
Shuckburgh, M.A. London: Elliot Stock, 1889.
Pp. [iii] iv-xii [1-18].

Anon.   #92

The A,B,C. With the Church of England Catechism. To which
is annexed, Prayers used in the academy of our Saviour;
and another for Easter-Day. Philadelphia: Printed by
Young, Stewart, and Mc Culloch, in Chestnut-Street, No. 7,
below Third-Street, 1785.

Coll: 12°: A⁶ 6 leaves (Approx. 18.8 X 11.8cm) Pp. [1-2,3]
        4-12

Illus: Engraved title
Binding: Rebound in boards
Notes: Uncut. Rosenbach #99

Abecedaire   #93

Nouvel Abecedaire, ou Alphabet Syllabique, Contenant les
premiers elemens de la lecture, les prières journalières,
les principes de la bonne education en douze strophes,
quelques historiettes et fables aussi intéressantes qu'instructives pour la jeunesse, et une fable pour apprendre
à compter. Nouvelle-Orleans: Chez Godin, Libraire, 1847.

Coll: 16° [1²⁴] 24 leaves (13.9 x 11.2cm) Pp. [1-3] 4-48

Illus: Engravings throughout

About, Edmond [Pseud of Francois Valentin] 1828-1885   #94

Le Roi Des Montagnes. Illustree par Gustave Doré.
Cinquième Edition. Paris: Librairie de L.
Hachette et Cie, 1861. Pp. [vi] +372].

Illus: Numerous engravings throughout text, including
      10 full-page.
Binding: By Chatelin in three-quarter morocco with
      gilt monogram of Duc de Chartres on spine.
Notes: First issue with Doré illustrations.

 # 15

Anon

An Account of the Constitution of the Present State of
Great Britain . . . . Adorn'd with cuts. a revision of
an earlier unknown edition. London: Pr. F. J. Newbery,
[1759?]

Coll: 12⁰   π A²B-2B⁶ 2C² 149 leaves (13.3 x 8.4cm)
[2]+iv+292pp.

Plates: Engraved frontispiece and title page +6.

Binding: Full calf

(cont'd)

An Account of the Constitution of the Present State of
Great Britain . . . .   (Cont'd)

Notes: Roscoe # 1(1); Muir gives 1765 as date, and
Welsh (p. 233) gives 1759.

 # 16

Adam, Alexander. 1741-1809

The Rudiments of Latin Grammar. By Alexander Adam, LL.D.
Rector of the high school of Edinburgh. Second Troy Edi-
tion, abridged from the Third Edinburgh Edition. Recom-
mended by the President and Trustees of Williams' College,
to be used by those who are intended for that seminary.
Published according to act of Congress. Troy: Printed by
Parker and Bliss, for Themselves, and for Obadiah Penniman,
Albany, 1809.
Coll: 12⁰: A-W⁶ 126 leaves (17.6 X 10.2cm) Pp. [1-5]
6-252

 # 97

Adams, Andy   1859-1935

The Log of a Cowboy: a narrative of the old trail
days. Illustrated by E. Boyd Smith. Boston and
New York: Houghton, Mifflin and Company, May 1903.
Pp.[x 1]2-387 [388: colophon for Riverside Press].

Plates: Frontispiece + 5 illustrations

Binding: Bound by Jas. MacDonald Co., N.Y. (boxed
first ed.)

 # 99

[Adams, William Taylor] Oliver Optic, pseud
1822-1897

The Boat Club; or, the Bunkers of Rippleton. A
Tale for Boys by Oliver Optic. Boston: Lee and
Shepard, 1869. Pp. [1-4] 5-8 [9-10] 11-252 [253-
54: blank].

Plates: Frontispiece

#100

[Adams, William Taylor] Oliver Optic, pseud., 1822-
1897

The Boat Club; or, The Bunkers of Rippleton. Boston:
Brown, Bazin, and Company, 1855.

Coll: 12⁰ 1-21⁶ 126 leaves (17 x 11cm) Pp. [1- 2]
3 [4] 5-8 [9-10] 11-252 [253-254: blank]
Plates: Frontispiece +3
Binding: Yellow free and paste-down endpapers.
Notes: Obsolete signings present

 # 101

[Adams, William Taylor] Oliver Optic, pseud., 1822-
1897
Field and Forest; or, the fortunes of a farmer. By
Oliver Optic. Illustrated [by S. C. Kilburn]. On-
ward and Upward Series. Boston: Lee and Shepard
Publishers; New York: Lee, Shepard, and Dillingham,
1871. Pp. [1-6] 7-288.

Plates: Frontispiece +13.

 # 102

[Adams, William Taylor] Oliver Optic, pseud
1822-1897

Hope and Have; or, Fanny Grant among the Indians.
By Oliver Optic. No. 5, "Woodville Stories" series.
Boston: Lee and Shepard, 1868. Pp. [1-4] 5-283;
[1-4: adverts].

Plates: Frontispiece & half-title vignette by
Champney.

 # 103

[Adams, William Taylor] Oliver Optic, pseud., 1822-
1897

In Doors and Out; or, Views from the Chimney Corner.
Boston: Brown, Bazin, and Company, 1855.

Coll: 12⁰ (signed in 6's, gathered in 12's) 1-13¹²
14¹⁰ 166 leaves. Pp. [1-4] 5-9 [10] 11-330
[331-332 are blank]. (19 x 11.9cm)
Plates: Frontispiece +5: signed "Baker."
Binding: Yellow free and paste-down endpapers.
Notes: First ed. Pp.[1-4: adverts.

 # 104

[Adams, William Taylor] Oliver Optic, pseud., 1822-
1897
Little by Little; or, the cruise of the Flyaway
. . . . By Oliver Optic. Boston: Crosby, Nichols,
Lee & Co.; Cincinnati: Rickey, Mallory & Co., 1861.
Pp. 280.

Plates: Frontispiece & half-title vignette by
Andrew Filmer.
Notes: First ed. ?

 # 105

[Adams, William Taylor] Oliver Optic, pseud., 1822-1897

On Time; or, the young captain of the Ucayga steamer. By Oliver Optic. [Illustrated.] Boston Lee and Shepard, 1870. Pp. [i-vi,] 7-282, [1-6 of adverts.]

Plates: Frontispiece, illustrated title page + 6.

 # 106

[Adams, William Taylor] Oliver Optic, pseud., 1822-1897

Switch Off; or, the war of the students. By Oliver Optic. [Illustrated.] Boston: Lee and Shepard, 1870. Pp. [i-v,] 6-288.

Plates: Frontispiece, illustrated title page + 6.

 # 107

[Adams, William Taylor] Oliver Optic, pseud., 1822-1897

The Yacht Club; or, the young boat-builder. By Oliver Optic. Illustrated [by John Andrewson ?] The Yacht Club Series. Boston: Lee and Shepard Publishers; New York: Lee, Shepard, and Dillingham, 1876. Pp. [1-2] 3-340; [1-4 adverts bound in at end.]

Plates: Frontispiece + 12.

 # 109

Ade, George   1866-1944

Fables in Slang. Illustrated by Clyde J. Newman. Chicago & New York: Herbert S. Stone and Company, 1900. Pp. [i-xii,] 1-205 [206].

Illus: 45 full-page cuts.

Notes: First edition.

 # 110

Ade, George   1866-1944

The Old Time Saloon. New York: Ray Long & Richard R. Smith, Inc., 1931. Pp. [i-xii], 1-174.

Plates: Frontispiece + 11 + illustrated endpapers:(by various artists).

Notes: First edition. #416 of a special edition signed by author.

 # 111

Anon

The Adventures of Little Dog Trim and His Funny Companions. London: Printed and Published by G. Martin, n.d. [1810?].

Coll: 8° [A^16] 16 leaves (15.6 x 10 cm) not paginated

Plates: 16 colored engravings, numbered.

Binding: Original orange wrappers: color engraving pasted to front; Martin adverts. on attached endpaper, front and back.

Notes: Printing and illustrations on facing pages, alternating with blank facing pages.

 # 113

Aesop.   619-564 BC

The Aesop for Children. With pictures by Milo Winter. Chicago: Rand McNally & Co., [1919]. Pp. [1]-112.

Illus: Frontispiece + several other illustrations.

 # 114

Aesop   619-564 B.C.

Aesop's Fables. Rev. T. James, M.A., ed. Philadelphia: J.B. Lippincott & Co., 1855.

Coll: 12° 1-17^6 [18]^2 104 leaves. (14.8 x 9.6cm) Pp. [i] ii-xx, 21-208.

Illus: "Frontispiece," engraved title page + cuts.

 # 115

Aesop   619-564 BC

Aesop's Fables. A new translation by V. S. Vernon Jones with an introduction by G. K. Chesterton and illustrations by Arthur Rackham. New York: Doubleday Page & Co.; London: William Heinemann, 1924. Pp. [i-iv] v-xi [xii] xiii-xxix [xxx] 1-223 [224].

Plates: Frontispiece + 12 color illustrations. Many pen and ink illustrations, including 19 full-page.

 # 116

Aesop   . 619-564 B.C.

Claude Dalbanne/ Livres a Gravures Imprimés a Lyon an XVe Siecle/ Les/ Subtiles Fables/ D'Esope/ Lyon Mathieu Husz/ 1486/ Notice de J. Bastin/ Lyon. Copyright by Claude Dalbanne, [1926]. Pp. [i-iv, 1] 2-191 [192].

Illus: Frontispiece + several other illustrations.

Notes: Unbound.

Aesop   619-564B.C.   **# 117**

La Morale Des Enfans, choix de Fables D'Esope a la
portée du jeune age; avec vingt figures en taille-
douce. A Paris: Chez Genets jeune, Libraire, rue
de Thionville, no. 1846, 1805.

<u>Coll</u>: Oblong 8° π⁴, A-B⁸   20 leaves. Pp. [i-iv] v-
viii, [1] 2-32.

<u>Plates</u>: 20 copper plate engravings bound in at end and
numbered.

<u>Binding</u>: Wrappers.

Aesop.   619-564 BC   **# 118**

Select Fables of Aesop and Others, with instructive applications. Embellished with numerous [13] cuts. London: Printed for E. Newbery, n.d. [1790?].

<u>Coll</u>: 16°   A-H⁸   64 leaves (10.9 x 7.7cm) vi +7-
127 + [1] pp.

<u>Binding</u>: Dutch floral boards. H8 forms rear paste-down
endpaper.

<u>Notes</u>: Roscoe # 7(2). Bookplate of Percival Merritt.

Anon   **# 119**

The Affecting History of the Children in the Wood.
Embellished with [wood] cuts. Hartford: Printed
by John Babcock, 1798.

<u>Coll</u>: [1]¹⁶ 16 leaves (11.9 x 6.5cm) Pp. [1, 2-5]
6-29 [30-31, 32].
<u>Contents</u>: [1·11ᵛ - 1·12ʳ]: "Story of Three Robbers"
[1·12ᵛ - 1·14ʳ]: "The Fox, the Cat and
the Spider, a Fable" ; [1·14ʳ - 1·15ᵛ]:
contains riddles.

                                           (cont'd)

The Affecting History of the Children . . . . (Cont'd)

<u>Illus</u>: 10 woodcuts.
<u>Binding</u>: Rose wrappers.
<u>Notes</u>: [1·1ʳ] and [1·16ᵛ] are pasted to blank
wrappers. A prose version of the tale, perhaps the first in America. Welch 169.2.
See also The Children in the Wood. An
Affecting Tale. Cooperstown . . . . 1837.

Agnew, Georgette   **#120**

Let's Pretend. Illustrated by Ernest H. Shepard.
London: J. Saville & Co., Ltd., 1927. Pp. [1-8], 9-
64

<u>Illus</u>: numerous illustrations throughout text.

<u>Binding</u>: Dust cover

[Aikin, Lucy 1781-1864 Mary Godolphin, pseud]   **# 121**

Robinson Crusoe in Words of One Syllable.
Illustrated. New York: McLoughlin Brothers,
Publishers, 1882. Pp. [11, 1] 2-93.

<u>Plates</u>: Color frontispiece: "Crusoe taking a
load from the ship to the shore."
(Illustrator unknown) + 5 illustrations
in color.
<u>Binding</u>: Cover (illustrated cloth over boards)
bears 1898 copyright of McLoughlin
Brothers.

[Aikin, Lucy] 1781-1864 Mary Godolphin, pseud   **# 122**

Sandford and Merton, in words of one syllable. By
Mary Godolphin. New York: McLoughlin Brothers,
Publishers, n.d. Pp. [1-5] 6-144 [145-146].

<u>Plates</u>: Frontispiece + 5 illustrations in color.

[Aikin, Lucy] 1781-1864 Mary Godolphin, pseud   **#123**

The Swiss Family Robinson in Words of One Syllable.
By Mary Godolphin. New York: George Routledge &
Sons, n.d. Pp. [1-iv, 1] 2-165 [166-72 : adverts].

<u>Plates</u>: Frontispiece + 7.

Ainsworth, William Harrison   1805-1882   **# 124**

The Flitch of Bacon: or, the custom of Dunmow. Illustrated by John Gilbert. London: George Routledge &
Co., 1854.

<u>Coll</u>: 8 A⁶B-AA⁸ BB⁴ 194 leaves (16.2 x 10.1cm)
Pp. [1]-xii, [1]-376.

<u>Plates</u>: Frontispiece + 7

<u>Binding</u>: Marbled free and paste-down endpaper; ¼ calf
over marbled boards.

Aladdin and the Wonderful Lamp

         see

                    The Story of Aladdin and the Wonderful
                    Lamp. Illustrated by John Kettelwell.
                    Knopf, 1928.

Alcott, Louisa M[ay]   1832-1888   # 125

An Old Fashioned Girl. With Illustrations. Boston:
Roberts Brothers, 1871. Pp. [1-3] 4 [5] 6 [1] 2-378.

Plates: 2 frontispieces +2, engraved by W. H. Morse.

Notes: Not a first printing. Blanck # 163. (1870)

Alcott, Louisa M[ay]   1832-1888   # 126

Little Men: life at Plumfield with Jo's Boys.
Boston: Roberts Brothers, 1871. Pp. [i-viii] 1-376.

Plates: Engraved frontispiece +3.

Notes: First American ed. Blanck # 167.

Alcott, Louisa M[ay]   1832-1888   # 127

Under the Lilacs. Illustrated by H. Wolf. Boston:
Roberts Brothers, 1878. Pp. [i-vi] 1-305 [306] 6:
adverts.

Plates: Engraved frontispiece +3. Picture facing
p. 260 is signed H. Wolf.

Notes: First ed. Blanck # 188.

Alcott, William A.

        see

        Confessions of a School Master, s.v., 'C'

Aldrich, Thomas Bailey   1836-1907   # 128

The Ballad of Babie Bell and Other Poems. New York:
Rudd and Carleton, 1859.

Coll: 12° π⁶[1]⁶ 2⁶ 3⁶ ... 60 leaves
(18.7 x 11.8cm) Pp. [i-v] vi [vii-x] 11-117 [118]
+ 2 blank.

Notes: McKell copy lacks π1.

Aldrich, Thomas Bailey   1836-1907   # 129

The Story of a Bad Boy. Illustrated by A. B. Frost.
Boston and New York: Houghton, Mifflin and Company,
1895. Pp. [1-2, i-iii] iv-viii [ix-xi] xii-xiii [xiv,
1] 2-286.

Illus: Frontispiece +8 full-page.

Notes: Preface by T[homas] B[ailey] A[ldrich], dated
1894.

Aldrich, Thomas Bailey (1836-1907

        see

                Our Young Folks; An Illustrated Magazine
                for Boys and Girls. No. 52 (April,
                1869 [contains "One Memorable Night,"
                Ch. VII, and "The Adventures of a
                Fourth," Ch. VIII of The Story of A
                Bad Boy]).

Alexander, Caleb, A.M. 1775-1828   # 131

The Young Ladies' and Gentlemen's Spelling Book: or a
new and improved plan; containing a criterion of rightly
spelling and pronouncing the English language: interspersed with many easy lessons, in reading, entertaining
fables and collections of moral sentences. Intended for
the use of common schools. [First Worcester Edition],
Worcester: Printed by I. Thomas & Son, Sold wholesale
and retail by them; also, by Thomas and Andrew, and
other booksellers in Boston, 1799.

Coll: 12°: A-M⁶ 72 leaves (16.3 X 10.2cm) Pp. [i-vi]
        vii-xii [13] 14-115 ('116' mispaginated 115) 117-144
                                                (Cont'd)

Alexander, Caleb, A.M. 1775-1828 (Cont'd)

The Young Ladies' and Gentlemen's Spelling Book. 1799.

Illus: Woodcut frontispiece +8 woodcuts in text

Notes: Frontispiece labeled "First Worcester Edition"

Alger, Horatio, Jr.   1832-1899   # 132

Ben, the Luggage Boy; or, among the wharves. [Vol. V
of 6 vols: "Ragged Dick Series."] Boston: Loring,
Publisher, 1870. Pp. [i-vii] viii [9] 10-290.

Plates: Engraved title +3, by Kinnersley.

133

Alger, Horatio, Jr.   1832-1899

Fame and Fortune; or, the progress of Richard Hunter. [Vol. II of 6 vols: "Ragged Dick Series."] Boston: Loring, Publisher, 1868. Pp. [i-vi] vii-viii, 9-279 [280].

Plates: Engraved title + 3, by N. Y. Kinnersley.

Notes: First ed.

134

Alger, Horatio, Jr.   1832-1899

Mark, the Match Boy; or, Richard Hunter's Ward. [Vol. III of 6 vols: "Ragged Dick Series."] Boston: Loring, Publisher, 1869. Pp. [i-vi] vii-viii, 9-276.

Plates: Engraved title + 3 by Kinnersley.

Notes: First ed.

135

Alger, Horatio, Jr.   1832-1899

Ragged Dick; or, street life in New York: with the boot-blacks. Decorative title page by N. Y. Kinnersley. [Vol. I of 6 vols: "Ragged Dick Series."] Boston: Loring, Publisher, 1868. Pp. [i-vi] vii-viii, 9-296.

Plates: Engraved title plus 2: by Kinnersley.

Notes: McKell copy lacks plate facing p. 48. First state of first ed. Plus another copy of same state with) missing plate. McKell # G-8-11-44-B

136

Alger, Horatio, Jr.   1832-1899

Rough and Ready; or, life among the New York newsboys. [Vol IV of 6 vols: "Ragged Dick Series."] Boston: Loring, Publisher, 1869. Pp. [1-8] 9-300.

Plates: Frontispiece + engraved title + 2, by Kinnersley.

137

Alger, Horatio Jr. 1832-1899

The Western Boy. [New York: Street and Smith, 1878].

Pagination: [1-9] 10-258 [259-260]

Notes: Front loose endpaper Recto bears author's autograph and erased pencil markings of which Blanck's letter to McKell [September 28, 1942] says "...my guess is that Alger or somebody in the publisher's office, made the notes since they refer to the possibility of making illustrations for the story."
First ed.; "appeared originally in the New York Weekly, June 30-September 15, 1873." (Jacob Blanck to McKell (September 15, 1942). "The first edition of Alger's...'Rags) to Riches' juveniles"

138

Alger, Horatio, Jr.   1832-1899

The Young Adventurer; or, Tom's trip across the plains. [The Pacific Series.] Boston: Loring, Publisher, 1878. Pp. [i-iv, 1-5] 6 [9] 10-293 [294].

Plates: Engraved frontispiece + series title, + 1, by Halm.

Notes: First ed.

139

Anon.

Ali Baba and the Forty Thieves; or The Wood-Cutter and his Female Slave. An Eastern Tale. With eight coloured engravings. A new Edition, corrected, and adapted for Juvenile readers of the present time, By a Lady. London: [Printed by Dean and Munday for] Dean and Munday, and A.K. Newman and Co. n.d.

Coll: 18°: [1^{18}] Archaic signatures are present 18 leaves (14.3 X 8.9^{cm}.) Pp. [1-3] 4-36

Plates: Fold out frontispiece with seven hand color engravings

Binding: Pink printed wrappers

140

Anon

Ali Baba; or the Forty Thieves. A tale for the nursery. With three copper plates. A new edition. London: Printed for Tabart and Co., [by J. Diggens, St. Ann's Lane] 1807.

Coll: 8° A^{16} 16 leaves $A2-A8 (12 x 7.8cm) Pp. [1-3] 4-33 [34-36: adverts]

Plates: Front + 2 on conjugate leaves included in pagination; all hand colored

Binding: Pink wrappers; initial and final pages as paste-   (cont'd)

Ali Baba; or the Forty Thieves 1807   (Cont'd)

down endpapers.

Notes: Horizontal chain lines; bookplate of E. C., which has inscription "Prodesse Quam Conspici."

141

Anon

Ali-Baba oujes Quarante Voleurs. Illustrations par H. Thiriet. Toulouse-Paris B. Sirven Éditeur, n.d.

Coll: Demy 4° 6 leaves (29.2 x 22.5cm) Pp. [1-12].
Illus: 8 pages in color
Binding: Stiff pictorial wrappers in color.
Notes: Text printed on verso of front cover and recto of rear cover.

Alice, Cousin (pseud)

    see

        Haven, Alice Bradley (Neal) 1826-1863

Almanack (Swiss, 1811)   # *145*

Alpenrosen. ein Schweizer-Almanack aus das Jahr 1811. Herausgegeben von Kuhn, Meisner, Wyk, u.a. mit Kupfern von König, u.a. Bern, bey S. S. Bergdorfer; Leipzig, bey Fried, Aug. Leo. Gedrucht bey Ludwig Albrecht Waller , n.d.

<u>Coll</u>: 16° 1^2, $\times^2$, $2-16^8$, 17^4 136 leaves (12.2 x 9.5cm) Pp. [1] ii-viii,[1] 2-247 [248].
<u>Plates</u>: Frontispiece+ title+ 9 (4 fold-outs + 5 woodengravings by König, Usteri, Volmar)
<u>Notes</u>: #S-12-29-54

Allen, Willis Boyd. 1855-1938   # *143*

The Sleeping Beauty. A Christmas story of to-day. By Willis Boyd Allen. Boston: 1899. Pp. [1]-[44].

Almanac

    see also

        The Comic Almanac for 1845.

Almanack, St. Nicholas (Dutch), 1798   # *144*

Nieuwen Aengenaemen En Nuttigen St. Nicholaes Almanach, Voor Het Jaer Ons Heere Jesu-Christi 1798. Dienende voor presenties der Kinderen, en voor opgroeyende Jeugd van beyde geflachten; inhoudende: .... Dit Werksen is vercierd met 45. Geestige Plaeties, konstig gesneden; als mede 23 kleyne Figuerkens, Seer vermaekelyk voor de Kinderen van allen ouderdom. Men Heeft'er bygevoegd het Leven van den Heyligen Nicolaus, Bisschop, seyne teere Liefde tot de Kinderen, syne Christelyke Deugden van mildaedigheyd, en goede Werken tot synen Evennaesten. Ersten (Deel. Den Prys is seven Stuyvers, in-   (cont'd)

Anon.   # *146*

[Alphabet Caricature, Diabolique et Grotesque. Paris: Chez Humbert. rue St. Jacques. 65. Litt. Vayron, Paris] [n.d.]

<u>Coll</u>: 16°; 13 foldout panels (14x 10.5 cm.).

<u>Illus</u>: Colored lithographs plus black on white lithographs.

Almanack, St. Nicholas (Dutch). (Cont'd)

genaeyd. Tot Maestricht. Men vind-se te koopen tot Gend, by Ph. en P. Gimblet, Gebroeders, Boekdruk. op de Koornmerkt.

<u>Coll</u>: oblong 4° A-G^4, G bis^2, H^4, I-L^4, M^2, A^4 56 leaves (10.1 x 17.8cm) Pp. i-viii, 1-56 (Gbis: 57 58-60) 57-64 65-92 , 1-8.

<u>Illus</u>: 47 woodcuts

<u>Binding</u>: Blue pictorial wrappers.   (cont'd)

    # *147*

Alphabet Imperial Militaire, Contenant: 1° L'art D'apprende a lire en encrivant. 2° Quelques Notions des premiens Klémens qui composent une Armée de Terre et de Mer. 3° Valeur des Nombres arabs et romains. 4° Nouveaux Poids et Mesures, etc. 5° Les Principes d'Arithmétique. Orné d'un Frontispice, et de huit Planches representant vingt-six Sujets. Paris: Chez Lebel et Guitel, Libraires. Rue des Prêtres-St.-Germain-l'Auxerrais, N$^{\circ}$ 27. 1810.

<u>Coll</u>: 12° 1-10^4, 11-124 (-12.2 and 12.4), 134   (cont'd)

Almanack, St. Nicholas (Dutch). (Cont'd)

<u>Notes</u>: McKell #s; S-3-1-49-B; 3-1-49-L. G bis is an insert; M^2 is pasted to a piece that is laid in to the binding. Horizontal chains.

Alphabet Imperial Militaire. (Cont'd)

70 leaves (16.9 x 9.7cm) Pp. [1] 2-40 (41-48 missing) 49-140.

<u>Plates</u>: Color front 15 engravings (14 color) on five plates. (These are all that are present in the McKell copy)
<u>Notes</u>: McKell copy missing gathering #4, hence some engravings may be missing. Leaf 12 misfolded; leaf 12.4 misfolded as well as cancelled.

Alphabets

see also

Baum, Lyman Frank. The Navy Alphabet.
1900.
Cook, Mrs. Harriet N. The Scripture Al-
phabet of Animals. 1842.
A History of the Big Letters, s.v., 'H'.
Maja's Alphabet. Philadelphia, 1852.
Nonsense Alphabet. Chicago, 1896.
(cont'd)

Alphabets (Cont'd)

see also

The Poetic Gift: or alphabet in rhyme.
New Haven, S. Babcock.
Welsh, Mrs. T. The Musical Alphabet . . . .
New York: Mesier, 1835.

 # 148

Altsheler, Joseph A[lexander]   1862-1919

The Lords of the Wild: a story of the old New York
border. Illustrated by Charles L. Wren. New York
and London: D. Appleton and Company, 1919. Pp. [i-x]
1-297 [298].

Plates: Frontispiece + 3.

Binding: Dust cover

Notes: Author presentation copy. Boxed first ed.

 # 149

Altsheler, Joseph A[lexander]   1862-1919

The Sun of Saratoga: a romance of Burgoyne's Surren-
der. New York: D. Appleton and Company, 1897. Pp.
[i-vi] 1-313 [314].

Notes: First ed.

American, an

see

Prime, Benjamin J. Muscipula Sive Cambromyomachia: the mouse trap. . . .
Entered 1840.

Anon   **# 150**

The American Musical Miscellany: a collection of the
newest and most approved songs, set to music. Northampton, Mass.: By Andrew Wright, for Daniel Wright and
Company. Sold by them, and S. Butler, in Northampton;
by I. Thomas, Jun. in Worcester; by F. Barker, in
Greenfield; and by the principal booksellers in Boston,
1798.

Coll: 12° A-D⁶ 2D-Z⁶ 150 leaves (16.5 x 10.5cm) Pp.
[i-v] vi [vii] viii-xii [13] 14-300.

Notes: Signatures J and V not used; D used twice

Anon.   **# 151**

The American Primer; or, An Easy Introduction to Spelling
and Reading. Fourth improved edition. Philadelphia:
Printed and sold by Mathew Carey..., 1813.

Coll: 12°: [A¹²] [B⁶] ([B⁶] folded inside [A¹²]) 18 leaves
(13.2 X 8.2cm) Pp. [1-2] 3-36

Illus: Woodcuts

Binding: Printed and illustrated mouse wrappers.

Notes: [B₁] signed "A₂" Evans #27716, Rosenbach #468

Anon   **# 152**

The American Star. Being a choice collection of the
most approved patriotic and other songs. Second
edition. Richmond: Peter Cottom, 1817.

Coll: 12° 2_A-S⁶ 110 leaves (14.2 x 8.5cm) Pp.
[1-iv, 1-3] 4-210 [211], 212-215 [216: advert for
Peter Cottom].
Plates: Fold-out plate opp. p. 6 ("Perry's Victory").
Illustrated title page.
Notes: Very early printing of "Star Spangled Banner."
Third verse follows wording of 1815 hand bill
printing.

American Sunday School Union   **# 153 - 202**

50 Vols. Philadelphia: American Sunday School Union,
n.d. [Ca 1845].

Coll: Each volume, except vol. 4, contains three
gatherings of 8 leaves (48pp.). Hence 24° ?

Binding: Uniformly bound in quarter red calf, gilt
lettering over marbled boards, and in a wooden
case with glass front.

(1) God Made the World, Cain and Abel, Adam and Eve,
The Fall of Man, Noah and the Flood, Abraham. Pp.
(cont'd)

American Sunday School Union   (Cont'd)

1-8, 1-8, 1-8, 1-8, 1-8, 1-8. Six woodcuts.
(2) Isaac, Jacob and Esau, Joseph-Part First, Joseph-
Part Second, Joseph-Part Third, Joseph-Part Fourth.
Pp. 1-8, 1-8, 1-8, 1-8, 1-8, 1-8. Six woodcuts.
(3) Moses-Part First, Moses-Part Second, Moses-Part
Third, Moses-Part Fourth, Moses-Part Fifth, Miriam.
Pp. 1-8, 1-8, 1-8, 1-8, 1-8, 1-8. Six woodcuts, 1
vignette.
(4) Aaron, Joshua, Jane and Her Brother William (No.
101-I Series), The Rainy Sunday (No. 102-I Series),
Scripture Stories for Young Children (No. 103-1
Series). Third gathering contains four leaves
only. Pp. 1-8, 1-8,   1-8, 1-8, 1-8. 18 wood-
(cont'd)

American Sunday School Union   (Cont'd)

cuts. Each of last three stories has separate title page.

(5) The Lost Child, The African Woman, The Lord's Day, Fighting, The Glass of Whiskey, The Child in the Bulrushes. Pp. 1-8, 1-8, 1-8, 1-8, 1-8, 1-8. 18 woodcuts. Title page for each story.

(6) Isaac, Who Loves Children?, The Sunday School Boy, The Sunday School Girl, Little Prayers for Little Children, My Father. Pp. 1-8, 1-8, 1-8, 1-8, 1-8, 1-8. 18 woodcuts. Title page for each story.

(7) The Loaf of Bread, Heaven, The Drowning Boy, Be Neat, A Visit to Father, The Sower. Pp. 1-8, 1-8 1-8, 1-8, 1-8, 1-8,   Nineteen woodcuts.

(cont'd)

American Sunday School Union   (Cont'd)

Title page for each story.

(8) The Stilts, Cain, Read and You Will Know, The Best Child, How to be Saved, The Sabbath Breaker. Pp. 1-8, 1-8, 1-8, 1-8, 1-8, 1-8. 18 woodcuts. Title page for each story.

(9) History of Birds (No. 201-II Series), The Shepherd Boy (No. 202-II Series), The Lily: A Pretty Book for Good Children (No. 203-II Series), Pp. [1] 2-15 [16], [1-3] 4-15 [16], [1] 2-15 [16]. Forty-two woodcuts. Each title page contains same woodcut.

(10) The Four Seasons (No. 204-II Series), History of

(cont'd)

American Sunday School Union   (Cont'd)

Beasts (No. 205-II Series), The Fourth Commandment with some account of Jack Riot and Will Mindful (No. 206-II Series). Pp. [1] 2-16, [1] 2-15 [16], 1-2] 3-16. Forty-two woodcuts. Each title page contains the same woodcut.

(11) James and His Little Sister (No. 207-II Series), The Kind Little Girl (No. 208-II Series), The Falsehood. Pp. [1-2] 3-16, [1-2] 3-15 [16, 1-2] 3-15 [16]. Thirty-three woodcuts. Each title page contains the same woodcut.

(12) Make Haste, The Old Box-Maker, The Drowning Boy Saved, Dr. Franklin's Loan, The Honest Boy, The

(cont'd)

American Sunday School Union   (Cont'd)

Glass of Gin, Questions for Self-Examination, Guilty! Guilty! Guilty!!!, Three Sisters in One Grave, Is It Worth Climbing For, The End of the World, Tribute to Elizabeth Baker. Pp. 1-48. Each story covers four pages. Gatherings signed Vol. I-A-C. 4 woodcuts. Only Is It Worth Climbing For has separate title page.

(13) Little Peter and His Library Book, To My Son on Leaving Home, Vanity, The New Bonnet, Work and Thrive, Serious Questions, A Dreadful Thing to Die!, An Address at the Grave of a Sunday-School Child, Short Sayings,   The Kink in the Engine

(cont'd)

American Sunday School Union   (Cont'd)

Rope, Take Care of Your Ears, Every Man in His Place. Pp. 49-96. Each story covers four pages. Eighteen woodcuts. The seventh, eighth, and tenth stories have separate title pages. Gatherings are signed Vol I-D-F.

(14) All the World's on Stilts, Signs, The Fourth Commandment Broken, Little Jane, A Deed of Love, The Lurking Enemy, The Grocery Ruined Him, Harvest Close Upon Seed Time, What is it for a Child to Know the Scriptures?, "Going Apprentice," Pull it up by the Root, The Fish Which Brought Money to Christ. Pp. 1-48. Each story covers four pages.

(cont'd)

American Sunday School Union   (Cont'd)

Twelve woodcuts. Gatherings are signed Vol II- A B-C.

(15) Daily Mercies, Death of Little Mary, The Fruitless Fig-Tree, The Great Canal, The Bible is True, The Home-Made Boy, The Baby is With God, The Wise Man, Traveller's Prayer, Give Us This Day Our Daily Bread, The Flower-Beds, Parental Anxiety. Pp. 49-96. Each story covers four pages. Twelve woodcuts. Gatherings signed Vol II-D-F.

(16) Identical with Vol. 15. Binder's Error.

(17) Short Stories, Anecdotes for Little Boys, The Wooly Bear, The Climber, Human Life, Going to Church.

(cont'd)

American Sunday School Union   (Cont'd)

Pp. [1-2] 3-8, [1-2] 3-8, [1] 2-8, [1] 2-8, [1] 2-8, [1] 2-8. Twenty-six woodcuts. First, second, fifth and sixth stories have separate title pages.

(18) The Fearful Child, The Still and the Spring, The Visit, The Shepherd, Singing, The Parrot. Pp. [1] 2-8, [1] 2-8, [1] 2-8, [1] 2-8, [1] 2-8, [1] 2-8. Twenty-seven woodcuts. Each story has separate title page.

(19) The Lame Dove, The Worth of a Penny, The Converted Child, Fear Not, The Staircase Window, The Free Gift. Pp. [1] 2-8, [1] 2-8, [1] 2-8, [1] 2-8, [1] 2-8, [1] 2-8. 18 woodcuts. Each of first

(cont'd)

American Sunday School Union   (Cont'd)

three stories has separate title page.

(20) Something in Return, Asking Questions, Take Advice, The Borrower, My First Slide, The Rosebud, Faithful Fido, Noah's Ark. Pp. [1] 2-8, [1] 2-8, [1] 2-8, 1-24. Seven woodcuts.

(21) Wisdom of More Value Than Gold, What are Tickets Today, The Bird's Nest, The Old Woodcutter, I miss Thee My Mother, Mistrust Yourself, Sililoquy of a Water-Wagtail, The Family Gathering, The Bird's Nest, "Hold On By The Ropes," The Glow-Worm, The Miser and the Mouse. Pp. 25-72. Fourteen woodcuts.

(cont'd)

American Sunday School Union   (Cont'd)

(22) "Cut Behind! Cut Behind!", Which Shall Give Up?, Home Comforts, Aunt Maria, Small Faults Often End in Great Sins, The Hen and Chickens, The Storm at Sea, Little Fanny, The Call of Samuel. Pp. 73-88, 9-40. Fourteen woodcuts.

(23) The Old Man and His Young Friends, The Pure in Heart, The Wise Choice, The Young Friends, Sabbath Morning, The Happy Child, The Gold of Potosi, The Crooked Fingers, The Copper Mines in Pery's Mountain, The Cricket, The Good Shepherd, Anna and Her Brother, Little Martha, A Little Child's Hymn. Pp. 41-88. Thirteen woodcuts.

(cont'd)

American Sunday School Union   (Cont'd)

(24) Flowers and Weeds, The Little Flower Gatherer, The Bible-Printers, The Unhappy Boy Made Happy, The Honest Cabin-Boy, The Marys of the Bible. Pp. 1-8, 1-8, 1-8, 1-8, 1-8. Six woodcuts.

(25) Nayah The Little Hindoo Convert, The Gold Mine, The Name in the Rock, The Plate of Cherries, The Rose Tree, Charles Dwight. Pp. 1-8, 1-8, 1-8, 1-8, 1-8, 1-8. Six woodcuts.

(26) Do Not Forget to Pray, The Ragged Scholar's Home Made Happy, A Traveller's Story, The Widow's Lamp, The Great Globe, The Serpent in the Garden. Pp. 1-8, 1-8, 1-8, 1-8, 1-8, 1-8. Six woodcuts.

(cont'd)

American Sunday School Union   (Cont'd)

(27) The Two Brothers, The Great Flood, The Favourite Son, The Boy in a Pit, The Captive Boy Who Became a Great Man, The Kind Brother. Pp. 1-8, 1-8, 1-8, 1-8, 1-8, 1-8. Six woodcuts.

(28) The Brickmakers, The Long Journey, The First Lie, Lame Susan. Pp. 1-8, 1-8, [1] 2-16, [1] 2-16. Four woodcuts.

(29) House of the Soul: My Eyes, House of the Soul: My Ears, House of the Soul: My Tongue, House of the Soul: My Heart, House of the Soul: My Hands, House of the Soul: My Feet. Pp. [1] 2-8, [1] 2-8, [1] 2-8, [1] 2-8, [1] 2-8, [1] 2-8. Seven woodcuts.

(cont'd)

American Sunday School Union   (Cont'd)

(30) Little Jane Rebuked, Selfish George, Fourth of July. Pp. [1-3] 4-15 [16], [1] 2-16, [1] 2-16. Three woodcuts. First story has separate title page. Has copyright page indicating 1845.

(31) The Dark Day, Read and Imitate, Vain Little Laura, Vanity in Dress, A Hymn for a Child. Pp. [1] 2-16, [1] 2-16, [1] 2-16. Three woodcuts.

(32) The Infant's Prayer, The Heathen and the Christian, Naomi: The Hindoo Widow. Pp. [1] 2-16, [1] 2-16, [1] 2-16. Three woodcuts. First story has separate title page.

(33) Are You Ready?, The Indian Sisters, The Broken Cup.

(cont'd)

American Sunday School Union   (Cont'd)

Pp. [1] 2-16, [1] 2-16, [1] 2-16. Four woodcuts.

(34) The Secret, James Stibbins; or, Bad Habits Resisted and Overcome, Too Easy. Pp. [1] 2-16, [1] 2-16, [1-2] 3-16. Four woodcuts. Third story has separate title page.

(35) Little Henry, The Wanderer, The Hidden Scissors. Pp. [1-2] 3-16, 1-16, [1-2] 3-16. Three woodcuts. First and third stories have separate title pages.

(36) The Murder, Mossetse The African Orphan Boy, A Little Sermon for a Little Child. Pp. 1-16, [1] 2-16, [1-2] 3-16. Three woodcuts. Third story has separate title page.

(cont'd)

American Sunday School Union   (Cont'd)

(37) Jennie McDowell, The Winter Morning Walk, Letter to My Young Cousin. Pp. [1-2] 3-16, [1-2] 3-16, [1-2] 3-15 [16]. Three woodcuts. Each story has a separate title page.

(38) The Four Seasons, To-Day and To-Morrow, The Pond on the Common. Pp. [1-3] 4-16, [1-2] 3-16, [1-2] 3-16. Three woodcuts. Each story has a separate title page.

(39) Love One Another, The Stranger. Pp. [1-2] 3-32, [1-3] 4-16. Two woodcuts. Each story has a separate title page.

(40) The Pearl-Fisher of Ceylon, Old Jessie The Hindoo

(cont'd)

American Sunday School Union   (Cont'd)

Mother. Pp. 1-32, 1-16. Four woodcuts.

(41) A Lamb of the Fold, Shesh Achurjya. Pp. 1-32, 1-16. Two woodcuts.

(42) Industry Exemplified in the Life of President Dwight, Truth. Pp. [1-4] 5-32, [1-2] 3-16. Frontispiece + one woodcut. Each story has separate title page.

(43) Story of William Tyndale, Congo's Kraal. Pp. 1-32, [1] 2-16. Two woodcuts.

(44) The Blind Beggar, It is Time to Seek the Lord. Pp. [1-4] 5-30 [31-32], 1-16. Two woodcuts. First story has separate title page.

(cont'd)

American Sunday School Union   (Cont'd)

(45) The Inward Monitor, Lessons for Infants in Truth and Duty . . . by W. F. Lloyd. Pp. [1-2] 3-32, 1-16. First story has separate title page.

(46) Mary Edwards. Pp. [1-2] 3 [4] 5-48. One woodcut repeated. Separate title page.

(47) Idle Dick; or, The History of Richard Watson From Didier, Le Vagabond, by Rev. C. Malan. Children Should Come to the Lord Jesus. Pp. [1-5] 6 [7] 8 [9] 10-40 [41-43] 44-47 [48]. Eighteen woodcuts, including three full-page. Title page for Idle Dick.

(48) Divine and Moral Songs for Children. Pp. [1-4] 5-
(cont'd)

American Sunday School Union   (Cont'd)

48. Fourteen woodcuts repeated from earlier volumes in series.

(49) Original Hymns for Sunday Schools. Pp. [1-5] 6-37 [38] 39-48. Two woodcuts.

(50) Wandering John; or, The Prodigal Boy. Pp. [1-4] 5-48. Frontispiece.

American Sunday School Union

see also

The Book of One Hundred Pictures.
Children's Offerings to Heathen Idols.
The First Lie.
George Wilson and His Friend.
The Infant-School Girl.
Kindness to Animals.
The Life of George Wishart, q.v., 'L'.
My Cousin Hester.

(cont'd)

American Sunday School Union   (Cont'd)

see also

Picture Lessons, illustrating moral truths.
The Second Book of One Hundred Pictures.
Slim Jack; or, the history of a circus boy.
Wheeler, Mrs. Charlotte Bickersteth. Memoir of John Lang Bickersteth.
Wonder of Vegetation.

Anon.   # 203.1-2

The American Toilet. New York: Printed and published at Imbert's Lithographic Office, 1827.

Coll: 16°. 20 lithographed leaves. ff [1] 2-20   (11.3 x 9.6cm)

Binding: stabbed

Notes: Lithos and text on Recto; verso blank. Inside rear cover: "S-1-20-45-L"/"S-7-2-46-B"   Plus another copy.

Anon.　　　　　　　　　　　　　　　# 204

The American Tutor's Assistant Revised; or, A Compendious
System of Practical Arithmetic....To which is added, a
course of book-keeping by single entry. Philadelphia:
Printed and sold by Joseph Crukshank, 1813.
Coll: 12°:π² A-R⁶ S¹ 105 leaves (17.45 X 10ᶜᵐ·)
　　　Pp. [i-iv] [1] 2-180. [1] 2-15 [16]. 1-10.
Notes: E₃ and E₄ are missing from the McKell copy.
　　　π1ᴿ: "John G. Dun"

Anon　　　　　　　　　　　　　　　# 205

The Amulet. A Christmas and New Year's present for
MDCCCXLVI. With nine beautiful steel engravings.
Boston: Otis, Broaders & Company, 1846.

Coll: 12° A⁴ B¹⁸ C-X⁶ 148 leaves (17.3 x 11.3cm)
　　　Pp. [i] - [viii, 9] -296.
Plates: Frontispiece (drawn by W. Boxall, engraved
　　　by W. H. Mote); engraved title page ≠ 6. R.
　　　Andrews, printer of engraved title page.
Notes: L. H. Bridgham, printer. McKell copy lacks
　　　plate for p. 227.

Andersen, Hans Christian　1805-1875　　# 206

The Christmas Tree and Other Stories. Illustrated by
G. A. Davis. New York: McLoughlin Bros., n.d.　Pp.[1-
ii, 1] 2-4b.

Illus: Frontispiece + several other illustrations.

Andrewes, Margaret (Hamer)　　　　　# 207

Two Old Ladies, Two Foolish Fairies, and a Tom Cat.
By Maggie Browne. Illustrated by Arthur Rackham [1867
1939], London, Paris & Melbourne: Cassell and Company,
Limited, 1897. Pp. [i] -viii, [9] -190, [1-18 adverts].

Plates: Frontispiece + several other colored
　　　illustrations.

Andrews, Jane　1833-1887　　　　　# 208

Ten Boys Who Lived on the Road From Long Ago to Now.
Boston: Ginn & Company, Publishers, 1903. Pp [i] - [xii]
1- [250].

Plates: Frontispiece + several other illustrations.

Anet, Claude

　　pseud. of

　　　　　Jean Schopfer　1868-1931

Anne de Bretagne　(1477-1514)

　　see

　　　Delaunay, M. L'Abbe.　Le Livre D'Heures
　　　　De La Reine . . . . Paris: MDCCCLXI.

Anon　　　　　　　　　　　　　　　# 211

Arabian Love Tales being romances drawn from the Book
of the Thousand Nights and One Night rendered into
English from the literal French translation of Dr. J. C.
Mardrus by Powys Mathers and illustrated by Lettice
Sandford. London: The Folio Society, 1949. Pp. [i-viii]
ix [x] 1-245 [246].

Illus: Frontispiece + 11 full page black and white line
　　　drawings.

Arabian Nights

　　see

　　　Ali Baba and the Forty Thieves; or the
　　　　woodcutter and his female slave. By
　　　　a Lady. Dean and Munday.

　　　Ali Baba; or the forty thieves. Tabart.

　　　Ali-Baba oujes quarante Voleurs. Paris:
　　　　B. Sirven.

　　　The History of Sinbad, the Sailor. Con-
　　　　　　　　　　　　　　　　　(cont'd)

　　　　　　　　　　　　　　　　　　　　.2

Arabian Nights (Cont'd)

　　see

　　　　taining an account of his seven sur-
　　　　　prising voyages. Glasgow, 1819.

　　　The History of Sinbad the Sailor; Con-
　　　　taining an Account of his several
　　　　surprising voyages and miraculous
　　　　escapes. Boston, 1829.

　　　Little Hunchback. J. Harris, 1817.

　　　　　　　　　　　　　　　　　(cont'd)

Arabian Nights (Cont'd)

  see

    Mathers, Edward Powys, trans. Arabian
    Love Tales being romances drawn
    from the Book of the Thousand
    Nights and One Night . . . .
    Folio Society, 1949.

    New Sinbad the Sailor. Illustrated by
    Barcoot. London: Cowan &
    Standring.

    Olcott, Frances Jenkins, ed. More Tales
                        (cont'd)

3

Arabian Nights (Cont'd)

  see

    from the Arabian Nights. Illustrated
    by Willy Pogany. Henry Holt, 1915.

    The Story of Aladdin and the Wonderful
    Lamp. Knopf, 1928. q.v., '3'.

4

Argus, Arabella (pseud) **# 213**

The Adventures of a Donkey. London: Printed by and
for William Darton, Jun. . . . , 1815.

Coll: 12° (6's) A² B-U⁶ X² 118 leaves (12.9 x
8.5cm) Pp. [1-2, i-ii, 1] 2-231 [232].

Plates: Frontispiece engraving

Notes: First ed.

Argus, Arabella (pseud) **# 214**

Ostentation and Liberality: a tale. By Arabella Argus,
author of "The Juvenile Spectator" ... London:William
Darton and Son, Holborn Hill. 2 Vols, in one 1821 .
Vol I:
Coll: 12° A-S⁶ 108 leaves (14.X 8.2^cm.) Pp. [i-ii,3]
4-216

Plates: Frontispiece dated "1821" + 2 copper engravings
Vol II:
Coll: 12°: B(-B1)-T⁶ 108 leaves (14 X 8.2^cm.) Pp.[1-3]
4-216

Plates: Frontispiece dated "1821" + 2 copper engravings.

Anon **# 215**

The Arithmetical Table Book: or, first lessons in
arithmetic. Newark, N.J.: Printed and Published by
Benjamin Olds. 1844. Pp. [1-3] 4-24.

Coll: 12° [A¹²] (11 x 9.5cm)

Binding: Rust printed wrappers.

[ANON.]. Arithmetic Made familiar and easy to **# 216**
Young Gentlemen and Ladies. Being the Second Volume
of the Circle of the Sciences, &c. The Third
Edition. London: Printed for Newbery and Carnan,
1769.

Coll.: 32° : A-N⁸O¹. 105 leaves (92 X 6.3cm).
[i-x]1-200 pp.

Binding: Blue boards, red leather spine.
Notes: Roscoe #61(3)
Bookplate of Percival Merritt.

Anon **# 217**

Arithmetic Made Familiar and Easy. Being the Second
Volume of the Circle of the Sciences. Fourth Edition.
London: Printed for T. Carnan and F. Newbery, Jr.,
1777.

Coll: 32° A-N⁸ 104 leaves (9.9 x 6.6cm) Pp. [4] +vi,
1-198 ("20-22" misnumbered in reverse order).

Binding: Marbled boards, green vellum spine with paper
label.

Notes: McKell copy lacks B4. Roscoe # 61(4). Book-
      plates of James   Losh and Percival Merritt.

Arnold, Matthew 1822-1888 **# 218**

The Scholar Gypsy & Thyrsis. Illustrated by W.
Russell Flint. London: Philip Lee Warner, 1910.
Pp. [i-x, 1] 2-67 [68].

Illus: Frontispiece +9.

Binding: Dust cover.

Arnold, Thomas James, Esq. 1795-1842 **# 219**

Reynard The Fox. After the German version of Goethe.
By Thomas James Arnold, Esq. With illustrations from
the designs of Wilhelm von Kaulbach. New York: D.
Appleton and Co., 1860. [London: Printed by Richard
Clay, Breadstreet Hill.]

Coll: Lge 8° A-FF⁴, GG² 118 leaves (24.3 x 16.2 cm)
Pp. [i-viii, 1-2] 3-12 [13] 14-19 [20] 21-25 [26]
27-35 [36] 37-60 [61] 62-74 [75] 76-87 [88] 89-90
[91] 92-108 [109] 110-112 [113] 114 [115] 116-128
[129] 130-143 [144] 145-151 [152] 153-160 [161]
                        (cont'd)

Arnold. Reynard. 1860. (Cont'd)

[162-168] 169 [170] 170-173 [174] 175-183 [184]
185-205 [206] 207-208 [209] 210-216 [217] 218-
219 [220] 221 [222] 223-226, [227]: colophon,
228: blank].
Illus: Title page, half title; numerous others, all
      black and white and splendidly pornographic.
Binding: Westley's & Co., London.
Notes: On title page in pencil: "Julia from 'Santa
      Claus' 1859."

Ashford, [Margaret Mary] "Daisy"   1891-   #220

The Young Visitors; or, Mr. Salteena's plan. Preface
by J. M. Barrie. New York: George H. Doran Company,
[1919]. Pp. [i]-[xx, 21]-[106].

Plates: Frontispiece

Notes: Margaret Mary "Daisy" Ashford Devlin supposedly
     wrote this book at the age of nine. Plus another
     copy.

Aunt Ella

     pseud of

           Amy Ella Blanchard   1856-1926

           q.v.

Anon   #224

Atlas Minimus Universalis, or a Geographical
Abridgement Ancient and Modern of the Several
Parts of the Earth. In Fifty-Five Maps. Composed principally for the Use of Schools. London: Wm. Faden, January 1st. 1798.

Coll: 58 unsigned leaves (13.7 x 18cm)
Plates: 55 engraved maps numbered successively in
     arabic (#30 tipped in to #31; "36" misnum-
     bered 26). Plates in color. Engraving done
                 (Cont'd)

Anon   #228

Aunt Louisa's Golden Gift: Comprising Dame Crump,
Hush-a-Bye Baby, Childhood's Delight. With
Eighteen Pages Of Illustrations, Printed In Colors
And Gold. Original Designs By Howard And Herrick.
New York: McLoughlin Bros., n.d. Ff. 23.

Plates: 18 illus. in color

Notes: Justin H. Howard (?) and Henry W. Herrick,
     1824-1906.

Atlas Minimus 1798   (Cont'd)

     by W. Palmer, Islington.

Notes: Ff.[1]: title; ff.[2-3]: contents.

Anon   #229

Aunt Mary's Stories for Children. Illustrated.
Boston: Phillips, Sampson, and Company; New York:
J.C. Derby, n.d. Pp. [i-iii] 4-143 [144].

Plates: Frontispiece + 4.

Atmore, Charles   #225

Serious advice, from a father to his Children, respecting their Conduct in the world; Civil, Moral, and religious. Philadelphia: Printed and sold by J. H. Cunningham, 1819.

Coll: 12° A-C⁶ 18 leaves (13.9 x 8.1cm) Pp. [1-iii]
     iv [5] 6-36.

Plate: Engraved frontispiece

Binding: Blue printed wrappers
Notes: Evans # 47024. v. 1819 [MM]

Austin, Sarah [Taylor], trans.   #231
                         1793-1867

The Story Without an End. Illustrated by William
Harvey. London: Effingham Wilson, Royal Exchange,
1834.

Coll: 8° A-H⁸ χ⁸ 2χ4: blank leaves (13.3 x 10.5cm)
     Pp. [1-v] vi [vii-viii] 9-[128, 1-16: advert
     for Effingham Wilson; 8pp. blank].
Plates: Illustrated title page +13. Thompson, engra-
     ver.
Binding: Blue paper over boards. Free and paste-
     down endpaper.
Notes: F7-F8ᵛ: Advert. for Mrs. Austin's Bible
     selections.

Aulnoy, Louise D'   (c. 1830-   )

     see

         Gouraud, Julie

Bailey, N[athaniel]   -d. 1742   #235

An Universal Etymological English Dictionary. . . .
London: E. Bell, etc., 1721.
Coll: 8° (4's) A⁴, a⁴ B- 1 Lllll⁴, (2)Lllll-(3)
     Lllll,⁴(4)Lllll², Mmmmm-Bbbbbb⁴, Cccccc²
     (20.2 x 12.5cm) Unfoliated, unpaginated.
     454 leaves. $1,2 (-A1, Cccccc2)
Contents: A: title; Aᵛ: blank; A2-A2ᵛ: dedication
     to Frederico Ludovico (prince of Wales);
     A3-A3ᵛ: introduction; a4: abbreviations;
     a4ᵛ: alphabets of the English, Saxon,
                 (cont'd)

Bailey. Universal Etymological . . . . 1721.(Cont'd)

Greek, and Hebrew; B-Cccccc2^v: text and
"Finis"; advert for "The Way to Reading
Made Easy and Delightful in Two Parts.";
erratum for "Gunpowder" i.e., for "Igna-
tius Loyola [whom Bailey said invented
gunpowder] read Bartoldus Schwartz" : :
Binding: Original full-calf.
Notes: BMC 12984, bbblb.

236

Bailey, N[athaniel]   -d.1742

The Universal Etymological Dictionary. The second
edition with many additions. Vol II. London:
Thomas Cox, MDCCXXXI.

Coll: 8° (4's) $1,2 (-A1,-Dd2) A-Sss^4 ,Ttt^2 ,4A-
(4Y2 missigned 4Q2)-5T^4 , 5V-5Y^4 ,52^2
(19.6 x 12cm) Unfoliated, unpaginated 440
leaves.
Contents: A: title; A1^v: blank; A2-A2^v: dedication
to Frederico Ludovico (prince of wales,
signed N.   Bailey; A3-A4: preface;
(cont'd)

(Cont'd) 2

Bailey. Universal Etymological . . . 2d. ed., Vol.
II, 1731. (Cont'd)

A4^v: Alphabets of the English, Saxon,
Greek, and Hebrew; B-5V1^v: text; 5V2-
5V4^v: An additional collection of words
and descriptions, which have occurred too
late to be inserted in their proper
places; 5X-522^v: an additional collection
of proper names of persons and places;
with their etymologies.
Illus: Woodcut on dedication page and over 500 cuts
(cont'd)

(Cont'd) 3

Bailey. Universal Etymological . . . . 2d ed, vol.
II, 1731. (Cont'd)

throughout the text.
Binding: Original full calf.
Notes: Last alphabet of 23 signatures omits U sig.
instead of customary V. BMC # 12984. ff2.

Anon.   # 237

Les Baisers, Précédés du mois de Mai, poème. A la Haye,
et se trouve à Paris, chez Lambert, Imprimeur rue de la
Harpe. Et Delalain, rue de la Comédie Française, 1770.

Coll: Royal 8°: A^8 B^8 ($\pm$ 'B7' misigned Aiii), C^8 ($\pm$ C2)
D-G^8 H^4 2A-2C^8 84 leaves Pp. [1-2] 3-24 [25-27] 28
('29' and '30' mispaginated 5 and 6) 31-32 ('33'
mispaginated 31) 34 ('35' and '36' mispaginated 11
and 12) 37-48 [49] 50-54 [55] 56-58 [59] 60 [61] 62-
65 [66] 67-68 [69] 70 [71] 72-73 [74] 75-77 [78] 79-
80 [81] 82-83 [84] 85-86 [87] 88-90 [91] 92-93 [94]
95 [96] 97 [98] 99-101 [102] 103-105 [106] 107-112
[113] 114 [115] 116-117 [118] 119 [120]
(Cont'd)

Anon.   (Cont'd)

Les Baisers, Précédés du mois de Mai, Poème.

Supplement: [1-3] 4-47

Illus: 2 engraved plates plus numerous other engravings
by Ch. Eisen.
Binding: Full red calf, gilt edged.

Notes: McKell # 2-12-51L (?)/S-12-9-52L/12-11-52B

238

Baldwin, James   1841-1925

The Sampo: hero adventures from the Finnish
Kalevala. New York: Charles Scribner's Sons,
October 1912. Pp.[x] 1-366, 367-368: notes.

Plates: Frontispiece +63: all color, by N. C. Wyeth.

Notes: First ed.

239

Baldwin, James   1841-1925

A Story of the Golden Age. Illustrated by Howard
Pyle. New York: Charles Scribner's Sons, 1887.

Pp.[xvi] 1-267 [268] 269-272, 273-277, [278], 279-
286 + 4 leaves adverts.

Plates: Frontispiece +11 +2 maps (2d is a fold-out)

Notes: First ed.

240

Baldwin, James   1841-1925

The Story of Siegfried. Illustrated by Howard Pyle.
New York: Charles Scribner's Sons, 1882. Pp.[xx] +
290, 291-293, 294-306 +2 leaves adverts.

Plates: Frontispiece +5.

Notes: First ed.

Ballads

see

A Collection of Old Ballads. 3 vols.
London, 1725-27.

Gilbert, Sir William Schwenk. Bab Ballads.

(Cont'd)

2

Ballads (Cont'd)

   see

      Lanier, Sidney, ed. The Boy's Percy:
      . . . . Scribner's, 1882.

      M., T. A New Book of Old Ballads.

      The Merry Ballads of the Olden Time.

      Percy, Thomas, Bishop. Reliques of
         Ancient English Poetry. J. Dodsley,
         1765.

                         (cont'd)

Ballads (Cont'd)

   see

      Pollard, Josephine. The Decorative
         Sisters: a modern ballad. New
         York, 1881.

      Rackham, Arthur. Some British Ballads.

#241

Ballantyne, R[obert] M[ichael] 1825-1894

Mee-a-ow! or, Good Advice to Cats and Kittens.
By R. M. Ballantyne, Author of "Three Little
Kittens," "Robber Kitten," Etc. London; Edinburgh
and New York: Thomas Nelson and Sons, 1859.

Coll: 4° A-D^4 16 leaves   (24.3 x 18.4cm)
Pp. [3-9] 10-34
Plates: Frontispiece + 7 colored woodcut plates
Notes: Osborne, see p. 323.

 # 242

[Ballantyne, Robert Michael] (Comus, pseud.) 1825-1894

My Mother. By Comus, author of "Three Kittens," "Mister
Fox," "Robber Kitten," Etc. New York: James Miller, 522
Broadway, n.d. [And] The Story of Reynard the Fox.
With six illustrations from designs by Kaulbach. New
York: James Miller, 522 Broadway, n.d.

Coll: sm 4° 1^b, 2^{10} 3^b, 4^{10} 32 leaves   (16.1 x
12.2cm)   Pp. [1-3] 4-7 [8] 9 [10] 11-12 [13] 14-16
[17] 18-19 [20] 21-22 [23] 24-25 [26] 27-31 [32],
[1-4] 5-6 [7-8] 9-10 [11-12] 13-16 [17-18] 19-20
[21-22] 23-31 [32].

                         (cont'd)

My Mother and Reynard the Fox. (Cont'd)

Illus: Front + 13 colored engravings. Last 5 engravings
on one side of page only.

Notes: Pages 26-27 in "Reynard" story are missing from
McKell copy.

#243

[Ballantyne, Robert Michael] 1825-1894
(Comus, pseudonym)
The Robber Kitten. By Comus, Author of "Three
Little Kittens," "Mister Fox," Etc. London,
Edinburgh and New York: Thomas Nelson and
Sons, 1858.

Coll: 4° π^5 (π.1, π.2-π.4), A-C^4 17 leaves
(24.3 x 18.4cm)   Pp. [1-11, 1-9] 10-32.
Plates: Frontispiece + 7 woodcut plates in color,
on one side of leaf only.
Notes: Gumuchian #449. First edition.

244

[Ballantyne, Robert Michael] 1825-1894
(Comus, pseudonym)
Three Little Kittens. By Comus, Author of
"Mister Fox," Etc. London, Edinburgh, and New
York: Thomas Nelson and Sons, 1857.

Coll: 4°; π^6 (π.1, π.2-π.4), A-B^4; 13 leaves;
pp. [1-11, 1-9] 10-24. (24.7 x 19.1cm)

Plates: Front. + 7 colored woodcut plates and
1 uncolored illustration (p. 24).

#245

[Ballantyne, Robert Michael] 1825-1894

Wonderful History of Three Little Kittens Who
Lost Their Mittens. "Good Little Pigs' Library
Vol. 2" Boston: Brown, Taggard & Chase, 1858.

Coll: Sm. 4°; 1^{16}; 16 leaves; op. [1] 2 [3] 4,
5-31 [32].

Plates: 10 in color.

Anon.   **#233**

The Babes in the Wood. Providence: Chauncey Shepard. n.d.

Coll: 8°; [1^8] 8 leaves (15.2 X 9.9cm) Pp. [1-3] 4-5
[6-7] 8-9 [10-11] 12-13 [14-15] 16

Illus: Hand-tinted woodcuts

Notes: Blank facing pages alternate with facing pages bearing engravings and text. Inscription on inside
front cover dated May 8, 1838.

#247

Bannerman, [Helen Brodie Cowan] 1862-3 - 1946

The Story of Little Black Sambo, [and] the Story of
Topsy from Uncle Tom's Cabin. Pictured by John R.
Neill. Chicago: The Reilly and Britton Co.,
Publishers, [1908]. Pp. 13-32 [33-34]; 35-36, 37-
57 [58-60: Advert for L. Frank Baum.]

Binding: Free and paste-down endpaper front and back.

Illus: "Frontispiece" + several full page color illus.
Notes: Title page for Topsy on p. [35].

Barbour, Ralph Henry. 1870-1944 **#249**

The Half-Back: a story of school, football, and golf. Illustrated by B. West Clinedinst. New York: D. Appleton and Company, 1899. Pp. [i-iv] v [vi-vii] 1-267 [268-274: 269-274 adverts.]
Notes: First ed.

Illus: Frontispiece + 9 black & white illus.

Barnum, Mrs. George Sherman

i.e.

Frances Courtenay Baylor   1848-1920

q.v.

Baron, Richard **#250**

Durch Nacht zum Licht. "Amerikanische Jugend bibliothek." Philadelphia: Morwitz & Co., n.d.

Coll: 8° 1-5⁸ 6⁴ 44 leaves (14.7 x 10.5cm)
      Pp. [1-2, 3] 4-85 [86, 87-8].
Illus: Frontispiece color engraving on front cover.
Binding: Paper over boards
Notes: Adverts on p. [86]; p. [87] is pasted down.
      Front cover bears title Aus Nacht Zum Licht.
      Plus another copy with adverts on p [86] but upside down.

Barr, Amelia E[dith Huddleston] 1831-1919 **#251**

A. L. S. 2 pages (20 x 12.3cm), Cornwell on Hudson, September 10, 1898, to Tudor Storrs Jenks, concerning her serial "The Bells of Trinity."

Barr, Amelia E [dith (Huddleston)] 1831-1919 **#252**

The Bow of Orange Ribbon: a romance of New York. New York: Dodd, Mead, and Company, 1886. Pp. [i-vi] 1-[446]

Barrie, J[ames] M[atthew] 1860-1937 **#253**

The Little Minister. New York: R. H. Russell, Publisher, 1898. Pp. [i-vi, 1] - [376].

Plates: Frontispiece + 24.

Barrie, J[ames] M[atthew]   1860-1937 **#254**

Peter Pan in Kensington Gardens from the Little White Bird. A new edition, illustrated by Arthur Rackham. London: Hodder & Stoughton, [1912]. Pp. [i-viii] 1-125 [126].

Plates: Frontispiece +55 (49 color drawings tipped to plate; 6 pen-and-ink drawings).

Barton, Bruce   1886- **#255**

Another Boy, The story of the birth at Bethlehem. Copyright [Minneapolis, Minn.: Buckbee-Brehn Co.,] n.d. Ff. [16].

Notes: Unopened; printed on one side of leaf only.

Barton, Lucy

see

Goodrich, Samuel Griswold. Peter Parley's Book of Bible Stories. Boston & New York: 1845. [Contains Bible Letters, etc., by Lucy Barton.]

Anon. **#258-274.2**

BATTLEDORES 1

The Cock, the Elephant, the Horse, Playing With Fire. n.d. 13.8 X 17.7cm. 4 engravings.   (258)

The ABC/ The New ABC. Printed by J.F. Shearcroft, Braintree, n.d. 13.3 X 21.6cm. 30 engravings. (259)

A Gift From London/ A Reward for Obedience. Published by W.&T. Darton, Nov. 20, 1807. 15.1 X 21.5cm. 4 engravings.   (260)

Gout and Doctor, This is the Cat, This is the Ark, (261)

Anon.

BATTLEDORES 2

The Camel. ca. 1810. 14.1 X 17cm. 4 engravings.

The Ship, This is the Cat, This is the Ark, Young
Lambs to Sell. ca. 1810. 14.1 X 17.2cm. 4 engravings.
Inside the fold (inner form?) contents agree exactly
with preceding number. This is earlier, for the engravings show less wear than in #3.   (262)

The Cock, This is the Cat, This is the Ark, Playing
with Fire. Published by J.G. Rusher, Banbury, ca. 1810.
14. X 17.1cm. 4 engravings. Outer form is precisely the   (263)

Anon.

BATTLEDORES 3

same as #1 above and imprinted later. Inner form is
precisely the same as #5 above and imprinted earlier.

The Good Boy, This is the Cat, This is the Ark, Chairs
To Mend. ca. 1810. 14.1 X 17.2cm. 4 engravings. Inner
form is precisely the same as #4, 5, 6 above and is
later than #6 but earlier than #4 and #5.   (264)

The Fallow Deer, the Elephant, the Horse, the Monkey
Turned Cook, ca. 1810. 14 X 17.6cm. 4 engravings.
Inner form precisely identical to inner form of #1
above, but later.   (265)

Anon.

BATTLEDORES 4

The Cake, The Gardener, The Vulture, Elephant and Child.
ca. 1810. 13.8 X 17.7cm. 4 engravings.   (266)

Notes: Nos. 4-9 in a cloth snap case with title "BATTLE-
DORES" in gilt lettering. Formerly in the Heath
and Merritt collections.

C.N. Wright's New & Improved Battledore. Nottingham:
C.N. Wright, n.d. 12.6 X 20.7cm. 9 engravings of
animals.   (267)

Anon.

BATTLEDORES 5

The Child's Battledore. Alnwick: W. Davison, n.d.
13.2 X 21.1cm. 6 engravings.   (268)

New Battledore. Alnwick: W. Davison, n.d. 13 X 21.2cm.
5 engravings.   (269)

Youth's Battledore. Alnwick: W. Davison, n.d. 13.1 X
21.2cm. 5 engravings. Inner form is identical to
that of #12, but printed later.   (270.1)

Another copy.   (270.2)

Anon.

BATTLEDORES 6

Union Battledore. Alnwick: W. Davison, n.d. 13 X
21.2cm. 6 engravings.   (271)

The British Battledore. Alnwick: W. Davison, n.d.
12.9 X 21.2cm. 6 engravings.   (272)

Another edition. Alnwick: W. Davison, n.d. 12.9 X
21.4cm. 4 engravings. Inner form is different from
#16.   (273.1)

Another copy. Same as #17 but on light tan rather than
yellow paper.   (273.2)

Anon.

BATTLEDORES 7

English Battledore. Alnwick: W. Davison, n.d.
13.1 X 21.3cm. 4 engravings.   (274.1)

Another copy, but on blue rather than yellow paper.
                                           (274.2)
#10-20 are in a brown slip case containing bookplate of
Percival Merritt.

Baum, L[yman] Frank   1856-1919   #275

Dorothy and the Wizard of Oz. Illustrated by
John R. Neill. Chicago: The Reilly & Lee Co.,
[1908]. Pp. [1-3] 4-256.

Plates: Frontispiece +15 + numerous decorations

Notes: First edition.

Baum, L[yman] Frank   1856-1919   #276

Dot and Tot of Merryland. Pictures by W.W. Denslow.
Indianapolis: The Bobbs-Merrill Company, [1901].
Pp. [1-7], 8-225 [226].

Illus: Numerous decorative illustrations

Notes: First ed.

Baum, L[yman] Frank   1856-1919   #277

The Marvelous Land of Oz. . . . a sequel to The
Wizard of Oz. Pictured by John R. Neill. Chicago:
The Reilly & Britton Co., 1904. Pp. [1], 2-287 [288].

Plates: Frontispiece +15 + numerous decorations
Binding: Dust cover, red cloth
Notes: First edition, first state.

Baum, L[yman] Frank   1856-1919   #278

The Marvelous Land of Oz. . . . a sequel to The
Wizard of Oz . . . . Pictured by John R. Neill.
Chicago: The Reilly & Britton Co., 1904. Pp. [1,]
2-287 [288].

Plates: Frontispiece +15 + decorations.
Binding: Red cloth
Notes: First edition, late issue. Word "marvelous"
omitted from front cover.

#278.1

Baum, L[yman] Frank   1856-1919

The Marvelous Land of Oz. . . . a sequel to The
Wizard of Oz. Pictured by John R. Neill. Chicago:
The Reilly & Britton Co., 1904. Pp.[1,] 2-287 [288].

Plates: Frontispiece +15 +decorations
Binding: Red cloth
Notes: First edition, late issue. Plates some-
       what blurred. Inscribed to "William
       and Mary from Aunt Eliza."

#278.2-3

Baum, L[yman] Frank   1856-1919

The Marvelous Land of Oz. . . . a sequel to the
Wizard of Oz. Pictured by John R. Neill. Chicago:
The Reilly & Britton Co., 1904. Pp.[1,] 2-287 [288].

Plates: Frontispiece +15 +decorations
Binding: Red cloth
Notes: First edition, late issue. Plus another
       copy.

#279

Baum, L. Frank. 1856-1919

Mother Goose in Prose. Chicago: Way and Williams [1897].

Pag: [1-8] 9-15 [16-18] 19-28 [29-30] 31-42 [43-44] 45-51
     [52-54] 55-61 [62-64] 65-72 [73-74] 75-86 [87-88]
     89-95 [96-98] 99-106 [107-108] 109-116 [117-118] 119-
     127 [128-130] 131-137 [138-140] 141-147 [148-150]
     151-159 [160-162] 163-171 [172-174] 175-180 [181-182]
     183-196 [197-198] 199-204 [205-206] 207-217 [218-220]
     221-229 [230-232] 233-241 [242-244] 245-254 [255-256]
     257-265 [266-268]

Plates: Frontispiece, title page, illustrator's page + 11
        lithographs by Maxfield Parrish.

[CONT'd]

[CONT'd]

Baum, L. Frank. 1856-1919

Mother Goose in Prose. [1897].

Notes: Presentation letter on fly leaf to author's sister
       Mary. T.L.S. Maxfield Parrish, Windsor, Vermont,
       October 30, 1944, to Don Bach, concerning the
       illustrator's part in the book. This is Baum's first
       for children and the first book illustrated by
       Parrish.

#280

Baum, L[yman] Frank   1856-1919

The Navy Alphabet. Pictures by Harry Kennedy.
Lettered by Charles Costello. Chicago and New York:
George M. Hill Company, 1900. Ff. 29.

Illus: Decorations throughout.

Notes: First ed.

#281

Baum, L[yman] Frank   1856-1919

The New Wizard of Oz. With pictures by W.W.
Denslow. Chicago: M.A. Donohue & Co., 1903 ? .
Pp.[1,] 2-261 [262].

Plates: Illustrated title page, + 15 + decorations

Notes: LC lists a "New Wizard of Oz" published by
       Bobbs-Merrill in Indianapolis, 1903.
       Word "new" omitted from front cover.

#282

Baum, L[yman] Frank   1856-1919

Queen Zixi of Ix: or, the story of the magic
cloak. Illustrated by Frederick Richardson. New
York: The Century Co., 1905. Pp.[i-viii, 1,] 2-
303 [304].

Plates: Frontispiece +15 +numerous monochrome illus.

Notes: First edition.

#283

Baum, L[yman] Frank   1856-1919

The Wonderful Wizard of Oz. With pictures by W.W.
Denslow. Chicago & New York: Geo. M. Hill Co.,
1900. Pp.[1-3,] 4-261 [262].

Plates: Illustrated title page +23 + decorations
Binding: Illustrated paste-down endpapers.
Notes: First edition, first state, early copy; see
       Blanck, PP. to P, pp. 111-112. Title page,
       state A. McKell copy lacks pp.[1-2,] which
       are torn out.

#285

Baylor, Frances Courtenay   1848-1920

Juan and Juanita. Illustrated by Henry Sandham.
Boston: Ticknor and Company, 1888. Pp.[i]-276,[1]
xvi (adverts).

Plates: 13 +cuts

Notes: McKell copy lacks frontispiece.
       Frances Courtenay Baylor is Mrs. George Sherman
       Barnum.

#286

The Bay Psalm Book, Being a Facsimile Reprint of the
First Edition, Printed by Stephen Daye at Cambridge, in
New England in 1640. Introduction by Wilberforce Eames.
New York: Dodd, Mead & Co., 1903. Pp. xvii [xviii] +
facsimile edition.

Notes: Bookplate of Ross County Historical Society.

Beadles Dime Tales Series (Nos. 6, 11)

see

Ellis, Edward S[ylvester]

Beebe, [Charles] William   1877-1962   #292

Beneath Tropic Seas: a record of diving among the coral reefs of Haiti. With sixty illustrations. New York-London: G.P. Putnam's Sons, 1928. Pp. [ ] ii-xiii [xiv] 1-234.

Plates: Frontispiece ≠19 of photographs.

Notes: First edition.

Beard, D[aniel] C[arter]   1850-1941   #288

The American Boy's Handy Book: what to do and how to do it. New York: Charles Scribner's Sons, 1882. Pp. [i] - [xiv, i] - [392], [1-1b: adverts].

Illus: Cuts

Anon.   #295

The Beggar's Petition. Dayton, Ohio: Published and Sold by B. F. Ells, n.d. [ca. 1836-1840].

Coll: 24°; [1⁸]; 8 leaves (10.3 x 6.9 cm.); pp. [1-2] 3-16.

Illus: Numerous woodcuts.

Notes: A long note concerning B. F. Ells' woodcuts will be found in Midland Notes No. 8.

Bechtel, John   1690-1777   #290

Kurzer Catechismus Vor etliche Gemeinen Jesu Aus der Reformirten Religion In Pennsylvania, Die sich zum alten Berner Synodo halten: Herausgegeben von Johannes Bechteln, Diener des Worts Gottes. Philadelphia, Gedrukt bey Benjamin Franklin, 1742.

Coll: 12° A-C⁶ D⁴ 22 leaves (12.7 x 7.6cm) Pp. [1-2] 3-42 [43-44.]

Binding: Bound by F. Bedford in full red morocco, gilt tooling, gilt edge.

Notes: Saban 4223, Rosenbach p. 15,

Les Belles Heures De Jean De France Duc De Berry.   #297

Reproduction integrale des enluminures precedee d' introduction de Jean Porcher conservateur du Cabinet des Manuscrits. Paris: Bibliotheque Nationale, MCMLIII. Pp. [5] 6-31 [32,] 33-34 [35,] 36-49 [50, 51, 52-54 [ff. I-CLVIII of color plates; ff. 1-6 black and white) 226] 227, 228 [229-230, 231-232].

Beckmann, Herrn Conr[ad]. Ludwig   1856-   #291

Reinke Fuchs. Das ist: Ein sehr Nutz-, Sinn- und Lehrreiches Büchlein, darein auf verblumte, jedach lobliche Schreibart der Thierwelt Wesen, Tugenden und Laster mercklich beschrieben. Aufs Neue, in jessiger Zeit üblichen Reimarten verarbeitet und mit sehr angenehmen Kupffern versehen. [8 lines poetry] Dusseldorf am Rhein: Druck und Verlag von Arnz & Comp. Palmarum, MDCCCLVI.

Coll: Demy 4° 1-4⁴ 16 leaves Pp. 1-30 [31 ; 32 is blank]

Plates: Front +title (page +8 chromolithos.

Belson, Mary

see

Elliott (Elliot, Eliot), Mary n.d.

Beckman, Josef Hermann

see

Picture Bible of the Late Middle Ages

Bennett, Charles Henry   1829-1867   #301

The Nine Lives of a Cat. London: Griffith and Farran, 1860.

Coll: 8° A⁹ (A2+1) B⁸ C⁷ (C1, C2-C7) D⁸ 32 leaves Ff. [1-3] 1-20 21; 1] 2-16 of adverts

Plates: 20 in color by Bennett; all 18.2 x 13.4cm

Notes: A3: Preface, dated 1859, tipped in.

Bennett, John. 1865-1956 # 302

Barnaby Lee. Illustrated by Clyde O. De Land. New York: The Century Co., 1902. Pp. [i]-x, [1]-454.

Plates: Front +33 included in pagination.

Notes: Front fly-leaf inscribed by author.

Bentley, Rensselaer ca. 1800-1870 # 304

The Pictorial Spelling Book. New York: Sheldon and Company, Publishers, n.d., [1845?].

Coll: 12° 1-7^{12} 84 leaves (17.7 x 11.2cm) Pp. [1-5] 6, 7-15, 16-168.
Plates: Frontispiece +cuts.
Binding: Stabbed
Notes: A blue back speller. Entered 1839.

Berquin, [Arnaud] 1749-1791 # 305

The Blossoms of Morality; Intended for the Amusement and Instruction of Young Ladies and Gentlemen. Trans from M. Berquin. By the Editor of The Looking Glass for the Mind. With Forty-seven cuts, Designed and Engraved by J. Bewick. 7th ed. London: Printed [by S. & R. Bentley...] for J. Harris and Son..., 1821.

Coll: 24°; A^3 (+A$_3$) B-U^6 X^4; 121 leaves (13.7 x 8.6 cm.); pp. [i-iii] iv-viii [1] 2-235 [236].

Illus: 47 wood engravings by John Bewick (1760-1795).

(Cont'd)

Berquin The Blossoms of Morality. 1821. p.2.

Notes: BMC gives 12°.
Front loose endpaper: "11.B.5289".
The Rev. J. Cooper, trans., (i.e., Richard Johnson).

Berquin, Mr. Arnaud 1749-1791 # 306

The Children's Friend. Translated from the French of Mr. Berquin by Lucas Williams, Esq. A New Corrected Edition with Addition, and Embellished with Forty-Four Copper Plates. In Six Volumes. . . . London: . . . J. Stockdale . . . ; F. and C. Rivington . . . ; B. Law and Son . . . ; J. Johnson . . . ; C. Dilly . . . ; J. Murray . . . ; J. Sewell . . . ; W. Creech . . . , 1793. (Not in BMC)
Vol. I:
Coll: 12° A^8 B-N^{12} O^4 156 leaves (16.9 x 10cm) Pp. [i-v] vi-xvi, [1] 2-296.
Plates: Frontispiece + 7 engravings
#S-4-25-49 (cont'd)

Berquin -2-

Vol. II:
Coll.: 12°: [A^2] B-M^{12}N^8. 142 leaves (16.7 X 10.1 cm). Pp. [i-iv][1] 2-278 [279-280].

Plates: Frontispiece + 7 engravings.

M6 and M7 missing from McKell copy.

Vol. III:
Coll.: 12°: [A^2] B-N12O^6. 152 leaves (16.8 X 9.9cm). Pp. [i-iv][1] 2-300.

Plates: Frontispiece + 8 engravings.
(cont'd)

Berquin -3-

Vol. IV:
Coll.: 12°: [A^2] B-O^{12}P^6. 164 leaves (16.8 X 10.4 cm). Pp. [i-iv], [1] 2-322 [323-324].

Plates: Frontispiece + 7 engravings.

Vol. V:
Coll.: 12°: [A^2] B-M^{12}N^8. 142 leaves (16.8 X 10.2 cm). Pp. [i-iv], [1] 2-278 [279-280].

Plates: Frontispiece + 5 engravings.

(cont'd)

Berquin -4-

Vol. VI:
Coll.: 12°: [A^2] B-M^{12}N^2. 136 leaves (16.9 X 10.4 cm). Pp. [i-iv], [1] 2-268.

Plates: Frontispiece + 4 engravings.

Berquin, [Arnaud] 1749-1791 # 307

Choix De Petits Drames Ed De Contes Tires De Berquin. Illustre de 30 vignettes par Faulquier et Forest. Paris Librairie. De L. Hachette et Cie rue Pierre-Sarrazin, No 14, 1856 Typograph of Charles LaHure .

Coll: 8° π^2, a-u^8 170 leaves Pp. [1-4, i] ii [1] 2-9 [10] 11-46 [47] 48-68 [69] 70-103 [104] 105- 112 [113] 114-136 [137] 138-140 [141] 142-167 [168] 169-241 [242] 243-276 [277] 278-334.

Illus: Numerous engravings.

Berquin, Arnaud 1749-1791 # 308

Idylles. [Paris: Quillan, 1775].

Coll: 16° a^4 A-C^8 D^{4}X^2[2] A-D^8 E^2 68 leaves [17 x 12cm] Pp. [i] ii-vi [vii-viii, 1] 2-55 [56], [i- iv, 1] 2-60 [61] 62-67 [68].
Plates: Engraved title page, plus 24 engravings by C. P. Marillieu.
Notes: Bookplates of W. Vernon and Cortland F. Bishop. BMC has 12°. McKell # S-5-12-1951 B.

[Berquin, Arnaud.]   (c. 1749-1791)   # 309

The Looking Glass for the Mind; or Intellectual
Mirror. Being an elegant Collection of the
most delightful little Stories, and Interesting
tales, Chiefly translated from that much admired work L'Ami Des Enfans. With elegant
engravings on wood, By Anderson. New York:
Printed for Campbell and Mitchell, Booksellers
and Stationers, 124 Pearl Street. M'Farlane and
Long, print., 1807.

Coll: 12⁰; π², A-R⁶; 104 leaves (17.3 x 10.2
     cm.); pp. [i-iii] iv [1] 2-203 [204].
                 (cont'd)

[Berquin] The Looking Glass for the Mind. 1807.
                       (Cont'd).

Illus: Several wood engravings.

Binding: By Riviere and Son.

Notes: Pagination on p. 16 is upside down.
       Welch 77.7 (the McKell Copy).
       π1, 2 signed. (All '3's are signed 2).

[Berquin, Arnaud]   1749-1791   # 310

The Looking-Glass for the Mind; or Intellectual
Mirror; Being an Elegant Collection of...Tales.
Chiefly translated from that much admired work
L'Ami Des Enfans   With Seventy-four
cuts, designed and engraved on wood by J[ohn]
Bewick. 16th ed. London: Printed [by S. & R.
Bentley] for John Harris..., 1825.

Coll: 12⁰; [A²] B-M¹² N⁴; 118 leaves (18 x 10.1
     cm.); pp. [1-iv] [1] 2-271 [272].

Illus: 74 woodcuts by J. Bewick. (1760-1795)
Notes: Edited. by J. Cooper (i.e., Richard Johnson).
       Trans. by The Rev. W.D. Cooper (Richard
       Johnson ?)

Bianco, Margery Williams   # 311

Poor Cecco. The wonderful story of a wonderful wooden
dog who was the jolliest toy in the house until he went
out to explore the world. By Margery Williams Bianco
author of "The Velveteen Rabbit." Illustrated by
Arthur Rackham. London: Chatto & Windus, 1925. Pp.
[i-viii] ix [x-xiv] 15-175, [176]

Plates: Frontispiece 6: all in color and all laid in.
       Plus several decorative cuts.

Notes: Bookplate of C. H. Waterland Mander on front
       paste down endpaper. A color plate is pasted to
       back paste-down endpaper.

[Bianco,] (Mrs.) Margery Williams   1881-1944   # 312

The Velveteen Rabbit: or how toys became real. Illustrated by William Nicholson. London: Heinemann, 1922.
Pp. [viii] 1-[20].

Plates: 10: the plates on pp. 3, 9, and 19 are two pages.

Notes: First ed.

The Bibelot

   see

       Lang, Andrew. Three Poets of French
         Bohemia. Xiv, No. 5 (May, 1908).

Bible

   see also under

       Old and New Testaments and under titles
       of the separate books.

Bible

   see also

       Kleine Biblische Historien aus dem Ulten
       und Neuen Testament. Harrisburg, Pa.:
       G.S. Peters, n.d.

       Schroth, Picture Bible of Late Middle
       Ages.

Bible (Apocrypha)   # 313

The Book of Tobit and the History of Susanna. Re-
printed from the Revised Version of the Apocrypha.
. . . Introduction by Dr. Montague R. James . . .
Four colour-plates after drawings by W. Russell
Flint. London: The Haymarket Press, 1929. Pp. [1]
ii-xvi [1] 2-47 [48].

Illus: Frontispiece +3.

Notes: #168 of 875.

Bible, (Apocrypha)   # 314

The History of Susanna. Engravings by Mallette
Dean. San Francisco: Grabhorn Press, n.d.

Pagination: ff. 21.

Illus: Numerous colored woodcuts throughout.

Bible (Apocryphal New Testament) # 315

The Apocryphal New Testament, being all the Gospels, Epistles, and other pieces now extant, attributed in the first four centuries to Jesus Christ, His Apostles and their companions, and not included in the New Testament by its compilers. Ravenna, Ohio: William Coolman, Jr., 1832.

Coll: 12° A-DD⁶ 174 leaves (16.8 x 10.3cm) Pp. i-ii, iii-x [11-12, 13] 14-348.
Binding: Green boards.
Notes: From London edition.

Bible (Apocryphal New Testament) # 316

The Apocryphal New Testament . . . . From the last London edition. Chillicothe, O.: Benj. J. Gray, 1835.

Coll: 12° 1-17⁶ 102 leaves (14.2 x 9.9cm) Pp. [i-iii] iv-vii [viii, 9] 10-202 [203-204].

Binding: Free and paste down endpapers. ¼ calf over boards.

Bible # 317

The Children's Bible: or, an History of the Holy Scriptures. . . . To which are added, the Principles of the Christian Religion, Adapted to the Minds of Children. By a Divine of the Church of England. Adorned with Copper and Metal Cuts. Dublin: Printed by and for Henry Saunders, in Castle-street. MDCCLXIII.

Coll: 16° A-M⁸ 96 leaves (13 x 9.4cm) Pp. [ii] +1-190+ [2].

Illus: Frontispiece + 5 engravings and woodcuts.

[ANON.]. A Curious Hieroglyphick Bible; or, Select # 318
Passages in the Old and New Testaments. Represented with Emblematical Figures, for the Amusement of Youth . . . to which are Subjoined, . . . the Lives of the Evangelists, and Other Pieces, Illustrated with Cuts. The Thirteenth Edition. London: Printed and Sold by Robert Bassam; H.D. Symonds; and Scatcherd and Whitaker, 1796.

Coll.: 12° (in 6's): A⁴B-M⁶N² 72 leaves (13.2 X 8.6cm). [8] + 136 pp.

Illustrations: Frontispiece (A1) + numerous cuts in text.
A1 forms front attached endpapers. Bookplate of Percival Merritt.

Bible, Hieroglyphical # 319

A New Hieroglyphical Bible: with devotional for youth. Containing four hundred cuts, by Adams. New York: Harper & Brothers, 1837.

Coll: 8° 1⁸ (-1,1) 2-13⁸ 103 leaves (16 x 13cm) Pp. [3-4, 5] 6, 7-208.
Plates: Frontispiece, vignette (engraved) title page + cuts.
Notes: McKell copy missing pp. 205-206.

Anon. # 320

The Hieroglyphick Bible; or select passages in the Old and New Testaments, represented with emblematical figures, for the amusement of youth: designed chiefly... to which are subjoined, a short account of the lives of the Evangelists, and other pieces. Illustrated with nearly five hundred cuts. Second edition. Boston: Published by Isaiah Thomas, Jr., No. 6 Marlborough Street. J.T. Buckingham, Printer, 1814.

Coll: 12°: (6s) A-M⁶ 72 leaves (13.9 X 9cm) Pp. [i-iv] vi-vii [viii-9] 10-144

Illus: Numerous cuts

Hieroglyphic Bibles

see also under

Clouston, William Alexander. Hieroglyphic Bibles, Their Origin and History: . . . contains also Frederick A. Laing. A New Hieroglyphic Bible told in stories. Glasgow; 1894.

Bible # 321

The Holy Bible Abridged . . . Illustrated With Notes, and adorned with Cuts. For the Use of Children. London: Printed for T. Carnan and F. Newbery, Junior, 1775.

Coll: 24° A-M⁸ 96 (9.7 x 6.3cm) Pp. [1-iv] v-vii + 9, +176.

Binding: Dutch floral boards

Notes: McKell copy lacks M1 and M8. Roscoe # 27(10). Bookplate of Percival Merritt.

Bible # 322

The Holy Bible Abridged; containing the history of the New Testament. Adorned with cuts. For the use of children. York: Printed by T. Wilson and R. Spence, 1803.

Coll: 12° A-G⁶ 42 leaves (10.2 x 7.5cm) Pp. [1-3] 4-55 [56] 57-84.

Illus: 31 woodcuts in text: one is a full-page cut, p. [56].

(cont'd)

The Holy Bible Abridged. (Cont'd)

Contents: History of Edward VI: E5-F2; The Prodigal son: F2ᵛ-F5ᵛ; Poem on Piety: F5ᵛ-F6ᵛ; Hymns: G-G6ᵛ.

Binding: Dutch flowery boards; wrap-around end paper in back.

Notes: Bookplate of Percival Merritt

The Holy Bible in Verse. London: B. Harris, Jr.
1717.

see under

Harris, Benjamin, Sr.

#323

Bible, Dutch　1772

De Kleine Print-Bybel, waar in door verscheide as-beel-
dingen een meenigte van Bybelsche spreuken verklaart
worden. Tot vermaak der jeugd, en om te leeren elke zaak
naauwkeurig of te schelzten, en by haaren regten naam
te noemen; ook de spreuken der H. Schrift by na zonder
moeite in het geheugen te brengen. Uit de Hoogduitsche
en de Hollandsche taal overgeget. Tot Amsterdam: By
Dirk onder de Linden en zoon, Boekverkopers, in de Kal-
verstraat, over de Nieuwezyds Kapel, 1772.

Coll: $8°$　1^6, 2-38^4, 39^2　156 leaves (13.8 x 9.2cm)
ff. [1, *1] *2-*4, 1-150 [151].

(cont'd)

De Kleine Print-Bybel. (Cont'd)

Illus: Engraving on title page plus leaves 1-150 engraved
on one side of leaf only.

Binding: Initial and final leaves are pasted down endpapers.

Notes: Leaf 90 missing from McKell copy. Leaves *2-*4
printed on both sides, remaining leaves printed
on one side of leaf only.

#324

[Bidpai] Pilpay

The Fables of Pilpay. Rev. Ed. New York: Hurd and
Houghton, 1872. Pp. [1] ii-xviii, 1-274.

Illus: Vignette title page ≠ cuts.

#325

[Bidpai] Pilpay

The Instructive and Entertaining Fables of Pilpay,
an Ancient Indian Philosopher. . . . The Sixth
Edition, Corrected, improved, and enlarged; and
adorned with nearly seventy Cuts neatly engraved.
London: Printed for J.F. and C. Rivington, S.
Crowder, T. Longman, B. Law, S. Bladon, G. and T.
Wilkie, and B. Collins, 1789.

Coll: $12°$　A^{10}　B-K^{12}　L^6　M^2　126 leaves (17.3 x
10.4cm) Pp. [1-2, i-xviii] 1-232.
Plates: 21 containing three engravings each (I.
Beckington ?)

#326

[Bidpai (Pilpay]

The Moral Philosophie of Doni [The Fables of Bidpai]:
drawn out of the aancient writers. A work first
compiled in the Indian tongue, and afterwards re-
duced into divers other languages: and now lastly
Englished out of Italian by Thomas North . . .
London: Henry Denham, 1570. Reprint ed. by Joseph
Jacobs, London: David Nutt, 1888. Pp. [1] ii-lxxx
[1] 2-259 [260].

Plates: Frontispiece ≠ 2 ≠ cuts.

#331

Bilderbuch für kleine artige Mädchen. Stuttgart:
Verlag von Rudolph Sheliuss. n.d.

Coll: A book of 8 leaves　(20.2 x 26.2cm)

Illus: Title +42 colored woodcuts on 7 leaves.

Binding: Rebound. Each plate pasted to new binding.

Notes: Printed on one side of the leaf only. McKell
S-5-12-45.

#332

Bildergalerie, welche vierundzwanzig Vorstellungen
von verschiedenen Kinder und andern Spielen, Uebungen
und Beschäftiggungen, so wie auch einem erklärenden
Lert enthalt zum Zeitvertreib für Kinder. Nürnberg:
in der Johan Trautnerischen Kunsthandlung, n.d.

Coll: oblong $4°$　π^1)(^{4})DC 1-3^8　31 leaves　Pp.
[1-ii] 3,5,7,9,11,13,15,17,19,21,23, [25], 1-24
(illustrations)

Illus: 24, one side of page only, numbered: some are
not colored, some partially, and some are fully
hand-colored.

(cont'd)

Bildergalerie. (Cont'd)

Notes: Title page pasted to)(.1 and the)(DC gathering
is pasted to)(.4.

#333

Anon.

Bilder-Zaubereien eine amüsante Unterhaltung
für Jung und Alt. Blow Book or Magic Picture
Book, amusing and interesting for young and
old. [Also in Swedish, Danish, Hungarian, and
Polish.] [n. d.]

Coll: $8°$ [1-4^8]; 32 leaves; ff. 32.

Binding: Stiff wrappers.

Illus: Numerous color and black and white
illustrations.

Notes: "It shows first only plain white leaves,
then changes into a stamp
(cont'd)

Anon.   Bilder-Zaubereien.   *(Cont'd)* ..

album, a picture Book, black Silhouettes,
Carricatures, animals, etc."

Anon.   The Blackbird's Nest. 1824. (cont'd)

relation to the subject matter or the
other illustrations. Back has advertisements.

Notes: Initial and final leaves pasted to
       wrapper. Final leaf, recto, has
       advertisement.

Birch, Reginald. [Bathhurst, illus.] 1856-   # 335

A. L. S. 5 pages (23.1 x 18.1 cm.), Juchen-
hausen, Ober Bayern, Germany, September 11,
1903 to William Fayal Clarke, with original
hand colored pen and ink sketch.

Notes: William Fayal Clarke 1855-1935

Blackmore, R[ichard] D[oddridge] 1825-1900   # 341

A. L. S.   One page (13.4 x 8.6cm), Teddington,
Middlesex, March 28, 1893, to Rev. Creighton
Spencer, concerning editions of Lorna Doone.

Bisset, J[ames]   1762? - 1832   # 339

Juvenile Reduplications: or, the new "House that
Jack Built." A Parody. With appropriate Cuts and
explanatory Notes. Birmingham: Printed by Grafton
& Reddell . . . for the author; Sold by Newbery
. . . ; T. Heptinstall . . . ; and T. Hurst . . . ,
London: 1800.

Coll: 8° A-B⁸ C² 18 leaves (15.6 x 9.3cm) Pp.
[1-iii] iv [5] 6-34 [35-36].
Plates: Frontispiece + engraved cuts.
Notes: Roscoe # 37. No. BMC no.

Blanchard, Edmund Forster   -1870

    see

        Brough, Robert Barnabas. Funny Dogs With
        Funny Tales.

Blackbeard, Gaffer

    see

        Perrault-D'armancour, Pierre. A New History
        of Blue Beard, written by Gaffer Blackbeard
        . . . . Philadelphia, John Adams, 1804.

Blanchard, Amy E[lla (Aunt Ella, pseud.)]1856- 1926   # 347

Wee Babies. Printed in colours from original designs
by Ida Waugh. Poetry by Amy E. Blanchard. New York:
E. P. Dutton & Co.; London: Griffith and Farren,
Copyright, 1882, E. P. Dutton & Co. Pp. [1] 2 [3] 4-16,
18-17, 19-22, 24-23, 25-48.

Illus: Several chromolithos.

Anon.   # 340

The Blackbird's Nest: A Tale for Children.
Published by J. Babcock and Son, New Haven, and
by S. Babcock and Co., Charleston: 1824.
[Sidney's Press]
Coll: 16°; [1¹⁶]; 16 leaves (13 x 10.4 cm.); [1-5]
6-30 [31-32].
Illus: Front. + 7 wood cuts.
Binding: Buff wrappers. Front has illustration
         of Bluebeard fighting with one of his
         wives, which seems to have no
                                    (cont'd)

Blanchard, Pierre. 1772-1856   # 348

Le Trésor des enfans; Ouvrage classique, Devisé en Trois
Parties: 1°. La Morale, 2°. La Vertu, 3°. La Civilité.
Par Pierre Blanchard. Orné de vignettes en taille-douce.
A Paris: Chez Le Prieur, Libraire, rue Saint-Jacques, No.
278. An XI, (1802).

Coll: 12°: A-S⁶ T⁴ [U²] 114 leaves (15.7 X 9.7cm)
Pp. [i-v] vi-xii [13] 14-155 ('156' mispaginated as
155) 157 ('158' mispaginated 153) 159-225 [226]
227-228

Illus: Frontispiece (not a plate) plus 14 engravings on
       7 plates.

351

[Bland,] E[dith] Nesbit   1858-1924

Rosy Cheeks and Golden Ringlets. "Our Children's
Book Case" series. London, Paris & New York:
Raphael Tuck & Sons. Designed at the Studios in
England and printed at the Fine Art works in
Germany. [c. 1907]. ff.[6].

Plates: 4 in color by M.G. + 4 +color cover.

Notes: No inside title page.

354

Boccaccio, Giovanni   1313-1375

Contes/ de Boccace . . ./ Lavis/ de/ Marc Chagall/
Textes/ de/ Jacques Prévert/ de/ Frantz Calot . . ./
et/ Légendes/ Verve. /Printed in France, Verve
copyright, 1950/. ff. 36.

355

[Boccaccio, Giovanni] Jean Bocace 1313-1375

Contes De Bocace; traduction nouvelle, augmentée de
divers contes et nouvelles en riens vens imités de ce
Poète célèbre, par La Fontaine, Passerat, Vergier,
Perrault, Dorat et autres; et enrichie de notes histori-
ques sur les principaux personnages que Bocace a mis sur
la scène, et sur les usages observés dans le siècle où
il vivoit. Par S. Sabatier De Castres auteur des trois
Siecles de la Littérature. Tome premier. a Paris:
chez Poncelin, imprimeur-libraire, rue du Hurepaix, No.
17, an X, -1801. [11 Vols.]

(cont'd)

Contes De Bocace. (Cont'd)

Vol I:
Coll: 8° π² ★⁸ ★★² 1-17⁸ 18² 150 leaves
    Pp. [1-4] i-xx, [1]-18 [19] 20-40 [41] 42-88 [89]
    90-126 [127] 128-132 [133] 134-156 [157] 158-
    168 [169] 170-192 [193] 194-200 [201] 202-209 [210]
    211-216 [217] 218-232 [233] 234-250 [251] 252-276.

Plates: Title page and front +16 others: all engravings

Vol II: [Same title page]
Coll: 8° π² 1-14⁸ 114 leaves Pp. [i-iv] [1]-8 ("9"
    (cont'd)

Contes De Bocace. (Cont'd)

mispaginated 6) 10-40 [41] 42-56 [57] 58-86 [87]
88-147 [148] 149-152 [153] 154-199 [200] 201-
223 [224].

Plates: Title page + 7 others: all engravings.

Vol III: [Same title page]
Coll: 8° π² 1-15⁸, 6⁴ 126 leaves Pp. [i-iv] [1]-76
    [77] 78-95 ("96" not paginated) 97-155 [156-157]
    158-236 [237] 238-247 [248].

Plates: Title page + 4 others: all engravings.

(cont'd)

Contes De Bocace. (Cont'd)

Vol IV: [Same title page]
Coll: 8° π², 1-24⁸ 194 leaves Pp. [i-iv] [1]-33 ("34"
    mispaginated 4) 35 [36] 37-60 [61] 62-66 [67] 68-
    98 [99] 100-106 [107] 108-123 [124] 125-140 ("141"
    not paginated) 142-154 [155] 156-194 [195] 196-
    265 [266] 267-270 [271] 272-304 [305] 306-374 [375]
    376-382 [383-384].

Plates: Title page +11 others: all engravings.

Vol V: [Same title page]
Coll: 8° π² 1-16⁸, 17⁴,   18² 136 leaves Pp. [i-iv]
    (cont'd)

Contes De Bocace. (Cont'd)

[1]-23 [24] 25-30 [31] 32-75 ("75" printed from
bottom to top instead of from left to right) 76-
97 [98] 99-226 [227] 228-267 [268].

Plates: Title page +12 others: all engravings.

Vol VI: [Same title page]
Coll: 8° π², 1-16⁸, 17² (17·1-17·6, 17·7) 137 leaves
    Pp. [i-iv] [1]-37 [38] 39-58 ("59" mispaginated 56)
    60 [61] 62-83 [84] 85-103 [104] 105-114 [115] 116-
    152 [153] 154-214 [215] 216-226 [227] 228-263 [264]
    265-269 [270].

(cont'd)

Contes De Bocace. (Cont'd)

Plates: Title page +12 others: all engravings.

Vol VII: [Same title page]
Coll: 8° π², 1-12⁸, 13⁴, 14² 104 leaves Pp. [i-iv] 1-
    18 [19] 20-24 ("25" mispaginated 57) 26-54 [55]
    56-58 [59] 60-64 [65] 66 [67] 68-132, 135-136,
    133-134, 139-140, 137-138, 141-142 143 150 [151-
    153] 154-189 [190] 191-202 [203-204].

Plates: Title page +11 others: all engravings.

Vol VIII: [Same title page]
Coll: 8° π² 1-16⁸, 17²   132 leaves Pp. [i-iv] [1]-
    (cont'd)

Contes De Bocace. (Cont'd)

30 [31] 32-34 [35] 36-66 [67] 68-100 [101] 102-
117 [118] 119-138 [139] 140-148 [149] 150-172
[173] 174-210 [211] 212-226 [227] 228-244 [245]
246-259 [260].

Plates: Title page +13 others: all engravings

Vol IX: [Same title page]
Coll: 8° π², 1-20⁸, 21² 164 leaves Pp. [i-iv] [1]-11 [12]
    13-71 [72] 73-89 [90] 91-208 [209] 267 [268] 269-
    276 [277] 278-318 [319] 320-321 [322-324].

(cont'd)

Contes De Bocace. (Cont'd)

Plates: Title page +12 others: all engravings.

Vol X: [Same title page]
Coll: 8° π², 1-15⁸, 16⁴, ★⁸ ★★⁸ 140 leaves Pp. [i-iv]
    [1]-32 [33] 34-105 [106] 107-146 [147] 148-150
    [151] 152-166 [167] 168-174 [175] 176-178 [179]
    180-248, [1] ii-xxvii [xxviii].

Plates: Title page+ front +12 others: all engravings

Vol XI: [Same title page]
Coll: 8° π², 1-25⁸, 26⁷   (26·1-26·6, 26·7) 209
    leaves Pp. [i-iv]   [1]-26 [27] 28-171 [172]
    (cont'd)

Contes De Bocace. (Cont'd)

173-259 [260] 261-294 [295] 296-307 [308-311]
312 [313] 314 [315] 316-341 ("342" mispaginated
32) 343-386 [387-389] 390-407 [408] 409-414.

Plates: Title page + 12 others; all engravings.

Notes: Volume numbers vary consecutively on each title
page. Vols. 1, 3-8, and 10 have an engraved
title page dated 1802. Vols. 2 and 9 are undated. Illustrations are drawn and sculpted by
many and various illustrators: principal de-
lineator is Gravelat, principal sculptors are
Delvaux and   ) Cochin. Uniform size:
(19.9 x 12.3cm)

#356

Boccaccio, Giovanni. 1313-1375

The Decameron. J. M. Rigg, trans. Illust. by Louis
Chalon. 2 vols. London: Henry F. Bumpus, 1906.

Vol.I:
Pagination: [i]-[xxii], [1]- 332
Illus: Front. + 7

Vol II:
Pagination: [i]-[xvi], [1]-404
Illus: 4 plates

Notes: James Macmullen   ) Rigg (1855-1926).
                                              (cont'd)

Boccaccio. Decameron. Rigg, trans. London, 1906.
(Cont'd)

Additional plates by Chalon meant to accompany
this edition: 8 illustrated plates in black
and white, laid in a plain red board container
with "Decameron" in black letters across the
front.

#358

Bohny, Niklaus

Neues Bilderbuch. Anleitung zum anschauen, denken,
rechnen und sprechen fur kinder von 2½ bis 7 jahren,
zum gebrauche in familien, kleine kinderschulen,
taubstummen-anstalten und auf der ersten stufe des
elementarunterrichts. Entworfen und bearbeitet von
Niklaus Bohny, lehrer. Stuttgart und Esslingen:
Schreiber und Schill [c. 1850].

Coll: Large 4° [A]⁴ 4 leaves Pp. [1-3] 4 [5] 6-8 +
Ff.1-37 of illustrations.

Illus: 37 leaves, engraved on recto only, foliated;
36 of which   ) are in color.

#359

Bond, A   L

The Child's Natural History. New York: George
Routledge & Sons, 1882. Pp. [i]-viii, [1]-100.

Plates: Front + cuts.

#360

Anon

Les Bons Examples ou Telics. Jolies Gravures
Morales Amusantes avec un petit coute pour chaque
sujet. Ce petit recueil Dedie aux Enfans des deus
Sexes est propre a jeller dans leur coeur le germe
des vertus sociales. Paris: Chez le Cerf,
Libraire, & Blanchard, Libraire, n.d.

Coll: Oblong 8°   1-3⁴   12 leaves Pp. 1-22
       [23-24].
Plates: Frontispiece + title + 10 engravings
Binding: Free and past-down end papers in front;
         paste-down end papers in rear.

Book of Common Prayer

see

A Pleasant and Useful Companion to the
Church of England; . . . exposition
of the Book of Common Prayer. . . .
London: 1764.

#362

Anon

The Book of Games: or, a History of the Juvenile
Sports, Practised at the Kingston Academy. Illustrated with twenty-four copper plates. London:
Printed by J. Adlard . . . for Tabart and Co. . . .,
1805.

Coll: 12° [A]² B-0⁶ 80 leaves (13.3 x 8.2cm) Pp.
       [1-iv, 1] 2-156.
Plates: Frontispiece + 23.
Notes: No BMC no.

#363

Anon

The Book of Games; or, A History of Juvenile Sports,
Practised at a Considerable Academy Near London:
Illustrated By Twenty-four Copper Plates. London:
Printed for Tabart & Co. . . . By B. McMillan, 1810.

Coll: 12° [A]² B-P⁶ 86 leaves (13.5 x 8.9cm) Pp.
       [1-iv, 1] 2-168.
Plates: Frontispiece + 23 dated variously July 13,
        1804; November 5, 1804; February 4, 1805.
Notes: BMC gives 24°. McKell # S-2-5-43B.

#364

The Book of Job, from the Translation Prepared at
Cambridge in 1611 for King James I. Preface by
Mary Ellen Chase. Illustrated by Arthur Szyk.
New York: Heritage Press, [1946]. Pp. [1-4], 5-
148.

Plates: Frontispiece + 7.

 # 365

Book of Kells. Evangeliorum Quattuor. Codex Cenannensis, Berne: Urs Graf-Verlag. Vol. I: 1950; Vol. II: 1950; Vol. III: 1951. Ff. 1-182; (2) 183-339; (3) Pp. 1-10 11-83 84

Binding: Vols. I-II in vellum; Vol. III in ¼ vellum.

Notes: Giant folios.

 # 366

Anon

The Book of One Hundred Pictures. Philadelphia: American Sunday-School Union, No. 1122 Chestnut Street; New York: 599 Broadway. [Entered 1861]. Pp. [1-4] 5-104; [1] 2-4 of adverts.

Illus: 100 engravings + title.

 # 367

Anon.

Ye Book of Sense, a Companion to The Book of Nonsense. Philadelphia: Porter and Coates, [n.d.]

Coll: Oblong 4°; [A⁴ (A·1 under front paste down end paper), B-I⁴]; 36 leaves (14.2 x 23.6 cm.); Leaves unnumbered.

Illus: 32 leaves illustrated in color; printed on recto only.

 # 368

Anon

The Book of Trades and Professions: or, familiar objects described. Embellished with twenty-four illustrations, by Croome. Philadelphia: Geo. S. Appleton; New York: D. Appleton, 1851.

Coll: 16 1-7⁸ 56 leaves (14 x 11.4cm) Pp. [i-ii, 1-2] 3 [iv] 5, vi [7-8] 11-100 [101-112 : advert]

Illus: half-title page + 23

 # 370

[Boreman, Thomas]

A Description of some curious and uncommon Creatures, Omitted in the Description of Three Hundred Animals, and likewise in the Supplement to that Book . . . . Illustrated with Sixteen Copper-Plates . . . . London: Printed for Richard Ware, . . . and Thomas Boreman . . . , 1739.

Coll: 12° [A]² B-H⁶ I⁴ 48 leaves (15.8 x 9.7cm) Pp.[iv,] 1-88 + [4].

Notes: I4: "Books printed for Richard Ware. . . ." Bookplate of John Walker Heneage. On loose end-paper verso: "From Wilbur Macy Stone Collection." McKell # S-3-9-51.

W 371

[Boulger, Dorothy Henrietta (Havers)]   d.1889

Cape Town Dicky; or, Colonel Jack's Boy. By Theo Gift. Illustrated by Alice Havers. Monotints by Ernest Wilson. London: Hildsheimer & Faulkner; New York: Geo. C. Whitney, [1888]. 64pp.

Plates: Frontispiece (recto and verso) + 15 color plates + 47 monotints.

Binding: Advertising on free endpapers (front end back).

Notes: First ed. See Osborne, p. 327. Inscription on front endpaper verso reads: "David McC. McKell. Christmas 1887."

 # 376

Anon.

The Boy's Own Book; A Complete Encyclopedia of All the Diversions Athletic, Scientific, and Recreative, of Boyhood and Youth. Sixth American Edition. Boston: Munroe and Francis; Joseph H. Francis; New York: Charles S. Francis, 1839.

Coll: 16°: [A⁸] B-Y⁸ Z⁴ AA⁸ BB⁴ CC⁸ 164 leaves (13.6 X 13.3cm) Pp. [1-2],[i-iii] iv [7] 8-316 [317-320], [1] 2 [3-4], [1-2] 3-4

Illus: Woodcuts

Notes: CC3ᴿ-CC8ⱽ advertisements. 4 leaves of advertisements bound in at end.   A.A.S. #123 Note of Vol 1 1818

 # 377

Anon.

The Boy's Treasury of Sports, Pastimes, and Recreations. With nearly four hundred engravings, Designed by Williams, and engraved by Gilbert. Fourth American Edition. New York: Clark, Austin & Smith, 1854.

Coll: 12°: 1-39⁶ 40² 236 leaves. Pp. [1-4] 5 [vi] vii [8] 9-472. (17.1 x 11.1cm)

Illus: "Frontispiece" plus numerous engravings.

Notes: Obsolete letter signings present, Signature #22 torn out of McKell copy. Pages 274-290 missing in McKell copy.

 # 378

Bradley, D[aniel] B[each] .   (1804-1873)

Evangelical Catechism. By D. B. Bradley. The 5th. Edition, 5000 copies. Bangkok: A.B.C.F.M. Press, 1846.

Coll: 12°: [1-4⁶]; 24 leaves (17.2 x 11.5 cm.) pp. [1-11, 3] 4-47 [48].

Illus: Ornamental woodcut on title page.

Notes: Title is also in Siamese on title page. Pagination is in Siamese.

 # 379

Bradley, D[aniel] Beach] .   (1804-1873)

History of Joseph. By D. B. Bradley. Second Edition, 2000 copies. Bangkok: A.B.C.F.M. Press, 1848.

Coll: 12°: [1-6⁶]; 36 leaves (16.8 x 11.5 cm.) pp. [1-11, 3] 4-72.

Notes: Title page contains title in Siamese as as well as above info. in English. Cropped at bottom. Pagination is in Siamese.

Bradley, D [an] B [each] (1804-1873) #380

History of Moses. 2000 copies. Bangkok:
A.B.C.F.M. Press, 1847. (Title also in Siamese)

Coll: 12°; [1-8⁶]; 48 leaves (16.8 x11.5 cm.);
    pp. [1-11, 1] 2-43 [44, 45-46].

Illus: 1 woodcut (p. 43).

Binding: Paper covered boards; final leaf as
    paste down end paper.

Notes: Book printed in Siamese.
    Pagination in Siamese.
    P. [44] is blank.

Briggs, [Clare A   ] 1875-1930   #384

Oh Skin-nay! The days of real sport. Verses by Wilbur
D. Nesbit. Chicago: P. F. Volland & Co., [1913]. Pp.
[124].

Illus: Cuts.

Bromholm Psalter

    see under

        Two East Anglian Psalters (also contains
           Ormesby Psalter)

#390

Brooks, Charles

Puck's Mighty Pranks. Illustrated by Paul Konewka.
Boston: Roberts Brothers, 1871. Ff. [1-12] I-IX;
[1-24pp.]

Illus: Silhouettes.
Binding: Light blue-green wrappers. Free and pastedown endpapers front and rear.

#391

Brooks, Noah   1830-1903

The Boy Emigrants: a tale of the American plains
and California gold mines. Illustrated. London:
The Religious Book Society, [1903?]. Pp. [i-]viii,
[9]-[416].

Plates: Frontispiece + five + cuts.

Notes: Several illustrations initialed "W.L.S."
    (William Ludlow Sheppard? illustrator of
    the 1877 Scribner's edition). McKell # SG
    6-1-55 B.

#392

Brooks, Noah   1830-1903

The Boy Settlers: a story of early times in Kansas.
Illustrated by W. A. Rogers. New York: Charles
Scribner's Sons, 1891. Pp. [i-x, 1] -252.

Plates: Frontispiece +15.

#393

Brooks, Noah   1830-1903

Our Baseball Club and How It Won the Championship.
Introduction by Al. G. Spalding. New York: E.P.
Dutton and Company, 1884. Pp. [i]-viii, [1] -202,
[1-2, adverts.]

Plates: Frontispiece + 9; signed by F.T. Merrill.

#394

Brough, Robert B [arnabas] (1828-1860); Alfred Elwes
(-1888); James Hannay (1827-1873); Edmund
F [orster] Blanchard (-1870).

Funny Dogs With Funny Tales. The Dogs from the
Pencil of Harrison Weir. The tales from the pens of
Robert B. Brough, Alfred Elwes, James Hannay, and
Edmund F. Blanchard. London: Addey and Co., MDCCC
LVII.

Coll: 4° A² B-C⁴ D² E-I⁴ 40 leaves (23.9 x 18.3cm)
    Pp. [1-5] 6-9 [10-14] 15-26 [27-28] 29-36 [37-
    38] 39-46 [47-48] 49-56 [57-58] 59-66 [67-68]
    69-76 [77-78]   79-86 [87-88] 89-96.
                          (cont'd)

Funny Dogs With Funny Tales. (Cont'd)

Illus: Front +7 engraved plates by Harrison Weir, which
    are included in the pagination.

Brown, Goold. 1791-1857   #395

The Institutes of English Grammar; Methodically arranged;
with examples for Parsing, Questions for Examinations,
False Syntax for correction, Exercises for Writing, Ob-
servations for the advanced Student, and a Key to the Oral
Exercises: to which are added Four Appendixes. Designed
for the use of Schools, Academies, and Private Learners.
By Goold Brown, Principal of an English and Classical
Academy, New-York ne quis igitur tanquam parva fastidint
Grammatices elements. Quintillian Fourth Edition. New-
York: Published by Samuel Wood & Sons, No. 261, Pearl-St.
R. & G.S. Wood, Printers, 1830.

(Cont'd)

Brown, Goold. 1791-1857   (CONT'D)

Coll: 12º: 1-27⁶ 162 leaves (18.1 x 10.3cm) PP. [i-iii]
iv-x ('xi' mispaginated ix) xii, [1] 2-260 [261]
262-284 [285] 286-293 [294] 295-304 [305] 306-307
[308] 309-311 [312].

Illus: None

Notes: Free and pasted down end papers.

#396

Brown, Paul   1893-

War Paint; an Indian Pony. Illustrated. New York:
Charles Scribner's Sons; London: Charles Scribner's
Ltd., 1936. Pp. [96].

Binding: Dust cover

#397

Browning, Elizabeth Barrett   1806-1861

Sonnets from the Portuguese. Illustrated by
Fred A. Mayer. New York: Illustrated Editions
Company, [1937]. Pp. [1] -xvi 17-110.

Illus: Frontispiece + decorative illustrations

Browne, Maggie

pseud. of

Margaret (Hamer) Andrewes, q.v. Two Old
Ladies . . . . London . . . 1897.

Brownell, Anna   1794-1860

see

Jameson, Mrs. (pseud)

#398

Browning, Elizabeth Barrett   1806-1861

Sonnets from the Portuguese. Illustrated by
Willy Pogany. New York: Thomas Y. Crowell Company, [1936]. Pp. [1-8,] 9-96.

Plates: Frontispiece + illustrated half-title,
+ 12 (7 in color).

#400

Browning, Robert   1812-1889

The Pied Piper of Hamelin: a child's story.
Illustrated by Hope Dunlap. [Chicago & New York]:
Rand McNally Co., [1910]. Pp. [1-10,] 11-56.

Plates: Frontispiece, illustrated title page, 9 full-
page colored illustrations + cuts.

#402

Browning, Robert   1812-1889

The Pied Piper of Hamelin, illustrated by Arthur
Rackham. London: George G. Harrap & Co. Ltd.,
[1934]. Pp. [1-6] 7 [8-10] 11-18 [19-22] 23-26
[27-28] 29-34 [35-40] 40-44 [45-48].

Plates: Frontispiece + 3.

#403

Browning, Robert   1812-1889

The Pied Piper of Hamelin. Illustrated by Kate
Greenaway. London and New York: Frederick Warne
and Co., [1910]. Pp. [1-3], 4-48.

Plates: Frontispiece + cuts.

Brownjohn, John

Pseud of

Talbot, Charles Remington (1851-1891), q.v.

Anon.   #407

The Bud of Promise and Other Books For
Children and Youth. New York: Published by
the American Tract Society. 8 pamphlets bound
as one book . [n.d.]

Coll: Sm. 8°: [1]⁴ (-1.1), 2⁸; 1⁸; 1⁸; 1⁸; 1⁸;
      1⁸, 1⁸, 1⁸] 70 leaves; pp. [i-vi, 1-2,
      3] 4-16; [-2, 3] 4-16; [-2, 3] 4-16;
      [-2, 3] 4-16; [-2, 3]4-16; [1-2, 3] 4-16;
      [-2, 3] 4-16; [-2, 3] 4-16.

Illus: Title page + 24 engravings.

)   (cont'd)

Anon. The Bud of Promise and Other Books. p. 2.

Contents: The Bud of Promise, #41;
          The Sea-Captain's Daughter, #42;
          The Twin Sisters, #43;
          Samuel, a Converted Malabar, #44;
          Joseph Tate Meredith, #45;
          The Treasure Laden Ship, #46;
          What Do You See?, #47;
          The Indian Girl, #48.

Bunner, H[enry] C[uyler] 1855-1896   #412

"Short Sixes": stories to be read while the candle
burns. Illustrated by C. J. Taylor, F. Opper and S. B.
Griffin. New York: Puck, Keppler & Schwartzmann, 1891.
Pp. [i-viii] 1-232.

Illus: Cuts

Bunyan, John.   (1628-1688) #413

A Book for Boys and Girls; or, Country Rhymes
for Children. By John Bunyan. Being a Facsimile
of the unique First Edition, Published in 1686,
Deposited in the British Museum. Intro. by Rev.
John Brown, D. D., author of "John Bunyan: His
Life, Times, and Work." London: Elliot Stock,
1890.

Pagination: [1-vi, vii] viii-xxviii, [1-viii] 1-79.

Notes: McKell # 8-12-10-49-B.

Bunyan, John   1628-1688   #414

Divine Emblems: or, Temporal Things Spiritualized.
Fitted for the Use of Boys and Girls. London:
Printed for J. Mawman . . . by John Abraham . . . .
1802.

Coll: 12° A-G⁶ 42 leaves (15.4 x 9.5cm). Pp.
      vi, 7-84.

Illus: 49 woodcuts.

[Bunyan, John]. 1628-1688   #415

Bunyan's Pilgrims Progress, from this world to that which
is to come: Exhibited in a metamorphosis or a transforma-
tion of pictures. Fifth edition, improved. New Haven, Ct.:
Published by E. Barber. T.J. Stafford, Printer, [n.d.]

Coll: (A Harlequinade or turn up) Sm 8°: [1]⁴ 4 leaves
      (13.9 X 9.3cm) Pp. [1-8]

Illus: 5 wood engravings

Contents: Back page has poem "A prospect of Heaven Makes
          Death Easy," by Dr. Watts

                                        #416

Bunyan, John   1628-1688

The Pilgrim's Progress . . . . Complete in Three
Parts. To which is added The Life and Death of
the Author. Embellished with Cuts. Exeter:
Printed for Henry Ranlet, And Sold at his Book-
store: And by Charles Pierce, Portsmouth; Angier
March, and Thomas & Whipple, Newburyport. 1804.

Coll: 12° A-Z2⁶ 174 leaves (17.6 x 10.7cm) Pp.
      [i-iv] v-x [11] 12-50 ("51" misnumbered 52)
      52-138 [139-143] 144-148 [149] 150-261 [262-
                                        (cont'd)

Bunyan. Pilgrim's Progress. . . . 1804 (Cont'd)

265] 266-334 [335] 336-345 [346] 347-348.

Illus:13 full-page woodcuts.

                                        #417

Bunyan, John   1628-1688

The Pilgrim's Progress From This World To That
Which Is To Come, Delivered Under The Similitude
of a Dream. Engraved by G.E. and J. Dalziel,
from Designs by William Harvey. London: David
Bogue, 1851.

Coll: 8°[a]³ b-m⁴ , A-3x⁴ 270 leaves (19.8 x
      13.3cm) Pp. [i-iii] iv [v] vi-xcii [xciii-
      c, 1] 2-440.

Plate: Engraved frontispiece, numerous in text en-
       gravings(wood).

                                        #418

Burgess, [Frank] Gelett 1866-1951

Goops and How to Be Them. A manual of manners for
polite infants inculcating many juvenile virtues both
by precept and example. With ninety drawings by
Gelett Burgess. New York: Frederick A. Stokes Company,
Publishers [University Press, John Wilson and Son.
Cambridge, U.S.A., 1900]. Pp. [i-viii, 1-88].

Notes: First ed.

Burgess, Thornton W[aldo]   1874-1965   # 419

The Adventures of Bob White. Illustrated by Harrison Cady. Boston: Little, Brown, and Company, 1919. Pp.[i]-[viii, 1] - [118].

Plates: Frontispiece+5

Burgess, Thornton W[aldo]   1874-1965   # 420

The Adventures of Peter Cottontail. Illustrated by Harrison Cady. Boston: Little, Brown, and Company, 1914. Pp.[i-viii], 1-120.

Plates: Frontispiece +5.

Burgess, Thornton W[aldo]   1874-1965   #421

Mother West Wind "How" Stories. Illustrated by Harrison Cady. Boston: Little, Brown, and Company, 1917. Pp.[i]-[x, 1] -228.

Plates: Frontispiece+7.

Burgess, Thornton W[aldo]   1874-1965   # 422

Mother West Wind "When" Stories. Illustrated by Harrison Cady. Boston: Little, Brown, and Company, 1917. Pp.[i]-[x, 1] - [228; 1-2, adverts.]

Plates: Frontispiece+7.

Burgess, Thornton W[aldo]   1874-1965   # 423

Mother West Wind "Where" stories. Illustrated by Harrison Cady. Boston: Little, Brown, and Company, 1918. Pp.[i]-[viii, 1] -244, [1-4, adverts.]

Plates: Frontispiece+7.

Burgess, Thornton W[aldo]   1874-1965   # 424

Mother West Wind "Why" Stories. Illustrated by Harrison Cady. Boston: Little, Brown, and Company, 1915. Pp.[i-viii, 1] -230, [1-2, adverts.]

Plates: Frontispiece+7

Notes: Front fly-leaf cut out of McKell copy.

Burnett, Frances Hodgson.   (1849 -1924) #426

A. L. S. One page (16.3 x 13.1), Plandome, Long Island, July 15, 1920, to a Mr. McGee, about autographing some books for him.

Burnett, Frances Hodgson   1849-1924   # 427

Editha's Burglar: a story for children. Illustrated by Henry Sandham. Boston: Jordan Marsh and Company, 1888. Pp.[1-10, 11] 12-64 +1 leaf advert on verso.

Plates: Front.+13 included in pagination. Front depicts a full-length Editha "hiding" behind a chair (photograph).
Binding: Maroon cover
Notes: First ed. Blanck # 2071. Owl device and Rand Avery device on copyright page.

Burnett, Frances Hodgson   1849-1924   # 428

Giovanni and the Other: children who have made stories. Illustrated by Reginald B. Birch. New York: Charles Scribner's Sons, 1892. Pp.[xii, 1] 2-193, [194: blank+8 leaves adverts.]

Plates: Front +8 included in pagination, but not numbered.
Contents: Giovanni and the Other; Illustrissimo Signor Bebe; The Daughter of the Custodian; A Pretty Roman Beggar; Eight Little Princes (cont'd)

Burnett   Giovanni and the Other   (Cont'd)

One Who Lived Long, Long Ago; The Little Faun; What Use is a Poet?; The Boy Who Became a Socialist; Birdie; The Tinker's Tom; The Quite True Story of an Old Hawthorn Tree.

Notes: First ed. Blanck: # 2082. Advert on verso of half-title page.

#429.1-2

Burnett, Frances Hodgson 1849-1924

Little Lord Fauntleroy. Illustrated from drawings by Reginald B. Birch. New York: Charles Scribner's Sons, 1886. Pp. [xii, 1] 2-209 [210: colophon] +7 leaves adverts.

Notes: First ed. Blanck # 2064. Plus another copy, same ed.

430.1-2

Burnett, Frances Hodgson 1849-1924

Little Saint Elizabeth and Other Stories. Illustrated by Reginald B. Birch. New York: Charles Scribner's Sons, 1890. Pp. [xiv, 15] 16-146 +8 leaves advert for Scribner's.

Contents: Little Saint Elizabeth; The Story of Prince Fairyfoot (3 parts); The Proud Little Grain of Wheat; Behind the White Brick.
Plates: Frontispiece +11
Notes: First ed. Blanck # 2077; advert on verso of half-title. Plus another copy, same ed.

431

Burnett, Frances Hodgson 1849-1924

Sara Crewe; or, what happened at Miss Minchin's. Illustrated by Henry Sandham from drawings by Frances Hodgson Burnett. New York: Charles Scribner's Sons, 1888. Pp. [1-10, 11] 12-64, + 1 leaf advert on verso.
Illus: Front + 13 included in pagination, but not numbered.

Binding: Green cover.
Notes: Second state of the first ed. Blanck # 2067. Advert on verso of half-title page.

432

Burns, Robert. 1759-1796

Robert Burns Rare Print Collection. 8 parts. Philadelphia: R. G. Kennedy & Co., 1900.

Plates: Each part contains loose plates in orange wrappers: I (4), II (5), III (5), IV (4), V (4), VI (4), VII (5), VIII (4).

Binding: Enclosed in stiff board portfolio.

Notes: Connoisseur edition, issued for private circulation. # 553.

433

Burroughs, Edgar Rice 1875-1950

The Return of Tarzan. Decorated by J. Allen St. John. Chicago: A. C. McClurg and Co., March 1915. Pp. [viii] 1-365, [366].

Illus: Decorations on chapter heading pages and title page.

Notes: First ed.

#434

Burroughs, Edgar Rice. 1875-1950

Tarzan and the Jewels of Opar. With Illustrations by J. Allen St. John. Chicago: A. C. McClurg and Co., April 1918. Pp. [viii] 1-350 +2 leaves adverts.

Illus: Frontispiece + 7

Notes: First ed.

435.1

Burroughs, Edgar Rice 1875-1950

Tarzan of the Apes. Chicago: A. C. McClurg & Co., [June] 1914. Pp. 1-[401, 402].

Illus: Title page

Binding: Red cover

Notes: First ed.; has half-title.

435.2

Burroughs, Edgar Rice 1875-1950

Tarzan of the Apes. Chicago: A. C. McClurg & Co., 1914. Pp. [1-viii,] 1-[401, 402].

Illus: Title page

Notes: First ed.

436

Burroughs, Edgar Rice 1875-1950

The Tarzan Twins. Illustrated by Douglas Grant. Joliet, Illinois, New York . . . Boston: The P. F. Volland Company, 1927. Pp. [1-5] 6, 7-126 [127-128: advert]

Illus: Free and paste-down endpapers, front and back, illustrated in color with African scene: lion and antelope. Numerous illus. in color in text, some full-page.
Notes: First ed.

437

[Burton, Rev. Warren] 1800-1866

The District School As It Was. By one who went to it. Rev. ed. Boston: Phillips, Sampson and Company, 1850.

Coll: 12° 1-17⁶ 18² 44 leaves (16.5 x 10.3cm) Pp. [i-v] vi [vii] viii-x [11] 12-206 [207-208: blank].

Busch, Wilhelm 1832-1908 #440

A Bushel of Merry-Thoughts by Wilhelm Busch. Described and Ornamented by W Harry Rogers. London: Sompson Low Son, and Marston, Milton House, Ludgate Hill, 1868.

Pagination: [1-iv, ff. 1] ff. 2-14; [ff. 1-2] ff. 3-16; [ff. 1] ff. 2-16; ff. 1-16
Illus: Numerous engravings and decorations
Contents: 1) The Terrible Punishment of the Naughty
   Boys of Corinth

      (cont'd)

Busch. . . . Merry-Thoughts (cont'd)

  2) The Exciting Story of the Cat and The
  the Mouse
  3) The Disobedient Children Who Stole
  Sugarbread
  4) The Fearful Tragedy of Ice Peter
Notes: The Table of Contents lists Ice Peter First
  and Boys of Corinth fourth. This is a
  book of plates.

Busch, Wilhelm 1832-1908 #441

Buzz a Buzz or the Bees. Done freely into English by the Author of My Bee Book from the German of Wilhelm Busch. London: Griffith and Farran; Chester: Phillipson & Golder, 1872. Pp. [1-iii] iv, [ff. 1,] ff. 1-72 [1-10pp. notes].

Illus: 136 hand-colored + 3 uncolored + engraved
  title
Notes: First English edition. Text is foliated
  and printed on one side of leaf only. Ff. 1
  is a plate printed on recto and titled
      (cont'd)

Busch . . . Buzz a Buzz (cont'd)

"Prelude," and is not paginated or foliated. Preface by the translator signed "W. C. C." and dated Sep. 1872. Cover title has "By W. C. C. author of My Bee Book."

Busch, Wilhelm 1832-1908 #442

Neues Wilhelm Busch Album: Sammlung lustiger Bildergeschichten mit 1500 zum Teil farbigen Bildern von Wilhelm Busch. Berlin: Grünewald Verlagsanstalt Hermann Klemm, n.d. Pp. [i] - [viii], 1] -488.

Plates: Frontispiece + cuts.

Notes: Bookplate of Helena M. Nye.

Busch, Wilhelm 1832-1908 #443

Schnaken & Schnurren. Eine Sammlung humoristischer kleiner Erzählungen in Bildern. 2 vols. München: Verlag von Braun und Schneider, [c. 1867-1872]. Pp. [1-2] Ff. 31.

Illus: Woodcuts

Notes: McKell # S-10-20-48 B

Busch, Wilhelm 1832-1908 #444

Wilhelm Busch Album: Humoristischer Hausschatz mit 1500 Bildern von Wilhelm Busch. 326. bis 335. Auflage München: Friedr. Bassermann'sche Verlagsbuchhandlung, 1929. Pp. [1-4], 1- [viii] 1- [356].

Plates: Frontispiece + cuts.

Binding: Dust cover

Notes: Bookplate of Helena M. Nye

Butler, Ellis Parker 1869-1937 #445

Pigs is Pigs. Illustrated by Will Crawford. New York: McClure, Phillips & Co., 1906. Pp. [1-iv], [1] - [38].

Plates: Frontispiece + 4.

[Butler, William Allen] 1853-1923 #447

Nothing To Wear: an episode of city life. (From Harper's Weekly). Illustrated by [A.] Hoppin. New York: Rudd & Carleton, 1857.

Coll: 12° [1-2¹²] 24 leaves (17.2 x 11.5cm) Pp. [1-6, 7] 8-68.

Plates: Frontispiece + 7.

Butler, William Allen 1825-1902 #448

Two Millions. New York: D. Appleton & Co., 1858.

Coll: 12° 1-4¹² 12 leaves (17.4 x 11.3cm) Pp. [i-ii, 1-2, 3] 4-5 [6-7] 8-36 [37] 38-45 [46] 47-55 [56] 57-83 [84] 85-93 [94].
Notes: First ed.

449

Anon.

The Butterfly's Funeral. A Sequel to the Butterfly's Ball and Grasshopper's Feast. By J.L.B. The embellishment designed and engraved by a Lady. London: Printed [by Brettell and Co., for] John Wallis, Jun., 1808.

Coll: 16°. [1², 2-6², 7² (7²=1-1⁴)] 16 leaves (12.5 X 10.3ᶜᵐ·) Pp. [1-3] 4-6 [7-32]

Illus: Frontispiece + 11 engravings

Binding: Blue wrappers.

Notes: [9-6-3-42 L]

450

Butterworth, Hezekiah   1839-1905

Zigzag Journeys in the British Isles; or, vacation rambles in historic lands. Boston: Estes and Lauriat, Publishers, 18 89. Pp. 11 [12], 13-320 1 leaf blank

Illus: Frontispiece + numerous black and white in text Color pictorial free and paste-down endpapers.

Notes: First ed.

451

Butterworth, Hezekiah   1839-1905

Zigzag Journeys in the Great Northwest; or, a trip to the American Switzerland. Boston: Estes and Lauriant, Publishers, 1890. Pp. xiv [15] 16-319 [320: blank].

Illus: Frontispiece + numerous black and white in text.
Binding: Pictorial free and paste-down endpapers.
Notes: First ed.

452

Butterworth, Hezekiah   1839-1905

Zigzag Journeys in the Occident. The Atlantic to the Pacific: a summer trip of the Zigzag Club from Boston to the Golden Gate. Boston: Estes and Lauriat, 1883. Pp. 12 [13-14, 15] 16-320.

Illus: Frontispiece numerous black and white in text Color pictorial free and paste-down endpapers.
Notes: First ed.

453

Byrne, [Brian Oswald] Donn-   (1889-1928)

Blind Raftery and His Wife, Hilaria. Illustrated by John Richard Flanagan. New York & London: The Century Co., [1924]. Pp. [i-vi, 1] 2-175 [176].

Plates: Frontispiece + 3.

454

Byrne, [Brian Oswald] Donn-   1889-1928

Crusade. Boston: Little, Brown, and Company, 1928. Pp. [i-vi], [1] -250.

Binding: Dust cover

Notes: No. "K" of a group of 15 copies not for sale of a limited edition of 365. Signed by the author.

455

Byrne, [Brian Oswald] Donn-   1889-1928

Crusade. Boston: Little, Brown, and Company, 1928. Pp. [i-iv], [1] -250.

456

Byrne, [Brian Oswald] Donn-   1889-1928

Destiny Bay. Boston: Little, Brown, and Company, 1928. Pp. [i-viii], [1] -350.

457

Byrne, [Brian Oswald] Donn-   1889-1928

Field of Honor. New York & London: The Century Co., [1929]. Pp. [i-vi], [1] -[436].

458

Byrne, [Brian Oswald] Donn-   1889-1928

Hangman's House. Illustrated by John Richard Flanagan. New York & London: The Century Co., [1926]. Pp. [i]-[xiv], [1] -466.

Plates: Frontispiece + 7.

Byrne, [Brian Oswald] Donn-   1889-1928   # 459

Messer Marco Polo. Illustrated by C. B. Falls. New York: The Century Co., [1921]. Pp.[i-vi],[1]-[148].

Plates: Frontispiece+3.

Byrne, [Brian Oswald] Donn-   1889-1928   # 460

The Wind Bloweth. Illustrated by George Bellows. New York: The Century Co., [1922]. Pp.[i-vi],[1]-394].

Plates: Frontispiece+7

Bysh's Edition of the History of Little Red Riding Hood, or the Deceitful Wolf.

see under

Perrault-D'armancour, Pierre (1678-1700)

Cabell, James Branch   1879-1958   # 462

Chivalry. Illustrated by Howard Pyle. New York and London: Harper and Brothers, Publishers, [October] 1909. Pp.[xii][1]-[224].

Plates: Color frontispiece: "I sing of Death."

Notes: First ed.

Cabell, James Branch   1879-1958   # 465

The Soul of Melicent. Illustrated by Howard Pyle. New York: Frederick A. Stokes Company, 1913. Pp.[i-viii, 1-2] 3-216.

Plates: Color Frontispiece+3 others in color.

Binding: Dark blue, horizontally ribbed, cloth.
Notes: On copyright page, lower left, "September, 1913."

Caldecott, R [andolph]   1846-1886   #466-481.1-2

"Picture Books." 16 vols. London: George Routledge & Sons [1878-1885].

[Oblong quartos, paper wrappers, colored engravings, advertisements on back.]

(466) The Babes in the Wood. Pp. 2-30. 8 full page colored illustrations. Hand dated Oct. 1879 on front wrapper.

(467.1-3) Come Lasses and Lads. Pp. [1-2] 3-22 [23-24]. 6 full page colored illustrations. Hand dated 7 Nov 1884 on front wrapper. Plus two other copies.
(cont'd)

Caldecott Picture Books   (Cont'd)

(468.1-3) Goldsmith, Oliver.   An Elegy on the Glory of her Sex: Mrs. Mary Blaize. Pp. [1-2] 3-22 [23-24]. 6 full page color illus. Hand dated Oct. 1885 on front wrapper. Plus two other copies.
(469.1-3) The Farmer's Boy. Pp. 3-30. 8 full page color illus. Plus two other copies.
(470.1-2) The Fox jumps over the Parson's Gate. Pp. [1-2] 3-22 [23-24]. 6 full page color illus. Hand dated Oct 1883 on half-title page. Plus another copy.
(471.1-3) A Frog he would a-Wooing go. Pp. [1-2] 3-22 [23-24] 6 full page color illus. Hand dated Oct 1883 on half-title page. Plus two other copies.
(cont'd)

Caldecott Picture Books   (Cont'd)

(472) The Great Panjandrum Himself. Pp. [1-2] 3-22 [23-24]. 6 full page color illus. Hand dated Oct 1885 on front wrapper.
(473.1-2) Hey Diddle Diddle and Baby Bunting. Pp. [1] 2-23 [24]. 6 full page color illus. Hand dated 18 Nov 1882 on front and back wrappers. Plus another copy
(474.1-3) The House That Jack Built. Pp. 2-29. 8 full page color illus. Plus two other copies.
(475.1-2) Cowper, William.   The Diverting History of John Gilpin. Pp. 3-31. 8 full page color illus. Plus another copy.
(476.1-3) Goldsmith, Oliver.   The Mad Dog. Pp.[3]
(cont'd)

Caldecott Picture Books   (Cont'd)

4-30. 8 full page color illus. Hand dated Oct 1879 on front wrapper. Plus two other copies.
(477.1-3) The Milkmaid. Pp. [1-3] 4-22 [23-24]. 6 full page color illus. Presentation copy signed by author. Dated 7 Oct. 1882. Plus two other copies.
(478.1-3) The Queen of Hearts. Pp. 3-30. 8 full page color illus. Hand dated Dec. 1881 on title page. Plus two other copies.
(479.1-2) Ride a-cock Horse to Banbury Cross & A Farmer Went Trotting Upon His Grey Mare. Pp. [1-2] 3-22 [23-24]. 6 full page color illus. Hand dated 7 Nov. 1884 on front cover. Plus another copy.
(cont'd)

Caldecott Picture Books   (Cont'd)

(480.1-2) Sing a Song for Sixpence. Pp. 3-30. 8 full page color illus. Hand dated Dec. 1880 on front cover. Plus another copy.
(481.1-2) The Three Jovial Huntsmen. Pp. 3-30. 8 full page color illus. Hand dated Dec. 1880 on front cover. Plus another copy.

Notes: See Juman invoice 4/7/58

482

Calender (Kalender Augsburg, 1490)

(No. 26) Gedruckt zu Augsburg von hannsen Schonsperger, und vollendet am montag vor sant Katherina Tag nach Christi begurt. M. CCCC. und in dem ye-jare. Diese Ausgabe der holzschnitte aus dem deutschen Kalender Augsburg 1490 bei Hans Schonsperger erschien mit einem Nachwort von Kurt Pfister im Roland-Verlag Dr. Albert Mundt München-Pasing im Fruhjahr 1922.

Coll: 12° [1-2⁸, 1⁴] 20 leaves (18 x 12.2cm) Fr. 20

Illus: The original numerous woodcuts reproduced.

Notes: Ltd. ed. #26.   McKell # S-3-4-55

483

Calhoun, Frances Boyd   1867-1909

Miss Minerva and William Green Hill. Illustrated by Angus Macdonall. Chicago: The Reilly and Britton Co., 1909. Pp. [1-4] 5-212.

Illus: Frontispiece +decorative cuts.

Notes: First ed.

484

Calkins, N[orman] A[llison]   1822-1895

Prang's Natural History Series for Schools and Families 14 Large Plates: Plants. Birds. Quadrupeds . . . Boston: L. Prang & Co., [Entered 1872]. Fr. 14

Plates: 14 Chromo-lithos

Notes: Lge folio size. See also Prang, Louis, comp. Folding Lithograph Series. Boston: 1865.

485

Campe, Joachim Heinrich]   1746-1818

The New Robinson Crusoe, Designed for the Amusement and Instruction of the Youth of Both Sexes. Translated from the original German. Embellished with Cuts [by John Bewick]. London: Printed for E. Newbery, 1790.

Coll: 16° B-I⁸ 64 leaves (10.7 x 7.1cm) Pp. 1-4[5] 6-128.

Illus: Frontispiece (Bl⁷) + 13 woodcuts in text.

Binding: Dutch floral boards
Notes: McKell copy lacks Bl. Roscoe # 49 (1).

486

Campe, Joachim Heinrich]   1746-1818

The New Robinson Crusoe; Designed for the Amusement and Instruction of the Youth of Both Sexes. Translated from original German. Embellished with Cuts [by John Bewick]. London: Printed for E. Newbery, 1797.

Coll: 16° B-I⁸ 64 leaves (11 x 7.7cm) Pp. 1-4 [5] 6-128.

Illus: Frontispiece (Bl) + 13 woodcuts in text.
Binding: Dutch floral boards.
Notes: Bookplate of Percival Merritt. Roscoe #49(2).

487

Candeze, Dr. Ernest [Charles Auguste]   1827-1898

The Curious Adventures of a Field Cricket. N. D'Anvers, trans. Illustrated by C. Renard. London: Sampson Low, Marston, Searle and Rivington, 1878. Pp. [viii, 1] - [320].

Plates: Frontispiece + 21.

Canfield, Dorothy

see

Fisher, Dorothea Frances Canfield   1879-1958

488

Le/ Cantique/ des/ Cantiques/ de/ Salomon/ Selon le français des Docteurs de Louvain/ 1550. Composé & gravé par R. Drouart/ à/ Paris/ MCMXXV. Fr. 40.

Binding: Unbound

Notes: See also The Song of Songs . . . . Golden Cockerel Press, 1925.

489

Cardell, William S[amuel]   1780-1828

Story of Jack Halyard, the Sailor Boy; or, the Virtuous Family. Sixth Edition revised by the author. Philadelphia: Uriah Hunt . . . . Stereotyped by L. Johnson, 1827.

Coll: 12° A-S⁶, T⁴ 112 leaves (14.1 x 8.2cm) Pp. [1-2, i-iii] iv-xviii [19] 20-224.

Illus: Woodcut frontispiece
Notes: Not in Rosenbach.

490

Carleton, Will   1845-1912

Farm Ballads. Illustrated [Howard Pyle, Charles Stanley Reinhart, Willard Poinsette Snyder, and others]. New York: Harper & Brothers, Publishers, 1873. Pp. [1-17] 18-108, + 1 of adverts.

Plates: Frontispiece +9 +decoraTions.

Notes: First edition.

Carlisle, Countess   # 491

Rudiments of Taste, in a series of letters from a mother
to her daughters, to which are added, Maxims addressed
to young ladies, by the Countess Dowager of Carlisle.
Philadelphia: Printed by William Spotswood, 1790.

Coll: 12°: [A²] B-M⁶ N⁴ 72 leaves (12.55 X 7.4cm.)
     Pp. [i-iv][1] 2-140

Notes: Bookplate of J.G.E. Hopkins

Anon.   # 492

The Carrier-Pigeon. New York: Published by the American
Tract Society, 150 Nassau-Street, n.d.

Coll: 8°: [1⁸] 8 leaves (13.9 X 9.1cm) Pp. [1-2, 3] 4-16

Illus: 3 engravings

Notes: Title page bears the number "-30-" beneath the en-
       graving.

Carroll, Lewis [Pseud of Charles Lutwidge Dodgson] — # 494
        1832-1898

A.L.S. One page (17.5 x 13.7cm), folded, written
front and back. Chirst Church, Oxford, Ja nuary 9,
1892 to "Dolly."

Notes : Has tongue-in-cheek criticism of "Dolly'S"
        fiance. Two other A.L.S.: one laid in
        Alice's Adventures in Wonderland, 1866, first
        ed., first issue, q.v. ; and one laid in the
        Hunting of the Snark, 1876, first ed., q.v.

Carroll, Lewis [Pseud of Charles Lutwidge Dodgson] . # 495
        1832-1898

Alice in Wunderland. Mit Zeichnungen und Acquarellen
von Robert Hogfeldt. Zurich: Artemis-Verlag, [1947].
Pp. [1-4] 5-123 [124].

Illus: 6 color plates + numerous smaller black on
       white illustrations.

Binding: Dust jacket illustrate with plate facing p.36.

Carroll, Lewis [Pseud of Charles Lutwidge Dodgson]   # 496
        1832-1898

Alice's Adventures in Wonderland. By Lewis Carroll. With forty-two illustrations by John Tenniel. New York: D. Appleton and Co., 455 Broadway, 1866. Pp. [i-xii, 1] 2-192.

Notes: First ed., first issue. A.L.S. to Miss # 497
       Lucy Walters, The Bungalow, Bourne Hall
       Road, Bushey Watford, England. Feb. 8, 1899,
       laid in. The letter has relevance to dating
                                          (cont'd)

Carroll. Alice's Adventures . . . . 1866. (Cont'd)

completion of the above work.
Leaves signed B-N.

Carroll, Lewis [Pseud of Charles Lutwidge Dodgson]   # 498
        1832-1898

Alice's Adventures in Wonderland . . . . Illustrations from drawings by Blanche McManus. New York:
M. F. Mansfield and A. Wessels, 1899. Pp. [4]+11-
121, [122].

Plates: Frontispiece +11: all color.

Carroll, Lewis [pseud. of Charles Lutwidge Dodgson,] # 499
        1832-1898

Alice's Adventures Under Ground. Being a Facsimile
of the Original Ms. Book afterwards developed into
"Alice's Adventures in Wonderland." Illustrated by
author. London & New York: Macmillan and Co. 1886.
Pp. [i] - [xvi], 1- [92], [93]- [96]; [1-4, adverts.].

Notes: Easter greeting by author, pp. [93-96].

Carroll, Lewis [pseud. of Charles Lutwidge Dodgson,] #500
        1832-1898

Alice's Adventures Under Ground. Being a Facsimile
of the Original Ms. Book afterwards developed into
"Alice's Adventures in Wonderland." Illustrated by
the Author. New York: The Macmillan Company, 1932.
Pp. [i-x], 1-92, [1-2, adverts.]

Illus: 14 full page + numerous smaller illus. [facs]

Binding: Has dust cover

Carroll, Lewis [Pseud of Charles Lutwidge Dodgson]   # 501
        1832-1898

The Hunting of the Snark: an agony in eight fits.
By Lewis Carroll author of "Alice's Adventures in
Wonderland," and "Through the Looking-Glass."
With nine illustrations by Henry Holiday. London:
Macmillan and Co., 1876. Pp. xi, [1-2] 3-83 [84].

Plates: Frontispiece +8
Binding: Original decorated blue-green cloth, en-
         closed in half morocco slipcase.
                                          (cont'd)

Carroll. Hunting of the Snark. 1876 (cont'd)

Notes: First ed. Presentation copy inscribed to
"Ellen Thorne from the Author. Mar. 19,
1892." A.L.S. Four pages, folded, written
front and back. Christ Church, Oxford, #502
April 27, 1892, to Elleanora Thorne.
Signed C.L. Dodgson.

#503

Carroll, Lewis [pseud. of Charles Lutwidge Dodgson,]
1832-1898

The Story of Sylvie and Bruno. Illustrated by
Harry Furniss. London: Macmillan and Co., Limited;
New York: The Macmillan Company, 1904. Pp. [i]-xii,
[1] -330, [1-2, adverts].

Plates: Frontispiece + cuts.

504

Carroll, Lewis (pseud) [Charles Lutwidge Dodgson] 1832-1898

Through the Looking-Glass, and what Alice found there. By
Lewis Carroll, author of "Alice's Adventures in Wonderland"
With fifty illustrations by John Tenniel. Boston: Lee
and Shepard. New York: Lee, Shepard, and Dillingham,
1872. Pp. [xii, 1] 2-25 [26] 27-45 [46] 47-65 [66] 67-90
[91] 92-112 [113] 114-136 [137] 138-156 [157] 158-184 [185]
186-212 [213-218] 219-224.

Illus: Numerous engravings.

Notes: First American edition. Title page has "(The
Right of Translation and Reproduction is reserved.)"

#505

Carroll, Lewis [Pseud of Charles Lutwidge Dodgson]
1832-1898

Through the Looking Glass . . . . With twelve full
page illustrations in color from drawings by
Blanche McManus. New York: M. F. Mansfield and A.
Wessels, 1899. Pp. [4] 11-139, [140].

Plates: Frontispiece + 11.

#506

Carruth, Hayden   1862-1932

The Voyage of the Rattletrap. Illustrated by H.
M. Wilder. New York: Harper and Brothers Publishers, 1897. Pp. [x] 1-207, [208].

Illus: Frontispiece + 36 other black and white included in pagination.

Notes: First ed.

#510

Castlemond, Harry [Pseud of Charles Austin Fosdick]
1842-1915

Frank on the Prairie by Harry Castlemond. Philadelphia: Porter and Coates; Cincinnati: R. W. Carroll
and Co., n.d. Pp. viii, 9-245 [246 + 8 pages adverts.]

Illus: Decorative title page
Notes: LC gives 1865.
        Title page has "Frank and Archie Series" but
        the decorative title page has "Gunboat Series."

#512

Anon.

A Catechism: Compiled and Recommended by the Worcester
Association of Ministers, for the Instruction and Improve-
ment of Children and Youth. Fifth edition, with Hymns.
Worcester: Published by George A. Trumbull, Manning and
Trumbull, Printers..., 1821.

Coll: 12°: A-C⁶ 18 leaves (13.9 X 8.5cm) Pp. [2-6] 7-34 [35]

Illus: Engraved frontispiece (inscribed "Trumbull's First
Edition")

Binding: Rebound over original blue wrappers

Notes: A_1^R and C_6^V pasted to wrappers. Bookplates of Howard
Pyle and John Stuart Groves.

#518

Catherwood, Mary Hartwell   1847-1902

The Chase of Saint-Castin and Other Stories of the
French in the New World. Boston and New York:
Houghton, Mifflin, and Company, 1895. Pp. [3] + 1 2-
266.

Contents: The Chase of Saint-Castin; The Beauport
Loup-Garou; The Mill at Petit Cap; Wolf's
Cave; The Windigo; The Kidnapped Bride;
Pontiac's Lookout.

Notes: First ed.

#519

Catherwood, Mary (Hartwell).   1847-1902

The Story of Tonty. Illustrated [by Enoch Ward].
Chicago: A. C. McClurg and Company, 1890. Pp. [1]-
vi, [7] - [228].

Plates: 10 + cuts.

#520

Catherwood, [Mrs.] Mary Hartwell   1847-1902

The White Islander. New York: The Century Co., 1893.
Pp. [i] - [xii], 1-164.

Plates: Frontispiece + 4.

Anon   #521

The Cat's Castle Besieged and Taken by the Rats.
Embellished with Fifteen Coloured Engravings.
London: Printed and Sold by John Marshall . . . ,
1819.

Coll: 8° A^16   16 leaves   (17.7 x 11cm)   Not
     paginated
Illus: Text and illustrations on facing pages
     alternating with blank facing pages
Binding: Rose paper boards with past-on title
     vignette
Notes: #S-;2-;0-49B

Anon.   #522

The Cat's Concert. For regardless at once both of wind
or of weather, there were guests of all sizes and nations
together. Philadelphia: Published and sold wholesale
and retail by Mary Charles, n.d.

Coll: 16°: [1-2^8] 16 leaves (12.7 X 10.2^cm·) ff 16

Illus: 14 hand colored engravings

Notes: Printed on one side of leaf only.

#527

Cervantes, [de Saavedra] Miguel   1547-1616

Don Quixote. [Illustrated by Jules Pelcoo.] [Ca 1870].
Ff. [12].

Notes: A book of colored engravings with captions
     in English, German, French, and Dutch.
     Captions are at the bottom of the page in
     double columns.

#528

Cervantes De Saavedra, Miguel   1547-1616

Don Quixote de la Mancha. Trans. Charles Jarvis,
Esq. Illustrated by Tony Johannot. 3 vols.
London: J. J. Dubochet & Co.

Vol I: 1837
Coll: 8° π^4 A^4 b-c^4 B-30^4 3H^5   245 leaves   (24.8 x
     15.5cm) Pp. [i-viii, 1] 2-8 [ix] x-liv [lv-
     lvi, 9] 10-434.
Contents: Pp. [ix]-liv: "Memoir of Cervantes with a
     Notice of His Works" based upon that of
     M. Viardot.   (cont'd)

Cervantes   Don Quixote   (3 vols.)   (Cont'd)

Vol II: 1838
Coll: 8° [A^4] B-3^4 268 leaves   (24.8 x 15.5cm)
     Pp. [1-9] 10-416, 415--534 (total of 536).

Vol III: 1839
Coll: 8° [A^4] B-30^4 3X^5 269 leaves   (24.8 x 15.5cm)
     Pp. [1-9] 10-538.

Illus: Hundreds of engravings by Johannot in texts.
Binding: Half morocco, brown and gilt tooled on
     backs, green on sides, top edges gilt.

Chadwick, Henry   1824-1908   #529

The Sports and Pastimes of American Boys: a guide
and text-book of games of the play-ground, the
parlor, and the field. Illustrated. New York:
George Routledge and Sons, [1884]. Pp. [i-iv,] [9]
10-303+[1].

Plates: Frontispiece +3 (full-page in color)

Notes: Probable first edition.

CHAPBOOK   #532

The Adventures of a Halfpenny; commonly called a
Birmingham Halfpenny, or Counterfeit; as related
by itself. Banbury: Printed and Sold by J.G.
Rusher, n.d. [ca. 1810].
8 leaves (11.1 x 6.8cm). 8 cuts. Bound in blue
wrappers, with cut and poem on back and advertisements
on the inside. From the Merritt Collection.

CHAPBOOK   #533

The Cheerful Warbler, or Juvenile Song Book. York:
Printed and Sold by J. Kendrew, Colliergate, n.d.
8 leaves (9.9 x 6.5cm). 14 cuts.

CHAPBOOK   #534

The Children in the Wood Restored, By Honestas, the
Hermit of the Forest; or Perfidy Detected. . . .
The Sequel to the History of the Children in the
Wood. Banbury: Printed by J.G. Rusher, n.d.
[ca. 1840].
8 leaves (9.8 X 6.5cm). 11 cuts. Unbound, unopened,
uncut. Unfolded sheet measures 26.2 X 19.6cm.
From the Merritt Collection.

CHAPBOOK   #535

The Child's Instructor, or Picture Alphabet.
Glasgow: Printed and sold, wholesale, by Lumsden &
Son, n.d.
16 leaves (10.5 X 6.6cm). 28 cuts. Bound in
brown wrappers.

CHAPBOOK #536

Cinderella; or the Little Glass Slipper. York: Printed by J. Kendrew, Colliergate, n.d. 8 leaves (9.8 X 6.5cm). 16 cuts.

CHAPBOOK #541

The Life of Jack Sprat. Banbury: Printed by J.G. Rusher, n.d. 16 leaves (9.4 X 6.3cm). 16 cuts. Unbound, unopened, uncut. From Merritt Collection.

CHAPBOOK #537

The Cries of Banbury and London, and Celebrated Stories. Banbury: Printed by J.G. Rusher, n.d. [ca. 1840]. 8 leaves (9.8 X 6.5cm). 16 cuts. Unbound, unopened, uncut. From Merritt Collection.

CHAPBOOK #542

Nursery Rhymes, from the Royal Collections. Banbury: Printed by J.G. Rusher. 8 leaves (9.8 X 6.5 cm). 14 cuts. Unbound, unopened, uncut. From Merritt Collection. [n.d.]

CHAPBOOK. #538

The Fairy and the Farmer. Smithfield: Printed by J.L. Marks, n.d. 4 leaves (10.7 X 6.5cm) unopened. Bound in lavender wrappers with "Paul Pry's Magic Lantern" on front.

CHAPBOOK #543

The Renowned History of Dame Trot and Her Cat. Banbury: J.G. Rusher, n.d. [ca. 1840]. 8 leaves (9.4 X 6.3cm). 11 cuts. Unbound, unopened, uncut. Unfolded sheet measures 25.3 X 19cm. From Merritt Collection.

CHAPBOOK #539

Gammer Gurton's Garland of Nursery Songs, and Toby Tickle's Collection of Riddles. Compiled by Peter Puzzlecap, Esq. Embellished with a variety of Cuts. Glasgow: Published and Sold Wholesale by Lumsden and Son, n.d. [ca. 1815]. 16 leaves (10.2 X 6.4cm). 26 cuts. Bound in tan wrappers with cuts front and back. Bookplate of Percival Merritt.

CHAPBOOK #544

Scripture Histories; from the Creation of the World, To the Death of Jesus Christ. With a Description of St. Paul's Church, London. Decorated with Cuts. Wellington: Printed by F. Houlston and Son, n.d. [ca. 1820]. 12 leaves (10.4 X 6.4cm). 8 cuts. Bound in blue wrappers. Advertisments. Bookplate of Percival Merritt.

CHAPBOOK #540

Jack & Jill And Old Dame Gill. Banbury: Printed by J.G. Rusher, n.d. [ca. 1840]. 8 leaves (9.8 X 6.5cm). 15 cuts. Unbound, unopened, uncut. From Merritt Collection.

CHAPBOOK #545

A Short History of Birds & Beasts, for the Amusement and Instruction of Children. Adorned with Cuts. Wellington, Salop: Printed by F. Houlston and Son, n.d. [ca. 1820]. 12 leaves (10.5 X 6.6cm). 13 cuts. Bound in tan wrappers, with advertisements in back. Bookplate of Percival Merritt.

CHAPBOOK #546

Tom, The Piper's Son. York: Printed by J. Kendrew, Colliergate, n.d.
8 leaves (9.8 X 6.6cm). 16 cuts.

Anon. #553-5

CHAPBOOKS A3 (ca. 1820).

Tom Tucker. London: Bishop & Co., Printers, n.d.
Coll: 16°: [A⁴]. 4 leaves (12.8 X 9.4cm). 8 cuts.

Jacky Dandy. London: Bishop & Co., Printers, n.d.
Coll: 16°: [A⁴]. 4 leaves (12.2 X 9.3cm). 8 cuts.

Jack Sprat and his Cat. London: Bishop & Co., n.d.
Coll: 16°: [A⁴]. 4 leaves (12.3 X 9.2cm). 8 cuts.

CHAPBOOK #547

The Waggon Load of Money. York: Printed and Sold by James Kendrew, Colliergate, n.d.
8 leaves (9.8 X 6.6cm). 19 cuts.

Anon. #556-7

CHAPBOOKS A4 (ca. 1820).

The Riddle Book. London: Bishop & Co., Printers, n.d.
Coll: 16°: [A⁴]. 4 leaves (12.8 X 9.3cm). 7 cuts.

Songs For Little Children. London: Bishop & Co., Printers, n.d.
Coll: 16°: [A⁴]. 4 leaves (12.6 X 9.4cm). 9 cuts. Contains:
The Great Bell at Bow; High diddle diddle; Bah, Bah, Black Sheep; Ride a Cock-Horse.

CHAPBOOK #548

The World Turned Upside Down; or, No News, and Strange News. York: Printed and Sold by J. Kendrew, Colliergate, n.d.
16 leaves (10 X 6.7cm). 29 cuts. Bound in yellow wrappers, with advertisements on back.

Anon. #558-9

CHAPBOOKS B1. The following six are bound together with original wrappers.

The House that Jack Built; To which is Added, Some Account of the Affectionate Little Arthur. Adorned with Cuts. Beverley: Printed by M. Turner, and sold by G. Turk (?) Hull (?), 1812.
16 leaves (10.1 X 6.1cm, all unsigned). 15 hand-color cuts. Bound in blue wrappers. Advertisements in final leaf.

Little Tom, the Huntsman's Boy. Second Edition. Wellington, Salop: Printed by and for Houlston and Son, 1827.
16 leaves (10.1 X 6.1cm, all unsigned). Frontispiece +

Anon. #549-550

CHAPBOOKS A1 (ca. 1820). All nine bound together in late 18th c. cloth.

History of Mary Ann. London: Bishop & Co., Printers, n.d.
Coll: 16°: [A⁴]. 4 leaves (12.5 X 9.4cm). 7 cuts.

The Tragical Death of An Apple Pie. London: Bishop & Co., Printers, n.d.
Coll: 16°: [A⁴]. 4 leaves (12.5 X 9.6cm). 2 cuts + alphabet.

Anon. #560-1

CHAPBOOKS B2.

6 hand-colored cuts. Bound in gray wrappers. Advertisements on back of wrapper.

Nothing at All. Wellington, Salop: Printed by and for F. Houlston and Son, 1824.
8 leaves (10.1 X 6.1cm). Frontispiece + 4 hand-colored cuts. Bound in light blue wrappers; advertisements on back, from lists "By the Author of Enquiries into Natural Causes and Effects."

The History of Three Silver Trouts. Decorated with Cuts.

Anon. #551-2

CHAPBOOKS A2 (ca. 1820).

Red Riding Hood. London: Bishop & Co., Printers, n.d.
Coll: 16°: [A⁴]. 4 leaves (12.6 X 9.5cm). 6 cuts + alphabet. A short version in verse.

The History of Dame Crump. London: Bishop & Co., Printers, n.d.
Coll: 16°: [A⁴]. 4 leaves (12.7 X 9.4cm). 9 cuts + alphabet.

Anon.

CHAPBOOKS B3.

Wellington, Salop: Printed by and for F. Houlston & Son, 1821.
16 leaves (10.1 X 6.1cm). Frontispiece + 6 hand-colored cuts. Bound in brown wrappers, advertisements on back.

#562
A Visit to an Infants-School. By Mrs. Cameron, author of "Emma and her Nurse,"--"Margaret Whyet,"--"The Two Lambs," &c. &c. London: Printed for Houlston and Son, 1831.
16 leaves (10.1 X 6.1cm). Frontispiece + 6 hand-colored cuts. Bound in blue wrappers, advertisements on back.

Anon.   # 563

CHAPBOOKS B4.

The Little Dog Dash. Wellington, Salop: Printed by and for
Houlston and Son, 1828.
24 leaves (10.1 X 6.1cm). Frontispiece + 6 hand-colored
cuts. Bound in orchid wrappers, advertisements on back.

Chapbooks

see also

The Merry Andrew . . . . Brentford,
printed by P. Norbury. n.d.

A New Riddle Book, or a whetstone for Dull
Wits. Derby: n.d.

Pearson, Edwin. Banbury Chap Books. Lon--
don, 1890.

Anon.   # 564-5

CHAPBOOKS C1. (ca. 1820).

Pretty Tales, Containing Five Entertaining Stories, For
the amusement and instruction of Little Children. By
Timothy Teachwell. Chelmsford: Printed and Sold by I.
Marsden.
12 leaves (12 X 7.1cm). Frontispiece + 8 cuts. Contains
Solomon Wiseman, Johny Badboy, Billy Blossom, The Cat and
Fish, Nancy Wheatley, and The Sad Effects of Quarreling.
Bound in gray wrappers, with woodcut on back. McKell copy
lacks leaves 1 and 12.

The History of Abou Casem, and His two remarkable Slippers

Chaucer, Geoffrey   1340-1400   # 570

The Canterbury Tales of Geoffrey Chaucer. Illustra-
ted after drawings by William Flint. Boston: Hale
Cushman & Flint; London: Jonathan Cape & The
Medior Society. [1928]. Pp. xv+ 1-637 [638].

Plates: Frontispiece in color +23 in color.

Anon.

CHAPBOOKS C2. (ca. 1820).

To which is added, The History of the Master Cat; or, Puss
in Boots. Chelmsford: Printed and Sold by I. Marsden.
12 leaves (12.5 X 7.1cm). 5 cuts. Bound in gray wrappers
with woodcut on back.

Juvenile Dialogues; or Recreations for School Boys, # 566
during thier Leisure Hours at Boarding School. By Billy
Merrythought. Chelmsford: Printed and sold by I. Marsden.
12 leaves (12.5 X 7.1cm). 14 cuts. Also contains Wise
Sayings for Children. Bound in green wrappers, with woodcuts on back and on the verso of the front.

Chester, George Randolph   1869-1924   # 572

Get-Rich-Quick Wallingford. [Illustrated.] Philadelphia: Henry Altemus Company, [1908]. Pp. [1]-
448.

Plates: Frontispiece +5.

Anon.   # 567-8

CHAPBOOKS C3. (ca. 1820).

The Cottage Piper or History of Edgar, The Itinerant
Musician; An Instructive Tale. Ornamented with Cuts.
Chelmsford: Printed and Sold by I. Marsden.
12 leaves (12.5 X 7.1cm). 3 woodcuts. Bound in gray
wrappers, with woodcut on back.

The Young Traveller's Delight; Containing the Lives of
Several Noted Characters, Likely to amuse All good Children. Chelmsford: Printed and Sold by I. Marsden.
12 leaves (12.5 X 7.1cm). 6 woodcuts. Contains Little
Tom the Traveller and The Lion, Nancy Tender, Sammy and

Chesterfield, [Philip Dormer Stanhope] Lord 1694-1773 ## 573

Lord Chesterfield's Maxims; or, A New Plan of Education
. . . . Being the Substance of the Earl of Chester-
field's Letters, to his Son . . . . London: Printed for
F. Newbery, 1774.

Coll: 24° A⁶B-C⁹D-H⁶   54 leaves (13.5 x 8.4cm) xii +
90 + 6pp.

Plates: Engraved frontispiece

Notes: H4: "Books printed for F. Newbery." Roscoe #
53(1). Bookplate of Percival Merritt.

Anon.   # 569

CHAPBOOKS C4. (ca. 1820).

Jeremy, George and The Dragon, and The Fortunate Suicide.
Bound in green wrappers, with woodcut in back.

Fat and Lean; or, The Fairy Queen, Exhibiting the Effects
of Moral Magic, By The Ring and The Three Mirrors. Chelmsford: Printed and Sold by I. Marsden.
12 leaves (12.5 X 7.1cm). 7 cuts. Also contains Nat and
Mat. Bound in gray wrappers.

The six preceding titles are bound together in their
original wrappers in the McKell copy.

Child, Mrs. [Lydia Maria (Francis)] 1802-1880 # 574

The Happy Grandmother. To which is added The White
Palfrey. [N. d.]

Coll: 18° A¹⁸   18 leaves (13.3 x 8.2cm) Pp. [3] 4-36.

Plates: Frontispiece signed "G.A." 2 plates.

Notes: Closely clipped at bottom.
Bound in with six others in Omnibus # 1, q.v.

#575

Child, Mrs. [Lydia Maria (Francis)] 1802-1880

The Little Girl's Own Book. By Mrs. Child. Author of "The Frugal Housewife". . . . New York: Clark, Austin & Co., 1849.

Coll: 8°: 1 -18⁸ 144 leaves (14.3 x 11.9cm) Pp. [i-iii] iv [v] vi-viii [ix-xii, 13] 14-288.

Plates: Frontispiece (hand-colored copper plate engraving) +cuts.

#579

Children's Literature, Books and Manuscripts: An exhibition November 19, 1954 through February 28, 1955. Foreword by Herbert Cahoon. New York: The Pierpont Morgan Library, 1954.

#576

Child, Mrs. [Lydia Maria (Francis)] 1802-1880

The Little Girl's Own Book. By Mrs. Child. Illustrated. Boston: American Stationers Company, John B. Russell, 1837.

Coll: 8°: [1]-18⁸ 144 leaves (13.8 x 11.6cm) Pp. [i-iii] iv [v] vi-viii [ix-xii, 13] 14-288.
Illus: Numerous cuts.

Notes: Entered 1833. LC lists an 1834 ed. only.

#580

The Children's Magazine. Vol. II for 1830. New York: Published by the General Protestant Episcopal Sunday School Union. Printed at the Protestant Episcopal Press..., 1830.

Coll: 12°: π² 1-11¹² 12¹⁰ 144 leaves (14.45 X 8.9cm) Pp. [i-iv][1] 2-284

Illus: 26 woodcuts

Notes: 10₇ and 8₇ are partially missing from McKell copy.

#577

Anon.

The Children in the Wood. An Affecting Tale. Cooperstown: Stereotyped, printed and sold by H.&E. Phinney, 1837.

Coll: 16°: [1¹⁶] 16 leaves (8.9 X 13.2cm) Pp. [1-5] 6-31 [32]

Binding: Bound in printed yellow wrappers

Notes: See also The Affecting History of the Children in the Wood. . . . Hartford. 1798.

#581

Anon.

Children's Offerings to Heathen Idols. Revised by the Committee of Publication Sunday-School Union. Philadelphia: American Sunday-School Union, . . . [1846?]

Coll: 12°: 1-2⁶ 12 leaves (14.2 X 9.1cm) Pp. [1-4] 5-24

Illus: Woodcut frontispiece

#578

Anon.

Children of Wood: to which is added, Tales of the Governess. York: Printed and Sold by Edw. Peck, 1802.

Coll: 32°: A⁴ B¹⁶ C⁴ (=A5-8) 24 leaves (10.3 X 6.6cm.) Pp.[1]2-5,6-47[48]

Illus: Engraved frontispiece
Binding: Pink wrappers; initial and final leaves serve as paste down endpapers.
Notes: C2ᵛ-C4: advertisements

#582

Childs, George. 1829-1894

Child's Drawing Book of Objects: Studies from Still Life, For Young Pupils and Drawing Classes in Schools. By George Childs. Philadelphia: John W. Moore, 1843. [Reprinted by Walter and Barbara Schatzki, 1950.]

Coll: 26 leaves (19.1 x 27.2 cm.).

Illus: 288 "objects" lithographed by Pinkerton, Wagner, & Mc Guiyon, Philadelphia, on 24 plates.

The Children in the Wood

see also under

Marks' Edition

and

CHAPBOOK

#583.1

Anon.

The Child's Grammar: or English Grammar Illustrated. Cadiz, Ohio: Published by H. Anderson, Engraver, Printer, & Publisher of Maps, Prints, & Juvenile Books. n.d.

Coll: 12°: [1¹²] 12 leaves (13.4 X 9.1cm.) Ff. [1]2-12

Notes: Blank facing pages alternate with facing pages containing text and hand-tinted engravings. Engraved conjugate leaves are pasted on paper boards to form title page and rear advertisement for the book. Inside rear cover: "M-5-23-44B"/ "QM-5-23-44L)"; [1¹²] of the McKell copy is missing.

Anon.   #*583,2*

The Child's Grammar, or English Grammar Illustrated.
Cadiz, Ohio: Published by H. Anderson, Engraver, Printer,
& Publisher of Maps, Prints, & Juvenile Books. n.d.

Coll: 12° [1¹²] 12 leaves (13.7 X 9.2^{cm}·) Ff. [1] 2-12

Notes: Blank facing pages alternate with facing pages
       containing text and hand-tinted engravings. En-
       graved conjugate leaves are pasted on blue paper
       boards to form title page and rear advertisement
       for the book. Inside rear cover: "(M-5-23-446)/
       S-6-20-47B/6-20-47-L" on [1₁^R] "A. N. Washburn,/
       presented by Emily Kilborn/Worthington,/1829.

Anon.   #*584*

The Child's Library. New York: Printed and sold by
Mahlon Day, at the Juvenile Book-store, 1825. [12 in
one volume].

Coll: 32° π² [1-12⁸]   96 leaves (9.3 X 5.5^{cm}·)

Contents: "The A,B,C, In Verse" Pp. [1] 2-16
          "The Good Child's Little Primer" Pp. [1] 2-16
          "Little Stories for Little Children" Pp. [1] 2-16
          "The New-York Cries" Pp. [1-2] 3-16
          "Picture of New-York" Pp. [1-2,3] 4-16
          "The Farm House" Pp. [1-2] 3-16
          "A Hymn on Creation" Pp. [1-2] 3-16
          "Youthful Sports" Pp. [1-2, 3] 4-16
                                        (cont'd)

Anon   (Cont'd)

The Child's Library. [Entered 9 April, 1825].
          "Travellers Mounted upon Curious and
           Wonderful Animals" Pp. [1-2] 3-16.
          "The Little Field Daisy" Pp. [1] 2-16
          "The Amusing Puzzling Book" Pp. [1] 2-16
          "Juvenile Pastimes, In Verse" Pp. [1-2] 3-
          16.
Illus: Numerous woodcuts.
Notes: Each has its own title page; Single title
       page for whole volume on π 1 (contents on
       π 2)
                                        (cont'd)

The Child's Library.   (Cont'd)

       In the table of contents number 2 is listed
       "The Good Child's Little Spelling Book";
       number 4 is listed "New-York Cries in Rhyme";
       and, number 7 "Hymn on Creation."

Anon.   #*585*

Child's Life of Washington, with Ten Illustrations. Philadelphia and Baltimore: Fisher and
Brother, [1860].

Coll: 64°; [1-9⁸] 10-12⁸; 96 leaves (7.2 X
      5.4 cm.); pp. [1-iv] v [vi], [7] 8-192.

Illus: Engravings.

Anon.   #*586*

The Child's Pictorial Geometry. Hartford, Conn. & Berea,
Ohio: E.B. & E.C. Kellogg, 1842.

Coll: 12° [1-12]² 24 leaves (14.45 X 11.1^{cm}·) Ff. [1-24]

Binding: stabbed

Notes: Printed from engraved plates. Blank facing pages
       alternate with facing engravings. Title page on
       cover. On front cover "36805." Bookplate of
       Caroline Maria Bewins. On rear attached end paper
       "M-A-L"/"S-1-20-45L"/ "S-12-10-49B"

Anon.   #*587*

The Child's Pictorial Music Book. Hartford, Conn. &
Berea, Ohio: Published by E.B. & E.C. Kellogg, n.d.

Coll: 12° [1-12]² 24 leaves (13.95 X 10.2^{cm}·) Ff. [1-24]

Binding: stabbed

Notes: Printed from engraved plates. Blank facing pages
       alternate with facing engravings. Title page on
       cover. On rear attached end-paper "S-12-10-49B"

Anon.   #*588*

The Child's Pictorial Preceptor. Hartford, Conn. & Berea,
Ohio: Published by E.B. & E.C. Kellogg. n.d.

Coll: 16°: 1², 2, 3², 4, 5², 6, 7², 8, 9², 10, 11², 12,
      13², 14   21 leaves (14.5 X 11.7^{cm}·) Ff. [1-21]

Plates: 21 engravings.

Notes: McKell #s: (M-A-L) S-9-13-44-L; S-1-20-45-L;
       S-9-18-44B. A book of plates. McKell copy lacks
       back cover.

                                         #*589*

Anon

A Choice Collection of Riddles, Charades, Rebusses,
&c. Part Second. By Peter Puzzlewell, Esq. London: Printed for E. Newbery, 1796.

Coll: 12° A-I⁶ 54 leaves (13.9 x 8.6cm) 108pp.

Plates: Engraved frontispiece

Notes: Bookplate of Percival Merritt. Roscoe #
       311(3).

Chroniques de France   #*592*

Joan the Maid of Orleans, Being that portion of the
Chronicle of St. Denis which deals with her life and
times, from the Chroniques de France printed in Paris
in 1493. Now translated by Pauline B. Sowers with reproductions of woodcuts from the original edition and a
bibliographical note on the work of Antoine Verard. San
Francisco: Roy Vernon Sowers, 1938. Pp. [8+ i-ii, iii]
iv-xxv.

 # 593

[ANON]. Chronology Made familiar and easy to Young Gentlemen and Ladies. To which is added, A Table of the most memorable Events from The Beginning of the World. Being the Seventh Volume of the Circle of the Sciences, &c. The Third Edition Corrected. London: Printed for Newbery and Carnan, 1770.

Coll.: 32°: A-S⁸. 144 leaves (9.2 X 6.3cm). [1-iv]v-xiv, xiv-xv[1]2-272 pp.

C1,2,3 missigned D2,3,4.

Binding: Blue boards, red leather spine.
Notes: Roscoe #62(3a); bookplate of Percival Merritt.

Anon   **# 594**

Chronology Made Familiar and Easy to Young Gentlemen and Ladies. To which is added, A Table of the most memorable Events from the Beginning of the World. Being the Seventh Volume of the Circle of the Sciences, &c. The Fourth Edition. London: . . . for T. Carnan and F. Newbery, Junior, 1778.

Coll: 24° A-S⁸ 144 leaves (9.8 x 6.5cm), Pp. xvi, 17-272.
Binding: Marbled boards, green vellum spine with paper label.
Notes: Roscoe #62(4)

Chukovskii, K[orn]   1882-   **#595**

Skazki.(Fairy Tales) Academia, 1935. Pp.[1-8,]9-158[159-161, 162 (blank), 163 (colophon), 164, blank].

Plates: 8 enameled (or oil) on thick morocco grain paper; with decorative cuts.
Notes: Stamped on title page "Printed in Soviet Union." See also under Skazka and Skazki: Russian children's books.

Anon   **# 598**

City Cries: or, a peep at scenes in town. By an observer. Illustrated with twenty-four designs by Croome. Philadelphia: George S. Appleton; New York: D. Appleton & Co., 1850.

Coll: 16° 1⁸ 2-6⁸ 7⁴ 52 leaves (14.1 x 11.4cm) Pp. [i-iii] iv-vi [7-8] 9-102 [103-104+1-16: adverts bound in at end].
Plates: Engraved half-title+23 full page illustrations in text.

Anon.   **# 599**

City Sights for Little Folks. [Tom Thumb Series]. New York: Clark, Austin & Smith, 3 Park Row & 3 Ann-Street, [ca..1852]

Coll: 24°: A-M⁸ 96 leaves (8.3 X 6.2cm) Pp. [i-iv] v-vii, 8-191 [192]
Illus: Numerous woodcuts (one every other leaf from A5 to M7)
Binding: Wrappers, stabbed
Notes: Illustration pages are not numbered on verso (from verso of p. 9 to verso of p. 189)

Clark, Adam   **# 600**

Epitome of the Jewish History, &c. Abridged from Dean Prideaux, by Dr. Adam Clark. New York: Published by B. Waugh and T. Mason, for the Methodist Episcopal Church, at the conference office, 14 Crosby-Street. J. Collard, Printer. [For the Sunday School Union of the Methodist Episcopal, etc.] 1832.

Coll: 8° 1-3⁸, 4⁶, 1-2⁸ 46 leaves (13.1 x 8.2cm) Pp. [1-2,3] 4-58 [59-60]; [1] 2-32.

               (cont'd)

Epitome of the Jewish History. (Cont'd)

Contents: Pp.[1]2-32: "African Valley."

Notes: Colophon on page 32 of "African Valley."

[Clemens, Samuel Langhorne]   1835-1910   **# 601**

Adventures of Huckleberry Finn (Tom Sawyer's Comrade). By Mark Twain. Illustrated [by Edward Windsor Kemble]. New York: Charles L. Webster and Company, 1885. Pp.[1] 2-366.

Plates: 2 frontispieces+174 illustrations

Notes: First American edition, first issue, first state (second ?); see Blanck #3415; Merle Johnson, p. 43ff. Portrait frontispiece: second state; p. 283: third state; p. 155: first state (Blank); leaf 238 pasted under terminal end paper.

[Clemens, Samuel Langhorne]   1835-1910   **# 602**

Adventures of Huckleberry Finn (Tom Sawyer's Comrade). By Mark Twain. Illustrated [by Edward Windsor Kemble]. New York: Charles L. Webster and Company, 1885. Pp.[1] 2-366, blank leaf.

Plates: 2 frontispieces+174 illustrations

Notes: First American edition, first issue, third state (Merle Johnson, p. 45; Blanck, Bibliography of American Lit., Vol. II, p. 99, #3415). First state of portrait frontispiece; p. 283: third state.

[Clemens, Samuel Langhorne]   1835-1910   **# 603**

Adventures of Huckleberry Finn (Tom Sawyer's Comrade). By Mark Twain. Illustrated [by Edward Windsor Kemble]. New York: Charles L. Webster and Company, 1885. Pp.[1] 2-367 [368].

Plates: Two frontispieces+ 174 illustrations
Notes: First American edition, second issue (Blanck #3415; Merle Johnson, p. 43ff.). Portrait frontispiece: third state; p. 283: fourth state. Errors on pp. [13], 57, 58, 59 have been corrected or agree with later states;

               (cont'd)

Clemens. Huckleberry Finn (First Am. Ed., second issue). (Cont'd)

    (See Blanck and Johnson. P. 155: third state).

#608

Clemens, Samuel Langhorne]   1835-1910

A Connecticut Yankee in King Arthur's Court. Intro. by Carl Van Doren. Illustrated by Honoré Guilbeau. New York: Limited Editions Club, 1949. Pf. 143.

Illus: Cuts

Notes: #565 of 1500. Signed by illustrator.

#604

[Clemens, Samuel Langhorne]   1835-1910

The Adventures of Huckleberry Finn (Tom Sawyer's Comrade). Illustrated [by Edward Windsor Kemble]. London: Chatto & Windus, 1884. Pp. xvi, [1] 2-438 + 2+34 of adverts bound in at end .

Plates: Frontispiece +174 illustrations.
Binding: State A
Notes: First English edition; See Blanck #3414.

#609

[Clemens, Samuel Langhorne]   1835-1910

Curious Dream and other sketches. By Mark Twain. London: George Routledge and Sons, Limited, [1872]. Pp.[1] 2-150; [1-8 of adverts].

#605

[Clemens, Samuel Langhorne]   1835-1910

The Adventures of Tom Sawyer. By Mark Twain. [Illustrated by True W. Williams]. Hartford, Conn.: Chicago, Ill.; Cincinnati, Ohio: The American Publishing Company. San Francisco, Cal.: A. Roman & Co., 1876. Pp.[i-xii, 17] 18-274 [275]+2+[1-4 of adverts].

Plates: Frontispiece +cuts.
Notes: First edition, second printing, issue A (Blanck #3369); ["ix"] mispaginated xii; ["x"] mispaginated xiii; ["xii"] mis   paginated xvi.

#610

Clemens, Samuel L[anghorne]   1835-1910

Following the Equator: a journey around the world. By Mark Twain. [Illustrated by Dan Beard, A.B. Frost, B.W. Clinedienst, Frederick Dielman, Peter Newell, F.M. Seinor, T.F. Fogarty, C.H. Warren, A.G. Reinhart, F. Berkeley Smith, C. Allan Gilbert. Photographs by Walter G. Chase, Major J.B. Pond, and F.R. Reynolds.] Hartford, Conn.: The American Publishing Company, 1897. Pp.[1] 2-712.

Plates: Frontispiece +numerous full-page plates included in pagination.

    (cont'd)

#606

[Clemens, Samuel Langhorne]   1835-1910

The Celebrated Jumping Frog of Calaveras County, and other sketches. By Mark Twain. ed. John Paul [Charles Henry Webb]. New York: C.H. Webb, Publisher, 1867. Pp.[1] 2-198+[2].

Notes: First edition, second issue (see Blanck #3310).

Clemens. Following the Equator.   (Cont'd)

Notes: First American edition (Blanck, #3451).

#607

[Clemens, Samuel Langhorne]   1835-1910

A Connecticut Yankee in King Arthur's Court. By Mark Twain. [Illustrated by Daniel Carter Beard.] New York: Charles L. Webster & Company, 1889. Pp. [i] ii-xv [xvi,] 17-575+ 1-2 of adverts.

Plates: Frontispiece + illustrations.

#611

Clemens, Samuel L[anghorne]   1835-1910

Holograph ms leaf (19.5 x 16.1cm) torn from ruled notebook.

(Clemens, Samuel L[anghorne])   1835-1910   #612

The Innocents Abroad, or the new Pilgrim's Progress.
By Mark Twain. Illustrated [by True W. Williams].
Hartford, Conn.: The American Publishing Company,
1898. Pp. [1-xviii, 19] 20-651.

Plates: 2 frontispieces + 13 (most are illustrations).

[Clemens, Samuel Langhorne]   1835-1910   #613

Life on the Mississippi. By Mark Twain. [Illustrated]
Boston: James R. Osgood and Company, 1883. Pp. [1]
2-624.

Plates: Frontispiece + "more than 300 illustrations."

Notes: First American edition, first state, intermediate A (Blanck, #3411).

[Clemens, Samuel Langhorne]   1835-1910   #614

The Prince and the Pauper: a tale for young people
of all ages. By Mark Twain. Illustrated [by Frank
Thayer Merrill]. Boston: James R. Osgood and
Company, 1882. Pp. [1] 2-411 + 2 blank leaves.

Illus: 192.
Notes: First American edition, binding is state A
(Blanck #3401).

[Clemens, Samuel Langhorne]   1835-1910   #615.1

The Prince and the Pauper: a tale for young people
of all ages. By Mark Twain. Illustrated [by Frank
Thayer Merrill]. Boston: James R. Osgood and
Company, 1882. Pp. [1] 2-411 + 2 blank leaves.

Illus: 192.
Notes: First American edition; binding is state B
(Blanck, #3402).

[Clemens, Samuel Langhorne]   1835-1910   #615.2

The Prince and the Pauper: a tale for young people
of all ages. By Mark Twain. Illustrated [by Frank
Thayer Merrill]. Boston: James R. Osgood and
Company, 1882. Pp. [1] 2-411 + 2 blank leaves.

Illus: 192.
Notes: First American edition; binding is state B
(Blanck, #3402).

[Clemens, Samuel Langhorne]   1835-1910   #616

The Prince and the Pauper: a tale for young people
of all ages. By Mark Twain. Illustrated [by Frank
Thayer Merrill]. New York: Charles L. Webster and
Company, 1885. Pp. [1] 2-411, + 1 blank leaf.

Illus: 192.

[Clemens, Samuel Langhorne]   1835-1910   #617

Punch, Brothers, Punch! and other sketches. New
York: Slote, Woodman & Co., 1878. Pp. [1-5,] 6-140
+ 1 + 3 of adverts.

Notes: First edition, second state; Blanck #3378;
Merle Johnson, pp. 31-32.

(Clemens, Samuel L[anghorne])   1835-1910   #618

Roughing It. By Mark Twain. Fully illustrated by
eminent artists. Hartford, Conn.: American Pub-
lishing Company; Chicago, Ill.: F.G. Gilman & Co.;
Toledo, Ohio: W.E. Bliss; Cincinnati, Ohio:
Nettleton & Co.; Philadelphia, Penn.: D. Ashmead;
New Orleans, La.: J.W. Goodspeed; San Francisco,
Cal.: A. Roman & Company, 1872. Pp. [1] ii-xviii,
[19] 20-591, + 1 of adverts.

Plates: 2 frontispieces +6.

                                        (cont'd)

(Clemens). Roughing It.   (Cont'd)

Binding: Library (i.e., sheep) covers.

Notes: First American edition (Blanck, #3337). With
adverts, p. [592]. P. 242: state B (Blanck;
State 2: Johnson).

[Clemens, Samuel Langhorne]   1835-1910   #619

Saint Joan of Arc. By Mark Twain. Illustrated by
Howard Pyle. Decorated by Wilfred J. Jones. New
York and London: Harper & Brothers Publishers,
1919. Pp. [1-xvi, 1] 2-32 + [6.]

Plates: Frontispiece + 3 colored illustrations.

[Clemens, Samuel Langhorne]   1835-1910   # 620

Saint Joan of Arc. By Mark Twain. With illustrations
in color by Howard Pyle. Decorations in tint by
Wilfred J. Jones. New York and London: Harper &
Brothers Publishers, 1919. Pp. [i-xvi, 1] 2-32 +[6].

Plates: Frontispiece +3 color illustrations.
Binding: Dust cover.
Notes: First edition. Pp. [35-38] unopened.

[Clemens, Samuel Langhorne]   1835-1910   # 621

Saint Joan of Arc. By Mark Twain. With illustrations
in color by Howard Pyle. Decorations in tint by
Wilfred J. Jones. New York & London: Harper &
Brothers Publishers, 1919. Pp. [i-xvi, 1] 2-32 +[6].

Plates: Frontispiece +3 color illustrations.

(Clemens, Samuel L[anghorne])   1835-1910   #622

A Tramp Abroad; Illustrated by W[alter] Fr[ancis].
Brown, True [W.] Williams, B. Day, and other artists
--with also three or four pictures made by the
author of this book, without outside help; in all
three hundred and twenty-eight illustrations. By
Mark Twain. Hartford, Conn.: American Publishing
Company; London: Chatto & Windus, 1880. Pp. [i] ii-
xvi, 17-631 + 1 page of adverts.

Plates: 2 frontispieces +28 (included in pagination)
+ 5.

(cont'd)

(Clemens) A Tramp Abroad.   (Cont'd)

Binding: With Library (i.e., sheep) binding.

Notes: First American edition (Blanck, #3386).
       Portrait frontispiece: second state (Blanck);
       frontispiece: first state.

Clouston, W[illiam] A[lexander]   1843-1896   #623

Hieroglypnic Bibles, Their Origin and History: a hitherto unwritten chapter of bibliography with Facsimile illustrations; also Frederick A. Laing. A New Hieroglyphic
Bible Told in Stories. Glasgow: David Bryce and Son,
1894. Pp. [xvi,1] 2-316 +184 plates [comprising Laing's
Hieroglyphic Bible].

Notes: McKell # S-7-6-4b-L

Cobb, Mrs. C. S.   ca. 1800-1880   #624

The Fire-Fly, a story for children. Translated from
the French, by Mrs. C. S. Cobb. Published by Lyman
Cobb, Jun., 1855.

Coll: 16° [1]16   16 leaves (14.3 x 9.1cm) Pp. [1-2]
[3] 4-27 [28] 29-30 [31] 32.

Binding: 1 sheet, partly unopened; uncut; unbound.

Cobb, Lyman   1800-1864   #625

Cobb's Expositor, or sequel to the Spelling-Book . . .
. New York: Collins and Hannay, 1833.

Coll: 12° 1-18⁶   108 leaves (14.3 x 9.1cm) Pp. [1-3]
4-216.

Notes: First ed. (?).

Cobb, Lyman, A. M.   1800-1864   #626

The North American Reader; containing a great variety
of pieces in prose and poetry, from very highly
esteemed American and English writes. Zanesville, O.:
J. R. & A. Lippitt, 1836.

Coll: 12° A-X¹²   (17.5 x 10.6cm) Pp. [i-xii, 23]
24-498, [499] -504: adverts.
Plates: Frontispiece wood engraving from a painting
by W. Wanx.

Cobb, Sylvanus, Jr.   1823-1887   #627

The Gunmaker of Moscow; or, Vladimir the Monk. New
York: Robert Bonner's Sons, 1888. Pp. [1-6, 7] 8-
196.
Plates: Frontispiece by Lumley.
Binding: Flamingo wrappers
Notes: Not a first ed. Published originally in The
       New York Ledger in 1856, and republished 3
       times.

Cock Robin

    see

    The Death and Burial of Cock Robin.
       Otley: W. Walker c. 1830.
    The Happy Courtship, Merry Marriage, and
       Pic Nic Dinner of Cock Robin and
       Jenny Wren. To Which Is Added, Alas!
       The Doleful Death of the Bridegroom.
       London: for J. Harris, 1806.
    The Life and Death of Cock Robin. Albany:
       Peese's . . . . n.d.

    (cont'd)

Cock Robin (Cont'd)

   see

      The Life and Death of Cock Robin. "Mark's
      Edition." New York: P.J. Cozans, n.d.

      The Tragi-Comic History of the Burial of
      Cock Robin; With the Lamentation of
      Jenny Wren; The Sparrow's Apprehen-
      sion; and the Cuckoo's Punishment.
      Being a sequel . . . of Robin Red-
      Breast and Jenny Wren. Philadelphia:
      Benjamin Warner . . . , 1821.

CODEX MANESSE (in German)   # 629

Fol 1: FRAV / RICARDAHVCH / ZUM FESTLICHEN / 18. JVLI
1934 / IN HOHER / VEREHRVNG / VND IN / ALTER /
VERBVNDENHEIT / VEBERREICHT / VOM / INSEL
VERLAG (12 lines)

      428 leaves numbered (in pencil) 2-428

Fol 429: DIESE FAKSIMILE-AUSGABE DER MANESSESCHEN LIEDER-
HANDSCHRIFT ERSCHIEN IN DEN JAHREN 1925 BIS 1927
IM INSEL-VERLAG ZU LEIPZIG. DIE WIEDERGABE ER-
FOLGTE MIT GENEHMIGUNG DES BADISCHEN MINISTER-

                             (cont'd)

CODEX MANESSE (Cont'd)

      IUMS DES KULTUS UND UNTERRICHTS NACH DEM IN DER
      HEIDELBERGER UNIVERSITATS-BIBLIOTHEK BEFINDLICHEN
      ORIGINAL IN FARBIGEM LICHTDRUCK DURCH DIE KUNSTAN-
      STALT ALBERT FRISCH IN BERLIN. HERGESTELLT WUR-
      DEN 320 NUMERIERTE EXEMPLARE. DIES IST NR. 200

      illuminated manuscript, rubricated capitols and
      headlines, decorative initials, 137 full page
      colored paintings, plus one uncolored drawing.

Coffin, Charles Carleton   1823-1896   # 630

The Boys of '76; a history of the battles of the Revolu-
tion. Illustrated by I. P. Pranishnikoff. New York:
Harper & Brothers, Publishers, Franklin Square, 1877.
Pp. [1]-398.

Plates: Frontispiece: "The Alarm."

Coffin, Charles Carleton   1823-1896   #631

Old Times in the Colonies. Illustrated. New York:
Harper & Brothers, 1880. Pp. [1-2, 3] 4-460; [1] 2-
4 of adverts.

Plates: Frontispiece (pp. 1-2) + 21 full-page
      illustrations included in pagination
      (several signed "Howard Pyle" 1853-1911).

Coffin, Charles Carleton   1823-1896   # 632

Winning His Way. Boston: Ticknor and Fields, 1866.
Pp. iv+ 1-258, [259-260: blank].

Plates: Frontispiece +1: wood engravings;+ woodcut
      on title page.
Notes: First ed.

Cole, William H   # 633

The Institute Reader and Normal Class-Book . . . .
Cincinnati & New York: Wilson, Hinkle & Co., n.d.
[1870?] . Pp. [1]-x, [11]-360.

Illus: Cuts

Notes: Adverts on endpapers. LC # PE 1121.C6 1870

Coleridge, Samuel Taylor   1772-1834   # 634

The Rime of the Ancient Mariner. Illustrated by
Edward [Arthur] Wilson. Introduction by John
Livingston Lowes. New York: The Limited Editions
Club, 1945. Pp. [1-6,] 7-69 [70].

Illus: 8 full-page in color + cuts.

Notes: #201 of 1500; signed by illustrator.

Anon   # 635

A Collection of Old Ballads. 3 vols. London:
J. Roberts et al, 1725-7.

Vol. I: 3d ed., 1727
Coll: 12° A⁶ B-N¹² 150 leaves (16.1 x 9.2cm)
      Pp. [1-2, i] ii-viii [ix-x, 1] 2-287[288:
      adverts]
Plates: 2 Frontispieces by J. Pine + 13; all
      copper engravings + numerous decorations

Vol II: 2d ed., 1726
Coll: 12° A⁸ 2B-F¹² G² H-N¹² 144 leaves
                     (cont'd)

Collection of Old Ballads (Cont'd)

      (16.1 x 9.2cm) Pp. [1-4, i] ii-xi [xii-
      xvi, 1] 2-267 [268: adverts]
Plates: 2 Frontispieces by J. Pine + 13; all
      copper engravings + numerous decorations
Vol III: 1st ed., 1625
Coll: 12° A¹¹ (A 10+1) B-M¹² 143 leaves (16.1 x
      9.2cm) Pp. [1-4, i] ii-xii [xiii, xiv-xviii, 1]
      2-263 264: adverts
Plates: 2 frontispieces by J. Pine + 13; all copper
      engravings + numerous decorations
Binding: Grained calf, gilt edged and tooled,
      boxed.   (cont'd)

Collection of Old Ballads (cony'd)

Notes: See Arthur E. Case, A Bibliography of
English Poetical Miscellanies 1521-
1750, Oxford, 1935. #326 (2) (b); (3) (a);
and, (1) (c).

Anon   #636

A Collection of the most approved Entertaining
Stories. Calculated for the Instruction and
Amusement of all the little Masters and Misses of
this vast Empire. By Solomon Winlove, Esq. London:
Printed for F. Newbery, 1770.

Coll: 24° [A²] B-I⁶ K⁴   54 leaves   (11 x 7.2cm)
Pp. [1-iv,] 1-99 + 5

Plates: Frontispiece +5.

                                        (cont'd)

A Collection of the Most Approved . . . Winlove,
Solomon. (Cont'd)

Notes: K3 —K4: Catalogue of other F. Newbery books.
Contains "Jack Horner," "Cinderella," "Little
Red Riding Hood," "Fortunatus," etc.--eleven
stories in all. Roscoe # 381 (1). McKell #s:
SG 1-5-55 L; SG 1-10-55 B.

Collodi, C[arlo] [Pseud of Carlo Lorenzini] 1826-
                                              1890

The Story of a Puppet; or, the adventures of
Pinocchio. Translated by M.A. Murray. Illustrated
by C. Mazzanti. "The Children's Library Series."
New York: Cassell Publishing Company, 1892. Pp.
[i-viii, 1] 2-232.

Illus: Numerous illustrations

Notes: Leaves B-Q signed.

Colum, Padraic   1881-   #640

The Adventures of Odysseus and the Tale of Troy. Illustrated by Willy Pogany. New York: The Macmillan Company, 1918. Pp. [xii]+[1] -254.

Plates: Color frontispiece; "Judgment of Paris."

Notes: First ed., Dec. 1918.

Colum, Padraic   1881-   #641

The Island of the Mighty. Illustrated by Wilfred
Jones. New York: The Macmillan Company, 1924.
Pp. [i] -xxiv, [1] - [266].

Plates: Frontispiece +21.

Anon   #643

The Comic Adventures of Old Mother Hubbard, and Her
Dog: in Which is Shewn the Wonderful Powers that
Good Old Lady Possessed in the Education of her
Favorite Animal. London: . . . for J. Harris and
Son, 1819.

Coll: 8° [A¹⁶] 16 leaves (17.9 x 10.7cm) Pp. [1-5]
6-7 [8-9] 10-11 [12-13] 14-15 [16-17] 18-19
[20-21] 22-23 (misnumbered 33) [24-25] 26-27
[28-29] 30-31 [32-33] 34+[1-2].

Illus: Text and colored engravings on facing pages
alternating with blank facing pages.
Binding: Rose paper   boards
Notes: #S1-11-43-B

Anon   #644

The Comic Almanac, for 1845: An Ephemeris in Jest
and Earnest, Containing 'All Things Fitting for
such a work.' By Rigdum Funnidos, Gent. Adorned
with numerous humourous illustrations:- and a
dozen of "Right Merry" Cuts pertaining to the
months. By George Cruikshank. London: Imprinted
for David Bogue, Bibliopolist, in Fleet Street.
Vizetelly Brothers & Co., Printers, Peterborough
Court, 135 Fleet Street.

Coll: 8° (in 8's) A-G⁸ D-J² K² 42 leaves.
                                        (cont'd)

The Comic Almanac for 1845.   (Cont'd)

(16.5 x 10.5cm) Pp. [1] 2-16; [1-] 2-63 [64].

Plates: 12 +several cuts.

Binding: Edward Baker, binders; stiff wrappers,
red pictorial stiff wrappers bound in.
16pp. of adverts bound in to front.

Anon   #645

The Common-place Book of Romantic Tales. [Illustrate
by Henry Inman, A. B. Durand, R. Westall, J. B. Long-
acre, W. Allston.] New York: Charles Wells, 1831.

Coll: 12° 1⁷ 2-23⁶ 24⁵ 144 leaves (15.3 x 9.3cm)
Pp. [1-ii, 1] -iv [5] -286.

Plates: Frontispiece, illustrated title page are in
color + 4 other steel engravings.

Comus

pseud of

Robert Michael Ballantyne 1825-1894

q.v.

Coolidge, Susan [Pseud of Sarah Chauncey Woolsey] 1835-1905   # 653

A Guernsey Lily; or, how the feud was healed. A story for girls and boys. Boston: Roberts Brothers, 1881. Pp. [iii-ix] x [xi-xii, 1] 2-238.

Illus: Frontispiece +130 including 36 full-page by various people.

Anon   # 646

Confessions of a School Master. Andover and New York: Gould, Newman and Saxton, 1839.

Coll: 12° π⁶ 14 2-26⁶ 27² 162 leaves (15.3 x 9.3cm)
        Pp. [i-iii] iv-v [vi-vii] viii-xx [13] 14-316.
Notes: Copyright by William A. Alcott

[Cooper, James Fenimore]   1789-1851   # 654

The Last of the Mohicans; a narrative of 1757. 3 vols. London: John Miller, 1826.

Vol I:
Coll: 12° [A]⁶ B-N¹² 150 leaves (17.6 x 10.3cm) Pp.
        [i-iii] iv-xi [xii, 1] 2-287 [288].
Vol II:
Coll: 12° [A]¹ B-M¹² N⁶ 139 leaves (17.6 x 10.3cm)
        Pp. [i-ii, 1] 2-276.
Vol III:
Coll: 12° [A]¹ B-N¹² O4 149 leaves (17.6 x 10.3cm)
                                        (cont'd)

Anon.   # 649

Continuation of old Dame Trudge and her Parrot. Illustrated with whimsical engravings. Philadelphia: Published by Morgan & Yeager, at their Juvenile Bookstore, [c. 1825].

Coll: 16°: [1⁸] 8 leaves (13.6 X 10.2cm) ff 8 Pp. [1-16]

Illus: 8 hand-colored engravings

Binding: Buff wrappers

Notes: Rosenbach 655

Cooper   Last of the Mohicans   (Cont'd)

    Pp. [i-ii, 1] 2-295 [296].

Binding: Dark blue half-calf over marbled boards.

Notes: First English ed. Blanck # 3833.

Cook, Mrs. Harriet N   # 650

The Scripture Alphabet of Animals. New York: The American Tract Society,   [1842].

Coll: 12° (6s)1-8⁶ 9⁴ 52 leaves (14.7 x 9.2cm) Pp. [1-4, 5] 6-98 [99-104 : blank].
Plates: 16
Binding: Stabbed; π⁴ composed of 2 free and 2 paste-down endpapers.

Anon   # 657

The Council of Dogs. Illustrated with suitable engravings. London: Printed [by H. Bryer] for J. Harris . . . , 1808.

Coll: 16° A⁸ 8 leaves (11.5 x 9.5cm) Pp. [1-3] 4-16.
Plates: Engraved frontispiece +7.

Notes: Bound in with six others in Omnibus #2, q.v.

Cooper, J. (The Rev. J., The Rev. Mr., The Rev. S.)

    Pseuds of

    Johnson, Richard (fl. 1770-c.1800)

Anon.   #658

The Court of Oberon, or Temple of the Fairies: A collection of tales of past times. Originally related by Mother Goose, Mother Bunch, and others, adapted to the language and manners of the present period. London: Printed [by S. and R. Bentley...] for J. Harris and Son, 1823.

Coll: 12°: A², B-M¹², N⁴ (-N⁴). 137 leaves (16.6 X 10.3cm.) Pp. [i-iii] iv [1] 2-72 [73] 74-147 [148] 149-269 [270]

Plates: Frontispiece + 23 hand-color engravings.

Notes: Frontispiece inscribed "published Aug. 20, 1823." First illustration in text inscribed "published Sep. 1, 1823."

Anon.   # 659

The Courtship and Marriage of Jerry and Kitty; Illus-
trated with elegant engravings. London: J. Harris,
Nov. 20, 1814.
Coll: 16⁰: 1-4⁴ 16 engraved leaves (13.2 X 10.2ᶜᵐ·)
     Pp. [32]

Plates: 15 hand colored engravings numbered

Binding: Buff wrappers. Stabbed in an outer wrapper.
        Printing on facing pages, alternating with
        blank facing pages

Notes: McKell copy lacks plates 12-13

Anon.   # 660

The Courtship and Marriage of Jerry and Kitty; Illustrated
with elegant engravings. London: J. Harris, Nov. 20, 1814.
Coll: 16⁰: [1-4⁴] 16 leaves (12.9 X 10.5ᶜᵐ·) Pp. [32]

Illus: 15 copper plate engravings, hand colored, numbered
      1-15, on facing pages alternating with blank facing
      pages.

Binding: Green morocco binding by Morrell, with original
        gray wrappers bound in.

Notes: Leaves 7 and 16 contain watermark date 1818.

Cowper, William   1731-1800   # 661
[COWPER, WILLIAM]. The Diverting History of John
Gilpin. Showing How He Went Farther than He
Intended, and Came Home Safe Again. Illustrated
with Humourous Engravings. London: Printed [by
H. Bryer] for J. Harris . . . . 1808.

Coll.: 16⁰: A⁸. 8 leaves (11.75 X 9.2cm). [1-3]4
-15[16] pp.

Plates: Engraved frontispiece + 7.

                              S-1-11-43

Cowper, William. 1731-1800   # 662

The Diverting History of John Gilpin: Showing How He Went
Farther Than He Intended And Came Safe Home Again. With
six illustrations by George Cruikshank. Engraved on wood
by Thompson, Branston, Wright, Slader, and White. London:
[Printed by Ibotson and Palmer for] Charles Tilt, 1828.

Coll: 16⁰: (eights) A⁴ B⁸ C⁴ (C4=A5-A8), 18 leaves (13.5
X 3cm) Pp. [iv, 5] 6-20 (Illustration leaves unnum-
bered).
Illus: Six vignettes
Binding: Buff wrappers. Two leaves (4pp) of advertisement
        tipped in at end.
Notes: "1st ed, rare" McKell

[Cowper, William]. 1731-1800   # 663

The Diverting History of John Gilpin: Showing how he went
farther than he intended, and came safe home again. With
six illustrations by George Cruikshank, engraved on wood
by Thompson, Branston, Wright, Slader, and White. London:
Charles Tilt [Ibotson and Palmer, Printers . . .], 1828.

Coll: 16⁰: A-D⁴ E² 22 leaves (12.7 X 10.5cm)
     Pp. [i-iv, 5] 6-20 [21-22]
Illus: Six unnumbered wood engravings not included in
      pagination.
Binding: Gray wrappers bound in green leather over half
        boards.
                              (Cont'd)

[Cowper, William]. 1731-1800   (Cont'd)

The Diverting History of John Gilpin.

Notes: Bookplate of Samuel F. Barger. E² is advertising

Cox, Marian [Emily] Roalfe   1860-1917 # 664

Cinderella. Three hundred and forty-five variants
of Cinderella, Catskin, and Cap o' rushes, abstracted a
and tabulated, with a discussion of mediaeval ana-
logues, and notes. Introduction by Andrew Lang, ...
London: For the Folk-lore Society by David Nutt,
1893. Pp. [1] -lxxx, [1] - [536].

Cox, Palmer. 1840-1924   #665

The Brownies Around the World. By Palmer Cox. New York:
Published by The Centruy Co. [1894]. [Copyright, 1892,
1893, by The Curtis Publishing Company; Copyright 1894,
by The Century Co.]

Pagination: [i-viii] ix-xi [xii] 1-144

Illus: Many illustrations by Palmer Cox

Notes: First edition in original dust wrapper

Cox, Palmer. 1840-1924   #666

"The Brownies Ride," (A Poem, illustrations by the
author) in St. Nicholas, an illustrated magazine for
young folks, Vol. X, No. 4, Pp. 263-266. Conducted by
Mary Mapes Dodge, New York: The Century Co., London:
Frederick Warne & Co., February 1883.

Coll: 8⁰

Illus: 3 by Cox

Binding: Original wrappers, uncut

Notes: First printing of Cox's poem

Cox, Palmer   1840-1924   # 667

Brownie Year Book. New York: McLoughlin Bro's,
Publishers, [1895]. Pp. [1-26].

Notes: Pasted on front paste-down endpaper: "Com-
      pliments of C.B. Jefferson, Klaw & Erlanger.
      600th Performance of "Palmer Cox's Brownies.
      English's Opera House, Monday Night, February
      17th."

Cox, Palmer (1840-1924)

see also

Wolson, A. Nouvelles aventures des mar-
mousets. George Cres. n.d.
Le Royaume des Marmousets. George
Cres. n.d.

(C

Anon.   #668

Crabbe's Familiar Tales for Children. Boston:
Published by Munroe and Francis...and C. S.
Francis....New York. [c. 1840]
Coll: 12⁰; π², 2π², A-E¹⁴; 74 leaves (14.9 x
8.8 cm.); pp. [] 2-4 [1-111] iv [1-4] 5-
14 [15-16] 17-26 [27-28] [1-5] 6-10
[1-13] 14-17 [18-20] 21-22 [23] 24-27
[28] [-5] 6-16.
Illus: Woodcuts.
Notes: On rear loose end paper recto: G-7-23-43
B.
No. 16 of Juve C aile Classics.

[Craik,] Dinah Maria Mulock   1826-1887   #669

John Halifax, Gentleman. Illustrated by Augustus
Hoppin. New York: Harper & Brothers, Publishers,
1860. Pp. [1-7] 8-[486, 1-2: adverts].

(C

Crane, Walter.   (1845 - 1915) #672

The Blue Beard Picture Book, Containing Blue
Beard, Little Red Riding Hood, Jack and the
Bean Stalk, Baby's Own ABC. With Thirty-Two
pages of Illustrations by Walter Crane.
Printed in colors by Edmund Evans. London &
New York: George Routledge and Sons. "Toy
Book" series. [1875].
Coll: 4⁰; [A⁹(A·1 tipped into A·2)] [B-D⁸]; 35
leaves printed on inner form.
Illus: 32 pages of colored illustrations by
Walter Crane printed on one side of page
only.

(C

Crane, Walter.   (1845-1915) #673

Goody Two Shoes' Picture Book; containing
Goody Two Shoes, Beauty and the Beast, The Frog
Prince, An Alphabet of Old Friends; with
Twenty-Four Pages of Illustrations By Walter
Crane. Printed in colours by Edmund Evans.
London and New York: George Routledge and Sons,
n.d. [c. 1875].
Pagination: 70 leaves (26.7 x 22.4 cm.); ff. 70.
Illus: 24 colored illustrations.
Notes: 70 leaves, printed on one side only.

(O

Anon   #676

The Cries of London, as They are daily exhibited in the
Streets . . . . . Embellished with sixty-two elegant Cuts
. . . . London: Printed for F. Newbery, 1775.
Coll: 32⁰ A-I⁸   72 leaves (10x 6.5cm) Pp. [4+1] 11-v,
6-133 [7]

Binding: Dutch floral boards

Notes: I3: A Description of London; I4ᵛ: A Song on the
City of London; I5ᵛ: Books printed for F. New-
bery. Roscoe # 86(2). Bookplate of Percival
Merritt.

(O

Anon.   # 677

Cries of London. Part Second. New York: Printed and sold
by Mahlon Day, at the New Juvenile Book Store, n.d.
Coll: Octavo, [1⁸] 8 leaves; ff 8
Illus: 8 colored woodcuts; one on each printed page
Notes: Printed on one side of leaf only. Pencil notes
on wrapper indicate publication date ca 1830.

( )

Cruikshank, George   1792-1878 #680

George Cruikshank's Fairy Library. Cinderella and the
Glass Slipper. Edited and illustrated with ten subjects
designed and etched on steel, by George Cruikshank.
London: David Bogue, 86 Fleet Street. [Printed by G.
Barclay, Castle St. Leicester Sq.] n.d.
Coll: sm 4⁰ A¹⁶ 16 leaves (17.1 x 13.3cm)
Pp. [1-4,5] 6-27 [28, 29] 30-31 [32]
Plates: Frontispiece+5: all steel etchings.
Binding: Light blue wrappers.
Notes: # 3 of series   (C

Cruikshank, George   1792-1878 #681.1-2

George Cruikshank's Fairy Library. The History of
Jack & the Bean-Stalk. Edited and illustrated with
six etchings by George Cruikshank. London: David
Bogue, 86 Fleet Street. [Printed by G. Barclay, Castle
St. Leicester Sq.] n.d.
Coll: sm 4⁰ A¹⁶ 16 leaves (17.1 x 13.3cm)
Pp. [1-4, 5] 6-32.
Plates: 6 steel etchings
Binding: Light blue wrappers
Notes: # 2 of series   ( ) Plus another copy

Cruikshank, George   1792-1878 #682.1-2

George Cruikshank's Fairy Library. Hop-O'-My-Thumb and
The Seven-League Boots. Edited and illustrated with
six etchings by George Cruikshank. London: David
Bogue, 86 Fleet Street. [Printed by G. Barclay, Castle
St. Leicester Sq.] n.d.
Coll: sm 4⁰ A¹⁶ 16 leaves (17.2 x 13.2cm)
Pp. [1-2, 3] 4-30 [31-32]
Plates: Frontispiece +5 wood engravings
Binding: Light blue wrappers

                                        (cont'd)

George Cruikshank's Fairy Library. Hop-O'My-Thumb
and The Seven-League Boots. (Cont'd)

Notes: #1 of series. List of illus. on p. [31].
Contains letter from Cruikshank to Kent, dated
Nov. 12, 1853. This is a signed presentation
copy to Isabella Alison Reynolds "Papa's eldest
girl" Sept. 4, 1853.
Plus another copy rebound in marbled boards.

 # 683

[Cummins, Maria Susanna]   1827-1866

The Lamplighter. Boston: John P. Jewett & Company.
Cleveland: Jewett, Proctor and Worthington, 1854.

Coll: 12° 1-44⁶ 259 leaves (19.2 x 12.3cm)
Pp.[1-4] 5-523 [524-8]
Binding: 44.5-6 as paste-down end papers
Notes: First page of each of 50 chapters not paginated.
First ed. See Blanck #4252

#684

[Cundall, Joseph]   1818-1895

Robin Hood and His Merry Forresters. By
Stephen Percy [pseud.]. New York: Henry G.
Langley; 1844.

Coll: 16° (8's) [1]-10⁸ 11-12⁴ 13² 90 leaves
[14.7x 11.2cm] Pp.[1-6, 7] 8-33 [34] 35-67
[68] 69-91 [92] 93-116 [117] 118-139 [140] 141-
158 [159] 160-179 [180].
Plates: Color frontispiece+7: all hand color copper engravings.
                                  (cont'd)

Cundall. Robin Hood. 1844.   (Cont'd)

Contents: A True Tale of Robin Hood in verse by
Martin Parker. The Life and Death of
Robert Earl of Huntingdon.

#685

Curtis, Mary

Memoirs of a Country Doll. Written by Herself.
Companion to the "Memoirs of a London Doll."
With illustrations by D. C. Johnston. Boston and
Cambridge: James Munroe & Company, 1808

Coll: 8° π⁴ 1-4⁸, 5⁴ 40 leaves Pp.[1-9,]10-
80. (16.7 x 11cm)

Plates: 4 engravings, one is hand-colored.

Daggett, Herman, M. A. 1766-1832   **#690**

The American Reader, Consisting of Familiar,
Instructive, and Entertaining Stories. Selec-
ted for the Use of Schools....Poughkeepsie:
Published by Paraclete Potter. R. & S. Potter,
Printers, 1818.

Coll: 12°; A-Z⁶; 148 leaves (13.8 x 8.5 cm.);
pp. [1-3] 4-5 [6], 7-31 [32] 33-286, 287-
288.

Notes: Copyright descr. has "Third Edition."
Folds D-F, P, R, Z, have vertical
chains, and are of different paper than
the other folds.

 # 691

Anon

[The Dairyman's Daughter. Printed by Thomas
Richardson, Friar-Gate, Derby,] n.d.

Coll: 12 leaves (13.3 x 8.4cm) Pp.[1]
2-12

Notes: Item is signed "Newport, Isle of Wight/
July, 1837." No title page. Bound in
with six others in Omnibus #1, q.v.

 # 692

Anon

Dame Truelove's Tales, Now first Published. Useful
Lessons for Little Misses & Masters, and Ornamented
With Appropriate Engravings. London: Published by
J. Harris [Printed by E. Hemsted], [1817?].

Coll: 16° A-E⁸ 40 leaves (12.8 x 10.6cm) Pp. 1-79
+[1]

Plates: Engraved frontispiece, title page, another
frontispiece +20 engravings. "Published
May 20, 1817," on engravings.
Notes: #S-1-11-43-B

#693

Dame Wiggins of Lee and Her Seven Wonderful Cats. A
humorous tale written principally by a Lady of Ninety.
Embellished with sixteen coloured engravings. London:
A. K. Newman & Co., n.d. [ca 1824].

Coll: 8° [1¹⁶] 16 leaves (17.7 x 10.5cm) Pp.[1-5] 6, 9
[1-11] 10-11 [12-13] 14-15 [16-17] 18-19 [20-21]
22-23 [24-25] 26-27 [28-29] 30-31 [32].

Illus: Hand colored wood engravings: Front+14

Binding: Rebound by Zaehnsdorf: green leather, gilt
                                  (cont'd)

Dame Wiggins of Lee 1824   (Cont'd)

borders. Original pink illustrated wrappers
bound in.

Notes: Blank facing pages alternate with facing pages of
text and illustration. "Frontispiece included in
pagination. McKell # S-1-23-43-B

Anon.   #694

Dame Wonder's Picture Books Master Rose. New York: John McLoughlin, Publisher, n.d.

Coll: 12°; [1⁴]; 4 leaves (19.5 x 11.4 cm.).
ff. 1-4.
Illus: 8 hand-colored woodcuts.

Binding: White wrappers. Illustration on front. Advertisement on back.

[Dana, Richard Henry]. 1815-1882.   #695

Two Years Before the Mast. A Personal Narrative of Life at Sea. New York: Harper & Brothers, 1840.

Coll: 12°: 1^6-40^6 41^2 242 leaves (14.9 X 8.7cm)
Pp. [1-3] 4-483 [484]

Notes: On second flyleaf "Henrietta M. Channing/From her Cousin-/The Author" 1st edition. Blanck 4434. Not in original binding

---

Anon.   #696

The Dandies' Ball; or, High Life in the City. Embellished with sixteen coloured engravings. London: Printed and sold by John Marshall..., 1821.
Coll: 8°: 1^{16} 16 leaves (18.3 X 11.4cm.) Pp. [1-32]
Illus: 16 hand-colored engravings
Notes: BMC gives 1819 and ascribes illustrations to Isaac Robert Cruikshank. Printed on one side of the leaf only.

Anon   #697

Daniel in the Den of Lions. Revised by the editor. New York: Lane & Scott, 1849.

Coll: 8° 1-2⁸ 16 leaves (13.5 x 8.3cm) Pp. [i-iv , 5] 6-32.

Plates: Frontispiece, vignette title page +cuts.

Darky, George A.B.   #698

A System of Popular Geometry; containing in a few lessons so much of the Elements of Euclid as is necessary and sufficient for a right understanding of every Art and Science in its leading truths and general principles. By George Darky, A.B. The second edition. London: Published for John Taylor...by James Duncan, sold by J.A. Hessey and John Hatchard and son..., 1827 [Printed by Thomas Davison, Whitefriars]
Coll: 12°: B^{12}, b^6, B-D^{12}(D^6+-) E-F^{12}, G^4, X^2 84 leaves (18.1 X 11cm.) Pp. [i-v] vi-vii[viii-ix] x-xx[xxi] xxii[xxiii]xxiv-xxxv[xxxvi], 1-2]3-118[119]120-124 [125]126 [127]128[1-4]
Notes: X^2= Advert.

[Darton, William] 1747-1819   # 700

Little Truths Better than Great Fables; Containing Information on Divers Subjects, for the Instruction of Children. Vol. II. Illustrated with Copper Plates. Philadelphia: Printed for, and to be sold by, J. and J. Crukshank . . . , 1800.
Coll: 16° A⁸, B-C^{12} 32 leaves (10.3 x 8.9cm) Pp. [1-3] 4-64.
Plates: Frontispiece+3
Notes: Another copy, identical except for differently illustrated blue wrappers and
                 (cont'd)

Darton. Little Truths . . . 1800 (cont'd)

unopened leaves C₁10, C₁11 in one copy
See Rosenbach #254, Evans #37291, Welch #248.3

[Darton, William]   1747-1819   # 701

Little Truths Better than Great Fables: In Variety of Instruction for Children from four to Eight Years Old. London: Printed for and Sold by, William Darton, 1787.

Coll: 16° A⁶ (± A²) B-G⁶ 42 leaves (10 x 9.9cm) Pp. vi, 7-84.
Plates: 3 engravings

Notes: McKell # S-11-21-47 B.

[Darton, William]   1747-1819   #702

A Present for a Little Girl. London: Printed by and for Darton and Harvey . . . , 1806.

Coll: 12° π¹A-C³ D⁶ E-G³ 2π¹ 26 leaves (15.6 x 9.8cm). One gathering. 52 unnumbered pages.
Illus: 3 full-page engravings and 24 others in text: 3 give date of June 12, 1805. Vignette on title page.
Binding: Original tan wrappers.
Notes: 2π: adverts. McKell # S-1-23-45.

Day, Clarence, [Jr.]   1874-1935   #708

Life With Father. New York & London: Alfred A. Knopf, 1935. Pp. [1-4, i] -vi, [1] - [260].

 # 709

Day, Clarence, Jr.   1874-1935

This Simian World. Illustrated by the author.
New York: Alfred A. Knopf, 1920. Pp. [i-vi, 1]
2-95 [96].

Illus: Cuts.

Day -3-

The History of Sanford and Merton (Cont'd)

Vol. III. [First Edition]. 1789.

Coll.: 12°: π^1B-N^{12}O^{10}. 155 leaves (16.5 X 9.6 cm).
[2] 308 pp.

Plates: Frontispiece.

Bound set, each volume containing the bookplate of
A. Edward Newton.

 # 710

Day, Thomas   1748-1789

The History of Sandford and Merton: a book for the
young. London: T. Nelson and sons, 1873. Pp. [5-8,
9] 10-429 [430].

Plates: Engraved title page +3: all color
Notes: Has half-title page and plain title page also.

 # 713

Day, Thomas   1748-1789

The History of Sandford and Merton; an Entertaining
and Instructive Tale. Embellished with a Neat
Coloured Frontispiece. London: Printed and Sold
by Dean and Munday, Threadneedle Street. Price
Six pence, n.d.

Coll.: 12° 1^4, 2^8, 3^4 16 leaves (13.9 x 8.5cm)
Pp. [3-4, 5] 6-34.

Plates: Fold-out, hand-colored woodcut frontispiece.
Binding: Pink wrappers bound in, by Stroogants.
Notes: Abridged edition

 # 711

Day, Thomas   1748-1789

DAY, THOMAS The History of Sandford and Merton
[Abridged]; A Work Intended for the Use of Children.
London: Printed [by Darton, Harvey, and Co.] for
F.C. and J. Rivington; Law and Whitaker; Longman,
Hurst, Rees, Orne, and Brown; Darton, Harvey, and
Co.; Baldwin, Cradock, and Joy: J. Harris; Sherwood,
Neely, and Jones: Gale and Fenner; and Ogle and Co.,
1815.

Coll.: 12°:[A^2]B-L^{12}M^{10}. 132 leaves (16.8 X 10.1cm).
$1, 2, 5 (except in Quire A which has no signatures).

Plates: Engraved frontispiece by Unwins.

 # 714

Day, Thomas   1748-1789

The History of Sandford and Merton. Illustrated by F.
Borders. New York: Published by Allen Brothers, 1870.
Pp. viii, 9-530, [1]-2: advert.

Plates: Frontispiece: "Timely Help." Engraved title
page laid in.

Notes: "The only Complete American Edition."

 # 712

[Day, Thomas]   1748-1789

[DAY, THOMAS.] The History of Sandford and Merton,
A Work Intended for the Use of Children. 3 vols.
London: John Stockdale. BMC 1031.

Vol. I Second Edition corrected. 1784.

Coll.: 12°: A-M^{12} (-M12). 143 leaves (16.5 X 9.6
cm). x, 11-286 pp.

Plates: Frontispiece.   (cont'd)

Day -2-

The History of Sanford and Merton (Cont'd)

Vol. II. [First Edition]. 1786.

Coll.: 12°: π^1 (=O12) B-O^{12} (-)12). 156 leaves
(16.5 x 9.6cm). [2] 306 + [4] pp.

Plates: Frontispiece.

(cont'd)

Day, Thomas (1748-1789)

    see also

        Aikin, Lucy. Sandford and Merton, in
            words of one syllable. McLoughlin
            Brothers, n.d.

 # 715

Anon.

[Dean's New Book of Dissolving Views. London:
Dean & Son, Publishers, Ludgate Hill.] n.d.

Coll: 8° 1^6 6 leaves (26.8 x 18.6cm) Fols. 1-6.
Illus: 12 color engravings, 2 moveable scenes on each
    leaf: by Calvert, sculp.
Notes: Free and pasted down endpapers are adverts.

Dearborn, Benjamin. 1755-1838   **#716**

The Columbian Grammar: or, An Essay For Reducing a
Grammatical Knowledge of the English Language to a Degree
of Simplicity, Which will render it easy for the In-
structor to Teach, and for the Pupil to learn. Accompanied
with Notes, Critical and Explanatory. For the Use of
Schools; and of young Gentlemen and Ladies, Natives or
Foreigners, who are desirous of attempting the Study with-
out a Tutor. Being designed as Part of a General System of
Education, in the most useful Branches of Literature, for
American Youth of Both Sexes. Boston: Printed by Samuel
Hall, for the author, 1795.

<u>Coll</u>: 12°: [A²] B-M⁶ N⁴   72 leaves (16.8 X 10cm)
    Pp. [4] + [i] ii   [iii-iv, 5] 6-140

[Cont'd]

Dearborn, Benjamin. 1755-1838

The Columbian Grammar (Cont'd)

<u>Notes</u>: Bookplate of E.B. Dearborn

Dearborn, Nath[anie]l   1786-1852   **#717**

American Text Book For Letters . . . . Boston: n.d.,
[1842?].

<u>Coll</u>: Half-quarto (oblong octavo) 1-6⁴ (plates); D-
G⁴ (12.1 x 19.9cm) Fr. [1-2] 3-24; pp. 27-
54 [55-56, 57-58: blank].
<u>Plates</u>: 24 on one side of leaf only.
<u>Notes</u>: One leaf pasted to 1.2 of plates; it contains
    a preface on the recto, and errata on verso.

Anon.   **#718**

The Death and Burial of Cock Robin. Otley: Printed by W.
Walker, [ca. 1830].
<u>Coll</u>: 32°: 1⁸   8 leaves (10.4 X 6.6ᶜᵐ·) Pp. [1-4] 5-15 [16]
<u>Illus</u>: Frontispiece + 15 cuts in text
<u>Binding</u>: Yellow pictorial wrappers. Initial and final
    leaves serve as paste down endpapers.

Anon   **#719**

Death Bed of a Modern Free Thinker. Exemplified in
the last hours of the Hon. Francis Newport, son to the
late Lord Newport, [Tract Society, Methodist Episcopal,
etc.], n.d.
<u>Coll</u>: 8° 1⁸, 2⁴   12 leaves (13.1 x 8.7cm) Pp. [1] 2-24.

<u>Illus</u>: Woodcut on p. [1].

<u>Notes</u>: No title page; no colophon on p. 24.
    Bound in with Epitome of Jewish History &
    African Valley

Anon   **#721**

Les Défauts Horribles histoires ebourifrantes et
morales pour les petits enfants de trois a six ans
Par Trim. I. Gourmands et malpropres. Paris:
Libraire Hachette Et Cⁱᵉ. [Coulommiers Imprimerie
Paul Brodard], [ca 1862]. ff. [1] 2-22 [plates].

<u>Illus</u>: Title page + 30 hand colored illustrations.

<u>Binding</u>: Gray boards. Color illustration on front;
    advertisement on back.

Defoe, Daniel 1660-1731   **#722**
[DEFOE, DANIEL.] The Adventures of Robinson Crusoe.
A New and Improved Edition. With Engravings. London:
J. Harris . . ., 1831. Printed by Samuel Bentley,
Dorset Street, Fleet Street.

<u>Coll.</u>: 12° (6's): A⁴B-P⁶O² .   96 leaves (13.9 X 8.9
cm). [i-viii] [1]-2-170 [171-172] pp.

<u>Plates</u>: 12 numbered. Stipple engravings (metal).
No. 5 used as frontispiece.

Frontispiece dated Nov. 1, 1818.

Defoe, Daniel. 1660. - 1731   **#723**

The Fortunes and Misfortunes of the Famous Moll Flanders.
Illust. . . . by Reginald Marsh. New York: The Heritage Press, n.d., [1942?]. Pp. [i]-[xvi], [1]-[356].

<u>Illus</u>: Frontispiece + numerous cuts & full page illustra-
tions.

[Defoe, Daniel]   1660-1731   **#724**

The Life and Adventures of Robinson Crusoe, of
York, mariner. Illustrated. Philadelphia: J.B.
Lippincott & Co., n.d. Pp. [i] -viii, 1-312, [1-4
adverts.]

<u>Illus</u>: Cuts.

[Defoe, Daniel]. 1660-1731   **#725**

The Life and Adventures of Robinson Crusoe of York, Mariner. Written by Himself [Abridged]. York: Printed and
sold by J. Kendrew, Colliergate, n.d. [1825?].

<u>Coll</u>: 32°: [1¹⁶] unsigned 16 leaves (10 X 6.4cm) Pp. [1-5]
6-31 [32]

<u>Illus</u>: 5 wood engravings

<u>Binding</u>: Blue wrappers, pictorial, advertising on back

[Defoe, Daniel]   #726
                                          1659-1731

The Life and Adventures of Robinson Crusoe . . . .
Philadelphia: J. & J. L. Gihon, 1853.

Coll: 12° $1^6 2$-21^6 126 leaves (15 x 9.5cm)
Pp. [1-2] 3-251 [252]; [1-12: adverts bound in
   at end.
Plates: Frontispiece + 7.

Defoe, Daniel   1660-1731   #727

The Life and Adventures of Robinson Crusoe. With
Seventy-nine Original Illustrations by Walter
Paget. New York: McLoughlin Brothers, n.d. Pp.
[1-ii, 1] 2-158.

Plates: Color frontispiece

[Defoe, Daniel] 1660-1731   # 728
[DEFOE, DANIEL.] The Life And Most Surprising
Adventures Of Robinson Crusoe, Of York, Mariner.
Who lived twenty-eight years in an uninhabited island
on the coast of America, Near the mouth of the great
River Oronoque, With an account of his deliverance
thence, and his after surprising adventures.
Twentieth Edition, With Cuts. Edinburgh: Printed
by W. Darling and Son Advocates Close, 1786.

Coll.: 12° (6's): A-Dd^6. 162 leaves (16.9 X 10cm).
[1-iii] iv [5] 6-324 pp.

Plates: Frontispiece woodcut + 3 wood engraved
plates.   (cont'd)

Defoe . . . Robinson Crusoe, 1786   (cont'd)

Notes: Bookplate of William R. Bailey. Back of
       plates are signed "W.R. Bailey" P. 203:
       the numeral 3 is raised one line; p. 272:
       the numeral 72 is raised.

[Defoe, Daniel] (1660-1751)   # 729
[DEFOE, DANIEL]. The Life and Strange Surprizing
Adventures of Robinson Crusoe, of York, Mariner
 . . . . 3 vols. London: Printed for W. Taylor, 1719-
1720.

Vol. I: . . . Robinson Crusoe, of York, Mariner:
Who lived Eight and Twenty Years, all alone in an
un-inhabited Island on the Coast of America, near
the Mouth of the Great River of Oroanoque; Having
been cast on Shore by Shipwreck, wherein all the
Men perished but himself. With an Account how he
was at last as strangely deliver'd by Pyrates.
Written by Himself. London: Printed for W. Taylor
 . . . . MDCCXIX.

                                           (cont'd)

The Life and Strange Surprizing Adventures of
   Robinson Crusoe (1719-20) (Cont'd)

Coll.: 8^c: [A^2]B-2A^8. 178 leaves. [iv] 364 + [4] pp.

Plates: Frontispiece.

Contents: 2A6^v: Errata. 2A7: advertisements.

Vol. II: The Farther Adventures of Robinson Crusoe;
Being the Second and Last Part of His Life, And of the
Strange Sruprizing Accounts of his Travels Round
three Parts of the Globe. Written by Himself. To
which is added, a Map of the World, in which is
delineated the Voyages of Robinson Crusoe. London:

                                           (cont'd)

The Life and Strange Surprizing Adventures of
   Robinson Crusoe (1719-20) (Cont'd)

Printed for W. Taylor . . . . MDCCXIX.

Coll.: 8°: A^{4}B-2B^8. 188 leaves. [viii] 294 (295
misnumbered 215), 296-373 + [11] pp.

Plates: Frontispiece: fold-out map.

Contents: 2B3: advertisements.

Vol. III: Serious Reflections During the Life and
Surprising Adventures of Robinson Crusoe: With His
Vision of the Angelick World. Written by Himself.

                                           (cont'd)

The Life and Strange Surprizing Adventures of
   Robinson Crusoe (1719-20) (Cont'd)

London: Printed for W. Taylor . . . . 1720.

Coll.: 8°: A-R^{8}S^8(×S^8)2A-2E^{8}2F^4. 187 leaves.
[xvi] 137 (138 misnumbered 118) 139-270, [1] 2-64
(65-66 misnumbered 63-64) 65-84 + [2] pp. (total of
374 pp.).

Plates: Frontispiece: relief map of Crusoe's
Island, dated 1719.

Contents: 2A: "A Vision of the Angelick World."
F4: Advertisments.

McKell set bound by   Rivere & Son.

[Defoe, Daniel]   (1660-1731) # 730

[Robinson Crusoe, "Dean's Moveable" London:
Dean & Son, 11 Ludgate Hill.] [n.d.]

Coll: 8°; [1^{12}]; 12 leaves (24 x 16.6 cm.);
   pp. [1-24].

Illus: 6 colored engravings; moveable illustra-
       tions.

Notes: Free and pasted down end papers front
       and back are advertisements.

[Defoe, Daniel]   1660-1731   #731

The Wonderful Life and Adventures of Robinson Crusoe.
Adorned with cuts. New Haven: Sidney's Press, 1807.

Coll: 32° [1^{16}] 16 leaves (10.4 x 6.15cm) Pp. [1-5]
6-31 [32].
Illus: Front +13 woodcuts.
Binding: Illustrated wrappers; initial and final leaves
         pasted down.

Notes: A.A.S. #260.56 [same as 260.44], Evans #12413.

Defoe, Daniel (1660-1731)

see also

Aikin, Lucy. Robinson Crusoe in Words of one syllable. McLoughlin Brothers, 1882.

De Joinville, John Lord. 1224?-1317?   #732

Memoirs of John Lord De Joinville, Grand Seneschal of Champagne, Written by Himself; containing A History of Part of the Life of Louis IX, King of France, Surnamed Saint Louis, Including an Account of that Kings Expedition to Egypt in the Year MCCXLVIII. To which are added,--the notes & Dissertations of M. Du Cange on the above; together with the dissertations of M. Le Baron de la Bastie on the life of St Louis, M. L'Evesque de la Ravaliere and M. Falconet on the assassins of Syria; From the 'Memoires de l'Académie de Belles Lettres et Inscriptions de France.' The whole translated by Thomas Johnes, Esq. 2 Vols. [Hafod: Printed] by James Henderson, at the Hafod Press, 1807.

(cont'd)

De Joinville, John Lord. 1224?-1317? (cont'd)

Memoires of John Lord De Joinville. 2 Vols. 1807.

Coll: 2°: I: A³B-3H⁴ 3I¹ 216 leaves Pp.[i-vi,1] 2-426
II: A³B-2T⁴ 167 leaves Pp.[i-vi, 1] 2-328

Plates: I: Frontispiece + 2, plus 2 foldout maps; II: map

Notes: Bookplates of B. Winthrop and Percival and Elizabeth Merritt.

---

de la Mare, Walter [John]   1873-1956   #737

Peacock Pie a Book of Rhymes. New York: Henry Holt and Company, n.d. Pp. x+1-78.

Notes: Peacock Pie was first published in 1913.

Delaunay, M. L'Abbe   #740

Le Livre D'Heures De La Reine Anne De Bretagne traduit Du Latin Et Accompagne De Notices Inedites par M. L'Abbé Delaunay. Paris: L. Curmer, Éditeur, MDCCCLXI.

Premiere Partie: A book of full color plates, no title page, paginated to 477 [478].

Seconde Partie: (Has title page transcribed above) Pp.[i-iv, 1] 2-12, [13-14,] 4-5 [6-7]; 34-38, 39-47 [48-49 missing] 50-52 [53] 54-94 [95] 96-102 [103] 104-116 [117] 118-221 (222-223 missing)
(cont'd)

2

Le Livre D'Heures . . . Anne De Bretagne   (Cont'd)

224-237 (238-239 missing) 238-474 [475; 1] 2-49 [50; 1] 2-7 [8; 1-4].

Plates: 1 copper engraving on title page laid in; several decorative engravings in text.
Notes: Pp. 317 & 319 on one page; 325 & 327, on one page; same for the following: 329 & 331; 333 & 335; 341 & 343; 345 & 347; 349 & 351; 357 & 359; 365 & 367; 369 & 371; 373 & 375; 381&383; 385 & 387; 389 & 391; 393 & 395;
(cont'd)

3

Le Livre D'Heure . . . Anne De Bretagne   (Cont'd)

401 & 403; 405 & 407; 413 & 415; 421 & 423; 443 & 445; 453 & 455.

Binding: Red morocco, gilt tooled, gilt edged.

Denslow, W[illiam] W[allace]. 1856-1915   #741

Denslow's Mother Goose: being the old familiar rhymes and jingles of Mother Goose. Edited and illustrated by W. W. Denslow. New York: McClure, Phillips & Company, 1901. Pp. [96].

Derrow, Nathan B.   V.D.M.   #743

A Catechetical Orthography; Introductory to a new Spelling Book Intended Hereafter to be Published. By Nathan B. Derrow, V. D. M.. In New Connecticut. Pittsburgh, Printed for the author, by Cramer, Spear and Eichbaum, 1813.

Coll: 12°; A⁹ (A4 + A5); 9 leaves (14 x 8.5 cm.); pp. [1-4, 5] 6-17 [18].

De Selincourt, Mrs. Basil

see

Anne Douglas Sedgwick   1873-1935

Devlin, Margaret Mary "Daisy" Ashford

see

Ashford, Margaret Mary "Daisy"

 # 748

Dickens, Charles   1812-1890

A Christmas Carol. In Prose. Being a Ghost Story of Christmas. By Charles Dickens with illustrations by John Leech. Eleventh Edition. London: Printed and Published for the author, By Bradbury and Evans, 90, Fleet Street, and Whitefriars. MDCCCXLVI.

Coll: 8° A^4 $B-L^8$ M^4 88 leaves (17 x 11.3cm) Pp. [i-viii, 1] 2-38 [39] 40-73 [74] 75-120 [121] 122-151 [152] 153-166 [167-168 of adverts].   (cont'd)

Dickens. Christmas Carol. 1846.   (Cont'd)

Plates: Frontispiece in color + 8 color by John Leech (1817-1864). Numerous woodcuts interspersed. Presentation copy: half-title page signed "Frederick Salmon Esquire/ from his friend/ Charles Dickens/ Twenty Eighth March/ 1846."

 # 749

Dickens, Charles   1812-1870

A Christmas Carol. Illustrated by Arthur Rackham. London: William Heinemann. Philadelphia; J. P. Lippincott, [1915]. Pp. [xii, 1-2] 3-147 [148: colophon]

Plates: Color frontispiece +11 in color+20 illus. in black and white.

 # 750

[Dickens, Charles]   1812-1870

Oliver Twist; or, the parish boy's progress. By "Boz". In three volumes. London: Richard Bentley, 1838.

Vol I:
Coll: 8° (12s) A^2 $B-P^{12}$ 170 leaves (20 x 12.4 cm) Pp. [i-iv, 1] 2-331, [332; 333-336: advert].

Plates: Frontispiece +9 by George Cruikshank.

Notes: McKell # S-5-)52-B. Uncut.   (cont'd)

Dickens   Oliver Twist, 1838   (Cont'd)

Vol II:
Coll: 8° A^2 $B-U^8$, X^2 156 leaves (20.2 x 12.6cm) Pp. [i-iv, 1] 2-307 [308].

Plates: Frontispiece +6 by Cruikshank

Notes: Advertisement on verso of half-title, p. [ii]. Uncut.

Vol III:
Coll: 8° (12s) A^2, $B-P^{12}$ 170 leaves (20 x 12.5cm) Pp. [i-iv, 1] 2-335 [336].   (cont'd)

Dickens   Oliver Twist, 1838 (Cont'd)

Plates: Frontispiece +7 by Cruikshank. Has cancelled plate facing p. 312, fireside scene: "Rose Maylie and Oliver."

Notes: Advertising for Bentley on pp. [i-ii]. Uncut.

 # 751

Dickens, Charles   1812-1870

Romance from the Pen of Miss Alice Rainbird Aged Seven [.] The Magic Fishbone. Illustrated by F. D. Bedford. London & New York: Frederick Warne and Co., [1922]. Pp. [i-ii, 1-22].

Plates: Title page+7 in color on conjugate leaves
Notes: Presentation copy--1921--to John Drinkwater from Francis D. Bedford. Bookplate of John Drinkwater. First printed in 1868.

 # 752

Dickinson, Rodolphus. 1787-1863

The Columbian Reader, comprising a new and various selection of elegant extracts in prose and poetry, for the use of schools in the United States, to which is prefixed an introduction on the arts of reading and speaking. By Rodolphus Dickinson, Esq. author of Geographical Publications, &c. Second edition. Boston: Published by R.P. & C. Williams; Hallowell: Ezekiel Goodale. For sale by them at their respective book-stores, and by most of the booksellers in New-England. E. Goodale, printer, 1818.

Coll: 12°: A-R^6 102 leaves (16.2 X 9.6cm) Pp. [i-v] vi-vii [viii-ix] x-xxxviii [39] 40-192 ("193" mispaginated 194) 194-204.

Binding: Wooden boards   covered with blue wrappers

Discreet Princess   **# 755**

[ANON.]. The Discreet Princess; or, the Adventures of Finetta. A Novel. London: Printed by R. Bassam, No. 53, St. John's-Street, West Smithfield, n.d.

Coll.: 32° (in 16's): [A^8] [B^8] C-D^8. 32 leaves (9.7 X 6.5cm), 61 + [3] pp.

Plates: Frontispiece.

          (cont'd)

Princess -2-

The Discreet Princess   (Cont'd)

D7^v: "A Catalogue of Books Printed and Sold by R. Bassam. . . ."

Bookplate of Percival Merritt.
BMC lists a different edition by Bassam, dated 1759.

Dodge, Mary Mapes.   (1831-1905) #763

MS of original eight-line verse, signed, to be used for a presentation copy of Hans Brinker.

Dobson, [Thomas.]   #759

First Lessons for Children. Philadelphia: Printed by T. Dobson..., 1797.

Coll: 12°; A-C^6; 18 leaves (15.5 x 8.9 cm.); pp. [1-2], 3-36.

Illus: 27 hand-tinted woodcuts.

Binding: Gray paper wrappers.

Notes: Welch #275.1.

Dodgson, Charles Lutwidge 1832-1898

see

Carroll, Lewis

[ANON.]. Doctor Birch and His Young Friends. By Mr. M.A. Titmarsh. London: Chapman and Hall, 186, Strand, 1849. [Bradbury and Evans, Printers: White-friars].   # 760

Coll.: 4° (4's): A^{2}B-F^{4}G5(4+1). 27 leaves (17.8 x 13.5cm). [i-iv][1]2-44[45]46-49[50] pp.

Plates: Frontispiece + engraved title + black and white vignette on printed title page (by Pierdon) + 14 hand-colored engraved plates.

Binding: Rebound.

First edition.

Dorey, Jacques   # 765

Three and the Moon: legendary stories of old Brittany, Normandy and Provence. Illustrated by Boris Artzy-basheff. New York: Alfred A. Knopf, 1929. Pp. [i-xii], 1-2] 3-7 [8-10] 11-22 [23-24] 25-34 [35-36] 37-46 [47-48] 49-65 [66-68] 69-97 [98-100] 101-103.

Plates: 8 in color.

Notes: LC# GR 161. D6

[ANON.]. Dr Last or the Devil upon Two Sticks [A Harlequinade, or "Turn-up]. London: Robert Sayer, Nov. 21, 1771.   # 761

Coll.: 4°: 2 leaves folded back to 18.5 X 8 cm. (making 4 panels). To each of these panels is pasted top and bottom and cut in the middle an engraving of identical size. Total of 8 tinted engravings: 2 each on A1^v and A2^z and 4 on paste-downs.

[Dorset, Catherine Ann (Turner)], A Lady (pseud) 1750?-1817?   # 766

The Authentic History of Whittington and His Cat. With Seven Coloured Engravings, A New Edition, Corrected and Adapted for Juvenile Readers, By a Lady. London: Dean and Munday, n.d.

Coll: 18° A^{18} 18 leaves (13.3 x 8.8cm) Pp. 3 4-36.

Plates: Fold-out frontispiece with seven hand-colored panels.

Notes: Bound in with six others in Omnibus # 1, q.v.

Dodge, M[ary] E[lizabeth] M[apes]. 1838-1905   #762

Hans Brinker; or, the silver skates. A story of life in Holland. Illustrated by F[elix] O[ctavius] C[arr] Darley and Thomas Nast. New York: James O. Kane, 1866. Pp. [iv] +[1] -347.

Plates: Frontispiece: "Once upon a time . . . ."

First ed. Blanck: # 4753

[Dorset, Catherine Ann (Turner)] A Lady (pseud) 1750?-1817?

The History and Adventures of Jack, the Giant Killer. With seven coloured engravings. A new edition. Corrected, and adapted for juvenile readers of the present times. By a Lady. London: [Printed by Dean and Munday for] Dean and Munday and A.K. Newman & Co. n.d.

Coll: 18°: [1^{18}] 18 leaves (13.9 X 9.2^{cm}.) Pp. [3-5] 6-38

Plates: Fold out frontispiece, containing seven colored engravings

Binding: Green pictorial wrappers, with advertisements on back. Advertising in front and back paste-down endpapers.

#767

[Dorset, Catherine Ann (Turner)] A Lady, pseud., *# 768*
1750 ? - 1817 ?

The Lioness's Rout; Being a Sequel to the Butter-
fly's Ball, The Grasshopper's Feast, and The Peacock
"At Home." By a Lady. London: Printed [by E.
Hemstead] for B. Tabart . . . , 1808.

Coll: 16° A-B⁸ 16 leaves (11.4 x 9.4cm) Pp. [1-3]
4-32.
Plates: Engraved frontispiece + 2.

Notes: Bound in with six others in *Omnibus #2*, q.v.

[Dorset, Catherine Ann (Turner)] A Lady (pseud) 1750?-1817?
The Lioness's Rout; Being a sequel to the Butterfly's
Ball, and the Peacock "At Home." Adorned with plates. By
a Lady. London: [Printed by E. Hemsted]. Published by
Tabart and Co. and J. Harris, 1808.
Coll: 16°: (eights) A-B⁸ 16 leaves (12.3 X 10.2cm·)
Pp. [1-3] 4-32
Plates: Frontispiece + 2 colored engravings
Binding: Orange wrappers, advertisements for Tabard on
back
Notes: [R-4-22-43L]   *# 769*

[Dorset, Catherine Ann (Turner)] A Lady, pseud., *# 770*
1750 ? - 1817 ?

The Lion's Masquerade. A Sequel To The Peacock At
Home. Written by a Lady. Illustrated With Elegant
Engravings. London: Printed [by H. Bryer] for J.
[ohn] Harris . . . ; and B. Tabart . . , 1807.

Coll: 16° A⁸ 8 leaves (11.4 x 9.2cm) Pp. [1-3]
4-16.
Plates: Engraved frontispiece (color) + 5 color
engravings (after Springsgutt by William
Mulready).
Notes: Bound in with 6 others in *Omnibus #2*, q.v.

[Dorset, Catherine Ann (Turner)]. A Lady (pseud) 1750?-
1817?
The Peacock "At Home:" a sequel to the Butterfly's Ball.
Written by a Lady. And illustrated with elegant engravings
London: Printed [by H. Bryer] for J. Harris, 1807.

Coll: 16°: A¹⁶ 8 leaves (12.5 X 10.1cm) Pp [1-3] 4-16
Plates: Frontispiece + 5 engraved plates (by W. Mulready?)
Binding: Blue wrappers
Notes: 1st issue   *# 770.1*

[Dorset, Catherine Ann (Turner)] A Lady (pseud) 1750?-
1817?
The Peacock "At Home:" A Sequel to the Butterfly's Ball.
Written by a Lady. And illustrated with elegant engravings
London: Printed [by H. Bryer] for J. Harris, 1807.

Coll: 16°: A¹⁶ 8 leaves (12.5 X 10.1cm) Pp. [1-3] 4-16

Plates: Frontispiece + 5 engraved plates (by W. Mulready?)

Binding: Buff wrappers and hand colored plates.

Notes: Another copy, later issue, McKell #SC 6-2-44-B

[Dorset, Catherine Ann (Turner)] 1750?-1817? *# 772*

The Peacock "At Home:" or Grand Assemblage of Birds.
Written by Roscoe. Illustrated with elegant engravings.
Philadelphia: Published and sold wholesale by Wm. Charles,
and may be had of all the booksellers, W. M'Culloch,
Printer, 1814.

Coll: 16°: [1⁸] 8 leaves (13.1 X 10.2cm) Pp. [1-3] 4-16

Plates: Frontispiece + 6

Binding: Yellow wrappers

Notes: Rosenbach #486, Welch #280.2

[Dorset, Catherine Ann (Turner)] 1750?-1817? *# 773*

Think Before You Speak: or, The Three Wishes. A Tale. By
the author of the Peacock at Home. London:Printed for M.J.
Godwin and Co., at the French and English Juvenile and
School Library..., [B. McMillan, Printer...] 1823.

Coll: 8°: (1¹⁰ 1⁶) B⁵ C⁶ χ⁵ (2⁵*B6-10) 16 leaves Pp.[1-4]
5 [6] 7-11 [12] 13-15 [16] 17-21 [22] 23-25 [26] 27-
29 [30] 31-32

Illus: 7 hand colored engravings

Doyle, Richard. 1824-1883 *# 778*

Homer for the Holidays by a Boy of Twelve. A Series of
Eighteen Original Drawings by Richard Doyle, 1837.

Pagination: 21 leaves (33.9 X 28.3cm) of heavy art board,
numbered [1-ii] 1-18 [19]

Illus: 18 matted watercolors (24.3 X 19.2cm) depicting
scenes from the Iliad.

Binding: Full brown morocco, gilt ruled, gilt edged, by
Riviere & Son.

Notes: This series of humorous watercolors of scenes from
the Iliad ostensibly was done by the precocious
Doyle during a vacation period from school. They
were never published.

Doyle, Richard   1824-1883 *# 779*

In Fairy Land: a series of pictures from the elf-
world. With a poem by William Allingham. Second
edition. London: Longmans, Green, and Co., 1875.
Fr. [1-37].

Binding: Cloth title page pasted to recto of f.[37]

Notes: Bookplate of James W. Ellsworth.

Doyle, Richard   1824-1883 *# 780*

Jack the Giant Killer. London: Eyre and Spot-
tiswoode, [1888]. Pp. [1-2] 3-48.

Illus: Each page illustrated in color by the author.

Binding: Free and paste-down endpapers front and
back.
Notes: Facsimile copy.

Draper, John   # *781*

The Young Student's Pocket Companion, or Arithmetic, Geometry, Trigonometry, and Mensuration . . . . White Haven, /Penn.] : Printed by Allason Foster for the Author, 1772.

Coll: 12° a⁶ b²a² B-U⁶ X⁴   128 leaves (16.1 x 10.4cm)
      Pp. [2]+xviii + 236.

Du Chaillu, Paul [Belloni] 1831-1903   # *782*

The Country of the Dwarfs. Illustrated by C[harles] S[tanley] R[einhart]. New York: Harper and Brothers, Aug., 1871. Pp. [x]+[ii] -314, [1] -8: advert.

Plates: Frontispiece: "Du Chaillu and King Quenqueza," by J.S.R.

Notes: First ed.

Du Chaillu, Paul [Belloni]   1831-1903   # *783*

Lost in the Jungle. Illustrated. New York: Harper and Brothers, 1870. Pp. [x]+[11] -260, [1] -4: advert.

Plates: Frontispiece: "Shooting a Leopard." +30 illus., illustrator unknown.

Notes: First ed.

Du Chaillu, Paul [Belloni]   1831-1903   # *784*

My Apengi Kingdom with Life in the Great Sahara. Illustrated. New York: Harper and Brothers, 1871. Pp. [xi] + [12] -254, [1] -4: advert.

Plates: Frontispiece: "African Forest." 32 illus., illustrator unknown.

Notes: First ed.

Du Chaillu, Paul [Belloni]   1831-1903   # *785*

A Wild Life Under the Equator. Illustrated. New York: Harper and Brother, 1869. Pp. [xii] 13-231, [1] -8: advert.

Plates: Frontispiece: "Under Way in Africa." +32 other engravings. Illustrator (engraver) unknown.

Notes: Presentation copy from Du Chaillu. First ed.

Dufresne, Abel   # *786*

Contes a Henri et a Henriette par Abel Dufresne. Illustrés de dessins imprimés en couleurs. Paris: a La Librairie De L'Enfance et de la jeunesse, P.-C. Le Huby, Rue De Seine, 55, Faubourg Saint-Germain, n.d. [ca 1845].

Coll: 12° π⁶, 1-18⁶, 19² 116 leaves (19 x 11cm)
      Pp. [1-6, i] ii-v [vi, 1] 2-7 [8] 9-15 [16] 17-
      20 [21] 22-38 [39] 40-44 [45] 46-50 [51] 52-77
      [78] 79-84 [85] 86-90 [91] 92-96 [97] 98-102
      [103] 104-116 [117] 118-157 [158] 159-178 [179]
      180-195 [196] 197-210 [211] 212-219 [220].
                                              (cont'd)

Contes a Henri et a Henriette.   (Cont'd)

Plates: Front +7 chromolithos

Notes: Gumuchian # 2309

Dulcken H [enry] W[illiam]   1832-1894   # *788*

The Golden Harp; hymns, rhymes, and songs for the young. Illustrated by J.D. Watson, T. Dalziel, & J. Wolf. London: Routledge, Warne, and Routledge, 1864. Pp. [i] -xii, 13- [160]; 1-4, adverts.

Plates: Frontispiece +cuts.

Dumas, Alexandre. 1802-1870   # *789*

The Black Tulip: a romance. S. J. Adair Fitz-Gerald, trans. Intro. by Ben Ray Redman. New York: The Limited Editions Club, 1951. Pp. [i] - xxiv, [1]-[328].

Illus: Cuts

Notes: # 788 of 1500

Dumas, Alexandre. 1802-1870   #*790*

The Three Musketeers. William Robson, trans. Intro. by Ben Ray Redman. Illust. by Pierre Falke. 2 vols. Maastricht: The Limited Editions Club, 1932.

Vol I:
Pagination: [i]-[xxviii], [1] - [372].
Illus: Front. + 14

Vol II:
Pagination: [1-6], 7-[370].
Illus: Front. + 18

Notes: # 216 of 1500; (   ) signed by illustrator

Dumas, Alexandre 1802-1870 **#791**

Les Trois Mousquetaires Avec Une Lettre d'Alexandre Dumas Fils. Compositions de Maurice Leloir. Gravures sur bois de J. Huyot. 2 vols. Paris: Calmann Lévy, Éditeur, Ancienne Maison Michel Lévy Frères, 1894. Pp. [i]-xx, 1-[480]; [i-iv] 1-[470].

Plates: Illustrated title page, frontispiece + cuts.

Echternach, Golden Gospels of

see under

Metz, Dr. Peter.

Edgeworth, Maria 1767-1849 **#798**

Lazy Lawrence; or, Industry and Idleness Contrasted. [Illustrated by William Croome]. Philadelphia: Geo. S. Appleton; New York: D. Appleton & Co., 1851.

Coll.: 4° A-D⁸ E⁸ 40 leaves (14 x 11.3cm) Pp. [1] 2-63 [64, 1-16 of adverts.]

Plates: Frontispiece + 1 + 1 woodcut on E1 of adverts; H.W. Herrick, sc.

Edgeworth, Maria 1767-1849 **#799**

Moral Tales. With Original Designs By [Felix Octavius Carr] Darley. A New Edition. Philadelphia: Duffield Ashmead, 1867. Pp. [i] ii-vii [viii,] 9-180.

Plates: Frontispiece + 5.

EDGEWORTH, MARIA. (1767-1849) The Parent's Assistant; or, Stories for Children. In Six Volumes. London: Printed for J. Johnson . . . by G. Woodfall + . . . 1800. **# 800**

Vol. I: 12°: a⁸A-L⁸. 96 leaves (15.7 X 9.7cm). xiv + [2]176 pp. (i-iii, 1-3, 69, 116, 117 unnumbered; 128 misnumbered 238.

Plate: Engraved frontispiece signed F.A.B.

a1: General title page, as above: . . . In Six Volumes. By Maria Edgeworth, author of Practical Education and Letters for Literary Ladies. Vol. I . . . . (cont'd)

The Parent's Assistant (Cont'd) Edgeworth -2-

a8: advertisement dated June 1, 1800.

A1: Title: Lazy Lawrence, Tarleton, False Key, Being the First Volume of The Parent's Assistant, or Stories for Children. By Maria Edgeworth . . . . The Third Edition. London: Printed for J. Johnson . . . by G. Woodfall . . . . 1800.

Vol. II: The Birth-Day Present, Simple Susan, Being the Second Volume of The Parent's Assistant, or Stories for Children. . . . The Third Edition, with Additions. London: Printed for J. Johnson . . . by G. Woodfall . . . . 1800. (cont'd)

The Parent's Assistant (Cont'd) Edgeworth -3-

Coll.: 12°: A-N⁸. 104 leaves (15.7 X 9.7cm). 208 pp. (1-3, 42, 43, 92, 115, 208 unnumbered; 199 misnumbered 196).

Plate: Engraved frontispiece, signed C.P.

Vol. III: The Bracelets, The Little Merchants, Being the Third Volume of The Parent's Assistant, or Stories for Children. . . . The Third Edition. London: Printed for J. Johnson . . . by G. Woodfall . . . . 1800. (cont'd)

Parent's Assistant Edgeworth -4-

Coll.: 12°: A-N⁸O⁴P². 110 leaves (15.8 X 9.3cm). 220 pp. (1-3, 36, 37, 76-77, 113, 154, 155, 181, 219, 220 unnumbered; 112 misnumbered 142).

Plate: Engraved frontispiece, signed C[harlotte] E[dgeworth].

Vol. IV: Old Poz, The Mimic, Mademoiselle Panache, Being the Fourth Volume of The Parent's Assistant, or Stories for Children. . . . The Third Edition, with Additions. London: Printed for J. Johnson . . . by G. Woodfall . . . . 1800. (cont'd)

Parent's Assistant (Cont'd) Edgeworth -5-

Coll.: 12°: A-L⁸M⁴. 92 leaves (15.8 X 9.4 cm). 184 pp. (1-3, 34, 35, 63, 89, 118, 119, 184 unnumbered)

Plate: Engraved frontispiece, signed F[rancis] B[eaufort].

Vol. V: The Basket-Woman, The White Pigeon, The Orphans, Waste Not, Want Not, Forgive and Forget, Being the Fifth of The Parent's Assistant, or Stories for Children. . . . The Third Edition, with Additions. London: Printed for J. Johnson . . . by G. Woodfall . . . . 1800. (cont'd)

Parent's Assistant (Cont'd Edgeworth -6-

Coll.: 12°: A-O⁸, P⁴(-P4). 115 leaves (15.8 X 9.5 cm). 230 pp. (1-3, 39, 65, 122, 123, 191, 193 unnumbered).

Plate: Engraved frontispiece, signed F.E.

Vol. VI: The Barring Out, Eton Montem, Being the Sixth Volume of The Parent's Assistant, or Stories for Children. . . . The Third Edition, with Additions. London: Printed for J. Johnson . . . by G. Woodfall . . . . 1800. (cont'd)

The Parent's Assistant (Cont'd)   edgeworth -7-

Coll: 12°: A-N⁸. 104 leaves (15.7 X 9.6cm). 208 pp.
[1-3], 106, 107, 115 unnumbered.

Plate: Engraved frontispiece, signed FAB.

On title page of each volume: "To Lady Crewe from
the author." On inside front cover of each volume is
the bookplate of Lady Frances Anne Crewe (d. 1818).
Obsolete signatures present: Vols. 1-6.
                    McKell # [SG+ND+L]

Eggleston, Edward 1837-1902   #802

The Circuit Rider: a tale of the heroic age. Illustrated. New York: J. B. Ford & Company, 1874. Pp.[viii,
9]-332.

Notes: First American printing: first issue, first ed.
       Blanck # 5106.

Eggleston, Edward   1837-1902   #803

The Schoolmaster's Stories for Boys and Girls. Illustrated. American Homes Series. Boston: Henry L.
Shepard and Co., (Late Shepard & Gill), 1874. Pp.[1]-
279.

Contents: The Schoolmaster's Stories; The Cellar Door
          Club; Queer Stories; The Chicken Little
          Stories; and, Modern Fables.

Notes: First ed. Illustrator unknown. Blanck # 5107.

Ehrlich, Bettina   1903-   #804

Cocolo Comes to America. New York: Harper &
Brothers, 1949. Pp.[1-32].

Illus: Cuts

Binding: Dust cover

[ANON.]. The Elephant's Ball, and Grand Fete   #805
Champetre. Intended as a Companion to those much
admired Pieces, The Butterfly's Ball, and The
Peacock "At Home." Illustrated with Elegant Engravings. By W.B. London: Printed [by H. Bryer]
for J. Harris. . . , 1807.

Coll.: 16°: A⁸. 8 leaves (11.5 X 9.5cm). [1-3]
4-16 pp.

Plates: Engraved frontispiece + 7 (all colored) [by
William Mulready?].

Notes: Bound in with six others in Omnibus # 2, q.v.

[ANON.]. Ellen, or The Naughty Girl Reclaimed, A   #806
Story Exemplified in A Series of Figures. London:
Printed for S. and J. Fuller [by D.N. Shury], 1811.

Coll.: 16°: [A¹²]. 12 leaves (12.6 X 10cm).
[2]+ 19 + [3] pp.
Contains nine loose figures (colored engravings).

Pp. 6,8,10, 12 are blank.

Bound in original gray wrappers, with title on front
and advertisements for S. and J. Fuller on back, in
original cardboard slip case.

No Bk -

Elliott, [Elliot, Eliot,] Mrs. [Mary Belson] #807

[From wrapper (no title page)]. Greedy Child
Cured. By Mrs. Elliott. New York:
Mc Laughlin Bros. Publishers, n.d. [c. 1880].

Coll: 4°; A¹⁶; 16 leaves; pp. [1-3] 4-6
[7-8] 9-12 [13-14] 15-18 [19-20] 21-24
[25-26] 27-31 [32].

Illus: Fine colored engravings printed on one
       side of page only.

Binding: Yellow wrappers. Colored illus. on
         front, advertisement on back.

Notes: Initial and   final leaves pasted to
       wrapper.

Elliott (Elliot, Eliot), Mary Belson   #808

Poetic Gift: containing Mrs.[Anna Letitia (Aiken)]
Barbauld's Hymns, in verse. New Haven: S. Babcock,
n.d. Pp. [1-5], 6-24.

Illus: Front + cuts.

Notes: "Babcock's Moral, Instructive And Amusing Toy
       Books." Mrs. Barbauld, 1743-1825.

[Elliott (Elliot, Eliot),] Mary Belson   #809

The Rambles of a Butterfly. London: Printed By and For
W. Darton, Jun., 1819.

Coll: 12° A¹ B-Q⁶ 91 leaves 13.9 x 8.8cm) [2] +177+
[3]pp.

Plates: Engraved presentation page; frontispiece + 2
        (dated August 2, 1819).

Notes: McKell # R-4-22-43-L

[Elliott (Elliot)] Eliot, Mary [Belson]   #810

Rustic Excursions To Aid Tarry-at-Home Travellers:
for the amusement and instruction of young persons.
London: William Darton and Son . . . , [1027?].[N.d.]
2 vols in one.

Part I:
Coll: 12° A-D¹² 48 leaves (17 x 10.5cm) Pp.[i-iii]
iv-vi [7] 8-96.

Plates: Front + 3 engravings.

(cont'd)

Rustic Excursions . . . .   (Cont'd)

Part II:
Coll: 12° A¹²(-A; A11+1) B-D¹² 47 leaves (17 x 10.5cm) Pp. [1-iii] iv [5] 6-9b.

Plates: 4 engravings

Notes: P. iv dated "London; April, 1627." Pp. [1-ii], (title page to Part II) missing from McKell copy.

[Elliott] Elliot [Eliot] Mary [Belson]   # *811*
ELLIOT, MARY. Useful Gossip for the Young Scholar; or Tell-Tale Pictures. London: William Darton, n.d.

Coll: 18°(in 36): A⁹B¹⁸[C⁹](=A10-18). 36 leaves (13.3 X 8.8cm). [3] 4-72 pp. 67 woodcuts.

Notes: Bound together with six others in one vol., Omnibus # 1, q.v.

Ellis, Edward S[ylvester]   ed. 1840-1916   # *812*

Tales, Traditions and Romance of Border and Revolutionary Times. The Chieftain's Appeal. The Implacable Governor. Mrs. Slocumb at Moore's Creek. Brady's Leap. ["Complete Beadle's Dime Tales. Number 6."] New York: Beadle and Company, Publishers, entered 1864. Pp. [1-5] 6-16 [17-18] 19-32 [33-34] 35-40 [41-42] 43-55 [56], [i-iii] iv [v] vi [vii-viii].

Illus: 4 engravings

Binding: Yellow wrappers: illustrated on front; advertisement on back.   (cont'd)

Tales, Traditions and Romance, etc. (Cont'd)

Notes: Additional title page, preface, and contents appear on pp. [i]-[viii]. Additional pagination occasionally present at bottom of page.

[Ellis, Edward Sylvester,] ed.   1840-1916   #*813*

Tales, Traditions and Romance of Border and Revolutionary Times. ["Beadles Dime Tales Series," Number 11, Published Monthly.] Serg't Champes' Recognition. Col. Crawford's Fate Decided. Davis Fixing Court Business. Miss Moncrieffe, the Female Spy. New York: Beadle and Co., Publishers, [July, 1864].

Coll: 8° 1⁸ 2⁴ 3⁸ 4⁴ 5⁶ 30 leaves (18.8 x 12.3cm) Pp. [1-4, 5] 6-24 [25-26] 27-40 [41-42] 43-48 [49-50] 51-60.

(cont'd)

Ellis. Tales, Traditions . . . . 1864.   (Cont'd)

Illus: 4 engravers: Taylor; Adams; Roberts; & Avery.
Binding: Yellow pictorial wrappers; advertisement on back.
Notes: Subscript pagination: Pp. 257-312.

Elmo (pseud)

see

Handford, Thomas W.

Elwes, Alfred   -1888

see

Brough, Robert Barnabas. Funny Dogs With Funny Tales.

Emanuel, Walter [Lewis] 1869-1915   # *814*

A Dog Day or The Angel in the House. Pictured by Cecil Aldin. New York: R. H. Russell, 1902. 60pp.

Illus: numerous decorations throughout by Aldin

Anon.   #*815*

Emblems of Mortality; Representing, in Upwards of Fifty Cuts, Death Seizing All Ranks and Degrees of People . . . . To which is Prefixed a Copious Preface . . . . London: Printed for T. Hodgson, 1789.

Coll: 12° π² A⁶a⁶b²B-z⁶r² 42 leaves (17.6 x 10.6cm) Pp. [4]+xxviii+52.

Illus: By John Bewick (1760-1795) and Thomas Bewick (1753-1828)

Notes: McKell # S-3-3-47

Emerson, B [enjamin] D [udley]   1781-1872   # 816

The First Class Reader: a selection for exercises in reading, from standard British and American Authors, in prose and verse. Philadelphia: Hogan and Thompson, 1836.

Coll: 12⁰ 1-23⁶ 138 leaves (18.1 x 11cm) Pp. [i-iii] iv [v] vi-viii [9] 10-276.

Anon.   #817

The Emigrants: and other Stories. New York: Leavitt & Allen, 1855.

Coll: 16⁰: 1-4⁸ 32 leaves (14.3 X 11.2cm) Pp. [1-4] 5-6 [7-8] 9-10 [11-12] 13-14 [15-16] 17-18 [19-20] 21-22 [23-24] 25-26 [27-28] 29-30 [31-32] 33-34 [35-36] 37-38 [39-40] 41-42 [43-44] 45-46 [47-48] 49-50 [51-52] 53-54 [55-56] 57-58 [59-62] 63-64

Illus: 16 engravings

Notes: Illustrations printed on one side of the page only

Anon   #818

An Entertaining and Instructive Description of Birds, Beasts, Fishes, Insects, and Reptiles. London: Printed for H. Turpin, 1776.

Coll: 24⁰ A-H⁸ 64 leaves (10.5 x 6cm) 128pp.

Plates: 37 engravings in text.

Anon.   #819

Entertaining Histories, for young Masters and Misses

Coll: 32⁰: (8s) A-H⁸ 64 leaves (11 X 6.6cm.) Pp. [1-2] (3-4 missing: title page) [5] 6 (7-8 missing) 9-126 [127-128]

Illus: Frontispiece woodcut + several woodcuts Vertical chains

Binding: Pp. [1] + [128] as paste down end papers. Flowery boards

Notes: No title page. Advert. inside back cover: "Ashbel Stoddard's Printing-Office, in Hudson, by the gross, dozen or single...." Stoddard flourished C. 1809. McKell copy lacks A2, A4. Welch #337 (Welch lists McKell copy)

Anon.   #820

The Entertaining History of Little Goody Goosecap. Containing a variety of adventures calculated to amuse and instruct. London: Printed by T. C. Hansard, for Baldwin, Cradock, and Joy,...and John Sharpe, 1818.

Coll: 12⁰: A-B¹² C⁶ 30 leaves (14.5 X 9.1cm.) Pp. [1-3] 4-60

Illus: 20 woodcuts in text

Binding: Orange wrappers

Notes: McKell #R-4-22-43-L. McKell copy lacks C6

[Everdingen, Allart van.] 1621-1675   #822

[History of Reynard the Fox, or the deceits of the fox.]

Coll: oblong 4⁰ (12.8 x 20.8cm) A book of plates.

Plates: 50 engravings by Everdingen, printed on one side of leaf only.

Notes: No title page; information taken from fly-leaf. Proofs made in early 19th century from original plates.

Ewing, Juliana Horatia [(Gatty)] 1841-1885   #824

Jackanapes. Illustrated by Randolph Caldecott. London: Society for Promoting Christian Knowledge; New York: E. and J.B. Young and Co., 1884. Pp. [1-4] 5- [48]

Plates: Frontispiece + cuts.

Anon.   #825

The Extraordinary Life and Adventures of Robin Hood, Captain of the Robbers of Sherwood Forest. Interspersed with the history of Little John and his merry men all. New York: Published by W. Borradaile, and sold wholesale and retail, at his Book-store, 1823.

Coll: 12⁰: [1², 2⁶,-3⁶] 14 leaves (18 X 10.5cm.) Pp. [5,6, 7] 8-32

Illus: Frontispiece hand coloured etching by Prud'homme.

Binding: Plain wrappers

Notes: Arbitrary signings present. Rosenbach #625

Fabre, J [ean] Henri   1823-1915   #826

The Life of the Caterpillar. Alexander Teixeira de Mattos. New York: Dodd, Mead and Company, 1916. Pp. [1] 2-376.

Fabre, J [ean] Henri   1823-1915   #827

The Life of the Fly. Alexander Teixeira de Mattos. New York: Dodd, Mead and Company, 1919. Pp. [1] 2-477.

Anon #828

Fabliaux et contes du moyen age. Illustrations de A. Robida. Édition pour la jeunesse précédée d'une introduction par M.L. Tarapt. Paris: Librarie Renouard, Henri Laurens, Editeur, n.d. Pp. [1-4, 1] ii-iv [1] 2-119 [120]

Illus: Numerous illustrations in balck and white and color throughtout.

Anon #829

The Fairing; or, a Golden Toy for Children of all Sizes and Denominations. . . . Adorned with Variety of Cuts from original Drawings. London: Printed for T. Carnan, 1784.

Coll: 32° A-I⁸ 72 leaves (9.5 x 6.55cm) Pp. vi, 7-141 [3: advert].

Plates: Frontispiece numerous cuts in text.

Binding: Buff paper covered boards, illustrated with
(cont'd)

The Fairing (Cont'd)

woodcuts. Spine is binding.

Notes: I7ᵛ: "Books for the Instruction and Amusement of Children, Printed for T. Carnan . . . ." Roscoe # 110 (5). Bookplate of Percival Merritt.

Anon. #830

Fairy Tales; or, a Present for Young People: containing Instructive and Diverting Stories of The White Cat, Beauty and the Beast, and Puss in Boots [3 vols. in one]; with a coloured engraving. Derby: Published by Thomas Richardson; Simpkin, Marshall, & Co., London n.d.

Coll: (1) The White Cat 12°: A⁶ (≠A) 6 leaves (14.4 X 8.6ᶜᵐ·) Pp. [1-3] 4-12
(2) The Interesting Story of Beauty and the Beast 12°: A⁶ 6 leaves (14.4 X 8.6ᶜᵐ·) A², A³ signed Pp. [1-3] 4-11 [12]
(3) The History of Puss in Boots 12°: A⁶ 6 leaves (14.4 X 8.6ᶜᵐ·) A², A³ signed Pp. [1-3] 4-12
(cont'd)

Anon.

Fairy Tales; or, a Present for Young People (cont'd)

Plates: Fold out colored, engraved frontispiece of Beauty and the Beast, originally published at London by J.L. Marks

Binding: Yellow wrappers, advertisements in back, stabbed, free endpapers

Notes: Last two stories have their own title pages. Each of the three title pages bears "With a Colored Engraving" but there is only one frontispiece tipped in to ≠A of Book I

Anon. #832

False Stories Corrected. New York: Printed and sold by Samuel Wood, at the Juvenile Book-Store, No. 357, Pearl Street, 1814.

Coll: 18°: 1²⁴ 24 leaves (13.3 X 7.1cm) Pp. [i-ii, 1-3] 4-44 [45-46]

Binding: Pink wrappers. Initial and final leaves as paste down end papers

Notes: Advertisement on 1·24 (P. 45) Rosenbach #487, Welch #362.2

Anon #833

Une Famille de Rouges-Gorges. 2.ᵉ edition. Paris, Strasbourg: Ve Berger-Levrault et Fils, Libraires, 1855.

Coll: 12° π2, 1¹², 1.6, 2¹², 2.6, 3¹², 3.6, 4¹², 4.6, 5¹², 5.4 90 leaves. (14.8 X 9.9cm) Pp. [1-iv, 1] 2-173 [174, 175-176].

Plates: Frontispiece-title, +3; all lithos+many decorative cuts.

Binding: Final leaf as paste-down endpaper.

Notes: P. [174]: blank

Anon. #834

The Famous Tommy Thumb's Little Story-Book: Containing His Life and Surprising Adventures. To which are added, Tommy Thumb's Fables, with Morals, and at the end, pretty stories, that may be either sung or told. Adorned with many curious pictures. London: Printed for S. Crowder, and sold by B. Collins, and by most booksellers n.d.

Coll: 32°: (in 4's) A-D⁴ 16 leaves (8.6 X 5.7ᶜᵐ·) Pp. [1]-2-32

Binding: Buff wrappers, plain

Illus: 8 woodcuts in text

Anon. #835

The Famous History of Tom Thumb. Three Parts. London: [ca 1780.]

Part I:
Title: The Famous History of | TOM THUMB. | Wherein is declared, | His marvellous Acts of Manhood.| Full of Wonder and Merriment.| [a rule] | PART the FIRST | [a rule] | [woodcut, 8 x 6.8cm] | [a double rule] | LONDON: Printed for the Booksellers.

Coll: 12° A¹² 12 leaves (14.6 x 8.7cm) Pp. 1 -24.
(cont'd)

The Famous History of Tom Thumb. ca 1780 (Cont'd)

Binding: Orange wrappers

Part II:
Title: The Famous History of | TOM THUMB. | Wherein is declared, | His marvellous Acts of Manhood. | Full of Wonder and Merriment. | Performed after his First Return from | FAIRY-LAND. | [a rule] | PART the SECOND | [a rule] | [woodcut, 7.8 x 7cm] | [a double rule] | LONDON: Printed for the Book- sellers.

Coll: as in first part

(cont'd)

The Famous History of Tom Thumb. ca 1780   (Cont'd)

Binding: Gray wrappers

Part III:
Title: The Famous History of | TOM THUMB. | Wherein is
       declar'd, | His marvellous Acts of Manhood. | Full
       of Wonder and Merriment. | [a rule] | PART THE
       THIRD. | [a rule] [woodcut, 6.8 x 7cm] | [a double
       rule] | LONDON: Printed for the Booksellers.

Coll: as in first part

Binding: Yellow wrappers.
                                          (cont'd)

The Famous History of Tom Thumb. ca 1780   (Cont'd)

_____

Notes: McKell copy contains the three parts with original
       wrappers bound together in 19th century mottled
       calf.

                                          #836
Fannie, Cousin (pseud)

Golden Hours for Good Children. [From cover.] [n.d.]

Coll: Oblong royal 8° [1², 2-5²] 9 leaves (23.9 x
      17.5cm) Pp. [1-3] 4 [5] 6 [7] 8 [9] 10 [11] 12
      [13] 14 [15] 16 [17] 18.

Plates: Frontispiece +6 hand-colored copper engravings
        +decorations.

Binding: Stabbed.
                                          (cont'd)

Golden Hours for Good Children   (Cont'd)

Notes: McKell copy missing title leaf, [1.1], pp. [1-2]
       Title page (?) pasted to cover. Dedicated to
       Mary and Fanny Appleton.

                                          #837
Fannie, Cousin (pseud)

Red Beard's Stories For Children: Translated
from the German, by Cousin Fannie. Boston:
Phillips, Sampson & Co., 1856.

Coll: Royal 8°; 34 individual leaves (24.1 x
      17.4 cm.); Recto only of each leaf num-
      bered 5-67.

Illus: 24 illustrations, black on white.

Notes: Printed on recto only.

Farquharson, Martha

        see

        Martha Finley   1828-1909

                                          #838
Fauser, Alois, ed.

Die Bamberger Apokalypse [Faksimile or Bibl. 140
(A II 42) in der Staatlichen Bibliothek Bamberg.]
Frankfurt am Main: Insel-Verlag, 1958. Pp. [i-
cxxiv, 1-2] 3-22 [23-24] 25-39 [40] 41 [42-44].

Plates: 59 containing reproductions in color of
        miniatures.
Notes: # 213 of 500.

                                          #839
Anon.

The Feast of the Fishes; or, The Whale's Invitation to His
Brethren of the Deep. London: Printed [by H. Bryer] for J.
Harris, 1808.

Coll: 16°: A⁸ 8 leaves (12.1 X 10.1cm·) Pp. [1-3] 4-14
      [15-16]

Plates: Frontispiece +4 colored engravings
Binding: Blue wrappers. A8: advertisements
Notes: S-6-3-42-L

Fenn, Lady Eleanor (Frere)   1743-1813

        see

        Lovechild, Mrs.

                                          #845
Field, Eugene. 1850-1895

Little Willie by Eugene Field. [October 19, 1895].

Coll: 4°? [1⁴] 4 leaves (11.2 X 15cm) Pp.[1-8]

Illus: Wood engraving on P. [8] + 5 engraved initials

Binding: Brown wrappers

Notes: Unnumbered copy. Ltd. to 75 copies only.

Field, Eugene 1850-1895 **#847**

Nonsense for Old and Young. Illustrated by John
G. Frohn. Boston: Henry A. Dickerman & Son, 1901.
Pp. [1-9,] 10-58; [1-16 of adverts]

Plates: Frontispiece + cuts.

)

Field, Eugene. 1850-1895 **#848**

Poems of Childhood. Illustrated by Maxfield Parrish.
New York: Charles Scribner's Sons, 1904. Pp. [i] - [xii],
1- [200].

Illus: Title page + 8

Notes: First ed.?

)

Field, Rachel [Lyman] 1894-1942 **#849**

Hepatica Hawks. Allen Lewis, engraver. New York: The
Macmillan Company, Oct. 1932. Pp. 1-239.

Plates: Frontispiece engraving in green, white and
black.

Notes: First ed. Half title.

)

Fielding, Henry 1707-1754 **#850**
FIELDING, HENRY, ESQ. The history of the adventures
of Joseph Andrews, and his friend Mr. Abraham Adams.
With a short biography by Thomas Roscoe, revised and
four illustrations by George Cruikshank. London:
George Bell and Sons, 1887. Pp. [i]-lxxxiv, 1-[350].

Plates: Frontispiece + 4.

Front paste-down endpaper + 3-15 advertisements.
Bound in at end: 12 pp. advertisements + paste-down
endpaper.

)

Fielding, Henry. 1707-1754 **#851**

The History of Joseph Andrews, and His Friend Mr Abraham
Adams. London: Printed for the Proprietors, by J.F. Dove,
1825.

Coll: 24°: B-Q^{12} 180 leaves (12.7 X 7cm) Pp. [1-3] 4-359
[360]

Plates: Engraved frontispiece + half-title vignette

⊃

Fielding, Henry 1707-1754 **#852**

The History of Tom Jones A Foundling. 2 vols.
Illustrated by George Cruikshank. London: James
Cochrane and Co., 1831.
Vol I:
Coll: 8° [a^4]b^8 A-2E^8 2F^3 (2f1+ 2F2-3) 239 leaves
(17.05 x 10.6cm) Pp. [i-vii] viii-xix
[xx-xxi] xxii-xiii[xxiv, 1] 2-454
Plates: Frontispiece + 4 by Cruikshank

Vol II: o
Coll: 8° π^2 A-2E^8 226 leaves (17.1 x 10.7cm)
(cont'd)

)

Fielding. History of Tom Jones (cont'd)

Pp. [i-v, 1] 2-448.
Plates: Frontispiece + 3 by Cruikshank

Notes: Vols. V and VI of The Novelist's Library,
edited by Thomas Roscoe. Bookplates of
Robert Hoe.

)

Fierens-Gevaert, Hippolyte 1870- **#853**

Les Très Belles Heures De Jean De France Duc De
Berry. Société Des Bibliophiles et Iconophiles de
Belgique. Bruxelles: Weckesser Frères; Leyde: A. W.
Sethoff; Paris: Maurice Rousseau. M. DCD. XXIV.
(i.e., 1924). Pp. [b] 7-59 [60,] 61-66 [67, 68; 69-
70;] Ff. I-XXIII (color plates); ff. [1]: blank; ff.
1-14 (black and white).

Notes: #587 of 710.

)

#854

Anon

The Fifteen Joys of Marriage. Translated from the
French by Elizabeth Abbott with illustrations by
René Ben Sussan. New York: Bramhall House, 1959.
Pp. [i-v] vi-vii [viii-x, 1-5] 6-221 [222].

Illus: 15 in color.

)

Figure Book

see

Ellen, or the naughty girl reclaimed, a story
exemplified in a series of figures.
(contains nine loose figures)

)

Anon. #855

Figures in Verse and Simple Rhymes, for Little Learners.
New York: Kiggins & Kellogg, 38 John Street, n.d.

Coll: 32°: [1⁸] 8 leaves (9.1 X 5.2cm) Pp. [1-2,3] 4-16

Illus: Numerous engravings

Binding: Blue wrappers

Notes: McKell copy missing back wrapper

Anon. #856

Filial Affection: or The Wonderful History of Little
Jack. Embellished with cuts. Birmingham: Printed by T.
Brandard, n.d.

Coll: 24°: [1¹²] unsigned 12 leaves (10.4 X 8.1^cm·)
Pp. [1-5] 6-23 [24]

Illus: Frontispiece wood cut on p. [2] +5 vignettes in
text

Binding: Blue plain wrappers; initial and final leaves
serve as paste down endpapers

Finley, Martha [Farquharson (pseud)] 1828-1909 #857

Elsie and Her Loved Ones. By Martha Finley. New York:
Dodd, Mead and Company, [1903]. Pp. [i-iv, 1] -300.

Plates: Frontispiece

Finley, Martha [Farquharson (pseud)] 1828-1909 #858

Elsie at Nantucket. A sequel to "Elsie's New Relations."
New York: Dodd, Mead & Company, Publishers [1884].
Pp. 334.

Plates: Frontispiece by Photo. Eng. Co., N.Y.

Finley, Martha (Farquharson [pseud]) 1828-1909 #859

Elsie's Children: a sequel to "Elsie's Motherhood."
New York: Dodd, Mead & Company, Publishers, [before
1881]. Pp. 340.

Plates: Frontispiece +decorative title page

Finley, Martha [Farquharson (pseud)] 1828-1909 #860

Elsie's Girlhood. A sequel to "Elsie Dinsmore," and
"Elsie's Holidays at Roselands." New York: Dodd, Mead
& Company, Publishers, 1872. Pp. 422.

Plates: Frontispiece by G.E. Durand

Finley, Martha [Farquharson (pseud)] 1828-1909 #861

Elsie's Girlhood: a sequel to "Elsie Dinsmore," and
"Elsie's Holidays at Roselands." New York: Dodd, Mead
& Company, Publishers, 1872. Pp. [viii, 1]-422 [423-424]

Plates: Frontispiece by John S. Davis +2

Notes: Prov. "Vesta Quackenbush from Eddie E. De Leon,
Christmas 1881."

Finley, Martha (Farquharson [pseud]) 1828-1909 #862

Elsie's Motherhood: a sequel to "Elsie's Womanhood."
New York: Dodd, Mead & Company, Publishers, [before
1881]. Pp. 376.

Plates: Frontispiece +decorative title page.

Finley, Martha [Farquharson (pseud)] 1828-1909 #863

Elsie's New Relations: what they did and how they
fared at Ion. A sequel to "Grandmother Elsie." New York
Dodd, Mead & Company, Publishers, [1883]. Pp. 324.

Plates: Frontispiece

Finley, Martha [Farquharson (pseud)] 1828-1909 #864

Elsie's Widowhood: a sequel to "Elsie's Children."
New York: Dodd, Mead & Company, 1880. Pp vi + 331.

Plates: Frontispiece +decorative title page.

[Finley], Martha Farquharson (pseud) 1828-1909 **#865**

Elsie's Womanhood: a sequel to "Elsie's Girlhood." New York: Dodd, Mead & Company, Publishers, [before 1881]. 406pp.

Plates: Frontispiece +decorative title page (with Cupid).

Finley, Martha (Farquharson [pseud]) 1828-1909 **#866**

Elsie's Womanhood: a sequel to "Elsie's Girlhood." New York: Dodd, Mead & Company, Publishers, n.d., Pp. 406.

Plates: Frontispiece

Finley, Martha [Farquharson (pseud)] 1828-1909 **#867**

Grandmother Elsie: a sequel to "Elsie's Widowhood." New York: Dodd, Mead & Company, Publishers, [1882]. Pp. 298.

Plates: Frontispiece, by V. E. Taylor

[Finley], Martha Farquharson(pseud)1828-1909 **#868**

Holidays at Roselands: with some after scenes in Elsie's life; being a sequel to Elsie Dinsmore. New York: M. M. Dodd, 1868.

Pagination: Pp. 367+10. Bound in at end: 16pp. advert numbered 1-7, 2-10 ("9" misnumbered 13).

Plates: Frontispiece engraved title page signed "Howland, Sc."

Notes: Chapters 1, 2 and 10 pp. at the beginning of 3 are taken verbatim, same plates from 2d ed. of Elsie Dinsmore, Chapters 13-15.

[Finley], Martha Farquharson (pseud) 1828-1909 **#869**

Holidays at Roselands: with some after scenes in Elsie's life; being a sequel to Elsie Dinsmore. New York: Dodd, Mead & Company, Publishers, [1881 or earlier]. Pp. [b, 7] -373.

Plates: Frontispiece by BEN. SC. Decorative title page.

Notes: Drops from beginning those chapters which eventually ended Elsie Dinsmore. Adds two chapters to 1868 ed. at the end.

(Finley, Martha) Farquharson (pseud) 1828-1909 **#870**

Holidays at Roselands: a sequel to "Elsie Dinsmore." New York: Dodd, Mead & Company Publishers, [1898]. Pp. 354.

Plates: Frontispiece by G.E. Durand.

Notes: Begins as undated ed., but revises the end of chapter 16 and adds 17.

[Finley], Martha Farquharson (pseud) 1828-1909 **#871**

An Old Fashioned Boy. Philadelphia: Evans, Stoddart & Co., [1871?]. Pp. [1-2] 3-346, [1-6: advert].

Plates: Frontispiece +4, by Schell.

Finney, Charles G [randison] 1905- **#872**

The Circus of Dr. Lao. Illustrated by Boris Artzybasheff. New York: The Viking Press, 1935. Pp. [1-8] 9-154.

Plates: 7

Binding: Dust cover.

#873

The First Christmas Story, by I.H. Meredith and Grant Colfax Tullar. Published Quarterly by Tullar-Meredith Co. 108 Washington St. Chicago, Illinois. New York House 50 Fifth Ave. [N. d.]

Coll: 8°: [1⁸] 8 leaves ff 8 (23 x 15.8cm)

Binding: Cream wrappers

Notes: Wrappers are included in the foliation. "Vol. 3, No. 3....November 15, 1900....Subcription, 15¢ Per Year" and "Prices: Single copy $0.05, Per Dozen .50, Per 100 4.00" on front cover.

Anon. **#874**

The First Lie. Written for the Am. S.S.U. and Revised by the Committee of Publication. Philadelphia: American Sunday-School Union, 1122 Chestnut Street, [n.d.].

Coll: 32°: [1⁸] 8 leaves (11.2 X 7.3cm) Pp. [1-2] 3-1o

Illus: Two woodcuts in text and two on wrappers.

Binding: Wrappers.

Fisher, Dorothy Canfield.   (1879-1958) #875

A. L. S. one page (16.1 x 11.7 cm.), Villa
Montmorency, Paris, September 16, 1916, to
William Fayal Clarke, offering "Understanding
Betsy" to St. Nicholas Magazine. "I feel a long
way from books and book-making just now. I'm
working with the French soldiers blinded in
battle."

(

Fisher, Dorothy Canfield.   (1879-1958) #876

T. L. S. one page (27.1 x 21.1 cm.), 6 Rue
Petrelle, Paris, November 20, 1916, to William
Fayal Clarke, concerning "Understanding Betsy"
and a misunderstanding with Mr. Boyden of the
American.

(

[Fisher, Dorothea] Dorothy [Frances] Canfield 1879-
1958   #877

Understood Betsy. Illustrated by Ada C. Williamson.
New York: Henry Holt and Company, [August] 1917.
Pp. [3]+[1] 2-271, 272-274 4 leaves.

Plates: Frontispiece + 10.
Binding: Jas. MacDonald Co., N.Y.: boxed; dust cover
Notes: First ed.

(

FitzGerald (Fitzgerald), Edward. 1809-1883   #880

Edward Fitzgerald's Rubaiyat of Omar Khayyam. With a
Persian text, a transliteration, and a close prose and
verse translation by Eben Francis Thomson. [Illust. by
S   A   Kinsley.] [Worcester,
Mass.]: Privately printed [The Commonwealth Press],
1907. Pp. [1] - [xiv], [1] - 148.

Illus: Front + 1

Notes: Frontispiece portrait signed by S. A. Kinsley;
       protective paper signed "Your Sincere Friend
((cont'd)

Edward Fitzgerald's Rubaiyat of Omar Khayyam. (Cont'd)

Edward Fitzgerald." Plate portrait, p. 139 signed:
"Faithfully yours Eben Francis Thomson"; also signed by
S. A. Kinsley. Presentation page signed "Eben Francis
Thomson." Private edition of 275 copies.

(

Fitzgerald, P   A   ca. 1800-1870 #881

The Exhibition Speaker: containing farces, dialogues,
and tableaux, with exercises for declamation in prose
and verse. Also, a treatise on oratory and elocution,
hints on dramatic characters, costumes, position on
the stage, making up, etc., etc. With illustrations.
Carefully compiled and arranged for school exhibitions,
by P. A. Fitzgerald, Esq.: to which is added a complete
system of calisthenics and gymnastics, with illustrations for teachers and pupils, illustrated with fifty
engravings. New York: Sheldon and Company; Cincinnati: Applegate & Co.; Chicago: W. B. Keen; Cleveland:
((cont'd)

The Exhibition Speaker: (Cont'd)

Ingham & Bragg; Detroit: Putnam, Smith & Co., 1856.

Coll: 12° 1-11¹², 12⁶ 138 leaves (18.2 x 11.7cm)
Pp. [i-iv, v] vi [vii] 8-10 [xi] xii-xiii [xiv],
[15] 16-36 [37-38] 39-46 [47-49] 50-166 [167] 168
[169-171] 172-178 [179-180] 181-184 [185-186]
187 [188-191] 192-198 [199-200] 201-209 [210-213]
214-218 ("217" mispaginated 21; "218" mispaginated
18) [219-221] 222 [223] 224-268, [1]2-8.

Illus: Fifty engravings

((cont'd)

The Exhibition Speaker: (Cont'd)

Notes: Stereotyped by J & C. E. Felton, Buffalo. Last
       eight pages are advertisements. Pp. 121-122 of
       McKell copy missing.
       LC# PN4305. S4F55

C

Fitz-gerald, S[hafto] J[ustin] Adair 1859-   #882

The Zankiwank and the Bletherwitch. With pictures
by A[rthur] Rackham. London: J.M. Dent & Co.,
1896. Pp. [1]-xii, [1] 2-188.

Plates: Frontispiece + 16 + cuts.

(

                                                #885
Anon

The Flights of a Lady-Bird; or, the History of the
Winged Rambler. Embellished with Cuts. London:
E. Newbery, 1794.

Coll: 32° (in 16's) A-B¹⁶ 32 leaves (9.9 x 6.4cm)
61+[3] pp.
Illus: Frontispiece (A1ᵛ) + 12 woodcuts in text.
Binding: Pink and Green wrappers with 2 figures: St.
         Petrus & St. Paulus. A1 and B16 form at-
         tached endpapers.
Notes: B15ᵛ -B16: adverts for E. Newbery. Bookplate
       of Percival (Merritt. Roscoe , 136 (3).

#886

Anon

The Flights of a Lady-Bird; or, The History of the Winged Rambler. Embellished with Cuts. London: Printed [by S. Gosnell] for E. Newbery, 1799.
Coll: 32⁰ (8's) A-D⁸ 32 leaves (10.1 x 6.4cm) 61+[3] pp.
Illus: Frontispiece (A1ᵛ)+12 woodcuts in text.
Binding: Greenish-blue floral wrappers. A1 and D8 form attached endpapers.
Notes: D7ᵛ- D8: adverts for E. Newbery. Bookplate of Percival Merritt. Roscoe # 136 (4).

 # 887

Anon.

Flora's Gala, Illustrated with elegant engravings. London: Printed [by H. Bryer] for J. Harris, 1808.
Coll: 16⁰: A¹⁶ 16 leaves (12.7 X 10.6ᶜᵐ·)
Pr. [1-3] 4-16
Plates: Frontispiece + 5 colored engravings
Binding: Blue wrappers, advertisements on back.
Notes: [S-1-11-43]

Florian

see

William Tell, or The Patriot of Switzerland. By Florian. And Hofer, The Tyrolese. J. Harris.

 # 888

Foldout leaflets published by W. Walker & Son, Otley, n.d. Sheet (37.8 X 12.5cm) folded twice in the same direction to form four foldout leaves, the recto of the first leaf containing a colored cut and serving as title page.
Jack and Jill. 8 cuts.
Jack and the Bean-Stalk. 5 cuts.
The History of Jack the Giant Killer. 6 cuts.
Old Mother Goose. 8 cuts.
Poor Cock Robin. 8 cuts.
Tom, The Piper's Son. 8 cuts.
The Fireside Traveller. 8 cuts.

(cont'd)

Foldout leaflets -2-

New London Cries. 8 cuts.
My Brother. 8 cuts.
The Remarkable History of Goody Two Shoes. 8 cuts.

#889

Anon.

Footsteps to Natural History of Beasts. New-Haven: Sidney's Press, 1809.
Coll: 12⁰: A-C⁶ 18 leaves (13.8 X 8.4cm) Pp. [1-2, 3] 4-36
Illus: Frontispiece + 17 other woodcuts
Binding: Original brown illustrated wrapper bound in. frontispiece as paste down endpaper.
Notes: Howard Pyle Bookplate. John Stuart Groves Bookplate. Wrapper lists I. Cooke & Co. New Haven as publishers
A.A.S. #387.4   Evans #17520

#890

Anon.

Footsteps to Natural History of Birds. New-Haven: From Sidney's Press, [Published by Increase Cook & Co.,] 1809.
Coll: 12⁰: A-C⁶ 18 leaves (13.9 X 8.4cm) Pp. [1-2, 3] 4-35 [36]
Illus: Woodcut frontispiece + 19 woodcuts in text
Binding: Original printed blue wrappers bound in; initial and final pages as paste down endpapers.
Notes: Bookplates of Howard Pyle and John Stuart Groves. Evans # 17521, A.A.S. #388.2

#891

Ford, Alla T. and Dick Martin

The Musical Fantasies of L[yman] Frank Baum . . . . Chicago: The Wizard, 1958. Pp. [1-3] 4-80.
Plates: Frontispiece +cuts.
Notes: Fly-leaf inscribed to Col. McKell.
LC# PS 3503. A923Z

#894

Ford, Paul Leicester, ed.   1865-1902

New England Primer: A reprint of the earliest known edition, with many facsimiles and reproductions, and an historical introduction. Ed. Paul Leicester Ford. New York: Dodd, Mead and Company, 1894. Pp. [i-iv] 1-113 [114]. +82 unnumbered pages, reprint of 1727 Boston primer.
Plates: Frontispiece + 30.

Fosdick, Charles Austin 1842-1915

see

Castlemond, Harry. Frank on the Prairie.

Anon   **#896**

The Fox and the Geese, an ancient nursery tale. Illustrated with six drawings by Harrison Weir. And the Story
of Tom the Piper's Son. Cleveland, Ohio: J. B. Cobb &
Co., 1856.

Coll: 12° [1¹²] 12 leaves (17 x 11.4cm) Pp. [1-2, 3-21]
22-24. (Subscript number 10 present on p. [13].)

Illus: 6 engravings

Binding: Illustrated buff wrappers; advert on back.

Fox, John, Jr.   1862-1919   **#897**

The Little Shepherd of Kingdom Come. Illustrated
by F. C. Yohn. New York: Charles Scribner's Sons,
1903. Pp. [x] +404.

Plates: Frontispiece + 7.

1964.70

Foxton, Thomas   **#899**

Moral Songs Composed for the Use of Children.
Third edition corrected. London: Richard Ford,
1737.

Coll: 12° A-C¹² 36 leaves (14.7 x 8.4cm) xii,
57+3 pp.

[Franklin, Benjamin]. 1706-1790   **#901**

The Art of Making Money Plenty, in every Man's Pocket. By
Dr Franklin. New York: Pub' Sold by S. Wood, 357 Pearl St,
n.d.

Coll: 16°: 1⁸ 8 leaves (13 X 10.4cm) Pp. [1-16]

Illus: Numerous cuts

Binding: Blue wrappers, initial and final pages as paste
down endpapers

Notes: Advert. on back cover for Samuel Wood's books for
Children illustrated   by Anderson

Fricero, Kate J   **#903**

Little French People : a picture book for little folk.
London, Glasgow, Dublin, Bombay: Blackie and Son
Limited; New York: Dodge Publishing Company, n.d.
[ca. 1909]. Pr. [48].

Illus: Cuts

Notes: Pages uncut

Froissart, Sir John (Jean Froissart, c.1337-1410?)   **#905**

Chronicles of England, France and the Adjoining
Countries, From the Latter Part of the Reign of
Edward II to the Coronation of Henry IV. Newly
translated by Thomas Johnes. 4 vols. [Hafod:
Printed] By James Henderson, At the Hafod Press,
1803-1805.

Vol I: 1803
Coll: Demy 4° π³b-r² B-5N⁴ O² 431 leaves $1 (-π1)
(28.3 x 23.5cm) Pp. [i-iii] iv [i] ii, [v] vi-
xxiv [1] 2-835 [836].

(cont'd)

Froissart. Chronicles. Hafod. 1803-5 (Cont'd)   2

Plates: Engraved vignette by Angus after Britton
on title page; 16 full-page etchings by
J. Harris (two are maps, Netherlands and
France)

Vol II: 1804
Coll: Demy 4° [a]-r², g¹ (tipped to f2ᵛ), B-5B⁴
$1 (- a1) 385 leaves (28.3 x 23.5cm) Pp.
[i-ii, iii] iv-xxvi [1] 2-744.
Plates: Same as vol i, except 18 etchings, no maps.

(cont'd)

Froissart. Chronicles. Hafod. 1803-5 (Cont'd)   3

Vol III: 1804
Coll: Demy 4° π, a, b-e² B-4O⁴ 338 leaves $1 (-π
-a) Pp. [i-ii, iii] iv-xx [1] 2-631 ("632"
mispaginated 532) 633-656.
Plates: Same as vol ii, except only 4 etchings.

Vol IV: 1805
Coll: Demy 4° π² b-e² B-4S⁴ 4T² 556 leaves $1(-π1)
(28.3 x 23.5cm) Pp. [i-ii, iii] iv-xx [1] 2-
525 ("526" mispaginated 226)

(cont'd)

Froissart. Chronicles. Hafod. 1803-5 (Cont'd)   4

Plates: Same as vol iii, except only 16 etchings.

Binding: All four vols in red calf, gilt edged,
marbled free and paste down endpapers
front and rear, with 1 additional free
endpaper front and rear.
Notes: Bookplate of Revd W. Shepherd on front paste-
down endpapers of Vols I, III, IV; but on
back paste-down endpaper of Vol II.

Froissart, Jean (c.1337-1410?)

see also

Humphreys, H.N., Esq. Illuminated
Illustrations of Froissart. 1844-45
Lanier, Sidney, ed. The Boy's Froissart.
Scribner's, 1879.

Funnidos, Rigdum, Gent.

    see

        The Comic Almanac, for 1845: . . . London:
            for David Bogue.

Games

    see

        The Book of Games; . . . . London: J.
           Adlard for Tabart and Co., 1805

        The Book of Games; . . . . London: for
           Tabart & Co., by B. McMillan, 1810.

        The Playground; or, out-door games for
           boys. New York, 1866?

                           (cont'd)

Galsworthy, John.   (1867-1933) #909

The Forsyte Saga. London: William Heinemann,
1922.

Pagination: pp. [i]-xvi, [1]-1104.

Notes: First Edition.
    "Rare first issue not recorded in
    Bibliography. Dedication to Edward
    Sa.?.ett not printed on reverse of
    Book I." (Note on end paper).
    Dust cover.

Games (Cont'd)

    see

        The Village Green, or sports of youth.
           New Haven: S. Babcock, 1840.

        Youthful Sports. New York: Mahlon Day.

Galsworthy, John   1867-1933   #910

The Forsyte Saga. New York: Charles Scribner's Sons,
1925. Pp. xvi [1-2] 3-870.

Plates: 1 fold-out chart at end: Forsyte Family Tree.

Anon.   #913

A Gaping-Wide-Mouth Waddling Frog. [Illustrated by Walter Crane.] London: George Routledge and Sons, [Edmund
Evans, engraver and printer,] [C. 1867.]

Pagination: ff 1-8

Illus: 8 pages of colored lithos, by Walter Crane

Binding: Orange, stiff pictorial wrappers, advertisements
        on back. Initial and final leaves are pasted
        down.

Notes: On one side of leaf only. "Price Sixpence: or
        Mounted on Linen, One Shilling" on front cover.
        "Routledge's New   Sixpenny Toy Books" on
        back cover.

Galsworthy, John. 1867-1933   #911

Old English: a play in three acts. London: Duckworth
and Co., . . . [1924]. Pp. [1-8], 9-118.

Illus: Cuts

Binding: Dust cover

Notes: First ed.

Gaskell, Mrs. [Elizabeth Cleghorn ?] 1810-1865 #915

Cranford. with a preface by Anne Thackeray Ritchie
and illustrations by Hugh Thomson. London and New
York: Macmillan and Co., 1891. Pp. [i-v] vi-xxx,
[1] 2-297 [298-300].

Illus: Original drawing by Hugh Thomson tipped into
        binder's leaf$_2$.

[ANON.]. Games and sports for young boys. With
ninety illustrations. London & New York: Routledge,
Warne, and Routledge, 1862. Pp. [i]-iv, [1]-106,
[83-86], 87-100 [advertising].

Plates: Frontispiece + cuts.

[Geisel, Theodor] Seuss, Dr.   1904-   #918

The Seven Lady Godivas. Written and illustrated by Dr.
Seuss. New York: Random House, [1939]. Fr. 40.

Illus: Cuts

Notes: First nd.

Geissler, P   G   #919

Neuester Orbis Pictus für die Jugend. Oder lehrriche und unterhaltende Bilderschau von Gegenstaenden aus der Natur, der Kunst und dem Menschenleben, mit beigefugter Erklarung in deutschen, franzosischer, italienischer u. englischer Sprache. 24 fein ausgemalte Folio-Tafeln mit entsprechenden Randverzierungen nach Original-Zeichnungen von P. G. Geissler. Nurnberg: C. H. Zeh'schen Buchhandlung, 1842.

Coll: 2⁰ 1-6² 12 leaves 24pp. (36.3 x 24.9cm)

Plates: 25 (engraved title page + 24 colored engravings).

(cont'd)

Neuester Orbis Pictus . . . . (Cont'd)

Notes: McKell # S-3-9-51-L; #-3-9-51-B

[ANON.]. The Geographical Guide; A Poetical Nautical Trip Round the Island of Great-Britain; With . . . . Notes, in Prose . . . . London: Printed [by J. Cundee] for J. Harris . . ., 1805. [No BMC no.]

Coll.: 12⁰, [A²]B-D¹² 38 leaves (16.8 X 10.5cm). pp. [i-iv][1-3] 4-69 [70-72].   #920

Frontispiece, vignettes and small engravings.

Bookplates of A.M. Broadley, Geraldi Ponsonby, and Percival Merritt.

Anon   #921.1

Geography Made familiar and easy to Young Gentlemen and Ladies. Being The Sixth Volume of The Circle of the Sciences, &c. The Fourth Edition. London: Printed for T. Carnan, and F. Newbery, Junior, 1776.

Coll: 32⁰ A-Y⁸ 176 leaves (9.8 x 6.5cm) Pp. xx + 319 + 13.

Binding: Marbled boards, green vellum spine with paper label.

Notes: Y2ᵛ: "Books printed for T. Carnan and F. New- (cont'd)

Geography Made Familiar . . . Sixth Volume of Circle of the Sciences. 1776. (Cont'd)

    bery, Junior." Bookplates of James Losh and Percival Merritt. Roscoe # 63(4)

Anon   # 921.2

[Geography Made Familiar and Easy to Young Gentlemen and Ladies. Being the Sixth Volume of the Circle of the Sciences, &c. The Fourth Edition. London: . . . for T. Carnan and F. Newbery, Junior, 1776].

Coll: 32⁰ A-X⁸ Y² 170 leaves (9.2 x 6.3cm) [20]+ [1] 2-319 [320].
Binding: Blue boards, red leather spine
Notes: Y2ᵛ: "Books printed for T. Carnan and F. Newbery, Junior" advert. Bookplate of Percival Merritt. Roscoe #63(4). McKell copy lacks A1: title page.

Anon.   # 923

George Wilson and His Friend. By the author of "Jane and her Teacher." Revised by the Committee of Publication. Stereotyped by L. Johnson. Philadelphia: American Sunday School Union., 1827.

Coll: 12⁰; A-G⁶, H³ (H-H.2, H.3); 45 leaves (13.4 x 8.6 cm.); pp. [1-2, 3] 4-89 [90 blank.]

Illus: Front. wood engraving.

Binding: Paper over boards.

Atlas Minimus   (cont'd)

Notes: McKell copy lacks [A3], [A5], [A6]. Bookplate of Percival Merritt. Roscoe # 146 A(1).

Gerstlinger, Hans, ed   #924

Die Wiener Genesis. [Facsimile] 2 vols. Wien: Benno Filser [1931].

Vol I: Pp. [i-vi] vii [viii] ix-x [xi-xii] xiii-xv [xvi] 1-229 [230-232].
Illus: 26 plates containing 152 illustrations.

Vol II: Pp. [1-48.]
Illus: 24 bound mats containing 48 leaves reproduced in full color.

Anon.   #925

Die Geschichte Joseph's und seiner Brüder. Eine biblische Erzahlung. Harrisburg, Pa: Geducht zu haben bey G.S. Peters, n.d.

Coll: 12⁰: [1]¹⁸ 18 leaves (14.2 X 8.9cm) ff 1-18

Illus: Hand-tinted woodcuts

Notes: Blank facing pages alternate with text and illustrations.

Gibson, J[ohn]   #926

Atlas Minimus, or a New Set of Pocket Maps of the
several Empires, Kingdoms and States of the Known
World, With Historical Extracts relative to each. . . .
Revis'd, Corrected and Improved By Eman[uel] Bowen.
London: J. Newbery, 1758.

Coll: 24° [A⁶ B-C²⁴] (all unsigned) 54 leaves (11.2 x
8.3cm).

Plates: Front +50 engraved maps.

Binding: Full calf

                                            (cont'd)

Gibson, J[ohn]   #927

Atlas Minimus Illustratus: containing fifty-two
pocket maps of the world. Drawn and engraved by J.
Gibson; revised, corrected, and improved by E. Bowen.
To which are added, a description of the several
empires . . . . : with a concise account of the air,
soil, and climate of each; and the government,
customs, religion, and manners of the inhabitants.
London: Printed for T. Carnan and F. Newbery, junior,
1779.

Coll: 16°(unsigned) [1² 2-7⁸ 84 9²] 56 leaves (11.1 x
8.7cm). Ff. [56]   (cont'd)

Atlas Minimus Illustratus. (Cont'd)

Plates: Frontispiece +55 engraved maps.

Notes: Bookplate of Percival Merritt. Roscoe # 146 A
        (5).

Gilbert, Mrs. Ann (Taylor). 1782-1866   #928

My Mother. A Poem By A Lady. Illustrated with engravings.
Philadelphia: Published and sold by Morgan and Yeager.
No. 114 Chesnut Street. First door below the post office.
n.d.

Coll: 16°: [1⁶] 6 leaves (13.3 X 10.1cm) Pp. [1-12]

Illus: 6 hand colored copper engravings
Binding: Yellow wrappers
Notes: Printed on one side of leaf only

Gilbert, Mrs. Ann (Taylor) 1782-1866   #929

Rhymes for the Nursery. Munroe and Francis' Edition.
[Stereotyped by Geo. A. & Curtis, Boston.] Boston:
J. H. Francis; New York: C. S. Francis, [1839].

Coll: 16° 1⁸ 2-7⁸ 56 leaves (14.2 x 11.1cm) Pp.[1-
2]3-112.

Illus: 73 Colored engravings

Notes: McKell # S-9-17-42 Contains "My Mother. A
        poem by a lady."

Gilbert, Mrs. Ann Taylor   1782-1866   #930
    Signor Topsy-Turvy's Wonderful Magic
Lantern; or, The World turned upside down. By the
Author of "My Mother," and Other Poems. Illustrated
with Twenty-four Engravings. London: Printed for
Tabart & Co. . . . By B. McMillan, 1810.

Coll.: 16⁸: B-C¹⁶D⁴. 36 leaves (13.9 X 10.3cm).
[4]5-71 + [1]pp.

Plates: Frontispiece + 23.

D4ᵛ: Advertisements for "Elementary Books Lately
published by R. Phillips." MWC 11645. de. 54.

See ercy Muir, English Children's Books, pp. 91,
99.

Gilbert, [Sir] W[illiam] S[chwenck] 1836-1911   #930.1

The "Bab" Ballads. Much sound and little sense.
Illustrated by the author. London & New York: George
Routledge & Sons, [1868]. Pp.[i]-viii, [9]-[310].

Plates: Frontispiece + cuts.

Gilbert, [Sir] W[illiam] S[chwenck] 1836-1911   #930.2

Bab Ballads: much sound and little sense. New York.&
London: G. P. Putnam's Sons, n.d. Pp. [i] -[viii] 1 -
[162].

Illus: cuts

Gilbert, [Sir] W[illiam] S[chwenck] 1836-1911   #930.3

Fifty "Bab" Ballads. Much sound and little sense.
With illustrations by the author. New York: Street &
Smith, n.d. Pp. [1-4, i] -iv, [11] -234, [1-10: adverts].

Plates: Frontispiece + cuts.

Notes: Back cover of McKell copy missing. Preface dated
        Aug., 1867.

Giles, Chauncey   1813-1893   #930.4

The Little Basket-Maker, and other stories. Wakefield: William Nicholson and Sons; London: E.D.
Ewins and Co., and W. Tegg, n.d. Pp. [3-7], 8-157
[1-3, adverts.]

Glaubrecht, Otto (pseud) [Rudolf Oeser].   #931

Die Schreckensjahre von Lindheim. ["Volksgeschichten."]
Philadelphia: Hoffman & Morwitz, 1873. Pp. [i]-iv, [5]
-70.

Notes: Adverts on back paste-down endpaper.

[ANON.]. Gockel and Scratchfoot or, the adventures   #933
of two chickens. Translated from the German.
Illustrated. Chicago: Henry A. Sumner and Company,
1882. Pp. [i-vi], 7-[112].

Plates: Frontispiece + 2 + cuts.

Godolphin, Mary

     pseud. of

       Lucy Aikin 1781-1864,
       q.v.

[Godwin, William] 1756-1836   #934

The Looking Glass. A true history of the early years of
an artist; calculated to awaken the emulation of young
persons of both sexes, in the pursuit of every laudable
attainment; particularly in the cultivation of the fine
arts. By Theophilus Marcliffe. [Illustrated by William
Mulready.] London: Printed for Thomas Hodgkins, 1805.

Coll: 12° a⁶ b4 A-K⁶ L² (a3 missigned a2; b2 missigned
b) 72 leaves (12.9 x 8.1cm) Pp. [2]+xviii+[b].

Plates: Frontispiece, I-IV

                     (cont'd)

The Looking Glass. (Cont'd)

Notes: Kb: "New Books. Published by Thomas Hodgkins
at the Juvenile Library. . . ." BMC identifies
W. Mulready as the illustrator/subject of the
book. McKell # S-2-5-43.

Goethe Johann Wolfgang Von. 1749-1832   #935

Reineke Fuchs...mit Zeichnungen von Wilhelm Von Kaulbach
gestochen von R. Rahn und A. Schleich. Stuttgart und
Tübingen. [also München]. J.G. Cotta'sche Verlag. 1846.

Coll: 2°: π² 1-32⁴ 33¹ 131 leaves Pp. [i-iv] 1-257 [258]

Plates: Engraved frontispiece, title page, register der
        stahlstiche, + 35.

Notes: Bookplate of Augustus Arthur Van Sittart.

Goldsmith, Oliver   1728-1774   #936

The History of Little Goody Two Shoes; Otherwise
called Mrs. Margery Two Shoes the means by which
she acquired her learning and wisdom, and in consequence thereof her estate; . . . "Heath's Home
and School Classics." ed. by Charles Welsh. With
28 illustrations after the woodcuts in the original
edition of 1765, by Marion L. Peabody. Boston:
D.C. Heath & Co., Publishers, [April 16] 1900. Pp.
[i-v] vi, vii-ix [x], 1-51 [52-54.]

Binding: Brown pictorial wrappers.

                     (cont'd)

Goldsmith. Goody Two Shoes. 1900.   (Cont'd)

Notes: Wrapper bears: "Heath's Home and School
       Classics, No. 8, Issued Fortnightly."

Goldsmith, [Oliver] 1728-1744   #937

The Vicar of Wakefield; a tale, by Doctor Goldsmith.
Illustrated with twenty-four designs, by Thomas Rowlandson. London: Published by R. Ackerman, at the Repository of Arts, 101, Strand. Printed by W. Clowes,
Northumberland-Court, [May] 1817.

Coll: royal 8° γ² A-3B-δR⁷ 132 leaves (25.3 x 16cm)
       Pp. [i-ii, 1-5] 6-8 [1] 2-254.

Plates: 24 hand-colored engravings by Rowlandson.

Binding: Original gray boards, orange paper label on
                     (cont'd)

The Vicar of Wakefield . . . . (Cont'd)

     spine; rebacked.

Notes: Bookplates of Edward Henry Hill and Lucius Fil-
merding. Leaves uncut.

Goldsmith, Oliver (1728-1774)

see

A Museum for Young Gentlemen and Ladies. London: 1806. (Goldsmith's authorship is not proved.)

Goodrich. Book of Ornithology. (Cont'd)

Society and The David McCandless McKell Collection. Back loose endpaper verso: "D. K. Webb/ Chillicothe, Ohio." On spine: "Parley's Ornithology." No LC no.

#940

Anon.

Good Child's Soliloquy. Published by the American Tract Society. n.d.

Coll: 32°: [1^8] 8 leaves (10.1 X 6.5cm) Pp. [1] 2-15 [16]

Illus: 14 engravings

Notes: Title page bears no. "-20-"

#944

[Goodrich, Samuel Griswold]   1793-1860

The First Book of History. For children and youth. By the author of Peter Parley's Tales. Boston: Richardson, Lord & Holbrook, 1831.

Coll: 12° 1-13^6 14^8 90 leaves (17.7 x 13cm) Pp. [1-2] i-iv, [7] 8, [9] 10-178 [179] 180.
Plates: Frontispiece +16
Notes: Obsolete signings present
       First ed?
       LC gives Cincinnati: C. D. Bradford & Co.; New York: Collins and Hennay, 1831.

#941

Goodrich, Rev. Charles A. [ugustus] 1788-1779.

A History of the United States of America, or a plan adapted to the capacity of youth . . . . Illustrated by engravings. 2d. ed. New York: Published by Collins & Co., 1824.

Coll: 12° [1]-26^b 160 leaves (14.6 x 8.85cm) Pp. [1-4] 5-296. [1] 2-20 [21-24].

#945

[Goodrich, Samuel Griswold]   1793-1860

The Garland; being a Selection of Interesting Stories. By the Author of Peter Parley. [Parley's Library.] New York: Cornish, Lamport & Co.; St. Louis, [Mo.]: McCartney & Lamport, [1841].

Coll: 12° [1-16^6 17^2] Obsolete signings present.
98 leaves (15.1 x 9.5cm) Pp. [5-9] 10-62 + [3-5] 6-119 [120] + [191] 192-200 + [233] 234-241 [242].
Plates: Chromolitho half-title. Stereotype ed.
Notes: P. 51: "An omitted Pickwick paper." No LC no.

#942

[Goodrich, Samuel Griswold]   1793-1860

Balloon Travels of Robert Merry and His Young Friends, over various countries in Europe. Edited by Peter Parley. Illustrated. New York: Derby and Jackson, Publishers; Cincinnati: A. W. Derby & Co., [1855].

Coll: 12° 1-13^{12} 56 leaves (18.3 x 12.4cm) Pp. [i-ii], iii-iv, [v] vi-viii [9] 10-312.
Plates: Frontispiece 6.
Notes: First ed.

#946

[Goodrich, Samuel Griswold]   1793-1860

The History of the Western States. Illustrated by Tales, Sketches and Anecdotes. By Lambert Lilly, Schoolmaster. Boston: William D. Ticknor, 1842.

Coll: 12° [1]^{b}2-14^b 84 leaves (15.4 x 9.2cm) Pp. [1-iii] 4- [168].

Illus: Numerous woodcuts in text.

#943

[Goodrich, Samuel Griswold]   1793-1860

A Book of Ornithology, for youth . . . . Illustrated by Numerous Engravings. [Parley's Ornithology.] Boston: William Hyde, and Co., 1832.

Coll: 12° 1^{*6} 3-28^6 162 leaves (15 x 9.3cm) Pp. [1-v] vi-x [xi] xii [13] 14-322 +[2].
Plates: Frontispiece numerous cuts (engravings). Frontispiece engraving on leaf [1*]; not a separate plate.
Notes: Bookplates of the Ross County Historical (cont'd)

#947

[Goodrich, Samuel Griswold]   1793-1860

Parley's Magazine for Children and Youth. Vol. 1, Nos. 1-7 (Saturday, March 16, 1833 to Saturday, June 8, 1833).

Coll: 8° [1-7]^8 56 leaves (17.3 x 13.5cm) Pp. [1-3] 4-16, [17-19] 20-32, [33] 34-48, [49] 50-64, [65] 66-80, [81] 82-96, [97] 98-112.

Illus: Numerous woodcuts in text.

#948

[Goodrich, Samuel Griswold] 1793-1860

Parley's Magazine. Parts XVII-XX, Vol. V. [Illustrated.] New York and Boston: Charles S. Francis, and Joseph H. Francis, [1837?].

Coll: $8°$ $¶4$ $[1^8]$ 2^8 $[3^8]$ $4-5^8$ 5^8 6^8 $[6^8]$ $6-^8$ χ^8 $2\chi^8$ 7^8 $7-^8$ 8^8 $8-^8$ 9^8 $9-^8$ $[10^8]$ $10-^8$ 11^8 $11-^8$ 11^8 $11-^8$

Plates: Numerous woodcuts in text, several full-page.

Notes: McKell copy lacks ¶1-¶3.

#949

[Goodrich, Samuel Griswold] 1793-1860

Peter Parley's Book of Anecdotes. Illustrated. Philadelphia: Thomas, Cowperthwait & Co., 1839.

Coll: $8°$ (12s) $[1-6]^{12}$ 72 leaves (13.2 x 11cm) Pp. [xiii] 14-144.

Plates: Frontispiece+12 full-page illus. included in pagination.

Notes: Entered 1835. Signed 1-9⁸ but sewn as above. BMC gives 1845 edition only.

#950

Goodrich, Samuel Griswold 1793-1860

Peter Parley's Book of Bible Stories For Children and Youth. With Engravings. Boston: Munroe & Francis; New York: Charles S. Francis, 1845.

Coll: $24°$ A-V⁴ (includes U signature) 128 leaves (14.2 x 11.8cm) Pp. xii, 13-256.

Plates: Frontispiece+18 engravings.

Notes: Contains Bible Letters, etc., by Lucy Barton; and Gospel Stories.

#951

[Goodrich, Samuel Griswold] 1793-1860

Peter Parley's Geography for Beginners. Illustrated. New York: Huntington and Savage, 1849.

Coll: $8°$ $1-6^8$ 7^8 8^8 $9-10^8$ 80 leaves (15.1 x 12.1cm) Pp. [i-v] 6-160.

Illus: 18 maps +150 illus.

Notes: Stereotyped at the Boston type and stereotype foundry. McKell copy missing pp. 87-90. BMC gives 1850 edition only

#952

[Goodrich, Samuel Griswold] 1793-1860

Peter Parley's Geography for Beginners. Illustrated New York: Sheldon, Blakeman & Company, 1857.

Coll: $12°$ (6s) $1-10^6$ 11^4 $12-[13]^8$ (16. x 12.3cm) Pp. [i-v] 6-160 80 leaves.

Plates: Frontispiece+18 color maps+150 illus.

Binding: Stabbed.

#953

[Goodrich, Samuel Griswold] 1793-1860

Peter Parley's Illustrations of the Vegetable Kingdom: Trees, Plants and Shrubs. Boston: B.B. Mussey, 1840.

Coll: $8°$ (mixed) $¶r^2$ A^6 $B-G^8$ $1-20^8$ 21^4 (-21·4). 21 (-¶r) 219 leaves. civ, 330+[4] pp. (i-iv, vii, ix, cii, 1, 23, 311, 326 are unnumbered) (16.5 x 13cm).

Illus:"Frontispiece" engraving on ¶1ᵛ.

Notes: BMC: # 7083. a.2.

#954

Goodrich, Samuel Griswold Peter Parley (pseud) 1793-1860

Peter Parley's Short Stories for Long Nights. With engravings. Boston: Allen and Ticknor, 1834.

Coll: $16°$ $[1^8]$ $2-4^8$ $[5-6^8]$ 7^8 $[8-9^8]$ 72 leaves (13.4 x 11.2cm) Pp. [1-3] 4 [5-7] 8-140 [141-144].

Illus: Seven hand-tinted copper plate engravings.

#955

[Goodrich, Samuel Griswold] 1793-1860

Peter Parley's Tales about the Islands in the Pacific Ocean. With a map and numerous engravings. Boston: Carter, Hendee, and Co., 1833.

Coll: $64°$ $[1]^8$ $2-9^8$ 72 leaves (13.1 x 11cm) Pp. [1-5] 6-144.

Plates: Map tipped in; published by Gray and Bowen, Boston.

#956

[Goodrich, Samuel Griswold] 1793-1860

Peter Parley's Tales About the Sun, Moon, and Stars. [Illustrated] Boston: Gray & Bowen and Carter & Hendee, 1832.

Coll: $16°$ $¶^2$ $1-7^8$ 58 leaves Pp. [i-ix] 10-116. (13.3 x 11.3cm)

Plates: 1+numerous full-page illustrations.

Binding: Stiff paper wrapper, leather spine. Stabbed

Notes: LC has 1842 ed. only; BMC only 1837,45,and 62 editions.

#957

[Goodrich, Samuel Griswold] 1793-1860

Right is Might, and other sketches. By the author of Peter Parley's Tales. Illustrated. New York: Sheldon, Lamport & Blakeman, 1855.

Coll: $12°$ $[1-3]^6$ 3^6 $[4-5]^6$ 7^6 $[8]^6$ 9^6 $[10]^6$ 11^6 $[12]^6$ $[13]^4$ $[4]^6$ 82 leaves (15.2 x 9.6cm) Obsolete signatures present. Pp. [i-v] 6-144+10 blank leaves bound in at end.

Plates: Frontispiece+9 full page illus. in text.

[Goodrich, Samuel Griswold]   1793-1860   #958

The Second Book of History, including the modern
history of Europe, Africa, and Asia by the author
of Peter Parley's Tales. Illustrated. Baltimore:
Joseph Jewett, 1832.

Coll: 8° 1-11⁸ 12²   90 leaves (17.5 x 13.5cm)
Pp. [i-iv, 5] 6-180 + 32 (16 map plates)

Plates: Frontispiece 16 map plates.
Notes: First ed. (?). LC gives "Boston: Carter,
       Hendee & Co., 1832."

[Goodrich, Samuel Griswold]   1793-1860   #959

Short Stories: or a selection of interesting
tales. By the Author of Peter Parley. New York:
Published by Mafis & Cornish, [1840?]

Coll: 12° (6's) 1-16⁶ (obsolete signings present)
96 leaves (15.3 x 9.8cm) Pp. [3] 4-191+[1]
Plates: Frontispiece from a painting by E. Landseer.
       (Sir Edwin Henry Landseer, 1802-1870,?)
Notes: Stereotyped edition. Obsolete signings,[1]⁸
       2-12⁶, do not agree with this edition, which
       is gathered (sewn) in 6's.

[Goodrich, Samuel Griswold]   1793-1860   #960

The Tales of Peter Parley about Europe. With engravings.
Boston: S. G. Goodrich, [June 5] 1828.

Coll: 16° π⁴[1] -8⁸ 9⁴   36 leaves (13.45 x 12.25cm)
Pp. [i-vii] viii [1-3] 4-136.

Plates: Frontispiece vignette

Notes: Bookplate of James Mason Hoppin."π3ᵛ"incorrectly
       signed"v".

Goodrich, S[amuel] G[riswold]   1793-1860 #961

The Token and Atlantic Souvenir. [Illustrated by
G. L. Brown, F. Alexander, Washington Allston, T.
Birch, W. Croome, A. Fisher, S. S. Osgood, J. Doughty
R. W. Weir.] Boston: Charles Bowen, 1836.

Coll: 12° (6s) 1-30⁶ 180 leaves (18 x 11.6cm) Pp.
viii, [9]-360.
Plates: Frontispiece, presentation plate, illustrated
       title page +9. (Illustration listed on p. 61
       is frontispiece; illustrated listed on p. 357
       is on p. 359.) Steel engravings.
                                    (cont'd)

Goodrich   Token and Atlantic Souvenir, 1836 (Cont'd)

Notes: Yearbook. Contains the first publication of
       three Hawthorne short stories: "The Wedding
       Knell; The May Pole of Merry Mount; The
       Minister's Black Veil."

Goodrich, S[amuel] G[riswold]   1793-1860   #962

The Token and Atlantic Souvenir. [Illustrated by
G.L. Brown, John G. Chapman, W.W. West, Leslie,
Thomas Cole, Washington Allston, F. Alexander, T.
Birch.] Boston: Charles Bowen, 1837.

Coll: 12° 1-29⁶ 174 leaves (18.1 x 11.5cm) Pp.
     viii, [9]-348.
Plates: Frontispiece, presentation plate, illustra-
       ted title page +9. (Plate listed on p. 129
       is frontispiece.) Steel engravings.
Notes : A Yearbook. First publication of 8 short
                                    (cont'd)

Goodrich.   Token and Atlantic Souvenir. 1837.
   (Cont'd)

       stories by Nathaniel Hawthorne (1804-1864):
       "Monsieur du Miroir," "Mrs. Bullfrog," "Sun-
       day at Home," "The Man of Adamant," "David
       Swan," "The Great Carbuncle," "Fancy's
       Show Box," "The Prophetic Pictures."

Goodrich, S[amuel] G[riswold]   1793-1860   #963

The Token and Atlantic Souvenir. [Illustrated by
J. G. Chapman, G. Stewart Newton, G.L. Brown, Healy,
Woolaston.] Boston: American Stationers' Company,
1838.

Coll: 12° (6's) A-Z⁶ 156 leaves (19.9 x 13cm)
     Pp. viii, [9]-312.
Plates: Frontispiece, presentation plate, illustra-
       ted title page +7. (Plate listed on p. 79
       is frontispiece.) Steel engravings.
Notes: A Yearbook. Contains first publication of 5
                                    (cont'd)

Goodrich.   The Token and Atlantic Souvenir. 1838
   (Cont'd)

       short stories of Nathaniel Hawthorne (1804-
       1864): "Sylph Etheredge," "Peter Gold-
       thwait's Treasure," "Endicott and the Red
       Cross," "Night Sketches Beneath an Umbrella,"
       "The Shaker Bridal."

Goodrich, S[amuel] G[riswold]   1793-1860   #964

The Token and Atlantic Souvenir. Illustrated by
J. G. Chapman, Inskip, Landseer, H. Liverseege, T. M.
Joy, Paris, Stephanoff. Boston: Otis, Broaders, &
Company, 1840.

Coll: 8° 1-19⁸ 152 leaves (17.3 x 11.5cm) Pp.
     viii [9]-304.
Plates: Frontispiece, presentation plate, illustrated
       title page+7. (Plate listed on p. 199 is
       frontispiece.)
Notes: Yearbook.

[Goodrich, Samuel Griswold]   1793-1860   #965

The Travels, Voyages and Adventures of Gilbert
Go-Ahead in Foreign Parts. Edited by Peter Parley
[William Martin?]. Illustrated . . . . New York:
J. C. Derby; Boston: Phillips Sampson & Co.; Cin-
cinnati: H.W. Derby, 1856.

Coll: 12° (6's) [1]⁶ 2-24⁶ (-25·6). 149 leaves
     (18.5 x 12.2cm) Pp. viii, [9] 10-295 +[3].
Plates: Frontispiece, engraved title page + 6.

[Goodrich, Samuel Griswold]   1793-1860 #966

[Parley's] Universal History on the Basis of
Geography. Illustrated by maps and engravings. Two
volumes in one. New York: Mark H. Newman & Co.;
Cincinnati: Wm. H. Moore & Co.; Auburn: J. C.
Ivison & Co.; Chicago: S. C. Griggs & Co., 1850.

Coll: 12° 1-32¹² 384 leaves (16.4 x 12cm) Pp.
     i-viii, [1] ii-vii [viii, 9] 10-380; [1-4, vii]
     viii-xii [13] 14-380 [381-382].
                                    (cont'd)

Goodrich   Parley's Universal History   (Cont'd)

Plates: Frontispiece, vignette title page, illus.
        title page + cuts; Frontispiece, vignette
        title page + cuts.

Notes: McKell copy missing top portion of title page
       of vol. I, and last leaf of vol. II. Chapter
       headings and full page illustrations not
       always paginated.

Goodrich, S[amuel] G[riswold]   1793-1860   #967

The Young American: or book of government and law;
showing their history, nature and necessity. For the
use of schools. Third edition. New York: William
Robinson, 1843.

Coll: 12° [1]⁴ 1-23⁶ 24⁴ 146 leaves (18.2 x 11.5)
     Pp. [8] vi, 7-282 [283-284].
Plates: Frontispiece + cuts
Notes: Stereotyped by Geo. A. Curtis.

Anon.   #968

The Good Scholar. Illustrated. Boston: Lee & Shepard,
Publishers; New York: Lee, Shepard & Dillingham, 49 Greene
Street. [Entered according to Act of Congress, 1863]
["Sunny Bank Stories."]

Pagination: [1-6] 7-64

Illus: Frontispiece plus sixteen woodcuts

Notes: Electrotyped at the Boston Stereotype Foundry. Free
       and pasted down end papers front and back.

Anon.   #970

Goody Two-Shoes. ["Hewet's Illuminated Household Stories
For Little Folks." Illuminated with ten pictures. [Illus-
trations by W.H. Thwaites. Engraved by the best artists.
Vol. X] New York: H.W. Hewet, Engraver and printer,
[Entered...1855.]

Coll: Sm 4°; π², [1-4⁴]χ² 20 leaves (17.1 X 13.4cm) Pp.
     [i-iv] 1-29 [30-32, 33-36]

Plates: Frontispiece (Printed in Oil Colors by Brown,
        Loomis & Co.) + engraved title page

Illus: Several engravings.
                                    (cont'd)

Anon.

Goody Two-Shoes. [Entered...1855].   (cont'd)

Binding: Pictorial wrappers

Notes: Leaves 1·1 and 3·1 are signed A and B respectively.
       Initial and final pages as paste down end papers.

Goulding, F[rancis] R[obert]   1810-1881 #972

Robert and Harold or the Young Marooners on the Florida
Coast. Philadelphia: William S. Martien..., [Stereotyped
by Slote & Mooney, Philadelphia,] 1852.

Coll: 12°: [1⁴] 2-35⁶ 36⁴ 212 leaves (16.7 X 10.6cm)
     Pp. [iv-v] vi-xii, 13-422 [423-424]

Illus: Fold-out map + 5 plates

Notes: 1st edition, Blanck, Parley to Penrod, p. 9. First
       American boys' story written without didacticism,
       solely to amuse.

Goulding, F[rancis] R[obert]   1810-1881 #973

The Young Marooners, on the Florida Coast; or,
Robert and Harold. [Illustrated.] New and Enlarged
Edition. Philadelphia: Claxton, Remsen, & Heffel-
finger, 1876. Pp. [i] ii-xii, 13-446.

Plates: Frontispiece + 5.

Gouraud, Julie [Pseud. of] Louise D'Aulnoy, c. 1830- #974

Mémoires D'Une Paupée contes Dédiés aux Petites
Filles par Mlle Julie Gouraud (Louise D'Aulnoy)
Quatrième Édition. Paris: Amédée Bedelet, Libraire-
Éditeur, Rue Des Grands-Augustins, 20. [N.d.]

Coll: 8° [1]¹ 2[1]⁴, 1-11⁸ 12² 95 leaves
     (19.6 x 13.3cm) Pp. [1-4, 1] ii-vi, [1] 2-4
     [5] 6-11 [12] 13-17 [18] 19-24 [25] 26-28 [29]
     30-33 [34] 35-46 [47] 48-55 [56] 57-63 [64]
     65-69 [70] 71-74 [75] 76-80 [81] 82-85 [86]
     87 [88] 89-100 [101] 102-107 [108] 109-120
     [121] 122-127 [128] 129-134 [135] 136-140 [141]
                                    (cont'd)

Gouraud. Memoires   (Cont'd)

142-149 [150] 151-160 [161] 162-168 [169] 170-180.

Plates: Frontispiece + 11 lithos by Lemercier, and numerous small engravings.

Binding: Free and paste-down endpapers.

Notes: See *Les Jeux De La Poupée*

Grammar Made Familiar and Easy.   (cont'd)

Newbery, junior . . . ." Bookplates of James Losh and Percival Merritt. Roscoe : 64(5).

Graham, Miss [Mary Jane]   1803-1830   #977

Histories From Scripture For Children: exemplified by appropriate domestic tales. By Miss Graham. Third edition. Embellished with elegant engravings, by S. Williams. London: Dean and Munday, n.d.

Coll: 16° B-P⁸ 112 leaves (13.7 x 10.5cm) Pp. [i] -[xii, 13] 14-216, + 4 leaves adverts.

Anon   #980.2

Grammar Made Familiar and Easy. Being the First Volume of the Circle of the Sciences, &c. The Fourth Edition. London: . . . for T. Carnan and F. Newbery, Jun., 1776.

Coll: 32° a⁸ A-I⁸ K⁶ 86 leaves (9.2 x 6.4cm) Pp. 4 + xvi, 17-152.
Binding: Blue Boards, red leather spine.
Notes: Roscoe #64(5); Bookplate of Percival Merritt.

Grahame, Kenneth   1859-1932   #978

The Reluctant Dragon. Illustrated by Ernest Howard Shepard. New York: Holiday House, 1938. Pf. 39.

Plates: 19 black and white

Anon.   #981

Grandmamma's Book of Rhymes for Children. Boston: Wm. J. Reynolds and Company, n.d.

Coll: 8°: [1-4⁸](obsolete signings present) 32 leaves Pp. [1-7] 8 [9] 10-56 [57] 68-70 [71] 94 [73-74] [-64] (16.5 x 10.7cm)
Illus: Woodcuts

Binding: Figured tan wrappers; yellow free and paste-down endpapers.
Notes: [4.8] and rear cover missing from McKell copy Nos. 58-67 not used in pegination.

Grahame, Kenneth   1859-1932   #979

The Wind in the Willows. Introd. by A. A. Milne. Illustrated by Arthur Rackham. New York: The Limited Editions Club, 1940. Pp. [1] 2-245 [246.]

Plates: Frontispiece + 15

Notes: McKell # G-1-30-45 B

Grandville, [J.J.] [Pseud of Jean Ignace Isidore Gérard] (1803-1847)   #982

The Flowers Personified. Being a translation of Grandville's "Les Fleurs Animees." By N. Cleaveland, Esq. Illustrated with steel engravings, beautifully colored. New York: Published by R. Martin, 1847.

Coll: 8° 1-6⁴, 8⁸, 9-35⁴ 140 leaves. (26.5 x 17.5cm) Pp. [1-5] 6-8 [9] 10-13 [14-15] 16-21 [22] 23-38 [39] 40-41 [42] 43-66 [67] 68-72 [73] 74-75 [76] 77-83 [84] 85-100 [101] 102-103 [104] 105-109 [110] 111-112 [113] 114-126 [127] 128 [129] 130-) 133 [134] 135 [136] 137- (cont'd)

Anon   #980.1

Grammar Made Familiar and Easy. Being the First Volume of the Circle of the Sciences. The Fourth Edition. London: Printed for T. Carnan and F. Newbery, Jun., 1776.

Coll: 32° a⁸ A-K⁸ 88 leaves (9.8 x 6.4cm) Pp. [4] + xvi, 152 + 4.

Binding: Marbled boards, green vellum spine with paper label.

Notes: K7: "Books printed for T. Carnan and F. (cont'd)

[Grandville.] The Flowers Personified, 1847.²
(Cont'd)

144 [145] 146 [147] 148-156 [157] 158 [159] 160-167 [168] 169 [170] 171-183 [184] 185 [186] 187-194 [195] 196-197 [198] 199-211 [212] 213 [214] 215-217 [218] 219 [220] 221-229 [230] 231 [232] 233-252 [253] 254 [255] 256-258 [259] 260 [261] 262-267 [268] 269 [270] 271-278 [279] 280.

Illus: Front. and title page + 25 colored engravings by J. N. Gimbrede, designed by J. J. Grandville.

                                    (cont'd)

.3

Grandville. The Flowers Personified. 1847.(Cont'd)

Notes: First and only American edition. McKell #
8-9-25-50-B. Cleaveland (1796-1877)

Grandville, J.J. (i.e., Jean Ignace Isidore Gérard)
1803-1847

     see also

       Perrault-Darmancour, Pierre. Contes de
       Perrault. Illustres par Grandville.
       Paris, 1851.

#985

Greenaway, Kate   1846-1901

A Apple Pie. Engraved and printed by Edmund Evans.
London and New York: George Routledge and Sons,
[1886]. Fr. [22].

Plates: 17 in color.

Notes: First ed. See Osborne, p. 90.

#986

Greenaway, Kate. 1846-1901

Kate Greenaway's Book of Games, with Twenty-
four Full-page Plates Engraved and Printed in
Colours by Edmund Evans. London, Glasgow,
Manchester, and New York: George Routledge &
Sons, n.d. [1889?]

Pagination: pp. [1-10] 11-12 [13] 14-16 [17] 18 [19]
            20 [21] 22 [23] 24-25 [26] 27 [28] 29 [30] 31
            [32] 33 [34] 35 [36] 37 [38] 39 [40-41] 42 [43]
            44 [45] 46 [47] 48-49 50 [51] 52 [53] 54 [55]
            56-57 [58] 59 [60] 61 [62] 63 [64].
Illus: 24 full-page color illus. by author.
Notes: First Edition.   BMC# 7913 f 35

#987.1

Greenaway, Kate   1846-1901

Kate Greenaway's Painting Book with outlines from
her various works for boys and girls to paint.
London and New York: Frederick Warne and Co.,
1900. Pp. [5-7,] 8-62.

Plates: 61 pages of plates, 8 of which are in color
         (i.e., Frontispiece + 7)
Binding: Blank paper dust cover.

Notes: Osborne (p. 220) gives date of 1900.

#987.2

Greenaway, Kate   1846-1901

Kate Greenaway's Painting Book . . . . London and
New York: Frederick Warne and Co., [1900]. Pp. [5-7,]
8-62.

Plates: 61 pages of plates, 8 of which are in color
         (i.e., Frontispiece + 7)

#988

Greenaway, Kate   1846-1901

Marigold Garden. Pictures and rhymes by Kate
Greenaway. London and New York: Frederick Warne
& Co., Ltd., n.d. Pp. 50.

Notes: Engraved and printed by Edmund Evans, Ltd.

#989

Greenaway, Kate   1846-1901

Marigold Garden: pictures and rhymes by Kate
Greenaway. Printed in colours by Edmund Evans.
London: George Routledge and Sons, [1885]. Pp.
[1-60].

Illus: 3 full page colored illus. + numerous half-
page illus. and decorations

#990

Greenaway, Kate   1846-1901

Under the Window: pictures and rhymes for children.
Engraved and printed by Edmund Evans. London and
New York: George Routledge & Sons, n.d. Pp. 64.

Plates: 63 in color

Notes: Osborne (p. 64) gives date 1878; Mahony (p.413)
        gives 1879; and BMC gives 1879.

#991

Greenwood, James

The Bear King: a narrative confided to the marines.
With illustrations by Ernest Griset. London: Griffith and Farran, 1868. Pp. [vi] + 98 + 6 pages adverts.

Illus: Front + 11 plates cuts.

Notes: First ed. See Osborne, p. 349.

 # 992

Greenwood, James

The Purgatory of Peter The Cruel. With thirty-six illustrations, drawn on wood, by Ernest Griset. London and New York: George Routledge & Sons, 1868. 164 pp.

Notes: 2 pages adverts bound in at end.
LC# PZ7. 6853P

 # 993

Greenwood, James

The Hatchet Throwers. With thirty-six illustrations, drawn on wood, by Ernest Griset, from his original designs. London: John Camden Hotten, Piccadilly, 1866. Pp. 164 + [16].

Notes: First ed. Bookplate of John Browne on front paste-down endpaper. See Osborne, p. 349.

 # 994

[Gregg, Mrs.] Mary Kirby
Kirby, Elizabeth   1823-1873

The Talking Bird; or, the little girl who knew what was going to happen. Illustrated by Hablot K. Browne. London: Grant & Griffith, 1856. Pp. [1-5], 6-96, [1]-32 (adverts).

Plates: Front +3 + woodcut on X 1

$B^2 - 6^8$, [X^{16}: adverts $^{1}/8 + 16/$
(16.9 x 12.4cm)

 # 996

Grimm, [Jakob Ludvig Karl (1785-1863), and Wilhelm Karl Grimm (1786-1859)]

German Popular Stories, Translated from the Kinder und Haus Marchen, Collected by M.M. Grimm, From Oral Tradition. 2 vols. London: 1823-1826.

Vol I: . . . London: Published by C. Baldwyn, 1823.
Coll: 12° π^2 A^6 B-L^{12} 128 leaves (17.1 x 10.1cm)
Pp. [2]+xii,+240.
Plates: 11 engravings by George Cruikshank (1792-1878).
Notes: First issue.

(cont'd)

[Grimm, Jakob Ludvig Karl (1785-1863) and Wilhelm Karl Grimm (1786-1859)]
 # 997

Hänsel & Gretel. Das Deutsche Bilderbuch Serie A: Märchen. No. 5. Gez. von Rich Scholz. München. Mainz: Verlag von Jos. Scholz, n.d.

Coll: oblong 8° [1^8] 8 leaves (22.2 x 29.1cm) Ff. 8.

Illus: 8 full-page chromolithos by "R.[ich]S.[cholz]," plus many other smaller illustrations.

Notes:"Scholz' Kunstler-Bilderbucher." F. 8^v: advert for Joseph Scholz, Mainz.

 # 998

Grimm, [Jakob Ludvig Karl (1785-1863), and Wilhelm Karl Grimm, (1786-1859)]

Kinder und Haus-Marchen. Gesammelt durch die Brüder Grimm. Kleine Ausgabe. Mit sieben kupfern. Berlin: Gedruct und verlegt bei G. Reimer, 1825.

Coll: 16° π^2 A-T^8 U^6 160 leaves (13.2 x 10.8cm)
Pp. [3] + iv, +1-316.
Plates: Frontispiece +6, four signed by L.E. Grimm.
Notes: McKell # S-5-23-60.

[Grimm, Jakob Ludvig Karl (1785-1863); and, Wilhelm Karl Grimm (1786-1859)]
 # 999

Schneewittchen. Ein Kinder-Märchen mit 17 Bildern. Berlin: Winckelmann und Söhne [Gedruct bei Karl August Wilhelm Schmidt, n.d.].

Coll: 8° 1-2^8 16 leaves (16.5 x 10.2cm) Pp. [1-2, 3] 4-31 [32].
Illus: 17 hand colored illustrations.
Binding: Stiff wrappers. Paste down endpapers front and back.

Grimm. German Popular Stories. 2 vols. 1823-26
(Cont'd)

Vol II: . . . London: James Robbins & Co.; Dublin: Joseph Robbins, Junr & Co. MMDCCCXXVI.
Coll: 12° A^3 B-L^{12} M^{10} 132 leaves (17.1 x 10.2cm)
Pp. [2]+iv,+256 +[2]
Plates: 9 engravings by George Cruikshank (1792-1878).
Binding: Bound by Riviere.
Notes: Bookplate of Frederick Locker (by Kate Greenaway). McKell # D-1-21-?-B

 # 1001

Groom, [Mrs.] G. Laurence

The Singing Sword: a poem . . . Foreword by Richard Le Gallienne. Cover & portrait by C. Buchel & decorations by the author. Leeds: at The Swan Press; London: Gay and Hancock, Ltd., 1927. Pp. [1] 2-63 [64].

Illus: Frontispiece +cuts.

Notes: Richard Le Gallienne, 1866-

 # 1002

Groom, [Mrs.] G. Laurence

The Singing Sword: a poem . . . foreword by Richard Le Gallienne. Drawings by Clinton Balmer. New York & London: Harper and Brothers, 1929. Pp. [1] ii-x, [1] 2-73 [74].

Illus: Frontispiece +3 +numerous decorative cuts.

Grumbo, the great giant, king of the country of
eagles.

see together with

> The Life and Death of Tom Thumb, the
> Little Giant. Together with some
> curious anecdotes respecting Grumbo
> the Great Giant, etc. York, 1804.

[Habberton, John]   1842-1921   **# 1004**

Helen's Babies. With some account of their ways
innocent, crafty, angelic, impish, witching, and
repulsive. Also, a partial record of their
actions during ten days of their existence. By
their latest. Boston: Loring, Publisher, 1876.
Pp. [1-4, 5] 6-206 [1-2 of adverts.]

Notes: See Peter Parley to Penrod.

Haggard, [Sir] H[enry] Rider 1856-1925   **# 1005**

King Solomon's Mines. London, Paris, New York &
Melbourne: Cassell & Company, Limited, 1885. Pp.
[2] +vi, [7] -320, + [16 pp. advert. bound in at end].

Plates: Fold-up map tipped in opposite title page.

Notes: Advert: "Selections from Cassell & Company's
Publications." Inscription on front endpaper
reads: "Gerard from A. Lang."

Hale, Lucretia P [eabody]   1820-1900   **#1006**

The Peterkin Papers. Illustrations. Boston: James
R. Osgood and Co., 1880. Pp. 246.

Plates: Frontispiece
Binding: Brown cloth
Notes: First ed.

Hale, E[dward] E[verett]   1822-1909   **# 1007**

In His Name. A Christmas story. [Old and New Series; No.
2.] Boston: Printed by the Proprietors of Old and New
as a Christmas gift to their subscribers, 1873. Pp. [i-
iii, 1-88] + [1-5: adverts].

Binding: Paperbound.

Notes: Brackets appear on title page around the series
information.

Hale, Mrs. Sarah Jane, ed.   1788-1879   **# 1008**

Spring Flowers. "Little Boy's and Girl's Library." Illustrated by J. H. Howard. Edited by Mrs. Sarah Jane
Hale. [New York]: McLoughlin Bro's, 24 Beekman, n.d.

Coll: sm 4° [1-6⁸] 48 leaves (16.8 x 13cm) Pp. [1-4,5]
6-8 [9-10] 11-18 [19-20] 21-28 [29-30] 31-38 [39-40]
41-52 [53-54] 55-64; [1-4,5] 6-8 [9-11] 12-14 [15]
16-18 [19-20] 21-22 [23] 24-26 [27] 28 [29-30] 31-
33 [34] 35-36 [37] 38 [39-40] 41 [42] 43-45 [46] 47-
48 [49-50] 51-52 [53] 54-57 [58-60] 61-63 [64: "conclusion"] .

(cont'd)

Spring Flowers. (Cont'd)

Plates: 16 hand colored engravings on conjugate leaves,
paginated with the text but engraved on one side
only.

Notes: Pagination includes the plates; collation does not.
Plates on heavier paper. Error: the conjugate
plates that should appear between pp. 52-55, and
after page 64, are placed between pp. 50-51, and
pp. 60-61. "Sketches of Little Girl's" has a "conclusion" signed by Thomas Lovechild, in which he
refers to "my sketches of little girls."

Hall, George Eli   1863-1911   **# 1009**

A Balloon Ascension at Midnight. With silhouettes
by Gordon Ross. San Francisco: Paul Elder and
Morgan Shepard, 1902. Pp. [i-x, 1] 2-25 [26].

Plates: Illustrated title page, 2 plates + cuts.

Notes: Author's autograph Edition. Copy "A" of
30 copies.

Hamilton, Gail

see

> Our Young Folks; An Illustrated Magazine
> for Boys and Girls.

Anon   **# 1012**

Hamlain; or, The Hermit of the Beach. A Moral
Reverie. Calculated for the Instruction and Amusement of Youth. London: Printed for E. Newbery,
1799.

Coll: 12° A-6R² 99 leaves (13.7 x 8.5cm) 3
4-198pp.

Plates: Engraved frontispiece

Binding: Marbled boards, red leather spine.
(cont'd)

Hamlain . . . .   (Cont'd)

Notes: Bookplate of Percival Merritt. Roscoe # 153.

Handford, Thomas W. . . ("Almo" pseud) # 1013

Merry Christmas 1891-2. Richly illustrated from original drawings by True W. Williams. Chicago: [Press of Illinois Printing and Binding Co.] [Copyright 1887.] Belford-Clarke & Co.

Pagination: [i-iv] vii-xii [13] 14 [15]16-122 [123]124-128

Illus: 50 full-page engravings from originals by True W. Williams

Notes: Wrappers are included in pagination

Handforth, Thomas   1897-   # 1014

Mei Li. [Illustrated by Thomas Handforth.] New York: Junior Books, Doubleday Doran & Company, Inc., 1938. Pp.[1-52].

Illus: Woodcuts throughout.

Binding: Dust cover.

Hannay, James   1827-1873

    see

        Brough, Robert Barnabas. Funny Dogs With
        Funny Tales.

Anon   # 1015

The Happy Courtship, Merry Marriage, and Pic Nic Dinner of Cock Robin and Jenny Wren. To Which Is Added, Alas! The Doleful Death of the Bridegroom. London: Printed for J. Harris, 1806.

Coll: 16° A⁸ B⁶ 14 leaves (12.7 x 9.3cm) 28pp.

Plates: 26 engravings.

Anon.   # 1016

The Hard Way: or, The End of Disobedience. An authentic Narrative. New York: Published by Carlton & Porter, Sunday-School Union, 200 Mulberry-Street, n.d.

Coll: 12°: 1⁸ 2⁶ 14 leaves (13.2 X 8.3cm) Pp. [1-7] 8-20 [21-28]

Illus: Frontispiece engraved

Notes: Pages 21-24 are advertisements

Anon.   # 1018

Mss. Harlequinade. Three hand drawn and painted Harlequin-ade, verse hand written. All evidently by the same hand. No author nor title. [N d.]

Format: (1) One sheet of 47.4 X 20cm. folded vertically
            from top and bottom toward the center, and
            then folded horizontally to form a harlequinade
            of two drawings and four flaps measuring 23.9
            X 9.8cm.
        (2) As above, sheet: 47.7 X 20.7cm.; harlequinade:
            24.1 X 10.3cm.
        (3) As above, sheet: 47.1 X 18.9cm; harlequinade:
            23.9 X 9.9cm.

Anon.

Mss. Harlequinade.

Binding: Enclosed in Dutch flowery wrappers

Harlequinade

    see

        Dr. Last or the Devil upon two sticks,
        s.v. 'D'

        La Nouvelle Omphale, Comédie, Représentée
            par les Comédiens Italiens Ordinaires
            du Roi, devant leurs Majestés le 22
            9bre 1782. Paris, 1783.

                                    (cont'd)

Harlequinade (Cont'd)

    see

        Perrault-D'armancour, Pierre. Blue Beard.
            McLoughlin Bros. n.d.

            Cinderella. McLoughlin Bros. n.d.

            Mother Goose Melodies with Magical
            Changes. G.W. Carleton, 1879.

#1020

Harris, Benjamin, Sr.

The Holy Bible in Verse. /London: B. Harris, Jr./
1717.

Coll: 8° /A/⁷⁸ B-D⁸   32 leaves (8.5 x 5.3cm)
         not paginated
Notes: B8ᵛ: A caution to the reader by B. Harris,
         Jr., dated March 15, 1712, warning against
         a plagiarized edition, same title and shape
         as this, printed by one Bradford.

#1021

Harris, Joel Chandler   1848-1908

On the Plantation: a story of a Georgia boy's adventures during the war. Illustrated by E.W. Kemble.
New York: D. Appleton and Company, 1892. Pp. xii
+233 +10 .

#1022

Harris, Joel Chandler   1848-1908

The Tar-baby and other rhymes of Uncle Remus.
Illustrated by A.B. Frost and E.W. Kemble. New York:
D. Appleton and Company, 1904. Pp. xiv +191 .

Plates: Frontispiece

Notes: First edition.

#1023

Harris, Joel Chandler   1848-1908

Uncle Remus, his songs and his sayings: the folk-
lore of the old plantation. Illustrated by
Frederick S. Church and James H. Moser. New York:
D. Appleton and Company, 1881. Pp. 231+/1-6 of
adverts/.

Plates: Frontispiece +7.

Notes: First edition.

#1024

Anon.

Harris's Cabinet of Amusement and Instruction. [London:
J. Harris, 1809/.

Coll: 16°: [1-4⁴] 16 engraved leaves (12.3 X 9.3ᶜᵐ·),
         printed on inner forme only. Pp. [1-32].
Plates: 16 hand colored engravings
Binding: Printed Buff wrappers
Notes: No title page inside. Publication information
         taken from first plate. A book of plates and
         Nursery (counting) rhymes: i.e. " 1-2 Come Buckle
         My Shoe" etc.

#1025

Harte, /Francis/ Bret [t]   1836-1902

Colonel Starbottle's Client and Some Other People.
Boston and New York: Houghton, Mifflin and Company, 1893. Pp. [i-iv, 1] 2-283 [284]

#1026

Harte, F/rancis/ Bret [t]   (1836-1902)

The Heathen Chinee /Plain Language from Truthful
James/ . Illustrated by Joseph Hull. Chicago:
The Western News Company, /1870/. Ff. 1-9.

Plates: 9 lithographed loose leaves with illustra-
         tion and text in verse on one side.
Binding: Unbound, in white envelope.
Notes: First printing. Blanck #7248.

#1027

Harte, /Francis/ Bret [t]   1836-1902

Poems. Boston: James R. Osgood And Company,
1871. Pp. [i] ii-vi, [7] 8-152.

Notes: First ed., late issue. "FO" monograph on
         spine. Blanck # 7253. Another copy with-
         out monograph of the same edition.

#1028

Harte, [Francis] Bret [t]   1836-1902

The Queen of the Pirate Isle. Illustrated by Kate
Greenaway. London: Chatto and Windus, [1886].
Pp. [1-9,] 10-58.

Plates: Frontispiece

Notes: First ed.

#1029

Harte, [Francis] Bret [t]   1836-1902

The Queen of the Pirate Isle. Illustrated by Kate
Greenaway. London: Chatto & Windus, [1886] . Pp.
[1-9] , 10-58.

Plates: Frontispiece +cuts
Binding: State B. Lacks end fly-leaf
Notes: First ed. Blanck # 7337

 # 1030

Harvey, T[homas] W., A.M.   1821-1892

The Graded-School Fourth Reader. Eclectic Educational Series. [Illustrated.] Cincinnati & New York: Wilson, Hinkle & Co., n.d. [1875?] Pp.[i] ii-vii [viii] 9-240.

Illus: Cuts.

 # 1031

Harvey, Tho[ma]s W., A.M.   1821-1892

A Practical Grammar of the English Language, for the Use of Schools of Every Grade. Cincinnati & New York: Wilson, Hinkle & Co., n.d. [1868?]. Pp.[i] ii-vi, 7-264.

Notes: First edition ? LC gives "rev. ed."[1878].

#1032

Hastings, Thomas   1784-1872

Elements of Vocal Music, arranged as a brief textbook for classes. New York: Published by Ezra Collier & Co., 1839.

Coll: 12° 1-3⁶ 18 leaves (18.8 x 11.4cm) Pp.[1-5] 6-36.

Notes: Bound in with The Mother's Nursery Song

 # 1033

Hastings, Thomas   1784-1872

The Mother's Nursery Song. New York: Published by Ezra Collier . . ., 1835.

Coll: 12° 1-6⁶ 36 leaves (18.8 x 11.4cm) Pp.[1-4] 5-72.

Notes: Bound together with Elements of Vocal Music

 # 1034

[Haven, Alice Bradley (Neal)] Cousin Alice, pseud., 1827-1863.

"All's Not Gold That Glitters"; or, The Young Californians. By Cousin Alice. [Illustrated by Devereux, J. McL., and others.] New York: D. Appleton & Company, 1854.

Coll: 12° 1-9¹² 108 leaves (17.1 x 11cm) Pp.[1-5] 6 [7,8,9] 10-214; [1-2] of adverts.
Plates: Color half-title; "front" + 3 (b & white)

Notes: Pp. 199-200 missing

 # 1035

Hawes, Charles Boardman   1889-1923

The Dark Frigate . . . . Illustrated. Boston: The Atlantic Monthly Press, 1923. 247 pp.

Plates: Frontispiece +8.

Binding: Dust cover.

#1036

Hawes, Charles Boardman   1889-1923

The Mutineers . . . . Illustrated. Boston: The Atlantic Monthly Press, 1920. 276 pp.

Plates: Frontispiece

Hawks, Francis Lister   1798-1866

see

        Philip, Uncle (The Good Child's Own Book)

 # 1037

Hawthorne, Nathaniel   1804-1864

Tanglewood Tales, for Girls and Boys; being a second wonder-book. Boston: Ticknor, Reed, and Fields, 1853.

Coll: 8° [1]⁸ 2-21⁸ 168 leaves 18.8 x 10.8cm) Pp.[1-4] 5 [6] 7-336.
Plates: Engraved title page +6.
Notes: First edition; boxed.
        BLANCK # 7614.

 # 1038

Hawthorne, Nathaniel   1804-1864

Tanglewood Tales. Illustrated by Edmund Dulac. London, New York, Toronto: Hodder and Stoughton, [1919?] Pp.[i-xii, 1] 2-245 [246].

Plates: Frontispiece +13

Notes: Tipped in preliminary page autographed by Edmund Dulac.

Hawthorne, Nathaniel. 1804-1864   # 1039

A Wonder-Book for Girls and Boys. By Nathaniel Hawthorne.
With engravings by [W.J.] Baker from designs by Billings.
Boston: Ticknor, Reed, and Fields. [Stereotyped by Hobart
& Robbins, Boston], 1852.

Coll: 8°: 1-16⁸ 128 leaves Pp. [i-iii] iv [v] vi [7] 14
[15] 16-53 [54] 55-56 [57] 58-61 [62] 63-88 [89] 90-92
[93] 94-97 [98] 99-124 [125] 126-127 [128] 129-135
[136] 137-168 [169]170-172 [173] 174-176 [177] 178-20
[208] 209 [210] 211-213 [214] 215-250 [251] 252-256
(16,8 x 10.6cm)
Plates: Frontispiece + 6 wood engravings

(cont'd)

Hawthorne, Nathaniel. 1804-1864   (cont'd)

A Wonder-Book for Girls and Boys. 1852.

Binding: Rebound in blue morocco by "Bayntun, Binder, Bath,
Eng." with original cloth covers and spine bound
in at end of text.

Notes: Entered 1851. 1st edition Blanck 7606.

Hawthorne, Nathaniel   1804-1864   #1040

A Wonder Book for Girls and Boys. Illustrated by
Walter Crane. Boston: Houghton Mifflin and Company, 1893. Pp. x+210.

Plates: Frontispiece

Notes: Edition de Luxe.

Hawthorne, Nathaniel   1804-1864   #1041

A Wonder Book for Girls and Boys. Illustrated by
Walter Crane. Boston: Houghton Mifflin and Company, 1893. Pp. x+210.

Plates: Frontispiece.

Hawthorne, Nathaniel   1804-1864   #1042

A Wonder Book and Tanglewood Tales for Girls and
Boys. Illustrated by Maxfield Parrish. New York:
Duffield and Company, 1910. Pp. ix + 358.

Plates: Frontispiece+9.

Hawthorne, Nathaniel   1804-1864

see also

Goodrich, Samuel Griswold. The Token and
Atlantic Souvenir. (Yearbook, for
the years 1836, 37, 38. Each contains first publications of short
stories by Hawthorne.)

Hay, John   1838-1905   #1043

Jim Bludso of the Prairie Belle, and Little Breeches.
Illustrated by S. Etyinge, Jr. Boston: James R.
Osgood and Company, 1871. Pp. [1] 2-23 [24].

Plates: Frontispiece+7 full-page cuts.

Hay, John   1838-1905   #1044

The Pike County Ballads. Illustrated by N[ewell]
C[onvers] Wyeth. Boston and New York: Houghton
Mifflin Company, 1912. 47 pp.

Notes: Preface by Wyeth.

Baydon, A[rthur] L[incoln]   1872-   #1046

Stories of King Arthur. Illustrated by Arthur
Rackham. New York: Funk and Wagnalls Company,
n.d. 94 pp.

Plates: Frontispiece.

Notes: On title page: "Thirty-third thousand."

Hayer, M   A   #1047

Little Bright Eyes. "Our Children's Book Case"
series. London, Paris, & New York: Raphael Tuck
& Sons. Designed at the Studios in England and
printed at the Fine Art Works in Germany. [c. 1900].
Fr. 6.

Illus: 4 in color by M.G. + 4 + color cover.

Notes: No inside title page.

 # 1048

Hayer, M   A

A Tale in the Twilight. "Our Children's Book Case" series. London, Paris, & New York: Raphael Tuck & Sons. Designed at the Studios in England and printed at the Fine Art Works in Germany. [c. 1900]. Ff. 6.

Illus: 4 in color by M.G. + 4 + cover.

Notes: No inside title page.

 # 1049

Hazard, Paul   1878-1944

Books Children and Men. Trans. by Marguerite Mitchell. Boston: The Horn Book, Inc., 1944. Pp. xiv + 176 [177-178].

 # 1051

Headley, Rev. P[hineas] C[amp].   1819-1903

The Miner Boy and His Monitor; or, the career and achievements of John Ericsson the engineer. New York: William H. Appleton, 1865. Pp. [1-5,] 6-[298].

Plates: Frontispiece, engraved title page + 3.

 # 1053

Heath, Henry

"Characteristics." A series of 54 original and unpublished drawings in color, executed in 1834, bound in 2 volumes. Each drawing is on heavy blue paper (25.2 x 17.2) tipped to folio leaves. Vol. I contains 27 drawings, Vol. II contains 27 drawings. Editorial pencilings on initial drawing in Vol. I indicate that it was meant to serve as a title page for publication by J. B. Brookes, London. Pencilings on the initial drawing in Vol. II indicate the same plan for publication by Brookes.

 # 1054

Hecht, Ben   1893-1964

The Cat That Jumped out of the Story. Illustrated by Peggy Bacon. Philadelphia and Toronto: John C. Winston Company, [1947]. Pp. [1-32].

Plates: Frontispiece + 5 full-page color engravings + cuts.
Binding: Dust cover
Notes: First edition.

 # 1055

Anon.

Heedless Girls and Boys; with Pictures of Accidents. New Haven: S. Babcock, 1836.

Coll: 32°: [1⁸] 8 leaves (9.15 X 5.3cm) Pp. [1] 2-16

Illus: 7 hand-tinted woodcuts; one plain

Binding: Printed blue wrappers.

 # 1056

Anon.

Heedless Johnny. "Peter Prim's Series." New York: McLoughlin Bros., Publishers, [n.d.]

Coll: 18°: [1⁶] 6 leaves (15.3 X 10cm) Pp. [1,2 - 11,1\overline{3}]

Illus: 8 colored engravings

Binding: Red paper wrappers, illustrations on front, advertisement on back, indicating "large 18°."

Notes: Initial and final leaves pasted to the wrapper. cloth leaves. Wrapper serves as title page.

Hegan, Alice Caldwell

    see

        Rice, Alice Caldwell (Hegan) 1870-1942

 # 1058

Hendley, George

A Memorial for Sunday School Boys, being the first part of an authentic account of the conversion, experience, and happy deaths of twenty-five children. By George Hendley, Minister of the Gospel. First American from the sixth English edition. Boston: Published by Samuel T. Armstrong, No. 50, Cornhill. U. Crocker, Printer, 1819.

Coll: 8°: A⁸, B⁵(B4+1), C⁶, D⁵(D1+1) 24 leaves (12.9 x 7cm) Pp. [i-iii] iv-vi [vii] viii [9] 10-40, (41-42 missing) 43-47 [48].

Binding: Red wrappers

(cont'd)

A Memorial for Sunday School Boys.   (Cont'd)

Notes: Preface dated January 1st, 1816.

 # 1059

Henkel, Ambrosius

Das Kleine ABC-Buch, oder erste Anfangs-Büchlein, mit Schonen bildern und deren namen, nach dem ABC, und den Kindern das Buch-Stabiren leichter zu machen. Von Ambrosius Henkel. Zweite auslage. Newmarket, Schenandoah County, Virginia: Gedrucht in Solomon Henkel's Druckerey, 1819.

Coll: 12⁰: (6s) A-C⁶ 18 leaves (13.7 X 8.6cm.)
Pp. [1-2,3] 4-36

Illus: Numerous cuts

Notes: Early German American Abcedarium

LC# PF3114. H38

 # 1063

Henty, G[eorge] A[lfred]   1832-1902

At Aboukir and Acre: a story of Napoleon's invasion of Egypt. With eight illustrations by William Rainey, R.I. and three plans. London: Blackie & Son, Limited, 1899. Pp. [x], 11-352; 1-32 of adverts bound in at end.

Plates: Frontispiece + 7.

Notes: First edition.

 # 1064

Henty, G[eorge] A[lfred]   1832-1902

At Agincourt: a tale of the white hoods of Paris. With twelve illustrations by Wal. Paget. London: Blackie & Son, 1897. Pp. [x], 11-384; [1] 2-32 of adverts for Blackie & Son.

Plates: Frontispiece + 11.

Notes: First edition, first issue.

 # 1065

Henty, G[eorge] A[lfred]   1832-1902

Beric the Briton: a story of the Roman invasion. Illustrated by W. Parkinson. London: Blackie & Son, Limited, n.d. Pp. [iii] - [x], [11] -383 [384; 1] 2-32 of adverts bound in at end.

Plates: Frontispiece + 11.

 # 1066

Henty, G[eorge] A[lfred]   1832-1902

By Right of Conquest; or, with Cortez in Mexico. Illustrated by W.S. Stacey. London: Blackie & Sons, Limited; New York: Charles Scribner's Sons, n.d. Pp. [iii] - [x], [11] -384; [1] 2-32 of adverts bound in at end.

Plates: Frontispiece + 9.

 # 1067

Henty, G[eorge] A[lfred]   1832-1902

The Cat of Bubastes: a tale of ancient Egypt. Illustrated by J.R. Weguelin. London: Blackie & Son, 1899. Pp. [viii], [9]-352; [1] 2-32 of adverts bound in at end.

Plates: Frontispiece + 7.

Notes: First edition, later issue (Kennedy & Farmer, p. 20). McKell copy has light gray cloth covered boards (rather than blue or brown) and lacks half-title.

 # 1068

Henty, G[eorge] A[lfred]   1832-1902

The Dash for Khartoum: a tale of the Nile expedition. Illustrated by Joseph Nash, R.I. and John Schönberg. New York: Charles Scribner's Sons, 1891. Pp. [1-5,] 6-382 [383-384; 1] 2-16 of adverts bound in at end.

Plates: Frontispiece + 11.

Notes: First American edition.

#1069

Henty, G[eorge] A[lfred]   1832-1902

For the Temple: a tale of the fall of Jerusalem. Illustrated by Solomon J. Solomon. London: Blackie & Son, 1888. Pp. [viii], [9] -384; [1] 2-32 of adverts bound in at end.

Plates: Frontispiece + 9.

Notes: First edition; later issue (see Kennedy & Farmer, p. 51.). McKell copy has red cloth-covered boards rather than light brown.
                                    (cont'd)

Henty. For the Temple. London: 1888.   (Cont'd)

Colored map (a plate) missing. On verso of front free endpaper: "For Jessica with mother's love. Xmas 1887."

#1070

Henty, G[eorge] A[lfred]   1832-1902

Friends though Divided: a tale of the Civil War. London: Griffith Farran Browne & Co. Ltd., n.d. Pp. [iii] -vi, [1] -384, +[1].

Plates: Frontispiece + 7.

Notes: On front free endpaper: "Armiger with love from Beatrice and Gladys Christmas 1905."

#1071

Henty, G[eorge] A[lfred]   1832-1902

Held Fast for England: a tale of the siege of
Gibraltar (1779-83). Illustrated by Gordon Browne.
London: Blackie & Son, Limited, 1892. Pp.[x],[11]
-352; [1] 2-32 of adverts bound in at end.

Plates: Frontispiece+7.

Notes: First edition.

#1076

Henty, G[eorge] A[lfred]   1832-1902

The Lion of St. Mark: a story of Venice in the
fourteenth century. Illustrated by Gordon Browne.
London: Blackie & Sons, Limited; New York:
Charles Scribner's Sons, [1889]. Pp.[iii]-[x],[11]
-384;[1] 2-32 of adverts bound in at end.

Plates: Frontispiece+9.

Notes: Plus another copy.

#1072

Henty, G[eorge] A[lfred]   1832-1902

In the Heart of the Rockies: a story of adventure
in Colorado. Illustrated by G.A. Hindley. New
York: Charles Scribner's Sons, 1894. Pp.[iv], 5-
353 [354]; 1-16 of adverts bound in at end.

Plates: Frontispiece+7.

Notes: First American edition.

#1077

Henty, G[eorge] A[lfred]   1832-1902

A March on London: being a story of Wat Tyler's
insurrection. Illustrated by W.H. Margetson.
London: Blackie & Son, Limited, 1898. Pp.[x],[11]
-352.

Plates: Frontispiece + 7.
Binding: New endpapers: yellow.
Notes: First edition.

#1073

Henty, G[eorge] A[lfred]   1832-1902

In Greek Waters: a story of the Grecian war of
independence (1821-1827). Illustrated by W.S.
Stacey. New York: Charles Scribner's Sons, 1892.
Pp.[iv], 5-408; [1] 2-16 of adverts bound in at end.

Plates: Frontispiece+11+map of Grecian archi-
         pelago, p. 9.

Notes: First American edition.

#1088

Henty, G[eorge] A[lfred]   1832-1902

On the Irrawaddy: a story of the first Burmese
war. Illustrated by W.H. Overend. New York:
Charles Scribner's Sons, 1896. Pp.[x],[11]-315
[316-319; 1] 2-32 of adverts bound in at end.

Plates: Frontispiece +7.

Notes: First American edition.

#1074

Henty, G[eorge] A[lfred]   1832-1902

In the Reign of Terror: the adventures of a
Westminster boy. Illustrated by J. Schönberg.
London: Blackie & Son, Limited; New York: Charles
Scribner's Sons, [1897?] Pp.[viii],[9]-351 [352; 1]
2-16 of adverts bound in at end.

Plates: Frontispiece+7.

#1079

Henty, G[eorge] A[lfred]   1832-1902

Redskin and Cow-boy: a tale of the western plains.
Illustrated by Alfred Pearse. New York: Charles
Scribner's Sons, 1900. Pp.[x],[11]-384;[1] 2-32
of adverts bound in at end.

Plates: Frontispiece +11.

#1075

Henty, G[eorge] A[lfred]   1832-1902

A Knight of the White Cross: a tale of the siege
of Rhodes. Illustrated by Ralph Peacock. New
York: Charles Scribner's Sons, 1895. Pp.[1-5],
6-400; 1-16 of adverts bound in at end.

Plates: Frontispiece +11.

Notes: First American edition.

#1080

Henty, G[eorge] A[lfred]   1832-1902

St. George for England: a tale of Cressy and
Poitiers. Illustrated by Gordon Browne. London:
Blackie & Sons, Limited; New York: Charles
Scribner's Sons, [1884?] Pp.[viii],[9]-352;[1]2-24
of adverts bound in at end.

Plates: Frontispiece + 7.

1081

Henty, G[eorge] A[lfred]   1832-1902

Tales of Daring and Danger. London: Blackie & Son, Limited, n.d. Pp. [vi], [7]-160; [1] 2-32 of adverts bound in at end.

Plates: Frontispiece +1.

1082

Henty, G[eorge] A[lfred]   1832-1902

The Tiger of Mysore: a story of the war with Tipoo Saib. Illustrated by W.H. Margetson. London: Blackie & Son, Limited, 1896. Pp. [x], [11]-379 [380]; [1] - [32] of adverts bound in at end.

Plates: Frontispiece +13 (includes one colored map and one plate of Henty).

Notes: First edition.

1083

Henty, G[eorge] A[lfred]   1832-1902

True to the Old Flag: a tale of the American war of independence. With twelve illustrations by Gordon Browne. London: Blackie & Son, Limited; New York: Charles Scribner's Sons, [1884?]. Pp. [iii]-[viii], [9]-390; 1-24 Scribner's catalogue bound in at end.

Plates: Frontispiece +1+6 maps.

Notes: On verso of frontispiece: "Clyde from George. Xmas, 1898."

1084

Henty, G[eorge] A[lfred]   1832-1902

Under Drake's Flag: a tale of the Spanish Main. With twelve full-page illustrations by Gordon Browne. London: Blackie & Son, Limited; New York: Charles Scribner's Sons, [1910?]. Pp. [9]+10-368; [1-2]3-24 of adverts bound in at end.

Plates: Frontispiece +11.

1085

Henty, G[eorge] A[lfred]   1832-1902

When London Burned: a story of Restoration times and the great fire. Illustrated by J. Finnemore. New York: Charles Scribner's Sons, 1894. Pp. [iv], 5-403 [404-405]; 1-16 of adverts bound in at end.

Plates: Frontispiece +11.

Notes: First American edition.

1086

Henty, G[eorge] A[lfred]   1832-1902

With Clive in India: or the beginnings of an empire. Illustrated by Gordon Browne. London: Blackie & Son, Limited, n.d. Pp. [viii], [9]-382 [383-384]; [1] 2-32 of adverts bound in at end.

Plates: Frontispiece +11+map plate on leaf conjugate with p. [9].

1087

Henty, G[eorge] A[lfred]   1832-1902

With Wolfe in Canada: or, the winning of a continent. With twelve full-page illustrations by Gordon Browne. London: Blackie and Son, [1886?] Pp. [viii], [9]-384; [1] 2-32 of "Blackie & Son's catalogue of books for young people."

Plates: Frontispiece +11; 2 maps.

1088

Henty, G[eorge] A[lfred]   1832-1902

Won by the Sword: a tale of the Thirty Years' War. With twelve illustrations by Charles M. Sheldon and four plans. New York: Charles Scribner's Sons, 1899. Pp. [x], 11-384; [1] 2-32 of Scribner's "list of books for young people."

Plates: Frontispiece +11+plans.
Binding: The leaf conjugate with p. [ix], the list of illustrations, was pasted under the endpaper by the binder.

Notes: First American edition.

1089

Henty, G[eorge] A[lfred]   1832-1902

Wulf the Saxon: a story of the Norman Conquest. With twelve illustrations by Ralph Peacock. New York: Charles Scribner's Sons, 1894. Pp. [x], 11-383 [384], 1-16 of adverts bound in at end.

Plates: Frontispiece +11.

Notes: First American ed.

1090

Henty, G[eorge] A[lfred]   1832-1902

The Young Carthaginian: or a struggle for empire. Illustrated by C.J. Staniland, R.I. London: Blackie & Son, 1887. Pp. [viii], [9]-384; [1] 2-48 of adverts bound in at end.

Plates: Frontispiece +11.

Notes: First edition; later issue (see Kennedy and Farmer, p. 87). McKell copy has light red cloth-covered boards rather than light blue.

1092

Herbert, J. A.

The Sherborne Missal. Oxford: Printed for . . .
The Roxburghe Club, 1920. Pp. [1-9] 10-34 [35-36]

Plates: Frontispiece (in color) 30 full-leaf
   reproductions.
Notes: McKell # Q-2-29-60-B

Hergest, Red Book of

   see

      Lanier, Sidney, ed. The Boy's Mabinogion:
      being the earliest Welsh tales of
      King Arthur in the famous Red Book
      of Hergest. Scribner's, 1881.

1093

Anon.
The Hermit of the Forest, and the wandering Infants, a
rural fragment. Adorned with cuts. London: Printed [by
J. Crowder and E. Hemsted,] for J. Harris, 1805.

Coll: 32°: (Eights) B-C⁸ 16 leaves (8.8 X 6.4ᶜᵐ·)
   Pp. [1-4] 5-31 [32]

Illus: 8 woodcuts

Binding: Orange wrappers. Initial and final leaves serve
   as paste down endpapers

Notes: Cover bears "From Harris's Juvenile Library"

1098

Hey, William

Fifty Fables for Children. Illustrated by Otto
Speckter. With a serious appendix. Translated into
English by Sophie Klingemann. Gotha: Friedrich
Andreas Perthes, n.d.

Coll: 8° 1-9⁸ 72 leaves (24.8 x 16.9cm) Pp. [1-2]
   Fr. 1-50 Pp. [1-2, 3] 4-36 [37] 38-40 [41-42:
   blank]
Plates: 50 wood engravings in text numbered 1-50, by
   Laufer, Sc.

1101

[ANON.]. L'Histoire de Plusieurs Petits Garcons &
Petites Filles. Pour L'Amusement de Les Bons Enfans
Ages de Quatre ou Cinq ans. [woodcuts] à Londres:
Jean Marshall & Co., n.d.

Coll: 24°: A¹²(-A1) B-C¹². 35 leaves.(10.2 X 8.9
cm). [5] + 7-69 + [3]pp.

Illustrated with 23 cuts.

C12 forms rear attached endpaper. Bookplate of
Percival Merritt. Vertical chain lines.

1102

[ANON.]. The History, Adventures, and Daring
Robberies, Committed on the High Seas by the follow-
ing Notorious Buccaniers: Anne Bonny [,] Capt.
Howel Davis [,] Capt. Bartho. Roberts . . . . London:
Printed [by MacDonald & Bailey] for T. Hughes . . . ,
1806.

Coll.: 12°: B-D⁶. 18 leaves (17.7 X 10.1cm). [1-3]
4-36 pp.

Plate: Engraved frontispiece.

1103

Anon.
The History of an Old Woman who had three sons, Jerry
James, and John, together with an account of what became
of them, her property, and last of all herself. Illu-
strated with sixteen beautiful engravings. London:
Printed for J. Harris, 1815.

Coll: 16°: 1-4⁴ unsigned 16 engraved leaves (13.1 X
10.8ᶜᵐ·) printed on inner forme only Pp. [1-32]

Illus: 16 engravings; first is partially colored
Binding: Buff wrappers, advertisements in back, stabbed
Notes: S-1-11-43. Only first plate has coloring; and
   that only partially

1105

Anon
The History of Goody Two-Shoes, Embellished with elegant
engravings. Cleveland, Ohio: Published by Sanford & Co.
1841.

Coll: 8° [1⁸] 8 leaves (12.4 x 7.8cm) Pp. [1-3] 4-16.

Illus: 4 engravings

Binding: Blue pictorial wrappers

1106

Anon
The History of Jenny Spinner, the Hertfordshire Ghost.
Written by Herself. Chatham: Printed [by and] for C. and
W. Townson..., [August 1, 1803].

Coll: 12°: B-D¹² E² 38 leaves (17 X 10cm) Pp. [1-3] 4-75
[76]

Plates: Copperplate frontispiece

Notes: Frontispiece inscribed ("Published as the Act directs
   Aug. 1, 1803 by S. Highley, 24 Fleet Street")
   Bookplate of Howard Pyle.

1107

Anon.
The History of Joseph and His Brethren. Ornamented with
Cut. New-Haven: Published by John Babcock and Son, and
S. and W.R. Babcock, Charleston, S.C. Sidney's Press,
1821.

Coll: 32°: 1¹⁶ 16 leaves (10.8 X 6.4ᶜᵐ·)
   Pp. [1-4, 5] 6-31, [32]

Binding: Dark green flowery wrappers. Initial and final
   pages as paste down end papers.

Anon.   # 1108

The History of Little Fanny, Exemplified in a Series of figures. Second edition. Philadelphia: Published by Morgan & Yeager, 1825.

Coll: 16°: 1⁸ 8 leaves Pp. [1-2, 3] 4-15 [16]

Plates: Frontispiece + 7 copper engravings, all hand colored.

Binding: Yellow wrappers bound in; calf with tooled figure on front.

Anon.

The History of Little Fanny. 1825.

Notes: Advertisement on back wrapper, title page on wrapper has "Published and sold wholesale and retail, by Mary Charles, No. 71, South Second Street. Price plain 18 3-4 cents, coloured, 25 cents. 1821." Rosenbach #672.

Anon. .   # 1109

The History of Little Goody Twoshoes; otherwise called Mrs. Margery Twoshoes with the means by which she acquired her learning and wisdom, and in consequence thereof her estate. Set forth at large for the benefit of those...See the original manuscript in the Vatican at Rome, and the cuts by Michael Angelo; illustrated with the comments of our great modern criticks. The first Worcester edition. Worcester, Mass: Printed by Isaiah Thomas, and sold, wholesale and retail, at his bookstore. 1787.

Coll: 32°: A-K⁸ 80 leaves (10.2 X 6.5cm) Pp. [1-5, 6] 7-66 [67] 68-142 [143] 144-156 [157] 158 [159-160]

Anon.

The History of Little Goody Twoshoes.

Illus: Several woodcuts

Binding: Cloth wrappers

Notes: Rosenbach #118, Welch #427.4

Anon.   # 1110

The History of Madamoiselle de St. Phale, giving a full account of the miraculous conversion of a noble French Lady and her daughter to the Reformed Religion. With the defeat of the intrigues of a Jesuit their confessor. Translated out of French by B. Star, late of Topsham in Devon. The third edition. Illustrated with copper cuts. London: Printed for F.H. and sold by B. Billingsly at the Printing-Press in Cornhill..., 1707.

Coll: 12°: A-G¹² H⁶ 90 leaves (15 X 8.8cm) Pp. [1-iv] 1-175 [176]

Anon.

The History of Madamoiselle de St. Phale, 1707.

Plates: Frontispiece + 5 woodcuts

Binding: Rebound

Notes: Bookplate of Howard Pyle

Anon   # 1110.1

The History of Our Blessed Lord, In Easy Verse, for Young Children. Illustrated. New York: H. W. Hewet, 1844.

Coll: 8° A-B⁴, C-E⁸, F⁴ 36 leaves (16.4 X 13 cm) Pp. [i-ii] iii-vii [8-10] 11 [13-14] 15-18 [19-20] 21-22 [23-24] 25-26 [27-28] 29-30 [31-32] 33-34 [35-36] 37-38 [39-40] 41-44 45-46 47-48 [49-50] 51-54 [55-56] 57-60 [61-62] 63-64 [65-66] 67-70 [71-72] 73-76 [77-78] 79-80 [81-82] 83- 84 [85-86] 87-90 [91-92]
(cont'd)

History of our Blessed Lord . . . (cont'd)

93-94 [95-96] 97-100 [101-102] 103-106 [107-108] 109-112 [113-114] 115-116

Plates: Frontispiece + 22 engravings.

Notes: Pagination includes engravings. McKell copy missing plates on pp. 108, 113. Introduction by Jona M. Wainright, dated Oct. 30, 1844, refers to the author as "she" and adds that this is an American edition of an English book.

Anon.   # 1111

The History of Primrose Prettyface; who, by her sweetness of temper, and love of learning, was raised from being the daughter of a poor cottager, to great riches, and the dignity of Lady of the Manor. New edition. London: Printed [by Samuel Bentley] for John Harris & Baldwin and Cradock, [Sept.], 1830.

Coll: 12°: A-F⁶ 36 leaves (16.5 X 10.1ᶜᵐ·) Pp. [1-3] 4-42 [43] 44-72

Plates: Frontispiece + 1, (hand colored, copper).

Notes: S-1-11-43 B

[ANON.]. The History of Prince Fatal, and Prince Fortunatus. To which is added, An Account of Astolpho's Journey to the Moon. Ornamented with Cuts. Third Edition. Wellington: Printed and Sold by Houlston and Son, n.d. [1800?].   # 1112

Coll.: 24°: A⁶B12[C6] ([c⁶]+ A7-A12). 24 leaves (13.7 X 7.8cm). 48 pp.

Illustrations: Frontispiece (A1) + 5 cuts in text.

Anon.   # 1113

The History of Prince Roslyn. The Story of the Old Man
and His Dog Trim. The Generous Pedlar. An Anecdote.
London: Printed and published by James Wallis, n.d.
Coll: 18°: A^{18} 18 leaves (13.5 X $8.8^{cm.}$)
      Pp. [1-2] 3-19 [20] 21-33 [34] 35 [36]

Illus: 3 woodcuts

Binding: Red printed wrappers

Notes: "Wallis's Juvenile Tales"

Anon.   # 1115

The History of Sinbad the Sailor: Containing an Account
of his Several Surprising Voyages and Miraculous Escapes.
Boston: Published by J.P. Clark, 1829.
Coll: 12°: π^2 [1 6+1] [2]^4 3^8 4^4 5^8 6^4 7^8 8^4 49 leaves
(13.4 X $7.3^{cm.}$) Pp. [i-ii] [1-3] 4-96

Illus: 5 engravings [+ engraved frontispiece and title
       page included in collation (π^2)]

Anon.   # 1114

The History of Sinbad, the Sailor. Containing an account
of his seven surprising voyages. Glasgow: Published by
J. Lumsden & Son, 1819.
Coll: 18°: A X A_1 X_2 A_3 X_3 A_4 X_4 A_5 B X_5 B_2-B_7
      [C^9 (=A_6, X_6, A_7, X_7, A_8, X_8, A_9, X_9, A_{10})].
      26 leaves (13.6 X $8.8^{cm.}$) Pp. [1-5] 6-50 [51-52]

Illus: Frontispiece + 7 full page woodcuts by John Bewick

Binding: Rust wrappers

                                           # 1116

The History of Sixteen Wonderful Old Women, Illustrated
by as many engravings; exhibiting their principal ec-
centricities and amusements. London: Printed by S.
and R. Bentley for J. Harris and Son, 1822.

Coll: 8° [1 18] 18 leaves (17.7 x 10.6cm) Pp. [1-ii]
      1-32 [33-34].

Illus: 16 hand colored engravings

Binding: Pink printed wrappers

Contents: l.1: title; 1.1^v: blank; 1.2-1.17: text;
          1.18: advert   ) for Harris listing 31 titles;
          1.18^v: blank

Anon.   # 1117

A History of the Big Letters: Intended for the Instruction
& Amusement of all the Little Children in the Nation. By
Edward Dogood, Little Boy Eight Years Old. Pittsburgh: Sold
at Z. Cramer's Bookstore, Market Street. Cramer & Spear,
Printer, n.d.
Coll: 32°: A^{16} 16 leaves (10.5 X 6.5cm) Pp. [1-4] 5-31 [32]

Illus: Several woodcuts

Binding: Blue wrappers; initial page pasted down

Notes: Preface by "The Author, Reading Valley, January, 1,
       1809."

[AMON.]. The History of the Family at Smiledale.   # 1118
Presented to all Little Boys and Girls who wish to
be good, and make their friends happy. London:
Printed for J. Harris, n.d. [1800?].
Coll.: 32^o(in 8's): A-H^8. 64 leaves (11.2 X 7.6cm).
128 pp.

Illustrations: Frontispiece (A^1) which forms front
endpaper + 12 cuts (all by Bewick).

Bookplate of Percival Merritt.

Anon.   # 1119

The History of the Holy Jesus...Being a pleasant and
profitable companion for Children; composed on purpose
for their use. By a lover of their precious souls. The
twenty-fifth edition. Boston: Printed and sold by John
Boyle..., 1774.
Coll: 16°: [$_A8$]B^8-C^8 24 leaves (9.9 X $7.7^{cm.}$) Pp. [1, 2-47,48]
Illus: Frontispiece ("The Author" with "IT" in upper right-
       hand corner) + 18 in text.
Binding: Blue-gray wrappers (On front: "Ruby Putnam her
         book. Given to her by Nancy Howes")
         [A_1^r] and C_8^v pasted to blank wrappers
Notes: Rosenbach #79   McKell # G-114-46B

Anon   # 1120

The History of the King of the Peacocks and The
Princess Rosetta. Embellished with an Engraving.
Cork: Printed by Charles Dillon, n.d.
Coll: 18° A^6 6 leaves (13.3 x 8.5cm) Pp. [3]
      4-12.

Plates: Frontispiece woodcut.

Notes: Bound in with six others in Omnibus # 1, q.v.

                                           # 1121

[AMON.]. An History of the Lives, Actions, Travels,
Sufferings and Deaths of the Apostles and Evangelists.
. . . . Adorned with Variety of Copper-plate Cuts.
London: Printed for J. Newbery, 1763.

Coll.: 24°: B^8 (B1 +X 2) C-Q^{8}R^6. 128 leaves (9.7
X 6.2 cm). vi, 246 + [6] pp.

[McKell # ??????]

Apostles -2-

X_2: An unsigned fold of two conjugate leaves inserted after B1 which contain the Preface.

R4^v: "Books just published by J. Newbery . . . . "

Plates: Frontispiece + 7 (copper engravings, some
tinted).

Bookplate of Percival Merritt.

Anon   # 1123

The History of Tom Thumb. "Mary Bell's Series." Cincinnati, Ohio: Peter G. Thompson, n.d.

Coll: an 4° [14] 4 leaves (19.6 x 14.1cm) ff. [4]

Illus: 4 full page colored engravings

Binding: Illustrated blue-grey wrappers: front serves as title page, back has adverts. Text printed on insides of wrappers. Text on one side of leaf, engraving on other.

[ANON.]. The History of Valentine and Orson. [Nottingham:] Printed for the Company of Walking Stationers, n.d. [c. 1796-1800].   # 1124

Coll.: 16° : [A⁸]. 8 leaves, 16pp.

An unbound, unopened, uncut chapbook. Imposition was on half-sheet. Original sheet measures 25" X 15 13/16".

2 copies.

[ANON.]. The History of Young Edwin and Little Jessy: Together with an Account of the Pleasant Walk which William and Winifred Took with Margery, Who Lives at the Foot of Parnassus. Written by the aforesaid Margery . . . . London: Printed [by Swan and Son] for J. Harris . . . , 1807.   # 1125

Coll.: 24° : A-I⁶. 54 leaves (13.6 X 8.65cm). [1-3]4-108 pp.

Plate: Engraved frontispiece xxtx by J.S. Sampsen (?) with original drawing facing.

R-4-22-43L

Hofer, the Tyrolese

see

William Tell, Or The Patriot of Switzerland. By Florian. And Hofer, The Tyrolese. J. Harris. n.d.

Hoffmann, E[rnst] T[heodor] A[madeus] 1776-1822   # 1127

Nutcracker and Mouse King and the Educated Cat. Translated by Ascott R. Hope. London: T. Fisher Unwin, 1892. Pp. viii + 198 .

Plates: Frontispiece

Hoffmann, Franz   1814-1882   # 1128

Der Henkeldukaten. / Der Schiffbruch. "Amerikanische Jugendbibliothek." Philadelphia: Morwitz & Co., n.d.

Coll: 8° 1-5⁸ 40 leaves (15 x 10) Pp. [1-2, 3] 4-45 [46]; 1-2, [3] 4-33 [34].

Illus: Color woodcut on front cover.

Binding: Paper over boards.

Hoffmann, Franz   1814-1882   # 1129

Neger und Weisse./ Der Treue Sachse.. "Amerikanische Jugendbibliothek." Philadelphia: Morwitz & Co., n.d.

Coll.: 8° 1-5⁸ 6⁴ 44 leaves (15.2 x 10.5cm) Pp. [1-2, 3] 4-61 [62]; 1-2, [3] 3-25 [26.]

Binding: Paper over boards, printed.

[Hoffman-Donner, Heinrich]   1809-1894 # 1130

The English Struwwelpeter or Pretty Stories and Funny Pictures. [N. P., n.d.]

Coll: 4°; 24 leaves (23.2 x 19 cm.); ff. 24.

Binding: Green boards, free and paste down end papers front and back.

Notes: ff. 11 is upside down.
McKell #S-7-13-48-B.
Printed on one side of leaf only.

Hoffman [-Donner], Dr. Heinrich   1809-1894   # 1131

Melodien zu Dr. Heinrich Hoffman's Struwwelpeter. Zusammengestellt von Andreas Hussla; Kais. Russischer Kapellmeister a. D. Eigentum und Verlag der literarischen Unstalt, Rutten & Loening, in Frankfurt am Main, n.d.

Coll: lge 4° [1-24] 8 leaves [1]2-16pp.

Illus: Color front cover.

Binding: Boards

                         (cont'd)

Melodien   (Cont'd)

Notes: A book of musical notation. No inside title page. Back cover has "Druck von Krebs-Schmitt Nachts. Aug. Weissbrod, Frankfurt a. M."

Hoffmann-Donner, [Dr] H[einrich] 1809-1894 # 1132

Prinz Grünewald und Perlenfein mit ihrem lieben Ese-
lein. Ein Bildermärchen verzeichnet und gereimt von
dem Verfasser des Struwwelpeter (H. Hoffmann-Donner).
Frankfurt a. M.: Literarische Anstalt. (Rütten &
Löning.), n.d.

Coll: 4° A book of plates numbered [1]2-24.

Illus: Each leaf engraved in color by "Ettl."

Notes: Pencil and ink drawings by artist laid in
front and back wrappers.

Hoffman-Donner, Heinrich. 1809-1894 # 1133
Slovenly Peter, or Pleasant Stories and Funny Pictures.
Translated from the German. [New York: C. Town?,1849].
Coll: 4°: 20 separate leaves, unnumbered, unsigned,
printed on recto side only.
Illus: Handcolored engravings on each leaf.
Binding: Printed and illustrated blue paper wrappers,
stabbed.
Notes: Only known copy of the first American edition of
Struwwelpeter. Lacks back wrapper. [S-9-15-54]
C. Town is the publisher, printer, or translator:
"Entered according to Act of Congress, in the
year 1849, by C. Town..." on front wrapper.

1134
Hoffman [-Donner] Heinrich, M.D. 1809-1894

"Der Struwwelpeter" sive Fabulae Lepidae Et Picturae
Iocosae Quas Invenit ac Depinxit Henricus Hoffman,
Doctor Medicinae. Picturas Secundum Hoffmani Exem-
plar Delineavit Et Lignis Incidit Friedericus Kredel.
Versiculos In Sermonem Latinum Transtulit Eduardus
Bornemann. Francofurti Moenani A. P. Chr. n. 1956.
In Aedibus Rütten & Loening Bibliopolarum Qui Iam
Originarium Hoffmani Librum Edenum Guraverunt. Fr.
27.

Illus: Numerous in color. (cont'd)

Hoffman-Donner. "Der Struwwelpeter." sive Fabulae
Lepidae .... 1956. (Cont'd)

Notes: "Nachwort" laid in, 12 page pamphlet. Ex-
cepting f. 1, printed on one side of leaf
only.

1135
Hofland, Mrs. [Barbara (Wreaks) Hoole] 1800-1844

The Young Cadet; or, Henry Delamere's Voyage to
India, his travels in Hindostan, his account of the
Burmese War, and the wonders of Klora. Boston:
Munroe & Francis; New York: C. S. Francis, 1829

Coll: 12° (6's) 1-15⁶ 90 leaves (14.9 x 9cm)
Pp.[i-ii, iii] iv [v] vi [vii] viii-xi [xiii,
13]14-179,[180;] advert.
Binding: Stabbed and sewn; free and paste-down endpapers front and rear.
(cont'd)

Hofland. Young Cadet. 1829. (Cont'd)

Notes: Advert: List of Mrs. Hofland's works for
sale by Munroe and Francis.

Neue Gesellschaftspiele .... (Cont'd)

[131-133] 134-164 [165-167] 168-258 [259] 260-
262.

Plates: 4 woodcuts bound in at end on four cancel-
substitution leaves (making four conjugate
leaves).

Binding: Stiff wrappers.

[Holbrook, Josiah]. 1788-1854 # 1136

Self Instructor, No. 1, Child's First Book, Drawing Series
by Josiah Holbrook. Hartford: Published by J.H. Mather &
Co.; New York: at the Exchange, 140 Grand Street, n.d.

Coll: Sm 4°: 1¹² 12 leaves (15.2 X 13.6cm) Pp. [i-iii]
iv, 5-24

Binding: Brown wrappers

1137
Holder, Louise

Neue Gesellschaftspiele und Unterhaltungen, zum Berg-
nugen und zur Uebung des Scharfsinns für die Jugend.
Enthaltend: Rathsel in Erzählungen. Gesellschaftspiele. Charaden dramatisch dramatisch vorzustellen
Pantomimische Wörterspiele. Dramatisirte Spruchworter
zur unvorbereiteten Aufführung in einem Zimmer ge-
eignet. Von Louise Holder. Ulm: In der I. Ebner'-
schen Buchhandlung, n.d.

Coll: 8° π,1-15⁸,16⁷(16.6+1),17⁴ 132 leaves Pp.[1
-2, i-ii, 3] 4-62 [63-65] 66-96 [97-99] 11-130
(cont'd)

1138
Holdich, L A

Food for Lambs; or, a guide to infant teachers and
parents in the religious instruction of young
children. New York: Carlton & Porter, n.d. 1856 ?

Coll: sm 8° [1-6⁸ 48 leaves (13.2 x 8.5cm) Pp.[1,
2,3] 4,[5-6, 7] 8-96.
Binding: 2 free and 2 paste-down endpapers front and
rear; paper over boards, advert on back,
printed front.
Notes: Missing ¼ of pp. 47-48, and all of 49-50.
"Sunday School Union 200 Mulberry St."

1139

[ANON.]. Holiday Gifts for Good Boys And Girls:
Containing the Surprising and Diverting Histories
of Blue Beard, Jack and the Bean-Stalk, and Tom
Thumb; With a coloured Engraving. Derby: Thomas
Richardson, n.d.

Coll.: 18°; A⁶2A⁶3A⁶. 18 leaves (13.3 X 8.4cm).
[3]4-12, [3]4-12, [3]4-12 pp.

Plates: Frontispiece, fold-out hand-colored
engraving by J.L. Marks.

Notes: Bound in with six others in Omnibus #1, q.v.

1143

Holmes, Oliver Wendell. 1809-1894

The One Hoss Shay, With its companion poems . . . .
Illust. by Howard Pyle. Boston and New York: Houghton,
Mifflin and Company, 1892. fr. [3]-[80].

Illus: Frontispiece +12 (included in foliation)+ cuts.

1145

Anon

Home Pictures. "Uncle Ned's Picture Books" Series.
New York: McLoughlin Bro's., [1864?]. Fr./1-8/
including plates.

Plates: 4 full-page in color.

Notes: See BMC. Title page information on front
cover. No inside title page.

1146

Honoré   fl c. 1250-1300

An Illuminated Manuscript of La Somme Le Roy, attributed
to the Parisian miniaturist Honoré. Intro. Eric George
Millar. Oxford: The Roxburghe Club, 1953. Pp. [i-xii,
1] 2-48 [49] 50-51 [52]
Illus: Photo reproductions (34)+ frontispiece

1149

[ANON.]. The Horse's Levee, or The Court of
Pegasus. Intended as a Companion to The Butterfly's
Ball, and The Peacock "At Home." Illustrated with
Elegant Engravings. London: Printed [by E. Hemstead]
for J. Harris . . . , 1808.

Coll.: 16°: A⁸. 8 leaves (11.45 X 9.5cm). [1-3]4-
16 pp.

Plates: Frontispiece + 7.

Notes: Bound in with six others in Omnibus #2, q.v.

1150

Hosemann, Th[eodor].   (1807-1875) 1150

Slovenly Kate; and Other Pleasing Stories and
Funny Pictures. "Slovenly Peter Series."
From the German of Th. Hosemann. A Companion to
"Slovenly Peter." Philadelphia: Willis. P.
Hazard, 1852.

Coll: Large 4°; Singles; ff. 22. (24.2 x 19.2cm)

Contents: Slovenly Kate; Envious Tom; Tell-tale
Jenny; Untidy Tom; Headstrong
Nancy; Charley, the Story-teller;
Screaming Annie; Sammy Sweet tooth;
(cont'd)

Hosemann.   Slovenly Kate.   1852.   p. 2.

Ned, the Toy Breaker; Prying Will.

Binding: Stabbed; boards.

Illus: Numerous hand colored illustrations.

Notes: Printed on one side of leaf only.
Title page from Slovenly Peter and title
page from Simple Hans, as well as 1 leaf
of ads., bound in at end, 20, 21, 22.

1157

Anon.

The House That Jack Built. [2 Vols.] Philadelphia: Pub-
lished and sold wholesale and retail by Morgan & Yeager.
n.d. [ca 1820].
[Vol. I]
Coll: 16°: [1⁸] 8 leaves (14.2 X 11.9cm)
Illus: 8 colored engravings by William Charles
Binding: Gray wrappers, probably by William Charles
Notes: Uncut edges; printed on one side of leaf only.
Notes on Charles in Weiss, Harry B. Bibliography of
Charles (New York Public Library).

Anon.

The House That Jack Built. 2.Vols. n.d.

[Vol II (Continuation)] Continuation of the House that
Jack Built

Coll: 16°: [1⁸] 8 leaves (14.2 X 10.4cm)

Illus: 8 colored engravings by William Charles.

Binding: Gray wrappers, probably by William Charles. The
fly-leaves pasted on the inside wrappers repre-
sent the labels for four drawing books published
by Charles.

Anon.

The House That Jack Built. 2 Vols. n.d.

Notes: Uncut edges; printed on one side of leaf only.
Morgan & Yeager fl. 1824. Charles (1776-1820c).

The House that Jack Built

see also

A Kid, a Kid. or the Jewish Origin of the
celebrated legend The House that Jack
built. Mahlon Day, 1835.

Pleasure Book for Children. The House that
Jack Built. Cleveland, 1956.

1167

[Hughes, Thomas]   1822-1896

The Scouring of the White Horse; or, the long vaca-
tion ramble of a London clerk. Illustrated by
Richard Doyle. Cambridge & London: Macmillan and
Co., 1859.

Coll: 8° [A]⁶ B-P⁸ Q² 120 leaves (17.5 x 13.5cm)
Pp. [v-ix] x-xv [xvi, 17] 18-244.+ [16pp adverts].
Plates: 2 frontispiece engravings by W. J. Lintot.

1158

[Howard, Justin H.]

Nothing to Do: an accompaniment to "Nothing to
Wear." By a Lady. With illustrations by the
author. New York: Wiley & Halstead, 1857.

Coll: 12° π²[1-5]⁶ 32 leaves (17.3 x11.7cm)
Pp.[1-4], 5-57 [58; 1-6 of adverts.]

Plates: Frontispiece+7.

Notes: Frontispiece signed "J.H. Howard." See
Butler, Wm. A., Nothing to Wear.

1168

Hughs, Mrs. [Mary (Robson)]. b 1790-05? - ret. 1839

The Proud Girl Humbled, or the two school-mates; for
little boys and little girls. Philadelphia: Lindsay
and Blakiston, n.d. Pp. [3-4], 5-56.

Plates: Frontispiece

Coll: 16 [1] 2-3⁸ 4⁴ 28 leaves (14.3 x 11.1cm)

1162

Howitt, [Mrs.] Mary [Botham]   1799-1888

Mary Howitt's Story Book: with illustrations. New York:
C. S. Francis & Co.; Boston: Crosby, Nichols, and
Co., 1853.

Coll: 12° [A]⁸[B]⁴ C-S⁴ T⁸ U¹² X-2P⁴ 236 leaves
(15.4 x 9.8cm) Pp. [i-v] vi [vii-viii] 9-160,
[5-6] 7-160, [5-6] 7-160 (totl of 572pp.)
Plates: Engraved frontispiece, title page+2.

1171

Humphreys, H.N., Esq.

Illuminated Illustrations of Froissart. Selected
From the MS. in The Bibliotheque Royale, Paris
and from other sources. By . . . . London:
William Smith, 113, Fleet Street. MDCCCXLV.
[Bradbury and Evans, Printers, Whitefriars]

Coll: 8° (4's) [1-9⁴, 10²] unsigned. 39 leaves
(24.6 x 17.5cm) Pp. [i-v] vi [1] 2 [3-11] 12
[13-67 ("68" mispaginated 307)].
Plates: Color half-title, 36 full-page in color.
(cont'd)

1163

Howitt, [Mrs.] Mary [Botham]   1799-1888

Tales in Verse. London: William Darton and Son,
n.d.

Coll: 12° [A]² B-S⁶ T² 108 leaves (15.8 x 9.9cm)
Pp. [i-iii] iv [1] 2-212.
Plates: Engraved frontispiece, title page +8.

Humphreys. Froissart. Bibliotheque Royale (Cont'd)

Each plate has protective leaf preceding.
Binding: Rebound in ¼ red morocco; marbled free
and paste-down endpapers front and rear,
with additional free endpaper front and
rear; gilt edged. Stabbed. Spine marked
"Vol. I."
Notes: Pp.[1-ii]: another half-title not illustrated;[v]-vi: list of plates refers to
Smith's edition of Froissart in two vols.

Howitt, Mary [Botham]   1799-1888

Tales in Verse. New York: Harper & Brothers, 1847.

Coll: 12° 1-15⁶ 90 leaves (15.2 x 9.7cm), Pp.
[1-5] 6 [7] 8 [9] 10-133 [134] 137-172, [1] 2-10:
adverts.

Plates: 3 +cuts.

1172

Humphreys, H.N., Esq.

Illuminated Illustrations of Froissart. Selected
from The MS. In The British Museum. By . . . .
London: William Smith, 113, Fleet Street.
MDCCCXLIV [Bradbury and Evans, Printers, Whitefriars.]

Coll: 8° (4's) [1-9⁴, 10²] unsigned. 39
leaves (24.6 x 17.5cm) Pp. [i-v] vi [1] 2
[3-21] 22 [23-27] 28 [29-31] 32 [33-37] 38 [39]
40 [41-43] 44 [45] 46 [47-49] 50 [51] 52 [53]
54 [55-63] 64 [65-71 ("72" mispaginated 70)]

Humphreys. Froissart. British Museum. (Cont'd)

Plates: Color half-title, 36 full-page in color;
each plate has a protective leaf preceding.
Binding: Rebound in ½ red morocco; marbled free
and paste-down endpapers front and rear,
with additional free endpaper front and
rear; gilt edged. Stabbed. Spine marked
"Vol. II."
Notes: Pp. [i-ii] : another half-title, not illustrated; [v]-vi: list of plates refers to
Smith's edition of Froissart in two vols.

Husz, Mathieu (Les Subtiles Fables D'Esope, 1486)

see

Aesop. Claude Dalbanne Livres a Gravures
Imprimes a Lyon an XV⁰ Siecle . . . .
1926.

1175

Anon

The Hyacinth: or, affection's gift. [Illustrated by
T. P. Davis, J. Neagle, R. Farrier, J. Northcote.]
Philadelphia: Henry F. Anners, 1847.

Coll: 12° 1-18⁶ 108 leaves (15.4 x 9.4cm) Pp. [1-
5] 6 [7] 8-215 [216]

Plates: Frontispiece +5

Notes: A yearbook

1176

Anon

Hymns for Little Children. New York: Published by
Samuel Wood & Sons, and Samuel S. Wood & Co., 1819.

Coll: 32° 1¹⁶ 16 leaves (10.6 x 6.5cm) Pp. [1-ii, 1-3]
4-26 [27-28, 29-30].

Binding: Blue-green flowery wrappers. Initial and final
leaves as paste-down endpapers.

Contents: Blank: 1; Alphabet and numbers: 1ᵛ; Title page:
1.2; Blank: 1.2ᵛ; Text: 1.3-1.14ᵛ; Blank: 1.15-
1.16ᵛ.

(cont'd)

Hymns for Little Children. (Cont'd)

Notes: Samuel Wood & Sons, No. 261 Pearl-Street; Samuel
S. Wood & Co., No. 212 Market-St. Baltimore.

1177

Ilias Ambrosiana Codex F. 205 P. INF. Biblio-
thecae Ambrosianae Mediolanensis Berne: Urs
Graf-Verlag, 1953. Pp. [i-viii] ix-xv [xvi] xvii-
lvii [lviii-lx]; Ff. 2b (i.e., 56 pp.) all but
first and last 2 contain photos of MS fragments.

1178

Anon

The Illuminated American Primer, being an introduction to Mrs. Sigourney's Pictorial Reader. For
the use of schools. Claremont, N.H., Manufacturing
Company, S. Ide, Ag't., n.d.

Coll: 12° 1-3⁶ 18 leaves (17.9 x 10.9cm) Pp. [1-2]
3-36.
Illus: Cuts
Binding: Stiff yellow pictorial wrappers; stabbed;
front and back paste-down endpapers.
Notes: 5th ed., copyright 1844.

1181

Anon

The Infant's Book. New York: Richard Marsh, n.d.
Pp. 1-12.

Illus: Cuts.

Binding: 6 leaves on 3 sheets, unbound.

1182

Anon.

The Infant's Grammar, or a Pic=nic Party of the Parts of
Speech. London: [Printed by S. And R. Bentley for] John
Harris, n.d.

Coll: 12°[?]: [1¹⁴] 14 leaves (17.7 X 10.8cm.)
Ff. [1-2] 3-13 [14]

Plates: Hand tinted engravings. Blank facing pages alter-
nated with facing pages containing text and illustration.

1183

Anon.

The Infant's Library. Bibliothèque des Enfants. London:
Printed and sold by John Marshall..., n.d. [15 vols.;
woodcuts + text on facing pages.]

Vol. I
Coll: 64°: A⁸-D⁸ 32 leaves (5.9 X 4.5cm·) Pp. [1-2] 3-63
[64]
Vol. II
Coll: 64°: A-D⁸ 32 leaves (5.95 X 4.5cm·) Pp. [1-2] 3-63
[64]
Vol. III
Coll: 64°: [1¹⁶] 16 leaves (5.8 X 4.425cm·) Pp. [1-4]
5-28 [29-32]

Anon.

The Infant's Library. Bibliothèque des Enfants.

Vol. IV
Coll: 64°: [1¹⁶] 16 leaves (5.7 X 4.3$^{cm.}$) Pp. [1-4] 5-28 [29-32]

Vol. V
Coll: 64°: [1¹⁶] 16 leaves (5.75 X 4.6$^{cm.}$) Pp. [1-4] 5-28 [29-32].

Vol. VI
Coll: 64°: [1¹⁶] 16 leaves (5.65 X 4.5$^{cm.}$) Pp. [1-4] 5-28 [29-32]

Vol. VII
Coll: 64°: [1¹⁶] 16 leaves (5.85 X 4.4$^{cm.}$) Pp. [1-4] 5-28 [29-32]

Anon.

The Infant's Library. Bibliotheque des Enfants.

Vol. VIII
Coll: 64°: [1¹⁶] 16 leaves (5.7 x 4.4cm) Pp. [1-4] 5-28 [29-32].

Vol. IX
Coll: 64°: [1¹⁶] 16 leaves (5.7 x 4.4cm) Pp. [1-4] 5-28 [29-32].

Vol. X
Coll: 64°: [1¹⁶] 16 leaves (6.4 x 4.05cm) Pp. [1-4] 5-28 [29-32].

Vol. XI
Coll: 64°: [1¹⁶] 16 leaves (5.5 x 4.2cm) Pp. [1-4] 5-28 [29-32].

Anon.

The Infant's Library. Bibliothèque des Enfants.

Vol. XII
Coll: 64°: [1¹⁶] 16 leaves (5.6 X 4.5$^{cm.}$) Pp. [1-4] 5-28 [29-32]

Vol. XIII
Coll: 64°: [1¹⁶] 16 leaves (5.9 X 4.5$^{cm.}$) Pp. [1-4] 5-28 [29-32]

Vol. XIV
Coll: 64°: [1¹⁶] 16 leaves (5.75 X 4.45$^{cm.}$) Pp. [1-4] 5-28 [29-32]

Vol. XV
Coll: 64°: [1¹⁶] 16 leaves (5.6 X 4.7$^{cm.}$) Pp. [1-4] 5-28 [29-32]

Anon.

The Infant's Library. Bibliothèque des Enfants.

Notes: Volumes in sliding-front wooden box; hand-tinted engraving of a glass enclosed bookcase with drawers pasted on the sliding front. Bookseller's emblem pasted to back panel: "Sold at/Whitleys (sic)/Toy and Teenbridge/Warehouse, N⁰ 12 Old Bond Street, London." Ram's horns top of sliding panel provide handle.

The Infant's Library

see also

A Short History of England for The Infant's Library. London: John Marshall . . . , n.d.

Anon.   # 1184

The Infant-School Girl; or, Memoir of Mary Elizabeth Crook, of Baltimore. Written for the American Sunday-School Union, and revised by the Committee of Publication. Philadelphia: American Sunday-School Union..., [1848].

Coll: 12°: [1⁶]2-3⁶ 18 leaves (14.2 X 9.1cm) Pp. [1-6] 7-36

Illus: Woodcut frontispiece

Anon   # 1186

Instructions for Children: intended for the use of The Methodist Societies. New-York: Published by J. Emory and B. Waugh, for the Tract Society of the Methodist Episcopal Church, at the conference office, 14 Crosby-Street, J. Collard, Printer. [For the Sunday School Union of the Methodist Episcopal, etc.] 1829.

Coll: sm 8°: 1-2⁸, 3-[4]⁶ 48 leaves (13.2 x 8.5cm) Pp. [1-2, 3] 4-43 [44], [1] 2-12.

(cont'd)

Instructions for Children. (Cont'd)

Illus: Woodcut vignette on title page

Contents: Lessons; "Reformed Edward" on pp. [1] 2-12.

Notes: McKell copy lacking 1·2-1·7, (pp. [3]-14).

Anon.   # 1187

Instructive Stories; Consisting of Arthur and George. "Cabinet of Lilliput" London: Printed [by H. Bryer] for J. Harris, 1802.

Coll: 64°: A-D¹² 48 leaves (6.6 X 6.2$^{cm.}$) Pp. [1-3] 4-61 [62-63] 64-93 [94] 95 [96]

Plates: Frontispiece + original drawing tipped in facing

Binding: Pink boards

Notes: #[R-4-22-436]

Irish Miniatures

see

Book of Kells

Irving, C[hristopher]   -d. 185b   # 1188

A Catechism of Botany, containing a description of the
most familiar and interesting plants, arranged
according to the Linnaean. With an appendix on the
formation of an herbarium. Adapted to the use of
schools in the United States. With engraved illustrations. By C. Irving, Ll. D., Holyrood-house, South-
hampton. Third American Edition, improved and enlarged. New York: Published by Collins and Hannay,
230 Pearl-Street. J. & J. Harper, printers, 1824.
[Second Part].

Coll: 12 A-F⁶ , G5 (G 1 - G 4, G 5) 41 leaves
                                        (cont'd)

A Catechism of Botany. (Cont'd)

          (13.4 x 8.4cm) Pp. [1-5] b-79 [80] 81-82.

Illus: Frontispiece engraved by G. B. King.

Binding: Original brown wrappers; advertisement on
         back.

Irving, Washington   1783-1859   # 1190

Old Christmas: from the Sketch Book of Washington
Irving. Illustrated by R. Caldecott and James D.
Cooper. London: Macmillan & Co., 1882. Pp. [xvi, 1]
165 [166-168].

Plates: Frontispiece +illustrated title page 103
        other illustrations.

Irving, Washington   1783-1859   # 1191

Rip Van Winkle, with drawings by Arthur Rackham.
London: William Heinemann, 1905. Pp. [i-iv] v-
viii, 1-57 [58-60] + Ff. 1-50.

Illus: Frontispiece +49 drawings tipped to rectos
       of Fols. 1-49.

Notes: #214 of limited ed. of 250, signed by
       illustrator.

Anon   # 1194

Jack and the Bean-Stalk. A New Version. To which is
added Little Jane and Her Mother. Boston: Wm. S. Reynolds & Co., No. 20 Cornhill, 1848.

Coll: 8° [1-4⁸] 32 leaves (17.3 x 11cm) Pp. [1-11] 12-
20 [22-25] 26-37 [38-41] 44-54 [55-58] 59 [60] 61-
70 [71-72].

Illus: Numerous wood engravings by Devereux, S.C., and
       others. Woodcuts by Striling.

Binding: Green pictorial wrappers

Jack and the Giants. London: Griffith and Farren,
1858

    see under

        The Story of Jack and the Giants.

Anon.   # 1196

Jack the Giant Killer, a Hero Celebrated by Ancient
Historians. Banbury: Printed by J.G. Rusher, n.d. [1820?]

Coll: 32°: [1⁸] 8 leaves (9 X 6.1ᶜᵐ·)
      Pp. [1-2] 3-15 [16]

Illus: 6 cuts in text

Binding: Buff pictorial wrappers

Anon   # 1197

Jack, The Giant Killer; "Hugh Thomson's Illustrated
Fairy Books." London & New York: Macmillan & Co., 1898.
[R.& R. Clark Limited Printers, Edinburgh]. [Hugh
Thomson illustrator].

Coll: 4°: Pp.[1-32]

Illus: 16 Chromo lithos and numerous other decorative
       illustrations by Hugh Thomson

Binding: Illustrated wrappers

Notes: Decorative illustrations are in the margin around
       the text.

Jack the Giant Killer. New York: Sheldon & Co.

        see

            Our Favorite Fairy Tales.

James, Montague Rhodes   # 1199

The Apocalypse in Latin and French (Bodleian MS
Douce 180) Described by Montague Rhodes James
. . . . Oxford: Printed for presentation to the
members of the Roxburghe Club, MCMXXII. Pp. [i-xii]
1-97 pagination for plates.

Plates: Repros in collotype of the MS, includes a
        frontispiece.

1201

James, Philip [Brutton] 1901-

Children's Books of Yesterday. Ed. C. Geoffrey Holme.
London: The Studio Ltd., 1933. Pp. [i-iv, 1-5] 6-128.

Notes: Holme, C. Geoffrey 1887-

James, Rev. T., M.A., ed.

see

Aesop's Fables. Philadelphia, 1855.

1202

James, Will   1892-1942

Sand. New York, London: Charles Scribner's Sons,
1929. Pp. [x] 328.

Plates: Frontispiece +42 other illustrations by
the author.

Notes: First ed. PZ 10.3 J 33 San.   29-921

1203

James, Will   1892-1942

Smoky the Cowhorse. New York and London: Charles
Scribner's Sons, 1926. Pp. [iv] v-xi+ 3, 310.

Illus: Pencil drawing of Smoky inscribed "To Robert
Cross from Will James '26'" tipped in to
front end paper.

Binding: Dust cover

Notes: Presentation copy to Robert Cross. First ed.
JL 795. H7J3.   26.16523.

Jameson, Mrs.(pseud)[Anna Brownell]   (1794-1860)
1204

Female Sovereigns. By Mrs. Jameson, authoress
of "The Diary of an Ennuyee," etc. 2 Vols.
Vol. I. New York: Harper & Brothers, Publishers,
1854.

Coll: 8° 8, A⁴, B-C⁸, D⁴, E-F⁸, G⁴, H-I⁸, K⁴,
L-M, N⁴, O-Q⁸, R⁹(R8+1).
117 leaves.
pp.[xiii-xiv, xv] xvi-xix [20-25] 26-245
[246]

Notes: Binding is speckled calf; plate on spine
has title and in gold below is stamped
"3d Series."

1205

Jamieson, Alexander

A Grammar of Rhetoric, and Polite Literature: compre-
hending the principles of language and style, the elements of taste and criticism; with rules, for the
study of composition and eloquence. Illustrated by
appropriate examples. Selected chiefly from the
British classics. For the use of schools, or private
instruction. By Alexander Jamieson, Ll. D. Fourth
Edition. New Haven: Printed and published by A. H.
Maltby and Co., 1826.

Coll: 12 14, 2-26⁶ 154 leaves (17.2 x 10.2cm)
(cont'd)

A Grammar of Rhetoric . . . . (Cont'd)

Pp. [1-iii] iv-vii [viii-ix] x-xi [xx], [19]
20-36 [37] 38-80 [81] 82-135 [136] 137-191 [192]
193-226 [227] 228-266 [267] 268-306 .

Binding: Free and pasted down endpapers.

Anon.   # 1206

Jane and Eliza. Newark: Printed for the publisher, 1840.

Coll: 12°: [1⁶] 6 leaves (18.7 X 11cm) Pp. [1-2] 3-12

Binding: Rebound over original printed blue wrappers

Notes: Bookplates of John Stuart Groves.

Janneway, Jacob [James Janeway]. (1636?-1674)

Geistliches Exempel=Buch Für Kinder. Das ist:
Ein ausführlicher Bericht von der Bekehrung,
heiligem und exemplerischem leben. Wie auch
Fröhlichem Tode unterschiedlicher junger Kinder,
vormals in Englischer Sprache zusammen getragen
durch Jacob Janneway. Unjebo aber In Hoffnung
eineges Nutzens sonderlich aber zur Beschämung
vieler alten, zur Reibung der Nachfolge, und
zum beweiss der Möglichkeit eines Thätigen
Christenthums aus dem Englischen ins Deutsche
überzetst Erster Teil. Basel: Gedruckt bey
(cont'd)   # 1217

Janneway. Geistliches Exempel-Buch. 1749. (Cont'd)

Joh. Heinrich Decker, c.1749.

Coll: 12° A-M¹², N⁶ ; 150 leaves.
Pp. [1-2] 3-300
Binding: Paste-down endpapers front and back.

Notes: Horizontal chains. Front endpaper has "1749."

Jaspert, Werner   #1212

Werner Jaspert erzählt die Geschichte des listenreichen Reineke Fuchs. Die Bilder dazu zeichnete C. Gefischer. [Frankfurt A.M.: H. Cobet Verlag. Auflage von 25000 Exemplaren gedruckt unter Lizenz Nr. 27 Heinrich Cobet Verlag, Frankfurt am Main. Typographie und Schriftgraphik von Hermann Zapf. Das Buch wurde gesetzt aus der Trajanus der Schriftgiesserei D. Stempel AG, Frankfurt am Main--Sud.], n.d. Pp. [1-4,5] 6-42 [43-44 colophon].

Illus: Numerous color vignettes by Gefischer (C. E. Fischer?)
Notes: McKell # S-12- (30-48-B

Jean de France, duc de Berry

    see

       Fierens-Gevaert. Les Tres Belles Heures
         De Jean De France . . . .

Jenks, Tudor Storrs. (1857-1922)   #1215

A. L. S. 2 pages (25.7 x 20.4 cm.), New York, May 16, 1887, to William Fayal Clarke, concerning revisions in "The Pigmy Fleet," with original pen and ink drawing.

Jenks, Tudor Storrs. (1857-1952)   #1216

A. L. S. 4 pages (25.7 x 20.5 cm.), New York, October 5, 1887, to William Fayal Clarke, concerning inheritance law and land economics, interspersed with original and humorous pen and ink sketches.

Jess, Zachariah, Compiler   #1220

The American Tutor's Assistant, Improved: or a compendious system of decimal, practical arithmetic...Containing also a course of book keeping, by single entry. Stereotyped by D. & G. Bruce, New York. Philadelphia: Printed and published by M'Carty & Davis, [June 3] 1821.

Coll: 12°: A-S⁶ 108 leaves (17.4 X 10.7cm) Pp. [1-5] 6-188. [i] ii, 1-10 [11] 1-10 [11][i] 1-3

Anon (Julie Gouraud? c.1830-)   #1221

Les Jeux De La Poupée Conversations D'une Petite Fille Avec Sa Poupée. Melées de contes, fables et historiettes. Illustres de gravures. Paris: Amédée Bédelet Editeur, Rue Des Grands-Augustins, 20, n.d.

Coll: 12°. 1-6, 7⁴ 40 leaves (18 x 11.9cm) Pp. [1-5] 6-8 [9] 10-13 [14] 15-16 [17] 18-20 [21] 22-27 [28] 29-30 [31] 32 [33] 34-42 [43] 44 [45] 46-50 [51] 52-58 [59] 60-60 .

Plates: Frontispiece +7 color engravings.

Notes: "Lectures Illustrees" series.

Jewett, Sarah Orne   1849-1909   #1222

Betty Leicester: a story for girls. Boston and New York: Houghton, Mifflin and Company, 1890. Pp. [x, 1] -287, [288-290].

Notes: First ed. PS 2132.B4 1890. 4-16142. 1904.70

John-The-Giant-Killer, Esq.

    see

       Newbery, John. Food for the Mind . . . .
         1759.

[Johnson, Richard].   #1228

False Alarms; or, the Mischievous Doctrine of Ghosts and Apparitions, of Spectres and Hobgoblin, Exploded. Philadelphia:Printed for Benjamin Johnson, No. 31 High-Street, and Jacob Johnson, No. 147 High-Street, 1802.

Coll: 16°: A¹⁶ A2, A3, A4 signed 16 leaves (12.7 X 10.1cm) Pp. [1-3] 4-31 [32]

Plates: Frontispiece engraving by J[ames] Akin.

Binding: Original marbled wrappers

Notes: Welch #613.1

[Johnson, Richard].   #1229

The Picture Exhibition; Containing the original drawings of Eighteen Disciples, to which are added moral and historical explanations. Published under the inspection of Mr. Peter Paul Rubens, Professor of Polite Arts. Worcester, Mass.: Printed by Isaiah Thomas...,1788.

Coll: 32°: A⁷ B-G⁸ H⁷ 62 leaves (10.2 X 6.4cm) Pp. [i-iii] iv-viii [9] 10-112 [113-124]

Illus: 18 woodcuts in text

Binding: Silver wrappers

Notes: H₂ᴿ-H₅ᴿ contain advertisements, H₅ᵛ-H₇ᵛ blank. On inside rear cover "S-11-9-42IL"/"See also 11-16-42L" Welch #627, Rosenbach (# 134

1230

[Johnson, Richard] 1573-1659

The Illustrious and Renown'd History of the Seven Famous Champions of Christendom. In Three Parts. London: Printed for T. Norris and A. Bettesworth, n.d. [1719?].

Coll: 12⁰ A-G¹² 84 leaves (13.9 x 8.3cm) Pp. [1]-162, +[6]

Plates: 47 woodcuts in text.

Notes: G10: "A Catalogue of Books, Printed by Tho. Norris . . . Just Publish'd . . . ."

1231

[Johnson, Richard,] 1734-1793 The Rev. Mr. Cooper (pseud)

The History of France, from the earliest period to the present time. . . . Embellished with copper-plate cuts. Designed for the use of young ladies and gentlemen. London: Printed for E. Newbery, MDCCLXXXVI.

Coll: 12⁰ π⁴ a⁶ b² B⁴ C-U⁶ X² 126 leaves (14.2 x 8.4cm) Pp. [8] xv [xvi, 1] 226.

Plates: Front +5

(Cont'd)

The History of France . . . (Cont'd)

Binding: Full calf

Notes: Roscoe # 83 (1)

1232

[Johnson, Richard] The Rev. Mr. Cooper (pseud) 1734-1793

The History of South America. Containing the discoveries of Columbus, the conquest of Mexico and Peru, and other transactions of the Spaniards in the New World. By the Rev. Mr. Cooper. London: Printed for E. Newbery, 1789.

Coll: 12⁰ A-P⁶ 90 leaves (13.5 x 8.1cm) Pp. [xii,] 1-168.

Plates: Front +3

Binding: Marbled boards. Green vellum spine.

(cont'd)

The History of South America. (Cont'd)

Notes: Bookplate of Percival Merritt. Roscoe # 172

1233

[Johnson, Richard] 1734-1793 The Rev. Mr. Cooper (pseud)

Letters between Master Tommy and Miss Nancy Goodwill; Containing the History of their Holiday Amusements. Embellished with Cuts. The Third Edition, corrected. Printed for T. Carnan and F. Newbery, Junior, 1776.

Coll: 12⁰ A-F⁶ G¹² 48 leaves (11.2 x 7.5cm) Pp. iv +92.

Plates: 15 cuts in text.

(cont'd)

Letters between Master Tommy . . . . (Cont'd)

Binding: Dutch floral boards

Notes: Bookplate of Percival Merritt. Roscoe # 214 (2).

1234

[Johnson, Richard] 1734-1793 The Rev. Mr. Cooper (pseud)

The Little Female Orators; or, Nine Evenings Entertainment. With Observations. Embellished with Cuts. London: Printed for T. Carnan, 1770.

Coll: 12⁰ [A]² B-I⁶ K⁴ 54 leaves (10.9x7.5cm) Pp. [iv] 1-104.

Notes: Bookplate of Percival Merritt. Roscoe #222 (1).

1235

J[ohnson], R[ichard] ,ed. The Rev. Mr. Cooper (pseud) 1734-1793

The Little Moralists; or the history of Amintor and Florella, the pretty little shepherd and shepherdess of the vale of Evesham. Embellished with cuts. London: Printed [by J. Crowder and E. Hemsted] for J. Harris, 1802.

Coll: 32⁰ A-E⁸ 48 leaves (9.8 x 6.2cm) Pp. [1, 2-7] 8-81 [82] 83-89 [90] 91-95 [96]

Illus: Front +12 woodcuts

(cont'd)

The Little Moralists . . . . (Cont'd)

Binding: Pink wrappers. Initial and final pages as paste-down endpapers

Notes: Bookplate of Percival Merritt

[Johnson, Richard] The Rev. Mr. Cooper (pseud) #1236
1734-1793
Poetical Blossoms, being a selection of short poems,
intended for young people to repeat from memory. By
The Rev. Mr. Cooper. London: Printed for E. Newbery,
1793.

Coll: 12° [A²] B-F⁶ G⁴ 90 leaves (11.7 x 7.8cm) iv,
1-76 pp.

Plates: Engraved frontispiece

Notes: Bookplate of Percival Merritt. Roscoe # 297

[Johnson, Richard] The Rev. Mr. Cooper (pseud) #1237
1734-1793
The Toy Shop; or, Sentimental Preceptor. Containing
some choice trifles, for the instruction and amusement of every little miss and master. Embellished
with cuts. London: Printed for E. Newbery, n.d.
[ca 1788].

Coll: 16° A-H⁸ 64 leaves (11.1 x 7.3cm) 127+[1] pp.

Illus: 13 woodcuts in text

Notes: McKell copy wanting A1 (Frontispiece?). H5-H8:
(cont'd)

The Toy Shop   (Cont'd)

advertisements for E. Newbery. H8ᵛ: pasted to
back cover as endpaper. Bookplate of Percival
Merritt. Roscoe # 357 (2)

Johnson, Richard (The Rev. J. Cooper), trans. & ed.

see under

Berquin, Arnaud. The Blossoms of
Morality. J. Harris and Son, 1821.
The Looking Glass for the Mind.
John Harris, 1825.

Johnson, Rossiter   1840-1931 #1238

Phaeton Rogers: a novel of boy life. [Illustrated
by I.W. Taber (with others)]. New York: Charles
Scribner's Sons, 1881. Pp. [iii-viii, 1] 2-344.

Plates: Frontispiece +10+many illustrations.

Notes: Bound in at end: adverts, pp. [1-16]. First
edition. McKell copy has marble endpapers
rather than yellow, as described in Blanck's
Peter Parley to Penrod, p. 60.

Jones, Mrs. Elizabeth C   #1240

Infantine Ditties. By Mrs. Elizabeth C. Jones, author
of 'Fugitive Poems,' &c., &c. Providence: Cory,
Marshall, and Hammond, 1830.

Coll: 12° 1¹² 12 leaves (15.7 x 9.8cm) Pp. [1-2,]
3-24.

Illus: Title page +4 hand colored engravings

Binding: Yellow wrappers

Notes: McKell # G7-23-   43-B

Jones, Lynds E [ugene]   1853-1902 #1241

Out-Door Sports for Boys (and Girls). Edited by Lynds
E. Jones. Copiously illustrated. New York, London,
Glasgow and Manchester: George Routledge and Sons,
Limited. [Copyrighted 1890 by Joseph L. Blamire].
Pp. [1-2, i-iii] iv, [1] 2-143 [144].

Illus: Many by various illustrators.

Jones, Manley H   , comp. #1242

Christmas is Coming. Selected by Manley H. Jones.
Illustrated by Charlotte Becker. Boston: [Published
by] Houghton Mifflin Co. [Printed by] Riverside
Press, Cambridge, 1939. Pp. [1-32].

Illus: Cuts by Becker

Jonny Newcome, in the Navy . . . . Turner and
Fischer, n.d.

see under

Turner and Fischer-Publishers of every
variety of colored toy books.

Jordan, David Starr   1851-1931 #1243

Eric's Book of Beasts. Done in water-colors and
accompanied with appropriate jingles by David
Starr Jordan. Interpreted in black and white by
Shimanda Sekko. San Francisco: Paul Elder and
Company, [1912]. Pp. [i-xii, 1] 2-115 [116].

Plates: Frontispiece +cuts.

Joseph and His Brethren

see

Die Geschichte Josephs und seiner Bruder.
Harrisburg, Pa.

The History of Joseph and His Brethren.
New Haven, 1821.

The Juvenile Miscellany   (Cont'd)

Vol IV:
Coll: 12° $1-27^{6}$ 162 leaves (14 x 8.8cm) Pp. [1-3] 4-324.

Plates: 3 frontispieces + several cuts

Notes: 3 numbers in one volume.

Anon.   # 1245

Julia Graham, or the Effects of Pride. A Tale for the Young. Philadelphia: Published by Henry Perkins; Boston: Perkins and Marvin, 1834.

Coll: 12°: π^{2} A-F^{6} G^{1} 39 leaves (14.5 X 8.6cm) Pp. [1-5] 6-78

Notes: Stamp of E.G. Sprague.

Anon.   # 1249

The Juvenile National Calendar or a Familiar Description of the U.S. Government. Baltimore: Published by Fielding Lucas Jr..., Philadelphia: Ash & Mason, n.d.

Coll: 12°: [1^{12}] 12 leaves (17.45 X 11.1cm) ff[1] 2-12

Illus: Blank facing pages alternate with facing pages containing text and hand tinted engravings

Binding: Tan conjugate sheets pasted onto paper boards form cover title page and rear advertisements for Fielding Lucas, Jr. Publisher.

Anon.   #1246

The Juvenile Miscellany. Boston: Printed and published by John Putnam. n.d.
Vol. I, 1826:
Coll: 12°: $1-9^{6}$ 54 leaves (14.2 X 8.5$^{cm.}$) Pp. [i-iv] [5]6-108

Plates: Frontispiece + 2 plates

Notes: Vols. 1 and 4 bound together

Anon.   # 1250

Juvenile Trials for Robbing Orchards, Telling Fibs, and Other offences. Philadelphia: Published by Benjamin Johnson, No. 22, North Second Street, 1814.

Coll: 16°: A-C^{16} 48 leaves (13 X 9.7cm) Pp. [i-iv, 5] 6-95 [96]

Illus: 3 hand-colored cuts

Anon.   # 1247

The Juvenile Miscellany. Boston: Printed and published by John Putnam. n.d.
Vol. IV, New Series, 1830:
Coll: 12°: $1-9^{6}$ 54 leaves (14.2 X 8.5$^{cm.}$) Pp. [1-3] 4-108

Plates: Frontispiece and woodcuts.

Notes: Vols. 1 and 4 bound together

[Kaler], James Otis   1848-1912   # 1251

Toby Tyler; or ten weeks with a circus. Illustrated [by William Allen Rogers]. New York: Harper & Brothers, 1881. Pp. [viii, 9] -265, [1] b; advert.

Plates: Frontispiece + 20. Most plates signed "W.A. Rogers," or "Rogers."

Notes: First ed. McKell copy has "Ten weeks with a circus" lettered in white on a black field, rather than lettered in red on a black field, as noted by Blanck, p. 59.

Anon   # 1248

The Juvenile Miscellany. New Series. Vols. I, IV. Boston: Press of Putnam and Hunt. 1828, 1830.

Vol I:
Coll: 12° $1-27^{6}$ 162 leaves (13.7 x 8.6cm) Pp. [1-3] 4-323 [324].

Plates: 2 frontispieces + several cuts

Notes: 3 numbers in one volume. McKell copy lacks Pp. 219-226, 231-238, 243-250. Signings are irregular.   (cont'd)

KAY, R. The New Preceptor, or Young Lady's & Gentleman's True Instructor in the Rudiments of the English Tongue. Containing Rules for Pronunciation . . . and adorned with Emblematical Cuts . . . . Newcastle: Printed by and for M. Angus & Sons . . . and for W. Charnley, 1801.   # 1252

Coll.: 12°: A-H6I^{4} 52 leaves (16.9 X 9.2cm). [5] vi-vii [2] 10-104.

Illustrations: 8 cuts in text.

In the McKell copy, conjugate leaves H3, [H4] (pp. 89-92) were in reverse order in the forme.

#1253

Keach, B[enjamin].   1640-1704

War with the Devil: or the Young Man's Conflict with
the Powers of Darkness . . . . 22nd ed. London:
Printed for E. Johnston in Ludgate Street, 1776.

Coll: 12⁰ A-F¹² Q⁶ 78 leaves (14.9 x 8.5cm) Pp. vi +
156.

Plates: 15 woodcuts in text.

#1259

Kellogg, Rev. Elijah   1813-1901

Lion Ben of Elm Island. Elm Island Stories [series].
Boston: Lee and Shepard, Publishers; New York:
Lee, Shepard & Dillingham, 1871. Pp. [1-4] 5-265;
[1-6, adverts bound in at end.]

Plates: Frontispiece, title page +2.

#1255

Kellogg, Rev. Elijah   1813-1901

The Ark of Elm Island. Elm Island Stories [series].
Boston: Lee & Shepard, 1869. Pp. [1-8] 9-288.

Plates: Frontispiece +3. (Plate facing p. 81
        signed "Harley.")

Notes: First ed.

#1260

Kellogg, Rev. Elijah   1813-1901

The Young Ship-Builders of Elm Island. Elm Island
Stories [series]. Boston: Lee and Shepard, 1870.
Pp. [1] 2-304.

Plates: Frontispiece +1.

Notes: First edition ?

#1256

Kellogg, Rev. Elijah   1813-1901

Boy Farmers of Elm Island. Elm Island Stories
[series]. Boston: Lee and Shepard, 1870. Pp. [1]
2-300; [1-4, adverts bound in at end.]

Plates: Frontispiece, title page +2.

#1261

[Kendall, Edward Augustus]   1776?-1842

Keeper's Travels in Search of His Master. London:
Printed for E. Newbery, 1798.

Coll: 12⁰ Aᵇ (A1+X3) B-Qᵇ 99 leaves (13.5 x
      8.3cm) Pp. viii [1] 2-190.

Plates: Engraved frontispiece

Binding: Marbled boards, green vellum spine.
Notes: Bookplate of Percival Merritt. Roscoe # 20b(1)

#1257

Kellogg, Elijah [Rev.]   1813-1901

Burying the Hatchet; or, the young brave of the
Delawares. Illustrated. The Forest Glen Series.
Boston: Lee and Shepard Publishers; New York:
Charles T. Dillingham, 1879. Pp. [1] 2-336.

Plates: Frontispiece, title page +2.

#1262

[Kendall, Edward Augustus]. 1776?-1842

Keeper's Travels in search of His Master. Philadelphia:
Published by James Thackara. R. Carr, Printer, 1801.

Coll: Sm 8⁰: A¹⁰ (A+X, A4+A5) B⁹ (B4+B5) C⁹ (C4+C5) D⁹ (D4+
      D5) E⁹ (E4+E5) F⁹ F4+F5) G⁹ (G4+G5) H⁸ $5 ('F6'
      signed F4-G5) 72 leaves (13.9 X 8.6cm) Pp. [1-ii,
      IX] X [iii] iv-viii [1] 2-130 [131-134]

Plates: Frontispiece

Contents: Blank H7-H8ᵛ

Notes: Vertical Chains. Pp. [ix], x = table of contents
       placed after P. ii. Welch # 663.2

#1258

Kellogg, Rev. Elijah   1813-1901

Charlie Bell, the waif of Elm Island. Elm Island
Stories [series]. Boston: Lee and Shepard, 1869.
Pp. [1] 2-325; [1-6, adverts bound in at end.]

Plates: Frontispiece, title page +2.

#1263

[Kerer, Johannes]   1430 ? -1507

Statuta Collegii Sapientiae. Freiburg, Breisgan,
1497. Complete Facsimile Edition. With 80
miniatures in full color reproduction. Jan Thorbecke Verlag Lindau & Konstanz/1957. Pp. [1-4 (an
advertising pamphlet laid in]; Ff. 54.

Notes: Translation accompanies Facsimile Edition
       in separate volume.

[Kerer, Johannes]   1430 ? - 1507   # 1264

Statuta Collegii Sapientiae: The Statutes of the
Collegium Sapientiae in Freiburg University,
Freiburg, Breisgan, 1497. Facsimile Edition.
Introduced and Edited by Joseph Hermann Beckmann.
Jan Thorbecke Verlag Lindau & Konstanz, [1957].
Pp.[1] 2-95 [96].

Plates: 2
Notes: This is the translation of the Facsimile
Edition, which is a separate volume.

Anon.   # 1265

A Kid, A Kid or, The Jewish Origin of The Celebrated Legend The House that Jack Built. New York: Printed and
sold by Mahlon Day..., 1835.

Coll: Sm 8°: [1⁸] 8 leaves (12.6 X 7.7cm) Pp. [1-3] 4-16

Illus: Woodcuts

Binding: Printed gold wrappers

Notes: Rosenbach #797

Kidgell, John   fl. 1766   # 1266

Original Fables. Two Vols. in one. London: Printed
for James Robson, MDCCLXIII.

Coll: 8° [A]⁶ B-I⁸ (-I8), *I⁸,2χ²χ⁶K-U⁸ (-U8) 170 leaves
(15.5 x 9.4cm) Pp. [xii], 1-128,+[xviii+8] 129-
272 ("273-278" mispaginated 217-222),+ xx+[4].

Plates: 94 engravings

Notes: French text on verso, English on recto.

Kiefer, Monica   # 1267

American Children through Their Books, 1700-1835. Foreword by Dorothy Canfield Fisher. Philadelphia: University of Pennsylvania Press, 1948. [2d printing, June,
1948.] Pp. [i-xiv,1] 2-248 [249-250].

Plates: Frontispiece +5.

[Kilner, Mary Jane]   b. 1753 -   # 1268

The Adventures of a Pincushion. Designed Chiefly
For the Use of Young Ladies. London: Printed for
John Marshall and Co., [c. 1785].

Coll: 24° A-I⁶ K⁸ 62 leaves (11.8 x 7.9cm)
Pp. x, 11-124.
Illus: 37 cuts.
Notes: McKell : S-3-3-47B.

Kilner, Dorothy   -d. 1836   # 1270

[KILNER, DOROTHY]. The Life and Perambulation of a
Mouse, 2 vols. London: Printed and Sold by John
Marshall and Co., n.d.

(1). [Vol. I]: The Life and Perambulation of a Mouse.
Coll.: 24°: [A] -I⁶K1. 55 leaves (11 X 7.7 cm).
xii, 13-110 pp.

Plates: Frontispiece + 24 cuts in text.

[A3]: "To the Reader," signed M.P.[pseud.] and dated
April 13, 1783. On front loose end paper: "Fanny
Kilner to Harry Loft 1842."

Anon   # 1271

Die Kinderwelt. Eine Wochenschrift zur Belohnung für
Fleik und Artigkeit. Carlsruhe: A. Bielefeld. Lith.
v. Creuzbauer, & Hasper, Carlsruhe, 1846. [Nos. 1-
26, 1846; 1-26, 1847.]

Coll: 4° 104ff.

Plates: Title plate + 52 chromolithos

Notes: 1846 appears at top of title page.

Kilner -2-

(2). [Vol. II]: The Life and Perambulation of a
Mouse. Vol. II.

Coll.: 24°: A-H⁶I⁴. 52 leaves (12 X 7.7cm).
x, 11-99 + [5] pp.

Plates: Frontispiece + 22 cuts in text.

A3ᵛ: Dedication signed M.P. dated April 13, 1784.
I3ⁿ: "New Books for the Instruction and Amusement
of Children: Printed and Sold by J. Marshall . . . ."
On front loose end paper: "Fanny Kilner to Harry
Loft 1842." McKell :   S-3-3-47-B

Anon.   # 1272

Kindness to Animals; or, the Sin of Cruelty exposed and
rebuked. Revised by the Committee of Publication of The
American Sunday School Union. Philadelphia: American
Sunday-School Union, 1122 Chestnut Street, [Entered 1845].

Coll: 12°: 1-9⁶ 54 leaves Pp.[1-6] 7-106 [107] [108: blank]
(13.6 x 8.6cm)
Illus: Frontispiece plus numerous other engravings.

Kingston, William H[enry] G[iles] ed. 1814-1880 # 1276

Adventures of Dick Onslow Among the Redskins. A
book for boys. Illustrated. Boston: J. E. Tilton
and Company, 1867. Pp.[i]-[viii,] 9-336.

Plates: Illustrated title page + 4.

Kip, John D. W.   # *1277*

The Union Speller. An English spelling book; for the use of schools in the United States: in four parts. Washington, C. H., Ohio: Printed by Hamilton Robb, 1830.

Coll: 12°   A-Q⁶, Q⁶, I-R⁶   102 leaves   (17.1 x 10.3cm)   Pp. [i-ii] iii [iv] v-vi [7] 8-204.

Kipling, [Rudyard] . 1865-1936   # *1284*

The City of Dreadful Night / American Notes. New York & Boston: H. M. Caldwell Co., n.d., [1899?] pp. [3-6], 7-168, [5] -140 .

Kipling, Rudyard   1865-1936   # *1280*

The Brushwood Boy. Illustrated by Orson Lowell. New York: Doubleday and McClure Company, 1899. Pp. [viii], 1-119 [120].

Plates: Frontispiece †17 (all the illustrations are not plates).

Notes: First American Edition.

Kipling, Rudyard   1865-1936   # *1285*

How the Camel Got His Hump. Illustrated by F[eodor] [Stepanovich] Rojankovsky. Just So Stories. Garden City, New York: Garden City Publishing Company, Inc., [1942]. 28 pp.

Notes: See Stewart, James McG., Rudyard Kipling: A Bibliographical Catalogue, # 272 B.

Kipling, Rudyard   1865-1936   # *1281*

The Butterfly That Stamped. Illustrated by F[eodor] [Stepanovich] Rojankovsky. Just So Stories. Garden City, New York: Garden City Publishing Company, Inc., [1947]. 28 pp.

Notes: See Stewart, Jas. McG., Rudyard Kipling: A Bibliographical Catalogue, #272 G.

Kipling, Rudyard   1865-1936   # *1286*

How the Leopard Got His Spots. Illustrated by F[eodor] [Stepanovich] Rojankovsky. Just So Stories. Garden City, New York: Garden City Publishing Company, Inc., [1942].

Notes: See Stewart, Jas. McG., Rudyard Kipling: A Bibliographical Catalogue, #272 A.

Kipling, Rudyard   1865-1936   # *1282*

Captains Courageous: a story of the grand banks. Illustrated. New York: The Century Co., 1897. [x]+233 pp.

Plates: Frontispiece +20.

Notes: First American edition.

Kipling, Rudyard   1865-1936   # *1287*

How the Rhinoceros Got His Skin. Illustrated by F[eodor] [Stepanovich] Rojankovsky. Just So Stories. Garden City, New York: Garden City Publishing Company, Inc., [1942]. 28 pp.

Notes: See Stewart, James McG., Rudyard Kipling: A Bibliographical Catalogue, # 272 D.

Kipling, Rudyard.   *(1865 - 1936)*   # *1283*

'Captains Courageous.' A Story of the Grand Banks. With Illustrations by I. W. Taber. London: Macmillan and Co., Limited; New York: The Macmillan Company, 1897. All rights reserved. [Copyright 1896, 1897 by Rudyard Kipling].

Coll: 8°   pp. viii-[1] 2-245 [246].

Illus: 22.

Notes: First English Edition. See #163 of Stewart, James Mc G. Rudyard Kipling: a Bibliographical Catalogue, ed. A. W. Yeats. Toronto, 1959.

Kipling, Rudyard   1865-1936   # *1288*

Just So Stories For Little Children. By Rudyard Kipling. Illustrated by the Author. London: Macmillan and Co., Limited, 1902. Pp. [1-iv, 1] 2-249 [250].

Illus: 22 full-page, printed on one side of leaf, numerous smaller illustrations and decorations.

Notes: First edition. Leaves signed B-R. See Jas. McG. Stewart, #260*. Bookplate of Efrem Zimbalist. McKell Nos. S-4-28-491; 4-28-49-3.

#1289

Kipling, Rudyard   1865-1939

Just So Stories for Little Children. Illustrated
by Rudyard Kipling. London: Macmillan and Co.,
Limited, 1902. Pp. [vi, 1] 2-249 [252].

Plates: 22

Notes: First edition.

#1290

Kipling, Rudyard.   1865-1936

Kim. By Rudyard Kipling, author of "Plain Tales
from the Hills," "The Seven Seas," "The Jungle
Books," "The Days Work," "Stalky & Co.," etc.
New York: Doubleday, Page & Company, 1901. Pp.
[i-vi], 1-460.

Plates: Frontispiece +9 full-page in sepia by
        John Lockwood Kipling, author's father.
Binding: Untrimmed edges.
Notes: First American edition. See Jas. McG.
       Stewart, #253*. Rudyard Kipling copyright,
       1900, 1901.

#1291

Kipling, Rudyard   1865-1936

Kim. Illustrated by John Lockwood Kipling. London:
Macmillan and Co., Limited, 1901. Pp. [vi, 1] 2-413;
[1-2 of adverts bound in at end.]
Plates: Frontispiece +9, and signed "J.L.K."

Notes: First edition. Illustrated by the author's
       father.

#1292

Kipling, Rudyard   1865-1936

The Man who Would Be King. New York: Doubleday
and McClure Company, 1899. Pp. [1-iv] 1-136.

Notes: First edition. First Kipling book with
       elephant on binding.

#1293

Kipling, Rudyard   1865-1936

Puck of Pook's Hill. Illustrated by Arthur Rackham.
New York: Doubleday, Page & Co., 1906. Pp. [i-vi, 1]
277 [278]

Plates: Frontispiece +3.

Notes: First American Edition. See Stewart, James
       McG. Rudyard Kipling: A Bibliographical
       Catalogue, pp. 248-249. McKell copy lacks π
       4-5: list of illustrations, sub-title.

#1294

Kipling, Rudyard   1865-1936

Rewards and Fairies. [Illustrated by Frank Craig.]
Garden City, New York: Doubleday, Page & Company,
1910. Pp. [1] ii-xiv, [1] 2-344.

Plates: First American Edition. See Stewart, Jas.
        McG., Rudyard Kipling: A Bibliographical
        Catalogue, p. 269. McKell copy lacks gilt
        top.

#1295

Kipling, Rudyard   1865-1936

Rewards and Fairies. Illustrated by Frank Craig.
London: Macmillan and Co., Limited, 1910. Pp. [1]
ii-xii, [1] 2-338; [1-10 adverts, unopened].

Plates: 4

Notes: First edition.

#1296

Kipling, Rudyard   1865-1936

Rudyard Kipling's Verse: Inclusive Edition, 1885-
1918. [in 3 vols.] London: Hodder & Stoughton, 1919.
Vol I: 6 leaves, [318] pp., 1 leaf; vol II, 6 leaves,
[324] pp.; vol III, 6 leaves, [292] pp.

Notes: First edition.

#1297

Kipling, R[udyard]   1865-1936

Skazki (Fairy Tales). Perevod S Angliayskogo
(trans. from English by Korn Chukovskii). Stihi V
Perevude (Poems in translation by S. Marshak)
Risunki N Pereplet (Color illustrations by) V.
Kurdov. Children's Literature Publishers, Moscow,
Leningrad, 1936. Pp. [1-4,] 5-78 [79, 80] colophon.

Plates: Frontispiece +4; all color lithos; several
        other decorative illustrations.
Binding: Color, pictorial free and paste-down end-
                                        (cont'd)

Kipling. Skazki. 1936   (Cont'd)

    papers front and rear.

Notes: Not all pages paginated.

Kipling, Rudyard   1865-1936   #1298

Stalky & Co. London: Macmillan and Co., Limited,
1899. Pp. [xii, 1] 2-272; [1-2 of adverts bound in
at end.]

Notes: First edition.

Kirkham, Samuel   #1299

English Grammar in Familiar Lectures, Accompanied by a
Compendium; embracing a new order of parsing, a new
system of punctuation, exercises in false syntax, and
a system of philosophical grammar in notes: to which
are added an appendix, and a key to the exercises designed for the use of schools and private learners.
Last edition, enlarged and improved. Cincinnati:
Published by Morgan and Sanxay, 1835. New York:
Stereotyped Wm. Hager & Co.

Coll: 12°: 1-19⁶ 114 leaves (17 x 10.1cm) Pp. [1-3]
4-228.

Anon.   #1300

Klapptibel für Artige Kinder. No. 4. Neu
Ruppin bei Oehmigke & Reimschneider. [ca 1820].

Coll: 12°: [1² (1·1-1·2), 2-3⁴, 4¹ (4¹=1·3)];
11 leaves (12.5 x 7.5 cm.); ff. 11.

Illus: 6 pages of plates, hand colored.

Binding: Blue pictorial boards.

Notes: 1·1 pasted to 1·2.
       Printed on one side of leaf only.
       Title page pasted to outer board.

Anon.   #1301

Kleine Biblische Historien aus dem Ulten und Neuen Testament. Mit vielen bunten bildern geziert. Harrisburg, Pa:
Gedruckt und zu haben bey G.S. Peters. n.d.

Coll: 12°: 1¹⁸ 18 leaves (14.5 x 8.8cm) ff. 18.

Illus: 18 hand color engravings

Binding: Orange wrappers

Notes: McKell #S-1-6-45-B

Anon.   #1302

Kleine Erzählungen über Ein Buch mit Kupfern; oder leichte
Geschichte für Kinder. Philadelphia: [Printed by Jacob
Meyer] for Johnson and Warner, 1809.

Coll: 12°: A-C³ D⁴ [E³](conjugate with C³) [F³](conjugate
with B³) [G³] (conjugate with A³) one gathering of
22 leaves (13.9 X 8.75cm). Ff. 1-44.

Illus: Woodcuts (19);

Binding: Marbled boards; paste-down endpapers are conjugate.

Notes: Evans #17875, Rosenbach #395

Anon.   #1302

Kleines Bilder Cabinet für Erlernung der Vier
Sprachen. I. Deutsch, II. Lateinisch, III.
Franczosisch und IV. Italianisch. Cum
Privileg: Sacrae Caes: Mai Augsburgh Verlege
Bey Martin Engelbrecht.

Coll: 8°; [1 (1.1, 1·2)-51²], 102 leaves; ff.
102.

Illus: 100 colored numbered engraved plates
       plus title page and frontispiece (1·1=
       frontispiece; 1·2=title page).

(cont'd)

Anon. Kleines Bilder Cabinet. n.d. (cont'd)

Notes: A book of plates printed on one side of
       leaf only.
       McKell #S-6-17-57.

Anon.   #1306

The Knife Grinder's Budget of Pictures & Poetry, for
boys and girls. London: Printed [by W.Walker] for T. and
J. Allman, 1829.

Coll: 32°: 1¹⁴ unsigned 14 leaves (9 X 5.7cm·)
       Pp. [1-5]6-27[28]

Illus: Frontispiece + 23 wood cuts

Binding: Yellow pictorial wrappers. Initial and final
         leaves serve as paste down endpapers.

Notes: Info re. printer on p. 27

Knoll, Remedius   1306.1

Vierzig Kupferstiche | für die | Katholische Normal-
schule| der | Taubstummen, | der Kinder und anderer
Einfältigen, | zum | gründlichen sowohl als leichten
Unterricht | in dem Christenthume. | Augsburg:
Nicholas Doll, [c. 1770].

Coll: Title page + 40 hand-colored, engraved plates
      (28.4 x 41.3cm) of biblical christian scenes.
      Numbered tabs on each plate.

(cont'd)

Knoll, Remedius (cont'd)

Binding: Contemporary calf, plates on stubs, four
         to a gathering, with title in gold on
         spine.

#1307

Knox, Thomas W[allace] 1835-1896

The Boy Travellers in the Far East: adventures of two youths in a journey to Japan and China. Illustrated. New York: Harper & Brothers, Publishers, 1880. Pp.[7] 8-421 [422; 1-2 of adverts bound in at end.]

Plates: Frontispiece+illustrations

Notes: First edition.

#1308

Knox, Thomas W[allace] 1835-1896

The Lost Army. Illustrated. New York: The Merriam Company, n.d. [1894]. Pp.[i] ii-iv,[5] 6-296.

Plates: Frontispiece+9.

#1309

Knox, Thomas W[allace] 1835-1896

The Young Nimrods in North America: a book for boys. Illustrated. New York: Harper and Brothers, 1881. Pp.[3] 4-299 [300]; [1-4 of adverts bound in at end.]

Plates: Frontispiece+illustrations.

Notes: Probable first edition.

#1310

Anon

Knudsen's Method of Drawing Instruction for Schools. Third Year's Drawing Instruction. Containing forty shading patterns. To be used by the ordinary teacher. "Pictures are the End, but not the means of Drawing instruction." New York: Published by C. W. Knudsen, 1864.

Notes: Following cards missing: 8,9,21,25,27,28, 39,40.

#1315

Kpäylov, I.A.

Basni (Fables) V' IX Knigah' (In IX books) S' Biografieu, Napisannoiu P. A. Plethebaym. (Illus.) Vtorue Polnoe Izdanie (Third Complete Edition). Saint Petersburg: Printer of Textbooks, Institute, 1847.

Coll: 12° (b's) I-II ᵇ III⁹ 2-24ᵇ 158 leaves (19.1 x 12.3cm) Pp.[1-2, i] ii-xxviii ,[3] 4-279 [280, I] II-X
Plates: Frontispiece+24 hand-color copperplates.
(cont'd)

(Cont'd)

Kpäylov, I.A. Fables. 1847.

Binding: Stabbed and sewn. Free and paste down endpapers front and rear.

 # 1316

Kreitschwert, W. V.

Das Wunderbare Bilderbuch. Ein Festgeschenk voll komischer Sachen, zum Staunen, und Sachen für heitere Kinder. 10. Auflage. Nach Originalzeichnungen von W. V. Kreitschwert. Stuttgart: Julius Hoffmann. (K. Thienemann's Verlag), n.d.

Coll: Demy 4° A book of 13 plates.

Illus: Title+12 Chromolithos by Emil Mocholanz. Each illustration has a flap pasted to it which makes it moveable.

Notes: Bookplate of Rose County Historical Society.

 # 1317

Kuwagata Keisai (1761-1824)

Raikin Zui. Kansei, 1790.

Coll: 34 leaves (25.5 x 18.9cm) Accordion fold, printed on one side only.
Illus: 12 hand-colored, double-leaf woodcuts.
Binding: Blue paper wrappers.

 # 1318

LACEY, HENRY. The Principal Events in the Life of Moses, and in the journey of the Israelites from Egypt to Canaan. London: Printed [by Darton, Harvey, and Co.] for Darton, Harvey, and Darton, 1815.

Coll.: 12°: A-D¹²E⁶F² . 56 leaves (15.6 X 9.7cm). [1-3]4-112 pp.

Plates: Frontispiece + 14 (2 woodcuts on each plate). Two plates state publishing date of December 31, 1814.

 # 1319

Lack, David

Robin Redbreast. Oxford: At the Clarendon Press, 1950. Pp.[i]-[xii], 1-[224].

Illus: Vignette title page+3 plates+numerous full page illustrations + cuts

Lady a

see

Ali Baba and the Forty Thieves . . . .
By a Lady. Dean and Munday and A.K.
Newman Co.
Dorset, Catherine Ann (Turner), 1750-1817
Gilbert, Mrs. Ann (Taylor), 1782-1866
Pinchard, Mrs. Elisabeth. The Blind
Child, 1793.
Poems For Children. By a Lady. Mahlon
Day, 1837.

(cont'd)

Lady, a (Cont'd)

see

Taylor, Jane (1783-1824), and Ann Taylor
Gilbert (1782-1866). Little Ann and
Other Poems. Frederick Warne, n.d.

Wishing; or, the fisherman and his wife.
A juvenile poem by a Lady. A.K.
Newman & Co., n.d.

#1320

[AVON.] Lady Grimalkin's Concert and Supper. London:
Printed [by H. Bryer] for J. Harris . . . , 1809.

Coll.: 16°: A⁸. 8 leaves (11.7 X 9.1cm). [1-3]4-16
pp.

Plates: Engraved frontispiece (colored) + 7 colored
engravings.

S-1-11-43

#1321

[AVON.] The Lady's Cabinet Album. [Illustrated by
various artists.] New York: Published [by Elisha
Sands] for the Booksellers, [1832]. Pp. [iii]-xii
[1]-348.

Plates: Frontispiece, engraved title page + 20.

McKell copy lacks plate p. 145.

Lamb, Charles   1775-1834   #1327

Beauty and the Beast. By Charles Lamb with an
Introduction by Andrew Lang. London: Field & Tuer,
The Leadenhall Press, E.C. Simpkin, Marshall & Co.;
New York: Scribner & Welford, 1866 or after. Pp.
[1-2, i] ii-xxiv, [1-2, 3] 4-42; [1-2 of adverts]

Plates: Frontispiece +7; all are steel engravings.
Notes: Autograph letter of Lang inserted. Lang's
preface mentions Hazlitt's letters of Charles
Lamb, 1866. Pp. [1-2] are the title leaf.

Lamb, Charles   1775-1834   #1328

[LAMB, CHARLES.] Beauty and the Beast. London:
Printed by B. M'Millan, Bow Street, Covent Garden,
1811.

Coll.: 16°: B¹⁶. 16 leaves (12.2 X 10.2cm). 32 pp.

Plates: 8 colored engravings.

BMC mentions fold-out   music sheet which McKell
copy lacks.

[Lamb, Charles]. 1775-1834   #1329

Beauty and the Beast. New York: McLoughlin Bros.,
Publishers, entered 1856. [Electrotyped by Vincent
Dill, New York.]

Coll: Lge 8° 1⁸ 8 leaves Ff. 8.

Illus: 8 colored woodcuts by W. Momberger

Binding: Yellow wrappers: illus. by Momberger on front,
advertisement on back. Initial and final
pages pasted to wrappers.

Lamb, Charles]. 1775-1834   #1330

Beauty and the Beast. W. Momberger, illustrator. New York:
John McLoughlin, publisher, 1856.

Coll: Royal 8°: [1⁸] Pp [1, 2-15, 1b].

Illus: 8 hand-colored wood engravings

Binding: Green pictorial wrappers, advertisement on back,
initial and final pages as paste down end papers

[Lamb, Charles] (1775-1834)   #1331

The King and Queen of Hearts, with the rogueries of the
Knave who stole the Queen's pies. Illustrated in fifteen
elegant engravings. London: Printed for M.J. Godwin, &
1809.

Coll.: 16°: (2s) 1, 2-7², 8 (8=1²) 16 leaves (13.9 X
9.6cm.) Fr.[1]2-15, [1b].

Illus: 13 copper plate engravings. Printing on facing
pages (outer forme) alternating with blank facing pages.

Binding: Yellow wrappers; initial and final leaves serve
as paste down endpapers. Stabbed

Notes: Leaves 2-7²ᵛ have text and illustrations only on

LAMB

The King and Queen of Hearts   (Cont'd)

outside, i.e., have blank inner pages. Page [2] bears
"Printed for The Hodgkins Hanway Street, Nov' 18, 1805.
See also Lucas, Edward Verral, "Introduction" to Charles
Lamb's The King and Queen of Hearts, 1805. Facsimile
edition. McClure, Phillips, 1902.

1332

[Lamb, Charles and Mary;] 1775-1834, 1764-1847

Mrs. Leicester's School: Or, The History Of
Several Young Ladies, Related By Themselves. Second
Edition: London: Printed for M.J. Godwin, at the
Juvenile Library . . . , 1809. [Printed by Richard
Taylor & Co. Shoelane.]
Coll: 12° A² B-H¹² I⁶   92 leaves (19 x 11cm)
   Pp. [1-2, 1] ii-viii[9] 10-30 [31] 32-45 [46]
   47-84 [85] 86-93 [94] 95-109 [110] 111-129
   [130] 131-144 [145] 146-153 [154] 155-167
                                    (cont'd)

Lamb.   Mrs. Leicester's School . . . . (Cont'd)

   [168] 169-179, [180 (advertising)].

Plates: Frontispiece (W. Hopwood, del.; J. Hopwood,
       sculp.)

Notes: Bookplate of A. Edward Newton. Uncut.

[Lamb, Charles and Mary]. 1775-1834 1764-1847   # 1333

Poetry for Children, Entirely Original. By the author of
"Mrs Leicester's School." Boston: Published by West and
Richardson, and Edward Cotton. [E.G. House, Printer, Court-
Street], 1812.

Coll: 12°: (6s) A⁴ B-M⁶ N²   72 leaves (14.5 X 8.7cm)
   Pp. [i-iii] iv-vi [7] 8-31 [32] 33-144

Notes: Mrs Leicester's School is attributed to Charles and
   Mary Lamb. Vertical chains. McKell copy has top of
   P. 15 (16) torn. Rosenbach #462, Welch # 683.

Lamb, Harold [Albert]   1892-1962   #1334

The Crusades: iron men and saints. Illustrated.
Garden City, New York: Doubleday, Doran & Company,
Inc., 1930. Pp. [1]-[xiv], [1]-368.

Illus: Front.+title page+7+cuts.

Notes: First ed.

Lamb, Harold [Albert]   1892-1962   1335.1

The Crusades: the flame of Islam. Illustrated.
Garden City, New York: Doubleday, Doran & Company, Inc.,
1931. Pp. [1]-[xiv, 1] -490.

Illus: Front.+7+1 full page cut+4 maps.

Notes: First ed.

Lamb, Harold [Albert]   1892-1962   # 1335.2

The Crusades: the flame of Islam. Illustrated.
Garden City, New York: Doubleday, Doran & Company, Inc.,
1931. Pp.[1]-[xiv], 490.

Illus: Frontispiece+7+1 full page cut+4 maps.

Notes: First ed.

Lamb, Harold [Albert]   1892-1962   # 1336

Cyrus the Great. Garden City, N.Y.; Doubleday &
Company, Inc., 1960. Pp. [1-7], 8-[310].

Illus: 4 plates + 1 cut

Binding: Dust cover

Notes: First ed.

Lamb, Harold [Albert]   1892-1962   #1337

Durandal a crusader in the horde. Illustrated by
Allan McNab. New York: Junior Literary Guild,
1931. Pp.[xii] 1-370, [371-372].

Plates: Color Frontispiece +6+cuts (full-page cut,
   p. [371]).

Binding: Dust cover

Lamb, Harold [Albert]   1892-1962   # 1338

Gengis Khan: the emperor of all men. Illustrated.
New York: Robert M. McBride & Company, 1928. Pp. [1-12],
13-270.

Illus: Frontispiece+5+5 two-page plates+2 maps included in pagination.

Notes: Half title page signed "Harold Lamb, March 14,
   1933." First ed., 9th printing.

Lamb, Harold [Albert]   1892-1962   # 1339

Tamerlane: the Earth shaker. Illustrated. New York:
Robert M. McBride & Company, 1928. Pp. [1]-[xiv], 15-
340.

Illus: Front + 11 + 6 two-page plates

Binding: Dust cover

Notes: First ed.

 # 1340

Lamb, Harold [Albert]   1892-1962

Theodora and the Emperor: the drama of Justinian.
Garden City, N.Y.: Doubleday & Company, Inc., 1952.
Pp. [i-xiv], [1]-336.

Illus: One map +illustrated end papers.

Binding: Dust cover

Notes: First ed.

 # 1341

Lamb, Harold [Albert]   1892-1962

Suleiman the Magnificent: Sultan of the East. Garden
City, N.Y.: Doubleday & Company, Inc., 1951. Pp. [i]-
[xii], 1-370.

Illus: Frontispiece

Binding: Dust cover

Notes: First ed.

 # 1342

Lamb, Harold [Albert]   1892-1962

White Falcon. New York: Robert M. McBride & Company,
[1926]. Pp. [i-vi, 1] -244.

 # 1343

Landells, E[benezer] (1808-1860; and Alice
Landells (1841-1913)

The Girl's Own Toy-Maker, and Book of Recreation.
Illustrated . . . London: Griffith and Farran,
1860. Pp. [i] ii-viii, [1] 2-154, [1] 2-32 of
adverts .

Plates: Frontispiece + cuts.

 # 1344

Ländlich, Sittlich?-? Ein Bilderbuch für fröhliche
Kinderherzen mit b feinen Bildern in Farbendruck
nebst einem kurzen erzählenden Text. Dritte Auflage.
Eßlingen: Verlag von I. F. Schreiber, n.d.

Coll: 4° [1⁶] b leaves Ff 6

Illus: Title page +5 full-page colored engravings

Notes: A bust of a man's head in wood is mounted on the
back board. Each page and the front cover
board are cut so that the head fits through.
Final page paste(to board.

 # 1347

Lang, Andrew, ed.   1844-1912

The Blue Fairy Book. Illustrated by H[enry] J[ustice]
Ford and G[eorge] P[ercy]. Jacomb Hood. London
and New York: Longmans, Green, and Co., 1889. Pp.
xxii, [1] 2-390.

Plates: Frontispiece + 7.

Notes: First edition. # 71 of 113 copies.

 # 1348

Lang, Andrew, ed.   1844-1912

The Green Fairy Book. Illustrated by H[enry]
J[ustice] Ford. London and New York: Longmans,
Green, and Co., 1892. Pp. xiv [1] 2-366, [1].

Plates: Frontispiece +12.

Notes: Limited edition; # 148 of 150 numbered
copies. Uncut.

 # 1352

Lang, Andrew   1844-1912

The Princess Nobody; a tale of fairy land, by
Andrew Lang after the drawings by Richard Doyle.
Printed in colours by Edmund Evans. London:
Longmans, Green and Co., [c. 1887]. Pp. [1-9] 10-12
[13] 14-20 [21-22] 23-29 [30-33] 34-37 [38-40] 41-56.

Illus: Frontispiece +5 full-page (colored and not)
plus many smaller (colored and not). Reproductions of illustrations by Richard Doyle.

Binding: Free and paste-down endpapers front and
back, illustrated (white on black).

Notes: Richard Doyle (1824-1883)

 # 1353

Lang, Andrew, ed.   1844-1912

The Nursery Rhyme Book. Illustrated by L. Leslie
Brooke. London & New York: Frederick Warne & Co.,
Ltd., 1897. Pp. [1-7,] 8-288.

Plates: Frontispiece +8 +cuts.

 # 1354

Lang, Andrew, ed.   1844-1912

The Red Fairy Book. Illustrated by H[enry] J[ustice]
Ford and Lancelot Speed. London and New York:
Longmans, Green, and Co., 1890. Pp. xvi [1] 2-
367 [368].

Plates: Frontispiece +3.

Notes: Ltd. edition; # 68 of 113 numbered copies.
Uncut.

#1355

Lang, Andrew   1844-1912

Three Poets of French Bohemia. In The Bibelot,
XIV, No. 5 (May, 1908). Pp. [6] +165-192 + [1-4].

Binding: Blue wrappers.

Notes: Reprint of article which first appeared in
       Dark Blue (May, 1871).

Larcom, Lucy (1824-1893)

        see

        Our Young Folks; An Illustrated Magazine
            for Boys and Girls.

#1356

Lanier, Sidney, ed.   1842-1881

The Boy's Froissart: being Sir John Froissart's
Chronicles of adventure, battle and custom in
England, France, Spain, etc. Illustrated by Alfred
Kappes. New York: Charles Scribner's Sons, 1879.
Pp. xxxi, 422; [1-6] of adverts bound in at end.

Plates: Frontispiece +11.

Notes: First edition (see Blanck, p. 283).

#1361

Lathbury, Mary A[rtemesa]   1841-1913

Seven Little Maids; or the birthday week. Illustrated by Mary A[rtemesa] Lathbury. New York: R.
Worthington, 1884. Fr. 8.

Plates: Frontispiece +7.

Notes: First ed.

#1357

Lanier, Sidney, ed.   1842-1881

The Boy's King Arthur; being Sir Thomas Malory's
History of King Arthur and his knights of the
Round Table. Illustrated by Alfred Kappes. New
York: Charles Scribner's Sons, 1880. Pp. xlviii ,
403 [404; 1-4] of adverts.

Plates: Color frontispiece + 11 black and white.

Notes: First edition. See Blanck, p. 283.

Anon.   #1363

Law Among the Birds. In Three Parts. To which is Added
The Sparrow's Ball. Boston: William Crosby and Co., 1841.

Coll: 12°: [1-6⁶] 36 leaves (16.1 X 10.1cm) Pp. [1-11]
      12-67 [68-72]

Illus: Engravings by Devereux

Notes: [1⁶] consists of one conjugate fold [1₁,1₆] en-
       closing two separate folds [1₂, 1₃; and 1₄, 1₅].

#1358

Lanier, Sidney, ed.   1842-1881

The Boy's Mabinogion: being the earliest Welsh
tales of King Arthur in the famous Red Book of
Hergest. Illustrated by Alfred Fredericks. New
York: Charles Scribner's Sons, 1881. Pp. [xxiv],
361; [1-16] of adverts bound in at end.

Plates: Frontispiece +11.
Notes: First edition.

#1366

Lear, Edward   1812-1888

Nonsense Books. Illustrated. Boston: Roberts
Brothers, 1888. Pp. [i] ii-xxii, [23]-[80], [1]-[80],
[1-12], 1-70, [i] ii-ix [x, 1] 2-107 [108, 1] 2-84,
[1] 2-16 of adverts.

Plates: Portrait frontispiece + cuts.

#1359

Lanier, Sidney, ed.   1842-1881

The Boy's Percy; being old ballads of war, adventure and love from Bishop Thomas Percy's Reliques
of Ancient English Poetry. Illustrated by E[dmund].
B[irckhead]. Bensell. New York: Charles Scribner's
Sons, 1882. Pp. xxxii, 1-441 [442; 1-2] of adverts.

Plates: Frontispiece +49.

Notes: First edition. See Blanck, p. 283. Bishop
       Thomas Percy (1729-1811).

Lear, Edward   (1812-1888)

        see also

        Our Young Folks; An Illustrated Magazine
            for Boys and Girls. Vol. VI. (con-
            tains possible first printing of
            three poems: "The Daddy Long Legs
            and the Fly," "The Duck and the Kan-
            garoos," "The Owl and the Pussycat.")

Leary, Grandfather (pseud.) #1367

Aladdin; or the wonderful lamp. By Grandfather Leary.
With eight splendid illustrations on wood. Philadel-
phia: Published by Jas. L. Gihon, No. 98 Chestnut
Street, n.d. [1846?].

Coll: 4° [1⁸] 8 leaves Ff. 8

Illus: Title page:- small woodcut in color; 6 full
page woodcuts; 1 small woodcut, black on white.

Binding: Blue wrappers: front has small woodcut,

(cont'd)

Aladdin; or the wonderful lamp. (Cont'd)

back has advertisements. Front has the follow-
ing: "Lovechild, Lawrence. Aladdin; or, the
wonderful lamp. "Grandfather Lovechild's
Nursery Stories." By Lawrence Lovechild.
With nine splendid illustrations on wood by
Gilbert, Gihon, Brightly, Waitt, and Downes,
from original designs by Darley. Philadelphia:
Published by J. & J. L. Gihon, No. 98 Chestnut
Street. Entered . . . 1846, by George B.
Zieber. E. B. Mears, stereotyped.

Leighton, William (1833-1911); and Eliza Garrett, #1371
trans.

The History of Oliver and Arthur. Boston and New
York: Houghton, Mifflin and Company, 1903.
Pp. [i-xvi, I] II-CVI, [1-6].

Notes: McKell # C-4-15-49-B.

Le Row, Caroline B , comp. #1375

English as She is Taught. Genuine answers to examina-
tion questions in our public schools. Collected by
Caroline B. Le Row. New York: Cassell Publishing
Company [copyright 1887]. Pp. [x]+1-109 [110].

Illus: Decorative woodcuts.
Binding: Stiff, buff wrappers with flowers.

Leslie, Miss [Eliza], ed. 1787-1858 #1377

The Violet: a Christmas and New-Year's gift, or
birthday present, 1839. Philadelphia: E.L.
Carney & A. Hart [1838].

Coll: 8° 1⁴ 2-13⁸ 14⁴ 104 leaves (14.9 x 9.4cm)
Pp. [i-x, 17] 18-216.
Plates: Engraved frontispiece, title page 5: by J.
L. Pease, J & W.W. Watt, A. Lawson, W.
Ellis, Oscar A. Lawson, Ed. Eldridge, and
G.H. Cushman after R. Farrier, Tucker, W.
Kidd, Fanny Corbeau, Baume, E. Landseer.
Notes: Yearbook.

Letters Between Master Tommy and Miss Nancy Goodwill. . . . T. Carnan and F. Newbery, Jun.
1776.

see under

Johnson, Richard

#1385

THE LIBRARY FOR YOUTH. 8 vols. London: Printed
for J. Wallis, Ludgate Street, By J. Cundee, Ivy-
Lane, 1801.
1. Geography and Astronomy Familiarized, for Youth
of Both Sexes.
Coll.: 32° (in 8's): A-D⁸. 32 leaves (9.3 X 5.5
cm). 64 pp. Colored frontispiece + 1 plate.

2. Short and Easy Rules for Attaining a Knowledge
of English Grammar. To which are added A few Letters
for the Formation of Juvenile Correspondence.
Coll.: 32° (in 8's): A-D⁸. 32 leaves (9.3 X 5.5cm).

LIBRARY -2-

64 pp. Frontispiece.

3. A Compendium of Simple Arithmetic; in which the
First Rules of that pleasing Science are made known
to the Capacities of Youth.
Coll.: 32° (in 8's): A-D⁸. 32 leaves (9.3 X 5.4
cm). 64 pp. Frontispiece.

4. Mythology, or Fabulous Histories of the Heathen
Deities.
Coll.: 32° (in 8's): A-D⁸. 32 leaves (9.3 X 5.4
cm). 63 + 1 pp. Frontispiece.

LIBRARY -3-

5. The History of England, from the Conquest to
the Death of George II.
Coll.: 32° (in 8's): A-D⁸. 32 leaves (9.3 X 5.5
cm). 64 pp. Frontispiece + 30 colored cuts in
text.

6. Scripture History; or, a Brief Account of the
Old and New Testament.
Coll.: 32° (in 8's): A-D⁸. 32 leaves (9.3 X 5.5
cm). 32, [2]3-32 pp. (total of 64 pp.). Frontispiece.

LIBRARY -4-

7. A Familiar Introduction to Botany. Illustrated
with Copper-Plates.
Coll.: 32° (in 8's): A-D⁸. 32 leaves (9.3 X 5.9
cm). 63 + 1 pp. Colored frontispiece + 3 colored
plates.

8. British Heroism: or Biographical Memoirs of some of
those Renowned Commanders, Who have extended the
Glory of the British Nation to the remotest Parts
of the World.
Coll.: 32° (in 8's): A-D⁸. 32 leaves (9.3 X 5.3cm).
64 pp. Frontispiece.

All 8 vols. contain the bookplate of Percival Merritt.

Anon. #1387

The Life and Adventures of Alexander Selkirk, the Real Robinson Crusoe. A Narrative founded on facts. Stereotyped by J.A. James, Cincinnati. Cincinnati: Published by U.P. James, 1834.

Coll: 24°: [A¹²] B¹² C⁶ 30 leaves (12.8 X 7.2cm) Pp. [1-5] 6-60

Illus: Woodcut frontispiece + 10 woodcuts in text.

Notes: Alexander Selkirk, 1676-1721.

Anon. #1388

The Life and Death of Cock Robin. Albany, New York: Published at Pease's Great Variety Store, n.d.

Coll: 8°: A⁴ 4 leaves (18.6 X 11.5cm.) Pp. 2-3, 6-7, 10-11, 14-15.

Binding: Illustrated blue paper wrappers, advertisements for R.H. Pease on back.

Anon. #1389

The Life and Death of Cock Robin. "Marks' Edition." New York: Published by P.J. Cozans, n.d.

Coll: 8°: [1⁴] 4 leaves (19 X 11.3cm) Pp. 2-3, 6-7, 10-11, 14-15

Illus: 14 hand-colored cuts.

Binding: Illustrated blue wrappers, advertisements on back

Notes: Same plates as those used in earlier edition published in Albany, N.Y. by R.H. Pease

---

Anon. #1390

The Life and Death of Tom Thumb, the Little Giant. Together with some curious anecdotes respecting Grumbo, the Great Giant, King of the country of Eagles. With cuts by Bewick. York: Printed by T. Wilson and R. Spence, 1804.

Coll: 32°: A¹⁶ 16 leaves (10 X 6.7cm.) Pp. [1-4] 5-30 [31-32]

Illus: Frontispiece +11 woodcuts by Thomas Bewick ?

Binding: Gray-green wrappers

Notes: Thomas Bewick (1753-1828)

Anon. #1391

The Life and History of A, Apple Pie who was cut to pieces and eaten by twenty-six young ladies and gentlemen, with whom little folks ought to be acquainted. Embellished with sixteen elegant coloured engravings. London: Dean & Munday and A. K. Newman & Co., n.d.

Coll: 8°: 1¹⁶ 16 leaves (17.6 X 10.4cm.) Pp. [1-5] 6-7 [8-9] 10-11 [12-13] 14-15 [16-17] 18-19 [20-21] 22-23 [24-25] 26-27 [28-29] 30-31 [32]

Illus: Frontispiece + 15 (hand-colored wood engravings)

Binding: Green wrappers bound in.

Anon. #1392

The Life of Christopher Columbus, The Discoverer of America. American Juvenile Biography. Boston: Benjamin H. Greene, 1840.

Coll: 12°; π², 2π², 1-18⁶, 19², 20³(20:2 + 1); 117 leaves (15.5 x 9.8 cm.); pp. [1-iv] v-viii [9] 10-233 [234].

Illus: Front. + 1; wood engravings.

Anon. #1393

Life of George Wishart (of Pitarrow) the Martyr. Revised by the Committee of Publication. Philadelphia: Am.S.S.U. American Sunday School Union, No. 146 Chestnut Street, n.d.

Coll: 12°: A-G⁶, H² ("H1" signed G3) 44 leaves (14 X 9.1cm) Pp. [1-4, 5] 6-86 [87-88]

Illus: 2 wood engravings

Anon. #1394

The Life of Lord Nelson. Embellished with neat Wood-Engravings. Edinburgh: Printed [by and] for Oliver & Boyd, n.d.

Coll: 18°: [1¹⁶] 16 leaves (13.2 X 8.1cm.) Pp. [1-3] 4-31 [32]

Illus: Frontispiece + 6 wood engravings

Binding: Light blue wrappers: advertising on back. Initial and final pages as paste down endpapers

---

Anon. #1395

Lights of Education or, Mr. Hope and his family: A narrative for young persons. By a Lady. Baltimore: Published by E. J. Coale, J. Robinson, Printer, 1825.

Coll: 12°: A², B-P⁶, Q² 86 leaves (14.2 X 8.2cm) Pp. [i-iii] iv [9] 10-179 [180]

Illus: Frontispiece, woodcut

Lilly, Lambert

see

Goodrich, Samuel Griswold. The History of the Western States.

Linden, Auguste   #1400

Children's Trials; or, the little rope-dancers and
other tales. Translated . . . by Traver Mantle.
Boston: Crosby, Nichols & Co., 1857. Pp. [1-6 , 7]
-238, [239-240].

Plates: Frontispiece

Binding: Yellow endpapers.

The Little Girl's Diamond.   (Cont'd)

Contents: The Pleasures of Winter, 6-15
            The Happy Children, 16-27
            Fanny and Her Doll, 30-39
            The Story of Little Bridgett, 42-51
            The Apple Tree, 54-63
            The Roe and Its Child, 66-75
            Julia's Squirrell, 76-85 [86].

[ANON.]. The Lioness's Ball; Being a Companion to   #1403
the Lion's Masquerade. London: Printed [by H.
Reynell] for C. Chopple . . . ; R. Tabart . . . ;
J. Harris . . . ; Darton and Harvey . . . , [1807].

Coll.: 16° : A⁸. 8 leaves (11.5 X 9.2cm). [1-iv]
5-5, 8-16.

Plates: Engraved frontispiece + 5 [by W. Mulready].

A5 missigned A4.

Notes: Bound in with six others in Omnibus # 2, q.v.

Anon.   #1406

Little Hunchback. From the Arabian Nights Entertainments.
In three cantos. London: Printed [by H. Bryer] for J.
Harris, 1817.

Coll: 16°: A¹⁶ 16 leaves (12.2 X 10.2cm.)
       Pp. [1-3] 4-12 [13] 14-21 [22] 23-31 [32]

Plates: Engraved frontispiece plate +3, hand colored

Binding: Orig. buff pictorial wrappers, with advertise-
         ments on back.

Notes: Frontispiece is dated Dec. 22, 1817.

[ANON.]. The Little Curricle of Yellow Pasteboard;   #1404
with a Variety of Infantile Tales; intended to
engage the tender mind to a love os study, and the
first ideas of mortality. London: Printed for
J. Harris, 1803.

Coll.: 12° : A²B-C¹²D¹⁰. 36 leaves (15.8 X 9.5cm).
[4], 68 pp.

Plates: Frontispiece, engraved and hand-colored.
Text contains 50 hand-colored vignettes.

                                          -S-1-11-43-B

Anon   #1407

[Little Jacob, and How He Became Fat. "Little Slovenly
Peter Series." New York: McLoughlin Bros., Publishers,]
n.d.

Coll: 18° [14] 4 leaves (17.2 x 11.5cm) Pp. [1-8].

Illus: 8 colored engravings by Cogger.

Binding: Yellow wrappers; colored illustration on front,
          advert on back which indicates "large 18°."

Notes: Title information from wrapper; no title page.

The Little Female Orators. . . . T. Carnan, 1770.

        see under

        Johnson, Richard

Anon   #1408

Little Songs for Little Folks. Illustrated.
Boston: George F. Boure and Co., Publishers, n.d.
Pp. [1] [vii] 8-108.

Plates: Frontispiece +many full-page illustrations
        included in pagination.

Anon.   #1405

The Little Girl's Diamond. Cincinnati: Published by
Otto Onken, [entered 1852]. [Stereotyped by A. C. James,
16 Walnut St., Cincinnati.]

Coll: 16° 1-6 72 leaves   (12.8 x 10.1cm) Pp. [i-
      iv, 5] 6-15 18-27 30-39 42-51 54-63 66-85 86.

Plates: Front +title (on conjugate leaves) +5: all
        color engravings. Plates are laid in and take
        up the gaps in pagination. Front +title are
        included in pagination.

                                          (cont'd)

Anon.   #1409

Little Tommy's Sled Ride. "Mary Bell's Series." Cincinnati, Ohio: Peter G.Thompson, n.d.

Coll: 4°: [1⁴] 4 leaves

Illus: 4 full page colored engravings

Binding: Illustrated gray paper wrappers; front serves as
         a title page, back has advertisements. Text
         printed on insides of wrappers.

#1410

Anon

Little Will and Other Stories; in ten parts. Sunshine Series No. 1. Oakland, Cal.: Pacific Press Publishing Association, n.d. Pp. [i-iv], 1-16, 1-16, 1-16, 1-16, 1-15 [16], 1-16, 1-16, 1-16 1-15 [16], 1-16, [1-4 of adverts.]

Plates: Frontispiece + 5.

#1412

Anon.

The Lives of Richard Turpin, and William Nevison, two notorious highwaymen: Containing a particular account of all their adventures until their trial and execution at York. York: James Kendrew, Printer, Colliergate, n.d.

Coll: 12°: A¹² 12 leaves (18.95 X 10.5cm) Pp. [5-7] 8-28

Illus: Engraved frontispiece

Binding: Original green wrappers bound in.

Notes: Bookplate of Howard Pyle. Richard (Dick) Turpin, 1706-1739. William Nevison (-).

#1417

Les Livres de l'enfants du XVᵉ au XIXᵉ Siecle. Preface by Paul Gavault. 2 vols. Paris: Gumuchian and Cᶦᵉ, [Catalogue XIII] n.d.

Vol I: Texte
Pagination: [xxiv + 1] 2-446 [447-450].

Vol II: Planches
Pagination: 15 [16]

Plates: 336

#1420

Lofting, Hugh   1886-1947

Doctor Dolittle's Caravan. Illustrated by Hugh Lofting. New York: Fredk. A. Stokes Co., 1926. Pp. [i-xii] 1-342.

Plates: Frontispiece + illustrations

Notes: First ed.; the illustration, "There were real tears in the housekeeper's eyes," is on p. 102 rather than p. 112.

#1421

Anon

Logic Made Familiar and Easy: To Which Is Added a Compendious System of Metaphysics, or Ontology. Being the Fifth Volume of the Circle of the Sciences, &c. The Fourth Edition. London: Printed for T. Carnan and F. Newbery, Jun., 1777.

Coll: 32° A-T⁸ 152 leaves   (10 x 6.4cm) Pp. xi 264.

Notes: Bookplates of James Losh and Percival Merritt. Roscoe # 66(4).   BMC # 944ddd. 10.

#1422

[ANON.]. Logic Made familiar and easy to Young Gentlemen and Ladies. To which is added, A Compendious System of Metaphysics, or Ontology. Being the Fifth Volume of the Circle of the Sciences, &c. The Third Edition Corrected. London: Printed for Newbery and Carnan, 1769.

Coll.: 32° : A-T⁸. 152 leaves (9.2 X 6.3cm). [40] + 1-264 pp.

Binding: Blue boards, red leather spine.

Bookplate of Percival Merritt. Roscoe # 66(3a).

#1423

Löhr, J[ohann] A[ndreas] C[hristian] 1764-1823

Der Weinachtsabend in der Familie Thalberg. Für Kinder beschrieben von J. A. C. Lohr. Zweyte verbesserte Auflage: mit 15 Kupfern. Leipzig: bey Gerhard Fleischer dem Jüngern, n.d.

Coll: Oblong 4° π²,A-Q⁶,R⁴ 102 leaves Pp. [i] ii [iii] iv, [1] 2-199 [200].

Plates: Front + 14 hand-colored copper-plate engravings + title page engraving.

Der Weinachtsabend . . . . (Cont'd)

Notes: Title page is a plate pasted to π¹ʳ. McKell #s: S-7-13-40-B; S-7-:3-40-L

#1424

London, Jack   1876-1916

The Abysmal Brute. New York: The Century Co., 1913. Pp. [i-iv], 1-2] 3-169 [170].

Plates: Frontispiece engraving by Gordon Grant

#1425

London, Jack. (1876-1916)

A. L. S. one page (28.x 21.5 cm.), Piedmont, Calif., May 7, 1902, to the Editor of St. Nicholas Magazine. Cover letter for ms. of "The Cruise of the Dazzler," published in St. Nicholas in July, 1902: "Story enclosed herewith is a true incident in my own life. I have merely given it story form and here & there omitted unimportant details."

#1426

London, Jack   1876-1916

Before Adam. Illustrated by Charles Livingston
Bull. New York: The Macmillan Company; London:
Macmillan & Co., Ltd., 1907. Pp. [i] ii-vii [viii,]
1-242; [1-4 of adverts, unopened.]

Plates: Frontispiece +7 +2 maps +cuts.

#1427

London, Jack   1876-1916

Before Adam. With numerous illustrations by
Charles Livingston Bull. New York: The Macmillan
Company; London: Macmillan & Co., Ltd., 1907.
Pp. [i-vi] vii [viii-xii] 1-242 +4: adverts.

#1428

London, Jack   1876-1916

The Call of the Wild. Illustrated by Philip R.
Goodwin and Charles Livingston Bull. New York:
The Macmillan Co.; London: Macmillan and Co.,
Ltd., 1903. Pp. [1-8] 9-231 [232]; 1-2 of adverts .

Binding: First binding.

#1429

London, Jack   1876-1916

Children of the Frost. With illustrations by
Raphael M. Reay. New York: The Macmillan Co.,
1902. Pp. [1-iv] v [vi] vii [viii, 1-2] 3-261 [262]
+3: adverts.

#1430

London, Jack   1876-1916

The Cruise of the Dazzler. New York: The Century
Co., 1902. Pp. [1-iv] v-vii [viii, 1-2] 3-250.

#1431

London, Jack   1876-1916

The Cruise of the Dazzler. "St. Nicholas Books."
New York: The Century Co., 1902. Pp. [i] ii-vii [viii
-1] 2-250.

Plates: Frontispiece +5 signed "Burns."

Notes: First edition. BLANCK #11872

#1432

London, Jack   1876-1916

A Daughter of the Snows. With illustrations in
color by Frederick C. Yohn. Philadelphia: J. B.
Lippincott Co., 1902. Pp. [1-6] 7-334 +2: adverts.

#1433

London, Jack   1876-1916

The Faith of Men and Other Stories. New York: The
Macmillan Co.; London: Macmillan and Co., Ltd.,
1904. Pp. [1-iv] v [vi, 1-2] 3-286 +2: adverts.

#1434

London, Jack   1876-1916

The Game. With illustrations and decorations by
Henry Hutt and T.C. Lawrence. New York: The
Macmillan Co.; London: Macmillan and Co., Ltd.,
1905. Pp. [1-14] 15-182 +1-6 of adverts.

Notes: First state.

#1435

London, Jack   1876-1916

The God of His Fathers and Other Stories. New
York: McClure, Phillips and Co., 1901. Pp. [1-x]
1-299 [300].

 # 1436

London, Jack   1876-1916

Jerry of the Islands. New York: The Macmillan Co., 1917. Pp. [i-iv] v-ix [x] 1-337 [338] + 1-8 of adverts.

 # 1437

London, Jack   1876-1916

John Barleycorn. Illustrated by H.T. Dunn. New York: The Century Co., 1913. Pp. [i-vi, 1-2] 3-343 [344].

 # 1438

London, Jack   1876-1916

On the Makaloa Mat. New York: The Macmillan Co., 1919. Pp. [i-vi] 1-299 [300].

 # 1439

London, Jack   1876-1916

The Scarlet Plague. Illustrated by Gordon Grant. New York: The Macmillan Co., 1915. Pp. [1-8] 9 [10] 11-181, [182] + 1-6 of adverts.

 # 1440

London, Jack   1876-1916

Scorn of Women. New York: The Macmillan Co.; London: Macmillan and Co., Ltd., 1906. Pp. [i-iv] v [vi] vii [viii] ix-x [1-2] 3-256 + 1-3 of adverts.

Binding: First binding.

 # 1441

London, Jack   1876-1916

The Sea-Wolf. With illustrations by W.J. Aylward. New York: The Macmillan Co.; London: Macmillan and Co., Ltd., 1904. Pp. [i-vi] vii [viii] 1-366 + 1-3 of adverts.

 # 1442

London, Jack   1876-1916

The Son of the Wolf: tales of the far North. Boston and New York: Houghton Mifflin and Company, 1900. Pp. [i-viii, 1] 2-251 [252].

Plates: Frontispiece by L. M[aynard] Dixon '99 (?).

Binding: First binding.

 # 1443

London, Jack   1876-1916

South Sea Tales. New York: The Macmillan Co., 1911. Pp. [i-iv] v [vi, 1-2] 3-327 [328] + 1-8 of adverts.

Plates: Color frontispiece (by Anton Fischer).

 # 1444

London, Jack   1876-1916

The Strength of the Strong. New York: The Macmillan Co., 1914. Pp. [i-iv] v [vi-viii] 1-257 [258] + 1 of adverts.

Plates: Frontispiece by Spaenkuch.

Contents: "South of the Slot," "The Unparalleled Invasion," "The Enemy of All the World," "The Dream of Debs," "The Sea-Farmer," and "Samuel."

 # 1445

London, Jack   1876-1914

The Valley of the Moon. With frontispiece in color by George Harper. New York: The Macmillan Co., 1913. Pp. [i-iv, 1-2] 3-530 + 1-6 of adverts.

#1446

London, Jack   1876-1916

White Fang. New York: The Macmillan Co.; London:
Macmillan and Co., Ltd., 1906. Pp. [i-iv] v-vii
[viii-x, 1-2] 3-327 [328] + 1-4 of adverts.

Anon.   #1447

London Cries for Children. With twenty elegant wood cuts.
Philadelphia: Published by Johnson & Warner, No. 147,
Market Street. John Bouvier, Printer, 1810.

Coll: 12°: 1²⁰ 20 leaves (14.2 X 8.9cm) Pp. [1-5] 6-40

Illus: Several woodcuts

Binding: Pink wrappers

Notes: Vertical chains. Bookplate of Percival Merritt; +
       another copy (with Merritt bookplate). Rosenbach
       #421, Welch # 237.12

Anon.   #1448

The London Primer: or Mother's Spelling Book. London:
Printed [by Maurice] for Sir Richard Phillips and Co.,
n.d. [1820?]
Coll: 12°: A³⁶ 36 leaves (13.5 X 8.7cm.)
       Pp. [1-12] 13-50 [51-61] 62-64 [65] 66-72
Illus: Woodcut in title page + 66 cuts in text
Binding: Marbled boards, leather spine
        A1ᵛ: Advertisements

#1449

[ANON.]. London Scenes: in Easy Lessons for
Children. London: Printed for Darton and Harvey
. . . , 1837.

Coll.: 12° (2's): A⁸. 8 leaves (15.3 X 10cm).
Pp. [1] 2 [3] 4 [5] 6 [7] 8-10 [11] 12 [13] 14 [15] 16 pp.

Illustrations: 8 hand-colored wood engravings.

Binding: Lavender wrappers.

#1450.1

Longfellow, Henry Wadsworth   1807-1882

The Courtship of Miles Standish, and Other Poems.
Boston: Ticknor and Fields, 1858.

Coll: 8° (6's) 1-18⁶ 108 leaves (18.5 x 11.8cm)
       Pp.[1-7] 8-215 [216] ; [1]-[12] of adverts dated
       October 1858 bound in at end.
Notes: First edition, first issue. Obsolete
       signings present.

#1450.2

Longfellow, Henry Wadsworth   1807-1882

The Courtship of Miles Standish, and Other Poems.
Boston: Ticknor and Fields, 1859.

Coll: 8° (6's) [1]⁶ 2-18⁶ 108 leaves (18.3 x 11.8cm)
       Pp.[1-7] 8-215 [216 ; 1] 2-16 of adverts
       bound in at end.
Notes: First edition, second state. Dated 1859.

1454

[LONGUEVILLE, PETER]. The English Hermit; or, the
Adventures of Philip Quarll, who was lately dis-
covered by Mr. Dorrington, a Bristol Merchant,
upon an uninhabited Island; where he has lived
above fifty Years, without any human assistance,
still continues to reside, and will not come away.
Adorned with Cuts, and a Map of the Island. London:
Printed and Sold at No. 4 Aldermary Church Yard,
in Bow Lane [John Marshall and Co.], n.d. [ca. 1790?]

Coll.: 12° (sixes): [A⁶]B-I⁶. 54 leaves (11.7 X 7.7
cm). [1-6] 7-78 [79-82] 83-106 + [2] pp.

Illustrations: A2: Frontispiece (wood engraving),
map on C4ᵛ, and 24   cuts in text.

Longueville, Peter   Hermit -2-

I6: advertisements.

McKell corresp. # S-8-23-44-R.
See Osborne, p. 277 for authorship and date.

Lord's Prayer

    see under

       A Series of Easy Lessons on the Lord's
          Prayer. Hartford: Robinson, 1829.

Lorenz, E[dmund] S[imon]   1854-1942 #1455

Our Christmas Gifts. "Festal Days No. 25, September
1899." Issued every two months. A Christmas service
by E. S. Lorenz assisted by Ida Scott Taylor. Dayton,
Ohio: Lorenz & Co. Publishers, Copyright 1899. Pp.[1-
2] 3-15 [16].

Binding: Cream wrappers: illustrations on front,
        advertisement on back; initial and final pages
        pasted down.

Lossing, Benson J [ohn]   1813-1891   #1456

A Primary History of the United States for Schools
and Families. Illustrated with numerous engravings.
New York: Mason Brothers; Boston: Mason & Hamlin;
Philadelphia: J. Lippincott & Co.; Cincinnati: W.B.
Smith & Co., 1863. Pp.[1-5,]6 -223 [224.]

Plates: Frontispiece+cuts.

[Lothrop, Harriet Mulford (Stone)], Margaret Sidney,
pseud., 1844-1924.   #1457

Five Little Peppers and How They Grew. By Margaret
Sidney. Illustrated. Boston: D. Lothrop Company,
[1880]. Pp.[1-2] 3-410, [1-4 of adverts.]

Plates: Frontispiece+ 17.

Notes: First edition, later issue. See Blanck, Peter
Parley to Penrod, p. 54.

Lovechild, Grandfather

   i.e.

      Thomas Lovechild

         see

            Hale, Mrs. Sarah Jane, ed.,
            Spring Flowers, esp. notes.
               and
            Leary, Grandfather (pseud), Aladdin
            (esp. Notes)

Lovechild, Mrs. [Pseud of Lady Eleanor (Frere) Fenn]
1743-1813   #1459

The Infant's Friend. Part I. A spelling book. By
Mrs. Lovechild. London: Printed for E. Newbery, 1797.

Coll: 12° π, A₁⁶x,B-H⁶, I⁴ 54 leaves (13 x 8.5cm) Pp.
[xvi, 1-5] 6-92.

Plates: Woodcut frontispiece.

Notes: Bookplate of Percival Merritt. Roscoe # 117,
BMC # 12906.

Lovechild, Nurse

   see

      Tommy Thumb's Song-Book. Lumsden, 1814.

Lucas, E[dward] V[erral]   1868-1938   #1464

"Introduction" to Charles Lamb's The King and Queen
of Hearts, 1805. Facsimile edition. New York:
McClure, Phillips & Company, 1902. Pp.[i]-xv.

Notes: See also Lamb, Charles (1775-1834), The King
and Queen of Hearts. London: for M.J. Godwin, 1809. Cf. notes.

Anon.   # 1465

Lucy's Pet, and other Books for young children. Published
by the American Tract Society, [Ca. 1860].

Coll: 32°π⁹[1-8⁸]66 leaves (10.2 X 6.5cm) Pp.[i-iv, 1-3]
4-15[16], [1-3] 4-15 [16], [1-3] 4-7 [8] 9-15 [16],
[1-3] 4-15 [16], [1-3] 4-15 [16], [1-3] 4-15 [16],
[1-3] 4-15 [16], [1-3] 4-15 [16].

Illus: Numerous illustrations

Contents: [1] Lucy's Pet   [4] Under the Oak-Tree
          [2] The Little Samaritan [5] Ned and Joe
          [3] The Ewe-Lamb   [6] The Baby Brother

Anon.

Lucy's Pet, [Ca. 1860]

          [7] Patty's Garden
          [8] The Cat-Bird's Nest

Notes: Each story is set up with a title page. Each is a
gathering of 8, and each is paginated [1-3] 4-15
[16] (except for "The Ewe-Lamb"). Free and pasted
down end papers front and back.

Lummis, Charles F [letcher] (1859-1928)   #1466

A. L. S. one page (27.9 x 21.5 cm.), Piru,
Calif., June 29, 1923, to William Fayal Clarke,
concerning Mesa, Cañon & Pueblo and a story
"a la Mayne Reid" that he hopes to write.

1859-1928

[M., T]   #1468

A New Book of Old Ballads. Edinburgh: MDCCCXLIV
[1844, Laurie and Co., Printers].

Coll: 8° (8's) π4,1-5⁸ (unsigned) (17.4 x 10.2cm)
Pp. [i-iii] iv-vi [vii-viii, 1] 2-78 [79-80].

Illus: Woodcut on title page colored white.

Notes: Ed. limited to 60 copies. Preface inscr.: "T.
M. 3, London Street, November 1843." Colophon
p. [79]: "Antiquarian and Historical Bookseller
87, Princes Street, Edinburgh."

MacDonald, George   1824-1905   #*1471*

At the Back of the North Wind. Illustrated by
Arthur Hughes. New York: George Routledge & Sons,
1882. Pp. [iii] iv-viii, 1-378.

Illus: Cuts.

Mace, Jean   1815-1894   #*1472*

Grand-Papa's Arithmetic: a story of two little
apple merchants. New York: P.S. Wynkoop & Son,
1868. Pp. [i] ii-xi [xii, 13] 14-142; [1-2 adverts.]

[Mack,] Lizzie Lawson.   #*1473*
Mack, Robert Ellice.

Under the Mistletoe. New York: E. P. Dutton & Company, n.d. Pp. [1-5], 6-40.

Plates: Front +13 full-page color engravings+cuts.

Mack, Robert Ellice   #*1474*

All Around the Clock. Illustrated by Harriet M. Bennett. New York: E. P. Dutton & Company, n.d. Pp. [1-
6], 7-64.

Plates: Front + 21 full-page color engravings+cuts.

Magazines

   see

      The Children's Magazine. Vol II, 1830
      Goodrich, Samuel Griswold. Parley's
         Magazine for Children and Youth.
         Vol I, nos. 1-7, Mar. 16, 1833-June 8,
         1833.
         Parley's Magazine. Parts XVII-XX, Vol
         V, 1837?
      The Nursery

                                   (cont'd)

Magazines (Cont'd)

   see

      Our Young Folks; an illustrated magazine
         for boys and girls. No. 13 (Jan. 1866),
         No. 27 (Mar. 1867), No. 52 (April, 1869),
         and, Vol. VI, 1870
      The Strand Magazine.
      The Student and Schoolmate.
      Wisdom in Miniature.

Anon   #*1475*

Maja's Alphabet. With twenty-six illustrations.
Philadelphia: G. G. Henderson & Co., 1852.

Coll: 16° [1-4]⁸   32 leaves   (13.9 x 11.1cm) Pp.
        [1-64]

Notes: Printing on inner forme only. 4.4-4.8 (pp. [55-
        64: adverts]). Front free endpaper missing.

Maja's Alphabet

   see also

      Pleasure Book for Children . . . . and
         Maja's Alphabet. Cleveland, 1856.

Marcliffe, Theophilus

   i.e.,

      William Godwin (1756-1836), q.v. The
         Looking Glass. . . . London: 1805.

Anon   #*1484*

Marks' Edition: Adventures of Goody Two Shoes.
London: Published by J.L. Marks, 91 Long Lane
Smithfield, n.d.

Coll: 8°   1⁸   unsigned   8 leaves (18.4 x 11.2cm)
      Pp. [1] 2-3 [4-5] 6-7 [8-9] 10-11 [12-13] 14-
      15 [16].
Illus: 8 hand-colored woodcuts.
Binding: Lavender wrappers. Initial and final pages
         on paste-down endpapers. Advertising.
Notes: Title on p. 2 is "History of Goody Two Shoes."

Marks' Edition of Cock Robin

see under

Life and Death of Cock Robin.

Anon #1490

Marmaduke Multiply. New York and Boston: C. S. Francis and Company, [1859?]

Coll: 16° 1-6¹² Ff.[1-2] 3-71 [72]. (13.9 x 11.2cm)

Illus: Woodcuts

Binding: Buff printed wrappers.
Notes: Boston Reprint Co. 1860.

Anon. #1485

[Marks' Edition of Mother Hubbard and Her Dog. New York: Published by D.S. Cogans, n.d.]

Coll: 8°: [1⁴] 4 leaves Pp. [2] 3, 6-7, 10-11, 14-15 (19 x 11.3cm)
Illus: Hand colored engravings on each leaf

Binding: Blue wrappers. Decorations on front, advertisements on back.

Anon #1491

Marmaduke Multiply's Merry Method of Making Minor Mathematicians; or, the multiplication table, illustrated by sixty-nine appropriate hand-tinted engravings. London: J. Harris and Son, 1824.

Coll: 16° π¹, [1]-6⁴, 7⁵ (7.4+1), 8-17⁴ 70 leaves (12.8 x 10.3cm) Ff. 1 1-69.

Illus: On one side only, numbered.

Binding: Red and green marbled boards, red leather spine.

Notes: McKell # S-1-11-43.

Anon #1486

Marks' Edition: The Children in the Wood. Published by J.L. Marks, 91, Long Lane Smithfield, n.d.
Coll: 8° 1⁸ unsigned 8 leaves (17.4 x 10.4cm) Pp.[1-16].
Illustrations: 8 hand-colored wood engravings.
Binding: Pink wrappers. Initial and final pages on paste-down endpapers.
Notes: Bookplate of Percival Merritt. Title on p. [2] is "The History of the Children in the Wood."

Martin, William #1498

Peter Parley's Annual. A Christmas & New Year's Present for Young People. ed. William Martin. [Illustrated.] London: Darton & Co., 1860. Pp.[i] ii-viii,[1] 2-295 [296; 1] 2-32 of adverts+1 fold out advertisement.

Plates: Frontispiece + illustrated title page + 6 color plates.

Anon #1487

Marks' Edition: The Peahen At Home, or the Swan's Bridal Day. London: Published by J.L. Marks, 91 Long Lane Smithfield 1840? .
Coll: 8° 1⁸ 8 leaves (17.7 x 11.3cm) Pp.[1-16].
Illus: 8 hand-colored woodcuts.
Binding: Pink wrappers, initial and final pages on paste-down endpapers.

Martin, William

see

Goodrich, Samuel Griswold. The Travels, Voyages and Adventures of Gilbert Go-Ahead.

Anon #1489

Marmaduke Multiply. Boston: Monroe and Francis, 1845.

Coll: 16° 1-9⁸ 72 leaves (14 x 11.6cm) Ff. [1-2] 3-71 [72].

Illus: 70 hand colored engravings numbered 3-71.

Binding: Red cloth wrappers

Notes: Bookplate of Percival Merritt. Reprint? A book of plates on one side of leaf only.

Marzials, Theo[philus Julius Henry] 1850- #1499

A Book of Old Songs, newly arranged, & with accompaniments by Theo: Marzials; set to pictures by Walter Crane; Engraved and printed in colours by Edmund Evans. London: George Routledge and Sons, 1883. Pp [1]-[52].

Illus: Cuts.

#1508

Mavor, William [Fordyce], L.L.D.   1758-1837

The English Spelling Book; Accompanied by a progressive Series of Easy and Familiar Lessons, intended as an introduction to the English Language . . . From the 241st London Edition. York, U.C.: Published by Lesslie & Sons, 1834.

Coll: 12° (6's)   A-D⁶ 84 leaves (16.4 x 9.9cm) Pp. [1-5] 6-167 [168].

Illus: Numerous woodcuts.

(cont'd)

Mavor.   English Spelling Book . . . .   (Cont'd)

Notes: McKell copy lacks page number for p. 139.

#1509

Mavor, William [Fordyce], L.L.D.   1758-1837

The English Spelling-Book. Accompanied by a progressive series of easy and familiar lessons. Illustrated by Kate Greenaway. Engraved and Printed by Edmund Evans. London and New York: George Routledge and Sons, 1885. Pp. [1-4, 5-9] 10-108.

Illus: Frontispiece + title page + numerous engravings.

 # 1510

May, Phil   1864-1903

Phil May's Guttersnipes: 50 original sketches in pen and ink. London: The Leadenhall Press, Limited, [1896]. Ff. 56 1 of adverts.

Anon.   **#1511**

May-Day Eve; or, the Royal Chaplet: Humbly subscribed to Her Royal Highness the Prince Charlotte of Wales. London: Printed [by Brettel & Co.] for John Wallis, Jun., 1808.

Coll: 16°: [A⁸] 8 leaves (11.6 X 10cm.) Pp. [1-5]6-16

Plates: Frontispiece+ 6, hand colored

Binding: Blue, brown, and white marbled boards

Mayhew, Henry   1812-1887   **#1512**

The Wonders of Science; or, Young Humphry Davy . . . . New York: Harper & Brothers, Publishers, 1856.

Coll: 8° [A]⁸ B-S⁸ [T]⁸ U-Z⁸ [2A]² 2B-2E ⁸ 2F² 226 leaves (16.7 x 10.7cm) Pp. [i-v] vi-xi [xii-xiii] xiv [15] 16-452. Illus: Frontispiece +7 + cuts.

McGuffey, William H[olmes]   1800-1873   **#1518**

Eclectic Educational Series. McGuffey's New Third Eclectic Reader, for young learners. By Wm. H. McGuffey LL.D. Cincinnati: Wilson, Hinkle & Co.; Phil'a: Claxton, Remsen & Hafflefinger; New Orleans: Stevens & Seymour; New York: Clark & Maynard, [ca 1865].

Coll: 8° ¶, 3d.Rd.1-3d.Rd.15⁸ 121 leaves. Pp. [i-ii, iii-v] vi-vii, [8] 9-12 [13] 14-242.

Illus: A few engravings

Notes: Electrotyped at the Franklin Type Foundry. Entered 1865.

McGuffey, [William Holmes]. 1800-1873   **#1519**

Eclectic Education series. McGuffey's Newly revised Ecletic Primer. With pictorial illustrations. Cincinnati: Published by Winthrop B. Smith & Co., 137 Walnut St. [1849].

Coll: 8°: [1-4⁸] 32 leaves Pp. [1-6, 7] 8-60 [61-64]

Illus: 173 engravings

Notes: Front and back leaves pasted to wrapper. McKell . . . #M-10-1-44L/M-10-5-44B.

McGuffey, William Holmes   1800-1873   **#1527**

McGuffey's New Eclectic Spelling-Book: embracing a progressive course of instruction in English orthography and ortheopy; including dictation exercises. Cincinnati and New York: Van Antwerp, Bragg & Co., [1865]. Pp. [1-3] 4-144.

McGuffey, William Holmes. 1800-1873   **#1528**

McGuffey's newly revised Eclectic First Reader: Containing progressive lessons in reading and spelling. Revised and improved by Wm. H. McGuffey, L.L.D. Revised stereotype edition. Eclectic Educational Series. Cincinnati: Published by Winthrop B. Smith & Co., [entered 1853].

Coll: 12°: 1⁸, 2⁴, 3⁶,4⁸, 5⁴, 6⁶, 7⁸, 8⁴, 9⁶ 54 leaves (15 X 9.7cm) Pp. [1-3] 4-5,vi,7-108

Illus: Several engravings

Notes: M-10-1-44-L, M-10-5-44-B

McGuffey, William Holmes, 1800-1873   #1529

McGuffey's Newly Revised Eclectic Second Reader: Containing Progressive lessons in reading and spelling. Revised and improved by Wm. H. McGuffey, L.L.D. Revised stereotype edition. Eclectic Educational Series. Cincinnati: Published by Winthrop B. Smith & Co., [Stereotyped by C.F. O'Driscoll, Cincinnati] Entered in 1853].

Coll:8°: 1-14⁸ 112 leaves Pp. [1-2] 3-7[8] 9-224 (16 x 10.5cm)

Illus: Several engravings
Notes: M-10-1-44-L, M-10-5-44-B

McGuffey, William H[olmes]. 1800-1873.   #1530

McGuffey's Third Reader. Revised and Improved Eclectic Third Reader. Containing Selections in Prose and Poetry, from the best American and English writers with Plain Rules for Reading and directions for avoiding common errors....Thirty Second Edition-110,000 copies. Cincinnati: Published by Winthrop B. Smith, 1843.

Coll: 12°: (6s) A-O⁶ 84 leaves (18 X 11.2cm) Pp. 1-4 [5] 6 [7-8] 9-10 (2 pages between 10-11), 11-37 [38] 39-165 [166]

Illus: 3 cuts.

Meeke, Mrs. [Mary]   #1531

The Birth-day Present; or, pleasing tales, of amusement and instruction. By Mrs. Meeke. Embellished with seventeen neat, coloured engravings. London: [Printed by Dean and Munday, for] A. K. Newman & Co., [ca. 1825].

Coll: 8° [1]18 18 leaves (16.8 x 10   cm) Pp. [1-5] 6-36.

Meggendorfer, Lothar   #1532

Reiseabenteuer des Malers Daumenlang und seines Dieners Damian. Ein Ziehbilderbuch von Lothar Meggendorfer. Esslingen bei Stuttgart: J. F. Schreiber, u.d.

Coll: Lge 4° π, [A]⁸

Plates: 8 movable colored illustrations attached to inner, top, and bottom edge of recto of each leaf in [A] gathering, with push-pull paper lever extending from outer edge.

Anon.   #1535

Memoir and Character of Sarah, a Pious Woman of Connecticut, who died in the year 1818. Bridgnorth: [W. Smith, Printer, Ironbridge] Published by Gitton & Smith, n.d.

Coll: 24°: A¹⁰ 10 leaves (12 X 6.6cm) Pp. [1-3] 4-20

Binding: Rebound over original wrappers

Notes: Bookplates of Howard Pyle and John Stuart Groves.

Anon.   #1536

Memoirs of the Little Man & Little Maid so wonderfully contrived as to be either sung or said. Illustrated with curious engravings. Salem, Mass.: Published by Henry Whipple, 1818.

Coll: 16°: 1⁶ 6 leaves (12.9 X 10.2cm) Pp. 1-12

Binding: Gray-green wrappers

Notes: Welch. (McKell's copy) 769.5, McKell #S-12-10-45-B No title page inside

---

Anon.   #1537

Memoirs of the Little Man and the Little Maid: With some interesting particulars of their lives never before published. London: [Printed by C. Squire] Published by B. Tabart, 1807.

Coll: 16°: (2's) [A] B-D², [E]([E]=A²), F-H² 14 leaves (13.3 X 12.3cm) Pp. [i-ii] 1-12 [13-26]

Plates: 12 colored engravings
Binding: Buff wrappers EI-EIᵛ: Advertisements

Notes: B.M.C. #C38. b.36.

Anon.   #1538

The Merry Andrew, Which contains a complete collection of riddles, calculated entirely for the amusement and improvement of youth. Adorned with cuts. Brentford: Printed by P. Norbury, and sold by all booksellers in Town and Country, n.d.

Coll: 32°: 1³² unsigned 32 leaves (9.7 X 6.1cm) Pp. [1-4] 5-62 [63-64]

Illus:"Frontispiece" + 21 woodcuts in text

Notes: Chapbook

Anon   #1539

The Merry Ballads of the Olden Time. Illustrated in Pictures & Rhyme. London: A. Warne & Co., n.d. Pp. [1-viii, 1-158].

Illus: 34 full-page chromolithos +numerous black and white lithos by Emrick and Binger, 15 Holborn Viaduct, London.

Anon.   #1544

Midnight Horrors; or The Bandits' Daughter. An original Romance. New York: Published by W. Borradaile, and sold wholesale and retail, at his Book-store, 1823.

Coll: 12°: A-D⁶ 24 leaves (19.5 X 11.2cm) Pp. [1-2, 3] 4-45 [46-48]

Illus: Frontispiece hand colored engraving.

Binding: Original blue wrappers

Notes: The English edition was published in 1810.

Mills, Alfred, illus.   1776-1883   #1548

Pictures of Roman History, in miniature, designed by Alfred Mills. With explanatory anecdotes. Philadelphia: Published by Johnson & Warner, No. 147 Market Street, J. Bouvier, printer, [Bellavista, Hamiltonville], 1811.

Coll: 64⁰ ¶4, A-I⁴,χ⁴ 56 leaves (6 x 5.3cm) Pp.[1-11 , 1] 2-96.

Plates: 48 on conjugate leaves, two plates each, sewn in

Notes: Endpapers: ¶-¶3;   Title page: ¶4; Endpapers: χ4; McKell # S-8- (23-44-B. Rosenbach # 441.

Mills, [Mrs.] Mary E[loise (Sales)]. 1875-   #1549

Truth, or Frank's Choice. London: Frederick Warne & Co., 1867. Pp.[i-iv, 1]-104.

Plates: Frontispiece

Milne, A[lan] A[lexander]   1882-1956   #1551

Now We Are Six. With Decorations by Ernest H. Shepard. London: Methuen and Co., Ltd., 1927. Pp.[i-vi] vii-x [xi-xii] 1-103 [104: colophon].

Illus: Illustrated in blue.

Binding: Pink free and paste-down endpaper front and back. Red boards.

Milne, A[lan] A[lexander]   1882-1956   #1550

The House at Pooh Corner. With decorations by Ernest H. Shepard. London: Methuen and Co. Ltd. [1928]. Pp [i-vi] vii-xi [xii] 1-178 [179-180: colophon].

Binding: Pictorial (silhouette) free and paste-down endpapers front and back. Flamingo boards.

Milne, A[lan] A[lexander]   1882-1956   #1552

The Red House Mystery. New York: E. P. Dutton & Company, [1922]. Pp.[i-x] 1-278.

Milne, A[lan] A[lexander]   1882-1956   #1553, 1-2

When We Were Very Young. With decorations by Ernest H. Shepard. London: Methuen and Co., Ltd., [1924]. Pp.[i-vi] vii-x [xi-xii] 1-99 [100].

Binding: Boxed. Blue boards. Dust cover. Free and paste-down endpapers front and back.

Notes: Two verses inscribed by Milne on front free endpaper. Explains why he wrote the poems. Signed "A. A. Milne" and dated 7/21/52. Plus another (copy of the same ed.

Milne, A[lan] A[lexander]   1882-1956   #1554

Winnie-the-Pooh. With decorations by Ernest H. Shepard. London: Methuen and Co. Ltd., 1926. Pp.[i-viii] ix-xi [xii-xvi] 1-158 [159-160: colophon].

Binding: Decorative maps on free and paste-down endpapers front and back. Green boards.

The Paradise Lost of Milton . . . . (Cont'd)

Vol II:
Coll: 2⁰ A²B²C-2I⁴ 2F³ 111 leaves (36.8 x 26cm)
Pp.[i-iv, 1-3] 4-27 [28-31] 32-56 [57-59] 60-105 [106-109] 110-151 [152-155] 156-190 [191-193] 194-218.

Plates: 9 engravings.

Notes: One of 50 L. P. copies.

Milton, John. 1608-1674   #1556

The Paradise Lost of Milton. With illustrations, designed and engraved by John Martin. 2 vols. London: Septimus Prowett, Thomas White, Printer, Crane Court, Fleet Street, 1827.

Vol I:
Coll: 2⁰ A³B⁴ C-2I⁴ 2G² 117 leaves (36.8 x 26cm)
Pp.[i-vi, 1-3] 4-34 [35-37] 38-77 [78-81] 82-109 [110-113] 114-152 [153-155] 156-190 [191-193] 194-228 [229-230].

Plates: 15 engravings.

(cont'd)

Anon   #1557

The Mirror of Witchcraft, or, Messenger of Darkness; being Invaluable and Authentic Communications from, and concerning The World of Spirits; Together with Relations of Apparitions, Witchcraft, Necromancy, &c. Together with Proofs of their Existence, from Distinguished Authors. Embellished with a Frontispiece. London: Printed [by J. G. Barnard] for Tegg & Castleman; . . ; Champante & Whitrow . . . ; B. Crosby & Co. . . . ; Wilmot & Hall . . . ; Howard & Evans . . . ; and T. Hughes . . . , [1803]?

(cont'd)

The Mirror of Witchcraft . . . .   (Cont'd)

Coll: 12° π¹ A-C⁶ D¹   20 leaves   (17.2 x 9.2cm)
Pp. [i-ii] 1-30.

Plates: Engraved frontispiece by H. Richter, listing
date of publication as April 21, 1803.

Notes: Not in BMC. Title page identifies J. G.
Barnard as printer; D1ᵛ identifies J. H. Hart
as printer.

#1560

Mitchel, O[rmsby] M[acKnight] A. M. 1809-1862

An Elementary Treatise on Algebra: designed to
facilitate the comprehension, demonstration and
application of the leading principles of that science.
Cincinnati: E. Morgan & Co., 1845.

Coll: 12° A-U⁶ X-2C⁶ .156 leaves (20.4 x 13cm)
Pp. [i-vi, vii] viii-xii, 13-306, [307-312].
Binding: Calf
Notes: Sewings in middle of A,'C gatherings: A1, 2, 3
are paste-down endpaper and free endpapers,
C4, 5, 6 are   free endpapers and paste-
down endpaper,) respectively.

#1561

Mitchell, S[ilas] Wier, M.D.   1829-1914

The Adventures of Francois. New York: The Century
Co., 1898. Pp. xi, 1-321.

#1562

Mitchell, S[ilas] Wier, M.D.   1829-1914

Hugh Wynne Free Quaker. 2 vols. New York: The
Century Co., 1897. Pp. 1-306; 1-261.

#1563

Mitchell, S[ilas] Weir, M.D., L.L.D.   1829-1914

The Red City: a novel of the second administration
of President George Washington. With illustrations
by Arthur I. Keller. New York: The Century Co.,
1908. Pp. [viii], +421.

Plates: Frontispiece +9

Notes: First ed.

#1564

[Mitchell, Silas Weir, M.D., L.L.D.] 1829-1914

The Wonderful Stories of Fuz-Buz the Fly and Mother
Grabem the Spider. Illustrated. Philadelphia:
J.B. Lippincott & Co., 1867. Pp. [1] 2-79.

Plates: Frontispiece +8.

Notes: First ed.

#1567

[Mogridge, George]   1787-1854

The Half-Day's Holiday. By the Author of "The Juvenile
Culprits," &c. London: Printed for Houlston And Son,
1830.

Coll: 16° (6's) A-C⁶ 18 leaves (14.4 x 9.1cm) Pp.
[1-5] 6 [7-8] 9-12 [13-14] 15-22 [23-24] 25-26
[27-28] 29-32 [33-34] 35-36.

Illus: Front +5 full-page cuts (unnumbered but included
in pagination).

Binding: Printed green   wrappers

#1568

[Mogridge, George]   1787-1854

Rural Pickings; or, attractive points in country
life and scenery. London: W. Tegg & Co.; Glasgow:
R. Griffin and Co.; Dublin: Cumming & Ferguson,
1846.

Coll: 8° A⁶ B-P⁸ 118 leaves (17.2 x 11cm) Pp. [i-
iv, v] vi-xii, [1] 2-222 [223-224: adverts].
Plates: Engraved half-title +4: all color
Notes: Has added half-title preceeding engraved one.

#1570

[Montagu, Lady B
Scott, Mrs. Sarah (Robinson)] 1723-1795

A Description of Millenium Hall, and the Country Adjacent
. . . by A Gentleman on his Travels. London: Printed
for J. Newbery, 1762.

Coll: 12° A² B-M¹² 134 leaves (16.8 x 10.2cm) Pp. [iv] 1-262+2.

Plate: Frontispiece

Binding: Full speckled calf.

Notes: Bookplate of Percival and Elisabeth Merritt.

#1571

Monteith, James   1829 or 30 - 1890

Manual of Geography Combined with History and Astronomy: designed for intermediate classes in public and
private schools. Rev. ed. "National Geographic Series." New York: A. S. Barnes & Co., 1871. Pp. [i-iv,
5]-124.

Illus: Half-title, frontispiece +cuts.

[Montolieu, MRS.] # 1571.1-2

The Enchanted Plants and Fables of Flora. Philadelphia: A. R. Poole, n.d.

Coll: 12° A⁴ B-M⁶ N² 72 leaves (13.4 x 8.1cm)
Pp. [i-iv, v] vi [vii] viii [9] 10-143 [144].
Illus: Title page
Notes: On back paste-down endpaper: "Elizabeth J. P.
Shields, 1829 [1819?]" New York ed. pub-
lished 1803. Plus another copy.

Montorqueil, G [eorges] # 1573

Louis XI [aquarelles de Job]. "Ancienne Librairie
Furne" Paris: Boivin & Cie-Editeurs [1905]. Pp. 4+
[I] II-IV [1] 2 [3] 4 [5] 6 [7] 8-9 10-11] 12 [13] 14-
18 19] 20-22 [23] 24-25 [26-27] 28 [29] 30 [31] 32 [33]
34 [35] 36-38 [39] 40 [41] 42 [43] 44 [45] 46-47 [48-49]
50 [51] 52 [53] 54 [55] 56 [57] 58-60 [61] 62-63 [64-65]
66 [67] 68 [69] 70 [71] 72 [73] 74 [75] 76 [77] 78 [79-
80].

Illus: 38 full-page aquarelles en chromotypogravure,
by Job, i.e., Jacques Marie Gaston Onfroy de
Breville, 1858-1931
Notes: Demy quarto

Moore, Clement C [larke], L.L.D. 1779-1863 #1576

Denslow's Night Before Christmas. Made into a
book and illustrated by W. W. Denslow. New York:
G. W. Dillingham Co., 1902. [64] pp.

Notes: Another copy.

Moore, Clement C [larke , L.L.D.] 1779-1863 # 1577

The Night Before Christmas. Illustrated by Arthur
Rackham. London: George G. Harrap & Co., Ltd.,
1931. Pp. [vii, 10] 11-35 [36].

Plates: Frontispiece+3. Plates are included in
pagination.
Binding: Dust cover
Notes: First edition.

Moore, Clement C [larke] 1779-1863 # 1578

The Night Before Christmas, illustrated by Arthur
Rackham. Philadelphia: J.B. Lippincott Co., n.d.
Pp. [1-32].

Moore, Clement Clarke. 1770-1863 #1579

The Night Before Christmas. Illustrated by Everett
Shinn. Chicago: The John C. Winston Co., [1942].
Pp. [1-28].

Binding: Dust cover.

Moore, Clement [Clarke] 1779-1863 # 1580

The Night Before Christmas. Illustrated by Roberta
Paflin. New York: E. P. Dutton & Co., Inc., 1944.
Pp. [1-16].

Binding: Dust cover

Moore, Clement C [larke] 1779-1863 #1581

The Night Before Christmas. Illustrated by
William T. Smedley, Frederic B. Schell, Alfred
Fredericks, and Henry R. Poore. Philadelphia:
Porter & Coates, [1883]. Ff. 26.

Moore, Clement Clark [e] 1779-1863 #1582

The Night Before Christmas. Illustrations and
animations by Julian Wehr. Duenewald Printing
Corp., 1949. Ff. [1-9].

Illus: Chromolithos on every page.
Notes: Ff. 3,6,8,9 are unopened double leaves
foliated as one leaf each. These leaves
are doubled to hold tabs that operate animated parts of the illustrations on these
same leaves.

Moore, Clement Clarke 1770-1863 # 1583

The Night Before Christmas. Woodcuts by Ilse
[Marthe] Bischoff. New York: Holiday House, n.d.
Pp. [1-32].

Binding: Paper bound.

Notes: Contains a history of the poem. See also
The New York Book, which contains the
first authorized printing of the poem.

#1584

Moore, Clement C[larke]   1779-1863

A Visit from St. Nicholas. Boston: The Atlantic
Monthly Press, 1921. Pp.[i-i, 1-10].

Illus: Woodcuts by Florence Wyman Ivins

Notes: Designed by Bruce Rogers and printed by
        William Rudge. Colophon signed by Bruce
        Rogers and Florence Ivins.

#1585

[Moore, Clement Clarke] 1779-1863

A Visit from Saint Nicholas. Illustrated by Aldren
Watson for the Peter Pauper Press, Mount Vernon, n.d.
Pp. [i-vi, 1]-[18].

Illus: Cuts

La Morale Des Enfans, choix de Fables D'Esope a la
          portee du jeune age; . . . . Paris, 1805.

          see under

                    Aesop (619-564B.C.)

Anon.   #1588

The Moralist; or Young Gentleman and Lady's Entertaining
Companion, Being a Collection of Moral Tales, and Stories,
Selected from the best Modern Authors. Glasgow: Printed
for the Booksellers, 1765.

Coll: 12° A-I⁶ 54 leaves (15.2 x 9.5cm) 108 pp. ("34"
       mispaginated 44; "66" mispaginated 65; "70-71" mis-
       paginated 69-70; "73" mispaginated 72 and so on to
       "81"; return to correct pagination with p. 82.

#1589

[ANON].Moral Lectures on the Following Subjects.
Pride, Envy, Avarice . . . Truth, Falshood, Education,
Industry . . . Happiness, Friendship, Mankind . . . .
By Solomon Winlove, Esq; Embellished with twenty-
eight curious Cuts. London: Printed for E.
Newbery, 1781.

Coll.: 24°: A-H⁸. 64 leaves (9.9 X 6.4cm).
[2], vi, 120 pp.

Bookplate of Percival Merritt.   Roscoe # 382 (4)

#1592

Morley, Henry   1822-1894

Oberon's Horn: a book of fairy tales. Illustrated
by Charles H. Bennett. London: Chapman and Hall,
1861. Pp.[1] ii-viii, [1] 2-221 [222; 1 of adverts.]

Plates: Frontispiece, illustrated title page +cuts.

#1593

anon.

Morozko (Mr. Frost). Illustrated by M[   ]G[   ]
Moscow: State Publishing House, 1923. Pp. [1] 2-3 [4]
5 [6] 7-8 [9] 10 [11-12].

Illus: Full page color illustration on unnumbered pages
        except pp. [1 & 12].

Binding: Pictorial Wrappers

Notes: A Russian fairy tale (Skazka).

#1597

Anon

The Mosaic Creation: or, Divine Wisdom Displayed in
the Works of the First Six Days. London: J. Newbery,
n.d. [1766?].

Coll: 32° A-F⁸ 48 leaves   (10.2 x 6.4cm) iv, 85
+[11] pp.

Plates: Frontispiece +6: (copper engravings)

                                        (cont'd)

Mosaic Creation   (Cont'd) -2-

Contents: A3: "A Pastoral Dialogue . . . by the late
. . . Mrs. Elizabeth Rowe." A4ᵛ: "The Mosaic
Creation. . . ." C⁵: "The Jewish Sabboth. . . ."
D4: "A Poetical Comment . . . By the late . . .
Mr. Addison." D5: "The Grateful Muse . . . . By
another Hand." D7: "Hymn of Praise . . . . By the
Late . . . Mrs. Rowe." E 1: "Mr. Pope's Universal
Prayer." E2ᵛ: "Seasonal Reflections Abridged from
Mr. Harvey's Descant on the Creation." E7: " . . .
                                        (cont'd)

Mosaic Creation   (Cont'd)   3

an Extract from the works of Dr. Beveridge. . . ."
F3ᵛ: "Books published for the Instruction of
Children, and sold by J. Newbery . . . ."
Binding: Dutch floral boards.
Notes: McKell copy lacks fols. F1, F7, F8 (pp. 81-82,
       93-96). Bookplate of Percival Merritt. Mss
       dates: "Wᵐ Smith 1766"; "Betsey Smith her
       Book 1780" Roscoe # 248 (2).

Mother Goose

    see under

        Perrault, Charles (1628-1703)

    and

        Perrault-D'armancour, Pierre (1678-1700)

Mother Goose in Prose

    see

        Baum, L[yman] Frank. (1856-1919)

[ANON]. The Mother's Fables, in Verse. Designed, #1599
Through the Medium of Amusement, to convey to The
Minds of Children. Some Useful Precepts of Virtue
and Benevolence. London: Printed [by and] for
Darton, Harvey, and Darton, 1818.

Coll: 12°: [A⁶⁻²]B-I⁶[K²(=A²)]. 54 leaves (13.6 X
8.8cm). [2] + vi + 96 + [4]pp.

Plates: Frontispiece + 11.

[K1][K2]: Advertisements for Darton, Harvey, and
Darton.

Anon.   #1600
The Moving Market; or, Cries of London: for the amuse-
ment and instruction of good children. Adorned with
cuts. Wellington: Printed by F. Houlston and Son, [1810?]
Coll: 32°: [1¹⁶] 16 leaves (10.2 X 6.5cm.)
    Pp. [1-5]6-31[32]
Illus: Frontispiece + 26 vignettes
Binding: Lavender wrappers, pictorial. Initial and final
leaves serve as paste down endpapers.
Notes: Percival Merritt Bookplate. McKell gives 1820
Muir gives 1810. B.M.C. gives [Salop., 1820?], #
012806 de. 29. (8)

Anon.   #1601
[M]rs. Prim and her Son Jim. Price 12½ cts.
Boston: Benjamin B. Munsey, 29 Cornhill]
Coll: 8°; [1⁸]; 8 leaves; ff. 8.
Illus: 8 colored woodcuts.
Binding: Cream colored wrappers. Decorations
    and title on front. Decorations and
    advertisements on back.
Notes: Printed on one side of page only.
    Initial and final pages pasted to
    wrapper.

Mulford, Clarence Edward   1883-1956   #1606

Bar-20. Illustrated by N.C. Wyeth and & F.E.
Schoonover. New York: The Outing Publishing
Company, 1907. Pp.[i]-[viii] 1-[384]

Mulford, Clarence E[dward]. 1883-1956   #1607

Hopalong Cassidy. Illustrated by Maynard Dixon.
Chicago: A. C. McClurg & Co., 1910. Pp.[x,]11-392.

Plates: Front + 4

Notes: First ed.

Mulock, Dinah Maria

    see

        Craik, Mrs. Dinah Maria (Mulock) 1826-1887

Munroe, Kirk   1850-1930   ## 1610,1-3

The Flamingo Feather. Illustrated, New York;
Harper & Brothers, 1887. Pp.[i]-vi, [1]-255 [256].

Plates: Frontispiece + 18: by Thur de Tholstrop.
    Plate on p. 109 is missing.

Notes: First ed. Blanck, p. 83.
    2 other copies: each has frontispiece + 19
    plates by de Thulstrop.

            #1611

Munroe, Kirk   1850-1930

The Fur-Seal's Tooth: a story of Alaskan adventure.
Illustrated by William Allen Rogers. New York:
Harper & Brothers Publishers, 1894. Pp.[viii],
267; [1-4]of adverts bound in at end.

Plates: Frontispiece + 32. Map plate after [viii] is
    not listed. Illustrations on pp. 30 and 67
    are not plates.

Notes: First edition.

#1612

Munroe, Kirk   1850-1930

The Painted Desert: a story of Northern Arizona.
Illustrated by F.H. Lungren. New York and London:
Harper & Brothers Publishers, 1897. Pp. [viii], 274;
[1-4] of adverts bound in at end.

Plates: Frontispiece +19.

Notes: First edition ?

#1613

Munroe, Kirk   1850-1930

Snow-Shoes and Sledges: a sequel to "The Fur-
Seal's Tooth." Illustrated [by William Allen
Rogers]. New York: Harper & Brothers Publishers,
1895. Pp. [viii], 271; [1-4] of adverts bound in at
end.

Plates: Frontispiece +25.

Notes: First edition.

#1614

Murray, Lindley   1745-1826

The English Reader; or pieces in prose and poetry.
Brunswick: Printed by J. Griffin, for T. Bedlington,
Boston, 1823.

Coll: 12° (6s) A-U⁶ X-Y⁶ 132 leaves (18 x 10.7cm)
Pp. [i-ii] iii-iv [v] vi-xv [xvi-xvii] xviii-
xix-xxi [xxii, 23] 24-264.

#1615

Murray, Lindley   1745-1826

The English Reader: or, Pieces in Prose and Poetry,
Selected from the best writers. Designed to assist young
persons to read with propriety and effect, to improve
their language and sentiments; and to inculcate some of
the most important principles of Piety and Virtue. With
a few preliminary observations on the principles of Good
Reading. By Lindley Murray, author of an English Grammar,
&c. &c. Cincinnati: Published by N. and G. Guilford. W.M.
and O. Farnsworth, Jun. Printers, 1828.

Coll: 12°: A-R⁶ 102 leaves (17.7 X 10.5cm) Pp. [i-iii] iv
[v] vi-xiii, [14] 15-16 [17] 18-51 ("52" mispaginated
42) [53] 54-138 [139] 140-204

Illus: none

Murray, Lindley. 1745-1826

Entick's New Spelling Dictionary, Teaching to Write and
Pronounce the English Tongue with Ease and Propriety;
in which each word is accented according to its just and
natural pronunciation; the part of speech is properly distinguished, and the various significations are in general
ranged in one line. The whole compiled and digested in a
manner intirely new, and adapted to the use of schools in
the United States: To which are added, an alphabetical
account of the heathen deities, a copious chronological
table of remarkable events, discoveries and inventions;
and a list of the principal post-towns in the United
States, with their distances from the seat of government.
To this work is prefixed, an abridgment of English

#1616

Murray, Lindley. 1745-1826

Entick's New Spelling Dictionary, 1812.

Grammar, designed for the younger classes of learners.
Fifth edition. New Haven: From. Sidney's Press. Printed
for Increase Cooke & Co., Book-sellers, 1812.

Coll: 16°: A-Aa⁸ 200 leaves (12.5 X 10.5cm) Pp. [1-5]
6-12 [13] 14-32 [33] 34-42 [43] 44-361 [362] 363-400

Murray, Lindley. 1745-1826   #1617

Introduction to the English Reader: or, a selection of
pieces, in prose and poetry; calculated to improve the
younger classes of learners in reading, and to imbue
their minds with the love of virtue. To which are added
rules and observations for assisting children to read
with propriety. (Stereotype Edition) From the last English edition. [2d English Ed] by Lindley Murray, author
of an English Grammar, etc, etc, New York: Published by
Collins and Co., 1820.

Coll: 12°: A-F⁶ [G⁶] H-I⁶ [K⁶] L⁶ [M⁶] N-O⁶ 84 leaves
(16.3 X 9.7cm). Pp. [i-iii] iv [v] vi-x [xi-xiii]
xiv-xvi [17] 18-24 [25] 26-71 [72] 73-75 [76] 77-110
[111] 112-142 [143] 144-162 [163] 164-166 [blank:167-
168]

Murray, [Lindley]   1745-1826   #1618

Key to the Exercises Adapted to Murray's English Grammar. Calculated to enable private learners to become
their own instructers [sic], in grammar and composition.
By the author of The Exercises. From the Ninth English
edition, improved by the author. New York: Printed and
sold by Collins and Perkins...,1808.

Coll: 12°: A-M⁶ 72 leaves (17.35 X 10.8cm·) Pp. [1-3]
4-144

Notes: McKell's insert: "Probably the first American
issue."

Murray, Lindley . 1745-1826   #1619

Key to the exercises adapted to Murray's English
Grammar. Calculated to enable private learners to be-
come their own instructors, for grammar and composition.
By the author of the Exercises. Stereotyped from the
last English edition, by B. & J. Collins, New York.
Philadelphia: Printed and published by S. Probasco, 1824.

Coll: 12°: A-O⁶, P⁴ 86 leaves (17.3 X 10.3cm·) Pp. [i-ii]
iii-iv [v] vi [vii] viii [1] 2-17 [18] 19-77 ('78'
mispaginated 87) 79-85 [86] ('87' mispaginated 78)
88-109 [110] 111-151 [152-153] 154-155 ('156' mispaginated 56) 157-168

Notes: Gatherings 'C' and 'F' are unsigned. No author's
name given in text

Anon   #1620

A Museum for Young Gentlemen and Ladies; Or, a
Private Tutor for little Masters and Misses . . . . .
Interpreted with Letters, Tales, and Fables for
Amusement and Instruction, and illustrated with
Cuts. (Being a Second Volume to the Pretty Book
for Children.) London: Printed for J. Hodges, on
the Bridge; J. Newbery, in St. Paul's - Church Yard;
and B. Collins in Salisbury, n.d. [1750 or earlier].

Coll: 16° A³ B-O⁸ P⁹ 116 leaves (10.8 x 8.4cm)
Pp. vi + 226.

Notes: Bookplate of Percival Merritt. See
Welsh, p. 273.   Roscoe H 253(i)

Anon.　　　　　　　　　　　　　　　　#1621

A Museum for Young Gentlemen and Ladies; or a Private
Tutor for Little Masters and Misses.　Containing a
Variety of useful Subjects . . . . Illustrated with Cuts.
13th ed.　London:　S. Crowder, and B.C. Collins, Salisbury, n.d.

Coll: 12° [A1] B-Q⁶, R⁵　　　　　　　　　　96 leaves
(12.7 x 6.5cm)　Pp. vi, [1] 2-166.

Notes: Bookplate of Percival Merritt.

[ANON. (Oliver Goldsmith?)]　A Museum for Young
Gentlemen and Ladies; Or, a Private Tutor for Little
Masters and Misses.　Containing a Variety of Useful
Subjects . . . with Letters, Tales, and Fables . . .
Illustrated with Cuts.　The Seventeenth Edition,
With Considerable Additions and Alterations.　London:
Printed [by B.C. Collins] for Darton and Harvey . . .
; Crosby and Letterman . . . ; J. Harris . . . ; and
B.C. Collins . . . , 1806.　　　　　　　　　　#1622

Coll:　12° : π² [A²] B-Q⁶ R⁹ (R4 + 1).　103 leaves (14 X
8.5cm).　[1-6][i-iii]iv-vi [1]2-194 pp.

R3 and R7(conjugate leaves) have their positions
exchanged.　　　　**See Osborne, p. 131.**
Bookplates of Julia　　Pass and Percival Merritt.

Anon　　　　　　　　　　　　　　　　#1623

My Cousin Hester.　Revised by the Committee of
Publication of the American Sunday School Union,
n.d. [1840?]

Coll: 12° 1-2⁶ 12 leaves　(14.5 x 9.1cm) Pp. 1-4
5-22, [23-24: blank].
Illus: "Frontispiece" and title page woodcuts.

Anon　　　　　　　　　　　　　　　　#1624

My Real Friend, or Incidents in Life, founded on
truth, For the Amusement of Children.　Second
Edition corrected.　London:　Printed by A. Darton,
Jun., 1812.

Coll: 12° A-D⁶ (4 quires stabbed) 24 leaves.
(15.8 x 9.9cm)　Pp. i-iv, 5-48.

Illus: 18 woodcuts, each containing "Published by
W. Darton Jun. Augˢᵗ. 19, 1812."

Binding: Original brown paper wrappers; advert for
Darton's children's books in back.

Notes: BMC # 12804.　f. 36. (4)

Anon.　　　　　　　　　　　　　　　#1625

My Tippoo. A Poem. Illustrated with engravings. Philadelphia: Published and sold by Wm Charles. [No. 32 South
Third Street], 1819.

Coll: 16°: [1⁶] 6 leaves (13 X 10.8cm) Pp. [1-12]

Illus: 6 hand-colored copper engravings

Binding: Gray wrappers. Printed on one side of leaf.

Notes: Evans, #48819, A.A.S. #839.3

Anon.　　　　　　　　　　　　　　　#1628

Natural History of Birds. Northampton: John Metcalf
[Published by J.H. Butler] 1838.

Coll: 12°: 1⁴, 2⁸ 12 leaves (13.5 X 7.3ᶜᵐ·) Pp. [1-4, 5]
6-24

Illus: Woodcut frontispiece +18 woodcuts in text

Binding: Wrappers bound in

Notes: Bookplate of Howard Pyle and John Stuart Groves

Anon.　　　　　　　　　　　　　　　#1629

The Natural History of Reptiles and Serpents. To which
is added, an appendix, containing an account of Worms,
of Corals, and of Sponges. Dublin: Printed by C.
Bentham, 1821.

Coll: 12°: A⁴, B¹², C⁶, D¹², E⁶, F¹², G⁶, H¹² K⁶, K¹²,
L² 90 leaves (13.9 x 8.8ᶜᵐ·) Pp. [i-v] vi [vii-
viii, 9] 10-39 [40] 41-44 [45] 46-75 [76] 77-80 [81]
82-94 [95] 96-127 [128] 129-155 [156] 157-173 [174]
175-178 [179-180]

Illus: Several full page and decorative woodcuts

Notes: McKell copy missing Pp. [179-180]

Anon.　　　　　　　　　　　　　　#1629.1

A Natural History of Reptiles, Serpents, and Insects.
Thirty-five engravings on wood. Alnwick: Printed and
sold wholesale and retail by W. Davison, [1815?].

Coll: 12°: A-C⁶ 18 leaves (13.8 X 8.6ᶜᵐ·)
Pp. [1-3] 5-14 [15] 16-36

Illus: 35 wood engravings [by Thomas Bewick?]

Binding: Brown wrappers, pictorial

Nesbit, E.

see

[Bland,] E[dith] Nesbit.　Rosy Cheeks and
Golden Ringlets. . . . 1900.

Anon.　　　　　　　　　　　　　　#1629.2

Neuer Lust=Weg Zum Vielmizlicher Künste und
Billenschaften.　Im Unterhaltendeß Lehrbuch
für Böglinge aus dem Kinder alter umihnen
durchbildliche Vorstellungen die Erlernung des
ABC.　Buchstabirens, Lesens und Schreibens,
Sowohl in Deutscher als in Lateinischer Sprache,
zu einer Spielbeschaftigung zu machen, u.
dadurch auf die angenehmste Viele zu erleich-
tern.　Mit emblematischen Kupferstichen und
Erklärungen derselben in vier verschiedenen
Sprachen.　Nürnberg:　bey Christoph Weigel,
Kunsthandlern gegen der K. R. Bost über,
n.d. [1710?]　　　　　　　　　　　(cont'd)

Anon. Neuer Lust=Weg   (1710)   p. 2.

Coll: 8°; A², B-Bb⁴, x², #⁴; 104 leaves;
    ff. 100 + pp. [1] 2-7 [8].

Illus: Numerous hand colored copper engravings.

Binding: Front and back: 1 paste down, 2 free
       end papers.

Notes: McKell #12-13-52L
       #S-12-13-52B
       #1-3-53
       All folds except #·4 are printed on one
       side of leaf only; blank pages are
) (cont'd)

Anon. Neuer Lust=Weg.   (1710?)   p. 3.

      pasted together so that each gathering
      appears as two leaves.
      x²= Frontispiece-title (conjugate).

Anon.   #1629.3

[Neues Spruchbüchlein mit Bildern von Fr.
Pocci] [1845.]

Coll: 32 separate leaves (10.1 x 13.2 cm.),
     each engraved on recto (verso blank)

Notes: Free and pasted down end papers.

Anon.   #1630

Neues unterhaltendes ABC Sillabir= und
Lesebuch von I. X. N. Nürnberg bey Christoph.
Fembo. 1820 mit königl. Baier allergn:
Freiheit.

Coll: 8°; A-D⁸; 32 leaves; ff. 5 + pp. 1-64.

Illus: Nine hand colored wood engravings by G.
     Roth bound in in front.

Binding: Marbled boards.

Notes: All plates conjugate on nine leaves
) (cont'd)

Anon. Neues unterhaltendes ABC. 1820. p. 2.

      folded and pasted to make nine color
      plates on five leaves; with a
      Nachschrift, p. 64.

Nevison, William

    see

       The Lives of Richard Turpin, and William
         Nevison. York: James Kendrew, n.d.

[ANON.]. The New Art of Hocus Pocus Revised; or,   #1631
The Whole Art of Legerdemain. Being the Best
Collection of Tricks on Slight of Hand, &c. . . .
Embellished with a Frontispiece . . . London:
Printed [by Dewick and Clarke] for T. & R. Hughes,
n.d.

Coll.: 12°: B-D6. 18 leaves (17.8 X 10.3cm).
[3-5]6-38 pp.

Plate: Engraved frontispiece (colored).

[Newbery, John] 1713-1767   #1632

A Collection of Pretty Poems for the Amusement of
Children. By Tommy Tagg, Esq. The sixteenth edition,
adorned with above sixty cuts. London: Printed for
the Booksellers in Town and Country, 1781

Coll: 24° B-E¹² F⁶ 54 leaves (10.6 x 8.3cm) 108pp

Plates: 62 cuts in text

Binding: Dutch floral boards, blue leather spine

Notes: Bookplate of Percival Merritt. Roscoe # 34b(9b)

[Newbery, John] 1713-1767   #1633

Food for the Mind, or a new riddle book compiled for
the use of the great and the little good boys and
girls . . . . By John-The-Giant-Killer, Esq. The
Third edition. London: Printed for the Booksellers of
Europe, Asia, Africa and America [by John Newbery],
1759.

Coll: 32° A-H⁸ 64 leaves (9.6 x 6.3cm) Pp. viii,
     112 + 8 pages of adverts]

Plates: 41+ woodcuts in text

                  (cont'd)

Food for the Mind . . . (Cont'd)

Notes: McKell copy wanting A8, B-B2, B7-C2, C7-E2,
     F8-G1, and H1. Bookplate of Percival Merritt.
     Roscoe # 190 B (3). H5ᵛ: "The following little
     books are printed for J. Newbery."

[Newbery, John] 1713-1767   #1634

The Newtonian System of Philosophy Adapted to the
Capacities of Young Gentlemen and Ladies. Being
. . . six lectures . . . by Tom Telescope, A.M.
London: Printed for J. Newbery, 1761.

Coll: 12° [A²], B-M⁶ N⁶ 72 leaves (11.6 x 7.6cm)
iv, 140pp.

Notes: Bookplate of Percival Merritt. Roscoe # 340 (1)

The Newtonian System . . . 7th ed. (Cont'd)

Notes: 15ᵛ-M6ᵛ: Advertisements for T. Carnan.
Bookplate of Percival Merritt. Roscoe # 340 (7)

[Newbery, John] 1713-1767   #1635

The Newtonian System of Philosophy . . . . The second
edition. London: Printed for J. Newbery, 1762.

Coll: 24° A-M⁶ 72 leaves (10.9 x 7.1cm) iv, 140pp.

Notes: Bookplate of Percival Merritt. Roscoe # 340 (2)

[Newbery, John, ed.]   1713-1767   #1639

The Newtonian System of Philosophy; . . . by Tom
Telescope, A.M. Illustrated with copper plates
and cuts. A New Improved Edition, with Many Al-
terations and Additions, to Explain the late New
Philosophical Discoveries, &c. &c. By William
Magnet, F.L.S. London: Ogilvy and Son; Vernor and
Hodd; J. Walker; Lackington, Allen, And Co., and
Darton and Harvey, 1798.

Coll: 12° (in 6's) A² B-M⁶ N⁴ 72 leaves. (13.5
x 8.6cm). Pp. [1-4], 1-137, [1-3].   (cont'd)

[Newbery, John] 1713-1767   #1636

The Newtonian System of Philosophy . . . . The third
edition. London: Printed for J. Newbery, 1766.

Coll: 12° A-M⁶ 72 leaves (11.5 x 7.5cm) iv, 140pp.

Plates: Frontispiece 8 engravings

Binding: Dutch flowery boards

Notes: Roscoe # 340 (3)

Newbery, John, ed. The Newtonian System of Philosophy; . . . . London: 1798. (Cont'd)

Plates: Frontispiece +4.

Notes: Bookplate of Percival Merritt.

[Newbery, John] 1713-1767   #1637

The Newtonian System of Philosophy Adapted to the
Capacities of Young Gentlemen and Ladies . . . By
Tom Telescope, A.M. . . . The sixth edition. London:
Printed for T. Carnan, 1784.

Coll: 24° A-M⁶ 72 leaves (11.6 x 7.3cm) [iv], 140

Plates: Frontispiece +7 copper engravings

Notes: 15ʳ-M6ᵛ: "Books for the instruction and amusement of children, printed for T. Carnan."
Bookplate of Percival Merritt. Roscoe # 340 (6)

A New Book of Old Ballads. Edinburgh: MDCCCXLIV.
1844, Laurie and Co., Printers .

see under M., T.

[Newbery, John] 1713-1767   #1638

The Newtonian System of Philosophy Adapted to the
Capacities of Young Gentlemen and Ladies. . . . Being
the substance of six lectures read to the Lilliputian
Society, by Tom Telescope, A.M. And collected . . .
by their old friend Mr. Newbery . . . who has also
added a variety of copper plate cuts. The seventh
edition. London: Printed for T. Carnan, 1787.

Coll: 24° (6's) A-M⁶ 72 leaves (11.7 x 7.6cm) [4] +
140pp.

Plates: Front + 8

        (cont'd)

[Newell, Peter Sheaf Hersey], illus. 1862-1924 #1640

The Hole Book. New York: Harper & Brothers, 1908.
Ff. 26.

Plates: 24 illus. on recto, text on verso.

Notes: First ed. Morgan, p. 294. The text
follows the progress of a bullet, which
has made a hole through the book!

Newell, Peter [Sheaf Hersey] 1862-1924   #1641

Peter Newell's Pictures and Rhymes. New York and Lond: Harper and Brothers Publishers, 1900. Ff. 56.

Anon.   #1642

The New England Primer, Enlarged and Improved: or, an easy and pleasant Guide to the Art of Reading. Adorned with cuts. Also the Catechism. Newburyport: Printed and Sold by John McCall; sold also by Isaiah Thomas, at his shops in Boston and Worcester. n.d. [?1790-1793].

Coll: sm 8°: [A8] B-E8 40 leaves (10.25 X 7.9cm.)

Illus: 48 alphabet woodcuts + 21 woodcuts in text

Binding: Blue paper over oak boards, brown calf spine Vertical chainlines. No pagination or foliation.

Anon.   #1643

The New-England Primer Improved. For the easy attaining the true reading of English. To which is added, the Assembly of Divines, and Mr. Cotton's Catechism, Boston: Printed by Kneeland and Adams, for John Perkins, 1767.

Coll: sm 16°: [A8] B-E8 40 leaves (9.4 X 7.4cm.)

Illus: Woodcut frontispiece (George III), 24 alphabet woodcuts, + 1

Binding: Contemporary tooled calf over oak boards Inside front board: "Samuel Frail His Primer; On frontispiece [A1]: 1769."

Notes: [G-3-28-51B]. No pagination or foliation.

Anon.   #1644

The New England Primer Improved. For the more easy attaining the true reading of English. To which is added, The Assembly of Divines, and Mr. Cotton's Catechism. Boston: Printed and Sold by John Boyle in Marlborough-Street, 1778.

Coll: sm 8°: [A8] B-E8 40 leaves (9.8 X 7.5cm.)

Illus: Woodcut frontispiece (John Hancock), 24 alphabet woodcuts + 1

Binding: Blue paper over oak boards, brown calf spine Vertical chainlines

Notes: 6-3-28-51   No pagination or foliation

Anon.   #1645

The New England Primer Improved, For the more easy attaining the true Reading of English. To which is added, The Assembly of Divines Catechism. New York: Printed and sold by James Parker, in Beaver-Street, 1768.

Coll: 16°: [A8] B-E8 40 leaves (9.8 X 7.6cm.)

Illus: Woodcut frontispiece (George III), 24 alphabet woodcuts, + 1

Binding: Original binding lacking
Notes: [A1]: "August th:5 [sic] 1772   Lydia White her Primer Keep it Clean and Neat And it always Will Look Sweet"

6-3-28-51B   No pagination or foliation

Anon.   #1646

The New England Primer; to which is added, the Shorter Catechism. Pittsburgh: Published by Cramer & Spear, Franklin Head, Wood Street, 1831.

Coll: 12°: [A-B12] 24 leaves (10.5 X 8.7cm.) Pp. [1-4] 5-46 [47] 48

Illus: 24 alphabet woodcuts + 2

Binding: Printed blue-gray paper wrappers, woodcut on back

Notes: G 12-17-48B

Anon.   #1649

A New Riddle Book, or a Whetstone for Dull Wits. Derby: Printed for the benefit of the travelling stationers, n.d.

Coll: 12°: 112 unsigned 12 leaves (14.4 X 8.9cm) Pp. [1] 2-24

Illus: 20 woodcuts in text

Binding: Yellow pictorial wrappers

Notes: BMC suggests a date of 1760. Chapbook

Anon.   #1650

The New Royal ABC Book, or the First Step to Learning. London: Printed and published by J.L. Marks, n.d.

Coll: 12°: 16 6 leaves (13.6 X 9.1cm.) Pp. [1 2 3-4] 5 [6-8] 9-12

Illus: 2 woodcuts

Binding: Green printed, pictorial wrappers

Anon   #1651

New Sinbad the Sailor. Illustrated by Barcoot. "The Album Series of Children's Picture Books." London: Gowan & Standring, n.d. Ff. 8 (includes plates).

Plates: 4 full-page in color.

Binding: First and last leaves are pasted down endpapers.

Anon.   #1652

New Story about Little Tom Thumb and His Mother. "Grandmamma Easy's Large Toy Books." Albany, N.Y.: Published and sold by Gray, Sprague & Co., 51 State-St., n.d.

Coll: Lrg. 8°: [18] 8 leaves Ff. 1-8 (27 x 18.1cm)

Illus: 8 colored woodcuts

Binding: Green wrappers. Illustration by Forbes and Pease on front, advertisement on back.

Notes: Printed on one side of leaf only. Initial and final pages pasted to wrappers.

Anon. #1653

New Testament Stories and Parables, for Children. New
Haven: Sidney's Press, 1808.

Coll: 16°: [A^{16}] B^{16} 32 leaves (10.5 X 6.4cm)
Pp. [1-3] 4-56 (? 57-64?)

Illus: Woodcuts

Binding: Tan printed and illustrated wrappers

Notes: McKell copy lacks covers and leaves B12-B16
A.A.S. #857.1

The New-York Book of Poetry. New-York: George
Dearborn, Publisher, 1837.

Coll: 8° [A]^3 B^2 1-32^4 133 leaves (23.2 x 14.7cm)
Pp. [1-vii] viii-x [1] 2-253 [254-256].

Plates: Engraved title page
Binding: Lavender covers
Notes: First ed. An annual containing the first
authorized printing of Clement Clarke Moore's
"Visit From St. Nicholas," i.e., "The Night
Before Christmas."

#1659.1

The New-York Book of Poetry. New-York: George
Dearborn, Publisher, 1837.

Coll: 8° [A]^4 B^2 1-32^4 134 leaves (22.6 x 14.5cm)
Pp. [1-2, i-vii] viii-x, 1-253 [254-256].

Plates: Engraved title page
Binding: Blue covers
Notes: First edition. An annual, containing the
first authorized printing of Clement Clarke
Moore's "Visit From St. Nicholas," i.e.,
"The Night Before Christmas."

#1659.2

Nieritz [Karl] Gustav   1795-1876

Die Maise. "Nieritz'sche Jugend-bibliothek."
Philadelphia: Morwitz & Co., n.d.

Coll: 8° 1-4^8 5^4 36 leaves (14.8 x 10.4cm) Pp.
[1-2, 3] 4-71 [72].
Binding: Paper over boards, printed.

#1661

Nieritz, [Karl] Gustav   1795-1876

Fünf Erzählungen für die Jugend. Nieritz'sche
Jugend-bibliothek." Philadelphia: Morwitz & Co.,
n.d.
Coll: 8° 1-6^8 7^{16} 8^4 68 leaves (15.1 x 10.5cm) Pp.
[1-2, 3] 4-31 [32], 33-34, 35] 36-61 [62-63, 64]
65-82 [83-84, 85] 86-115 [116] 117-118] 119-
134 [135-136].
Illus: Color woodcut on cover + plain woodcut on title
page
Contents: Five tales including Schwesterliebe; Der
(cont'd)

#1662

Nieritz   Fünf Erzählungen   (Cont'd)

Todsengraber; Das Reh Halsband; Backermädchen
Binding: Paper over boards. Adverts on back paste-
down endpaper.
Notes: Each story has half-title page and chapter
heading, except Backermädchen which lacks
both.

Nieritz, [Karl] Gustav   1795-1876

Schneider und Geiger. "Nieritz'sche Jugend-bibliothek." Philadelphia: Morwitz & Co., n.d.

Coll: 8° 1-8^8 64 leaves (14.8 x 10.2cm) Pp. [1-2,
3] 4-126 [127-128].
Illus: Color woodcut on front cover and plain woodcut
on title page.
Binding: Paper over boards.

#1663

Nieritz, [Karl] Gustav   1795-1876

Unrecht Gedicht Nicht. "Nieritz'sche Jugend-
bibliothek." Philadelphia: Morwitz & Co., n.d.

Coll: 8° 1-6^8 48 leaves (15.1 x 8.9cm) Pp. [1-2,
3] 4-96.
Illus: Color woodcut on front cover and plain woodcut
on title page.
Binding: Paper over boards. Advert on back paste-
down endpapers.

#1664

Nishikawa Sukenobu   (1671-1751)

Ehon Nishikawa Azuma warabe. 3 vols. Kioto, 1767.

Coll: 80 leaves. (22.9 x 16cm) accordion fold.
Printed on one side only.
Illus: 52 woodcuts, illustrating Japanese children's
lives in a year: 31 single-leaf; 21 double-
leaf (discrete border for each leaf).
Binding: Contemporary flowered wrappers; all within
a modern flowered cloth case.
Notes: Table of illustrations, in English translation, inserted in case.

#1665

Anon   #1667

Nonsense Alphabet. Nonsense Book Series. Chicago:
Donohue-Henneberry & Co. Copyright 1896 by Koerner &
Hayes. Ff. 8.

Illus: Numerous colored pictures throughout

Binding: Stiff wrappers, stapled. Initial and final
pages as paste down end papers.

Northend, Charles, A.M.   1814-1895   #1621

The Little Speaker, and Juvenile Reader; being a
collection of pieces in prose, poetry, and dialogue.
New York: Collins & Brother, n.d., [1849?]

Coll: 12⁰   1-13⁶ 14⁴   82 leaves   (15 x 9.6cm) Pp.
[1-5] 6-162 [163-164].

Illus: Engraved "frontispiece"

[ANON.]. A Nosegay, for the Trouble of Culling, or
Sports of Childhood. London: Printed by W. Darton,
Jun., 1813.   #1622

Coll.: 12⁰ : [A⁶] B¹² [C⁶(=A7-12)]. 24 leaves
(16.8 x 9.9cm). iv, 5-48 pp.

Illustrations: 36 woodcuts.

Bound in original blue wrappers, with advertisements
on back.
BMC # 7911. d. 45 indicates 8⁰

Anon.   #1623

La Nouvelle Omphale, Comédie, Représentée par
les Comédiens Italiens Ordinaires du Roi,
devant leurs Majestés le 22 9bre 1782. eta
Paris le 28 du même mois. Dédié aux Femmes
Vertueuses. [Paris: 1783]

Coll: 12⁰; [1⁴]; 4 leaves (11.2 x 8.7 cm.);
ff. 4.

Illus: Each leaf illust. in color, one side only.

Notes: First Edition.
       The center part of this small booklet
                    (continued)

Anon. La Nouvelle Omphale.   1783.   p. 2.

forms a harlequinade or turn-up of four parts,
each picture divided in the center, so that,
when opened, new pictures are formed.

#1674
The Nursery. A monthly magazine for youngest
readers. Boston: John L. Shorey, 36 Bromfield
St. John Anderson (illustrators, engravers).
Vol. X, No. 60, December, 1871-Vol. XXIII, No. 132,
December, 1877.

Notes: McKell collection lacking Vol. XII, No. 70,
       October 1872 and Vol. XXI, No. 125, May,
       1877.

Nutting, Judge [Newton Wright]   1840-1889   #1675

The History of One Day out of Seventeen Thousand.
Illustrated by Caroline S. King. Oswego, N.Y.:
R. J. Oliphant, 1889. Pp. [1]-[54].

Plates: 3 +cuts.

Nutting, William   #1676

The Juvenile Choir, for the use of Sabbath Schools,
Bible Classes, and the Social Circle. Philadelphia:
Joseph Whetham, 1840.

Coll: 16⁰ π²[1]-6 ⁸ 50 leaves (14.2 x 12cm) Pp. [1-4,
5] 6-96 [97-100].

Notes: First ed. (?). Pp. 97-98 are a free endpaper;
       pp. 99-100 are pasted down under another
       gathering of two leaves serving as free and
       paste-down endpapers. Gatherings 1, 3, 5 are
       not signed.

Observer, An

     see

        City Cries 1850

O'Keeffe, Miss [Adelaide]   1776-1855 ?   #1677

National Characters Exhibited in Forty Geographical
Poems, with plates. Printed by R. Galpine, Lyming-
ton. Printed for Darton, Harvey, & Darton, London.
1818.

Coll: 12⁰ A⁴ B-M ⁶ N 4   74 leaves (13.5 x 8.2cm)
      Pp. [1-2, 1-iii] iv [v] vi [1] 2-139, [140 : ads].
Plates: Frontispiece +7 copper engravings.

Okumura Masanobu   (1690-1768)   #1678

Yugashiki [i.e., Pictures of Ukiyoye Fancy.] 3
vols. Toto: Suharaya Mohei, 1820.

Coll: 132 leaves. (29.5 x 20.3cm) Accordion fold,
      printed on one side only.
Illus: 60 double-leaf woodcuts (20 in vol. I are
       hand-colored).
Binding: Orange (vol. I), grey (vol. II), and blue
         (vol. III) paper wrappers.
Notes: Table of illustrations, in English transla-
       tion, inserted in each volume.

Anon.   #1680

Old Dame Trot and her comical cat. Published by G. Martin, 6 Great St. Thomas Apostle, n.d.

Coll: 16°: (in 4s): 1-4⁴   16 leaves (12.8 X 9.7cm·)
printed on inner forme only. Pp.[1-32]

Illus: Engraved colored frontispiece (pasted to front
wrapper) 16 colored engravings.

Binding: Wrappers, gray front and buff back. Except for
the front wrapper and frontispiece-title page,
this seems to be an edition published by J. Harris. The first engraving in the text contains
"Publish'd Oct. 6, 1806, by J. Harris, corner
of St Paul's Church Yard, London." Martin's

Anon.

Old Dame Trot and her comical cat.

front wrapper is smaller (13.1 x 6cm) than the
leaves, and tipped in to the first leaf. A
possible replacement for a lost original wrapper.

Anon.   #1681

Old Dame Trott and Her Comical Cat. "Uncle Frank's Series."
New York: McLoughlin Bros., 30 Beekman, n.d.

Coll: 16°: [1⁴] 4 leaves (14.1 X 11.6cm). Pp. [1-8]

Illus: 8 colored woodcuts

Binding: Yellow wrappers colored in red. Illustrated on
front, advertisement on back.

Olney, J[esse], A.M.   1798-1872   #1682

Practical System of Modern Geography; or a view of
the present state of the world. 20th edition. New
York: Robinson, Pratt & Co., 1835.

Coll: 12° 1-24⁶   144 leaves (14.9 x 8.8cm) Pp.[1-v]
vi [7] 8-288.

Illus: Frontispiece + numerous engravings in text.

Olney, J[esse], A.M.   1798-1872 #1683

A Practical System of Modern Geography . . . .
Revised and Illustrated . . . . Eightieth edition.
New York: Pratt, Woodford & Co., 1853.

Coll: 12° 1-24⁶ 25⁴ 148 leaves (15.8 x 10.1cm)
Pp.[1-v] vi [7] 8-296.

Illus: Frontispiece + numerous illustrations in text.

Notes: Free endpapers torn out of McKell copy.

Olney's School Atlas. Pratt, Woodford, 1844.

see under

Robinson, Daniel T.

Omnibus # 1

Seven items bound together in one volume

Contents: (1) [Elliott] Elliot [Eliot] Mary [Belson],
Useful Gossip for the Young Scholar, q.v.
(2) Child, Mrs. [Lydia Maria (Francis)], The
Happy Grandmother . . . The White Palfrey,
q.v.
(3) Holiday Gifts for Good Boys And Girls, q.v
(4) [Dorset, Catherine Ann (Turner)] A Lady
(pseud) The Authentic History of Whittington and His Cat, q.v.

(cont'd)

Omnibus # 1   (Cont'd)

(5) Sleeping Beauty in the Wood, The History
of . . . ., q.v.
(6) King of the Peacocks and the Princess
Rosetta, The History of the . . . ., q.v.
(7) The Dairyman's Daughter., q.v.

Omnibus # 2

Seven items bound together in one volume. Front
attached endpaper has "Allen Terry To her Teddums,"
i.e., Edmund Gordon Craig] 10 March 1914."

Contents: (1) [Dorset, Catherine Ann (Turner)] 1750?-
1817?, The Lioness's Rout . . . sequel to
the Butterfly's Ball . . . . 1808 ., q.v.
(2) [Dorset (as above)] The Lion's Masquerade.
A Sequel to the Peacock at Home . . . .
1807., q.v.
(3) The Lioness's Ball; 1807 , q.v.

(cont'd)

Omnibus # 2   (Cont'd)

(4) The Horse's Levee, or The Court of
Pegasus . . . . 1808, q.v.
(5) The Council of Dogs, 1808, q.v.
(6) The Elephant's Ball, 1807, q.v.
(7) Roscoe, William . The Butterfly's Ball, an
the Grasshopper's Feast, Jan 1, 1807, q.v.

Notes: All of the above, except # (1), printed for
John Harris and associates. #(1) printed for
B. Tabart.

#1684

1,000 quaint Cuts from Books of Other Days including amusing illustrations from children's story books, fables, chap-books, etc., a selection of pictorial initial letters and curious designs and ornaments from original wooden blocks belonging to the Leadenhall Press. London: Field & Tuer, The Leadenhall Press, E. C. Simpkin, Marshall & Co.; Hamilton, Adams & Co.; New York: Scribner & Welford, n.d. Pp. vi 1-170.

Notes: McKell, G-9-28-43-B

Optic, Oliver

    pseud. of

        William Taylor Adams. 1822-1897

        q.v.

Anon   **#1688**

The Oracles: Containing Some Particulars of the History of Billy and Kitty Wilson; Including Anecdotes of their Playfellows . . . . and illustrated by Engravings. London: Printed for E. Newbery, [1795?].

Coll: 16° A-H⁸ 64 leaves (11 x 7.8cm) Pp. [1-7] 8-124 [125-128].

Plates: 14 wood engravings (John Bewick ?).

        (cont'd)

The Oracles   (Cont'd)

Binding: Dutch floral boards

Notes: H7-H8ᵛ: Advertisements of books printed for E. Newbery. Bookplate of Percival Merritt. McKell # S-1-23-43-B. Roscoe # 271

Ormesby Psalter

    see under

        Two East Anglian Psalters (also contains Bromholm Psalter)

Osgood, Lucius   **#1689**

Osgood's Progressive Second Reader: embracing progressive lessons in reading and spelling. Progressive Series. Pittsburg: A. H. English & Co., n.d., [1855?]

Coll: 12° 1-18⁶ 108 leaves (16.6 x 10.5cm) Pp. [1-2] 3-216.

Illus: Cuts.

Otis, James

    see

        Kaler, James Otis 1848-1912

Anon.   **#1691**

Our Favorite Fairy Tales. Jack the Giant Killer. New York: Sheldon & Co., n.d.

Coll: Sm 4°: [1¹²] 24 leaves Pp. [1-3] 4-24

Illus: 9 colored engravings

Binding: Yellow wrappers, front illustrated in color, advertisement on back

---

#1692

Our Young Folks: An Illustrated Magazine For Boys and Girls, No. 13 (January, 1866). Edited by J.T. Trowbridge, Gail Hamilton, and Lucy Larcom. Boston: Ticknor and Fields; New York: The American News Company; Philadelphia: T.B. Pugh; Chicago: John R. Walsh.

Coll: 8°: Pp. 1-[64]+ 1-4: advert.

Illus: Numerous plain engravings

Binding: Pictorial orange wrappers; advert on back.

Notes: Contains Harriet Beecher Stowe's "The Hen that Hatched Ducks." Pp. 35-41. John Townsend Trowbridge (1827-1916), Gail Hamilton (-), Lucy Larcom (1824-1893)

#1693

Our Young Folks: An Illustrated Magazine for Boys and Girls. Number 27, (March, 1867). Edited by J.T. Trowbridge, Gail Hamilton, and Lucy Larcum. Boston: Ticknor and Fields. Subscription office for New York City and Brooklyn.

Coll: 8° Pp. 9-192 + advertisement 1-4.

Illus: Several uncolored, plain engravings.

Binding: Pictorial orange wrappers. Advertisement on back.

Notes: Contains Harriet Beecher Stowe's "What Pussy Did with her Winters" Pp. 136-139. John Townsend Trowbridge (1827-1916), Gail Hamilton (-) Larcom (1824-1893)

#1694

Our Young Folks. An. Illustrated Magazine for Boys and
Girls. Number 52, (April, 1869). Boston: Fields, Osgood, &
Co., Successors to Ticknor and Fields. Subscription office
for New York City and Brooklyn.

Coll: 8° Pp. 15-272 + 1-8 advertisements

Illus: Numerous plain engravings.

Binding: Orange pictorial wrappers; advertisement on back.

Notes: Contains T.B. Aldrich's "The Story of a Bad Boy"
        Ch. VII, "One Memorable Night" VIII, "The Adventures
        of a Fourth" (accomp/by) "With a full page illus-
                                                (cont'd)

Our Young Folks. (Cont'd)

tration and two smaller designs by S. Eytinge, Jr."
Pp. 205-216.

#1695

Our Young Folks; An Illustrated Magazine for Boys
and Girls. Edited by J.T. Trowbridge and Lucy
Larcom. Vol. VI. Boston: Fields, Osgood, & Co.,
1870. Pp. 1-776.

Illus: Many full-page plates and smaller engravings.

Notes: A Bound Volume of Nos. i-xii, Vol. VI. This
        volume contains three poems by Edward Lear:
        "The Daddy Long-Legs and the Fly," "The
        Duck and the Kangaroos," "The Owl and the
        Pussycat." Possible first of these poems in
        print. John Townsend Trowbridge (1827-1916),
        Lucy Larcom   (1824-1893).

#1700

Paget-Fredericks, J[oseph Rous-Marten] 1908-

Miss Pert's Christmas Tree. Written and pictured by
J. Paget-Fredericks. New York: Macmillan, 1929. Pp.
[i-x]. 1-[30].

Illus: Front + 5 + cuts

Binding: Dust cover

Notes: Presentation page inscr. & signed by Author-
        illustrator.

#1701

Page, Thomas Nelson   1853-1922

Two Little Confederates. Illustrated [by Allan C.
Redwood and Edward Windsor Kemble]. New York:
Charles Scribner's Sons, 1888. Pp. [i-vi] 1-156; [1-8
of adverts bound in at end].

Plates: Frontispiece + 7.

Notes: First ed.

#1704

[Paltook, Robert]   1697-1767

The Life and Adventures of Peter Wilkins, a Cornish
Man . . . Embellished with Cuts. London: Printed
for E. Newbery, 1793.

Coll: 16° A-H⁸ 64 leaves (10.9 x 7.4cm) 128pp.

Illus: "Frontispiece"+12 other woodcuts in text
Binding: Dutch floral boards.
Notes: Bookplate of Percival Merritt. Roscoe #276(2).

#1705

Anon.

The Parents' Present to Their Happy Family; Containing
the Poems of My Father, Mother, Sister, & Brother, In
Imitation of Cowper's Mary. Embellished with Fifty Five
Engravings. Published by Johnson & Warner, and sold at
their bookstores, Philadelphia, and Richmond, Virginia.
A. Fagan, Printer, 1813.

Coll: 12° (6s) A-I⁶ 54 leaves
      Pp. [1-4, 5-6] 7-101 [102-108]

Illus: Frontispiece + 58 wood engravings

Binding: Pink wrappers; initial and final pages as paste
         down end papers
Notes: Only odd numbered   pages are paginated
       Welch 880

#1706

[Paris, John Ayrton]   1785-1856

Philosophy in Sport Made Science in Earnest, being
an attempt to illustrate the first principles of
natural philosophy by the aid of popular toys and
sports. In two volumes. Vol. II. [Illustrated.]
Philadelphia: Carey, Lea & Carey, 1828.

Coll: 12° A⁴ B-E⁶ Ff⁸ 174 leaves (14.4 x
      8.7cm) Pp. [i-iv, v] vi-viii [13] 14-351 [352].

Binding: Free and paste down endpapers front and
         back.
Notes: Chapter headin gs are not numbered.

Parley, Peter

    see titles under

        Goodrich, Samuel Griswold (1793-1860)

            and see

        Martin, William.

            and

        The Story of Captain Riley . . . .

#1707

[ANON]. The Pathetic tale of Poor Mary the Maid
of the Inn. London: Printed, and Published, by
J. Catnach, 2, & 3, Monmouthcourt, 7 Dials. n.d.

Coll.: 8° (4's): 1⁴ unsigned. 4 leaves (18 X 10.6
cm). [1-8]pp.

Illustrations: 5 hand-colored wood engravings + 1
uncolored.

Binding: yellow wrappers.

Page 1 title page has "Poor Mary the Maid of the Inn."
Inside front wrapper has C. Cousins 1845.

Anon

#1708

The Paths of Learning Strewed with Flowers or English Grammar Illustrated. Published September 25th 1820, by [John] Harris and Son . . . .

Coll: 8° 1^16 16 leaves (17.4 x 10.5cm) Ff. 1, 2-16.

Illus: 16 hand-colored copper engravings.

Anon.

#1709

The Path to Wealth and Wisdom. London: Printed and published by Edw.d Langley, May 1,1804.

Coll: 12°: [1^18] 18 leaves (13.7 X 8.7cm.) Pp. [1,2-35,36].

Illus: 34 colored woodcuts

Binding: Brown wrappers; front reads: "Printed and sold by Langley and Belch." Initial and final leaves serve as paste down end papers

Notes: [SC 8-27-47 B]

[ANON.]. Paul Preston's Voyages, Travels, and Remarkable Adventures; as related by himself. With engravings. London: John Harris, . . . 1838. [Printed by Samuel Bentley, Dorset Street, Fleet Street].

#1712

Coll.: 16° : A^4B-8^8. 118 leaves (13.4 X 10.4cm). [i-iii] iv-viii [1] 2-12 [13-14] 15-237 [238,1-16]pp.

Plates: Frontispiece, Orrin Smith, sc[ulptor]; de Rudrier, [del.] + 16 woodcut plates + various woodcut illustrations.

R^8 (16 pp.):J. Harris advertisements.

#1713

Anon

Paul Pry's Magic Lantern. Smithfield: Printed by J.L. Marks, [c. 1825].

Coll: 32° 1^4 4 leaves (10.6 x 6.3cm) Pp. [1] 2 [3] 4-8

Illus: 8 hand-colored cuts.

Binding: Peach pictorial wrappers; unopened.

The Peahen At Home, or the Swan's Bridal Day.

see under

Marks' Edition.

Pearson, Edwin

#1715

Banbury Chap Books and Nursery Toy Book Literature [of the XVIII and early XIX Centuries] . . . . London: Arthur Reader, 1890. Pp. [1-4, 1] ii-v [vi,1] 2-11b.

Illus: Reproduced illustrations on each page.

Peck, William G [uy] L.L.D.　　　1820-1892

#1716

Introductory Course of Natural Philosophy for the Use of Schools and Academies. Illustrated. New York & Chicago: A.S. Barnes & Co., 1873. Pp. [1] ii-viii, [9] 10-504.

Plates: Frontispiece + cuts.

Binding: Endpapers printed with advertising.

Anon.

#1718

The Pence Table Playfully Paraphrased, by Peter Pennyless. [London:] J. Harris, [1818?].

Coll: 16°: (4s) 1-4^4 unsigned 16 engraved leaves (12.9 X 10.6cm.) printed on inner forme only Pp. [1-32]

Illus: 16 hand colored engravings

Binding: Buff wrappers, pictorial, advertisements on back

Notes: B.M.C. #12807-AAA-60

Penn, James.　　1727-1800

#1719

Life of Miss Davis, the Farmer's daughter of Essex, who was seduced by her Lover, under a promise of marriage; and by him forced from her virtuous parents; Her grandeur while in keeping and extreme miseries she underwent till her return to her father. By James Penn. York: Printed by J. Kendrew, n.d.

Coll: 12°: A-C^6 18 leaves (16.9 X 10cm.) Pp. [1-4, 5] 6-36

Illus: "Frontispiece" woodcut

Notes: Bookplate of Howard Pyle. Title page has after James Penn "Vicar of Clavening cum Langley, in Essex, Lecturer of St. Ann and Agnes, Aldersgate.

Percy, Stephen (Pseud)

see

Cundall, Joseph　　1818-1895

[Percy, Thomas] 1729-1811   #*1720*

Reliques of Ancient English Poetry: Consisting of Old Heroic Ballads, Songs, and other Pieces of our earlier Poets, (Chiefly of the Lyric kind.) Together with some few of later Date. 3 vols. London: Printed for J. Dodsley in Pall-Mall. MDCCLXV.

Vol I:
Coll: 8° $A^8 b^6 B-Y^8 Z^4$ 186 leaves
Pp. [i-v] vi-xxiii [xxiv-xxviii,1] 2-344.

Plates: Engraved frontispiece+4 engravings.
Notes: McKell copy lacks A1 (half-title).

Reliques of Ancient English Poetry   (Cont'd)

Vol II:
Coll: 8° $A^4 B-2A^8 2B^2$ 190 leaves
Pp. [4]+i-iii [iv,1] 2-112, 129-144 ("145" mispaginated 451) 146-191 ("192" mispaginated 219) 193-384 [385-386].

Plates: 4 engravings.

Notes: [2B1] contains music notation for "For the Victory at Agincourt" (verso blank); [2B2] blank.

Vol III:
Coll: 8° $A^4 b^8 c^4 B-P^8$ (F3) $2P^8 - T^8$ (T6) $U^8 X^8 Y^5 2^8 **2$
        (cont'd)

Reliques of Ancient English Poetry   (Cont'd)

149 leaves. (   ) Pp. [4]+i-iii [iv, 1] ii-xxiv [1] 2-118,("119" mispaginated 153) 120-136 ("137" mispaginated 173) 174-240, 225-323 [324] 325-346 [347-350].

Plates: 4 engravings

Notes: Ms. leaf containing "L'Amore et Glycere (traduit de l'Anglois)" inserted after G3.

Notes: Back paste-down endpaper in each volume contains the bookplate of De Burgh, Marquis of Clanricarde, dated 1783.

[Perkins], Louise Saunders   1893-   #*1721*

The Knave of Hearts. With pictures by Maxfield Parrish. New York: Charles Scribner's Sons, 1925. Pp. [i-iv, 1] -[48].

Plates: Front+illustrated presentation page+title page+12 included in pagination.

Perrault, Charles. 1628-1703   #*1722*

Contes Des Fées, par Charles Perrault. Paris: Chez Le Fuel, Libraire, [ca. 1825].

Coll: oblong 4° 1-16⁸, 17   129 leaves (10.4 x 13.5cm)
Pp. [1-3] 4-6 [7] 8-78 [79] 80-94 [95] 96-171 [172] 173 [174] 175-178 ("179" mispaginated 779) 180-251 ("252" mispaginated 152) 253-258.

Plates: Front+title page+12 others by Sebastien Leray engraved by Noël. All in color.

        (cont'd)

Contes Des Fées. (Cont'd)

Binding: Red morocco with gold-tooled border. Has a hasp. Front and back free endpapers are of a paper different from the text.

Notes: Vertical chain lines. McKell #s SG-1-5-55-L; SG-1-10-55-B.

Perrault, Charles. 1628-1703   #*1723*

Contes Du Temps Passé par Charles Perrault. Contenant Les Fées, le Petit Chaperon-Rouge, Barbe-Blue, le Chat botté, la Belle au bois dormant, Cendrillon, le Petit-Poucet, Riquet à la Houpe et Peau d'Ane. Precédés d'une lettre sur les contes des fées par M. Le Marquis De Varennes, et illustrés par MM. Pauquet, Marvy, Jeanron, Jacque et Beauce. Texte gravé par M. Blanchard. Paris: Bertin, Libraire-Editeur, 1854.

Coll: 8° $1-4^4 5^2, 6^4, 7^2, 8^4, 9^2, 9-11^4, 12^2, 13-15^4, 16^3$ (16.1 pasted to 16.2-16.3) 59 leaves
(26.7 x 17cm)   (cont'd)

Contes Du Temps Passe (1854) (Cont'd)

Pp. [i-v] vi-xxxi [xxxii, 1-2] 3-6 [7-8] 9-16 [17-18] 19-22 [23-24] 25-36 [37-38] [39-46] [47-48] 49-56 [57-58] [59-70] 71-72 [73-82] [83-84] 85-104.

Plates: Engraved title page+9 others by various artists. Plates included in pagination. Each page of text beginning with [1] is illustrated with engraving and/or decorations.

Notes: McKell # S-7-11-47-B. Authorship of the above tales is now generally accorded to Pierre Perrault-D'armancour.

Perrault, Charles, comp.-   1628-1703   #*1724*

The Original Mother Goose's Melody. As issued by John Newbery, of London, circa 1760; Isaiah Thomas, of Worcester, Mass., circa 1785, and Munroe & Francis, of Boston, circa 1825. Reproduced in fac-simile, from the first Worcester edition, with introductory notes by William H. Whitmore. To which are added the Fairy Tales of Mother Goose, first collected by Perrault in 1696 reprinted from the original translation into English, by R. Samber in 1729. Boston: Parnell & Upham, The Old Corner Bookstore; London: Griffith Farran & Co., Limited, Newbery House, 1892. Copyrighted by W. H. Whitmore.   (cont'd)

The Original Mother Goose's Melody. (Cont'd)

Pagination: Pp. [1] 2-34, [35] 36-67 [68], [69-71] 72-78 [79] 80 [81] 82 [83] 84-86 [87] 88-94 [95] 96-98 [99] 100-104 [105] 106-109 [110] 111-117 [118].

Illus: Front+reprints of original woodcuts

Binding: Free and pasted down endpapers front and back.

[Perrault-D'armancour, Pierre].   #1725

Aschenputtel. Ein Altes Märchen neu erzählt von Gustav
Holting. Berlin: Windelmann und Söhne, [Druck von W.
Bormetter, Reue Grunstrasse 30.] n.d.

Coll: 12° 1⁸, 2⁴ (24=1·9-1·12) 12 leaves (17.9 x
    10.9cm) Pp. [1-2, 3] 4-24.

Illus: 14 hand-colored woodcuts

Notes: McKell # S-9-25-50-B

[Perrault-D'armancour, Pierre]   1678-1700   #1726

La Belle Au Bois Dormant Conte. , F.J. Paris:
Librairie Furne Jouvet Et Cie, Editeurs, 1885. Pp.
[1-2, 3] 4-32; [1] 2-16 of adverts.

Plates: Frontispiece +5 in color by C. Offterdinger.

Notes: Bookplate of Paul Gavault.

[Perrault-D'armancour, Pierre]   1678-1700   #1727

Blue Beard. "Pantomime Toy Books" New York: Mc-
Loughlin Bros., n.d.

Coll: 8° [1]⁸ 8 leaves (25 x18.2cm) Ff. [8].

Illus: A centerfold in oils

Notes: Centerfold like a harlequinade but turns from
    left to right.

[Perrault-D'armancour, Pierre]   1678-1700 #1728
Blue Beard; or, the Fatal Effect of Curiosity and Disobedience. Illustrated with elegant and appropriate engravings. London: Printed [by H. Bryer] for J. Harris, 1808.
Coll: 16°: A⁸ 8 leaves (12.X 9.8cm·) Pp. [1-3] 4-16

Plates: Frontispiece + 7, hand colored copper engravings.

Binding: Lavender boards with blue and white flowers.

Notes: "Sc 8-27-47-B

[Perrault-D'armancour, Pierre]   1678-1700   #1729

Bysh's Edition of the History of Little Red Riding Hood,
or the Deceitful Wolf. . . . Embellished with Eight
Coloured Engravings. London: Printed by T. Richardson
for J. Bysh, n.d.

Coll: 12° A-C⁶ 18 leaves (13.8 x 8.8cm) Pp. 36.

Plates: Foldout frontispiece contains eight tinted en-
    gravings.

Binding: Brown wrappers.

                                    (cont'd)

Bysh's Edition of Little Red Riding Hood.   (Cont'd)

Contents: A1: title; A1ᵛ: blank; A2-A3ᵛ: Introduction;
    A4-B4ᵛ: Little Red Riding Hood; B5-C6ᵛ: "The
    History of King Pippin and his Golden Crown."

[Perrault-D'armancour, Pierre]   1678-1700   #1730

Cendrillon. Conte ancien nouvellement raconte
par Gustave Holting traduit de l'allemand par
Emilie Mein. Berlin: Chez Winckelmann et fils.

Coll: 12°; [1¹²]; 12 leaves (16.1 x 10.1 cm.);
    [1-3] 4-24.

Illus: One full page colored illustration (p.16)
    plus numerous smaller colored illustra-
    tions.

Notes: Obsolete signatures present.

[Perrault-D'armancour, Pierre]   1678-1700 #1731

Cendrillon, Ou Le Petit Soulier Vert; Conte Imite De
Perrault. Paris: Chez De Laure, Libraire; Lille-
Chez, Libraire, Grande Place. [Lille: Imprimerie De
Blacquel. 1820.]

Coll: oblong 4° 1-4², 5⁴ 12 leaves (10.6 x 14.9cm)
    Ff. 12

Plates: Eight engravings on four plates

Binding: Initial and final leaves pasted to wrappers.

[Perrault-D'armancour, Pierre]   1678-1700   #1732

Cendrillon ou Le Petit Soulier Vert. Paris: Chez
Le Fuel, Libraire, Rue St. Jacques, No. 54. Vente,
Libraire, Boulevard Des Italiens, No. 7.

Coll: 32° π², 1-2⁸ [3⁴], [4⁸] 30 leaves (9.2 x
    6.1cm) Pp. [1-IV, 1] 2-32, 1-8 [9-24].

Plates: Frontispiece +8 engraved plates †one en-
    graving per page on pp. [11-22].
Binding: Free and paste-down endpapers.
                                    (cont'd)

Cendrillon ou Le Petit Soulier vert.   (Cont'd)

Notes: Pp. 1-8 at end of text are music supplement
    and pp. [11-22] are a calendar supplement.
    Pp. [9-10] and [23-24] are blank.

[Perrault-D'armancour, Pierre]   1678-1700   **# 1733**

Cinderella. Hamburg: Published by Gustav A. Seitz, n.d.

<u>Coll</u>: 8°   8 leaves.   Fr. 8.

<u>Illus</u>: Numerous in color on both sides of each leaf by Adolph Mosengel.

<u>Notes</u>: Book is bottle-shaped, with wrapper also shaped, colored, and illustrated. McKell Nos. S-11-19-46-L; and S-11-29-46-B

[Perrault-D'armancour, Pierre]   1678-1700

Cinderella or the Glass Slipper. New York: Published by Solomon King. n.d.   **# 1734**

<u>Coll</u>: 12°   1¹²   12 leaves   (17.7 x 10.2cm) Ff. [12].

<u>Illus</u>: 12 color cuts.

<u>Notes</u>: McKell copy has missing wrappers. #S-9-25-50-B.

[Perrault-D'armancour, Pierre]   1678-1700 **#1735**

Cinderella; or, the glass slipper. With original illustrations by H. L. Stephens. Printed in oil colours by J. Bien. London: Simpson Low, Son, & Marston, 1866. Pp. [1-11, 1] 2-13 [14].

<u>Plates</u>: Frontispiece +5 oil colors.

<u>Binding</u>: Bound by Bone & Son, 76 Fleet Street, London.

[Perrault-D'armancour, Pierre]   1678-1700 **#1736**

Cinderella; or the little glass slipper. A tale for the nursery. From the French of C. Perrault. Sixth edition with three copper plates. London: Printed [by Taylor] for Tabart and Co., No. 157, 1804.

<u>Coll</u>: 12° [B]-D⁶ 18 leaves Pp. 1-3 4-36.

<u>Plates</u>: Engrav. front +2, hand colored

<u>Binding</u>: Gray-green wrappers, paste-down endpapers

[Perrault-D'armancourr, Pierre]   1678-1700   **#1737**

[Cinderella, or the Little Glass Slipper. Philadelphia: Davis, Porter & Co.] n.d.

<u>Coll</u>: Large 8° [1-2]⁸ 18 leaves Pp. [1-2] 3-14 [14] 15-16 [17] 18-22 [23] 24-29 [30] 31 [32].

<u>Plates</u>: 4 engraved in color + engraved decorations on each printed page.

<u>Binding</u>: Yellow wrappers. Illus. on front, adverts on back. Initial page as paste-down endpaper; final page pasted to wrapper.

<u>Notes</u>: Plates printed on one side only. No inside title page.

[Perrault,-Darmancour, Pierre]   1678-1700 **# 1738**

Cinderella. "Pantomime Toy Books." N[ew] Y[ork]: McLoughlin Bros., n.d.

<u>Coll</u>: 8° [1⁸] 8 leaves [1-16pp] (24 x 18.5cm)

<u>Illus</u>: Center fold is a chromolitho harlequinade, turns from left to right.

<u>Binding</u>: Blue boards: color illustrations front; illustrated back. Initial and final pages pasted down.

Perrault[-D'armancour, Pierre]   1678-1700 **# 1739**

Les Contes de Perrault. Illustrés par A. Courboin, Fraipont, Geoffroy, Gerbault, Joh. L. Lorin, Robida, Vimar, Vogel, Fier. Introduction par M. Gustave Larroumet, de l'Institut. Paris: Librairie Renouard, Henri Laurens, Editeur, n.d. Pp. [1-4] i-[iv] 1-[116].

<u>Illus</u>: Cuts.

Perrault [-Darmancour, Pierre]   1678-1700 **# 1740**

Contes de Perrault. Illustrés par Grandville, Gérard-Séguin, Gigaux Lorents, Gavarne et Bertall. Paris: Publié par E. Blanchard ancienne Librairie Hetzel, Rue Richelieu, 78, 1851.

<u>Coll</u>: 8° 1-14⁴, 15³ (15.1, 15.2-15.3), 16-25⁴ 99 leaves. Pp. [1-9] 10-13 [14-15] 16-22 [23] 24-40 [41] 42-60 [61] 62-72 [73] 74-88 [89] 90-101 102-103] 104-118 [119] 120-190 [191] 192-197, [198, table of contents]   (19 x 13.5cm)

<u>Illus</u>: Frontispiece by Grandville + many other illustrations.   (cont'd)

Contes de Perrault (1851) (Cont'd)

<u>Notes</u>: Bookplate designated only by a crest: center or crest has embossed orange shield with three quarter-moons in silver; above are two swans (necks and heads only) in silver drinking from a gold chalice; number "18" in lower left corner. McKell # S-11-21-47-B. Gumuchian #4445.

[Perrault-D'armancour, Pierre]   1678-1700 **#1741**

The Entertaining Tales of Mother Goose for the amusement of youth, embellished with elegant engravings. Glasgow: Published by James Lumsden & Son, n.d., [1815?].

<u>Coll</u>: 18° A¹⁸ (archaic signatures present) 18 leaves (13.9 x 8.8cm) Pp. [1] 2-36.

<u>Illus</u>: engrav. front +title page +b

<u>Binding</u>: Blue-gray wrappers

<u>Notes</u>: McKell # S-6-28-45.

[Perrault-D'armancour, Pierre]   1678-1700 #1742
Fairy Tales of Past times from Mother Goose. Glasgow:
Published by J. Lumsden & Son. 1814..

Coll: 32°: (eights) A-C⁸ 24 leaves (9.85 X 6.1 ᶜᵐ·)
      Pp. [1-5] 6-10 [11] 12-23 [24] 25-30 [31] 32-47 [48]

Illus: Frontispiece woodcut + 5 vignettes in text

Binding: Lavender wrappers. Initial and final leaves
         serve as paste down endpapers.

Notes: "From Ross's Juvenile Library" on front

[Perrault-D'armancour, Pierre]   1678-1700 #1743

Histoire De Barbe-Bleue Qui Engonged Ses Femmes. Ornée
De 10 Gravures Coloriées. Leipsic: Chez Baumgaertner.
[ca. 1835].

Coll: oblong 8° 1⁸ 8 leaves Pp. [1-2] 3-16 (10.6 x
      16.2cm)

Illus: Front + 9 engraved plates in color.

Notes: Bookplate of Sznafranski no. 4035. Another copy:
       cropped (10.1 x 16.3cm). McKell # S-8-23-44-B;
       Gumuchian # 4455.

[Perrault-D'armancour, Pierre]   1678-1700 #1744

Histoires ou Contes du temps passé. Avec des moralitez.
Par le fils de Monsieur Perreault (sic) de l'Academie
Francois (sic). Suivant la Copie, a Paris. [Amsterdam:
Jaques Desbordes?], 1700.

Coll: 12° π4 A-G¹² H⁴ 92 leaves (13.9 x 7.4cm) Pp.
      [1-viii, 1] 2-175 [176].

Illus: Engraved Front + 8 engravings in text

Notes: Unauthorized ed., based upon the Barbin Paris
       ed. of 1697.

Perrault-D'armancour, Pierre]   1678-1700 #1745

Histoires ou Contes du tems passé. Avec des
Moralitez. Par Mr. Perrault. Nouvelle Edition
augmentée d'une Nouvelle, à la fin. Suivant la
Copie de Paris. Amsterdam: Jaques Desbordes, 1742.

Coll: 12° π4 A-G¹² H⁸ 96 leaves (14.4 x 8.1cm)
      Pp. [1-viii, 1] 2-184.
Illus: Engraved frontispiece + 8 engravings in text.
Notes: A reprint of Desbordes' 1729 edition.

Perrault [-D'armancour,] M. [Pierre]   1678-1700 #1746

The Histories of Passed Times, or the Tales of Mother
Goose. . . . [translated by Guy Miege and Robert Samber]
A New Edition, to which are added . . . The Discreet
Princess, and the Widow and her two Daughters. Adorned
with fine Cuts. 2 vols. London printed; and sold at
Brussels, By B. Le Francq, Bookseller. M.DCC. LXXXV.

Vol I:
Coll: 16° π4(-π4), A-K¹²+L⁴ 97 leaves (13.2 x 8cm)
      Pp. [iv] + 190.

Plates: Frontispiece + 7: engravings, numbered consecu-
        tively 1-8.
                                          (cont'd)

Histories of Passed Times (MDCCLXXXV)   (cont'd)

Vol II:
Coll: 16° π4(-π4), A¹²B²C-L¹²(-L11) 100 leaves (13.4 x
      8cm) Pp. [iv,1]-194 (= 196: B2 and C1 are both
      numbered 29-30).

Plates: Frontispiece + 1: engravings, numbered 9-10.

Notes: French text (verso) and English translation on
       facing pages. McKell #s SG-1-5-55-L; SG-1-10-
       55-B.

Perrault [-D'armancour] M. [Pierre]   1678-1700 #1747

Histories, or Tales of Passed Times with Morals. Written
in French by M. Perrault, And Englished by R[obert]. S
[amber]. Gent. Glasgow: Printed by Robert Duncan and
sold at his shop at Pope's Head Salt-mercat, 1769.

Coll: 12° A-I⁶ 54 leaves (14.9 x 9cm) Pp. vi,7-108.

Contents: G2-I6: The Discreet Princess; or, The Adven-
          tures of Finetta, A Novel.

Notes: McKell #s S-2-7-49-B; S-2-7-49-L.

[Perrault-D'Armancour, Pierre]   1678-1700 #1748

The History of the Sleeping Beauty in the Wood.
[Cork]: Printed by Charles Dillon, n.d.

Coll: 18° A⁶ 6 leaves (13.3 x 8.6cm) Pp. [3]
      4-12
Plates: Woodcut frontispiece
Notes: Bound in with six others in Omnibus # 1, q.v.

[Perrault-D'armancour, Pierre]   (1678-1700 #1749

Mother Goose: A comprehensive collection of the
rhymes made by William Rose Benét. Arranged and
illustrated by Roger Duvoisin. New York: The
Heritage Bookshelf, [1943]. Pp. [1-6] 7-112.

Illus: decorated throughout by Duvoisin
Binding: Dust cover
Notes: William Rose Benét (1886-1950)

[Perrault-D'armancour, Pierre]   1678-1700 #1750

Mother Goose Melodies with Magical Changes. "Star 2 Series
Fables." New York: G. W. Carleton & Co., Publishers. Copyright 1879 by Donaldson Brothers. Patent applied for.

Coll: Sm 4°: 1-8² 16 leaves (18.4 X 14cm) ff 16

Illus: 8 colored, by W.L.S. (+ 8 "half illustrations" on
       each leaf #1)

Binding: Wrappers

Notes: Every first leaf is only a half, so that it folds
       over half of leaf #2.   Both leaves have illus-
                                          (cont'd)

Perrault-D'armancour, Pierre

Mother Goose Melodies with Magical Changes. 1879. (Cont'd)

trations and text and operate in the manner of a
Harlequinade; the pages open in normal book order.
Illustrations and/or text on both sides of leaf.

#1755

Perrault [-D'armancour, Pierre]   1678-1700

Perrault's Tales of Mother Goose. The Dedication
Manuscript of 1695 Reproduced in Collotype Facsimile with introduction and critical text by
Jacques Barchilon. [2 vols]. New York: The Pierpont Morgan Library, 1956. Pp. [1-12, 13] 14-162;
(vol. 2) Ff. 67.

Illus: Vol. I: Frontispiece +7; Vol. II: Frontis-
      piece +7.

Notes: Vol. I: critical commentary; Vol. II: fac-
       simile of the (   ) 1695 MS. #42 of 600.

#1751

[Perrault-D'armancour , Pierre]   1678-1700

Mother Goose's Fairy Tales with two-hundred and
twenty illustrations by E.H. Corbould, Alfred
Crowquill [Pseud of Alfred Henry Forrester], W.
McConnell, and others. London and New York:
George Routledge and Sons, 1878. Pp. 320.

Illus: Frontispiece +illustrations.

Notes: Bookplate of Angus Waddle, #197. BMC: 12803.
       dd2.

Perrault-D'armancour, Pierre]   1678-1700 #1756

Puss in Boots. Illuminated With Ten Pictures. "Loomis'
Fairy Tales for Little Ones." New York: Brown, Loomis & Co.;
Boston: Brown, Bazin & Co., n.d. [1857?]

Coll: 16°: [A^14] 14 leaves (15.7 X 12.2cm), obsolete sig-
      natures present. Pp. [i-ii] 1-26

Plates: Engraved frontispiece, engraved title page (both
        tipped in following [A1]).

Illus: 8 engravings in text

Binding: Illustrated red wrappers, advertisements on back.
         Paste-down end-   (   ) papers.

#1752

[Perrault-D'armancour , Pierre]   1678-1700

Mother Goose's Melodies. Illustrated . . . from
original designs. Philadelphia: J.B. Lippincott &
Co., 1879. Pp. [1] 2-48 .

Illus: Cuts.

Perrault - D'armancour, Pierre]   1678-1700 #1757

Puss in Boots. Mounted on Linen. "Aunt Louisa's Big
Picture Series." New York: McLoughlin Bros., n.d.

Coll: Demy 4° [1^6] 6 leaves Ff [1] 2-6 (27 x 23cm)

Illus: 6 full-page plates, oil color, on linen.

Binding: Yellow wrappers on linen; illustration on
         front, advert on back. Initial and final leaves
         pasted down.

Notes: Printed on one side of leaf only.

1253

[Perrault-D'armancour, Pierre]   1678-1700

Mother Goose's Menagerie. By Carolyn Wells.
Pictured by Peter [Sheaf Hersey] Newell. Boston:
Noyes, Platt, & Company, 1901. Pp. [1] ii-x, 1-111
[112].

Plates: Frontispiece +11.

Notes: Carolyn Wells (act 1896-1942).

#1758

[Perrault-D'armancour, Pierre]   1678-1700

Puss in Boots. With original illustrations by H.
L. Stephens. Printed in oil colours by J. Bien.
London: Sampson Low, Son, & Marston, 1866. Pp.
[1-11, I] 2-11 [12].

Plates: Frontispiece +5 oil colors.

Binding: Bound by Bone & Son, 76 Fleet Street,
         London.

[Perrault-D'armancour, Pierre]   1678-1700 #1754

A New History of Blue Beard, Written by Gaffer Blackbeard,
for the Amusement of Little Lock Beard and his Pretty
Sisters. Adorned with cuts. Philadelphia: Printed by John
Adams, 1804.

Coll: 32°: [1^16] 16 leaves (10.1 X 6.1cm) Pp [2-5] 6-31

Binding: Greenish wrappers, [1_1^R] and [1_16^V] pasted to
         wrappers

Notes: Rosenbach 298, A.A.S. 895.4, Evans # 7025

#1759

[Perrault -D'armancour, Pierre]   1678-1700

Ritter Blaubart. Kindermärchen. Berlin: Verlag von
August Reise, n.d., [ca.1855].

Coll: 8° [1^8] 8 leaves Ff. [8] (20 x 14.1cm)

Illus: 8 colored woodcuts.

Notes: McKell # S-11-15-50-B

[Perrault-D'armancour, Pierre]   1678-1700   #1760
Sleeping Beauty in the Woods. "Fairy Moonbeam's Series."
New York: McLoughlin Bros., n.d.

Coll: 8°: [A⁴] 4 leaves (17.1 X 11.8cm) Pp. [1-8]

Illus: 7 colored engravings

Binding: Illustrated green paper wrappers, advertisements
    on back.

[Perrault-D'armancour, Pierre]   1678-1700   #1761
The Sleeping Beauty, Told by C.S. Evans and Illustrated
by Arthur Rackham. London: William Heinemann; Philadelphia:
J.B. Lippincott, Co., [1920].

Pagination: [1-9] 10-11 [12-13] 14 [15] 16 [17-19] 20 [21]
    22 [23] 24 [25] 26-30 [31] 32 [33-36] 37-38
    [39] 40-42 [43] 44-45 [46-47] 48-51 [52] 53
    [54] 55-63 [64-66] 67 [68-69] 70-74 [75-76] 77
    [78] 79 [80-81] 82 [83-87] 88 [89] 90-94 [95]
    96 [97] 98-100 [101-104] 105-110 [111-112]

Plates: 8 (silhouettes in color)
Illus: 16 full-page silhouettes + numerous silhouette fig-
    ures with text; color drawing of Sleeping Beauty
    laid on one page.

[Perrault - D'armancour, Pierre]   1678-1700   #1762
The Surprising Adventures of Puss in Boots, or the
Master-Cat. London:[Printed by S. and R. Bentley for] John
Harris,[ ].
Coll: 8°: 1¹⁶ 16 leaves (17.6 X 10.6cm.)
    Pp. [i, 1-3] 4-14 [15]

Illus: 14 hand colored engravings. Text and engravings on
    facing pages, alternating with blank facing pages.
    Leaf 16: Advertisement

Binding: Gray wrappers

Notes: Watermark on leaf 8 contains the date 1827.

[Perrault - D'armancour, Pierre] (in Russian) #1763
(1678-1700)
Volshebnyia Skazki Ilia Detei (Magic Fairy Tales for
Children). St. Petersburg, Izd. A. A. Pliusharom;
1839. (Two volumes in one)

Coll: 16° 1⁷ (1.1-1.6, 1.7), 2-10⁸ 11²(11.1 pasted
    to 10.8), 1-11⁸, 12⁹ (12.1-12.8, 12.9) 97
    leaves (13 x 10.6cm) Pp. [1-9] 10-15 [16-17]
    18-50 [51] 52-95 [96-97] 98-121 [122-123] 124-
    141 [142-143] 144-161 [162-164]; [1-9] 10-17
    ("18" mispaginated 81) 19-34 [35] 36-103 [104]
    105-114 [115] 116-122 [123] 124-178 [179] 180-
    192 [193-194].
                                         (cont'd)

Volshebnyia Skazki Ilia Detei.   (Cont'd)

Illus: Frontispiece +title page ; plus numerous other
    engravings.

Notes: Most of the tales are translations from the
    French tales of Perrault.

[Perrault-D'armancour, Pierre]   1678-1700   #1764
Walter Crane's Picture Books: Re-issue. Blue
Beard. London and New York: John Lane. Comp.
"Large Series" engraved and printed by Edmund
Evans. n.d.

Coll: 4° [1]⁸ 8 leaves (27 x 23cm) Ff.[8].
Illus: 8 color plate reprints by Crane.
Binding: Illustrated free and pasted down endpapers.

Perrault-D'armancour, Pierre (1678-1700)

    see also

        Cox, Marian. Cinderella. Three hun-
            dred and forty-five variants . . . .
            Folk-lore Society, 1893.
        Crane, Walter
        Cruikshank, George.

                                                  #1765
[ANON.]. The Peruvian Daemon; or Conjugal Crimes.
Containing Scenes of Terror in the Moorish Castle
of Honardo, and the Banditti Chamber of the
Alpine Mountains. London: Printed [by Lewis and
Hamblin] for T. and R. Hughes. . . . 1807.

Coll.: 12 : A-C⁶. 18 leaves (17.7 X 10.2cm).
[5-7]8-40 pp.

Plate: Engraved frontispiece.

Anon.   #1766
Peter Piper's Practical Principles of Plain and Perfect
Pronunciation. Philadelphia: Willard Johnson..., 1836.

Coll: 16°: [1-2⁸] 16 leaves (13.4 X 10.1cm) Ff. 1-16

Illus: Hand-tinted woodcuts (one on 1.1ᵛ)

Notes: [1₁ᴿ] and [2₈ᵛ] pasted to printed rose wrappers
    Rosenbach #813, (Rosenbach gives sm. octavo,
    A-B⁸)

Anon.   #1767
Peter Pipers Practical Principles of Plain and Perfect
Pronunciation to which is added a collection of entertaining Conundrums. London: [Printed by Samuel Bentley
and Co. for] Grant and Griffith, [1840?]

Coll: 8°: A¹⁶ 16 leaves (18.3 X 10.8cm.)
    Pp. [1-4] 5-28 [29] 30-32

Illus: 22 hand colored cuts
Binding: Yellow wrappers, advertisements on back.
Notes: [McKell # S-6-28-45]

Phelps, Elizabeth Stuart

see

Ward, Elizabeth Stuart Phelps 1844-1911

#1760

Philip, Uncle [Pseud of Francis Lister Hawks] 1798-1866

The Good Child's Own Book of Moral and Instructive Stories. "Franklin Lays." By Uncle Philip. New York: Philip J. Cozans, Publisher, 1856.

Coll: 8° 1¹² 12 leaves (18.8 x 12.4cm) Title page not paginated, but its verso is paginated "1" and the numbering is consecutive until 1·9ᵛ, which is p. 17 (then numbered consec., concluding on 1·12ᵛ which is p. 24).

Illus: 12 woodcuts

(cont'd)

Philip, Uncle   Good Child's Own Book   (Cont'd)

Binding: Cream colored wrappers: Illustrations on front, ABC's and numbers on back.

Anon.   #1770

Phoebe, The Cottage Maid, being a poetical tale, for the amusement and instruction of children of all ages. Embellished with eight coloured copper plates. New York: Published by S. King, of whom may be had the greatest variety of Toy Books in the United States. R. Tynell, Printer, 1824.

Coll: Octavo [1¹⁶] 16 leaves   Pp. [1-4, 5] 6 [7-8] 9-10 [11-12] 13-14 [15-18] 19-20 [21-22] 23-24 [25-26] 27-28 [29-30] 31-32   (16.1 x 9.9cm)

Illus: 8 colored copper plates, each illustration printed on one side of the leaf only

Binding: Orange wrappers

Notes: Percival Merritt bookplate

Picart, Mons. B

see

Young Clerk's Assistant. (Contains Picart's "A New Drawing Book of Modes")

Picket, A.[lbert]   1763-1850   #1771

Picket's Juvenile Spelling Book, or, analogical pronouncer of the English Language; conformable to the standard orthography of Johnson, and classic pronunciation of Walker; with appropriate definitions and reading lessons. Comprising a systematic, progressive, and practical course of instruction for primary schools. Last corrected edition New York: Printed and published by R. Bartlett and S. Raynor, 1835.

Coll: 12°: [1]-18⁶ 108 leaves (14.6 X 9.3cm) Pp. [1-5] 6-214 [215-216]

#1772

Picket, A.[lbert]   1763-1850
Picket, John M   , A.M.

Picket's Primer, or first book for children: designed to precede the Spelling Book. Cincinnati: U. P. James, n.d., [1863?]. Pp. [3-4] 5-31.

Illus: Frontispiece (inside front cover) + cuts.

Notes: P. 31 is the inside back cover.

Picton, Thomas   (1822-1891)

see

Preston, Paul

#1773

Picture Bible of the Late Middle Ages . . . Edited by Josef Hermann Beckmann and Ingeborg Schroth. Jan Thorbecke Verlag Konstanz. Bodensee. [Copyright 1960 Jan Thorbecke Verlag KG Konstanz]. Pp. 1-31 [32] (introduction laid in). Ff. 3, I-X, [1] 2-46.

Anon   #1774

Picture Lessons, Illustrating Moral Truths. For the use of infant-schools, nurseries, "Sunday Schools and family circles." Philadelphia: American Sunday-school Union, 146 Chesnut Street, [Ca. 1850].

Coll: Large 2° Ff. 18 (single leaves) (39.5 x 29.3cm)

Illus: Frontispiece + 9: full page hand colored lithos.

Pidgin, Cha[rle]s Felton   1844-1923   #1775

Quincy Adams Sawyer and Mason's Corner Folks.
Boston: G.M. Clark Publishing Company, 1900. Pp.
[i]-[xii], 1-586;[1] of adverts.

Plates: Frontispiece +1 fold-out map.

Pierpont, John   1785-1866   #1776

The National Reader; a selection of exercises in
reading and speaking . . . . Twenty-eighth edition.
Boston: Published by Charles Bowen, 1836.

Coll: 12° 1-23⁶ 138 leaves (18.7 x 10.8cm) Pp.
[1-iii] iv [v] vi-vii [viii, 9] 10-276.

Notes: First American text to include readings from
Shakespeare.

Pilkington, Mrs. [Mary Hopkins]   1766-1839   #1778

Biography for Girls;, Moral and Instructive
Examples for the Female Sex. Third Edition.
London: Printed for Vernor and Hood, Poultry;
and Newbery, St. Paul's Church Yard; By J. Cundee,
Ivy-Lane. 1800.

Coll: 24° [A]² B-S⁶ T4 108 leaves (12 x 8cm)
Pp. [i-iv, 1] 2-207 [208; 1-4] of adverts
for Vernor and Hood; "Books for Youth . . . ."

Plates: Frontispiece by Thurston.
(cont'd)

Pilkington. Biography for Girls. (Cont'd)

Bookplate of Percival Merritt. Roscoe
282 (3).

Pilkington, Mrs. [Mary Hopkins]   1766-1839   #1779

Tales of the Cottage; or, Stories Moral and
Amusing, for Young Persons. Third Edition.
London: Printed for J. Harris, 1803.

Coll: 24° A-S⁶ 108 leaves (12.8 x 7.8cm) Pp.
[iii-v] vi-viii, 1-6, 13-212; [1-4] of adverts.
(totals 216pp.)

Illus: Frontispiece (McKell copy lacking)

Notes: Bookplate of Percival Merritt.

[Pinchard, Mrs. Elizabeth]   #1780

The Blind Child, or anecdotes of the Wyndham family
written for the use of young people by a Lady. [2d.
ed.] London: Printed for E. Newbery, 1793.

Coll: 12° A-O¹²H⁶ (-H6)   89 leaves (16.5 x 9.6cm)
[viii, 9]-178pp.

Plates: Frontispiece (tinted engraving)

Notes: Bookplate of Percival Merritt. See Catalogue of
Osborne Collection, p. 289; Roscoe # 289 (2).
First ed. was 1791.

[Pinchard, Mrs. Elizabeth]   #1781

The Two Cousins, a moral story for the use of young
persons. . . . By the author of The Blind Child and
Dramatic Dialogues. London: Printed for E. Newbery,
MDCCXCIV.

Coll: 12° [A⁴] B-G¹² 76 leaves (16.7 x 10.4cm) [viii]
1-144 pp.

Plates: Frontispiece

Notes: 2 leaves adverts bound in at end. Bookplate of
Percival Merritt. Roscoe # 291 (1)

Pinnock, [William]. 1782-1843   #1783

A Catechism of Electricity, being a short introduction
to that science; written in easy and familiar language. Intended for the use of young people. Third
edition. London: Printed for G. and W. B. Whittaker
[by Shackell and Arrowsmith , 1822].

Coll: 12° (6's) π² A-F⁶ 38 leaves (13.8 x 8.8cm)
Pp. [1-iv, 1-3] 4-72.

Illus: Front +numerous steel engravings

Binding: Brown wrappers with adverts. Stabbed.

Planche, J[ames] R[obinson] 1796-1880   #1784

An Old Fairy Tale Told Anew in Pictures and Verse.
Illustrated by Richard Doyle. London: George
Routledge and Sons, [1865]. Pp. vi +1-51; [52:
bookplate];[53-56: advert for "Dalziels' Fine Art
Giftbook for 1866 . . . ."]

Illus: Frontispiece +18.

Binding: Blue and gold cloth, gold edges.

Notes: 4°   (4s) A-H⁴

Anon   #1785

The Playground; or, out-door games for boys.
Splendidly illustrated with 124 wood-cuts. New
York: Dick & Fitzgerald, Publishers, [186?] Pp.
[1-6 of adverts; 1] 2-4, [11] 12-120; [1-20] of adverts

Illus: Cuts.

Anon   #1786

A Pleasant and Useful Companion to the Church of
England; or, A Short, Plain, and Practical Ex-
position of the Book of Common-Prayer. . . .
London: Printed for J. Newbery, 1764.

Coll: 24° A-D⁸, I⁴ 116 leaves (9.6 x 6.4cm)
        Pp. 228+4.
Plates: Frontispiece+7 (copper engravings, some
        tinted).
Notes: P3: "Books Printed for J. Newbery . . . ."
        Bookplate of Percival Merritt. Roscoe #
        40(1).

[ANON]. The Pleasing Moralist: or, Young Gentlemen
and Ladies Preceptor. Containing Essays . . . To
which are added Advice to a Young Man . . . by
Solomon Winlove, Esq. Cuts by Bewick. London:
Printed for A. Millar, W. Law, and R. Cater.and for
Wilson, Spence, and Mawman, York, 1798. ["Advice to
a Young Man" by The Rev. Dr. Watts .]
Coll.: 32 (in 8's): A-F⁸. 48 leaves (11.1 X 8.2cm).
96 pp.

Illustrations: 31 woodcuts in text.

McKell copy Jacks A1.

Anon.   #1788

Pleasure Book for Children. The House That Jack Built.
Illustrated with twelve drawings, by John Absolon &
Harrison Wier, and Maja's Alphabet. Cleveland, Ohio: J.B.
Cobb & Co., 1856.

Coll: 12°: [1¹²] 12 leaves (17 X 11.3cm) Pp. [1-22] 23-24

Illus: 12 engravings

Binding: Buff wrappers, illustrations on front, advertise-
        ment on back.

Pletsch, Oscar (1830-1888)

        see

        Richter, Adrian Ludwig, and Oscar Pletsch,
            Nursery Carols. Bell and Daldy,
            1862.

Anon.   #1789

Poems for Children. By a Lady. New York: Mahlon Day...,
1837.

Coll: 16°: [1⁴] 2-5⁸ [6-7]⁸ 8⁴ 56 leaves (9.6 X 7.5cm)
        Pp. [1-5] 6-111 [112]

Illus: 34 woodcuts in text.

Anon.   #1790

The Poetic Gift: or Alphabet in Rhyme. New Haven: Published by S. Babcock. n.d.

Coll: 32°: [1]⁸ 8 leaves (8.9 X 5.5cm.) Pp. [1] 2-16

Plates: Woodcut illustrations.

Anon (L.C.)   #1791

Poetry for Young Children. Boston: Lilly, Wait,
Colman, and Holden, 1833.

Coll: 16° 1⁴ 2-6⁸ 7⁴ 48 leaves (13.8 x 11.3cm)
        Pp.[1-8, 9] 10-94 95-96.
Illus: "Frontispiece" and one other, hand colored
        woodcuts; + 2 decorative woodcuts on pp. 64 &
        82 (elephants).
Binding: Red cloth over boards; free and paste-down
        endpapers.
Notes: Adverts for Lilly, Wait & Co., on 7.4

[ANON]. Poetry Made familiar and easy to Young   #1792
Gentlemen and Ladies . . . . Being The Fourth Volume
of the Circle of the Sciences. The Third Edition.
London: Printed for Newbery and Carnan, 1769.

Coll.: 32° A-O⁸P2. 114 leaves (9.2 X 6.3cm).
4 + [i] ii-vi, 7-224 pp.

Contents: A6: "The Art of Poetry."

Binding: Blue boards, red leather spine.

Bookplate of Percival Merritt. Roscoe # 68 (3)

B6 missigned B4, E6 missigned E4, H5 missigned H3,
H6-H4, L5-L3, L6-L4.

Anon   #1793

Poetry Made Familiar and Easy. . . . Being the
Fourth Volume of the Circle of the Sciences, &c.
The Fourth Edition. London: Printed for T.
Carnan and F. Newbery, Jun., 1776.

Coll: 32° A-S⁸ 144 leaves (9.9 x 6.4cm)
        Pp. [1-4] i-vi, 7-281+[1-3].
Binding: Marbled boards, green vellum spine with
        paper label.
Contents: A6: "The Art of Poetry"; P3: "A
        Dictionary of Rhymes"; S7ᵛ: "Books
                                    (cont'd)

Poetry Made Familiar and Easy.   1776.   (Cont'd)

            sold by T. Carnan and F. Newbery,
            Jun. . . . . "
Notes: Bookplates of James Losh and Percival
        Merritt. Roscoe #68 (4).

Pogány, Elaine [Cox]   #1794

The Golden Cockerel from the original Russian fairy tale of Alexander Pushkin with pictures by Willy Pogány [William Andrew Pogany, 1882-1955]. New York: Thomas Nelson and Sons, 1938. Pp. [40].

Illus: Cuts

Binding: Dust cover

Pollard, Josephine   1834-1892   #1796

The Decorative Sisters: a modern ballad. Illustrated by Walter Satterlee. New York: Anson D.F. Randolph & Co., 1881. Ff. [1-18].

Illus: 18 on recto only

Notes: Text on versos. First edition.

Pollard, Josephine   1834-1892   #1797

Our Naval Heroes: in words of easy syllables. Illustrated by Edwin Forbes. New York: McLoughlin Bros, Publishers, [1886]. Pp. [vii], 8-192.

Plates: Frontispiece, vignette title page + 14.

Anon   #1798

The Poor Heathen or Missionary Sketches for Children. Philadelphia: Presbyterian Board of Publication. Paul T. Jones, Publishing Agent, n.d., [1850?].

Coll: 32°: [1]⁸ 2-6⁸ 7⁴ 52 leaves (10.9 x 7cm) Pp. [1-3] 4-104

Plates: Woodcut frontispiece + 7

Anon.   #1802.1-17

Popular Fairy Tales or a Lilliputian Library. 3 Vols. Baltimore: Published by Fielding Lucas Jr., John D. Toy, Printer, n.d.

Vol.1: The Discreet Princess
Coll: 12°: 1-2⁶, 3⁸ 20 leaves (14.2 X 9cm) Pp. [1-3] 4-40

Illus: Engraved, hand-tinted frontispiece and title vignette.
     Aladdin, or the Wonderful Lamp/The Three Wishes
Coll: 12°: 1-3⁶ 18 leaves (14.2 x 9cm) Pp. [1-3] 4-36
Illus: One hand-tinted engraving

Anon.   2

Popular Fairy Tales, 3 Vols.
     Jack and the Bean Stalk/Puss in Boots
Coll: 12°: 1-3⁶ 18 leaves (14.2 X 9cm·) Pp. [1-3] 4-35 [36]

Illus: Engraved, hand-tinted frontispiece
     Jack the Giant-Killer
Coll: 12°: 1⁴ 2-3⁶ 18 leaves (14.2 X 9cm·) Pp. [1-3] 4-31 [32]

Illus: Engraved, hand-tinted frontispiece
     The White Cat/Little Red Riding Hood
Coll: 12°: 1-3⁶ 18 leaves (14.2 X 9cm·) Pp. [1-3] 4-36

Anon.   3

Popular Fairy Tales, 3 Vols.

Illus: Engraved, hand-tinted frontispiece and plate.
     Riquet with the Tuft/Hop o' My Thumb
Coll: 12°: [1]² 2-4⁶ 20 leaves (14.2 X 9cm·) Pp. [1-3] 4-39 [40]

Illus: Engraved, hand-tinted frontispiece and plate
Notes: Advertisements bound in at end of volume
Vol. 2: Engraved, hand-tinted frontispiece and title page predede volume.
     Blue Beard/Cinderella, or the Little Glass Slipper

Anon.   4

Popular Fairy Tales, 3 Vols.
Coll: 12°: 1-2⁶ 3⁴ 16 leaves (14.2 X 8.9cm·) Pp. [1-3] 4-30 [31-32]

Illus: One hand-tinted engraving
     Fortunatus and the Wishing Cap
Coll: 12°: 1-3⁶ 18 leaves (14.2 X 8.9cm·) Pp. [1-3] 4-34 [35-36]

     The Fair One with Golden Locks
Coll: 12°: 1⁴ 26 3⁴ 14 leaves (14.2 X 8.9cm·) Pp. [1-3] 4-28

Anon.   5

Popular Fairy Tales, 3 Vols.
     Beauty and the Beast/Blanch and Rosalinda
Coll: 12°: 1² 2-3⁶ 4⁴ 18 leaves (14.2X8.9cm) Pp. [1-3] 4-36

Illus: Engraved, hand-tinted frontispiece and one plate
     The Invisible Prince
Coll: 12°: 1-5⁶ 6² 32 leaves (14.2 X 8.9cm) Pp. [1-3] 4-64

Illus: Engraved, hand-tinted frontispiece
     Fortunio
Coll: 12°: 1-2⁶ 3² 14 leaves (14.2 X 8.9cm) Pp. [1-3] 4-28

Anon.   6

Popular Fairy Tales, 3 Vols.

Illus: Engraved, hand-tinted frontispiece
Vol. III: Engraved, hand-tinted frontispiece and title page precede volume
     Prince Fatal and Prince Fortune/Tom Thumb/Toads and Diamonds
Coll: 12°: 1-3⁶ 18 leaves (14.3 X 8.9cm·) Pp. [1-3] 4-35 [36]

Illus: 2 hand-tinted engravings
     The Sleeping Beauty in the Wood/Peronella, or the Vanity of Human Wishes

Anon.   7

Popular Fairy Tales, 3 Vols.

Coll: 12°: 1-3⁶ 18 leaves (14.3 X 8.9ᶜᵐ·) Pp. [1-3] 4-36

Illus: Engraved, hand-tinted frontispiece and plate

Nourjahad, An Eastern Tale

Coll: 12°: 1-3⁶ 18 leaves (14.3 X 8.9ᶜᵐ·) Pp. [1-3] 4-35 [36]

Illus: Engraved, hand-tinted frontispiece.

Graciosa and Percinet

Coll: 12°: 1⁴ 2-4⁶ 22 leaves (14.3 X 8.9ᶜᵐ·) Pp.[1-3]4-44

Anon.   8

Popular Fairy Tales, 3 Vols.

Illus: Engraved, hand-tinted frontispiece

The Blue Bird

Coll: 12°: 1-5⁶ 6⁴ 34 leaves (14.3 X 8.9ᶜᵐ·) Pp. [1-3] 4-66 [67-68]

Illus: Engraved, hand-tinted frontispiece

#1803

Porter, Miss C. B.

The Silver Cup of Sparkling Drops, from many fountains for the friends of temperance. Buffalo: Geo. H. Derby and Co., 1852.

Coll: 8° 1-13¹² 156 leaves (18.5 x 12cm) Pp. [1-v] vi [7] 8-312.

Plates: Engraved title page

#1804

Porter, Jane   1776-1850

The Scottish Chiefs. Edited by Kate Douglas Wiggin and Nora A. Smith. Illustrated by N[ewell] C[onvers] Wyeth. New York: Charles Scribner's Sons, 1921. Pp.[xviii], 503+1.

Plates: 14.

#1805

[ANON.]. Portraits of Curious Characters in London, &c. &c. With Descriptive & Entertaining Anecdotes. . . . London: Printed By and For W. and T. Darton, . . . 1809.

Coll.: A-I⁶(-I6). 53 leaves (13.8 X 8.3cm). [1]2-105[106] pp.

Illustrations: 19 engravings in the text.

McKell copy lacks I6 (probably originally blank). I5ᵛ: advertisements.

Potter, Beatrix.[Mrs. William Heelis] 1866-1943 #1810

"An Old Woman who Lived in a Shoe" manuscript, unpublished..

Coll: 3 leaves (11.4 X 17.7ᶜᵐ·)

Illus: Pen-and-ink watercolor

Notes: Written and illustrated by Beatrix Potter and meant as a personal Christmas greeting.
Fol. 1: "Wishing you a Merry Christmas/and a Happy New Year--/Dec. 24th 97."
Fol. 2-3: Text of the nursery rhyme with two drawings. [S-4-17-48-B]. See Also Quinby, Jane. Beatrix Potter; a bibliographical checklist.

#1811

Potter, Beatrix (Mrs. William Heelis) 1866-1943

Twelve autograph illustrated letters, dated from April 11, 1892-March 13, 1900. Eleven are addressed to Noel Moore, one to "My dear Marjory." Positive and negative photostat copies.

Notes: Originals presented to Pierpont Morgan Library. Together with an epitaph, "In affectionate remembrance of poor old Peter Rabbit." Positive and negative photostats.

[Prang, Louis] comp.   1824-1909   #1814

[Folding Lithograph Series]. Boston: Published by L. Prang & Co. [4 Vols.] [Entered 1865].

Coll: 32°: [1⁸, 2⁴] 12 leaves ff 12 (glued; single fold out)

Contents: "Dame Duck's Lecture", "Who Stole the Bird's Nest", "A Farm Yard Story", "The Story of Hans the Swapper"

Illus: 48 colored lithographs (12 each)

Binding: Cardboard wrappers.

         (cont'd)

Prang, Louis   (Cont'd)

[Folding Lithograph Series, 1865.]

Notes: The four above are identical in format and printed on one side of page only. Only "Story of Hans the Swapper" has internal title page; that title page has "Entered...1864." See also Calkins, Norman Allison. Prang's Natural History Series . . . . Plants. Birds. Quadrupeds. Boston: 1872.

Presbyterian Board of Publication

     see

         Poor Heathen or Missionary Sketches for Children.

 # 1815.1-2

[ANON.]. Present from My Father; Containing Histories, Voyages, Travels, &c. Embellished with appropriate wood engravings. Derby: published by Thomas Richardson; Simpkin, Marshall, and Co., London. 1835. [Thomas Richardson, Derby, printer.] [3 vols. in one.]
Vol. I.: "Adventures of Robinson Crusoe."
Coll.: 12° (12's): A-B¹². 24 leaves (17.8 X 10.4cm). [1-5]6-47[48] pp.

Illustrations: Hand-colored, wood-engraved frontis-piece + several cuts.

Vol.II. Sinbad the Sailor."
Coll.: 12° (12's): A(-A,A2)-B¹². 22 leaves

Father –?–

(17.8 X 10.4cm). [5]-6-47[48]pp.

Illustrations: several woodcuts.

Vol.III.: "Little Red Riding Hood" and "The History of King Pippin and his Golden Crown."
Coll.: 12° (12's): A(-A,A2)-B¹². 22 leaves (17.8 X 10.4cm). [5]6-26[27]-47[48]pp.

pp.-312: "King Pippen."

 # 1819

Preston, Paul [pseud of Thomas Picton] 1822-1891

Paul Preston's Book of Gymnastics: or sports for youth. A legacy to promote the health and long life of his youthful friends. Boston: Munroe and Francis, 1842.

Coll: 16° 1-14⁴ 84 leaves (13.9 x 11.5cm) Pp.[1-4] 5[6-7]8-9[10-11]12-166.

Plates: Frontispiece + title page + numerous cuts.

Notes: Front + title page are conjugate plates not in-cluded in the pagination. Obsolete signings present.

 # 1820

[ANON.]. The Pretty Fortress Of Windsor Lodge; Or, Filial Affection Rewarded, In The Instance Of A Royal Protegee. A Moral Tale. Illustrated With Copper-Plates. London: William Darton [printer] . . . Sold also by Harvey and Darton . . . and John Harris . . . , n.d.

Coll.: 12°: A-I⁶. 54 leaves (13.8 X 8.6cm). [i-iii] iv[5]6-108 pp.

Plates: Frontispiece + 2 (laid in).

Osborne (p. 201) gives a fly-leaf date of 1832.
BMC: [1820?].

 # 1821

Anon
Pretty Tales for the Nursery. London: The Religious Tract Society, [ca. 1863].[London: Benjamin Pardon, Printer, Paternoster Row]. Pp.[1-3] 4-80.

Plates: 4 chromolithos by J. M. Kronheim & Co.+17 illustrations.

 # 1822

Prime, Benjamin Young 1733-1791

Muscipula Sive Cambromyomachia: the mouse-trap, or the battle of the Welsh and the mice; in Latin and English: with other poems, in different languages. By an American. New-York: Published by M. Dodd. Albany: W.C. Little. Boston: Crocker & Brewster. Philadelphia: J. Whetham. [Entered 1840.]

Coll: 8° [A]⁴,[B]-T⁸ O⁴ 48 leaves (16.7 x 11.2cm) Pp.[1-4, 5] 6-8[9],10[11]12-96.
Plate: Frontispiece [ ] (map). (cont'd)

Prime. Muscipula . . . . 1840. (Cont'd)

Binding: Stabbed and sewn. 2 free and 2 paste-down endpapers front and rear.

Primer
see also
The London Primer. London: Sir Richard Phillips, 1820?
The Royal Primer. J. Newbery, 1767?
The Tract Primer. American Tract Society, 1848?

Primrose Prettyface
see
The History of Primrose Prettyface . . . . John Harris, 1850.

 # 1824

Anon.
The Prize for Youthful Obedience. Parts I and II, in 2 Vols. Philadelphia: Published by Jacob Johnson, No. 147 Market Street. John Bioren, Printer, 1807.

Part I:
Coll: 12°: (6s) B⁶ B-D⁶ E⁴ 28 leaves (16.3 X 9.6cm) $1 (-B + all φ'3' leaves are signed 2) signed. Pp. [i-ii, 1-52][53-54]
Illus: Various woodcuts
Binding: Hard wrappers, final pages as paste down endpapers
Notes: Merritt bookplate. Rosenbach #352 (Cont'd)

Anon.

The Prize for Youthful Obedience, 1807. 2 Vols. *(Cont'd)*

Part II:

Coll: 12°: (6s) A² B-E⁶ 26 leaves (16 X 9.5cm) $1 (-A + all #'3' leaves signed 2) signed. Pp. [i-ii, 1-50]

Illus: Various woodcuts

Binding: Hard wrappers

Notes: Merritt bookplate

Anon.   # 1825

The Progress of the Dairy; Descriptive of the Method of Making Butter & Cheese; for the Information of Youth. New York: Published by Samuel Wood and Sons, No. 261, Pearl-Street; Baltimore: Samuel S. Wood & Co., No. 212, Market-Street, n.d.

Coll: 16°: 1¹⁴ 14 leaves (12.9 X 10.4cm) Pp. [1-4, 5] 6 [7-10] 11-12 [13-16] 17-18 [19-20] 21-22 [23-24] 25-27 [28]

Illus: 7 engravings

Binding: Blue wrappers

Psalms, the Book of   # 1826

The Book of Psalms from the version of Miles Coverdale as published in the "Great Bible" of 1539. With an introduction by Francis Jormald . . . and facsimile reproductions of eight illuminated folios from the fourteenth century manuscript known as Queen Mary's Psalter. Westminster: The Hay-market Press, 1930. Pp. [i]-[xviii], 1-157 [158].

Illus: Frontispiece + 7 included in pagination.

Notes: See also Queen Mary's Psalter.

Psalters

    see under

      Queen Mary's Psalter

      Two East Anglian Psalters (contains Ormesby and Bromholm Psalters)

Anon.   # 1827

Pug's Tour Through Europe as related by himself. Baltimore: Published by F. Lucas Jr., Philadelphia: Ash & Mason, n.d.

Coll: 8°: [1¹⁸] 18 leaves, Ff. [i] 1-16 [17]

Illus: Title page plus sixteen: all hand colored copper plates.

Binding: Wrappers (missing)

Notes: Printed on one side of leaf only. McKell #S-16-45B

Anon   # 1828.1

Punctuation Personified: or pointing made easy. by Mr. Stops. London: J. Harris and Son, 1824.

Coll: 8° π [1¹⁶] χ 18 leaves (17.7 x 10.6 cm) Ff. [i] 1-16 [17-18]

Illus: Colored engravings

Notes: Title page of McKell copy missing. Advertisements for "Harris' Cabinet of Amusement and Instruction" on χ.

     # 1828.2-3

Punctuation Personified: or pointing made easy. By Mr. Stops. London: J. Harris and Son, 1824.

Coll: 8° π¹, [1¹⁶] 17 leaves (17.7 x 10.6cm) Pp. [1-ii] ff. 1-16.

Illus: 16 hand colored engravings

Binding: Blue printed wrappers

Notes: One of Harris's "Cabinet of Amusement and Instruction." Plus another copy: lacking title

               (cont'd)

Punctuation Personified. 1824 (Cont'd)

     page; numbered ff. 1-16, + 1 leaf advertisement, on recto, for Harris's Cabinet of Amusement and Instruction listing 52 titles; has bookplate of Percival Merritt. Both copies printed on one side of leaf only.

Pushkin, Aleksandr Sergeyevich. 1799-1837   # 1830

Le Coq D'Or et d'autres contes de A. S. Pouchkine Illustres par B. Zworykine. L'edition d'art. Paris: H. Piazza, [1925]. Pp. [1-5] 6-76 [77-82].

Plates: 20 full-page lithos + decorations every page.

Anon   # 1829

Punctuation Personified; or painting made easy: by Mr. Stops. Published by H. Anderson, Cadiz, Ohio. Sold by J. & B. Turnbull: Steubenville, 1829.

Coll: 8° [1⁸] Ff. [8] (17.5 x 11cm)

Illus: Hand-colored woodcuts, one or more on each leaf.

Notes: Each leaf printed on one side only.

Pushkin, Aleksandr Sergeyevich 1799-1837   ## 1831

Pesn' O Veshchem Olege (Song of Oleg The Wise). Illustrations [and colored lettering] by V[ictor][M] Vasnetsov. [Text of the Song and the cover page done by V( ) D( ) Zamiraylo.] By authority of the High Commission established by the Imperial Acadmy of Sciences to honor the memory of A[leksandr] S[ergeyevich] Pushkin. A publication of the Office for the Publication of State Documents. In honor of the 100th anniversary of Pushkin's birth. May 26, 1899. Pf. [6].

Illus: Color illustrations - - on each leaf.

Binding: Unbound; one piece, uncut, accordion folds.

Pushkin, [Aleksandr Sergeyevich] 1799-1837   ## 1832

Skazka (Fairy Tale) O Zolotom Petushke (Of the Golden Cock). [Pushkin's Fairy Tales.] Illustrations by I[van] Y[akovlevich] Bilibin . . [A publication of the Office for the Publication of State Documents,] 1907. Pp. [1-2], 3-11, [12].

Illus: Color illustrations and decorations every page. Each illustration dated 1906 or 1907, but one on back of title page is dated 1910.

Binding: Pictorial wrappers bound in. Rebound in one volume with "Tale of Czar Sultan . . . ."

Pushkin, [Aleksandr Sergeyevich] 1799-1837   ## 1833

Skazki Pushkina (Pushkin's Fairy Tales). Skazka O Tsare Saltane, o sine ego, slavnom i moguchem vogatire knyaze Gvidone Saltanoviche, i o prekrasnoi tsarevne Lebedi. (The Tale of Czar Sultan, about his son, the glorious and powerful knight, Prince Gvidon Saltanovich, and of the beautiful Swan Princess). Risunki I. Ya. Bilibina. (Drawings by I[van] Y[akovlevich] Bilibin . Izdaniye Ekspeditsi Zagotovleniya Gosudarstvennika Bumag (A Publication of the Office for the Publication of State Documents), 1906. Pp. [1-2, 3] 4-20.

Illus: Several illustrations (5 full page) and decorations, all color.

Binding: Pictorial wrappers bound in. Second title

Pushkin, Aleksandr Sergeyevich 1799-1837

Tale of Czar Sultan . . . .

page on [1]. Rebound in one volume with "Tale of the Golden Cock."

Pushkin, Aleksandr Sergeyevich (1799-1837)

see also

Pogany, Elaine Cox. The Golden Cockerel . . . . Nelson and Sons, 1938.

Anon   ## 1834

Put's Original California Songster . . . . 4th ed. San Francisco: D. E. Appleton & Co., 1868. Pp. [i] - vi [7] -54.

Notes: Copyright 1854 by John A. Stone

Puzzlewell, Peter

see

A Choice Collection of Riddles, Charades, Rebusses, &c. . . . . E. Newbery

---

Pyle, Howard   1853-1911   # 1835

Men of Iron. Illustrated [by Howard Pyle]. New York: Harper & Brothers, 1892. Pp. [i-iv] v-vi, 1-328.

Plates: Frontispiece ≠ 20.

Notes: First ed. Blanck, p. 391.

Pyle, Howard   1853-1911   #1836.1

Otto of the Silver Hand. Illustrated by Howard Pyle. New York: Charles Scribner's Sons, 1888. Pp. xiii, [1-] 2-170 [171;1-16 of adverts].

Plates: Frontispiece ≠ 24 full-page plates ≠ vignettes.

Notes: First edition. Blanck, p. 391. Advertising pp. [9-16] are upside down.

Pyle, Howard   1853-1911   #1836.2-3

Otto of the Silver Hand. Illustrated by Howard Pyle. New York: Charles Scribner's Sons, 1888. Pp. xiii [1] 2-170 [171; 1-16 of adverts.]

Plates: Frontispiece ≠ 24 full-page ≠ vignettes.

Notes: First edition. Plus another copy.

Pyle, Howard   1853-1911   #1837

Pepper & Salt, or seasoning for young folk. Prepared by Howard Pyle. New York: Harper and Brothers, 1881. Pp. [1] ii-xiii [xiv] 1-121 [122; 1-2 of adverts].

Plates: Frontispiece + cuts.

Pyle, Howard   1853-1911   #1838

The Rose of Paradise . . . . Illustrated [by Howard Pyle]. New York: Harper & Brothers, 1888. Pp. [i-vi], 1-232.

Plates: Frontispiece + 7.

Notes: First edition. Blanck, p. 391.

Pyle, Howard   1853-1911   #1839

The Ruby of Kishmoor. [Illustrated by Howard Pyle]. New York and London: Harper & Brothers Publishers, 1908. Pp. [i-viii] 1-74.

Plates: Frontispiece + 9 (all color).

Binding: Uncut.

Notes: First edition. Blanck, p. 391.

Pyle, Howard   1853-1911   #1840

Stolen Treasure. Illustrated by the author. New York & London: Harper and Brothers Publishers, 1907. Pp. [i-vi, 1] 2-253 [254].

Plates: Frontispiece + 6.

Notes: Plate listed for page 40 torn out of McKell copy.

Pyle, Howard   1853-1911   #1841

The Story of Jack Ballister's Fortunes. [Illustrated by Howard Pyle]. New York: The Century Co., 1895. Pp. [i-vi] vii-ix [x-xii] 1-420.

Plates: Frontispiece + 13.

Notes: First edition. Blanck, p. 391.

Pyle, Howard   1853-1911   #1841, 1-2

The Wonder Clock or Four & Twenty Marvelous Tales, being one for each hour of the day; written and illustrated by Howard Pyle. Embellished with verses by Katherine Pyle. New York: Harper & Brothers, 1888. Pp. [i-v] vi-xiv [1-3] 4-318+[1-2].

Plates: Frontispiece + 24 by Katherine Pyle; numerous, some full-page, illustrations by Howard Pyle.

Notes: First edition. Blanck, p. 391. McKell # 0-1-30-45B.   Plus another copy.

Pyrnelle, Louise-Clarke   1852-   #1843

Diddie, Dumps, and Tot; or, plantation child-life. Illustrated. New York: Harper & Brothers, 1882. Pp. [xii] 13-217, [218-222].

Plates: Front + 11.

Notes: Bookplate of John Stuart Groves.

Quarll, Philip

see

         Longueville, Peter. The English Hermit . . . Philip Quarll. Marshall, c. 1790.

#1845

Queen Mary's Psalter: miniatures and drawings by an English artist of the fourteenth century reproduced from Royal MS. 2B VII in the British Museum. Introduction by Sir George Warner. London: British Museum, 1912. Pp. vi [1] 2-92 + 315 [316] of plates of reproductions of the Psalter.

Notes: Photo-facsimile; presentation copy from the British Museum to Miss Belle da Costa Greene, first librarian and confidential art secretary to Pierpont Mor-
(cont'd)

Queen Mary's Psalter   (Cont'd)

gan, and later first Director of the Pierpont Morgan Library. See also The Bay Psalm Book; and under Psalms, The Book of . . . . With . . . repros from . . . Queen Mary's Psalter. Haymarket Press, 1930.

Quinby, Jane 1901- # 1846

Beatrix Potter; a bibliographical check list. New York: [No publisher other than Quinby] 1954. Pp. 7-121.

Notes: Beatrix Potter, i.e., Mrs. William Heelis, 1866-1943. See also under Potter, Beatrix. "An Old Woman Who Lived in a Shoe." (an unpublished manuscript.)

Rabelais, François. 1490-1553 # 1847

Oeuvres...précédées d'une notice historique sur la vie... par P.L. Jacob...et accompagnée de Notes succinctes et d'un Glossaire par Louis Barré...illustrations par Gustave Doré. Paris: J. Bry Ainé, Libraire-Éditeur,... 1854.

Coll: 2°: [1⁶]2-42⁴ 43² 172 leaves Pp. [i-iv, 1-5] 6-339 [340]. (26.9 x 19.6cm),
Plates: 14 engravings by Doré (with numerous additional engravings in the text.

Binding: Red half-calf over red and black marbled boards; original paper wrappers bound in.
Notes: [S-5-12-51B]

Rabier, Benjamin [Armand] (1869-) # 1848

L'Esprit à 4 Pattes par Benjamin Rabier. Série universelle. Épinal: Imagerie Pellerin. n.d.

Coll: lge 4° [1⁸] 8 leaves Pp. [1-16]. (30.9 x 24.4cm)

Illus: Several chromolithos on every page

Binding: Stiff, pictorial wrappers; stapled.

Rackham, Arthur (1867-1939) # 1849

Peter Pan Pictures from Peter Pan in Kensington Gardens. Illustrated by Arthur Rackham. Woman at Home Supplement. Christmas, 1907. London: Hodder & Stoughton, n.d. Pp. [1-36: includes 32 Rackham illustrations].

Rackham, Arthur (1867-1939) # 1850

Some British Ballads. Illustrated by Arthur Rackham. New York: Dodd Mead & Co., n.d. Pp. [1-5] 6 [7] 8 [9-10,1] 2-170 [171-172].

Plates: Frontispiece + 15 color illustrations.

Rackham, Arthur (1867-1939) # 1851

Some British Ballads. Illustrated by Arthur Rackham. New York: Dodd Mead & Co., n.d. Pp. [1-5] 6 [7] 8 9-10, 1] 2-170 [171-172].

Plates: 16 small color plates, captioned, laid on heavy gray backing paper numerous cuts and decorations.
Binding: Decorative endpapers.
Notes: Published also by Constable, 1919. Colophon p. [171]; p. [172] is blank.

[Raspe, Rudolf Erich] 1737-1794 # 1852

Adventures du Baron de Münchhausen; traduction nouvelle par Théophile Gautier fils, illustrées par Gustave Doré. Paris: Charles Furne, Libraire-Éditeur [1862].

Coll: 2° [1]⁴ 2-29⁴ 30³ 119 leaves Pp. [1-5] 6-238 (leaves containing full-page illustrations are not paginated.)
Illus: 153 engravings (30 full-page) by Doré.
Notes: S-11-15-50-B.

[Raspe, Rudolph Eric] 1737-1794 # 1853

The Adventures of Baron Munchausen. From the best English and German editions. With eighteen illustrations printed in colours from original designs by A. Richard. London: Frederick Warne and Co., [1878]. Pp. [i] ii-vii [viii,] 1 - 103 [104]

Plates: Frontispiece + 33.

Raspe, Rudolf Erich] 1737-1794 # 1854

The Bravo of Perth: or, Voorn, the robber. Containing the uncommon adventures, depredations, and miraculous escapes, of a bold and resolute Scotch outlaw, of the fourteenth century. Cincinnati: Stereotyped and Published by J. A. James & Co., 1835.

Coll: 12° A-C⁶ 18 leaves (15.2 x 9.5cm) Pp. [1-5] 6-36.

Illus: Woodcut frontispiece

Notes: Bound together with "The Surprising Adventures of the Renowned Baron Munchausen."

Raspe, Rudolf Erich] 1737-1794 # 1855

The Surprising Adventures of the Renowned Baron Munchausen: containing his singular travels, miraculous escapes, and wonderful voyages and campaigns. Cincinnati: Published by J. A. James & Co., 1835.

Coll: 12° A-C⁶ 18 leaves (15.2 x 9.6cm) Pp. [1-4] 5-35 [36].

Illus: Woodcut frontispiece + cuts

Notes: C2ʳ-C8ʳ: "A Sermon Preached at Red River, Kentucky. By Mr. K-ly, a Drunkard." Bound together with "The Bravo of Perth."

1856

Rawlings, Marjorie Kinnan   1896-1953

The Yearling. Decorations by Edward Shenton. New York:
Charles Scribner's Sons, 1938. Pp. [i-viii], 1-428.

Illus: Vignette title page + cuts.

Notes: First ed.

1858

Anon

Rebus ABC. New York: McLoughlin Bros., n.d.

Coll: sm 4° [1⁸] 8 leaves (16.7 x 3.5cm) Pp. [1,2,3-
15,16]. (includes wrappers)

Illus: 26 colored engravings signed with monogram W.S.

Binding: Red wrappers. Illustrated on front; advert
on back. Preface on inside front wrapper,
text illustrations on inside back wrapper.

Notes: Front wrapper serves as title page.

1859

[ANON.]. The Recluse: or Haunted Castle in
Shropshire. . . . with The Wonderful Discovery
Made by a Young Officer, who Ventured Therein
. . . . Illustrated with a Beautiful Engraving.
London: [Printed by J.H. Hart] Published by
John Fairburn, [1806?].

Coll.: 12° : A-C⁶. 18 leaves (17.7 X 10.4 cm).
[1-3] 4-36.pp.

Plate: Engraved frontispiece, dated Mar. 28, 1806.

1860,1-3

Record of deposit for copyright claim, District
of Massachusetts, by the Boston publishing firm of
Hilliard, Gray, Little and Wilkins:

1. M.T. Ciceronis, Orationes quaedam selectae
. . . ed. by Charles Folsom, deposited on March
8, 1828; also contains handwritten receipt by
Charles Folsom of $500. as payment in full for
copyright. LC lists earliest edition as 1834.
2. James Robinson, Elementary Lessons in Intellectual Arithmetic . . . ; deposited on November
22, 1830. LC gives 1831 date of publication.
3. The Children's Robinson Crusoe . . . By A Lady
. . . Embellished w[ith] Cuts; deposited on December 11, 1830.

1861

Anon

Recreations Instructives Et Amusantes; ou, choix D'
historiettes morales, tirés des ouvrages de Mesdames
De Choiseul, De Renneville, Jauffret, &c. A l'usage
de la jeunesse. Philadelphie: Henry Perkins; Boston:
Perkins, Marvin, & Co., 1835.

Coll: 12° [1-16⁶, 17⁴ 102 leaves (17.2 x 10.4cm)
Pp. [1-5] 6-10 [11] 12-34 [35] 36-58 [59] 60-80
[81] 82-104 [105] 106-131 [132] 133-154 [155]
156-173 [174] 175-185 [186] 187-204.

1862

Reid, Captain [Thomas] Mayne   1818-1883

The Boy Slaves. With illustrations. Boston:
Ticknor and Fields, 1865. Pp. [i-iii] iv-v [vi]
1-321 [322-324].

Plates: Frontispiece + 7 ?

Notes: McKell copy lacking pp. 299-302.

1863

Reid, Captain [Thomas] Mayne   1818-1883

The Boy's Tar; or, a voyage in the dark. Illustrated
by Charles S. Keene. Boston: Ticknor and Fields,
1860. Pp. [i]-iv [1] -356.

Plates: Frontispiece + 11.

1864

Reid, Captain [Thomas] Mayne 1818-1883

The Plant Hunters; or, adventures among the Himalaya.
Illustrated. Boston: Ticknor and Fields, 1860.
Pp. [i]-vi [1] -353, [1: advert].

Plates: Frontispiece + 11.

1865

Reid, Captain [Thomas] Mayne   1818-1883

The Young Voyageurs or the Boy Hunters in the
North. With twelve illustrations by W[illiam]
Harvey. Boston: Ticknor and Fields, 1857.

Coll: 8° [1] -22⁸ , 23⁵ $1 (-1signed). (17.1 x
10.3cm). Pp. [1-7] 8-360, 361-362.

Plates: Frontispiece + 11.
Notes: Stereotyped edition.

1866

Remington, Frederic   1861-1909

Pony Tracks. Illustrated by Frederic Remington.
New York: Harper & Brothers Publishers, 1895.
Pp. [i-vii] viii [ix-x] 1-269; [1 of adverts].

Plates: Frontispiece + 69 illustrations.

1867

[ANON]. Rhetoric Made familiar and easy to Young Gentlemen and Ladies . . . . Being the Third Volume of the Circle of the Sciences, &c. The Third Edition. London: Printed for Newbery and Carnan, 1769.

Coll.: 32° : A-S⁸. 144 leaves. 144 leaves (9.2 X 6.3cm) [1-iv] v-x, 11-286 + [2] pp.

Binding: Blue boards, red leather spine.

S7-S7ᵛ: "Books Printed for Newbery and Carnan."

Bookplate of Percival Merritt. Roscoe # 69 (4)

1868

Anon

Rhetoric Made Familiar and Easy . . . . Being the Third Volume of the Circle of the Sciences, &c. The Fourth Edition. London: Printed for T. Carnan, and F. Newbery, Jun., 1777.

Coll: 32° A-S⁸ 144 leaves (9.9 x 6.5cm) Pp. i-x, 1-285 [286 misnumbered 280]; [1-2].
Binding: Marbled boards, green vellum spine with paper label.
Notes: S8ʳ: "Books printed for T. Carnan and F. Newbery, Junior . . . ." Bookplates of James Losh and Percival Merritt. Roscoe#69(5).

1869

[Rice] Alice Caldwell Hegan   1870-1942

Mrs. Wiggs of the Cabbage Patch. New York: The Century Co., 1901. Pp. 153.

Notes: First ed.

1870

Anon.

Rich Mrs. Duck, Dog's Dinner Party. New York: Mc-Loughlin Bros. Publishers [Entered 1867] Ff. 17

Illus: 16 full color: "Wevill, Sc."

Notes: Sm 4°

1872

Richards, Laura E [lizabeth Howe]   1850-1943

The Joyous Story of Toto. Illustrated by E.H. Garrett. Boston: Roberts Brothers, 1885. Pp. [1-4.] 5-226 [1-2].

Notes: First ed.

1873

Richards, Laura E [lizabeth Howe]   1850-1943

Sketches & Scraps by Laura E. Richards; with pictures by Henry Richards. Boston: Estes & Lauriat, 1881. [Printed in color by M. Benche, N.Y.] Pp. [1] 2-3 [4] 5-64.

Illus: Each leaf illustrated in color on both sides.

1874

Richardson, Samuel   1689-1761

The History of Pamela; or, Virtue Rewarded. Abridged from the Works of Samuel Richardson, Esq. Adorned with Copper Plates [by G. Lodge]. London: Printed for E. Newbery, n.d. [1789?].

Coll: 24° (6's) A⁴ B-O⁶ P⁷ 89 leaves (11.6 x 7.7cm) Pp. [i-viii] 1-161 [1-9].
Plates: Frontispiece + 5 engravings by Lodge.
Binding: Dutch floral boards.
Notes: P4-P7: adverts for E. Newbery. Bookplate of Percival Merritt. Roscoe #316 (4).

1875

Richardson, Samuel   1689-1761

The History of Sir Charles Grandison, Abridged from The Works of Samuel Richardson, Esq. . . . A New Edition, adorned with Copper Plates. London: Printed for E. Newbery, 1783.

Coll: 24° B-Q⁶ R¹ 91 leaves (11.5 x 7.4cm) 182pp.
Plates: Frontispiece + 5.
Notes: McKell copy lacking I6, N1, N6. Bookplate of Percival Merritt. Roscoe # 317(4)

1876

Richardson, Samuel. 1689-1761

The History of Sir Charles Grandison. Abridged from the works of Samuel Richardson Esq. author of Pamela and Clarisa. Tenth Edition. New Haven: From Sidney's Press, For Increase Cooke & Co. Book-Sellers, 1810.

Coll: 12°: (6s) A-L⁶ 66 leaves (13.3 X 8.1cm) Pp. [1-3] 4-132

Binding: Paper over thin oak sides.

1878

[Richardson, Samuel]   1689-1761

The Paths of Virtue delineated; Or, The History in Miniature of the Celebrated Pamela, Clarissa Harlowe, and Sir Charles Grandison, Familiarized and Adapted To the Capacities of Youth. London: Printed for R. Baldwin, in Paternoster-Row, 1756.

Coll: 12° [A]⁴ B-K¹² L⁸ 120 leaves (16.4 x 10cm) Pp. viii + 232.

Notes: Bookplate of Percival Merritt. McKell # G-7-23-43 -B.

1879

Richmond, Rev. Legh, A.M.   1772-1827

Annals Of The Poor: Containing The Dairyman's
Daughter, The Negro Servant, And Young Cottager, &c.
&c. A New Edition, Enlarged and Illustrated, With
An Introductory Sketch Of The Author. By The Rev.
John Ayre, A.M. Boston: Crocker & Brewster . . . ;
New York: J. Leavitt . . . , 1829.

Coll: 12° [1]⁴ 2-25⁶ 26² 150 leaves (14.9 x 9.1cm)
      Pp. [i-viii; xiii] xiv-xxx [31] 32-304 [1-6 of
      adverts].
Plates: Frontispiece, engraved title page +2.
        Plates signed ("R.B. Harraden."

1880

Richter, [Adrian] Ludwig 1803-1884   and
Pletsch, Oscar   1830-1888

Nursery Carols. Illustrated by the authors. London:
Bell and Daldy, 1862. Pp. [viii] 1-112.

Plates: Frontispiece + cuts.

Rigg, James Macmullen (1855-1926), trans.

    see

        Boccaccio. The Decameron. London: 1906.

1881

[Riggs], Kate Douglas Wiggin   1856-1923

Rebecca of Sunnybrook Farm. Boston and New York:
Houghton, Mifflin and Company, 1903. Pp. [2]+[1]-x
[1]-[327].

Notes: Kate Douglas was Mrs. Samuel Bradley Wiggin
       and Mrs. George Christopher Riggs.

1882

Riley, James Whitcomb   1849-1916

Old Fashioned Roses. Fourth Edition. London:
Longmans, Green, and Co., 1892. Pp. [i]-[x, 1] 2-
145.

Notes: Presentation page signed by author with
       accompanying verses. Address card tipped-
       in on fly-leaf, to "R.E. Town, Esq./ Care
       'The Star'/ Kansas City, Mo."

1883

Riley, James Whitcomb   1849-1916

Rhymes of Childhood. Indianapolis: The Bowen-
Merrill Co., 1891. Pp. [i-xiv, 1] 2-186.

Plates: Frontispiece

1885

[Ritchie, Leitch] ed.   1800 ? - 1865

Friendship's Offering; and winter's wreath: a
Christmas and New Year's present, for MDCCCXL.
[Illustrated by various artists.] London: Smith,
Elder and Co., 1840.

Coll: 12° A-KK⁶ 198 leaves (15.6 x 9.8cm) Pp. [i-
      iv, v] vi-vii [viii-ix] x [xi] xii [1] 2-384.
Plates: Frontispiece, engraved presentation page + 8.
Notes: McKell copy lacks the frontispiece.

1887

Anon

The Rival Pupils; or, A New Holiday Gift for a
Boarding-School. London: Printed for F. Newbery,
n.d. [1770?].

Coll: 12° A-O⁶ 2I⁶ 90 leaves (11.3 x 7.2cm)
      Pp. [4] xii + 152, 81-92 (totals 180pp).

Plates: Frontispiece + 4 copper engravings
                                          (cont'd)

The Rival Pupils   (Cont'd)

Contents: 2I: "Addenda. The Two Butterflies. A
          Fable. By a Lady."; 2Iv: The Hare and
          Partridge. A Fable." Roscoe # 319(4).

Binding: Dutch floral boards

Notes: Bookplate of Percival Merritt.

Robin Hood

    see

        Gundall, Joseph. Robin Hood and His
            Merry Forresters. By Stephen
            Percy. Langley, 1844. (Contains
            Martin Parker's "A True Tale of
            Robin Hood in Verse,")
        The Extraordinary Life and Adventures
            of Robin Hood . . . . W. Bor-
            radaile,   1823.

Anon.   # 1892

Robin Hood's Garland. Being a Complete History of all
the Notable and Merry Exploits performed By Him and His
Men on many Occasions. To which is added A Preface,
giving a more full and particular account of his Birth
&c. than any hitherto Published. . . . Adorned with
Twenty-Seven neat and curious Cuts adapted to the Subject
of each Song. London: Printed and Sold by R. Marshall,
in Aldermary Church-yard, Bow-Lane. n.d. [before Dec.,
1781].

Coll: 4° A-E⁸ F⁴ G² 46 leaves (19.1 x 13cm) 92pp.

                                              (cont'd)

Robin Hood's Garland.   (Cont'd)

Notes: G2: "A New Robin Hood Song, Sung by Mr. Beard."
       Manuscript date on title page: "December 10, 1781."
       Osborne, p. 13, lists a later edition of 1789.

Anon.   # 1893

The Robin's Christmas Eve. "Uncle Nel's Picture Books"
New-York: McLoughlin Bros, C. 1880

Coll: Royal 8° Pp. [1] 2-7 [8]

Plates: 4 oil colors on conjugate leaves

Binding: Pictorial wrappers, paste down endpapers. Ad-
         vertisement on rear.

Robinson, C[harles] H[enry]. 1843-1920?   # 1894

Longhead: the story of the first fire. Illustrated
by Charles Livingston Bull. Boston: L. C. Page &
Company, 1913. Pp. [1-viii], 1-126, [1-7 adverts].

Plates: Front + 3.

Robinson, D[aniel] T   1777-   # 1895

Olney's School Atlas. New York: Pratt, Woodford
and Co., 1844.

Coll: 2° [1-15]² 30 leaves (30.6 x 24.7cm) Pp.
      [i-iv] + 26 leaves (maps, printed on one side
      only).

Binding: Buff pictorial wrappers.

Robinson, Geraldine   # 1896

Three Kittens in a Boat. London and New York:
Frederick Warne & Co. Ltd., n.d. Pp. [1] - [54].

Plates: Front + 14 tipped in, but included in pagination

Robinson Crusoe

    see also under

            Defoe, Daniel (1660-1731)

    and

            The Life and Adventures of Alexander
                Selkirk, the Real Robinson Crusoe.

Robinson Crusoe, in words of one syllable

    see under

            Aikin, Lucy (Mary Godolphin, pseud.)

Anon.   # 1904

Romance of Indian History; or thrilling incidents in
the early settlement of America. New York: Published
by Kiggins & Kellogg, n.d.

Coll: 12°: 1¹² 24 leaves (15.9 X 10cm·) Pp. [1-3] 4-11
      [12] 13 [14] 15-24

Illus: 8 woodcuts

[Roscoe, William]   1753-1831   # 1909.1

The Butterfly's Ball, and The Grasshopper's Feast.
London: Printed for J. Harris, Corner of St. Paul's
Church Yard, Jan⸗ 1ˢᵗ, 1807.

Coll: 16° 1-4⁴ 16 leaves Pp. [1-32]. (12.8 x 9.5cm)

Illus: 14 hand colored copper engravings, printed with
       text on facing pages, alternating with blank
       facing pages.

Binding: Yellow wrappers with adverts on back. Paste-
         down endpaper in front; final page is also
         pasted down.

Notes: McKell # SC-6-2-44-3

[Roscoe, William]   1753-1831   # 1909.2

The Butterfly's Ball, and The Grasshopper's Feast.
London: J[ohn] Harris . . . , Jan. 1, 1807.

Coll: 16° 1-4⁴ 16 leaves (11.55 x 9.3cm) Pp.[1-32].

Illus:14 colored engravings (after William Mulready).
     Engravings and text appear on facing pages
     alternating with blank facing pages.

Notes: Bound in with six others in Omnibus #2, q.v.

Anon.   # 1910

The Rose-Bud; or Poetic Garland of Unfading Flowers. Embellished with numerous engravings. New Haven: Printed and published by S. Babcock, 1841.

Coll: 12°: [1¹²] 12 leaves (15.2 X 9cm) Pp. [1-3] 4-24

Binding: Yellow printed wrappers.

Anon.   # 1911

Rose Merton, The Little Orphan. "Dean's New Dress Book" London: Dean & Son, [C. 1863].

Coll: 8°: [1¹²] 12 leaves Pp.[1] 2 (1 blank unnumbered leaf) 3 (1 blank unnumbered leaf) 4-5 (1 blank unnumbered leaf) 6 (1 blank unnumbered leaf) 7-8 (1 blank unnumbered leaf)

Illus: 6 colored engravings by Calvert

Notes: Free and pasted down end papers, front and back are advertisements, cloth "dresses" are pasted on illustrations of Rose Merton. Plus another copy.

Anon.   # 1913.1

The Rose's Breakfast. Illustrated with elegant engravings. London: Printed [by H. Byer] for J. Harris, 1808.

Coll: 16°: A¹⁶ 16 leaves (11.6 X 9.4ᶜᵐ·) Pp. [1-3]4-32

Plates: Engraved frontispiece, colored plates

Binding: Buff-flowered printed wrappers, advertisements in back

Notes: [R-4-22-43 L]

Anon.   # 1913.2

The Rose's Breakfast. Illustrated with elegant engravings. London: Printed [by H. Byer] for J. Harris, 1808.

Coll: 16°: A¹⁶ 16 leaves (11.6 X 9.4ᶜᵐ·) Pp. [1-3]4-32

Plates: Engraved frontispiece+7

Binding: Gray printed wrappers, advertisements in back

Notes: [S-6-3-42 B]

Rossetti, Christina [Georgina]. 1830-1894   # 1914

Goblin Market. Illust. by Laurence Housman. London: Macmillan & Co., Dec. 1893. Pp.[1-viii, 1] [3-4] 5-6 [7-10] 11-12 [13-16] 17-18 [19-20] 21-28 [29-30] 31-32 [33-34] 35-42 [43-46] 47-50 [51-54] 55-63 [64: colophon].

Illus: On half-title and title pages +12 full page+ numerous cuts and decorations+colophon.

Notes: Uncut. "One hundred and sixty copies of this large paper edition were printed December 1893."

[ANON.]. The Royal Guide; or, an Easy Introduction to Reading English. Embellished with a great variety of Cuts. London: Printed for E. Newbery, n.d. [1790?].   # 1918

Coll.: 32°: [A⁸(-A1)] [B⁸] C-H⁸. 63 leaves (10.95 X 7.15cm). [3-28] 31-128 pp.

Illustrations: Frontispiece + 26 pps of engraved alphabet illustrations and text + woodcuts elsewhere in text.

Binding: Dutch flowered boards. McKell copy resewn with calf spine added with "Royal Guide.-Goldsmith" in gold lettering.

Bookplate of Percival Merritt. Roscoe # 323 (6 or 7)

Anon   # 1919

The Royal Primer; Or, an easy and pleasant Guide to the Art of Reading. London: Printed for J. Newbery and B. Collins, [1767?]

Coll: 12° A-C¹² 36 leaves (8.3 x 7.8cm) 72pp.

Illus: 26 cuts.

Notes: Roscoe #324 (5).

Rubens, Mr. Peter Paul, Professor of Polite Arts.

     see

          Johnson, Richard. The Picture Exhibition; Worcester, Mass: Isaiah Thomas, 1788.

Anon.   # 1920

The Rural Songster: A collection of national and sentimental songs for rural life. Dayton, Ohio: Published by B.F. Ells, 1850.

Coll: 8°: [1⁸] 2-7⁸ 56 leaves Pp. [i-v] vi-viii [9] 10-110 [111-112] (16.8 x 10.9cm)

Illus: Numerous engravings

Notes: Musical notations for many of the songs. Front leaf pasted to wrapper.

Rusher, W[illiam] # 1921

Reading Made Most Easy, consisting of a variety of useful lessons . . . the ninety-ninth edition. Recommended for the use of schools. Banbury: Printed by J. Rusher] for and sold by the Author, n.d., ca. 1810].

Coll: 18°. A9, B18, C9 (C9 = A18), B signed 36 leaves (13.2 x 8.9cm) Pp. [1-9] 1--71 [72].

Illus: Frontispiece woodcut

Binding: Blue wrappers;) initial and final pages as
paste-down) endpapers.
(cont'd)

Reading Made Most Easy . . . . (Cont'd)

Notes: Percival Merritt bookplate. BMC gives a date of 1830 for the 220th ed.: see T. 1430. (4).

Ruskin, John 1819-1900 # 1922

The King of the Golden River. Illustrated by Arthur Rackham. London: George Harrap & Co., Ltd., 1932. Pp. [1-4] 5-4B.

Plates: Frontispiece +3 color plates

Notes: Autographed by Arthur Rackham. No. 351 of an edition of 570 Copies.

Ruskin, John 1819-1900 # 1923

The King of the Golden River: or, the black brothers: a legend of Stiria. Illustrated by Richard Doyle. London: Smith, Elder & Co., 1851.

Coll: 8° A,4 B-D,4 E,4 32 leaves (17.9 x 13.5cm) Pp. [i-viii, 1] 2-56 [57, 58].

Illus: Frontispiece, title page + numerous engravings by Doyle.

Notes: 2 leaves of adverts. laid in, 1 leaf of advert. bound in at end of book. Bookplates of Edith Barbara Tranter and Frank Fletcher.

SADLER, _____. A calligraphic arithmetic manuscript. # 1928
4°. 90 leaves (14 blank) written on recto only. England, 1721.

This is a Commercial Arithmetic, executed by a master calligraphist named Sadler, who has identified himself on fol. 8 and 24. The latter is dated: "Sadler S[cripsit] 1721." The manuscript is divided under headings; e.g. Numeration Tables, Addition, Pence Tables, Money, Avoirdupois Weights, Troy Weight, Liquid Measure, Dry Measure, Substraction, Multiplication, Division, Barter, etc. Title pages of each heading is elaborately calligraphed with scrolls, birds, human heads and figures in highly decorative and fantastic manner. Bound in contemporary vellum.
(cont'd)

Sadler. Calligraphic arithmetic manuscript. 1721. (Cont'd)

The DNB gives a John Sadler (1813-1892), engraver, treasurer of Artists Amicable Fund, who was an amateur prevaricator, capable of forgery, and subject to temporary insanity. If done in 1721, the MS may be attributable to Thomas Sadler's (c.1650-1700) son, Thomas Sadler the younger. The father, educated at Lincoln's Inn, was an artist, once painted a portrait of John Bunyan.

St. Lambert, [Jean Francois] 1716-1803 # 1929

Les Saisons, Poeme. A Amsterdam: 1769.

Coll: 8° a8, b6, A-B8(-+B), C-L8("L1" missigned V), M-Z8 aa1 199 leaves (19.3 x 12.4cm) Pp. [i-v] vi-xxviii[1] 2 [3] 4-44 [45] 46-88 [89] 90-130 [131] 132-184 [185-186] 187-260 [261-263] 264-302 [303-305] 306-369 [370].

Plates: Frontispiece ("J. B. le Prince, del. Aug. de St. Aubin, Sculp. 1768") 5: all metal engravings.

Notes: Signatures J, U,) and W not used.

Anon. # 1931

Sammy Tickletooth, "Little Slovenly Peter Series." New York: McLoughlin Bros., Publishers, [n.d.]

Coll: 18°: [1⁴] 4 leaves (17.1 X 11.2cm) Pp. 1-8

Illus: 8 colored engravings

Binding: Pink wrappers. Illustrated on front; advertisement on back.

Notes: Wrapper serves as title page.

Sandburg, Carl 1878-1967 # 1932

Rootabaga Pigeons. Illustrations and decorations by Maud and Miska Petersham. New York: Harcourt, Brace, and Company, [1923]. Pp. [i-x, 1-2] 3-218.

Plates: Colored frontispiece + 7 full-page illustrations.

Notes: First ed.

Sandburg, Carl 1878-1967 # 1933

Rootabaga Stories. Illustrations and decorations by Maud and Miska Petersham. New York: Harcourt, Brace, and Company, [1922]. Pp. [i-x, 1-2] 3-230.

Plates: Colored frontispiece + 11 full-page illustrations.

Notes: First ed. bookplate of Elizabeth Ann Jacobs.

Sandford and Merton, in words of one syllable.

   see under

      Aikin, Lucy (Mary Godolphin, pseud.)

Sargent, Epes (1813-1880); and Amasa May   # 1934

The New American Fifth Reader. [Illustrated.]
Philadelphia: J.H. Butler & Company, n.d. [1871 ?]
Pp. [i-iv], 5-312.

Plates: Frontispiece + cuts.

Binding: All free end-papers cut out of McKell copy;
        Advertising on paste-down end-papers.

Saunders, Louise

   see

      Louise Saunders Perkins 1893-

Savigny, l'abbé [Laurence] de   # 1936

La Civilité en Images et In Action, ou la politesse,
le usages et les convenances enseignes aux enfants.
Par M. l'abbé De Savigny, Ouvrage illustré de 50 vignettes Par H. Valentin. Paris: Soulié, Éditeur,
. . . 1844.

Coll: 12° 1-19⁶, 20² (20.1 - 20.2, 20.3) 117 leaves
    (18.5 x 11cm) Pp. [1-9] 10-22 [23-25] 26-40
    [41-43] 44-54 [55-57] 58-72 [73-75] 76-92 [93-
    95] 96-114 [115-117] 118-132 [133-135] 136-156
    [157-159] 160-176 [177-179] 180-194 [195-197]
    198-212 [213-215] 216-230, [1-4].

                      (cont'd)

La Civilité . . . . (Cont'd)

Illus: Numerous engravings by Valentin. 50 are full-
      page illustrations, printed on one side of page
      only.

Binding: Deckled edges. Engraved title page bound in
        front; page of adverts bound in at back

Notes: Bookplate of F. Renaud.

1938

Scannell, F[lorence]

A Christmas Visit. "Our Children's Book Case"
series. London, Paris & New York: Raphael Tuck
& Sons. Designed at the Studios in England and
printed at the Fine Art Works in Germany. [c.1900].
Ff. 6.

Illus: 4 in color by M.G. + 4 + cover.
Notes: No inside title page.

Schmauk, J[ohn] G   # 1940

Erstes Buch für Deutsche Schulen. Philadelphia:
Mentz und Rovoudt, 1844.

Coll: 12° 1-6¹², 7⁶ 78 leaves (16.5 x 10.4cm)
    Pp. [1-3] 4, [5] 6-156.

Illus: Cuts

1941

[Schmid, Chanoene Christopher]   1768-1854

La Chapelle De La Fôret. Conte pour les enfans, par
l'auteur des Oeufs de Paquer; traduit de l'allemand.
Paris: Chez Levrault, . . . a Strasbourg, 1829
[Strasbourg, de l'imprimerie de F. G. Levrault].

Coll: 12 1⁷ (1.2+1), 2-3⁶, 4³ (4.1+1) 22 leaves
    (13.2 x 8.4cm) Pp. [1-11, 1-3] 4-42.

Illus: Title page + 2 colored plates: lithographs by
    F. G. Levrault. Wraparound endpapers (endpapers
    pasted to boards front and back).

                      (cont'd)

La Chapelle De La Foret. (Cont'd)

Notes: 1.2 is pasted to 1.3; 4.2 is pasted to 4.3

[Schmid, Chanoene Christopher]   1768-1854 # 1942

Les Oeufs De Paques. Conte pour les enfants, par l'auteur de l'historie de Henri d'Eichenfels. Autorise par
le conseil de l'instruction publique Veuve Berger-
Levrault et fils, Libraires. Paris, Strasbourg, 1858.

Coll: 12° π², 2π¹², 1⁶, 2¹², 2.⁶, 3.¹², 3.⁶, 4¹²
    68 leaves (14.9 x 8.9cm) Pp. [1-4, 1-iii] iv, [5]
    6-128 [129-132].

Illus: Front + 3 lithograph plates by Berger-Levrault.

Binding: Front endpaper is a wraparound. Final page
      pasted to board. π² pasted to 2π 1.

1943

Schmid, Christoph von   1768-1854

Die Feuersbrunst./ Die Wasserfluth am Rhein [On two separate title pages.] "Christoph von Schmid's Jugend-bibliothek." Philadelphia: Morwitz & Co., n.d.

Coll: 8° [A-D⁸ E⁴] 36 leaves (15.4 x 11cm) Pp. [1-3] 4-30 [31-32, 1-3] 4-37 [38-40].
Illus: Woodcut in color on front cover and black and white woodcut on title page.
Binding: Paper over boards. Final leaf serves as paste-down endpaper.

1944

[Schmid, Christoph von]   1768-1854

Die Kleine Lautenspielerin. ["Christoph von Schmid's Jugend-bibliothek." Philadelphia: Morwitz & Co., n.d.

Coll: 8° [A-D⁸ E⁴] 37 leaves (15.4 x 11.2cm) Pp. [1-3] 4-74.
Illus: Woodcut in color on front cover and black and white woodcut on title page.
Binding: Paper over boards.

1945

Anon

The Scholar's Companion; containing excercises in the orthography, derivation, and classification of English words. A new edition, enlarged and improved. Philadelphia: Perkins & Purves, 1844.

Coll: 12° 1-25⁶ 150 leaves (18.9 x 10.8cm) Pp. [1-2] 3-299 [300].

1946

Anon.

The School of Good Manners. Composed for the Help of Parents in Teaching their Children how to carry it in their places during their minority. Boston: Printed and sold by John Boyle in Marlborough, 1775.

Coll: Sm 8°: A-E⁸(?) 40 leaves (11.6 X 8.8cm) approx. Pp. [1-iv, 5] 6-66 [67-80?]

Binding: Leather over thin boards.

Notes: McKell #S-5-12-51-B. McKell copy missing E7-8 (?)

Schroth, Ingeborg

see

(Picture Bible of the Late Middle Ages)

1948

[Scott, Sir Walter]   1771-1832

Tales of a Grandfather; being stories taken from Scottish History. Vol. I. [Illustrations by Sir William Allen.] Edinburgh: Cadell and Co.; London: Simpkin and Marshall; Dublin: John Cumming, 1828.

Coll: 12° π³ A-U⁶ 123 leaves (14 x 8.7cm) Pp. [1-2] [i] ii [iii] iv [1-3] 4-239 [240].
Plates: Frontispiece + engraved title page.
Binding: Red calf back over marbled boards.
Notes: First ed. See) Osborne p. 172. Preface dated "Abbots-) ford, 10th. Oct. 1827."
(cont'd)

Tales of a Grandfather . . . Vol II (cont'd)

Tales of a Grandfather; being stories taken from Scottish History. Vol. II. [Illustrations by Henry Corbould and W. H. Lizars.] Edinburgh: Cadell and Co.; London: Simpkin and Marshall; Dublin: John Cumming, 1828.

Coll: 12° π³ A-T⁶ U⁷ (U6+π4) 124 leaves (14 x 8.7cm) Pp. [1-2, 1] ii-iv [1-3] 4-241 [242].

Plates: Frontispiece + engraved title page
Binding: Red calf back over marbled boards.
Notes: First ed. See) Osborne, p. 172. (cont'd)

Tales of a Grandfather . . . Vol III (cont'd)

Tales of a Grandfather; being stories taken from Scottish History. Vol. III. [Illustrations by W. H. Lizars.] Edinburgh: Cadell and Co.; London: Simpkin and Marshall; Dublin: John Cumming, 1828.

Coll: 12° π³ A-2C⁶ 2D⁴ 163 leaves (14 x 8.7cm) Pp. [1-2, 1] ii-iv [1-3] 4-320.

Plates: Frontispiece + engraved title page.
Binding: Red calf back over marbled boards.
Notes: First ed. See Osborne, p. 172.

1949

Scott, Sir Walter   1771-1832
SCOTT, SIR WALTER. Tales of A Grandfather; Being Stories taken from the History of France. Inscribed to Master John Hugh Lockhart. In Three Vols. . . . Printed for Robert Cadell, Edinburgh; Whittaker and Co London; and John Cumming, Dublin, 1831. [Printed by Ballantyne and Company, Paul's Work, Canengate.]

Vol. I:
Coll.: 12° (8's): π⁸χ4₁-T⁸U⁴2χ². 170 leaves (14 X 8.7cm). [1-2-16[a-- -i] ii-vi [1-3] 4-8[9] 10-315[316].

Plates: Steel engraved title page.

π⁸: Advertising.

Scott . . . Grandfather(cont'd)

Vol. II.
Coll.: 12° (8's): π⁴χ₁-U⁸χ5(b+1). 169 leaves (14.1 X 9cm). [1-2-i]ii-vi [1-3] 4-322[330] pp.

Plates: Frontispiece + title page, both steel engravings by W.H. Lizars(drawer and engraver).

Vol. III.
Coll.: 12° (8's): π⁶A-U⁸χ⁴Y-Z⁸. 126 leaves (14.1 X 9.1 cm). [1-2,i]ii-ix[x, 1-3] 4-360.

Plates: Frontispiece + title, both steel engraved, drawn and engraved by W.H. Lizars.

Anon.   # 1950

Scripture History or interesting narratives, recorded
in the lives of the prophets and apostles: Compiled
from the Old and New Testament, for the instruction
of youth. By a Clergyman. Embellished with twelve
coloured engravings. Steubenville: Published by J.& B.
Turnbull, 1830.

Coll: Octavo A-F² 12 leaves (17.6 X 10^cm) Pp. [1-2, 3]
4-24.

Plates: 12 colored engravings on six plates

Binding: Yellow wrappers

Notes: McKell #8-815-52-L/8-27-52B

[Scudder, Horace Elisha]   1838-1902   # 1951

The Bodleys Afoot. With illustrations. Boston:
Houghton, Osgood, and Company, 1880. Pp. i-viii,
[9] 10-202 [1-6 adverts bound in at end].

Plates: Frontispiece +10.

[Scudder, Horace Elisha]   1838-1902   # 1952

The Bodleys on Wheels. With illustrations. Boston:
Houghton, Osgood and Company, 1879. Pp. i-viii, [9]
10-222; [1-2 of adverts.]

Plates: Frontispiece +13

[Scudder, Horace Elisha]   1838-1902   # 1953

Doings of the Bodley Family in Town and Country.
With 77 illustrations [by Henry W. Herrick with
Bensell, Darley, Nast, M.L. Stone and others.]
New York: Published by Hurd and Houghton, 1875.
Pp. i-viii, [1] 2-250.

Plates: Frontispiece +17.

Notes: See Peter Parley to Penrod, p. 41: does not
match Blanck's description of the first ed.
in several particulars.

[Scudder, Horace Elisha]   1838-1902   #1954

Mr. Bodley Abroad. Illustrated. Boston: Houghton
Mifflin and Company, 1881. Pp. i-viii, [9] 10-210;
[1-2 of adverts.]

Plates: Frontispiece + 20 +cuts.

Anon   # 1957

The Second Book of 100 Pictures. [Illustrated.]
Philadelphia: American Sunday-School Union, n.d.
[1862?]. Pp. [1-iv] 5-104; [1] 2-4 of adverts.

Plates: Frontispiece.

Sedgwick, Anne Douglas (Mrs. Basil De Selincourt)   # 1958
1873-1935

The Little French Girl. Boston and New York:
Houghton Mifflin Company, 1924. Pp. [i-iv,] 1-508.

Notes: First ed.

Selkirk, Alexander (1676-1721)

see

The Life and Adventures of Alexander
Selkirk, the Real Robinson Crusoe.
Cincinnati: U.P. James, 1834.

Anon.   # 1959

A Series of Easy Lessons on the Lord's Prayer. Hartford:
Published by D.F. Robinson & Co., P. Canfield, Printer,
1829.

Coll: 16°: π² 1-2⁸ 3⁶ 24 leaves (12.4 X 10.3cm) Pp.
[i-iv, 5] 6-44 [45-48]

Illus: Frontispiece

Binding: Wrappers

Notes: Frontispiece: π2^v, Blank: 3·7-3·8^v, Rosenbach #731

Service, Robert W[illiam]. 1874-1958   #1960

Songs of a Sourdough. Author's edition. Toronto:
William Briggs, 1907. Pp. [1-11] iii-iv, 5-82 [83-84].

Notes: First ed. Bookplate of Jean Hersholt.

Seton, Ernest Thompson   1860-1946   # 1961

Two Little Savages; being the adventures of two boys
who lived as Indians and what they learned. With
over two hundred drawings. Illustrated by Ernest
Thompson Seton. New York: Doubleday Page & Company,
1903. Pp. [i] -[xviii] 19-552.

Plates: 29

Notes: First ed.

Seuss, Dr. (pseud)

        see

        Geisel, Theodor Seuss   1904-

Sforza, Galeazzo Maria (1444-1476)

        see

        Smital, Ottokar, ed. Nationalbibliothek
                in Wien Handschrift 1856: . . .
                Sforza . . . . Faksimileband. Wien,
                1930.

Shannon, Terry (pseud of Jessie Mercer)   # 1965

Jumper Santa's Little Reindeer. By Terry Shannon
illustrations by Charles Payzant. Jolly Books. New
York: [Anon Publishing Co., 1952]. Pp. [1-32].

Sherwood, Mary Martha (Butt).. 1775-1851   # 1971

The History of Little Henry and His Bearer. Third American edition. Catskill: Published by Nathan Elliott.
Croswell & Son, Printers, 1818.

Coll: 12°: A-C⁹ ($5 regularly inserted in each quire.)
        27 leaves (13.7 X 9.5 cm.)
        Pp. 1-3 [4-54]

Notes: Buff printed wrappers.
        Evans #45704, A.A.S. #1066.1, Rosenbach #571

Sherwood, Mrs. [Mary Martha Butt] 1775-1851   # 1972

The Little Girl's Keepsake. London: Darton and
Clark, n.d.

Coll: 12 ° (6s)   A² B-Q⁶ R⁴   (96 leaves (14.3 x
        9.2cm) Pp.[i-iv, 1] 2-188.
Plates: Frontispiece by J. Dadley, Sc. +3.

[Sherwood, Mrs.] Rosina Emmet (illustrator). 1854-   # 1973

Pretty Peggy and other Ballads. New York: Dodd, Mead
and Company, Publishers, 1880. Pp. [1]-64.

Illus: Several in color.

Notes: First ed.

[Shopfer, Jean] Claude Anet (pseud) 1868-1931   # 1974

The End of a World. Trans. from the French by
Jeffery E. Jeffery. New York & London: Alfred A.
Knopf, 1927. Pp.[iv, 1-2] 3-268.

Illus: Numerous illus. and cuts.

Notes: 1 p. advert. bound in at end.

Anon.   # 1976

A Short History of England for The Infant' [s] Library.
[London] : Printed and Sold by John Marshall . . . . n.d.

Coll: 64° A-D⁸   32 leaves 5.6 x 4.4cm) Pp.[1] 2-63 [64].

Plates: Woodcuts and text on facing pages.

Notes: Text in French. McKell # S-4-b-43.

Shute, Henry Augustus]   1856-1943   # 1977

The Real Diary of a Real Boy. Boston: The Everett
Press, 1903. Pp. [i-vi] 1-154, +1 leaf advertising.

Anon   #1981

Simples Contes Pour Les Petits Enfants. Tours: a^d
Mame Et Cie, Imprimeurs-Libraires, 1854.

Coll: 8° 1-8^8 64 leaves (12.2 x 7.6cm) Pp. [1-5] 6-
10 [11] 12-24 [25] 26-40 [41] 42-50 [51] 52-57
[58] 59-74 [75] 76-90 [91] 92-107 [108] 109-119
[120] 121-126 [127-128].

Illus: Frontispiece engraving signed, "Pisan."

Binding: Free and pasted-down endpapers.

Sigourney, Mrs. L [ydia] H [oward] [Huntley] 1791-1895   #1982

Pocahontas, and other poems. London: Robert Tyas,
1841.

Coll: 8° [A]^6 B-U^8 X^2 160 leaves (15.8 x 10.2cm)
Pp. [i-vii] viii-x [xi-xii, 1] 2-308.

Notes: First ed.

#1983

The Singer's Own Book: A well-selected collection
of the most popular sentimental, amatory, patriotic,
naval, and comic songs. Philadelphia: Key & Biddle,
[1832].

Coll: 8° A-U^8 160 leaves (12.4 x 8.1cm) Pp. 1-2
[3-4] 5-320.
Plates: 2 engraved frontispieces by George B. Ellis.
Notes: A1: adverts

Anon   #1984

The Sister's Gift, or The Naughty Boy Reformed.
Published for the Advantage of the rising Generation.
London: Printed for E. Newbery, 1793.

Coll: 32° (16's) A-[B]^8 . 16 leaves (10.3 x6.3cm)
32pp.
Illus: 8 woodcuts.
Binding: Red and black floral wrappers.
Notes: A1 and [B8] form attached endpapers. Bookplate
of Percival Merritt. Roscoe #335 (4).

---

anon.   #1985

Skazki [Fairy Tales]. Mariya Morevna. Illustrated by
I [van] Y[akovlevich] Bilibin. A publication of the
Office for the Publication or State Documents. [Passed
by the censor. St. Petersburg, 8 November 1903.] Pp. 1-12

Illus: Several illustrations (3 full page) and decorations, all color.

Binding: Pictorial wrappers. Bound in omnibus volume
with title on spine: I Bilibin. Fairy Tales.
St. Petersburg, 1901-1903.

Skazka (Maria Morevna, translation)   #1986

Translation for the Russian Story of Maria Morevna.
Illustrated by Ivan Y[akovlevich] Bilibin. Russian
Peasant Industries: 41 Old Bond Street, London, W. Pp 1-4

Notes: Contains advertisements on the last page
for the following: "Vasilisa the Fair," "Maria
Morevna," "Ivan Czarevich and the Gray Wolf,"
"Finist-the-Bright-Falcon," "The Frog Czarevna,"
"Alenushka and Ivanushka," "The Story of the
Golden Cock," "The Story of Czar Sultan," "Volga,"
"Illustr: Victor Vasnetsof, "The Song of Wise Oleg.'"

---

anon.   #1987

Skazka [Fairy Tale] O Raznotsvetnikh Ribakh [Of the
Multi-Colored Fishes]. Drawings by H [ ]
Oulyanoff. Edition I [ ] Kebel. Moscow, n.d.,
[ca. 1915]. Pp. [1], 2-11, [12].

Illus: Several illustrations (2 full page), all color.

Binding: Initial and final pages pasted to original
pictorial wrappers.

---

anon.   #1988

Skazki [Fairy Tales]. Perishko Phinista Yasna-Sokola
[The Feather of Phinist the Bright Falcon]. Illustrated
by I [van] Y[akovlevich] Bilibin . A publication or the
Office for the publication or State Documents. [Passed by
the censor. St. Petersburg, 18 March , 1902.] Pp. 1-12.

Illus: Several illustrations (2 full page) and decorations, all color.

Binding: Pictorial wrappers. Bound in omnibus volume
with title on spine: I Bilibin. Fairy Tales.
St. Petersburg, 1901-1903.

---

anon.   #1989

Skazki [Fairy Tales]. Sestritsa Alenushka I Bratets
Ivanushka [Little Sister Alenushka and Little Brother
Ivanushka]. Belaya Utochka [The Little White Duck].
Illustrated by I [van] Y[akovlevich] Bilibin. A pub-
lication of the Office for the Publication of State
Documents. [Passed by the censor. St. Petersburg, 8
November, 1903.] Pp. 1-12.

Illus: Several illustrations (3 full page) and decorations, all color.

Binding: Pictorial wrappers. Bound in omnibus volume
with title on spine: I Bilibin. Fairy
Tales. St. Petersburg, 1901-1903.

---

anon.   #1990

Skazki [Fairy Tales]. Skazka Ob Ivane-Tsareviche, Zhar-
Ptitse I O Serom Volke (The Tale of Ivan Czarevich,
The Fire Bird , and the Gray Wolf). Illustrated by
I [van] Y[akovlevich] Bilibin . A publication of the
Office for the publication or State Documents. [Passed
by the censor. St. Petersburg, May 3, 1901.] Pp. 1-12.

Illus: Several (3 full page) illustrations and decorations, all color.

Binding: Pictorial wrappers. Bound in omnibus volume
with title on spine: I. Bilibin. Fairy Tales.
St. Petersburg, 1901-1903.

#1991

Anon.

Skazki (Fairy Tales). Tsarevna Lyagushka (The Frog Princess). Illustrated by I[van] I[akovlevich] Bilibin . A publication for the Office for the Publication of State Documents. [Passed by the censor. St. Petersburg, 17 December 1901.] Pp. 1-9 [10-12].

Illus: Several illustrations (2 full page) and decorations, all in color.

Binding: Pictorial wrappers. Bound in omnibus with title on spine: I Bilibin. Fairy Tales. St. Petersburg, 1901-1903.

#1992

anon.

Skazki (Fairy Tales). Vasilisa Prekrasnaya (Vasilisa the Fair). Illustrated by I[van] Y[akovlevich] Bilibin. A publication of the Office for the publication of State Documents. [Passed by the censor. St. Petersburg, 3 December , 1902.] Pp. 1-12.

Illus: Several illustrations (4 full page) and decorations, all color.

Binding: Pictorial wrappers. Bound in omnibus volume with title on spine: I Bilibin. Fairy Tales. St. Petersburg, 1901-1903.

Skazki (Russian Fairy Tales)

see also

Chukovskii, Korn. Skazki. Academia, 1935.
Morozko (Mr. Frost) 1923
Pushkin, Aleksandr Sergeyevich 1799-1837
Czar Sultan
The Golden Cock
Oleg The Wise

and

Kipling, Rudyard

#1993

Anon

Sketches of Doll Life. A Christmas story for doll mammas. No. 2. Sunset Stories. Boston: Loring, Publisher, [1863]. Pp. [i-iii,]4-160.

#1994

Anon.

Slate pictures for the useful selfemployment of young children.

Coll: 8°; [1²-2⁸] 10 leaves (16.6 x 10.3cm) Pf. 10.

Illus: Numerous illustrations.

Binding: Printed wrappers, green on front only.

Notes: White on black paper.

#1995

Anon

Slim Jack: or, the history of a circus boy. Philadelphia: American Sunday-school Union, n.d., [1847?]

Coll: 12° 1-8⁶ 9² 54 leaves (14.9 x 9.5cm) Pp. [1-4] 5-107 [108].

Illus: Frontispiece †4 plates included in pagination.
Binding: Free and paste-down endpaper.

#1996

Anon.

The Slovenly Boy. Aunt Rhoda's Series. Cincinnati: Published by Peter G. Thomson, Copyright 1802 by Peter G. Thomson.

Coll: 8°: [1⁶] 6 leaves Pp. [1-3] 4-5 [6-7] 8-9 [10] 11 [12] (18.5 x 12.5cm)

Illus: 4 hand-colored engravings

Binding: Wrappers illustrated and colored

Notes: Wrappers included in pagination

#1997

Anon.

Slovenly Peter Reformed Shewing how he became a neat scholar. Translated from the German. With six illustrations. Philadelphia: Willis P. Hazard, Lith. of A. Brett & Co., 1853.

Coll: 8° (17 single leaves) Pf. [1, 1-4,5] 6-15 [16]. (26 x 14.3cm)

Plates: 6 hand-colored copper plate engravings.

Binding: Boards: decorations on front, advert on back. Yellow free and paste-down endpapers. Stabbed.

#1998

Smart, James H[enry]   1841-1900

A Manual of Free Gymnastic and Dumb-bell exercises: for the school-room and the parlor. Cincinnati: Sargent, Wilson & Hinkle; Chicago: Cobb, Pritchard & Co.; New York: Clark & Maynard, n.d. [1864]. Pp. [1-7] ii-iv, 5-64.

Illus: Cuts.

#1999

Smiley, Thomas T[ucker]   -d.1879

An Easy Introduction Into the Study of Geography, on an improved plan: compiled for the use of schools. Accompanied by an improved atlas. 5th ed., improved. Philadelphia: Printed by Clark & Raser for the Author, and for sale at J. Gregg's . . . and by booksellers and Country Merchants generally in the United States, 1827.

Coll: 12° A-X⁶ 126 leaves (14.2 x 8.7cm) Pp. [i-iii] iv-vi [vii] viii-ix [x-xi] xii [13] 14-252.

Smital, Ottokar, ed.   # 2000

Nationalbibliothek in Wien Handschrift 1856: Das
Schwarze Gebetbuch Des Herzogs Galiazzo Maria Sforza
Miniaturen Hereausgegeben und Erlairtert von O. Smital.
Faksimileband mit 61 Farbtafeln und 15 Lichtdructafeln
im Textband. Wien: Druck und Verlag Der Osterreichi-
schen Staatsdrukerei, 1930.

Pagination: Pp. [I-VI] VII [VIII] IX [X] 1-80 [81]
82-103 [104-106] 107-111 [112-114] (Plates
I-XV), [115-118].

Illus: 15 plates of 24 photo-reproduced illustrations.

(cont'd)

Nationalbibliothek in Wien Handschrift: (Cont'd)

Binding: Red velvet cloth; decorated front and back
with brass teardrops and sunbursts; closes
by two brass hasps, each with inlaid enamel
medallion on outer surfaces.

Notes: Edition consists of two books; the second is a
facsimile photo-reprint in color of Handschrift
1856: Nationalbibliothek in Wien. The facsimile
consists of 100 plates on 50 leaves plus single
blank plates front and rear. BMC # MS Fac 370.
Galeazzo Maria Sforza (1444-1476).

Smith, Kate Douglas   # 2004

The Story of Patsy: a reminiscence. San Francisco:
C. A. Murdock & Co., 1883. Pp. [1]-[28].

[Smith, Sarah (pseud of Hesba Stretton)] 1832-1911   # 2005.1-2

Jessica's First Prayer. Illustrated by Alfred Walter
Bayes. "The Sunday School Series of Juvenile Religious
Works." From the Religious Tract Society, London:
Boston: Henry Hoyt, 1867. Pp. i-vi, [7]-[122].

Plates: Frontispiece, illustrated title page+ 7.

Notes: First American ed. (?).
Plus another copy.

Smith, Rev. Thomas [of SPA Field's Chapel] (pseud).   # 2006

Lucinda; or, virtue triumphant; a moral tale. De-
signed for the instruction of youth. By the Rev.
Thomas Smith. London: Printed by G. Ault . . . for
E. Newbery . . . 1801.

Coll: 24° A² B-Q⁶ R⁴ 96 leaves (13.7 x 8.1cm) [4]+187
+[1] pp.

Plates: Frontispiece, inscribed: "Published by E.
Newbery, April 20, 1801."

(cont'd)

Lucinda. (Cont'd)

Notes: Bookplate of Percival Merritt. Roscoe # 339.
BMC indicates two editions of 1801: D12806. i.
17 (which is a 24°), and 12835.C.4 (a 12°).

Smith, Rev. Thomas (pseud.)   # 2007

The Shepherd's Son; or the wish accomplished. A moral
tale. Interspersed with poetical effusions, designed
for the improvement of youth. By the Rev. Thomas
Smith. London: Printed for E. Newbery . . . . By G.
Woodfall, 1800.

Coll: 24° A-P⁶ 90 leaves (13.2 x 8.6cm) iv, 5-
179 +[1].

Plates: Frontispiece, inscribed "Published by E. Newbery . . . ."

Notes: Bookplate of Percival Merritt. Roscoe #
340.

Anon   # 2009

The Snow Flake: A holiday gift, for MDCCCL.
[Illustrated by Stephanoff, Creswick, Stowe, Perning,
(H.?) Howard, Court, Miss Sharp, & [J.?] Jackson.]
Philadelphia: E. H. Butler & Co., 1850.

Coll: 12° [1⁴] 2-26⁶ 27² 156 leaves (18.2 x 12cm)
Pp. [viii, 13]-330 (includes plates; total 312pp.)

Plates: Engraved frontispiece, illustrated title page,
+7.

[ANON.]. The Songster's Repository; Being a choice
selection of the most Esteemed Songs Many of which
have not heretofore been Published. New York:
Published by Nath [ania]l Dearborn . . . , 1811.   # 2010

Coll: 12°: π²1⁴2-22⁶23². 134 leaves (17X 10.4cm).
[1-8]9-12[13]14-70 (71 misnumbered 70) 72-157 (158
misnumbered 851) 159-168; 187-211 (212 misnumbered
120) 213-267(268 misnumbered 286) 269-286.

Illustrations: Engraved frontispiece and title page.

Anon.   # 2112

The Sparrow. Philadelphia: Printed for Benjamin Johnson,
No. 31 High-Street and Jacob Johnson, No. 147 High-Street,
1802.

Coll: 16°: (8s) A-C⁸ 56 leaves (12.5 X 10.2cm) Pp.
[1-2, 3] 4-17 [18] 19-111 [112]

Plates: Frontispiece, "Thurston, del....Tanner, sc."

Spearman, Frank H[amilton]   1859-1937   #2013

Whispering Smith. Illustrated by N. C. Wyeth. New York: Charles Scribner's Sons, 1906. Pp.[1]-[xii] 1-442, [1-2: adverts].

Plates: Frontispiece+3.

Fables for Children . . . (Cont'd)

Binding: Rebound in calf by Riviere & Son; original red cloth wrappers bound in at end.

Notes: Bookplate of Gordon Abbott. Preface signed "the author, London, 1848."

Spinner, Jenny, The Hertfordshire Ghost

   see

   The History of Jenny Spinner, the Hertfordshire Ghost. Written by Herself. Chatham, 1803.

#2022

Steele, Joel Dorman, Ph.D., F.G.S. (1836-1886), and Esther Baker Steele, Litt. D.

Barnes's School History of The United States: Being a Revision of A Brief History of The United States. [Illustrated.] New York: Cincinnati, Chicago: American Book Company, n.d. [1903]. Pp.[1-4,] 5-372, i-lxii.

Plates: Frontispiece, 8 full-page portraits, 16 colored maps, +cuts.

[Spyri, Johanna]   1827-1901   #2016

Heidi's Lehr-und Wanderjahre. Eine Geschichte für Kinder und auch für Solche, welche die Kinder Lied haben. Von der Verfasserin von "Ein Blatt auf Vorny's Grab." Gotha: Friedrich Andreas Berthis, 1880. Pp.[1-iv, 1] 2-240.

Notes: First edition. Leaves 1-15 signed. McKell # S-6-22-59.

Stennet, R   #2024

Aldiborontiphoskyphorniostikos; a round game, for merry parties; with rules for playing the game. Embellished with sixteen elegantly coloured engravings, London: Dean & Munday, [ca. 1825].

Coll: 8°. 16 leaves printed on inner forme only. 1-2[8] Pp. [5-9] 10-11 [12-13] 14-15 [16-17] 18-19 [20-21] 22-23 [24-25] 26-27 [28-29] 30-31 [32-33] 34-35 [36]. (17.6 x 10.2cm)
Binding: Stiff light blue wrappers. Paste down endpapers front and rear. Rules of game on rear cover.

[Spyri, Johanna]   1827-1901   #2017

Heidi: Her Years of Wandering and Learning. A story for children and those who love children. Louise Brooks, trans. 2 vols. Boston: Cupples, Upham & Company, 1885. Pp.[1-ii, 1-4] 5-269 [270; 1-22 of adverts bound in at end]; [1-ii, 1-5] 6-269 [270]; 1-22 of adverts bound in at end].

Illus: Adverts on last three pages of vol. ii are engravings.
Notes: Both vols. are first american edition.

#2025

Stephens, C[harles] A[sbury]   1844-1931

The Young Moose Hunters, a backwoods-boy's story. Illustrated by Merrill. Boston: Henry L. Shepard & Co., 1874. Pp.[1-4], 5-288.

Plates: Frontispiece

Notes: First ed.

Staite, W   Edwards   #2019

Fables for Children, Young and Old in Humorous Verse. Second edition with additions. London: E. Churton . . .[ca 1848]. J. Billing, printer and stereotyper. Woking, Surrey.

Coll: sm4° (8's) π² A-H⁸ 66 leaves (15.7 x 12.3 cm) Pp. 1-4, 1-6, 7 8-10 11 12-126 127-128 .

Plates: Front+ engraved title page+6 hand-colored by T. H. Jones.

   (cont'd)

Stephens, Peter, Esq.   #2027

Racolta di Alcune Velle piu Belle Vedute D'Italia. 150 views of Italy Etch'd by various Artists, chiefly designed on the Spot by Peter Stephens, Esq. Published in July, 1767.

Coll: Single sheets. 405 leaves (17.1 x 26.2 cm.); ff. 405.

Illus: 2 title plates + 200 plates; all wood engravings.

Notes: Blank leaf between plates. Loundes gives "oblong quarto" Plate leaves have
   (cont'd)

Stephens, Peter, Esq. *(Cont'd)*

vertical chains, no watermark; blank
leaves have horizontal chains, all have
watermarks. Plate leaves are thicker
than blanks.

Sternau, Felix, Dr.   #*2031*

Palamedes. Oder erwecnende, belehrende und warnende
Erzählungen für Söhne und Töchter von sechs bis
zwolf Jahren. Von Dr. Felix Sternau. Berlin: Verlag
der Buchhandlung von C. Fr. Amelang. [Gedricht bei
Carl Friedrich Amelang], n.d.

Coll: 16° π⁴,1-11¹², 12² 130 leaves (14 x 12.8cm)
      Pp.[i] ii-iv [v] vi-vii [viii], 1-262, [263] 264-
      268.

Plates: Front+title page +6; all hand colored copper
        plate engravings.
Notes: Vertical chain (lines

Stevenson, Burton [Egburt]   1872-1962   # *2033*

The Red Carnation: an Anthony Bigelow Story.   New
York: Dodd, Mead & Company, 1939. Pp.[i]-[x] 1-296.

Binding: Dust cover

                                              # *2034*

Stevenson, Burton Egbert   1872-1962

Tommy Remington's Battle. [Illustrated.] "St.
Nicholas Books." New York: The Century Co.,
1902. Pp.[i] ii-ix [x, 1] 2-257 [258].

Plates: Frontispiece +6.

                                              # *2035*

Stevenson, Robert Louis   1850-1894

Kidnapped; being memoirs of the adventures of
David Balfour in the year 1751 written by himself and now set forth by Robert Louis Stevenson
with over one hundred illustrations and decorations by Louis Rhead. New York and London:
Harper & Brothers Publishers, 1921. Pp.[i-xii]
1-301 [302; 1-4].
Plates: Frontispiece in color +30 full-page en-
        gravings.
Binding: Front endpapers: "Sketch of the cruise
         of the brig (Covenant and the probable
         course of   David Balfour's wanderings."

Stevenson, Robert Louis   #*2038*

Treasure Island. By Robert Louis Stevenson. Intro. by
Angelo Patri. Illustr. by Charles Banks Wilson. Philadelphia and New York: J. B. Lippincott Company [Copy-
right 1948] Pp.[xviii,1-2] 3-268 [269-270].

Illus: Frontispiece +6: color. Several others in black
       and white.

Note: First impression.

                                              #*2039*

Stevenson, Robert Louis   1850-1894

Treasure Island. Illustrated by Edmund Dulac.
London: Ernest Benn Limited, 1927. Pp.[i] ii-
xiii [xiv,] 15-255 [256].

Plates: Frontispiece +11 +cuts.

Stevenson, Robert Louis   1850-1894   #*2040*

Treasure Island. London, Paris, & New York:
Cassell & Company, Limited, 1883. Pp.[i-vii] viii
[1] 2-126 (127 mispaginated "12") 128-292; 1-3 [4]
5-8 of adverts.

Plate: Frontispiece in color.

Notes: First edition. Leaves signed B-T. McKell
       Nos. #S-2-23-45; 12-16-47.

Stöber, K   #*2043*

Der Mühlartzt. Der Birkhof. "Amerikanische Jugend-
bibliothek." Philadelphia: Morwitz & Co., n.d.

Coll: 8° [A-E]⁸ 40 leaves (14.8 x 10.4cm) Pp.
      [1-3] 4-61 [62-64] 65-78 [79-80]
Illus: Woodcut in color on front; black and white
       woodcut on title page.
Binding: Paper over boards. Adverts on back
         paste-down endpapers.

Stoddard, John F., A.M.   1825-1873   #*2047*

The American Intellectual Arithmetic; containing
an extensive collection of practical questions on the
general principles of arithmetic. New York &
Chicago: Sheldon & Company, [1860 ?] Pp.[i-vii,]
8-176.

Binding: Front and back free endpapers torn out of
         McKell copy.
Notes: Revised edition. L.C.: [1860 ?]

Stoddard, William O[sborn]   1835-1925   #2048

Little Smoke: a tale of the Sioux. Illustrated by Frederic S. Dellenbaugh. New York: D. Appleton and Company, 1891. Pp.[i-ii, 1] 2-295 [296; 1-4 of adverts.]

Plates: Frontispiece +13.

Notes: First edition.

Stoddard, William O[sborn]   1835-1925   #2049

Two Arrows: a story of red and white. Illustrated. New York: Harper & Brothers, 1886. Pp.[1-3,]4-239.

Plates: Frontispiece +22.

Notes: First edition ?

Stops, Mr.

    see

        Punctuation Personified

Anon   #2052

Stories about Arnold, the Traitor, Andre, the Spy, and Champe, the Patriot: for the children of the United States. With engravings. Second edition. New Haven: Published by A. H. Maltby, 1831.

Coll: 16° [14] 2-5⁸ 36 leaves (13.5 x 11cm) Pp. [1-3] 4-72.

Illus: Front wrapper +14: engravings

Binding: Chartreuse wrappers. Free and paste-down endpapers.

Anon   #2053

The Story of Aladdin and the Wonderful Lamp. Illustrated by John Kettelwell. Preface by Hugh Walpole. London & New York: Alfred A. Knopf, 1928. Pp.[viii], 1- 109 [110; 1-2].

Plates: Frontispiece +6.

Notes: Sir Hugh Seymour Walpole (1884-1941).

Anon   #2054

The Story of Aleck, or Pitcairn's Island. Being a true account of a very singular and interesting colony. Amherst, Mass.: Published by J. S. & C. Adams, 1829.

Coll: sm 8° 1⁹ (1.4+1) 2⁹ (2.4+1) 3⁹ (3.4+1) 27 leaves (14.2 x 8.9cm) Pp.[1-iv, 5] 6-54.

Binding: Brown wrappers; free and paste-down endpapers front and back.

Anon   #2055

The Story of Captain Riley, and His Adventures in Africa. With engravings. ["Peter Parley's Little Library of True Stories."] New York: J.P. Peaslee, 1835.

Coll: 8° [1]⁸ 2-3 ⁸[4]⁸ 5-8 ⁸[9]⁸ 10-15⁸ 120 leaves (13.6 x 11.2cm) Pp.[viii] 9-240

Illus: 10 engravings +2 vignettes.

[ANON.]. The Story of Jack and the Giants. #2056
Illustrated with Thirty-Five Drawings by Richard Doyle. Engraved by G. and E. Dalziel. New Edition. London: [Printed by Livey, Robson, and Franklyn for] Griffith and Farran, 1858.

Coll.: 4°: [A² B-E⁴ F²]. 20 leaves. [v-vi] vii-viii [9] 10, 13-20, 23-32, 35-38, 41-46, 49-52, 55-56 pp.

Plates: Frontispiece, engraved title page, + 6.

Binding: Full green crushed morocco by Riviere and Son.

Two leaves (4 pages) of advertisements and original pictorial wrappers bound in at end.

Anon.   #2057

The Story of Little Mary and Her Cat, in words not exceeding two syllables. London: [Printed by Joseph Masters for] Darton and Clark, [1830?]

Coll: 18°: A¹⁸ 18 leaves (13.9 x 9cm.) Pp.[1-3] 4-35 [36]

Plates: Engraved frontispiece + 5

Binding: Buff printed wrappers

Notes: Frontispiece dated Mar 30, 1830.
       A18ᵛ: Advertisements

Stowe, Harriet Beecher (1811-1896)

    see

        Our Young Folks; An Illustrated Magazine for Boys and Girls. No. 13 (Jan., 1866 [contains "The Hen That Hatched Ducks"]) and No. 27 (Mar., 1867 [contains "What Pussy Did With Her Winters"]).

#2061

The Strand Magazine: an illustrated monthly.
George Newnes, ed. London: Burleigh Street,
Strand, Vol. II, July 1891 to Vol. VI, December,
1893.

Illus: Photographs and drawings.

Notes: Contain first appearances of Sir Arthur
Conan Doyle's Sherlock Holmes. See also
under Doyle (1859-1930).

#2067

The Student and Schoolmate: an illustrated
monthly for all our boys and girls. Vols., XIX-
XX. Boston: Joseph Hallen, 1867. Pp. [1-iv, 1]
2-240; [1] 2-244.

Illus: Numerous woodcuts in text.

Contents: Includes Horatio Alger Jr.'s "Ragged
Dick, or, Street Life in New York" in
12 chapter-installments.

Stratton, Hesba   1832-1911

see

Smith, Sarah. Jessica's First Prayer.

Summer Dew Drops. Turner & Fischer, n.d.

see under

Turner & Fischer's Selection of Large and
Showy Toys.

#2063

[Strickland, Agnes]   1796-1874

The Aviary. A reward for good children. London:
Houlston and Son, 1832.

Coll: 12° A-E⁶ 36 leaves (14.4 x 8.7 cm)
Pp. [1-6] 7-8, [9] 10-70 71-72.

Plates: "Frontispiece"+cuts.
Binding: Printed blue paper over boards, leather
spine.

#2069

[Swift, Jonathan]. 1667-1745

Adventures of Captain Gulliver in a voyage to Lilliput
[Abridged]. Edinburgh: Printed and published by G. Ross,
n.d.

Coll: 32°: (eights) [A]-C⁸ 24 leaves (9.8 X 6.1cm)
Pp. [1-5] 6-47 [48]

Illus: Woodcut frontispiece + 12 cuts (vignettes) in text

Binding: Buff, printed wrappers, initial and final pages
as paste down endpapers.

Strickland, Agnes. 1796-1874   #2064

Historical Tales of Illustrious Children. By Agnes
Strickland, authoress of "The Rival Crusoes," Etc. etc.
With engravings. Boston: Munroe and Francis. J.H. Francis,
128 Washington-Street, Boston. New York: C.S. Francis &
Co., n.d.

Coll: 12°: 1² 2-3⁸ 4-21 ⁴⁄₈ 22-23⁴ 24² 136 leaves (15.7 X
9.6cm) Pp. [3-5, 6] (7-8 skipped) [9] 10-43 [44-45]
46-276

Plates: Frontispiece + 7, + a few cuts; all engravings.

Swift, Jonathan. 1667-1745   #2070

The Adventures of Captain Gulliver, in a Voyage to the
Islands of Lilliput & Brobdingnag. Abridged from the Works
of the Celebrated Dean Swift. Adorned with [Wood] cuts.
Boston: Printed and sold by S. Hall...,1794.

Coll: 32°: [A⁸] B-G⁸ H⁷ 63 leaves (10.5 X 6.7cm) Pp. [1-6]
7-119 [120-126]

Illus: Woodcut frontispiece + 19 in text

Binding: Red and blue flowered boards.

Notes: [A₁] missing from McKell copy. H₄ᴿ-H₇ᵛ contains
advertisements. A condensation of Bks. I-II.

#2065

[Strickland, Agnes]   1796-1874

The Little Tradesman: or, a Peep into English
Industry. Accompanied with Forty-Eight Copper-
Plates. By the author of "The Moss-House,"
"The Aviary," "The Youthful Travellers," &c.
&c. London: William Darton, [After 1832]

Coll: 12°; A-D¹² 48 leaves(17.5 x 10.7 cm.);
pp. [1-2, 3] 4-95 [96(ads.)].

Illus: 48 copper plates on twelve conjugate
leaves not included in the pagination or
signatures.

#2071

Swift, Jonathan. 1667-1745

Le Gulliver Des Enfants ou Aventures Les Plus Curieuses
De Ce Voyageur. "Lectures Illustrées," [Series] Paris:
Amédée Bédelet, Libraire [ca 1860] [Paris-Imp. Simon
Raçon Et. Comp.]

Coll: 12° π² 1-8⁶, 9⁴ 54 leaves (17.8 x 11.4cm)
Pp. [1-5] 6-17 [18] 19-25 [26] 27-29 [30] 31-32
[33] 34-36 [37] 38-39 [40] 41-42 [43] 44-48 [49]
50-58 [59] 60-63 [64] 65-72 [73] 74-78 [79] 80-85
[86] 87-88 [89] 90-92 [93] 94-106 [107] 108.

Illus: 8 colored woodcuts.

(cont'd)

Le Gulliver Des Enfants. (Cont'd)

Binding: Pasted down endpapers. Boards.

Notes: Gumuchian # 5494

The Swiss Family Robinson, in words of one syllable

see under

Aikin, Lucy (Mary Godolphin, pseud.)

Swift, Jonathan. 1667-1745   #2072

Gullivers Reizen Naar Liliput en andre vreemde landen.
Door Jonathan Swift. Voor de jeugd bewerkt door J. J.
A. Goeverneur. Met 6 gekleurde platen naar acquarellen
van C. Offterdinger. Leiden: D. Noothoven Van Goor.
n.d., [1850?].

Coll: $8°$ π^2, 1-8^8 9^2 136 leaves Pp. [i-iv, i] 2-71
[72] 73-131 [132]. (20.5 x 14.5cm)

Plates: Frontispiece +5; in color by Offterdinger.

Anon.   #2075

[2 Syllabaire Série 5. Jeux De Garçons Francais
et Anglais. Paris: D. Marchand Editeur A. de
Saintonge 64] [ca. 1850.]

Coll: 23 separate leaves (9.2 x 12.7 cm.), each
     lithographed in color on recto (verso
     blank).

Binding: White wrappers; decoration on front
     recto (verso blank). Illustration
     (lithographed in color) on back verso
     (recto blank).

Notes: McKell #S-1-6-) 45B.

Swift, Jonathan   1667-1745   #2073

Gulliver's Travels. Illustrated. New York:
Leavitt & Allen, n.d.

Coll: $12°$ (b's) (obsolete signings present)[1-18^6
193](19·2 $\pm$ 1) (15.1 x 9.2cm) Pp. [i-iv, 81]
82-100 [101] 102-117 [118] 119-131 [132] 133-
140 [141] 142-151 [152] 153-167 [168] 169-180 [181]
182-190 [191] 192 - 194 [195] 196-216 [217]
218-225 [226] 227-241 [242] 243-249 [250] 251-
264 [265] 266-281 [282] 283-291 [292].
111 leaves.   (cont'd)

Anon.   #2076

[3 Syllabaire Série 5. Comtes Des Fees Francais
et Anglais. Paris: D. Marchand Editeur. Rue de
Saintonge 64. Lith. Vayron R. Galande 51 Paris]

Coll: 23 separate leaves (9.1 x 12.1 cm.), each
     lithographed in color on recto (verso
     blank). Illustration on back verso (recto
     blank).

Notes: McKell#S-1-6-45B.

Swift. Gulliver's Travels. Leavitt & Allen (Cont'd)

Illus: Half-title,"frontispiece," title other
     woodcuts in text.
Contents: Books I & II only.
Notes: P. 274 has broken type in the pagination.

Anon.   #2077

[Syllabaire 4 Série 5. Metiers, Feminin Francais
et Anglais. Paris: D. Marchand Editeur. Rue
de Saintonge 64. Lith. Vayron R. Galande, 51]
[ca. 1850.]

Coll: 23 separate leaves (9.2 x 12.5 cm.), each
     lithographed in color on recto (verso
     blank).

Binding: White wrappers; decorations on front
     recto (verso blank). Illustration lith-
     ographed in color on back verso (recto
     blank).

Notes: McKell #S-1-6-) 45-B.

Swinburne, Algernon Charles 1837-1909   #2074

The Springtide of Life: poems of my childhood. By
Algernon Charles Swinburne. With a preface by Edmund
Gosse. Illustrated by Arthur Rackham. London; William
Heinemann [1918]. Pp. [i-iv] v-ix [x] 1-132 [133,134].

Plates: Frontispiece+7: all in color +numerous
     decorative cuts. Decorative sketching in green
     ink on endpapers.

Notes: Colophon on p. [134]. Sir Edmund William
     Gosse (1849-1928)

[T., N. K.]   #2080

Good Tidings of Great Joy. London: T. Nelson and Sons,
Paternoster Row, and Edinburgh MCCCLVII.

Coll: $64°$ (eights) A-H^8 64 leaves (7.3 x 5.9cm) Pp.
     [1-4,1] 11, 7-128.

Binding: Green Calf, tooled.

Notes: $1 (+F2)

#2081

[ANON.]. Tabart's Collection of Popular Stories for
the Nursery: From the French, Italian, and Old
English Writers, Newly Translated and Revised, 3
vols. Adorned with Numerous Plates. London: Printed [by R. Taylor & Co.] for Tabart & Co. . . . ,
1804. No EMC no.

Part I:
Coll.: 24°: [A²]B-2⁶R⁴. 96 leaves (13.6 X 8.5cm).
Pp. [i-iv], [1] 2-187 [188].

R4ᵛ contains advertisements of Tabart's books.

Plates: Frontispiece + 5 illustrations, hand-tinted
copper plates.
Bookplate of Frederica(Christina Hastings.

Tabart -2-

Part II:
Coll.: 24°: [A²]B-2⁶R². 94 leaves (13.5 X 8.4cm).
Pp. [i-iv] [1]2-181 [182-184].

Plates: Copper plate frontispiece + 5 hand-tinted
copper plate illustrations.

R₁ᵛ-K₂ᵛ contain advertisements of Tabart's books.

Bookplate of Sophia Frederica Christina Hastings.

Tabart -3-

Part III:
Coll.: 24°: [A²]B-R⁶. 96 leaves (13.4 X 8.6cm).
Pp. [i-iv], [1] 2-188 [189-192].

Plates: Frontispiece + 6; copperplate, hand-tinted.

R₅ᴿ-R6ᵛ contains advertisements of Tabart's books.

Bookplate of Sophia Frederica Christina Hastings.

Tagg, Tommy

see

Newbery, John. A Collection of Pretty Poems
. . . . 1781

#2082

Taishoku Kan [i.e., Story of a Diver Girl.] Tokyo,
1711.

Coll: 18 leaves   (18.5 x 13cm) Accordion fold,
printed on one side only.
Illus: 3 double-leaf, Moronobu-style woodcuts.
Binding: Gray paper wrappers.

#2083

[Talbot, Charles Remington]   1851-1891

Miltiades Peterkin Paul. His adventures. By
John Brownjohn. With illustrations by L. Hopkins.
Boston: D. Lathrop & Co., Publishers, [1877]. Pp.
[i-vi, 1-26 ; 1] leaf of adverts laid in at end.

Illus: Frontispiece + numerous black and white.
Notes: First edition. McKell # G-7-23-43-B.

#2084

ANON. . The Tale of Saint Mary of Egypt. [Weston,
Connecticut, 1933].

Coll.: 9°: 1⁸. 8 leaves (10.5 X 8.5cm). [1-4] 5-12
[13-16]pp.

Vertical chains. Bookplate of Porter Garnett.

#2085

Anon.

Tales for all Seasons; or Stories and Dialogues for
Little Folks by Thomas Teller. New Haven: Published by
S. Babcock, n.d.

Coll: 16°: 1¹⁰, 2¹², 3¹⁰   32 leaves (13.9 X 11.1ᶜᵐ·)
Pp. [1-2, 3] 4 [5] 6-15 [16] 17-20 [21] 22-26 [27] 28-37
[38] 39-43 [44] 45-49 [50] 51-58 [59] 60-64

Illus: Several engravings

Binding: Pink wrappers

Notes: Dedication by "Thomas Teller, Roseville Hall,
1845."

#2086

Anon

Tales of Instruction and Amusement. William and
Lucy's trip to London. Beautifully coloured.
London: Published by A. Park, 47, Leonard Street,
Finsbury [1840 ?]
Coll: 8° 1⁸ unsigned 8 leaves (18 x 12.1cm)
Pp. [1-16]
Illus: 8 hand-colored wood-engravings.
Binding: Buff wrappers. Initial and final pages as
paste-down endpapers.

#2087

Anon.

Tales, uniting Instruction with Amusement: Consisting of
Throwing Squibs; and the Boy with a Bundle. Ornamented
with copper plate engravings. Philadelphia: Printed for
Bennett and Walton, No. 31, Market Street, 1808.

Coll: 12°: (6s) A-B⁶ $1,2 (-A, all threes signed 2) signed
12 leaves (13.7 X 8.8cm) Pp. [1-2] 3-22 [23-24]

Plates: Frontispiece + 1
Binding: Blue wrappers, stabbed
Notes: Advertisement for Bennett and Walton on p. 23.

Anon. #2088

The Talking Bird: or, Dame Trudge and Her Parrot. London: Printed [by H. Bryer] for J. Harris, 1806.

Coll: 16°: A⁸ 8 leaves (12.6 X 9.7ᶜᵐ·) Pp.·-vi [7]8-15[16]

Binding: Half calf over Brown cloth boards by Riviere & Son

Notes: McKell # S-1-11-43

Taylor, Isaac   1787-1865   #2098

The Linnet's Life. Twelve poems with a copper plate engraving to each. London: Printed for G. and W. B. Whittaker . . . and B. J. Holdsworth, 1822.

Coll: 12° A-C⁶ 18 leaves (15.7 x 9.7cm) Pp. [i-iv, 5] 6-36.

Plates: Front +11

Tarkington, [Newton] Booth   1869-1946   #2092

Penrod and Sam. Illustrated by Worth Brehm. Garden City, New York: Doubleday, Page & Company, 1916. Pp.[i]-[x, 1] - [350].

Plates: Frontispiece +7.

Notes: First ed., but not first state.

Taylor, The Rev. Isaac   1759-1829   #2099

Scenes in Europe, For the Amusement and Instruction of Little Tarry-at-Home Travellers. Second Edition. London: Printed by E. Hamstead. . . for J. Harris . . ., 1819.

Coll: 12° [A]⁴ B-I⁶ 52 leaves (15.8 x 9.1cm) Pp. [i-v] vi-viii [1] 2-93; [1-3] of adverts.

Plates: Frontispiece (fold-out hand-colored engraved map) + 28, each containing 3 color engravings. Plates dated Jan. 20, 1818 or Feb. 20, 1818.

Notes: S-1-11-43-B.

Tarkington, [Newton] Booth   1869-1946   #2093

Penrod. Illustrated by Gordon Grant. Garden City, New York: Doubleday, Page & Company, 1914. Pp.[x, 1 2] 3-[348].

Notes: First ed., but not first state.

Taylor, Jane   1783-1824   and
Ann Taylor [Gilbert]   1782-1866   #2100

Little Ann and Other Poems. Illustrated by Kate Greenaway. London & New York: Frederick Warne & Co., n.d. 64pp.

Tarkington, [Newton] Booth   1869-1946   #2094

Penrod Jashber. Illustrated by Gordon Grant. Garden City, New York: Doubleday, Doran & Company, Inc., 1929. Pp.[i]-[xii] 1-[322].

Notes: First ed.

Taylor, Jefferys   1792-1853   #2101

The Young Islanders. A tale of the last century. New York: D. Appleton and Company, 1842.

Coll: 12° [1]⁶ 2-25⁶ 26³ 153 leaves (16.9 x 10.3cm) Pp. [i-v] vi-vii [viii, 9] 10-306; [1-16 pp. of adverts bound in at end].

Plates: Engraved frontispiece +7
Notes: McKell copy lacks [1.1]

Taylor, G. B.   #2095

A Universal History of The United States of America, embracing the whole period, from the earliest discoveries, down to the present time. New York: Ezra Strong, 1842.

Coll: 12° 1⁶ 2-51⁶ 306 leaves (18.6 x 11.6cm) Pp. [1-3] 4 [5] 6-606 [1] ii-vi (totl of 612pp)

Plates: 2 frontispieces +18 engravings.

Anon.   #2102

A Teacher's Offering. Boston: Fred K.A. Brown & Co., Publishers, Printed by George C. Rand & Avery , 1862.

Pagination: [1-4] 5-48 (10.6 x 7.2cm)

Illus: Frontispiece plus 13 woodcuts plus 3 floral decorations.

Notes: Electrotyped at the Boston Stereotype Foundry. Free and pasted down end papers front and back.

Anon.   #2103

A Teacher's Offering. "Teacher's Tokens" [Compiled by Asa Bullard] Boston: Thompson, Bigelow & Brown, [Entered according to act of Congress, 1857].

Coll: 32°: 1-3⁸ 24 leaves (10.2 X 6.9cm) Pp. [1-4] 5-48

Illus: 10 woodcuts plus 4 floral illustrations.

Notes: Electrotyped at the Boston Stereotype Foundry. Free and pasted down end papers front and back.

(

Telescope, Tom

see

Newbery, John. The Newtonian System of Philosophy . . . .
(1) 1761
(2) 2nd ed. 1762
(3) 3rd ed. 1766
(4) 6th ed. 1784
(5) 7th ed. 1787
(6) A new improved ed. 1798

(

Teller, Thomas

see

Tales for all Seasons; . . . by Thomas Teller. New Haven, S. Babcock, n.d.

(

Anon   #2104

The Tell-Tale: an original collection of moral and amusing stories. London: Harris and Son. [Printed by Cox and Baylis, Great Queen Street.] 1823.

Coll: 12° A², B-P⁶, Q⁴ 90 leaves (16.4 x 10.2cm) Pp. [i-iv, 1] 2-174 [175-176 adverts]

Plates: Front +5 copper plate engravings

Notes: Frontispiece dated "Published April 20, From "Harris & Son's Original Juvenile Library."

(

Anon. (Thai Children's Book)   #2107

[MSS. Children's Picture Book]. 19th century. Thailand.

Foliation: 14 leaves. (14.1 x 10.3cm) First and last leaves blank.

Illus: Fr. [2-13] each contains, tipped to recto, a watercolor within a decorative border.

Binding: Paper boards

Notes: Paintings show strong Chinese influence.

(

Thompson, Maurice   1844-1901   #2112

Alice of Old Vincennes. Illustrations by F[rederick] C[offay] Yohn. Indianapolis: The Bowen-Merrill Company, Publishers, 1900. Pp. [x] 1-[442, 1-10: advert].

Plates: Frontispiece + 5.

Notes: First ed.

( )

Anon.   #2113

[From wrapper (No title page)] [Three Little Kittens and Mr. Fox. "Susie Sunshine's Series." New York: McLoughlin Bros., Publishers. n.d.]

Coll: 18°: [1⁶] 6 leaves (17.1 X 11.8cm) Fr. 6.

Illus: Eight colored engravings + first and last pages printed in color.

Binding: Illustrated orange paper wrappers, advertisements in back.

Notes: All leaves are cloth. Initial and final leaves pasted to wrapper.

(

Titmarsh, Mr. M.A.

see

Doctor Birch and His Young Friends. By Mr. M.A. Titmarsh. London: 1849.

( )

Todd, John   1800-1873   #2115

The Mountain Cottage. By John Todd. "Sabbath School Series." Pittsfield, Mass.: E. B Little, 1844.

Coll: 16° [1¹⁶ 2²] 18 leaves (10.7 x 7.7cm) Pp. [1-3] 4-35 [36]

Binding: Free and pasted down endpapers front and back.

(

Anon.   #2116

The Token. Boston: Brown, Taggard & Chase, (Successors to W.J. Reynolds & Co.), [Printed by George C. Rand & Avery, Electrotyped at the Boston Stereotype Foundry, 1857].

Coll: Sm 8°: 1-3⁸ 24 leaves (12 X 7.7cm) Pp. [1-4, 5] 6-48

Illus: Numerous woodcuts

Notes: Cover has "A Teacher's Token"

( )

#2118

Tomlinson, Everett T[itsworth] 1859-1931

The Boy Officers of 1812. [Illustrated by A. Burnham Shute.] "War of 1812 Series." Boston: Lee and Shepard Publishers, 1890. Pp. [1-5] 6-[336].

Plates: Frontispiece +7.

#2119

Tomlinson, Everett T[itsworth] 1859-1931

The Search for Andrew Field: a story of the times of 1812. [Illustrated by A. Burnham Shute]. Boston: Lee and Shepard, [1884]. Pp [i-viii, 9] 10-313 [314]; 1-6 of adverts.

Plates: Frontispiece +7

Notes: First ed.

Anon. #2120

Tommy Thumb's Song-Book, for all little Masters and Misses. To be sung to them by their nurses till they can sing them themselves, by Nurse Lovechild. To which is prefixed a letter from a lady on nursing. Glasgow: Published by J. Lumsden & Son, 1814.

Coll: 32⁰: (eights) [1-2⁸] 16 leaves (9.9 X 6.3^{cm}.) Pp. [1-4] 5-6 [7] 8 [9] 10-31 [32]

Illus: Frontispiece + 27 cuts in text

Binding: Blue wrappers. Initial and final leaves serve as paste down endpapers.

Notes: "From Ross'a Juvenile Library" on front

Anon. #2121

Tom Tearabout. "Father's Series." New York: McLoughlin Bros. & Co., [n.d.]

Coll: 16⁰: [1⁴] 4 leaves (15 X 12.1cm) Pp. [1-8]

Illus: 8 colored engravings.

Binding: Yellow wrappers, colored in red. Illustration on front. Advertisements on back.

Notes: Wrapper serves as title page.

Anon #2122

Tom the Thief. "Little Slovenly Peter Series." New York: McLoughlin Bros., Publishers, n.d.

Coll: 18 [1⁴] 4 leaves (17.1 x 11.5cm) Pp. [1-8]

Illus: 8 colored engravings

Binding: Yellow wrappers. Illustrations on front. Advert on back which indicates "large 18⁰."

Notes: Front wrapper serves as title page.

Anon. #2123

Tom Thumb. "Grandpapa Pease's [Series]" Albany: Published by Fisk & Little, Booksellers & Stationers, n.d.

Coll: Lg 8⁰: [1⁸] 8 leaves Ff. [1-2] 3-8. (26.8 x 18cm)

Illus: 8 colored woodcuts

Binding: Green wrappers. Illustrated on front, advertisement on back

Notes: Printed on one side of the page only. Initial and final pages pasted to wrapper

---

Anon. #2124

Tom Thumb Illuminated with Ten Pictures. New York: Loomis & Co., Engravers & Printers. [From Wrapper:] "Hewet's Illuminated Household Stories, for Little Folks." With illustrations by W.H. Thwaites. Engraved by the Best Artists. Tom Thumb Vol. VI. New York. Hewet Publisher, [Entered 1855].

Coll: Sm 4⁰: [1-4⁴] 16 leaves. Pp. [i-iv] 1-24 [25-26, 27-28] (17.5 x 13.5cm)

Plates: frontispiece and title page + Numerous other engravings. Frontispiece colored in oils.

Tom Thumb Illuminated with Ten Pictures. (Cont'd)

Binding: Buff illustrated wrappers. Stabbed. Initial and final leaves serve as paste-down endpapers.

Notes: P. 1 signed A, p. 17 signed B.

Tom Thumb

see also

The Famous History of Tom Thumb. London: c. 1780.
The Famous Tommy Thumb's Little Story-Book; containing his life and surprising adventures. London: for S. Crowder, n.d.
The Life and Death of Tom Thumb, the Little Giant . . . with Grumbo . . . York, 1804.

Anon. (Tom Thumb) #2125

Tom Thumb's Folio, or, a New Play-Thing for Little Giants. To which is prefixed, an Abstract of the Life of Mr. Thumb. And an Historical account of the Wonderful deeds he performed. Together with some anecdotes respecting Grumbo, the Great Giant. Hudson: Printed by Ashbel Stoddard, and sold wholesale and retail, at his Book-Store, Corner of Warren and Third Streets, 1806.

Coll: 32⁰: (8s) A⁴, B⁸, C⁴ (C⁴ = A5-8) 16 leaves (B1 is signed) (10.8 X 6.3cm) Pp. [1-4, 5] 6-28 [29] 30-31 [32]

Illus: 8 woodcuts

Anon.

Tom Thumb's Folio. 1806.

Binding: Brown wrappers, initial and final pages as paste-
down endpapers.

Anon. **#2126.1**

Tom Thumb's Play-Book, to teach Children their letters as
soon as they can speak: or, Easy Lessons for Little Children and Beginners. Being a new and pleasant method to
allure little ones into the first principle of learning.
Newcastle: Printed by G. Angus, 1824.

Coll: 16º: [A8] B8, [C8 (C8=A9-A16)] 24 leaves (9.8 X
8.5cm.) Pp. [1-3] 4-48

Illus: 26 cuts by Bewick

Binding: Blue wrappers, pictorial

Notes: Percival Merritt bookplate

Anon. **#2126.2**

Tom Thumb's Play-Book to teach Children their letters as
soon as they can speak: or, Easy Lessons for Little
Children and Beginners. Being a new and pleasant method
to allure little ones into the first principle of learning. Union Street: Printed [by G. Angus] for T. Bell,
1824.

Coll: 16º: [A8] B8, [C8 (C8=A9-A16)] 24 leaves (9.8 X 8.5cm.)
Pp. [1-3] 4-48

Illus: 26 cuts by Bewick

Binding: Blue wrappers, pictorial

Notes: Percival Merritt bookplate

#2127

Anon

Tom Trip's Museum: or, A Peep at the Quadruped
Race. 3 parts. London: John Harris, [1810 ?]

Part I:

Coll: 8º π, A16 17 leaves (16.4 x 10.4cm) Ff.
[1] 2-17.

Illus: 16 color woodcuts. (By Thomas Bewick ?)

Notes: Printing and cuts on facing pages alternating
with blank facing pages. (Bewick, 1753-1828)

Parts II and III have same collation and description.

#2129

Anon

The Tract Primer. New York: American Tract Society,
n.d., [1848?].

Coll: 12º 1-96 54 leaves (15.7 x 10.3cm) Pp. [1-4,
5] 6-108.

Illus: "Frontispiece" +vignette title page.

Anon. **#2131**

The Tragi-Comic History of the Burial of Cock Robin;
With the lamentation of Jenny Wren; The Sparrow's
Apprehension; and the Cuckoo's Punishment. Being a
Sequel to the Courtship, Marriage, and Pic-nic Dinner of
Robin Red-Breast and Jenny Wren. Philadelphia: Published
by Benjamin Warner, S. Probasco, Printer, 1821.

Coll: 16º: 18 8 leaves (12.3 X 10.3cm.) Pp. [1-2,3-4,5] 6-16

Plates: Frontispiece + 7

Binding: Pink wrappers, stabbed

Notes: Rosenbach #616. Has half-title page.

Traite de la Forme et Devis d'un Tournoi. Paris:
1946

see

Von Anjou, Herzog Rene d' 1409-1480

Anon. **#2132**

The Travels and Extraordinary Adventures of Bob the
Squirrel. Illustrated with twelve engravings by distin-
guished artists. Philadelphia: Geo. S. Appleton; New York:
D. Appleton & Co., 1847.

Coll: 16º: A-F8 48 leaves (14 X 11.5cm) Pp. [i-v] vi-viii
[9] 10-82 [83-96]

Illus: 12 engraved plates, colored

Notes: McKell # C-7-23-43B

Anon. **#2133**

The Trifle; or, Tales and Fables in words of one syllable. Embellished with coloured engravings. London:
Printed and sold by John Marshall, 1821.

Coll: 16º: [116] unsigned. 16 leaves (11,6 x 9.4cm.)
Pp. [1-3] 4 [5-6] 7-8 [9-10] 11-12 [13-14] 15-18 [19-20]
21-22 [23-24] 25-26 [27-28] 29-30 [31-32]

Illus: Frontispiece+7; all hand colored; all with im-
plied pagination.

Binding: Orange spotted wrappers with flower surrounded
book decal, bearing the title.

Trimmer, Sarah [Kirby] 1741-1810 **#2134**

TRIMMER, SARAH. Fabulous Histories. Designed for
the Instruction of Children, respecting Their
Treatment of Animals. The Two Volumes Comprised in
One. Tenth Edition. London: Printed [by T. Bensley]
for Whittingham and Arliss, Juvenile Library, 1815.

Coll.: 12 (in 8's): [A5] B-K8 2B8(+B1) 2C-2L8M2.
159 leaves (15.1 X 9.2cm). iii-xii, 144, 164 pp.

Illustrations: 18 Bewick woodcuts.

Binding: Full mottled calf, gilt tooled borders,
gilt edge, by Riviere & Son.

#2135

Trimmer, Mrs. [Sarah (Kirby)] 1741-1810

A New Series of Prints, Accompanied by Easy Lessons:
Consisting of Subjects Taken from the New Testament
[Part II]. London: Printed by J. Brettel for J.
Harris . . . and J. Harchard. . . 1805.

Coll: 16° A-G⁸ 56 leaves (11.4 x 9.1cm) Pp.[i-
iii] iv [5] 6-111 [112].

Notes: Part II is the "Lessons" to accompany the
"Prints" of Part I.

#2136

[ANON]. The Triumph of Goodnature, Exhibited in
the History of Master Harry Fairborn and Master
Trueworth. Interspersed with Tales and Fables, and
Ornamented with Cuts [by Bewick]. London: Printed
[by H. Bryer] for J. Harris, n.d. [1800?].

Coll.: 24° A-H⁸ 64 leaves (10.8 X 7.3cm).
117 + [11] pp.

Illustrations: Frontispiece (A1) + 12 woodcuts in
text.

Bookplates of Sophia Frederica Christina Hastings
and Percival Merritt.

#2137

Trowbridge, J[ohn] T[ownsend] 1826-1916

Cudjo's Cave. Boston: J.E. Tilton and Company,
1864. Pp.[1-2] 3-504.

Plates: Engraved half-title page.

Notes: First ed.; second state ?

#2138

Trowbridge, J[ohn] T[ownsend] 1827-1916

Jack Hazard and His Fortunes. Philadelphia:
Porter & Coates, [1899]. Pp.[i] ii-iv, 1-254.

Plates: Frontispiece +cuts.

#2139

Trowbridge, John Townsend] 1827-1916

Lawrence's Adventures Among the Ice-Cutters, Glass-
Makers, Coal-Miners, Iron-Men, and Ship-Builders.
Boston: Fields, Osgood, & Co., 1871. Pp. [i] -vi,
1-[243].

Plates: Frontispiece by John Andrew-Son +cuts.

#2140

Trowbridge, J[ohn] T[ownsend] 1827-1916

The Lottery Ticket. Illustrated. Boston: Lee and
Shepard Publishers, 1896. Pp.[i-iv] 5-202; 1-4 of
adverts.

Plates: Frontispiece +7.

Notes: First ed.

#2141

Trowbridge, J[ohn] Townsend] 1827-1916

A Start in Life: a story of the Genesee Country.
Illustrated by W. A. Rogers. Boston: Lee and
Shepard Publishers; New York: Charles T. Dillingham, 1889. Pp. [1-iv] 5-[164,+12 bound in at end,
7pp. adverts].

Plates: Frontispiece +7.

Trowbridge, John Townsend (1827-1916)

see

Our Young Folks; An Illustrated Magazine
for Boys and Girls.

#2144

Trusler, The Rev. J[ohn] 1735-1820

Proverbs Exemplified, and Illustrated . . . . Prints by
John Bewick. London: J. Trusler, May 1, 1790.

Coll: 12° A⁴ B-R⁶ S² 102 leaves (16.1 x 8.5cm) Pp.
viii, 1-196.

Plates: 51 woodcuts.

Notes: BMC # 12201.
John Bewick 1760-1795

#2142

Anon.

A True History of a Little Old Woman, Who Found a Silver
Penny. London: Printed [by W. Marchant] for Tabart and
Co, 1808.

Coll: 16°: 1⁴, 2², 3⁴, 4⁶ 16 leaves (12.5 X 10.5ᶜᵐ·)
Pp. [1] 2-20[21-32]

Plates: 16 hand colored engravings, the last four are a
fold out sequence of one scene. 12 pages of advertising bound in at end. Plates are dated May
27, 1806.

Binding: Yellow printed wrappers, with advertisements
front and back.

Notes: [S-2-11-44]

Trusler, [Rev.] John　1735-1820　　#2143

The Progress of Man and Society. Illustrated by upwards of One Hundred and Twenty cuts [by John Bewick]. London: John Trusler, 1791.

Coll: 12° A-Z⁶　130 leaves　(16 x 9.6cm)　Pp. [4] +iii+ v+[1] 2-264.

Notes: Bound in at end is a gathering of six leaves (signed Bl, pp. [1] 2-11 [12]) containing "A list of books, published by the Rev. Dr. Trusler, at the Literary Press . . . 1790." John Bewick (1760-1795)

Tuer, Andrew W[hite], F.S.A.　1838-1900　#2145

History of the Horn Book. 2 vols. London: The Leaden-hall Press, Ltd., 1896.

Vol I:
Pagination: [i-vi] vii [viii] ix-x [xi-xii] xiii [xiv] 1-179 [180].

Plates: Frontispiece

Vol II:
Pagination: [i-vi] vii-viii [ix-x] 1-278 [279-280].

Plates: Frontispiece.

(cont'd)

History of the Horn Book.　(Cont'd)

_____

Contents: Vol I: three hornbooks in modern facsimile;
Vol II: four hornbooks in modern facsimile.

Tuer, Andrew W[hite]　　1838-1900　#2146

Old London Street Cries and the cries of to-day with Heaps of Quaint Cuts including Hand-coloured Frontispiece. London: Field & Tuer, The Leadenhall Press; Simpkin, Marshall & Co.; Hamilton, Adams & Co.; New York: Scribner & Welford. 1885

Coll: 16°　A² B-K⁸　74 leaves　(12.4 x 9.8cm)
Pp. [i-iv][1-4,] 5-137 [138]; [1-6.]
Plates: Color woodcut frontispiece+many facsimiles of earlier cuts in text.

(cont'd)

Tuer. Old London Street Cries　(Cont'd)

Contents: Pp. 117-120: identification of artists
Pp. 131-137: index
Pp. [138]ff.: adverts.

Tuer, Andrew W[hite], F.S.A., comp.　1838-1900　#2147

Pages and Pictures from Forgotten Children's Books. London: The Leadenhall Press, Ltd., 1898-1899. Pp. 5-510+[12 leaves adverts].

Contents: Pp. 5-10: introduction; pp. 11-510: text, i.e., various illustrations and texts.

Tuer, Andrew W[hite], F.S.A., comp.　1838-1900　#2148

Stories from Old-Fashioned Children's Books. London: The Leadenhall Press, Ltd., 1899-1900. Pp. vii-xv 1-439, [3]+1-19+[4]+[7].

Illus: "Adorned with 250 amusing cuts."

Contents: Pp. vii-xv: introductory; pp. 1-432: text;
pp. 433-439: title index; pp. [3] 1-19 [4]:
advertising; pp. [7]: publisher's note/

Tullar, Grant Colfax, and I.H. Meredith

see

　　The First Christmas Story. . . . Tullar-
　　　Meredith Co.

Turnbull, James　　fl. 1830　　#2149

History of Animals, being a comprehensive selection from Goldsmith's Animated Nature, with anecdotes of animals, illustrative of their habits and characters. Embellished with twelve pages of [hand-tinted] copper-plate engravings by H. Anderson. Steubenville: [Printed by] James Wilson for J.&B. Turnbull, 1831.

Coll: 12°　A-R⁶　102 leaves　(18.1 x 10.2cm)　Pp. [i-iii]
iv [v] vi [vii] viii-xii [13] 14-204.

Binding: Paste-down endpaper in back

(cont'd)

History of Animals.　(Cont'd)

Notes: Parts of A6 and G6 torn out of McKell copy.
McKell # M-1-5-53-L.

[Turner, Elizabeth]   -1846   # 2150

The Cowslip; or, more cautionary stories, in verse. By
the author of that much-admired little work entitled
The Daisy. The Sixteenth edition. With new engravings.
London: [Printed by Samuel Bentley for] John Harris,
and Baldwin and Cradock, MDCCCXXXVI.

Coll: 12° (6s) A-X⁶ 36 leaves (14.1 x 9cm) Pp. [1-
5] 6-67 [68-69] 70-72.

Illus: 30 engravings

Binding: Gray wrappers,   printed.
                                                        (cont'd)

The Cowslip. (Cont'd)

Notes: F5-F6ᵛ: advertising. BMC does not give the
       1836 ed. But see BMC 11641. de. 51. (2).

[Turner, Elizabeth]   -d. 1846   #2151

The Cowslip; or, More Cautionary Stories in
Verse. A companion to that much admired little
work, entitled The Daisy. A New Edition with
Additional Poems. New York: C. S. Francis &
Co; Boston: J. H. Francis, [n.d.]

Coll: 16°   1⁸, 2⁴, 3⁸, 4⁴, 5⁸, 6⁴, [7 ⁸][8⁴]
       48 leaves (14.1 x 11.2 cm.).
       pp. [1-v] vi, [7]-96.

Illus: Several hand colored cuts.

                                                        # 2152
Turner, J[oseph] M[allord] W[illiam] 1775-1857

No. _____ of Liber Studiorum; illustrative of landscape compositions, viz. historical, mountainous,
pastoral, marine, and architectural, by J.M.W.
Turner, R.A. [London]: [a. 1819].

Coll: 1° 76 leaves (26.6 x 40cm) Unnumbered.
Illus: 73 engravings.
Binding: Each leaf stabbed.
Notes: Printed on recto only.

Anon.   #2153

Turner and Fischer-Publishers of every variety of colored
toy books. Adventures of Jonny Newcome, in the Navy.
Philadelphia and New York: Published by Turner and
Fischer, n.d.

Coll: 8°: [1⁴] 4 leaves (19.5 X 11.5ᶜᵐ·) Pp. [1-8]

Illus: 8 hand-colored woodcuts

Binding: Green wrappers. Illustration on front; adver-
         tisement on back.

Anon.   # 2154

Turner & Fischer's Eclection of Large and Showy Toys.
Summer Dew Drops. Philadelphia and New York: Published
by Turner & Fischer, n.d.

Coll: 16°: [1¹⁶] 16 leaves (16 X 12.7ᶜᵐ·)   Ff. [16]
Illus: 8 hand-colored woodcuts
Binding: White wrappers; front illustrated in color;
         back plain illustration
Notes: Initial and final leaves pasted to wrappers.
       Printed on one side of leaf only.

Turnley, Joseph   # 2155

The Language of the Eye. Illustrated by Gilbert,
Anelay, Etc. London: Partridge and Co., 1856.

Coll: 8° [A]³ B-H⁸ I⁴ 63 leaves (21.1 x 13.4cm)
      Pp. [1-vi, 1] 2-118 [119-120].

Plates: Engraved frontispiece †9

Turpin, Richard (Dick) 1706-1739

        see

                The Lives of Richard Turpin and William
                Nevison. York: James Kendrew, n.d.

                                                       # 2156
Anon

The Twelfth-Day Gift: or, The Grand Exhibition.
Containing a curious Collection of Pieces in
Prose and Verse .... London: Printed for
J. Newbery, 1767.

Coll: 24° [A]³ B-3⁶ T² 107 leaves (11.2 x
      7.2cm) Pp. [1-vi] 1-208.
Plates: Frontispiece †7.
Notes: McKell # SG 6-1-55 B; Roscoe #366 (2)

                                                       #2157,1-2

Two East Anglian Psalters at the Bodleian Library,
Oxford: The Ormesby Psalter, MS. Douce 366,
described by Sydney Carlyle Cockerell; The Bromholm Psalter, MS. Ashmole 1523, described by Montague Rhodes James. Oxford: The Roxburghe Club,
1926. Pp. viii [1] 2-37 [38-39] 40-46 [47-48] +
33 Ormesby plates +10 Bromholm plates + XVIpp.

Anon.   #2158

Uncle John's Little Rhymer. Philadelphia: George S.
Appleton, 1849.

Coll: 16°: [1-6⁴] 24 leaves (14.2 X 11.2ᶜᵐ·) ff 24

Illus: Hand-colored engravings on each leaf

Binding: Hand-colored engraving on front wrapper

Notes: Fold-out. All gatherings joined. Printed on one
       side of leaf only. First leaf pasted to front of
       wrapper. Engravings by N.B. Devereux, S. Herrick,
       and others

Anon.   #2159

The Uncle's Present, a new Battledoor. Philadelphia: Published by Jacob Johnson, 147 Market-Street, [1810].

Coll: 12°: 1⁴ 4 leaves (16.8 X 9.5cm)

Illus: 24 woodcuts

Binding: Pictorial wrappers

Notes: Uncut; folded to make three leaves, opens like a
       book. Rosenbach # 428.

Upton, Bertha [Hudson]   1849-1912   #2160

The Adventures of Two Dutch Dolls and a "Golliwog."
Pictures by Florence Upton. Words by Bertha Upton.
London & New York: Longmans, Green, & Co. [Spot-
tiswood & Co., Lith., London. [1895]. Pp. [1] 2 [3]
4 [5] 6 [7] 8-9 [10] 11 [12] 13 [14] 15 [16] 17 [18]
19 [20] 21 [22] 23 [24] 23*-24* [25] 26 [27] 28 [29]
30 [31] 32 [33] 34 [35] 36 [37] 38 [39] 40-41 [42]
43 [44] 45 [46] 47 [48] 49 [50] 51 [52] 53 [54] 55
[56] 55*-56*[57] 58 [59] 60 [61] 62 [63] 64.

                                         (cont'd)

Upton. Two Dutch Dolls. 1895.   (Cont'd)

Illus: 32 full-page chromolithos plus numerous
       lithographed decorations and illustrations.
Notes: Oblong book (leaf size is 21.6 x 27.6cm)
       BMC # 12809. t. 1.

Upton, Bertha [Hudson] 1849-1912   #2161

The Golliwogg's Air-Ship. Pictured by Florence K.
Upton. London, New York & Bombay: Longmans, Green
& Co., n.d. Pp. [1]-[68].

Upton, Bertha [Hudson]   1849-1912   #2162

The Golliwogg's Christmas. Pictures by Florence K.
Upton. London, New York, Bombay, & Calcutta: Longmans, Green & Co., 1907. Pp. [1]-[64].

Upton, Mr.   #2163

The Poem of My Childhood. With coloured engravings.
London: William Darton, n.d., [1812?].

Coll: 16° [1⁶] 6 leaves (11 x 9.4cm) Ff. [6].

Plates: 6 hand colored engravings

Binding: Pink wrappers, stabbed.

Notes: Separate leaves, engraved on recto, verso blank.
       Leaf [5] dated February 7, 1812. McKell # 3-1-
       23-43-B

Valade-Gabel, Jean Jacques   #2164

Picture Lessons for Boys and Girls. Translated and
adapted from the French . . . by C. Baker. London:
[1856].

Coll: 8° 1-9⁸ 72 leaves (15.8 x 10cm) Pp. [i-iii]
      iv [v], 6- [142, 143-144: blank]
Illus: A woodcut on nearly every page.
Notes: See BMC. McKell copy lacking title page and
       all pages before [iii]. Preface, [iii]-iv,
       signed C. B[aker].

Valentin, Francois   1825-1885

       see

       About, Edmond

Van Dyke, Henry   1852-1933   #2170

The First Christmas Tree. By Henry Van Dyke. Illustrated by Howard Pyle. New York: Charles
Scribner's Sons, MDCCCXCVII, [University Press, John
Wilson and Son, Cambridge, U.S.A.] Pp. [i-viii] 1
[2] 3-22 [23-24] 25 [26] 27-38 [39-40] 41 [42] 43-58
[59-60] 61 [62] 63-76.

Illus: Front + 3 plates, all in single color tint +
       decorative marginal ornamentation.

[Van Waters, George]   #2179

[The Poetical Geography. Cincinnati: 1849.]

Coll: 8° [1]⁸ 2-5⁸ 6⁶   46 leaves (23.7 x 16.9cm)
     Pp. [1] ii-vi, 7-92.

Notes: McKell copy lacks 1.1-1.4.

Van Waters, George   #2180

The Poetical Geography, designed to accompany outline
of maps or school atlases. To which are added the
rules of arithmetic in rhyme. By George Van Waters.
Published at Louisville, Philadelphia, Hartford, New
York, and Boston: 1850.

Coll: 4° 1-4⁸, 5⁴   36 leaves Pp. [i]ii-vi, 7-72.

Illus: Numerous engravings

Binding: Brown wrappers

Notes: Stereotyped by   James & Co., Cincinnati.

Van Waters, George   #2181

The Poetical Geography, designed to accompany outline
maps or school atlases. Cincinnati: "Sold by Agents
Only," 1853.

Coll: 8 [1]⁸ 2-5⁸   40 leaves (22.8 x 16.4cm) Pp. [i]
     ii-iii [iv] v-vi, 7-80.
Illus: Cuts
Notes: McKell copy missing back cover.

Vedder, David   1790-1854   #2183

The Story of Reynard the Fox. A new version by David
Vedder author of Arcadian Sketches--Poems, Legendary,
Lyrical and Descriptive, Pictorial Giftbook, etc.
Illust. by Gustav Canton of Munich and Dusseldorf.
London: W. S. Orr & Co., Paternoster Row; Edinburgh:
John Menzies; Dublin: James McGlashan. Schenck &
McFarlane, Lith.ʳˢ Edinburgh. Edinburgh: Printed by
R. & R. Clark. [ca. 1852].

Coll: Lge 4° A², B⁵ (B5 pasted to B4), C-L⁴, M².
     45 leaves. (26   x 20.3   cm) Pp. [i-v] vi-
                                          (cont'd)

The Story of Reynard the Fox. (Cont'd)

xiv, [1]2-76.

Illus: Frontispiece, title, and dedication pages +13
     other lithographed plates by Gustav Canton +
     numerous illustrations

Binding: Dark blue boards with "Reynard the Fox" and a
     foxhead on the front in gold. Back plain.
     Binding by John Gray, Edinburgh.

Venable, William Henry   1836-1920   #2184

Santa Claus and the Black Cat or, Who is Your
Master. Illustrations by John Ward Dunsmore.
Cincinnati: William Mayo Venable [Press of Mc-
Donald & Co., Copyright, 1899]. Pp. [1-11, 1-2] 3-
12 [13] 14-24 [25] 26-29 [30] 31 [32, 33-34].

Illus: 3 full-page lithos by G. G. McF. Co. + several
     decorative cuts.

Notes: 1 gathering of 16.

[Venning, Mary Anne]   #2185

Rudiments of Conchology: designed as a familiar introduction to the science, for the use of young persons.
With explanatory Plates, and references to the collection of shells in the British Museum. London:
Printed [by and] for Harvey and Darton, 1826.

Coll: 12° [A⁴] B-E¹² F⁴   56 leaves (17.45 x 10.4cm)
     Pp. [i-v] vi-vii [viii, 1] 2-103 [104].

Plates: Front + 9

Notes: McKell # S-7-13-   48-B

Anon   #2187

Very Little Tales for Very Little Children; in single
syllables of three and four letters. Philadelphia:
Geo. S. Appleton & Co., 1844.

Coll: 16° [1-12]⁸ 96 leaves (12.1 x 9.9cm) Pp. [1-4]
     5-192.
Notes: Signed [A]⁴ B-2A⁴, regularly gathered 2 signa-
     tures to the gathering. McKell copy lacks 1.1,
     1.4, 1.5, 12.8 [A1, A4, B1, 2A4]. First
     American edition, from sixth London edition.

Anon   #2188

Victor's Stories for Boys and Girls. By the writer
of "Uncle Paul's Stories." Boston: The American
Tract Society, n.d., [1867].

Coll: 8° 1-9⁸   72 leaves (19.1 x 15.2cm) Pp. [1-iii]
     iv [5] - 144.

Plates: Hand colored frontispiece + cuts.

Vieth, Gerhard Ulrich Anthony [(Anton)] 1763-1836   #2189

The Pleasing Preceptor; or Familiar Instructions in
Natural History and Physics, adapted to the Capaci-
ties of Youth, . . . Taken Chiefly from the German
of Gerhard Ulrich Anthony Vieth, Mathematical
Teacher at Dessau; intended for the Use of Schools,
and Illustrated with Cuts. 2 vols. London:
Printed for G.G. and J. Robinson . . . by George
Woodfall . . . 1800-1801.

Vol. I: 1800
Coll.: 12° A⁶ B-L¹² M⁶ N² 134 leaves (17 x
     10.3cm). Pp. iv -viii [ix] x-xi [xii] [1] 2-
     40 [41] 42-164 ("165" misnumbered 561) 166
     -256.
                                          (cont'd)

Vieth. The Pleasing Preceptor.   (Cont'd)

Illus: 7 cuts in text

Vol. II: Printed for G. and J. Robinson . . . by
G. Woodfall. . . . 1801.

Coll: 12° [A]² B-K¹² L⁶ 118 leaves (16.7 x 10.3cm)
Pp. [1-2] 1-11, 1-232.

Plates: 2+1 fold-out. 3 cuts in text.

Anon.   #2190

The Village Green; or Sports of Youth. New Haven: Published by S. Babcock, 1840.

Coll: 32°: [1⁴] 4 leaves (7.4 X 4.3cm) Pp. [1]2-8

Illus: 7 woodcuts

Binding: Yellow printed wrappers.

Virgil (Publius Vergilius Maro). 70-19 B.C. #2191

The Pastorals of Virgil, with a course of English
reading, adapted for schools: in which all the proper
facilities are given, enabling youth to acquire the
Latin language, in the shortest period of time. Il-
lustrated by 230 engravings, By Robert John Thornton,
M.D., Member of the University of Cambridge, &c., &c.
Third edition. 2 vols. London: Stereotyped and
Printed by J. Mc Gowan, 1821.

Vol I:
Coll: 12° A¹² (-A), a (-a,'a2') - b⁶, B-T⁶ (-Tb)
     128 leaves.   (17.2 x 10.1cm)

                             (cont'd)

The Pastorals of Virgil.   (Cont'd)

    Pp. [i-v] vi (vii+viii do not appear) [ix-x]
    xi-xii, [1] 2-12, [v-xxiv, 1] 2-214.

Plates: Front.+engravings by W. Blake, Cruikshank,
      Bewick, etc. Front. on wood by Hughes.

Notes: "The illustrations to the First Pastoral are
      drawn on wood and engraved by Blake, the only
      woodcuts he ever did; the heads are etched by
      him."--Chatzki.

                            (cont'd)

The Pastorals of Virgil.   (Cont'd)

Vol II:
Coll: 12° ⲧ, T6, U-3D⁶, 3E² 190 leaves (17.3 x
    9.9cm) Pp. [1-11,] 215-592 [593-595].

Plates: Front. by Cruikshank;+engravings

———

Binding: By F. Bedford

Notes: In vol. I all '3's are signed 2 except in sig-
      natures AELM; same with vol. II except -3E2.

Anon.   #2192

A Visit to the Bazaar: By the author of Juliet, or the
Reward of Filial Affection; and the Port Folio of a
school girl. The third edition. London: Printed [by
H. Bryer, Printer...] for Harris and Son..., 1820.

Coll: 16°: A², B-F⁸, G⁶ 48 leaves (12.6 X 10cm.)
Pp. [i-11,1] 2-92 [93-94].

Plates: Frontispiece + 31 hand-coloured copper-plate
      engravings

Binding: Bound by Wallis

Notes: Frontispiece has date, "Feb. 20, 1818 by J. Harris,
      corner of St. Paul's"
      S-2-4-43-B

---

anon.   #2193

VOL'GA. Bylini (Epic Poems). Illustrations by I [van]
J [akovlevich] Bilibin. Petrograd: I. I. Bilibin, 1904.
[Printed by] R. Golike & A. Bialborg, St. Petersburg.
Pp. [1-2], 3-4 [5] 6-8 [9] 10 [11] 12 [13] 14 [15] 16.

Illus: Full page color illustrations on unnumbered pages;
      other illustrations and decorations, some in color.

Binding: Pictorial wrappers. Rebound: "Geo. A. Flohr Co.,
      June 15, 1960, Cincinnati, O."

Notes: The title Vol'ga is the name of a character; the
      Bilini are Russian   epic poems.

Von Anjou, Herzog René 1409-1480   #2194

Livre du Cuer d'Amoure Espris. Miniaturen und text
heraus gegeben und erläutert von O. Smital und E. Wink-
ler. 3 vols. Wien: Druck und Verlag Der Österreich-
ischen Staatsdruckerei, 1926.

Vol I: Einleitung
Pagination: [x, 1-2] 3-117 [118] + 23 numbered plates +
    1 leaf with table of contents on recto.

Vol II: Text und Anmerkungen
Pagination: viii, 1-208 [209-214].

                             (cont'd)

Von Anjou. Livre du Cuer. 3 vols. 1926. (Cont'd)

Vol III: Tafeln
Pagination: [1-12]
Plates: 26, including 24 full-leaf repros in color.

[Von] Anjou [Herzog] René d'   1409-1480 #2195

Traité de la Forme et Devis d'un Tournoi. Afterword
by Edward Pognon. Vol. IV, No. 16 of Verve Revue ar-
tistique et litteraire Directeur: Teriade. Paris:
Editions de la Revue Verve, 1946. Pp. 1-70.

Notes: Text and illustrations compiled from 6 mss.,
      one in the Bibliotheque royale de Dresde, one
      in the Bibliotheque Mazarine, and four others:
      mss. francais 2692, 2693, 2694, and 2695.

Anon   #2196

Voyages & Glorieuses Découvertes des Grands
Navigateurs & Explorateurs Français. Illustré
par Edy Legrand. Paris: Tolmer, n.d. Pp. [1-32].

Plates: 2 fold-out color maps + cuts.

Ward, J   , comp.   #2203

The Instructing Gipsy; or, the universal fortune
teller; containing astrology, chartology, charms, . . .
unfortunate days. To which is added other useful information. London: Printed by Dewick and Clark . . .
for T. Hughes . . . , 1806.

Coll: 12° B-D⁶ 18 leaves (17.7 x 10cm) [3-5] 6-38 pp.

Plates: Engraved color frontispiece

Vrendenburg, Edric   #2197

Pets and Playmates. "Our Children's Book Case."
London, Paris & New: Raphael Tuck & Sons. Designed at the studios in England and printed at
the Fine Art works in Germany. [c. 1900]. Ff. 6.

Illus: 4 color by J. H. (or H. J.: monogram " HJ ")
+ 4 others plus cover.
Notes: No inside title page.

Ward, William   #2204

Jesse James' Blackest Crime: or, the destruction
of the overland stage. Adventure Series No. 34
Cleveland: The Arthur Westbrook Company, [copy-
right 1909]. Pp. [1-6, 7] 8-170; [1-11, 7] 8-24pp.
bound in at end.

Plates: Frontispiece

Contents: Pp. [1-11, 7] 8-24: First two chapters
of Jesse James' Nerve: or, the hold-
up of the Missouri Pacific Train.

Anon.   #2200

A Walk to Weller's Wood; or The Old Apple-Man.
From a London Copy. By the Author of "Nothing
at All," &c. New York: Printed and Sold by
Mahlon Day, at the New Juvenile Book-store,
No. 376, Pearl Street, 1832.
Coll: 12°; [1¹²]; 12 leaves (14.2 x 8.7 cm.);
[1-5] 6-23 [24].
Illus: Front. + 9 woodcuts.
Binding: Yellow wrappers. Illust. on front,
advertisement on back.
Notes: Initial and final leaves pasted to
wrapper.

Warner, Charles Dudley.   1829-1900   #2205

Being a Boy. Illustrated by "Champ" [James Wells
Champney]. Boston: James R. Osgood and Company,
1878. Pp. [vi, 1] -244.

Notes: First ed. (?)

Wallace, Lew [is]. 1827-1905   #2201

Ben-Hur: A tale of the Christ. New York: Harper &
Brothers, 1880. Pp. [1-5], 6-552, [1] -12 [adverts].

Notes: First ed. Presentation copy: autograph presentation slip tipped to front fly-leaf. Also inscribed
on dedication page.

Warner, Susan Bogert   1819-1885

   see also

      Wetherell, Elizabeth

[Ward,] Elizabeth Stuart Phelps 1844-1911

The Gates Ajar. Boston: Fields, Osgood, Co.,
Successors to Ticknor and Fields, 1869. i-iv
248pp.

Notes: Second issue

Warner, Susan Bogert   1819-1885 and
Warner, Anna Bartlet   1827-1915   #2207

Ma. Rutherford's Children. New York: George P.
Putnam & Co., 1853.

Coll: 12° π² 2π⁴ 1¹⁴ 2¹³ 3-6¹⁴ 7¹³ 8¹⁴ 9¹³ [10]⁴
133 leaves (17.1 x 10.8cm) Pp. [1-5] 6-265
[266].
Illus: Cuts
Notes: First ed.

#2208

Warren, Thomas, comp.

Little Master's Miscellany: or, Divine and Moral Essays in Prose and Verse; Adapted to the Capacities, and design'd for the Improvement of Youth, of both Sexes. Containing Dialogues . . . Select Fables, Moral Songs, and useful Maxims. The Third Edition. Illustrated with Copper-Plates. Birmingham: Printed by T. Warren, in the Bull-Ring; and sold by J. Robinson, Bookseller, in Ludgate-street, London. 1750.

Coll: 8° [A]-I⁶ 48 leaves (15.5 x 9.5cm) Pp. [viii]9-96.

Plates: 7 copper engravings

Notes: Bookplate of Percival Merritt.

#2209

Waterloo, Stanley　　　1846-1913

The Story of Ab. Chicago: Way & Williams, 1897. Pp. [i-x,] 1-351 [352]

Plates: Frontispiece

Notes: On front fly-leaf: "To Mrs. George Jordan, with the earnest good wishes of Stanley Waterloo. Chicago, October 22, 1897." First edition. McKell # SG 4-30-52 B.

#2210

[Waters,

Poetical Flower Garden: With Moral Reflections for the Amusement of Children. Embellished with Cuts. London: Printed for T. Carnan, 1778.

Coll: 12° π² A² B-C⁶E⁶ 48 leaves (11.5 x 7.2cm) Pp. [6], ii, iv, 5-88.

Binding: Dutch floral boards

Notes: Bookplate of Percival Merritt. Roscoe # 377(2). McKell　# 3-4-6-43

#2212

[Watts, Mrs. Alaric Alexander, i.e., Priscilla Maden (Wiffen) Watts] ed.　　1797-1873

The New Year's Gift and Juvenile Souvenir. [Illustrated by various artists.] London: Longman, Rees, Orme, Brown & Green, [1833]

Coll: 12° A² B-X⁶ 122 leaves (14.5 x 9.2cm) Pp. [iv] x [xi-xii, 1] 2-240.
Plates: Frontispiece, engraved title page +9.
Notes: Lacking preface ?

#2213

Watts, I[saac]. 1674-1748

The Cradle Hymn. With the evening and morning hymns, and Sunday morning. Beautifully embellished with fourteen elegantly coloured engravings. London: Printed [by Dean and Munday] for Dean and Munday...and A.K. Newman & Co....[1830].

Coll: 12°: [1¹][2]-[8²][9²] 16 leaves (16.1 x 9.9cm.) Pp. [1-5] 6-7 [8-9] 10-11 [12-13] 14-15 [16-17] 18 [19-21] 22-23 [24-25] 26-27 [28-29] 30-31 [32]

Plates: Hand tinted engravings

Notes: Blank facing pages alternate with facing pages containing text and illustration

---

#2214

Watts, Isaac, D.D.　1674-1748

Divine and Moral Songs, Attempted in Easy Language for the use of Children. Revised and Corrected. Boston: Printed and sold by Samuel Hall, 1799.

Coll: 16°: [A]⁸ B⁴ C⁸ D⁴ E⁸ F⁴ 36 leaves (10.3 X 8cm) Pp. [1-2] [i-iii] iv-vi [7] 8-70

Woodcuts: Frontispiece + 20 in text

Binding: Flowered wrappers

Notes: On envelope: "8-15-52L"/"S-8-27-52B"

#2215

Watts, Isaac D.D.　1674-1748

Divine and Moral Songs for Children. London: T. Nelson and Sons...Edinburgh; and New York, 1864.

Coll: 8°: 1-5⁸ 40 leaves (16.4 X 10.1cm) Pp. [i-iii] iv [5] 6-43 [44] 45-50

Illus: Title page + 15 engraved pages.

Notes: Done in purple ink and gold trim throughout; engraved pages are not paginated.

#2216

Watts, I[saac]. 1674-1748

Divine Songs, in easy language, for the use of children. Glasgow: Published by J. Lumsden & Son, 1814.

Coll: 32°: 1¹⁶ unsigned 16 leaves (10.15 X 6.3cm.) Pp. [1-5] 6-30 [31-32]

Illus: Frontispiece + 8 cuts in text

Binding: Buff wrappers. Initial and final leaves serve as paste down endpapers

Notes: "From Ross's Juvenile Library" on cover

#2217,1-2

Watts, Isaac. 1674-1748

Watt's Songs. Early Religion. New York: McLoughlin Bros., Publishers. n.d.

Coll: 12°: [1⁸] 8 leaves (14.3 x 9.6cm.) Pp. [1-16]

Illus: 4 hand-colored engravings

Binding: Wrappers, engraved

Notes: Another copy lacking pages 1 and 2 of above. Tops of inside pages bear Watt's Divine and Moral Songs."

#2218

Watts, Isaac. 1674-1748

Watt's Songs. Good Resolutions. New York: McLoughlin Bros., Publishers, n.d.

Coll: 12°: [1⁶] 6 leaves (14.4 X 9.7cm.) Pp. [1-12]

Illus: 4 hand-colored engravings

Binding: Wrappers, stabbed

Notes: Tops of inside pages bear title "Watt's Divine and Moral Songs."

Waugh, Ida (-1919)   #2219

Holly Berries. With original illustrations by Ida Waugh. New York: E. P. Dutton & Co.; London: Griffith & Farran, [1881]. Pp. [48].

Illus: Cuts

Weatherly, F [rederick] E [dward] 1848-1929   #2220

The Maids of Lee. Written by F. E. Weatherly. Illustrated by W   J   Hodgson. London: Hildesheimer & Faulkner, 41 Lewin St. Set to Music by J. E. Roeckel and published by Enoch & Son, n.d.

Coll: Oblong 4° [1^{12}] 12 leaves Pp. [1, 2-23, 24].
      (18.6 x 23.9cm)
Illus: Picture on each page; 6 engravings in color.

Binding: Stiff wrappers; initial and final pages as paste-down endpapers. Illus. on front wrapper.

Weatherly, Frederic E [dward]   1848-1929   #2221

Rhymes and Roses. Illustrated by St. Clair Simmons & Ernest Wilson. London: Hildesheimer & Faulkner; New York: Geo. C. Whitney. n.d. Pp. 1-32.

Illus: 7 in color + 23 tinted + color cover illustration.
Notes: Hildesheimer & Faulkner fl. 1883-1888. See Osborne, p. 478).

Webster, Noah L.. D.   1758-1843   #2222

A Dictionary for Primary Schools. New York: N. & J. White . . . 1836. [Stereotyped by A. Chandler, New York]

Coll: 16° [1]-21^8 22^4 172 leaves (13.3 x 10.3cm) Pp. [i-iii] iv-vi, [7] 8-341 [342-344].

Notes: Testimonials: 22·4-22·4^v.

Weems, M [ason]. L [ocke]. 1759-1825   #2228

The Life of George Washington; with Curious Anecdotes, Equally Honourable to Himself and Exemplary to his countrymen....Tenth Edition....Greatly Improved. Embellished with Seven Engravings. Philadelphia: Printed for Mathew Carey, 1810.

Coll: 12°: A-T^6 114 leaves (17 X 10cm) Pp. [1-3] 4-288

Plates: Frontispiece + 6

Notes: Bookplate of A. Edward Newton

Webster, Noah, L.L.D.   1758-1843   #2223

The Elementary Spelling Book; being an improvement on The American Spelling Book. [Edited by W.G. Webster.] The Last Revised Edition. Cleveland, Ohio: M.C. Younglove & Co. [1857].

Coll: 12° 1^{14} 2-5^{16} 6^6 84 leaves (17.s x 10.7cm) Pp. [1-5] 6-168.

Illus: Engraved title page, frontispiece woodcut on 1^2.

Webster, Noah, Jun.   1758-1843   #2225

Elements of Useful Knowledge. Volume I. Containing a historical and geographical account of the United States; for the use of schools. Hartford: Printed and sold by Hudson and Goodwin. 1802.

Coll: 12° A^4 B-R^6 S^2 102 leaves (16.1 x 10.5 cm) Pp. [5-12, 13] 14-206 [207-208].

Notes: BMC gives 1806 for first edition date.

Webster, Noah, Jun., Esq.   1758-1843   #2226

History of Animals; Being The Fourth Volume Of Elements Of Useful Knowledge. For The Use Of Schools, And Young Persons Of Both Sexes. New Haven, Published and Sold by Howe & Deforest, and Walter & Steele. 1812.

Coll: 12° A-W^6 126 leaves (17.6 x 10.1cm) Pp. [1-5] 6-247 [248-252].

Webster, Noah.   1758-1843   #2227

The Pictorial Elementary Spelling Book; being an improvement of the American Spelling Book by Noah Webster, L.L. D., with about one hundred and sixty original illustrations. Designed and engraved by W. P. Morgan and A. Anderson. The last revised edition. New York: Published by George F. Coolidge & Brother, Booksellers and Publishers, 323 Pearl Street. Proprietors of the copyright of Webster's Elementary Spelling Book (Copyright secured), n.d. [ca. 1848].

Coll: 12° [1^{10}, 2^{14}, 3^{10}, 4^{13}, 5^{12}, 6^{12}, 7^{12}, 8^6] 89 leaves (18.6x11.5)cm) Pp. [1-vi, 1-5] 6-168 [169-172]
(cont'd)

The Pictorial Elementary Spelling Book. (Cont'd)

Illus: 159 engravings by Morgan and Anderson.

Binding: Brown wrapper; initial and final pages pasted down.

Notes: Stereotyped by Charles G. Savage, 13 Chambers Street, New York. Advertisement on verso of title page dated May 1848.

Wells, Carolyn act 1896 - d. 1942 # 2230

The Merry-Go-Round. With drawings by Peter Newell. New York: R.H. Russell, Publisher, 1901. Pp. [i-viii,] 1-152.

Plates: Frontispiece + 10 f cuts.

Wells, Carolyn, comp. act 1896 - d. 1942 # 2231

A Nonsense Anthology. New York: Charles Scribner's Sons, 1903. Pp. [i] ii-xxxiii [xxxiv, 1] 2-289 [290].

Notes: Poem cut from newspaper or magazine pasted to p. [290].

Wells, Carolyn (-d. 1942)

see

Perrault-D'armancour, Pierre. Mother Goose's Menagerie.

Welsford, Mary Adams. # 2234

The Widow's Son, and Other Familiar Tales: for young children. By Mary Adams Welsford. New York: William Kerr & Co., 1842. [Printed by A. Hanford, Xylographic Printer, No. 26 Ann Street, N. York.]

Coll: 12° 1-5⁶, 6⁴ (-6·4) 33 leaves Pp. [1-5] 6-22, [23-25] 26-40 [41-43] 44-49 [50-53] 54-66. (14.9 x 9.3cm)

Illus: One woodcut on p. 61.

Welsh, Charles 1850-1914 # 2235

A Bookseller of the Last Century: being some account of the life of John Newbery, and of the books he published, with a notice of the later Newberys. London: Griffith, Farran, Okeden and Welsh, 1885. Pp. [xii, 1] 2-373.

Notes: Bookplate of Percival and Elisabeth Merritt.

Welsh, Charles (1850-1914), ed.

see

Goldsmith, Oliver. The History of Little Goody Two Shoes. 1900.

Welsh, Mrs. T # 2236.1-2

The Musical Alphabet Arranged Expressly for the Instruction and Amusement of Children by Mrs. T. Welsh. New York: Published by E. S. Mesier [ca 1835].

Coll: 2° [1²] Pp. [1] 2-3 [4] (32.9 x 24.9cm)

Illus: 31 small engravings illustrating letters of the alphabet.

Notes: The original; with facsimile "Reprinted for the friends of Walter and Barbara Schatzki, Christmas 1947."

Wetherell, Elizabeth [Pseud of Susan Bogert Warner] 1819-1885 # 2238

Queechy. By Elizabeth Wetherell. 2 Vols. New York: George P. Putnam, 1852.
Vol. I:
Coll: 8° [1-16¹² 17¹³ (17·12 +1)] 205 leaves (18.6 x 12.4cm) Pp. [1-5] 6-410.
Notes: First American ed. Signed in 6s.

Vol II:
Coll: 8° [1-16¹² 17⁶] 198 leaves (18.6 x 12.4cm)
Notes: First American ed. Signed in 6s. Archaic signatures in   first gathering.

Wetherell, Elizabeth [Pseud of Susan Bogert Warner] 1819-1885 # 2239

The Wide, Wide World. By Elizabeth Wetherell. In two volumes. New York: George P. Putnam, 1851.
Vol I:
Coll: 8° [1²] 2-15¹² 16⁸ 178 leaves (18.4 x 12.5cm) Pp. [1-iii] iv [9] 10-360.
Vol II:
Coll: 8° 1¹³ 2-13¹² 14⁸ [15²] 167 leaves (18.4 x 12.5cm) Pp. [i-iii] iv [3] 4-330 [331-332].

Notes: On I, p. 157 and II, pp. 34, pagination is placed at inner   margin of headline.

Wetzell, # 2240

Contes a Mes Eleves par Mᵐᵉ Wetzell. [Orné de Jolies Figures.] Paris: Theodore Lefevre, Éditeur [Carbeil, typogr. et stereat. de Crete.], n.d., [ca1860].

Coll: 12° II², 1-7¹², 8¹⁰ 96 leaves (17.4 x 10.7cm) Pp. [1-4, i] [i, II], [3] 4-27 [28] 29-35 [36] 37-44 [45] 46-53 [54] 55-59 [60] 61-64 [65] 65-81 [82] 83-86 [87] 88-95 [96] 97-101 [102] 103-127 [128] 129-136 [137] 138-146 [147] 148-159 [160] 161-186 [187] 188.

Illus: Front + title page are colored engraved plates. + 20 colored   engravings on 10 plates.
(cont'd)

Contes a Mes Kleves par Mme Wetzell. (Cont'd)

Binding: Free and pasted down endpapers. Yellow boards
decorated front and back with lithographies by
G. Paulon..

Notes: Qumuchian # 5824

#2246

White, William Allen   1868-1944

In Our Town. Illustrated by F.R. Gruger and
W[illiam James] Glackens. New York: McClure, Phillips & Co., 1906. Pp. [i-viii, 1] 2-269 [270].

Plates: 15

Notes: William James Glackens, 1870-1938.

#2242

[Wheeler, Mrs. Charlotte Bickersteth], comp.

Memoir of John Lang Bickersteth, Late of Rugby School.
Philadelphia: American Sunday-school Union, [1850].

Coll: 12° (6s) 1-6^6 36 leaves (14.2 x 9.2cm) Pp.
[i-vi], 7-71 [72].
Plates: Frontispiece
Binding: Calf spine, marbled boards.

#2250

Anon.

Whittington and his cat. London: Dean & Son, Publishers,
[Ca 1882].
Coll: 8°: [1^4] 4 leaves ff 4
Illus: 3 colored lithographs
Binding: Cream wrappers. Illustration on the front,
advertisements on the back.
Notes: Printed on one side of the page only.

#2247

Anon.

The White Kitten: A Sequel to Mary and Her Cat.
Published by Munroe and Francis, n.d. [ca. 1823].
Coll: 12°: A^4, B^2, C^6, D^2 (=B3, B4), E^4 (=A5-A8)
18 leaves (14.1 X 9^cm:) Pp. [1-4,5] 6-35 [36]

Illus: Several cuts

Binding: Yellow wrappers, initial and final pages as
paste down endpapers

Notes: Entered 21 November 1823. Title on wrappers has
"With Cuts."

#2251

Anon.

Whittington and His Cat. London: [Printed by Samuel Bent-
ley and Co, for] Grant and Griffith, [1845?]
Coll: 8°: A-B^12 24 leaves (18 X 10.5^cm.)
Pp. [1-3] 4-46 +[2]

Illus: 14 hand colored engravings

Binding: Yellow wrappers printed by H. W. Hutchings, which
on front list publishers as "Griffith and Farran,
Late Grant and Griffith." On back are advertisements. B12: Advertisements

Notes: McKell # [S 6-8-45]

#2244

White, Stewart Edward   1873-1946

Daniel Boone: wilderness scout. Illustrated by
Remington Schuyler. Garden City, New York:
Doubleday, Page and Company, 1922. Pp. [i-viii,]
1-308; [1-4].

Plates: Frontispiece +4.

Binding: Dust cover

Notes: First ed.

Wiggin, Kate Douglas

    see

        Riggs, Kate Douglas Wiggin

#2245

White, William Allen   1868-1944

The Court of Boyville. Illustrated by Orson
Lowell & Gustav Verbeck. New York: Doubleday &
McClure Co., 1899. Pp. i-xxx, 1-358; [1-2].

Plates: Frontispiece +70 included in pagination.

Notes: First ed.

William and Lucy's Trip to London

    see

        Tales of Instruction and Amusement. William
        and Lucy's, etc. London: A. Park, 1840?

Anon   #2256

William Tell, Or The Patriot of Switzerland. By
Florian. And Hofer, The Tyrolese. By The Author Of
Claudine, &c. New edition. London: [Printed by
S and R Bentley for] J. Harris, n.d.

Coll: 12° [A]² B-L¹² M⁶ 128 leaves (17 x 10.4cm)
      Pp. [i-vi][3] -252.
Plates: Engraved title +11: 1st plate dated Nov.20,1823
Binding: Gray printed boards and leather spine.

Williams, Margery

            see

         Mrs. Margery Williams Bianco
                 1881-1944

Anon   #2259

Willy the Wanderer. [Illustrated.] Salem: D.B.
Brooks and Brother, 1860. Pp. [i-v,] 6-144.

Plates: Frontispiece +6.

Wilson, Harry Leon   1867-1939   #2261

The Boss of Little Arcady. Illust. by Rose Cecil O'Neill.
Boston: Lothrop, Lee & Shepard Co., n.d., [1905?] Pp.
[1] - [x], [1] - [372].

Illus: Frontispiece + 3 + cuts

Notes: First ed. Mrs. Rose Cecil O'Neil Wilson, 1874-

Wilson, Harry Leon   1867-1939   #2262.1-3

Bunker Bean. Illust. by F[rederic] R   Gruger.
Garden City, New York: Doubleday, Page & Company, 1913.
Pp. [i-viii], [1] - [308].

Illus: Frontispiece + 7

Notes: First ed. Flyleaf inscribed by author. Another
       two copies, same as above but without inscription
       on flyleaf.

Wilson, Harry Leon   1867-1939   #2263

Cousin Jane. New York: Cosmopolitan Book Corporation,
1925. Pp. [i-vi], 1-388.

Notes: First ed.

Wilson, Harry Leon   1867-1939   #2264

The Lions of the Lord : a tale of the old West.
Illustrated by Rose Cecil O'Neill. Boston: Lothrop
Publishing Company, [1903]. Pp. [xii] 11-520.

Plates: Frontispiece +5 illustrations

Notes: List of illustrations not counted in the
       pagination: appears on p. [xi]. Four pages
       of adverts unopened and bound in at end.

Wilson, Harry Leon   1867-1939   #2265

Lone Tree. New York: Cosmopolitan Book Corporation,
1929. Pp. [i-vi], 1- [332].

Notes: First ed.

Wilson, Harry Leon   1867-1939   #2266

Ma Pettingill. Garden City, New York: Doubleday, Page
& Company, 1919. Pp. [i-viii], [1] - [328].

Notes: First ed.

Wilson, Harry Leon   1867-1939   #2267

Merton of the Movies. Garden City, N.Y., And Toronto:
Doubleday, Page & Company, 1922. Pp. [i-x], 1-336].

Notes: First ed.

Wilson, Barry Leon   1867-1939   #2268

Oh, Doctor! Illust. by Henry Raleigh. New York: Cosmopolitan Book Corporation, 1923. Pp. [i-vi], 1-384.

Illus: Frontispiece + 3

Notes: First ed.

Wilson, Barry Leon   1867-1939   #2269

Professor, How Could You! New York: Cosmopolitan Book Corporation, 1924. Pp. [i-vi], 1-340.

Notes: First ed.

Wilson, Barry Leon   1867-1939   #2270,1-2

Ruggles of Red Gap. Illust. by F[rederic] R Gruger. Garden City, New York: Doubleday, Page & Company, 1915. Pp. [i-viii], [1]-[372].

Illus: Frontispiece + 7

Notes: First ed. Plus another copy

Wilson, Barry Leon   1867-1939   #2271

The Seeker. Illust. by Rose Cecil O'Neill. New York: Doubleday, Page & Company, 1904. Pp. [i-xvi], 1-[342].

Illus: Frontispiece + 3 + cuts

Notes: First ed.

Wilson, Barry Leon   1867-1939   #2272

Somewhere in Red Gap. Garden City, New York: Doubleday, Page & Company, 1916. Pp. [i-x], [1]-[410].

Illus: Frontispiece + 7

Notes: First ed.

Wilson, Barry Leon   1867-1939   #2273

So This Is Golf. Illust. by M L Blumenthal. New York: Cosmopolitan Book Corporation, 1923. Pp. [1-10], 11-46.

Wilson, Harry Leon   1867-1939   #2274

The Spenders: A tale of the third generation. Illust. by O'Neill Latham. Boston: Lothrop Publishing Company, n.d., [1902?]. Pp. [i-x], 11-512.

Illus: Frontispiece + 5

Notes: First ed.

Wilson, Barry Leon   1867-1939   #2275

Two Black Sheep. New York: Cosmopolitan Book Corporation, 1931. Pp. [i-vi], 1-336.

Notes: First ed.

Wilson, Harry Leon   1867-1939   #2276

The Wrong Twin. Illust. by Frederic R Gruger. Garden City, N.Y., and Toronto: Doubleday, Page & Company, 1921. Pp. [i-viii], [1]-[362].

Illus: Frontispiece + 3

Notes: First ed.

Wilson, H[arry] L[eon]   1867-1939   #2277

Zig Zag Tales From the East to the West. Illust. by C[harles] Jay Taylor. New York: Keppler & Schwarzmann, 1894. Pp. [i-vi], [1]-[168], [1-7 adverts].

Illus: Frontispiece + cuts

Notes: First ed.

Wilson, Marcius   #2278

The Fifth Reader of the School and Family Series.
New York: Harper & Brothers, n.d., [1861?]. Pp. [i]-
x, [11]-[540].

Illus: Title page+cuts.

Notes: Front fly-leaf torn out of McKell copy.

Winlove, Solomon

          see

          A Collection of the Most Approved Enter-
              taining Stories .... for F. New-
              bery, 1770.

          Moral Lectures on the Following Subjects.
              Pride, Envy, Avarice .... E.
              Newbery, 1781.

          The Pleasing Moralist. London, 1798.

Winslow, Horatio   1882-   #2282

The Lost Halo. A Christmas Tale by Horatio Winslow.
Philadelphia: Franklin Printing Company, [1950].
Pp. [1-32].

Illus: Cuts

Anon.   #2285

Wisdom in Miniature: or the Young Gentleman and Lady's
Magazine. Being a collection of sentences, divine and
moral. Embellished with cuts. Philadelphia: Printed by
John Adams, 1805.

Coll: 32°: [1 ^{16}]16 leaves (10.1 X 6.2^{cm}·) Pp.[1,2-5]
6-30 [31,32].

Binding: Greenish-grey.[1$_1$^{R}] And [1$_{16}$^{v}] pasted to
          wrappers

Notes: Rosenbach #225, Evans #9752

Anon.   #2286

Wishing; or, the Fisherman and His Wife. A juvenile poem
by a Lady. London: Printed for A.K. Newman & Co. Leaden-
hall Street. n.d.
Coll: 18°: (18) 1^{18} (-1) 17 leaves (13.3 X 8.2^{cm}·),
          printed on outer forme only.
          Pp. [3-5] 6-7[8-9] 10-11[12-13]14-15[16-17] 18-19
          [20-21]22-23[24-25] 26-27[28-29] 30-31[32-33] 34-35[36]
Illus: 16 hand colored cuts
Binding: Blue wrappers, stabbed
Notes: McKell copy lacks first leaf.

Wolson, A   #2296

Nouvelles Aventures des Marmousets. A. Borissowitch,
trans. 74 illustrations de P. Cox. Paris: Georges
Crès & Cie, n.d. Pp. [1]-109, [110-112 adverts].

Illus: Cuts

Wolson, A   #2297

Le Royaume des Marmousets. A. Borissowitch, trans.
81 illustrations de P. Cox. Paris: Georges Crès &
Cie. n.d. Pp. [1]-156.

Illus: Numerous illustrations by Palmer Cox (1820-
       1924)

Anon.   #2298

Wonders! Descriptive of Some of the Most Remarkable of
Nature and Art. Baltimore: Published by Fielding Lucus
Jr.; Philadelphia: Ash and Mason, n.d.
Coll: 12°: [1^{12}] 12 leaves (16.0 X 10.6^{cm}·), printing
          on inner forme only. Ff.[1-12].

Illus: 12 engravings in text

Binding: Printed buff wrappers, advertisements for John
          Murphy on back. Front: Baltimore: Sold by J.
          Murphy. Initial and final leaves pasted down.

Notes: Bookplate of Percival Merritt

[ANON.]. The Wonders of the Microscope; or, An   #2299
Explanation of the Wisdom of the Creator in Objects
Comparatively Minute: Adapted to the Understanding
of Young Persons. Illustrated with Copper-plates.
London: Printed (by Assignment) [to G. Smallfield]
.... for William Darton ...., 1823.

Coll.: 24°: A^6-M^6 (72 leaves (13.9 X 8.7cm).
          [i-iii] iv-x[11] 12-144.

Plates: Four-fold-out engravings and one full-page
        engraving.

Engraved advertisement page tipped in at end.
M4^v-M6^R: advertising.   BMC gives 12°.

Anon   #2300

The Wonders of Vegetation: The flower. Philadelphia:
American Sunday-school Union, n.d., [1846?]

Coll: 12°   1-6^6 36 leaves (13.3 x 9cm) Pp.[1-iv]
      5-72

Illus: Vignette half-title+numerous cuts in text.

Woolsey, Sarah Chauncey (1835-1905)

see under pseud

Coolidge, Susan

Anon.   #2301

The World Displayed; or, a Curious Collection of Voyages and Travels, Selected from the Writers of all Nations. In which the Conjectures and Interpolations of Several vain Editors and Translators are expunged, Every relation is made concise and plain, and the Divisions of Countries and Kingdoms are clearly and distinctly noted. Illustrated and Embellished with Variety of Maps and prints by the best hands. The Second Edition [Mixed]. 20 vols. in 10. London: Printed for J. Newbery, at the Bible and Sun, in St. Paul's Church-Yard. 1760-62.

12° (half-sheets)

(cont'd)

World Displayed (Cont'd)

Vol I: 1760
Coll: A^6, a-b^6, B-Q^6 108 leaves (13.6 x 8.5cm) Pp.[i-iii] iv-xxxii [xxxiii-xxxvi,1] 2-179 [180].

Plates: Frontispiece, fold-out map+8: all engravings.

Vol II: 1761
Coll: A4 B-Y^6 130 leaves (13.6 x 8.5cm) Pp.[i-viii] 1-252 ("222" misnumbered 122).

Plates: Frontispiece+9: engravings

(cont'd)

World Displayed. (Cont'd)

Vol III: 1760
Coll: A4 B-T^6 112 leaves (13.7 x 8.2cm) Pp.[i-viii,1] 2-216.

Plates: Foldout map+9: engravings

Vol IV: 1761
Coll: A4 B-T^6 112 leaves (13.7 x 8.2 cm) Pp.[i-viii, 1] 2-214 [215-216].

Plates: 9 engravings.

Notes: T6-T6^v: adverts   ) for J. Newbery.

(cont'd)

World Displayed. (Cont'd)

Vol V: 1761
Coll: A4 B-S^6 106 leaves (13.7 x 8.4cm) Pp.[i-viii, 1] 2-57 [58] 59-107 [108] 109-126 [127] 128-129 [130-133] 134-164 [165] 166-203 [204].

Plates: 8 engravings

Vol VI: 1761
Coll: A4 B-R^6 S^2 102 leaves (13.7 x 8.4cm) Pp.[i-viii, 1] 2-110 [111] 112-195 [196].

Plates: 9 engravings

(cont'd)

World Displayed. (Cont'd)

Vol VII: 1762
Coll: A^3 B-T^6 U^3 114 leaves (13.6 x 8.4cm) Pp.[i-vi, 1] 2-221 [222].

Plates: 9 engravings

Vol VIII: 1761
Coll: A4 B-T^6 U^2 114 leaves (13.6 x 8.4 cm) Pp.[i-viii, 1] 2-53 [54] 55-87 [88] 89-121 [122] 123-220.

Plates: 9 engravings

(cont'd)

World Displayed. (Cont'd)

Vol IX: 1760
Coll: A4 B-T^6 112 leaves (13.6 x 8.3cm) Pp.[i-viii,1] 2-72 [73] 74-97 [98] 99-211 [212-216].

Plates: 9 engravings

Notes: T4^v-T6^v: Adverts for J. Newbery.

Vol X: 1760
Coll: A4 χ^2 B-Y^6 Z^3 135 leaves (13.6 x 8.3cm) Pp.[i-xii, 1] 2-43 [44] 45-122 [123] 124-150 [151] 152-202 [203] 204-258.

(cont'd)

World Displayed. (Cont'd)

Plates: 9 engravings

Notes: χ^2: Adverts for J. Newbery.

Vol XI: 1760
Coll: A4 B-S^6 T^2 108 leaves (13.5 x 8.4cm) Pp.[i-viii, 1] 2-119 [120] 121-128 [129] 130-166 [167] 168-208.

Plates: 7 engravings, one is a foldout.

Vol XII: 1760
Coll: A^2 B-S^6 T^4 108 leaves (13.5 x 8.4cm) Pp.[i-iv,1] 2-51 [52] 53-211)[212].

(cont'd)

World Displayed. (Cont'd)

Plates: Foldout map+9: engravings

Vol XIII: 1760
Coll: A^3 B-R^6 99 leaves (13.5 x 8.4cm) Pp.[i-vi, 1] 2-27 [28] 29-62 [63] 64-103 [104] 105-191 ("152" mispaginated 52) [192].

Plates: Foldout map+5 (3 are foldouts): engravings.

Vol XIV: 1760
Coll: A4 B-X^6 124 leaves (13.5 x 8.4cm) Pp.[i-viii,1] 2-124 [125] 126-240 ("238" mispaginated 233).

Plates: 6 (one a foldout)): engravings.

(cont'd)

World Displayed. (Cont'd)

Vol XV: 1760
Coll: A^3 B-T^6 U^2 113 leaves (13.6 x 8.4cm) Pp.[i-vi, 1] 2-82 [83] 84-220.

Plates: 7 engravings, one is a foldout; 3 woodcuts.

Vol XVI: 1760
Coll: A^2 B-R^6 S^3 101 leaves (13.6 x 8.4cm) Pp.[i-iv,1] 2-18 [19] 20-114 [115] 116-198.

Plates: 9 engravings

(cont'd)

World Displayed. (Cont'd)

Vol XVII: 1760
Coll: A³ B-R⁶ S⁷ (S6+1) 106 leaves (13.7 x 8.4cm)
Pp. [i-vi, 1] 2-11 [12] 13-68 [69] 70-118 [119] 120-
123 [124] 125-148 [149] 150-179 [180] 181-205 [206].

Plates: 7 engravings, two are foldouts.

Vol XVIII: 1761
Coll: A³ B-Y⁶ 129 leaves (13.5 x 8.4cm) Pp. [i-vi, 1]
2-84 [85] 86-251 [252].

Plates: 7 engravings, two are foldouts.

(cont'd)

World Displayed. (Cont'd)

Vol XIX: 1761
Coll: A⁴ B-X⁶ Y² 126 leaves (13.6 x 8.4cm) Pp. [i-viii,
1] 2-44 [45] 46-170 [171] 172-216 [217] 218-244.

Plates: 7 engravings, two are foldouts.

Vol XX: 1761
Coll: A³ B-S⁶ T³ 106 leaves (13.6 x 8.4cm) Pp. [i-vi, 1]
2-33 [34] 35-53 [54] 55-73 [74] 75-102 [103] 104-
186 [187] 188-209 [210].

Plates: 6 engravings, two are foldouts.

(cont'd)

World Displayed. (Cont'd)

Notes: Preface attributed to Samuel Johnson (1709-1784).

Wright, Albert D   # 2303

Primary Lessons: being a speller and reader, on an
original plan. Illustrated . New York: D. Appleton
& Co.; Philadelphia: G. S. Appleton, 1846.

Coll: 12ᶜ [1-9]⁸ 72 leaves Pp. [1-iv] 5-144.

Notes: First ed. Obsolete signings present. Half of
title page torn out.

Wyeth, N[ewell] C[onvers]   1882-1945   #2304

A Portfolio of 16 Colored Plates (25.9 x 18.7cm)
from Homer's *Odyssey*, published by Houghton in
1929.

Wynne, J[ohn] H[uddlestone]   1743-1788   #2305

Amusing and Instructive Tales for Youth: in Thirty
Poems, with Moral Applications in Prose . . . .
Ornamented with Cuts . . . engraved in wood by
Bewick. London: J. Harris . . . ; B. Crosby and
Co.; Darton and Harvey; and Longman, Hurst, Rees,
and Orme. 1809.

Coll: 12⁰ A-P⁶ 90 leaves (13.4 x 8.2cm) Pp. [1-
iii] iv-viii, 9-178 [179-180]

Illus: Numerous woodcuts in text by John Bewick

[Wynne, John Huddlestone]   1743-1788   # 2306

Choice Emblems, Natural, Historical, Fabulous, Moral and
Divine; For the Improvement and Pastime of Youth . . . .
Second Edition. London: Printed by J. Chapman, Fleet-
street; For George Riley, Curzon-street, May Fair, 1775.

Coll: 12⁰ A⁶ (-A6) B-I¹² K⁶ 107 leaves (13.9 x 8.4cm)
Pp. x+[1] -196+6 .

Plates: 53 wood engravings in text.

[Wynne, John Huddlestone]   1743-1788   #2307

Choice Emblems, Natural, Historical, Fabulous, Moral,
and Divine; For the Improvement and Pastime of
Youth: Displaying the Beauties and Morals of the
Ancient Fabulists . . . For the Use of Schools.
Seventh Edition. London: J. Chapman for E. Newbery,
MDCXCIII.

Coll: 12⁰ A-I¹² 108 leaves (15.7 x 8.9cm). Pp.
xxiv+192.

Plates: Engraved frontispiece+64 woodcut emblems.

(cont'd)

Wynne. Choice Emblems . . . 1793   (Cont'd)

Notes: On front loose endpaper: a mss. note by
George Daniel referring to William Pickering,
dated Canonburg, 1834. Horizontal chain lines
in H gathering; all others vertical. Bookplate of Percival Merritt. Roscoe # 389(b).
William Pickering (1796-1854).

[Wyss, Johann Rudolf]   1781-1830   #2308

The Family Robinson Crusoe; or, Journal of a Father
Shipwrecked, with his Wife and Children, on an Un-
inhabited Island. Translated from the German of
M. Wiss. 2 vols. London: Printed for M. J. Godwin
and Co., at the Juvenile Library . . . . 1816.

Vol I:
Coll: 12⁰ A-P¹² Q⁶ 186 leaves (16.8 x 10.1cm) Pp.
[7] viii-xxiv,+346+[2].

Plates: Frontispiece + 3, by H. Corbould.

(cont'd)

yss   Family Robinson Crusoe   (Cont'd)

Vol. II,
Coll.: 12°:[A²]B-Q¹²R¹⁰. 192 leaves. [3]iv, 380 pp.

Plates: Frontispiece (fold-out map) + 2 by H. Corbould.

Bookplates of T.M.E. Poore and A. Edward Newton.

McKell notes that in A.E. Newton's Book Collecting Games (p. 60) are described his copies.

2

Wyss. Schweizerische Robinson 1812-13
(Cont'd)

Plates: Frontispiece + 2 wood engravings by Corbould, del. and Springsgutt, sc.
Notes: Bookplates of J.M.E. Poore and A. Edward Newton.

Vol II: . . . Zweytes Bändchen. Mit einer karte. Zürich, 1813.
Coll: 8° π4, 1 -25⁸ 26⁴ 208 leaves (16.8 x 10. 4cm) Pp.[111] iv-v [vi-viii][3] 4-406+[2].
Plates: Fold-out map facing 2b·3ᵛ + 2 by Corbould & Springsgutt
                                              (cont'd)

1781-1830   #2309
[WYSS, JOHANN RUDOLF]. Le Robinson Suisse, ou Journal D'un Père de Famille Naufragé avec ses Enfans, traduit de l'Allemand de M. Viss, par M.ᵐᵉ De Montolieu. Troisième Edition, Orné de douze Figures en Toille-douce et de la Carte de l'Ile déserte. 3 vols. Paris: Arthus Bertrand, 1820.

Vol. I:
Coll.: 12°. π⁴(-π1) 1*²1**⁴ 1-22⁸/⁴236. 147 leaves (16.3 X 9.7cm). [iii-v] vi-[xx]274 + [2]pp.

Plates: 6 engravings, by Ch. Chasselat.
                                              (CONT'd)

3

Wyss. Schweizerische Robinson 1812-13
(Cont'd)

Notes: 2b·4: blank; Bookplate of A. Edward Newton.

Binding: ¾ calf over blue marbled boards. McKell Nos. S-12-9-52-L; 12-11-52-B.

Robinson Suisse (*Cont'd*)

Vol. II: Coll.: 12°. π¹1-22⁸/⁴. 133 leaves (16.3 X 9.7cm). [2]263 + [1] pp.

Plates: 4 engravings, by Ch. Chasselot.

Vol. III
Coll.: 12°. π¹1-20⁸/⁴21⁶. 127 leaves (16.3 X 9.7cm). [2]250 +[2] pp.

Plates: Frontispiece (fold-out map) + 2 engravings, by Chasselot.

McKell copy bound by) Baynton, Bath.

Wyss, Johann Rudolf (1781-1830)

   see also

        Aikin, Lucy. The Swiss Family Robinson, in words of one syllable. Routledge.

Wyss, [Johann Rudolf]   1781-1830   #2310

Le Robinson Suisse. Traduit De l'allemand de Wyss. Par Mᵐᵉ Elise Voiart. Précédé d' une introduction par Charles Nodier. Orné de nombreures vignettes a près dessins de M. Ch. Le Mercier. Paris: Garnier Frères, Libraires-Editeurs C, Rue des Saints-Peres 6 [ca. 1870. Paris - Imprimerie Charles Balt, Rue Bleue, 7. Pp.[1-8,][2] ii-viii, 1-48 [49] 50-150 ("151" mispaginated 11) 152-422.

Illus: Numerous engravings, sketches by Le Mercier.

Notes: Pp. [1-8] belong) to a π⁴ gathering.

#2313
Anon

Yankee Doodle: an old friend in a new dress. Pictured by Howard Pyle. New York: Dodd, Mead and Company, 1881. Pp.[1]2-31[32].

Plates: Frontispiece + 7 included in pagination.

Binding: Dust cover.

Wyss, Joh[ann] Rudolf   1781-1830   #2311

Der Schweizerische Robinson, oder der shiffbrüchige Schweizer Brediger und seine Familie. Ein lehr-reiches Buch für Kinder und Kinder-freunde zu Stadt und Land. herausgegeben von Joh. Rudolf Wyss. 2 vols. Zürich: Orell, Fussli und Compagnie, 1812-1813.

Vol I: . . . Erstes Bändchen. Zürich, 1812.
Coll: 8° π⁶ 2 π [1] -20⁸, 21⁸ (-21·8) 174 leaves (16.8 x 10.4cm) Pp.[xiv]+334.
                                              (cont'd)

Yearbook

   see

        Youth's Keepsake. . . . 1836.

        and

        Leslie, Miss Eliza

Anon   # 2315

The Young Captives: a narrative of the shipwreck and sufferings of John and William Doyley. New Haven: Published by S. Babcock, 1850.

Coll: 16° [1⁴] 4 leaves (9.4 x 8.2cm) Pp. [1] 2 [3] 4-5 [6] 7-8

Illus: 3 engravings

Binding: Yellow pictorial wrappers.

Anon.   # 2316

The Young Child's A,B,C; or, First Book. New York: Published by Samuel Wood & Sons; Baltimore: Samuel S. Wood & Co., [C. 1820].

Coll: 16°: [1⁸] 8 leaves (10.6 X 8.9cm) Pp. [1] 2-16

Illus: Woodcuts

Binding: Tan printed and illustrated wrappers

Notes: Evans #4363, V 1820 [N.N.,PP.], Rosenbach #596

    #2317

The Young Clerk's Assistant; or penmanship made easy, instructive and entertaining: being a compleat pocket-copy-book, curiously engrav'd for the practice of youth in the art of writing. London: Printed for Richard Ware, at the Bible and Sun in Amen-Corner, Warwick Lane [MDCCXXXIII].

Coll: 8° 74 single leaves Ff. [1-2] 3-8 [9] ("10" missing) 11-36 [37-38] 39-54 [55] ("56" missing) 57-61 [62] 63-74.

Plates: A book of 74 numbered plates with a frontispiece by "G. ( ) Bickham, sculp." Frontis- (cont'd)

Young Clerk's Assistant   (Cont'd)

piece= [1], stg.
A second frontispiece, ff. [37] : "Gheron, del. Bickham, Sc."

Contents: Ff. [38] : 2d title page, "The Virgin Muse; or select poems on several occasions moral and devine: engrav'd for the particular practice and amusement of the fair sex. [Two lines quote, Roscommon.] London: Printed for Richard Ware at the Bible & (cont'd)

Young Clerk's Assistant   (Cont'd)

Sun in Amen-Corner, Warwick Lane."

Ff. [62]: 3d title page, "A New Drawing Book of Modes. By Mons. B. Picart. Londn: Printed for Richard Ware at the Bible & Sun in Amen Corner, Warwick Lane, London."

Notes: Unnumbered plate, ff. [55] , first appears as plate ff. [9].

The Young Lady's Book; a manual of elegant recreations, arts, sciences, and accomplishments. [Illustrated by Abel Bowen, Alexander Anderson, and others.] London: Henry G. Bohn, n.d.   # 2318

Coll: 8° π⁴A-2M⁸ 2N⁷ 291 leaves (18.2 x 11.8cm) Pp. [i-v] vi [vii-viii, 9] 10-580 [581-582] + 16 adverts at beginning, and 13 pp. adverts at end.

Plates: Frontispiece †10.
Binding: Front and back paste-down endpapers.
Notes: Adverts at end dated 1877.

The Young Lady's Book; a manual of elegant recreations, excercises, and pursuits. [Illustrated by Abel Bowen, Alexander Anderson, and others.] Second edition. Boston: Carter, Hendee and Babcock, and Abel Bowen, n.d., [1830].   # 2319

Coll: 12° [1⁶] 2-42⁶ 252 leaves (17.1 x 11.2cm) Pp. [3-9] 10-504 [505-506] ;+1 leaf advert in front.

Plates: Engraved frontispiece, illustrated presentation page, illustrated title page †5.
Notes: First American ed.
Binding: Publisher's stamped red morocco, gilt edged.

Anon   #2320

The Young Man's Own Book: a manual of politeness, intellectual improvement, and moral deportment, calculated to form the character on a solid basis, and to insure respectability and success in life. Philadelphia: Desilver, Thomas, and Co., 1835.

Coll: 8° [A]⁸ B-U⁸ 160 leaves (13.4 x 8.3cm) Pp. x, [11] 12-320.

Plates: Frontispiece drawn by C.R. Leslie and engraved by Geo. B. Ellis; illustrated title page by H. ( ) Corbould and G.B. Ellis.

Anon   #2321

"Young Troublesome": or, Master Jacky's Holidays. London: Bradbury & Evans, 11 Bouverie Street. [c. 1865]. Pp. [1] 2-11 [12].

Illus: 12 in color by John Leech printed on one side of leaf only.
Notes: Oblong book. Leaf size: (17.2 x 26.2cm).

Anon.   #2322

Youthful Sports. Stereotyped by James Conner, New York. New York: Printed and sold by Mahlon Day, n.d.
Coll: 32°: [1⁸] 8 leaves (8.75 X 5cm.) Pp. [1-2] 3-16
Illus: Woodcut vignettes

Binding: Yellow wrappers: contain on front "Juvenile Pastimes in verse," on rear, an advertisement for "Books for sale by M. Day"

Notes: Rosenbach #739

Anon.   #2323

The Youth's Cabinet of Nature, for the Year; Containing
Curious Particulars Characteristic of Each Month. New
York: Printed and sold by Samuel Wood..., 1814.

Coll: 18°: $[1^{18}]$ $[2^8]$ $(C2^8]$ inserted in fold of $[1^{18}]$)
      26 leaves (13.6 X 8.5cm) Pp. $[1-3]$ 4-52

Illus: woodcuts

Binding: Light tan wrappers

Notes: Evans #33755, Rosenbach #516

                                                  #2324

Youth's Keepsake. A Christmas and New Year's Gift
for Young People. Illustrated by Singleton, A.
Fisher, and others. Boston: John Allen & Co.,
1836.

Coll: 12° 1-18⁶ 108 leaves (15.3 x 9.5cm) Pp.
      $[1-7]$ 8, 9-214 $[215-216]$.
Plates: "Frontispiece" + 5.
Binding: Stabbed
Notes: Frontispiece included in pagination. A Year-
       book. LC has two editions: (1) Boston:
       Carter & Hendee, 18__. and (2) New York:
       Leavitt &   Allen, $[185_]$.

Adams, Oscar Fay. A Dictionary of American Authors. 5th ed., rev. & enl. Boston: Houghton, Mifflin and Company, 1905. [Reprint. University of Michigan Microfilms, Inc., 1960.]

Allibone, S. Austin. A Critical Dictionary of English Literature and British and American Authors Living and Deceased, from the Earliest Accounts to the Latter Half of the Nineteenth Century. 3 vols.+2 vols. Supplement by John Foster Kirk, Philadelphia: J. B. Lippincott & Co., 1872-4, 1891.

Blanck, Jacob. A Bibliography of American Literature . . . for The Bibliographical Society of America. 5 vols. New Haven: Yale University Press, 1955-69.

_____. Peter Parley to Penrod: a Bibliographical Description of the Best-loved American Juvenile Books. New York: R.R. Bowker Company, 1938.

Burke, W.J., and Will. D. Howe. American Authors and Books, 1640 to the Present Day. Augmented and revised by Irving R. Weiss. New York: Crown Publishers, Inc., [1962].

Carr, James F., comp. Mantle Fielding's Dictionary of American Painters, Sculptors and Engravers. With an Addendum Containing Corrections and Additional Material on the Original Entries. New York: James F. Carr, 1965.

Evans, Charles. American Bibliography. A Chronological Dictionary of All Books, Pamphlets and Periodical Publications Printed in The United States of America from the Genesis of Printing in 1639 down to and Including the Year 1820. With Bibliographical and Biographical Notes. 14 vols.+ Supplement. New York: Peter Smith, 1941-59.

Gesamtkatalog der wiegendrucke; herausgegeben von den Kommission für den Gesamtkatalog der wiegendrucke. Leipzig: K.W. Hiersemann, 1925.

Green, Roger. Andrew Lang, a Critical Bibliography with a Short-title Bibliography of the Works of Andrew Lang. Leicester: E. Ward, 1946.

Groce, George C., and David H. Wallace. The New-York Historical Society's Dictionary of Artists in America, 1564-1860. New Haven: Yale University Press, 1957.

Gumuchian et Cie. Les Livres de l'enfants du XVe au XIXe Siécle. Preface by Paul Gavault. 2 vols. Paris: Gumuchian et Cie, [Catalogue XIII, 1930].

Johnson, Merle De Vore. A Bibliography of the Works of Mark Twain, Samuel Langhorne Clemens; a List of First Editions in Book Form and of First Printings in Periodicals and Occasional Publications of his Varied Literary Activities. Rev. and enl. New York: Harper and Brothers, 1935.

_____, ed. Merle Johnson's American First Editions; a Bibliographical Check-List of the Works of 199 American Authors. 3d ed., [rev. by Jacob Blanck]. New York: R.R. Bowker Company, 1936.

Kennedy, Roderick Stuart. A Bibliography of G.A. Henty and Hentyana. London: B.J. Farmer, 1957.

Kingman, Lee, Joanna Foster, and Ruth Giles Lontoft, comps. Illustrators of Children's Books, 1957-1966. Boston: The Horn Book, Inc., 1968.

Mahoney, Bertha E., Louise P. Latimer, and Beulah Folmsbee, comps. Illustrators of Children's Books, 1744-1945. Boston: Horn Book, Inc.,1947.

Pollard, A.W., G.R. Redgrave, G.F. Barwick, et al, comps. A Short-title Catalogue of Books Printed in England, Scotland and Ireland and of English Books Printed Abroad. 1475-1640. London: The Bibliographical Society, 1969

Roscoe, S. A Provisional Check-List of Books for the Entertainment, Instruction and Education of Children and Young People, Issued Under the Imprints of John Newbery and his Family in the Period 1742-1802. 1966.

Rosenbach, A.S.W. Early American Children's Books with Bibliographical Descriptions of the Books in his Private Collection. Foreword by A. Edward

Newton. Portland, Maine: The South-
     worth Press, 1933.

St. John, Judith, comp. The Osborne
     Collection of Early Children's Books
     1566-1910; a Catalogue Prepared at
     Boy's and Girl's House . . . . With
     an Introduction by Edgar Osborne.
     Toronto: Toronto Public Library,
     1958.

Stewart, James McG. Rudyard Kipling, a
     Bibliographical Catalogue. Ed. by
     A.W. Yeats. Toronto: Dalhousie
     University Press, 1959.

Thieme, Ulrich, Felix Becker, Hans
     Vollmer, et al, eds. Allgemeines
     Lexicon der Bildenden Künstler von
     der Antike bis zur Gegenwart. Unter
     Mitwirkung von 300 Fachgelehrten.
     Des in- und Auslandes. Vol I,
     Leipzig: Wilhelm Engelmann, 1907.
     Vols. II-XXXVII + I-VI der XX Jahr-
     hunderts, Leipzig: E.A. Seeman,
     Verlag, 1908-62.

Viguers, Ruth Hill, Marcia Dalphin, and
     Bertha Mahoney Miller, comps. Illus-
     trators of Children's Books, 1946-
     1956. Boston: The Horn Book, Inc.,
     1958.

Welch, d'Alté. "A Bibliography of Amer-
     ican Children's Books Printed Prior
     to 1821," Proceedings of the American
     Antiquarian Society. Vol. 73 (April,
     Oct., 1963); vol. 74 (Oct., 1964);
     vol. 75 (Oct., 1965); and, vol. 77
     (April, Oct., 1967).

Wing, Donald Goddard, comp. Short-
     title Catalogue of Books Printed in
     England, Scotland, Ireland, Wales,
     and British America and of English
     Books Printed in Other Countries,
     1641-1700. 3 vols. New York: The
     Index Society, Columbia University
     Press, 1945-51.

Robin Hood Stories: 684, 822, 825, 935,
    1892, 2183
Rollo Books: 82-90
Rule Books: 28, 30

Sandford and Merton Stories: 122, 710-
    14
Slovenly Peter (Struwwelpeter) Stories:
    1130-4, 1150, 1407, 1931, 1996-7,
    2122
Song Books: 150, 152, 512, 539, 557,
    587, 788, 891, 899, 1032-3, 1176,
    1408, 1499, 1753, 1834, 1892, 1920,
    1960, 1983, 2110, 2120, 2213-8, 2220,
    2236
Sports and Pastimes Books: 288, 362-3,
    276-7, 384, 393, 529, 566, 589, 912,
    986, 1343, 1633, 1649, 1706, 1785,
    1819, 1961, 1998, 2024, 2322
Swiss Family Robinson Books: 123,
    2308-11

Text Books: 36, 43, 58, 60, 65, 74,
    80-1, 96, 131, 151, 204, 215-7, 304,
    395, 512, 583-4, 586, 588, 625-6,
    633, 690, 698, 716-7, 743, 752, 781,
    815, 829, 881, 920-1, 980.1-2, 1030-
    1, 1136, 1182, 1186-8, 1205, 1207,
    1220, 1252, 1277, 1299, 1302, 1310,
    1375, 1385, 1421-2, 1489-91, 1508-9,
    1518-9, 1527-30, 1560, 1571, 1614-8,
    1642-6, 1662, 1694, 1771, 1776, 1783,
    1825, 1828-9, 1860.2, 1867-8, 1918,
    1921, 1928, 1934, 1945, 1999, 2047,
    2179-81, 2191, 2123, 2225-7, 2303,
    2306, 2317
Thai Books: 378-80, 2107
Tom Thumb Tales: 834-5, 1123, 1139, 1390,
    1652, 1802.13, 2123-26.2

Carr, R., printer: 1262
Carter, Hendee & Co.: 955-6
Carter & Porter: 1138
Carleton, G.W., & Co.: 1750
Cassell & Co., Ltd.: 207, 2040
Cater, R.: 1787
Catnach, J.: 1707
Century Co.: 665-6, 1841
Champante & Whitrow: 1557
Chapman and Hall: 760, 1592
Chapman, J.: 2306-7
Charles, Mary: 522
Charles, William: 772, 1625
Charnley, E.: 1252
Chiswell, R.: 65
Chopple, C.: 1403
Churton, E.: 2019
Clark, Austin and Company: 575
Clark, Austin and Smith: 377, 599
Clark & Maynard: 1518, 1998
Clark & Raser: 1999
Clark, J.P: 1115
Clark, R. & R., Ltd., printers: 1197
Claxton, Remsen & Heffelfinger: 973, 1518
Coale, E.J.: 1395
Cobb, J.B., &Co.: 896
Cobb, Lyman: 624
Cochrane, James, & Co.: 852
Collier, Ezra, & Co.: 1032-3
Collins & Brother: 1671
Collins & Co.: 941
Collins and Hannay: 625, 1188
Collins, B.C.: 1620-2, 1919
Collins, Thomas, bookseller: 62
Conner, James: 2322
Coolman, William, Jr.: 315
Cornish, Lamport, & Co.: 945
Cosmopolitan Book Corporation: 2263, 2265, 2268-9, 2273, 2275
Cottom, Peter: 152
Cox, Thomas: 236
Cozans, Philip J.: 1389, 1768
Cramer & Spear: 1117, 1646
Cramer, Spear and Eichbaum, printers: 743
Cramer's, Z., bookseller: 1117
Creech, W.: 306
Cres, Georges, et Cie: 2296-7
Crocker & Brewster: 1822, 1879
Crosby & Letterman: 1622
Crosby, Nichols & Company: 1162, 1400
Crosby, Nichols, Lee & Co.: 104
Crosby, B., & Co.: 1557, 2305
Crosby, William and Company: 90, 1363
Crowder, S.: 834, 1621
Crukshank, J. & J.: 700
Crukshank, Joseph: 204
Cumberland, R.: 71
Cumming & Ferguson: 1568
Cumming, John: 1949

Cundee, J.: 1778
Cunningham, J.H.: 225
Cupples, Upham and Company: 2017
Curmer, L.: 740

Dalbanne, Claude: 116
Darling, W., & Son, printers: 1728
Darton & Clark: 1972, 2057
Darton & Co.: 1498
Darton and Harvey: 702, 1403, 1449, 1622, 1639, 2185, 2305
Darton, Harvey & Co.: 711
Darton, Harvey and Darton: 1318, 1599, 1677
Darton, W.: 213, 701, 809, 811, 1624, 1820, 2065, 2163, 2299
Darton, W., Jr.: 809
Darton, W. & T.: 260, 1805
Darton, William, and Son: 810, 214
Davis, Porter & Co.: 1737
Davison, W.: 268-74.2
Day, John, printer: 43
Day, Mahlon: 584, 677, 1265, 1789, 2200, 2322
Dean and Munday: 139, 713, 766-7, 977, 1391, 2024, 2213
Dean and Son: 715, 2250
Dearborn, George: 1659
Dearborn, Nathaniel: 2010
Decker, Joh. Heinrich: 1207
Delalain: 237
De Laure, Chez: 1731
Denham, Henry: 326
Derby and Jackson: 942
Derby, A.W., & Co.: 942
Derby, George H., & Co.: 1803
Derby, H.W.: 965
Derby, J.C.: 229, 965
Desbourdes, Jacques: 1744-5
Desilver, Thomas, & Co.: 2320
Dick and Fitzgerald: 1785
Dillingham, Charles T.: 1257, 2141
Dillingham, G.W.: 1576
Dillon, Charles: 1748
Dilly, C.: 306
Dirk: 323
Dodd, M.: 1822
Dodsley, J.: 1720
Doll, Nicolas: 1306.1
Doran, George H. Co.: 220
Dubochet, J.J. & Co.: 528
Duchnes, Philip, bookseller: 5
Du Fresne, Raphael: 56.1
Duncan, James: 698
Duncan, Robert: 1747

Ebner Buchhandlung: 1137
Edwin, John, bookseller: 62
Elliott, Nathan: 1971